# EVOLUTIONARY PSYCHOLOGY

FOURTH EDITION

## The New Science of the Mind

David M

*The Univer*

**Allyn & Bacon**

Boston   Columbus   Indianapolis   New York   San Francisco
Upper Saddle River   Amsterdam   Cape Town   Dubai   London
Madrid   Milan   Munich   Paris   Montreal   Toronto   Delhi   Mexico City
São Paulo   Sydney   Hong Kong   Seoul   Singapore   Taipei   Tokyo

**Executive Editor:** Susan Hartman
**Marketing Manager:** Nicole Kunzmann
**Production Manager:** Meghan DeMaio
**Photo Researcher:** Martha Shethar
**Cover Designer:** Jodi Notowitz
**Editorial Production and Composition Service:** Revathi Viswanathan/PreMediaGlobal
**Printer/Binder:** Courier Companies
**Cover Printer:** Lehigh-Phoenix Color

10 9 8 7 6 5 4 3 2 1 15 14 13 12 11

**Allyn & Bacon
is an imprint of**

ISBN-10:  0-205-00278-1
ISBN-13: 978-0-205-00278-8

*This book is dedicated to:*
*Charles Darwin*
*Francis Galton*
*Gregor Mendel*
*R. A. Fisher*
*W. D. Hamilton*
*George C. Williams*
*John Maynard Smith*
*Robert Trivers*
*E. O. Wilson*
*Richard Dawkins*
*Donald Symons*
*Martin Daly*
*Margo Wilson*
*Leda Cosmides*
*John Tooby*
*And to all students of evolutionary psychology,*
*past, present, and future*

# ABOUT THE AUTHOR

**David M. Buss** received his Ph.D. from the University of California at Berkeley in 1981. He began his career in academics at Harvard, later moving to the University of Michigan before accepting his current position as professor of psychology at the University of Texas. His primary research interests include human sexuality, mating strategies, conflict between the sexes, homicide, stalking, and sexual victimization. The author of more than 200 scientific articles

and 6 books, Buss has won numerous awards including the *American Psychological Association (APA) Distinguished Scientific Award for Early Career Contribution to Psychology* (1988), the *APA G. Stanley Hall Lectureship* (1990), the *APA Distinguished Scientist Lecturer Award* (2001), and a *Robert W. Hamilton Book Award* (2000) for the first edition of *Evolutionary Psychology: The New Science of the Mind.* He is also the editor of the first comprehensive *Handbook of Evolutionary Psychology* (2005, Wiley) and co-editor (with Patricia Hawley) of *The Evolution of Personality and Individual Differences* (2011). He enjoys extensive cross-cultural research collaborations and lectures widely within the United States and abroad. His hobbies include tennis, squash, and disc golf, and he is an avid film buff.

# CONTENTS

# PREFACE

It is especially exciting to be an evolutionary psychologist during this time in the history of science. Most scientists operate within long-established paradigms. Evolutionary psychology, in contrast, is a revolutionary new science, a true synthesis of modern principles of psychology and evolutionary biology. By taking stock of the field at this time, I hope this book contributes in some modest measure to the fulfillment of a scientific revolution that will provide the foundation for psychology in the future. Since the publication of the award-winning first edition of *Evolutionary Psychology: The New Science of the Mind* in 1999, there has been an explosion of new research within the field. New journals in evolutionary psychology have been started, and the volume of evolutionary publications in mainstream psychology journals has steadily increased. New courses in evolutionary psychology are being taught in colleges and universities throughout the world. Many gaps in scientific knowledge remain, and each new discovery brings fresh questions and new domains to explore. The field of evolutionary psychology is vibrant, exciting, and brimming with empirical discoveries and theoretical innovations. Indeed, as Harvard Professor Steven Pinker notes, "In the study of humans, there are major spheres of human experience—beauty, motherhood, kinship, morality, cooperation, sexuality, violence—in which evolutionary psychology provides the only coherent theory" (Pinker, 2002, p. 135).

Charles Darwin must be considered the first evolutionary psychologist for this prophesy at the end of his classic treatise, *On the Origin of Species* (1859): "In the distant future I see open fields for far more important researches. Psychology will be based on a new foundation." More than 150 years later, after some false starts and halting steps, the science of evolutionary psychology is finally emerging. The purpose of this book is to showcase the foundations of this new science and the fascinating discoveries of its practitioners.

When I first started to conduct research in evolutionary psychology as an assistant professor at Harvard University in 1981, evolutionary speculations about humans abounded, but practically no empirical research had been conducted to back them up. Part of the problem was that scientists who were interested in evolutionary questions could not bridge the gap between the grand evolutionary theories and the actual scientific study of human behavior. Today that gap has closed considerably, because of both conceptual breakthroughs and an avalanche of hard-won empirical achievements. Many exciting questions still cry out for empirical scrutiny, of course, but the existing base of findings is currently so large that the problem I faced was how to keep this book to a reasonable length while still doing justice to the dazzling array of theoretical and empirical insights. Although it is written with undergraduates in mind, it is also designed to appeal to a wider audience of laypersons, graduate students, and professionals who seek an up-to-date overview of evolutionary psychology.

I wrote the first edition of this book with another purpose as well—frankly, a revolutionary one. I wrote it so that the hundreds of professors at colleges and universities throughout the world who have been thinking and writing about evolution and human behavior would be motivated to teach formal courses in evolutionary psychology and get those courses established as part of required psychology curricula. Already evolutionary psychology is attracting the best and the brightest young minds. I hope that this book helps to accelerate the trend and in some small way contribute to the fulfillment of Darwin's prophesy.

In revising this book for the second, third, and fourth editions, I had two goals in mind. First, I sought to provide a major update of new discoveries. Toward this end, more than 200 new references have been added to the second edition, and roughly 400 each to the third and fourth editions. Second, I sought to fill in important omissions. Coverage of topics in cognitive psychology, for example, is now more extensive. For the fourth edition, new sections have also been added on cross-cultural, physiological, genetic, and brain-imaging methods; evolved navigation theory; fire and cooking; homicide; mate copying; the effects of men's mate preferences on their actual mating behavior; hooking up; mother-child conflict; costly signaling; the recalibration theory of anger; and prestige signaling. The fundamental organization of the book, however, remains intact—an organization around clusters of adaptive problems such as survival, mating, parenting, kinship, and group living.

I have received many inspiring letters and emails from teachers and students who have used previous editions of *Evolutionary Psychology* and hope that future readers will also share their enthusiasm. The quest for understanding the human mind is a noble undertaking. As the field of evolutionary psychology matures, we are beginning to gain answers to the mysteries that have probably intrigued humans for hundreds of thousands of years: Where did we come from? What is our connection with other life forms? And what are the mechanisms of mind that define what it means to be a human being?

**Supplements:**

Pearson Education is pleased to offer the following supplements to qualified adopters:

> *Instructor's Manual and Test Bank (ISBN 0205015662).* The instructor's manual is a wonderful tool for classroom preparation and management.

> Each chapter in the teaching aids section includes a chapter overview, detailed outline, lecture suggestions, discussion questions, class activities, and media resources. The test bank contains a set of questions for each chapter, including multiple choice, true/false, short-answer, and essay questions. The tests are also available in the MyTest computerized version for ease in creating tests for the classroom.

> *PowerPoint Presentation (ISBN 0205015638).* The PowerPoint Presentation is an exciting interactive tool for use in the classroom. Each chapter pairs key concepts with images from the textbook to reinforce student learning.

# ■ ACKNOWLEDGMENTS

The acknowledgments for this book must include not only colleagues who have directly commented on its contents, but also those who have influenced my personal evolutionary odyssey, which has spanned more than twenty-five years. My interest in evolution began in an undergraduate geology class in the mid-1970s, when I first realized that there were theories designed specifically to explain the origins of things. My first evolutionary groping was a term paper for a course in 1975 in which I speculated, drawing on now-laughable primate comparisons, that the main reason men have evolved a status-striving motive is because higher status produced increased sexual opportunities.

My interest in evolution and human behavior grew when I was in graduate school at the University of California at Berkeley, but I found the most fertile evolutionary soil at Harvard University, which offered me a position as assistant professor of psychology in 1981. There I began teaching a course on human motivation using evolutionary principles, although the text scarcely mentioned evolution. My lectures were based on the works of Charles Darwin,

W. D. Hamilton, Robert Trivers, and Don Symons. I started corresponding with Don Symons, whose 1979 book is considered by many the first modern treatise on human evolutionary psychology. I owe Don special thanks; his friendship and insightful commentary have informed practically everything that I've written on the subject of evolutionary psychology. Influenced by Don's ideas, in 1982 I designed my first evolutionary research project on human mating, which eventually mushroomed into a cross-cultural study of 10,047 participants from thirty-seven cultures around the world.

After word got around about my evolutionary interests, a brilliant young Harvard graduate student named Leda Cosmides rapped on my office door and introduced herself. We had the first of many discussions (actually arguments) about evolution and human behavior. Leda introduced me to her equally brilliant husband and collaborator John Tooby, and together they tried to correct some of the more egregious errors in my thinking—something they continue to do to this day. Through Leda and John, I met Irv DeVore, a prominent Harvard anthropologist who conducted "simian seminars" at his Cambridge home, and Martin Daly and Margo Wilson, who came to Harvard on sabbatical. At that point, the early to mid-1980s, Leda and John had not yet published anything on evolutionary psychology, and no one was called an evolutionary psychologist.

The next pivotal event in my evolutionary quest occurred when I was elected to be a fellow at the Center for Advanced Study in the Behavioral Sciences in Palo Alto. Thanks to the encouragement of Director Gardner Lindzey, I proposed a special center project entitled "Foundations of Evolutionary Psychology." The acceptance of this proposal led Leda Cosmides, John Tooby, Martin Daly, Margo Wilson, and me to spend 1989 and 1990 at the center working on the foundations of evolutionary psychology, even through the earthquake that rocked the Bay area. In writing this book, I owe the greatest intellectual debt to Leda Cosmides, John Tooby, Don Symons, Martin Daly, and Margo Wilson, pioneers and founders of the emerging field of evolutionary psychology.

Harvard on one coast and the Center for Advanced Study on the other provided a bounty for budding evolutionary scholars, but I must also thank two other institutions and their inhabitants. First, the University of Michigan supported the evolution and human behavior group between 1986 and 1994. I owe special thanks to Al Cain, Richard Nisbett, Richard Alexander, Robert Axelrod, Barb Smuts, Randolph Nesse, Richard Wrangham, Bobbi Low, Kim Hill, Warren Holmes, Laura Betzig, Paul Turke, Eugene Burnstein, and John Mitani for playing key roles at Michigan. Second, I thank the Department of Psychology at the University of Texas at Austin, which had the prescience to form one of the first graduate programs in evolutionary psychology in the world under the heading of Individual Differences and Evolutionary Psychology. Special thanks go to Joe Horn, Dev Singh, Del Thiessen, Lee Willerman, Peter MacNeilage, David Cohen, and the department chairs, Randy Diehl, Mike Domjan, and Jamie Pennebaker for their roles at UT.

I owe tremendous thanks to friends and colleagues who have contributed to the ideas in this book in one form or another: Dick Alexander, Bob Axelrod, Robin Baker, Jerry Barkow, Jay Belsky, Laura Betzig, George Bittner, Don Brown, Eugene Burnstein, Arnold Buss, Bram Buunk, Liz Cashdan, Nap Chagnon, Jim Chisholm, Helena Cronin, Michael Cunningham, Richard Dawkins, Irv DeVore, Frans de Waal, Mike Domjan, Paul Ekman, Steve Emlen, Mark Flinn, Robin Fox, Robert Frank, Steve Gangestad, Karl Grammer, W. D. Hamilton, Kim Hill, Warren Holmes, Sarah Hrdy, Bill Jankowiak, Doug Jones, Doug Kenrick, Lee Kirkpatrick, Judy Langlois, Bobbi Low, Kevin MacDonald, Neil Malamuth, Janet Mann, Linda Mealey, Geoffrey Miller, Randolph Nesse, Dick Nisbett, Steve Pinker, David Rowe, Paul Rozin, Joanna Scheib, Paul Sherman, Irwin Silverman, Jeff Simpson, Dev Singh, Barb Smuts, Michael Studd, Frank Sulloway, Del Thiessen, Nancy Thornhill, Randy Thornhill, Lionel Tiger, Bill Tooke, John Townsend, Robert Trivers, Jerry Wakefield, Lee Willerman, George Williams, D. S. Wilson, E. O. Wilson, and Richard Wrangham.

I would like to thank the following reviewers for their feedback on the first edition: Clifford R. Mynatt, Bowling Green State University; Richard C. Keefe, Scottsdale College; Paul M. Bronstein, University of Michigan-Flint; Margo Wilson, McMaster University; W. Jake Jacobs, University of Arizona; and A. J. Figueredo, University of Arizona; as well as the reviewers for the second edition: John A. Johnson, Penn State, DuBois; Kevin MacDonald, California State University, Long Beach; and Todd K. Shackelford, Florida Atlantic University. Also, a special thank you to the third edition reviewers: Brad Duchaine, Harvard University; Heide Island, University of Central Arkansas; Angelina Mackewn, University of Tennessee at Martin; Roger Mellgren, University of Texas at Arlington; Amy R. Pearce, Arkansas State University; and Thomas Sawyer, North Central College.

The creation of the second edition benefited from the exceptionally thoughtful comments and suggestions by, and discussions with, a number of friends and colleagues: Petr Bakalar, Clark Barrett, Leda Cosmides, Martin Daly, Richard Dawkins, Todd DeKay, Josh Duntley, Mark Flinn, Barry Friedman, Steve Gangestad, Joonghwan Jeon, Doug Kenrick, Martie Haselton, Bill von Hippel, Rob Kurzban, Peter MacNeilage, Geoffrey Miller, Steve Pinker, David Rakison, Kern Reeve, Paul Sherman, Valerie Stone, Larry Sugiyama, Candace Taylor, John Tooby, Glenn Weisfeld, and Margo Wilson. Josh Duntley must be singled out for sharing his encyclopedic knowledge and keen insights. I would also like to thank Carolyn Merrill of Allyn & Bacon for wise counsel, persistence, and prescience.

I would like to thank the following individuals for help making additions and improvements to the third edition: Leda Cosmides, Josh Duntley, Ernst Fehr, Herbert Gintis, Anne Gordon, Ed Hagen, Martie Haselton, Joe Henrich, Joonghwan Jeon, Mark Flinn, Barry X. Kuhle, Rob Kurzban, Dan O'Connell, John Patton, Steve Pinker, David Rakison, Pete Richardson, Andy Thompson, and Wade Rowatt.

## ■ ACKNOWLEDGMENTS FOR THE FOURTH EDITION

I would like to thank the following individuals for insightful comments and suggestions on the fourth edition: Alice Andrews, Ayla Arslan, Sean Bocklebank, Joseph Carroll, Elizabeth Cashdan, Lee Cronk, John Edlund, Bruce Ellis, A. J. Figueredo, Aaron Goetz, Joe Henrich, Sarah Hill, Russell Jackson, Peter Karl Jonason, Jeremy Koster, Barry Kuhle, David Lewis, Frank McAndrew, David McCord, Geoffrey Miller, David Rakison, Brad Sagarin, David Schmitt, Todd Shackelford, Candace Taylor, and Gregory Webster.

Thanks go to my students past and present who are making major contributions to the field of evolutionary psychology: Laith Al-Shawaf, April Bleske, Mike Botwin, Jaime Confer, Sean Conlan, Todd DeKay, Josh Duntley, Judith Easton, Bruce Ellis, Diana Fleischman, Cari Goetz, Aaron Goetz, Heidi Greiling, Arlette Greer, Martie Haselton, Sarah Hill, Russell Jackson, Joonghwan Jeon, Barry Kuhle, Liisa Kyl-Heku, David Lewis, Anne McGuire, Carin Perilloux, David Schmitt, and Todd Shackelford. Special thanks also to Kevin Daly, Todd DeKay, Josh Duntley, A. J. Figueredo, Barry Kuhle, Martie Haselton, Rebecca Sage, Todd Shackelford, and W. Jake Jacobs for generously providing detailed comments on the entire book. I would also like to thank my wonderful editor, Susan Hartman, who provided support and enthusiasm throughout several editions of this book, and my superb and meticulous Production Editors, Aparna Yellai and Revathi Viswanathan.

And to Cindy.

# PART 1

# FOUNDATIONS OF EVOLUTIONARY PSYCHOLOGY

Two chapters introduce the foundations of evolutionary psychology. Chapter 1 traces the scientific movements leading to evolutionary psychology. First, the landmarks in the history of evolutionary theory are described, starting with theories of evolution developed before Charles Darwin and ending with modern formulations of evolutionary theory widely accepted in the biological sciences today. Next, three common misunderstandings about evolutionary theory are examined. Finally, we trace landmarks in the field of psychology, starting with the influence Darwin had on the psychoanalytic theories of Sigmund Freud and ending with modern formulations of cognitive psychology.

Chapter 2 provides the conceptual foundations of modern evolutionary psychology and introduces the scientific tools used to test evolutionary psychological hypotheses. The first section examines theories about the origins of human nature. Then we turn to a definition of the core concept of an evolved psychological mechanism and outline the properties of these mechanisms. The middle portion of Chapter 2 describes the major methods used to test evolutionary psychological hypotheses and the sources of evidence on which these tests are based. Because the remainder of the book is organized around human adaptive problems, the end of Chapter 2 focuses on the tools evolutionary psychologists use to identify adaptive problems, starting with survival and ending with the problems of group living.

# CHAPTER 1

*In the distant future I see open fields for more important researches. Psychology will be based on a new foundation, that of the necessary acquirement of each mental power and capacity by gradation.*

—Charles Darwin, 1859

# THE SCIENTIFIC MOVEMENTS LEADING TO EVOLUTIONARY PSYCHOLOGY

*A*s the archeologist dusted off the dirt and debris from the skeleton, she noticed something strange: The left side of the skull had a large dent, apparently from a ferocious blow, and the rib cage—also on the left side—had the head of a spear lodged in it. Back in the laboratory, scientists determined that the skeleton was that of a Neanderthal man who had died roughly 50,000 years ago, the earliest known homicide victim. His killer, judging from the damage to the skull and rib cage, bore the lethal weapon in his right hand.

The fossil record of injuries to bones reveals two strikingly common patterns (Jurmain et al., 2009; Trinkaus & Zimmerman, 1982; Walker, 1995). First, the skeletons of men contain far more fractures and dents than do the skeletons of women. Second, the injuries are located mainly on the left frontal sides of the skulls and skeletons, suggesting right-handed attackers. The bone record alone cannot tell us with certainty that combat among men was a central feature of human ancestral life. Nor can it tell us with certainty that men evolved to be the more physically aggressive sex. But skeletal remains provide clues that yield a fascinating piece of the puzzle of where we came from, the forces that shaped who we are, and the nature of our minds today.

The huge human brain, approximately 1,350 cubic centimeters, is the most complex organic structure in the known world. Understanding the human mind/brain mechanisms in evolutionary perspective is the goal of the new scientific discipline called *evolutionary psychology*. Evolutionary psychology focuses on four key questions: (1) *Why* is the mind designed the way it is—that is, what causal processes created, fashioned, or shaped the human mind into its current form? (2) *How* is the human mind designed—what are its mechanisms or component parts, and how are they organized? (3) *What are the functions of the component parts and their organized structure—that is, what is the mind designed to do?* (4) *How* does input from the current environment interact with the design of the human mind to produce observable behavior?

Contemplating the mysteries of the human mind is not new. Ancient Greeks such as Aristotle and Plato wrote manifestos on the subject. More recently, theories of the human mind such as the Freudian theory of psychoanalysis, the Skinnerian theory of reinforcement, and connectionism have vied for the attention of psychologists.

Only within the past few decades have we acquired the conceptual tools to synthesize our understanding of the human mind under one unifying theoretical framework—that of evolutionary psychology. This discipline pulls together findings from all disciplines of the mind, including those of brain imaging; learning and memory; attention, emotion, and passion; attraction, jealousy, and sex; self-esteem, status, and self-sacrifice; parenting, persuasion, and perception; kinship, warfare, and aggression; cooperation, altruism, and helping; ethics, morality, and medicine; and commitment, culture, and consciousness. This book offers an introduction to evolutionary psychology and provides a road map to this new science of the mind.

This chapter starts by tracing the major landmarks in the history of evolutionary biology that were critical in the emergence of evolutionary psychology. Then we turn to the history of the field of psychology and show the progression of accomplishments that led to the need for integrating evolutionary theory with modern psychology.

## ■ LANDMARKS IN THE HISTORY OF EVOLUTIONARY THINKING

We begin our examination of the history of evolutionary thinking well before the contributions of Charles Darwin and then consider the various milestones in its development through the end of the twentieth century.

### Evolution before Darwin

Evolution refers to change over time. Change in life forms was postulated by scientists to have occurred long before Darwin published his classic 1859 book, *On the Origin of Species* (see Glass, Temekin, & Straus, 1959; and Harris, 1992, for historical treatments).

Jean Baptiste Pierre Antoine de Monet Chevalier de Lamarck (1744–1829) was one of the first scientists to use the word *biologie*, thus recognizing the study of life as a distinct science. Lamarck believed in two major causes of species change: first, a natural tendency for each species to progress toward a higher form and, second, the inheritance of acquired characteristics. Lamarck said that animals must struggle to survive and this struggle causes their nerves to secrete a fluid that enlarges the organs involved in the struggle. Giraffes evolved long necks, he thought, through their attempts to eat from higher and higher leaves (recent evidence suggests that long necks may also play a role in mate competition). Lamarck believed that the neck changes that came about from these strivings were passed down to succeeding generations of giraffes, hence the phrase "the inheritance of acquired characteristics." Another theory of change in life forms was developed by Baron Georges Léopold Chrétien Frédérick Dagobert Cuvier

(1769–1832). Cuvier proposed a theory called *catastrophism*, according to which species are extinguished periodically by sudden catastrophes, such as meteorites, and then replaced by different species.

Biologists before Darwin also noticed the bewildering variety of species, some with astonishing structural similarities. Humans, chimpanzees, and orangutans, for example, all have exactly five digits on each hand and foot. The wings of birds are similar to the flippers of seals, perhaps suggesting that one was modified from the other (Daly & Wilson, 1983). Comparisons among these species suggested that life was not static, as some scientists and theologians had argued. Further evidence suggesting change over time also came from the fossil record. Bones from older geological strata were not the same as bones from more recent geological strata. These bones would not be different, scientists reasoned, unless there had been a change in organic structure over time.

Another source of evidence came from comparing the embryological development of different species (Mayr, 1982). Biologists noticed that such development was strikingly similar in species that otherwise seemed very different from one another. An unusual loop-like pattern of arteries close to the bronchial slits characterizes the embryos of mammals, birds, and frogs. This evidence suggested, perhaps, that these species might have come from the same ancestors millions of years ago. All these pieces of evidence, present before 1859, suggested that life was not fixed or unchanging. The biologists who believed that organic structure changed over time called themselves evolutionists.

Another key observation had been made by various evolutionists before Darwin: Many species possess characteristics that seem to have a purpose. The porcupine's quills help it fend off predators. The turtle's shell helps to protect its tender organs from the hostile forces of nature. The beaks of many birds are designed to aid in cracking nuts. This apparent functionality, so abundant in nature, required an explanation.

Missing from the evolutionists' accounts before Darwin, however, was a theory to explain how change might take place over time and how such seemingly purposeful structures such as the giraffe's long neck and the porcupine's sharp quills could have come about. A causal mechanism or process to explain these biological phenomena was needed. Charles Darwin provided the theory of just such a mechanism.

## Darwin's Theory of Natural Selection

Darwin's task was more difficult than it might at first appear. He wanted not only to explain why change takes place over time in life forms, but also to account for the particular ways it proceeds. He wanted to determine how new species emerge (hence the title of his book *On the Origin of Species*), as well as how others vanish. Darwin wanted to explain why the component parts of animals—the long necks of giraffes, the wings of birds, and the trunks of elephants—existed in those particular forms. And he wanted to explain the apparent purposive quality of those forms, or why they seem to function to help organisms accomplish specific tasks.

The answers to these puzzles can be traced to a voyage Darwin took after graduating from Cambridge University. He traveled the world as a naturalist on a ship, the *Beagle*, for a five-year period, from 1831 to 1836. During this voyage, he collected dozens of samples of birds and other animals from the Galápagos Islands in the Pacific Ocean. On returning from his voyage, he discovered that the Galápagos finches, which he had presumed were all of the same species,

*Charles Darwin created a scientific revolution in biology with his theory of natural selection. His book* On the Origin of Species *(1859) is packed with theoretical arguments and detailed empirical data that he amassed over the twenty-five years prior to the book's publication.*

actually varied so much that they constituted different species. Indeed, each island in the Galápagos had a distinct species of finch. Darwin determined that these different finches had a common ancestor but had diverged from each other because of the local ecological conditions on each island. This geographic variation was pivotal to Darwin's conclusion that species are not immutable but can change over time.

What could account for why species change? Darwin struggled with several different theories of the origins of change, but rejected all of them because they failed to explain a critical fact: the existence of adaptations. Darwin wanted to account for change, of course, but he also wanted to account for why organisms appeared so well designed for their local environments.

> It was . . . evident that [these other theories] could [not] account for the innumerable cases in which organisms of every kind are beautifully adapted to their habits of life—for instance, a woodpecker or tree-frog to climb trees, or a seed for dispersal by hooks and plumes. I had always been much struck by such adaptations, and until these could be explained it seemed to me almost useless to endeavour to prove by indirect evidence that species have been modified. (Darwin, from his autobiography; cited in Ridley, 1996, p. 9)

Darwin unearthed a key to the puzzle of adaptations in Thomas Malthus's *An Essay on the Principle of Population* (published in 1798), which introduced Darwin to the notion that organisms exist in numbers far greater than can survive and reproduce. The result must be a "struggle for existence," in which favorable variations tend to be preserved and unfavorable ones tend to die out. When this process is repeated generation after generation, the end result is the formation of new adaptation.

More formally, Darwin's answer to all these puzzles of life was the theory of *natural selection* and its three essential ingredients: *variation, inheritance,* and *selection.*[1] First, organisms vary in all sorts of ways, such as in wing length, trunk strength, bone mass, cell structure, fighting ability, defensive ability, and social cunning. Variation is essential for the process of evolution to operate—it provides the "raw materials" for evolution.

Second, only some of these variations are inherited—that is, passed down reliably from parents to their offspring, which then pass them on to their offspring down through the generations. Other variations, such as a wing deformity caused by an environmental accident, are not inherited by offspring. Only those variations that are inherited play a role in the evolutionary process.

The third critical ingredient of Darwin's theory is selection. Organisms with some heritable variants leave more offspring *because* those attributes help with the tasks of *survival* or

---

[1]The theory of natural selection was discovered independently by Alfred Russel Wallace (Wallace, 1858); Darwin and Wallace co-presented the theory at a meeting of the Linnaen Society.

*reproduction.* In an environment in which the primary food source might be nut-bearing trees or bushes, some finches with a particular shape of beak, for example, might be better able to crack nuts and get at their meat than finches with other shapes of beaks. More finches who have beaks better shaped for nut cracking survive than those with beaks poorly shaped for nut cracking.

An organism can survive for many years, however, and still not pass on its inherited qualities to future generations. To pass its inherited qualities to future generations, it must reproduce. Thus, *differential reproductive success*, brought about by the possession of heritable variants that increase or decrease an individual's chances of surviving and reproducing, is the "bottom line" of evolution by natural selection. Differential reproductive success or failure is defined by reproductive success relative to others. The characteristics of organisms that reproduce more than others, therefore, get passed down to future generations at a relatively greater frequency. Because survival is usually necessary for reproduction, it took on a critical role in Darwin's theory of natural selection.

## Darwin's Theory of Sexual Selection

Darwin had a wonderful scientific habit of noticing facts that seemed inconsistent with his theories. He observed several that seemed to contradict his theory of natural selection, also called "survival selection." First he noticed weird structures that seemed to have absolutely nothing to do with survival; the brilliant plumage of peacocks was a prime example. How could this strange luminescent structure possibly have evolved? The plumage is obviously metabolically costly to the peacock. Furthermore, it seems like an open invitation to predators. Darwin became so obsessed with this apparent anomaly that he once commented, "The sight of a feather in a peacock's tail, whenever I gaze at it makes me sick!" (quoted in Cronin, 1991, p. 113). Darwin also observed that in some species, the sexes differed dramatically in size and structure. Why would the sexes differ so much, Darwin pondered, when both have essentially the same problems of survival, such as eating, fending off predators, and combating diseases?

*Darwin got sick at the sight of a peacock because, initially, the brilliant plumage seemed to have no obvious survival value and hence could not be explained by his original theory of natural selection. He eventually developed the theory of sexual selection, which could explain the peacock's plumage, and presumably he stopped getting sick when he witnessed one.*

Darwin's answer to these apparent embarrassments to the theory of natural selection was to devise a second evolutionary theory: the theory of *sexual selection.* In contrast to the theory of natural selection, which focused on adaptations that have arisen as a consequence of successful survival, the theory of sexual selection focused on adaptations that arose as a consequence of successful mating. Darwin envisioned two primary means by which sexual selection could operate. The first is *intrasexual competition*—competition between members of one sex, the outcomes of which contributed to mating access to the other sex. The prototype of intrasexual competition is two stags locking horns in combat. The victor gains

*Stags locking horns in combat is a form of sexual selection called intrasexual competition. The qualities that lead to success in these same-sex combats get passed on in greater numbers to succeeding generations because the victors gain increased mating access to members of the opposite sex.*

sexual access to a female either directly or through controlling territory or resources desired by the female. The loser typically fails to mate. Whatever qualities lead to success in the same-sex contests, such as greater size, strength, or athletic ability, will be passed on to the next generation by virtue of the mating success of the victors. Qualities that are linked with losing fail to get passed on. So evolution—change over time—can occur simply as a consequence of intrasexual competition.

The second means by which sexual selection could operate is *intersexual selection*, or preferential mate choice. If members of one sex have some consensus about the qualities that are desired in members of the opposite sex, then individuals of the opposite sex who possess those qualities will be preferentially chosen as mates. Those who lack the desired qualities fail to get mates. In this case, evolutionary change occurs simply because the qualities that are desired in a mate increase in frequency with the passing of each generation. If females prefer to mate with males who give them nuptial gifts, for example, then males with qualities that lead to success in acquiring nuptial gifts will increase in frequency over time. Darwin called the process of intersexual selection *female choice* because he observed that throughout the animal world, females of many species were discriminating or choosy about whom they mated with.

Darwin's theory of sexual selection succeeded in explaining the anomalies that worried him. The peacock's tail, for example, evolved because of the process of intersexual selection: Peahens prefer to mate with males who have the most brilliant and luminescent plumage. Males are often larger than females in species in which males engage in physical combat with other males for sexual access to females—the process of intrasexual competition.

## The Role of Natural Selection and Sexual Selection in Evolutionary Theory

Darwin's theories of natural and sexual selection are relatively simple to describe, but many sources of confusion surround them even to this day. This section clarifies some important aspects of selection and its place in understanding evolution.

First, natural selection and sexual selection are not the only causes of evolutionary change. Some changes, for example, can occur because of a process called *genetic drift*, which is defined as random changes in the genetic makeup of a population. Random changes come about through several processes, including mutation (a random hereditary change in the DNA), founder effects, and genetic bottlenecks. Random changes can arise through a *founder effect*, which occurs when a small portion of a population establishes a new colony and the founders of the new colony are not entirely genetically representative of the original population. Imagine, for example, that the 200 colonizers who migrate to a new island happen by chance to include an unusually large number of redheads. As the population on the island grows, say, to 2,000 people, it will contain a larger proportion of redheads than did the original population from which the colonizers came. Thus, founder effects can produce evolutionary change—in this example, an increase in genes coding for red hair. A similar random change can occur through genetic bottlenecks, which happen when a population shrinks, perhaps owing to a random catastrophe such as an earthquake. The survivors of the random catastrophe carry only a subset of the genes of the original population. In sum, although natural selection is the *primary* cause of evolutionary change and the only known cause of adaptations, it is not the only cause of evolutionary change. Genetic drift—through mutations, founder effects, and genetic bottlenecks—can also produce change in the genetic makeup of a population.

Second, evolution by natural selection is not forward-looking and is not "intentional." The giraffe does not spy the juicy leaves stirring high in the tree and "evolve" a longer neck. Rather, those giraffes that, owing to an inherited variant, happen to have longer necks have an advantage over other giraffes in getting to those leaves. Hence they have a greater chance of surviving and thus of passing on their slightly longer necks to their offspring. Natural selection merely acts on those variants that happen to exist. Evolution is not intentional and cannot look into the future and foresee distant needs.

Another critical feature of selection is that it is *gradual*, at least when evaluated relative to the human life span. The short-necked ancestors of giraffes did not evolve long necks overnight or even over the course of a few generations. It has taken dozens, hundreds, thousands, and in some cases millions of generations for the process of selection to gradually shape the organic mechanisms we see today. Of course, some changes occur extremely slowly, others more rapidly. And there can be long periods of no change, followed by a relatively sudden change, a phenomenon known as "punctuated equilibrium" (Gould & Eldredge, 1977). But even these "rapid" changes occur in tiny increments in each generation and take hundreds or thousands of generations to occur.

Darwin's theory of natural selection offered a powerful explanation for many baffling aspects of life, especially the origin of new species (although Darwin failed to recognize the full importance of geographic isolation as a precursor to natural selection in the formation of new species; see Cronin, 1991). It accounted for the modification of organic structures over time. It also accounted for the apparent purposive quality of the component parts of those structures—that is, they seem "designed" to serve particular functions linked with survival and reproduction.

Perhaps most astonishing to some (but appalling to others), in 1859 Darwin's natural selection united all species into one grand tree of descent in one bold stroke. For the first time in recorded history, each species was viewed as being connected with all other species through a common ancestry. Human beings and chimpanzees, for example, share more than

98 percent of each other's DNA and shared a common ancestor roughly 6 million years ago (Wrangham & Peterson, 1996). Even more startling is the finding that many human genes turn out to have counterpart genes in a transparent worm called *Caenorhabditis elegans*. They are highly similar in chemical structure, suggesting that humans and this worm evolved from a distant common ancestor (Wade, 1997). In short, Darwin's theory made it possible to locate humans in the grand tree of life, showing their place in nature and their links with all other living creatures.

Darwin's theory of natural selection created a storm of controversy. Lady Ashley, a contemporary of Darwin, remarked on hearing his theory that human beings descended from apes: "Let's hope it's not true; but if it is true, let's hope that it does not become widely known." In a famous debate at Oxford University, Bishop Wilberforce bitingly asked his rival debater Thomas Huxley whether the "ape" from which Huxley descended was on his grandmother's or his grandfather's side.

Even biologists at the time were highly skeptical of Darwin's theory of natural selection. One objection was that Darwinian evolution lacked a coherent theory of inheritance. Darwin himself preferred a "blending" theory of inheritance, in which offspring are mixtures of their parents, much like pink paint is a mixture of red paint and white paint. This theory of inheritance is now known to be wrong, so early critics were correct in the objection that the theory of natural selection lacked a solid theory of heredity.

Another objection was that some biologists could not imagine how the early stages of the evolution of an adaptation could be useful to an organism. How could a partial wing help a bird, if a partial wing is insufficient for flight? How could a partial eye help a reptile, if a partial eye is insufficient for sight? Darwin's theory of natural selection requires that each and every step in the gradual evolution of an adaptation be advantageous in the currency of reproduction. Thus, partial wings and eyes must yield an adaptive advantage, even before they evolve into fully developed wings and eyes. For now, it is sufficient to note that partial forms can indeed offer adaptive advantages; partial wings, for example, can keep a bird warm and aid in mobility for catching prey or avoiding predators, even if they don't afford full flight. This objection to Darwin's theory is therefore surmountable (Dawkins, 1986). Further, it is important to stress that just because biologists or other scientists have difficulty imagining certain forms of evolution, such as how a partial wing might be useful, that is not a good argument against such forms having evolved. This "argument from ignorance," or as Dawkins (1982) calls it, "the argument from personal incredulity," is not good science, however intuitively compelling it might sound.

A third objection came from religious creationists, many of whom viewed species as immutable (unchanging) and created by a deity rather than by the gradual process of evolution by selection. Furthermore, Darwin's theory implied that the emergence of humans and other species was "blind," resulting from the slow, unplanned, cumulative process of selection. This contrasted with the view that creationists held of humans (and other species) as part of God's grand plan or intentional design. Darwin had anticipated this reaction, and apparently delayed the publication of his theory in part because he was worried about upsetting his wife, Emma, who was deeply religious.

The controversy continues to this day. Although Darwin's theory of evolution, with some important modifications, is the unifying and nearly universally accepted theory within the biological sciences, its application to humans, which Darwin clearly envisioned, still meets some resistance. But humans are not exempt from the evolutionary process. We finally have the conceptual tools to complete Darwin's revolution and forge an evolutionary psychology of the human species.

Evolutionary psychology is able to take advantage of key theoretical insights and scientific discoveries that were not known in Darwin's day. The first among these is the physical basis of inheritance—the gene.

## The Modern Synthesis: Genes and Particulate Inheritance

When Darwin published *On the Origin of Species*, he did not know the nature of the mechanism by which inheritance occurred. An Austrian monk named Gregor Mendel showed that inheritance was "particulate," and not blended. That is, the qualities of the parents are not blended with each other, but rather are passed on intact to their offspring in distinct packets called *genes*. Furthermore, parents must be born with the genes they pass on; genes cannot be acquired by experience.

Mendel's discovery that inheritance is particulate, which he demonstrated by crossbreeding different strains of pea plants, remained unknown to most of the scientific community for some thirty years. Mendel had sent Darwin copies of his papers, but either they remained unread or their significance was not recognized.

A *gene* is defined as the smallest discrete unit that is inherited by offspring intact, without being broken up or blended—this was Mendel's critical insight. *Genotypes*, in contrast, refer to the entire collection of genes within an individual. Genotypes, unlike genes, are not passed down to offspring intact. Rather, in sexually reproducing species such as our own, genotypes are broken up with each generation. Thus, each of us inherits a random half of genes from our mother's genotype and a random half from our father's genotype. The specific half of the genes we inherit from each parent, however, is identical to half of those possessed by that parent because they get transmitted as a discrete bundle, without modification.

The unification of Darwin's theory of evolution by natural selection with the discovery of particulate gene inheritance culminated in a movement in the 1930s and 1940s called the "Modern Synthesis" (Dobzhansky, 1937; Huxley, 1942; Mayr, 1942; Simpson, 1944). The Modern Synthesis discarded a number of misconceptions in biology, including Lamarck's theory of inheritance of acquired characteristics and the blending theory of inheritance. It confirmed the importance of Darwin's theory of natural selection, but put it on a firmer footing with a well-articulated understanding of the nature of inheritance.

## The Ethology Movement

To some people, evolution is most clearly envisioned when it applies to physical structures. We can easily see how a turtle's shell is an adaptation for protection and a bird's wings an adaptation for flight. We recognize similarities between ourselves and chimpanzees, and so most people find it relatively easy to believe that human beings and chimps have a common ancestry. The paleontological record of skulls, although incomplete, shows enough evidence of physical evolution that most concede reveals that change has taken place over time. The evolution of behavior, however, has historically been more difficult for scientists and laypeople to imagine. Behavior, after all, leaves no fossils.

Darwin clearly envisioned his theory of natural selection as being just as applicable to behavior, including social behavior, as to physical structures. Several lines of evidence support this view. First, all behavior requires underlying physical structures. Bipedal locomotion is a behavior, for example, and requires the physical structures of two legs and a multitude of muscles to support those legs. Second, species can be bred for certain behavioral characteristics using the principle of selection. Dogs, for example, can be bred (artificial selection) for aggressiveness or passivity. These lines of evidence all point to the conclusion that behavior is not exempt from the sculpting hand of evolution. The first major discipline to form around the study of behavior from an evolutionary perspective was the field of ethology, and one of the first phenomena the ethologists documented was imprinting.

Ducklings *imprint* on the first moving object they observe in life—forming an association during a critical period of development. Usually this object is the duck's mother. After imprinting, the baby ducks follow the object of their imprinting wherever it goes. Imprinting is clearly a form of learning—an association is formed between the duckling and the mother that was not there before the exposure to her motion. This form of learning, however, is "preprogrammed" and clearly part of the evolved structures of the duckling's biology. Although many have seen pictures of a line of baby ducks following their mother, the fact is that if the first object a duck sees is a human leg, it will follow that person instead. Konrad Lorenz was the first to demonstrate this imprinting phenomenon by showing that baby ducks would follow him rather than their mother if exposed to his leg during the critical period shortly after birth. Lorenz (1965) started a new branch of evolutionary biology called *ethology*, and imprinting in birds was a vivid phenomenon used to launch this new field. Ethology is defined as "the study of the proximate mechanisms and adaptive value of animal behavior" (Alcock, 1989, p. 548).

The ethology movement was in part a reaction to the extreme environmentalism in U.S. psychology. Ethologists were interested in four key issues, which have become known as the four "whys" of behavior advanced by one of the founders of ethology, Nikolaas Tinbergen (1951): (1) the *immediate influences* on behavior (e.g., the movement of the mother); (2) the

... was one of the founders Konrad ... ethology. He is most well of th ... r discovering the phenomenon ... inting, whereby ducklings will ... me attached to, and follow, the first ... ject they see moving. In most cases, ducklings get imprinted on their mothers, not the legs of a scientist.

*developmental influences* on behavior (e.g., the events during the duck's lifetime that cause changes); (3) the *function* of behavior, or the "adaptive purpose" it fulfills (e.g., keeping the baby duck close to the mother, which helps it to survive), and (4) the *evolutionary* or *phylogenetic origins* of behavior (e.g., what sequence of evolutionary events led to the origins of an imprinting mechanism in the duck).

Ethologists developed an array of concepts to describe what they believed to be the innate properties of animals. *Fixed action patterns,* for example, are the stereotypic behavioral sequences an animal follows after being triggered by a well-defined stimulus (Tinbergen, 1951). Once a fixed action pattern is triggered, the animal performs it to completion. Showing certain male ducks a plastic facsimile of a female duck, for example, will trigger a rigid sequence of courting behavior. Concepts such as fixed action patterns were useful in allowing ethologists to partition the ongoing stream of behavior into discrete units for analysis.

The ethology movement went a long way toward orienting biologists to focus on the importance of adaptation. Indeed, the glimmerings of evolutionary psychology itself may be seen in the early writings of Lorenz, who wrote, "our cognitive and perceptual categories, given to us prior to individual experience, are adapted to the environment for the same reasons that the horse's hoof is suited for the plains before the horse is born, and the fin of a fish is adapted for water before the fish hatches from its egg" (Lorenz, 1941, p. 99; translated from the original German by I. Eibl-Eibesfeldt, 1989, p. 8).

Ethology also forced psychologists to reconsider the role of biology in the study of human behavior. This set the stage for an important scientific revolution, brought about by a fundamental reformulation of Darwin's theory of natural selection.

*William D. Hamilton revolu[...] evolutionary biology with his [...] inclusive fitness, published in 19[...] continued to make profound theore[...] contributions on topics as diverse as the evolution of spite and the origins of sexual reproduction.*

## The Inclusive Fitness Revolution

In the early 1960s, a young graduate student named William D. Hamilton was working on his doctoral dissertation at University College, London. Hamilton proposed a radical new revision of evolutionary theory, which he termed "inclusive fitness theory." Legend has it that his professors failed to understand the dissertation or its significance (perhaps because it was highly mathematical), and so his work was initially rejected. When it was finally accepted and published in 1964 in the *Journal of Theoretical Biology*, however, Hamilton's theory sparked a revolution that transformed the entire field of biology.

Hamilton reasoned that *classical fitness*—the measure of an individual's direct reproductive success in passing on genes through the production of offspring—was too narrow to describe the process of evolution by selection. He theorized that natural selection favors characteristics that cause an organism's genes to be passed on, regardless of whether the organism produces offspring directly. [...]tal care—investing in one's own children—was rein[...]d as merely a special case of caring for kin who [...]s of parent's genes in their bodies. An organism can also increase the reproduction of its genes by helping brothers, sisters, nieces, or nephews to survive and reproduce. All these relatives have some probability of carrying copies of the organism's genes. Hamilton's genius was in the recognition that the definition of classical fitness was too narrow and should be broadened to be *inclusive fitness.*

Technically, inclusive fitness is not a property of an individual or an organism but rather a property of its *actions* or *effects.* Thus, inclusive fitness can be viewed as the sum of an individual's own reproductive success (classical fitness) *plus the effects* the individual's actions have on the re-productive success of his or her genetic relatives. For this second component, the effects on relatives must be weighted by the appropriate degree of genetic relatedness to the target organism—for example, 0.50 for brothers and sisters (because they are genetically related by 50 percent with the target organism), 0.25 for grandparents and grandchildren (25 percent genetic relatedness), 0.125 for first cousins (12.5 percent genetic relatedness), and so on (see Figure 1.1).

The inclusive fitness revolution marshaled a new era that may be called "gene's eye thinking." If you were a gene, what would facilitate your replication? First, you might try to ensure the well-being of the "vehicle" or body in which you reside (survival). Second, you might try to induce the vehicle to reproduce. Third, you might want to help the survival and reproduction of vehicles that contain copies of you. Genes, of course, do not have thoughts,

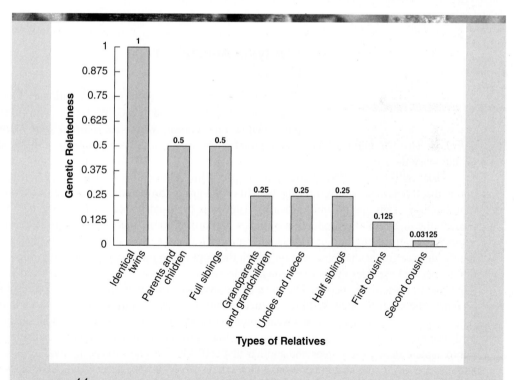

FIGURE *1.1* **Genetic Relatedness among Different Types of Relatives.** One implication of inclusive fitness theory is that acts of altruism will be directed more toward closely related individuals than more distantly related individuals.

*George C. Williams was one of the most important biologists of the twentieth century. His book* Adaptation and Natural Selection *is most widely known for the downfall of group selection, clarifying the central evolutionary concept of adaptation and marshaling new thinking based on genic-level selection.*

and none of this occurs with consciousness or intentionality. The key point is that the gene is the fundamental unit of inheritance, the unit that is passed on intact in the process of reproduction. Genes producing effects that increase their replicative success will replace other genes, producing evolution over time. Adaptations are selected and evolve because they promote inclusive fitness.

Thinking about selection from the perspective of the gene offered a wealth of insights unknown in Darwin's day (Buss, 2009a). The theory of inclusive fitness has profound consequences for how we think about the psychology of the family, altruism, helping, the formation of groups, and even aggression—topics we explore in later chapters. As for W. D. Hamilton himself, after a stint at the University of Michigan, Oxford University made him an offer he couldn't refuse. Unfortunately, Hamilton met an untimely death in 2000 from a disease acquired in the Congo jungle, where he had traveled to gather evidence for a novel theory on the origins of the virus that causes AIDS.

## Clarifying Adaptation and Natural Selection

The rapid inclusive fitness revolution in evolutionary biology owes part of its debt to George C. Williams, who in 1966 published a now-classic work, *Adaptation and Natural Selection*. This seminal book contributed to at least three key shifts in thinking in the field of evolutionary theory.

First, Williams (1966) challenged the prevailing endorsement of *group selection*, the notion that adaptations evolved for the benefit of the group through the differential survival and reproduction of groups (Wynne-Edwards, 1962), as opposed to benefit for the gene arising through the differential reproduction of genes. According to the theory of group selection, for example, an animal might limit its personal reproduction to keep the population low, thus avoiding the destruction of the food base on which the population relied. According to group selection theory, only species that possessed characteristics beneficial to their group survived. Those that acted more selfishly perished because of the overexploitation of the critical food resources on which the species relied. Williams argued persuasively that group selection, although theoretically possible, was likely to be a weak force in evolution, for the following reason. Imagine a bird species with two types of individuals—one that sacrifices itself by committing suicide so as not to deplete its food resources and another that selfishly continues to eat the food, even when supplies are low. In the next generation, which type is likely to have descendants? The answer is that the suicidal birds will have died out and failed to reproduce, whereas those who refused to sacrifice themselves for the group will have survived and left descendants. Selection operating on individual differences *within* a group, in other words, undermines the power of selection operating at the level of the group. Within five years of the book's publication, most biologists had relinquished their subscription to group selection, although recently there has been a resurgence of interest in the potential potency of group selection (Sober & Wilson, 1998; Wilson, Van Vugt, & O'Gorman, 2008; Wilson & Sober, 1994).

Williams's second contribution was in translating Hamilton's highly quantitative theory of inclusive fitness into clear prose that could be comprehended by everyone. Once biologists understood inclusive fitness, they began vigorously researching its implications. To mention one prominent example, inclusive fitness theory partially solved the "problem of altruism": How could altruism evolve—incurring reproductive costs to oneself to benefit the reproduction of others—if evolution favors genes that have the effect of self-replication? Inclusive fitness theory solved this problem (in part) because altruism could evolve if the recipients of help were one's genetic kin. Parents, for example, might sacrifice their own lives to save the lives of their children, who carry copies of the parents' genes within them. The same logic applies to making sacrifices for other genetic relatives, such as sisters or cousins. The benefit to one's relatives in fitness currencies must be greater than the costs to the self. If this condition is satisfied, then kin altruism can evolve. In later chapters, we review evidence showing that genetic relatedness is indeed a powerful predictor of helping among humans.

The third contribution of *Adaptation and Natural Selection* was Williams's careful analysis of adaptation, which he referred to as "an onerous concept." *Adaptations* may be defined as evolved solutions to specific problems that contribute either directly or indirectly to successful reproduction. Sweat glands, for example, may be adaptations that help solve the survival problem of thermal regulation. Taste preferences may be adaptations that guide the successful consumption of nutritious food. Mate preferences may be adaptations that guide the successful selection of mates. The problem is how to determine which attributes of organisms are adaptations. Williams established several standards for invoking adaptation and believed that it should be invoked only when necessary to explain the phenomenon at hand. When a flying fish leaps out of a wave and falls back into the water, for example, we do not have to invoke an adaptation for "getting back to water." This behavior is explained more simply by the physical law of gravity.

Williams provided criteria for determining when we should invoke the concept of adaptation: *reliability, efficiency*, and *economy*. Does the mechanism regularly develop in most or all members of the species across all "normal" environments and perform dependably in the contexts in which it is designed to function (reliability)? Does the mechanism solve a particular adaptive problem well (efficiency)? Does the mechanism solve the adaptive problem without extorting huge costs from the organism (economy)? In other words, adaptation is invoked not merely to explain the usefulness of a biological mechanism, but to explain *improbable usefulness* (i.e., too precisely functional to have arisen by chance alone) (Pinker, 1997). Hypotheses about adaptations are, in essence, probability statements about why a reliable, efficient, and economic set of design features could not have arisen by chance alone (Tooby & Cosmides, 1992, 2005; Williams, 1966).

In Chapter 2, we explore the key concept of adaptation in greater depth. For now, it is sufficient to note that Williams's book brought the scientific community one step closer to the Darwinian revolution by creating the downfall of group selection as a preferred and dominant explanation, by illuminating Hamilton's theory of inclusive fitness, and by putting the concept of adaptation on a more rigorous and scientific footing. Williams was extremely influential in showing that understanding adaptations requires being "gene-centered." As put eloquently by Helena Cronin in a recent volume dedicated to George Williams, "The purpose of adaptations is to further the replication of genes. . . . Genes have been designed by natural selection to exploit properties of the world that promote their self-replication; genes are ultimately machines for turning out more genes" (Cronin, 2005, pp. 19–20).

## Trivers's Seminal Theories

In the late 1960s and early 1970s, a graduate student at Harvard University, Robert Trivers, studied William's 1966 book on adaptation. He was struck by the revolutionary consequences that gene-level thinking had for conceptualizing entire domains. A sentence or brief paragraph in Williams's book or Hamilton's articles might contain the seed of an idea that could blossom into a full theory if nurtured properly.

Trivers contributed three seminal papers, all published in the early 1970s. The first was the theory of reciprocal altruism among nonkin—the conditions under which mutually beneficial exchange relationships or transactions could evolve (Trivers, 1971). The second was parental investment theory, which provided a powerful statement of the conditions under which sexual selection would occur for each sex (1972). The third was the theory of parent–offspring conflict—the notion that even parents and their progeny will get into predictable sorts of conflicts because they share only 50 percent of their genes (1974). Parents may try to wean children before the children want to be weaned, for example, in order to free up resources to invest in other children. More generally, what might be optimal for a child (e.g., securing a larger share of parental resources) might not be optimal for the parents (e.g., distributing resources more equally across children). We explore these theories in greater depth in Chapter 4 (theory of parental investment), Chapter 7 (theory of parent–offspring conflict), and Chapter 9 (theory of reciprocal altruism) because they have influenced literally thousands of empirical research projects, including many on humans.

*Robert Trivers is most well known for theories that provide the foundation of several chapters of this book—the theory of parental investment (Chapter 4), the theory of parent–offspring conflict (Chapter 7), and the theory of reciprocal altruism (Chapter 9).*

## The Sociobiology Controversy

Eleven years after Hamilton's pivotal paper on inclusive fitness was published, a Harvard biologist named Edward O. Wilson caused a scientific and public uproar that rivaled the outrage caused by Charles Darwin in 1859. Wilson's 1975 book, *Sociobiology: The New Synthesis*, was monumental in both size and scope, at nearly 700 double-column pages. It offered a synthesis of cellular biology, integrative neurophysiology, ethology, comparative psychology, population biology, and behavioral ecology. Further, it examined species from ants to humans, proclaiming that the same fundamental explanatory principles could be applied to all.

*Sociobiology* is not generally regarded as containing fundamentally new theoretical contributions to evolutionary theory. The bulk of its theoretical tools—such as inclusive fitness theory, parental investment theory, parent–offspring conflict theory, and reciprocal altruism theory—had already been developed by others (Hamilton, 1964; Trivers, 1972, 1974). What it did do is synthesize under one umbrella a tremendous diversity of scientific endeavors and give the emerging field a visible name.

The chapter on humans, the last in Wilson's book and running a mere twenty-nine pages, created the most controversy. At public talks, audience members shouted him down, and once a pitcher of water was dumped on his head. His work sparked attacks from Marxists, radicals, creationists, other scientists, and even members of his own department at Harvard. Part of the controversy stemmed from the nature of Wilson's claims. He asserted that sociobiology would "cannibalize psychology," which of course was not greeted with warmth by most psychologists. Further, he speculated that many cherished human phenomena, such as culture, religion, ethics, and even aesthetics, would ultimately be explained by the new synthesis. These assertions strongly contradicted the dominant theories in the social sciences. Culture, learning, socialization, rationality, and consciousness, not evolutionary biology, were presumed by most social scientists to explain the uniqueness of humans.

Despite Wilson's grand claims for a new synthesis that would explain human nature, he had little empirical evidence on humans to support his views. The bulk of the scientific evidence came from nonhuman animals, many far removed phylogenetically from humans. Most social scientists could not see what ants and fruit flies had to do with people. Although scientific revolutions always meet resistance, often from within the ranks of established scientists (Sulloway, 1996), Wilson's lack of relevant scientific data on humans did not help.

Furthermore, the tremendous resistance to Wilson's inclusion of humans within the purview of evolutionary theory was based on several common misunderstandings about evolutionary theory and its application to humans. It is worth highlighting a few of these before turning to movements within psychology that laid the groundwork for evolutionary psychology.

## ■ COMMON MISUNDERSTANDINGS ABOUT EVOLUTIONARY THEORY

The theory of evolution by selection, although elegant in its simplicity, generates a number of common misunderstandings (Confer et al., 2010). Perhaps its very simplicity leads people to think that they can understand it completely after only brief exposure to it—after reading an article or two in the popular press, for example. Even professors and researchers in the field sometimes get mired in these misunderstandings.

### Misunderstanding 1: Human Behavior Is Genetically Determined

*Genetic determinism* is the doctrine that argues that behavior is controlled exclusively by genes, with little or no role for environmental influence. Much of the resistance to applying evolutionary theory to the understanding of human behavior stems from the misconception that evolutionary theory implies genetic determinism. Contrary to this misunderstanding, evolutionary theory represents a truly interactionist framework. Human behavior cannot occur without two ingredients: (1) evolved adaptations and (2) environmental input that triggers the development and activation of these adaptations. Consider calluses as an illustration. Calluses cannot occur without an evolved callus-producing adaptation, combined with the environmental influence of repeated friction to the skin. Therefore to invoke evolutionary theory as an explanation for calluses, we would never say "calluses are genetically determined and occur regardless of input from the environment." Instead, calluses are the result of a specific form of interaction between an environmental input (repeated friction to the skin) and an adaptation that is sensitive to repeated friction and contains instructions to grow extra new skin cells when the skin experiences repeated friction. Indeed, the reason that adaptations evolve is that they afford organisms tools to grapple with the problems posed by the environment.

So notions of genetic determinism—behaviors caused by genes without input or influence from the environment—are simply false. They are in no way implied by the evolutionary theory.

## Misunderstanding 2: If It's Evolutionary, We Can't Change It

A second misunderstanding is that evolutionary theory implies that human behavior is impervious to change. Consider the simple example of calluses again. Humans can and do create physical environments that are relatively free of friction. These friction-free environments mean that we have designed change—a change that prevents the activation of the underlying callus-producing mechanisms. Knowledge of these mechanisms and the environmental input that triggers their activation give us the power to decrease callus production.

In a similar manner, knowledge of our evolved social psychological adaptations along with the social inputs that activate them gives us power to alter social behavior, if that is the desired goal. Consider the following example. There is evidence that men have lower thresholds than women for inferring sexual intent. When a woman smiles at a man, male observers are more likely than female observers to infer that the woman is sexually interested (Abbey, 1982). This is most likely part of an evolved psychological mechanism in men that motivates them to seek casual sexual opportunities (Buss, 2003).

Knowledge of this mechanism, however, allows for the possibility of change. Men, for example, can be educated with the information that they have lower thresholds for inferring sexual intent when a woman smiles at them. This knowledge can then be used by men, in principle, to reduce the number of times they act on their faulty inferences of sexual interest and decrease the number of unwanted sexual advances they make toward women.

Knowledge about our evolved psychological adaptations along with the social inputs that they were designed to be responsive to, far from dooming us to an unchangeable fate, can have the liberating effect of changing behavior in areas in which change is desired. This does *not* mean that changing behavior is simple or easy. More knowledge about our evolved psychology, however, gives us more power to change.

## Misunderstanding 3: Current Mechanisms Are Optimally Designed

The concept of adaptation, the notion that mechanisms have evolved functions, has led to many outstanding discoveries over the past century (Dawkins, 1982). This does not mean, however, that the current collection of adaptive mechanisms that make up humans is in any way "optimally designed." An engineer might cringe at some of the ways that our mechanisms are structured, which sometimes appear to be assembled with a piece here and a bit there. In fact, many factors cause the existing design of our adaptations to be far from optimal. Let's consider two of them (see Dawkins, 1982, Chapter 3).

One constraint on optimal design is *evolutionary time lags*. Recall that evolution refers to change over time. Each change in the environment brings new selection pressures. Because evolutionary change occurs slowly, requiring thousands of generations of recurrent selection pressure, existing humans are necessarily designed for the previous environments of which they are a product. Stated differently, we carry around a Stone Age brain in a modern environment. A strong desire for fat, adaptive in a past environment of scarce food resources, now leads to clogged arteries and heart attacks. The lag in time between the environment that fashioned our mechanisms (the hunter-gatherer past that formed much of our selective environment) and today's environment means that our existing evolved mechanisms may not be optimally designed for the current environment.

A second constraint on optimal design pertains to the *costs of adaptations*. Consider as an analogy the risk of being killed while driving a car. In principle, we could reduce this risk to near zero if we imposed a ten-mile-per-hour speed limit and forced everyone to drive in armored trucks with ten feet of padding on the inside (Symons, 1993). But we consider the costs of this solution to be ridiculously high. Similarly, we might consider a hypothetical example in which natural selection built into humans such a severe terror of snakes that people never ventured outdoors. Such a fear would surely reduce the incidence of snake bites, but it would carry a prohibitively high cost. Further, it would prevent people from solving other adaptive problems, such as gathering fruits, plants, and other food resources necessary for survival. In short, the existing fear of snakes that characterizes humans is not optimally designed—after all, thousands of people do get bitten by snakes every year, and some die as a result. But it works reasonably well, on average.

All adaptations carry costs. Selection favors a mechanism when the benefits outweigh the costs relative to other designs. Thus we have evolved mechanisms that are reasonably good at solving adaptive problems efficiently, but they are not designed as optimally as they might be if costs were not a constraint. Evolutionary time lags and the costs of adaptations are just two of the many reasons why adaptations are not optimally designed (Williams, 1992).

In summary, part of the resistance to the application of evolutionary theory to humans is based on several common misconceptions. Contrary to these misconceptions, evolutionary theory does not imply genetic determinism. It does not imply that we are powerless to change things. It does not mean that our existing adaptations are optimally designed. With these common misunderstandings about evolutionary theory clarified, let's turn now to the origins of modern humans, the development of the field of psychology, and an examination of the landmarks that led to the emergence of evolutionary psychology.

## ■ MILESTONES IN THE ORIGINS OF MODERN HUMANS

One of the most fascinating endeavors for those struggling to understand the modern human mind is to explore what is known about the critical historical developments that eventually contributed to who we are today. Table 1.1 shows some of these milestones. The first interesting item to note is the enormity of the timescale. It took roughly 3.7 billion years to get from the origins of the first life on earth to modern humans in the twenty-first century.

TABLE *1.1* **Milestones in Human Evolutionary History**

| Time | Event |
|------|-------|
| 15 billion years ago (bya) | The Big Bang—Origin of Universe |
| 4.7 bya | Earth forms |
| 3.7 bya | First life emerges |
| 1.2 bya | Sexual reproduction evolves |
| 500–450 million years ago (mya) | First vertebrates |
| 365 mya | Fish evolve lungs and walk on land |
| 248–208 mya | First small mammals and dinosaurs evolved |
| 208–65 mya | Large dinosaurs flourished |
| 114 mya | Placental mammals evolve |
| 85 mya | First primates evolve |
| 65 mya | Dinosaurs go extinct; mammals then increase in size and diversity |
| 35 mya | First apes evolve |
| 6–8 mya | Common ancestor of humans and African apes evolves |
| 4.4 mya | First primate with bipedal locomotion (*Ardipithecus ramidus*) evolves |
| 3.0 mya | The australopithecines evolve in savannas of Africa |
| 2.5 mya | Earliest stone tools developed—Oldowan (found in Ethiopia and Kenya, Africa); used to butcher carcasses for meat and to extract marrow from bones; linked with *Homo habilis* |
| 1.8 mya | Hominids (*Homo erectus*) spread beyond Africa to Asia—first major migration |
| 1.6 mya | Fire evidence; likely hearths; linked with African *Homo erectus* |
| 1.5 mya | Invention of Acheulean hand axe; linked with *Homo ergaster*—tall stature, long limbs |
| 1.2 mya | Brain expansion in *Homo* line begins |
| 1.0 mya | Hominids spread to Europe |
| 800 thousand years ago (kya) | Crude stone tool kit used—found in Spain, linked with *Homo antecessor* |
| 600–400 kya | Long, crafted wooden spears and early hearths used; linked with *Homo heidelbergensis* found in Germany |
| 500–100 kya | Period of most rapid brain expansion in *Homo* line |
| 200–30 kya | Neanderthals flourish in Europe and western Asia |
| 150–120 kya | Common ancestor for all modern humans (Africa) evolved |
| 100–50 kya | Exodus from Africa—second major migration ["Out of Africa"] |
| 50–35 kya | Explosion of diverse stone tools, bone tools, blade tools, well-designed fireplaces, elaborate art; found only among *Homo sapiens*, not among Neanderthals |
| 40–35 kya | *Homo sapiens* (Cro-Magnons) arrive in Europe |
| 30 kya | Neanderthals go extinct |
| 27 kya–present | *Homo sapiens* colonize entire planet; all other hominid species are now extinct |

*Note:* These dates are based in part on information from a variety of sources, including Johanson & Edgar (1996), Klein (2000), Lewin (1993), Tattersall (2000), Wrangham, Jones, Laden, Pilbeam, & Conklin-Brittain (1999), and the references contained therein.

Humans are *mammals;* the first mammals originated more than 200 million years ago. Mammals are warm-blooded, having evolved mechanisms that regulate internal body temperature to maintain a constant warm level despite environmental perturbations. Warm-bloodedness gave mammals the advantage of being able to run metabolic processes at a constant temperature. Except for some marine mammals such as whales, mammals are usually covered with fur, an adaptation that helps to keep body temperature constant. Mammals are also distinguished by a unique method of feeding their young: through secretions via mammary glands. Indeed, the term *mammal* comes from "mamma," the Latin word for *breast.* Mammary glands exist in both males and females but become functional for feeding only in females. Human breasts are merely one modern form of an adaptation whose origins can be traced back more than 200 million years. Another major development was the evolution of placental mammals around 114 million years ago, as contrasted with egg-laying nonplacentals. In placental mammals, the fetus attaches to the mother inside her uterus through a placenta, which allows the direct delivery of nutrients. The fetus remains attached to the mother's placenta until it is born alive, unlike its egg-laying predecessors, whose prebirth development was limited by the amount of nutrients that could be stored in an egg. These initially small, warm-blooded, furry mammals began a line that eventually led to modern humans.

Roughly 85 million years ago, a new line of mammals evolved: *primates.* Early primates were small, perhaps the size of squirrels. They developed hands and feet that contained nails instead of claws and opposable digits on hands (and sometimes feet) that enabled increased grasping and manipulative abilities. Primates have well-developed stereoscopic vision with eyes facing forward, which gave them an advantage in jumping from branch to branch. Their brains are large in relation to their bodies (compared to nonprimate mammals), and their mammary glands have been reduced to two (rather than several pairs).

One of the most critical developments of the primate line that led to modern humans occurred roughly 4.4 million years ago: *bipedal locomotion*, the ability to walk, stride, and run on two feet rather than on four. Although no one knows the precise evolutionary impetus for bipedalism, it undoubtedly offered a bounty of benefits on the African savanna where it evolved. It afforded the ability to rapidly cover long distances in an energetically efficient manner, enabled a greater visual angle for the detection of predators and prey, decreased the surface area of the body that was pelted by harmful sun rays, and freed up the hands. The liberation of hands from the work of walking not only enabled this early ancestor to carry food from place to place, but also opened up a niche for the subsequent evolution of tool making and tool use. It is in these bipedal primates that we first recognize the glimmerings of early humans (see Figure 1.2). Many scientists believe that the evolution of bipedalism paved the way for many subsequent developments in human evolution, such as tool making, large game hunting, and the enlargement of the brain.

It took roughly 2 million years of additional evolution, however, before the first crude tools appear in the paleontological record about 2.5 million years ago. These were Oldowan stone tools, fashioned by stone flaking to create a sharp edge (see Figure 1.2). These tools were used to separate meat from bone on carcasses, and to extract the nutritious marrow from the larger bones. Although Oldowan stone tools are simple and crude when viewed from today's modern perspective, making them required a level of skill and technological mastery that even a well-trained chimpanzee cannot duplicate (Klein, 2000). Oldowan stone tools apparently were so successful as a technology that they remained essentially unchanged for more than a million years. And they were linked with the first group in the genus *Homo*, called *Homo habilis*, or "handy man," which existed between 2.5 and 1.5 million years ago.

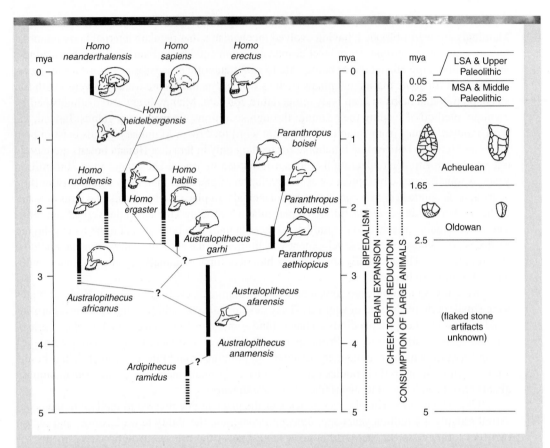

FIGURE *1.2*    **Left:** A tentative phylogeny of the human family (or subfamily, if it is accepted that the African great apes and people should be assigned to the same family) (modified after Strait, Grine, & Moniz, 1997, p. 55). **Right:** The temporal span of key anatomical and behavioral traits and of major Paleolithic culture-stratigraphic units in Africa and western Eurasia. The least controversial aspect of the phylogeny is probably the separation, between 3 mya and 2.5 mya, of the lines that culminated in *Paranthropus* (the "robust" australopithecines) and *Homo*. The number of human species that existed at any one time is highly controversial, and the phylogeny here presents an intermediate position.

*Source:* Klein, R. G. (2000). Archeology and the evolution of human behavior. *Evolutionary Anthropology, 9.*

Roughly 1.8 million years ago, bipedal tool-making primates evolved into a successful branch known as *Homo erectus* and started to migrate out of Africa and into Asia. Fossils dated at 1.8 million years old have been found in both Java and China (Tattersall, 2000). The term "migration" might be a bit misleading, in that it implies setting out on a quest to colonize a distant land. More likely, the "migration" occurred through gradual population expansion into lands with abundant resources. It is not clear whether this expanding *Homo erectus* group knew how to use fire. Although the earliest traces of controlled fire are found in Africa 1.6 million years ago, clear evidence of fire in Europe does not appear until a million years later. The descendants of this first major migration out of Africa ended up colonizing many parts of Asia and eventually Europe and later evolved into the Neanderthals.

The next major technological advancement was the Acheulean hand axe 1.5 million years ago. These axes varied considerably in size and shape, and little is known about their precise uses. Their common quality is the flaking on two opposing surfaces, resulting in a sharp edge around the periphery of the implement. These axes took considerably more skill to produce than the crude Oldowan stone tools, and they often show symmetry of design and standardization of production that are not seen with the earlier stone tools.

Around 1.2 million years ago, brains in the *Homo* line began to expand rapidly, more than doubling in size to the modern human level of approximately 1,350 cubic centimeters. The period of most rapid brain expansion occurred between 500,000 and 100,000 years ago. There are many speculations about the causes of this rapid brain size increase, such as the rise of tool making, tool use, complex communication, cooperative large game hunting, climate, and social competition. It is possible that all these factors played some role in the expansion of the human brain (Bailey & Geary, 2009).

Around 200,000 years ago, *Neanderthals* dominated many parts of Europe and western Asia. Neanderthals had weak chins and receding foreheads, but their thick skulls encased a large brain of 1,450 cubic centimeters. They were built for tough living and cold climates; short limbed and stocky, their solid bodies housed a thick skeletal structure, which was needed for muscles far more powerful than those of modern humans. Their tools were advanced, their hunting skills formidable. Their teeth bore the marks of heavy wear and tear, suggesting frequent chewing of tough foods or the use of teeth to soften leather for clothing. There is evidence that Neanderthals buried their dead. They lived through ice and cold, thriving all over Europe and the Middle East. Then something dramatic happened 30,000 years ago. Neanderthals suddenly went extinct, after having flourished through ice ages and sudden changes in resources for more than 170,000 years. Their disappearance strangely coincided with another key event: the sudden arrival of anatomically modern *Homo sapiens*, called *Homo sapiens sapiens*. Why? (See Box 1.1.)

# ■ LANDMARKS IN THE FIELD OF PSYCHOLOGY

*W*hereas changes have been taking place in evolutionary biology since Darwin's 1859 book, psychology proceeded along a different path. Sigmund Freud, whose contributions came a few decades after Darwin, was significantly influenced by Darwin's theory of evolution by natural selection. So was William James. In the 1920s, however, psychology took a sharp turn away from evolutionary theory and embraced a radical behaviorism that reigned for half a century. Then important empirical discoveries made radical behaviorism untenable, encouraging a turn back to evolutionary theory. In this section, we briefly trace the historical influence—and lack of influence—of evolutionary theory on the field of psychology.

## Freud's Psychoanalytic Theory

In the late 1800s, Sigmund Freud rocked the scientific community by proposing a theory of psychology that had a foundation in sexuality. To the Victorian culture, Freud's theory was shocking. Not only was sexuality a motivating force for adults, Freud proposed that it was *the* driving

BOX *1.1*

# Out of Africa versus Multiregional Origins: The Origins of Modern Humans

A hundred thousand years ago, three distinct groups of hominids roamed the world: *Homo neanderthalensis* in Europe, *Homo erectus* in Asia, and *Homo sapiens* in Africa (Johanson, 2001). By 30,000 years ago, this diversity had been drastically reduced. All human fossils from 30,000 years ago to today share the same modern anatomical form: a distinct skull shape, a large brain (1,350 cubic centimeters), a chin, and a lightly built skeleton. Precisely what caused this radical transformation to a singular human form has been the subject of contentious debate among scientists. There are two competing theories: the *multiregional continuity theory* (MRC) and the *Out of Africa theory* (OOA).

According to the MRC, after the first migration from Africa 1.8 million years ago, the different groups of humans in different parts of the world slowly evolved in parallel with each other, all gradually becoming modern humans (Wolpoff & Caspari, 1996; Wolpoff, Hawks, Frayer, & Huntley, 2001). According to this theory, the emergence of modern humans did not occur in a single area, but rather occurred in different regions of the world wherever humans lived (hence the term *multiregional*). The multiregional evolution of the different groups into the anatomically modern human form occurred, according to MRC, as a consequence of gene flow between the different groups, which mated enough to prevent divergence into separate species.

In sharp contrast, the OOA proposes that modern humans evolved quite recently in one location—Africa—and then migrated into Europe and Asia, replacing all previous populations, including the Neanderthals (Stringer & McKie, 1996). OOA contends, in other words, that modern humans arose in one place, not in multiple regions, and displaced all other humans, including the ones who had already been living in Asia and Europe. According to OOA, the different existing groups, such as the Neanderthals and *Homo sapiens*, had evolved into essentially different species, so interbreeding

was unlikely or trivially rare. In short, OOA posits a single location of modern human origins that occurred only recently, during the past 100,000 years, as contrasted with multiple regions of human origins posited by MRC.

Scientists have brought three fundamental sources of evidence to bear in testing which of these theories is correct: anatomical evidence, archeological evidence, and genetic evidence. The *anatomical* evidence suggests that Neanderthals and *Homo sapiens* differed dramatically. The Neanderthals had a large cranial vault; pronounced brow ridges; a massive facial skeleton; large, heavily worn incisors; a protruding mid-face; no chin; short stature; and a thick-boned, stocky body build. The early *Homo sapiens*, in contrast, looked like modern humans: a cranial vault with a vertical (rather than sloping) forehead; a reduced facial skeleton without the protruding mid-face; a lower jaw with a clearly pronounced chin; and more slightly built, less robust, bones. These large anatomic differences suggest that Neanderthals and early modern humans were isolated from each other, rather than mating with each other, and possibly evolved into two separate species—findings that support the OOA.

The *archeological* evidence—the tools and other artifacts left behind—shows that 100,000 years ago, Neanderthals and *Homo sapiens* were quite similar. Both had stone tools but virtually lacked tools of bone, ivory, or antler; hunting was limited to less dangerous species; population densities were low; fireplaces were rudimentary; and neither showed a penchant for art or decoration. Then, 40,000 to 50,000 years ago, a massive transformation occurred, sometimes described as "a creative explosion" (Johanson, 2001; Klein, 2000; Tattersall, 2000). Tools became diverse and tailored for different functions, expanding to include bone, antler, and ivory. Burials became elaborate, with grave goods entombed with the dead. Hunters began to target dangerous large animals. Population densities mushroomed. Art and decoration flowered. No one knows precisely why this radical transformation in cultural artifacts occurred. Perhaps a new brain adaptation led to the explosion of art and technology. But one thing is known with reasonable certainty: The Neanderthals did *not* partake. The "creative explosion" was almost exclusively limited to *Homo sapiens*. The archeological evidence, in short, supports the OOA (Klein, 2008).

New *genetic* techniques permit tests that were not possible a mere decade ago. We can now literally study the DNA of Neanderthal and *Homo sapiens* skeletons, for example, as well as comparing patterns of genetic variation among different modern populations. The oldest Neanderthal from which DNA has been extracted lived in a site in Croatia 42,000 years ago—undoubtedly not realizing the future scientific use to which his bones would be put. First, the DNA evidence reveals that Neanderthal DNA is distinct from that of modern humans, and it implies that the two lineages diverged perhaps 400,000 years ago or longer. This finding suggests that substantial interbreeding between the two groups was unlikely, although recent evidence points to a little interbreeding (Green et al., 2010). Second, if the DNA of modern humans contained Neanderthal DNA, we would expect it to be most similar to living Europeans, who currently reside in the Neanderthals' former territory. But the Neanderthal DNA is no closer to that of living Europeans than it is to the DNA of modern people living in other parts of the world. Third, modern human populations show an exceptionally low amount of genetic variation, suggesting that we all came from a relatively small population of more genetically homogeneous founding ancestors. Fourth, there is more genetic variation among modern African populations than among populations elsewhere in the world. This is consistent with the view that modern *Homo sapiens* first evolved in Africa, where it had a longer time to accumulate genetic diversity, and then a subset migrated and colonized the new lands. Much of the genetic evidence, in short, supports the OOA.

Most, although not all, scientists now favor some version of the single-origin OOA. All modern humans appear to share a common ancestry with Africans who lived perhaps 120,000 to 220,000 years ago. In the words of one prominent OOA author, we are all "Africans under the skin" (Stringer, 2002). The battle over modern human origins, however, continues to this day. Proponents of the MRC, for example, challenge the interpretation of the genetic evidence, and there are enough anomalies, such as in Australian fossil sites, to raise legitimate concerns about the OOA (Hawks & Wolpoff, 2001; Wolpoff, Hawks, Frayer, & Huntley, 2001). Some scientists suggest that the genetic evidence is compatible with *both* the OOA and the MRC (e.g., Relethford, 1998), and recent genetic evidence might cause the balance to shift more to the MRC (Marth et al., 2003; Templeton, 2007). Indeed, the genetic evidence appears to refute an *exclusive* version of the African origins of humans, because there is some evidence of interbreeding between the most recent African arrivals and the more ancient populations occupying Europe and Asia (Eswaran, Harpending, & Rogers, 2005; Templeton, 2005). Many questions remain unanswered by all the theories. No one knows, for example, precisely why the Neanderthals disappeared so rapidly. Did our superior technology allow us to outcompete them for access to critical survival resources? Did we evolve more complex language and hence better organizational skills that permitted more efficient utilization of resources? Did we develop more effective clothing and sophisticated dwellings to combat climatic fluctuations? Did we mate with any of the Neanderthals? Did we drive them out of the most bountiful plots of land to the peripheral low-resource areas? More ominously, did we kill them off with sophisticated weapons against which they were defenseless, even with their more robust body builds? Advances in science might someday allow us to answer the question of why we, and not the Neanderthals, are around today to ponder our past.

force of human behavior regardless of age, from the smallest newborn infant to the oldest senior citizen. All of our psychological structures, according to Freud, are merely ways of channeling our sexuality.

At the core of Freud's initial theory of psychoanalysis was his proposal of the *instinctual system*, which included two fundamental classes of instincts. The first were the *life-preservative instincts*. These included the needs for air, food, water, and shelter and the fears of snakes, heights, and dangerous humans. These instincts served the function of survival. Freud's second major class of motivators consisted of the *sexual instincts*. "Mature sexuality" for Freud culminated in the final stage of adult development—the genital stage, which led directly to reproduction, the essential feature of Freud's mature sexuality.

Astute readers might sense an eerie familiarity. Freud's two major classes of instincts correspond almost precisely to Darwin's two major theories of evolution. Freud's life-preservative instincts correspond to Darwin's theory of natural selection, which many refer to as "survival selection." And his theory of the sexual instincts corresponds closely to Darwin's theory of sexual selection.

Freud eventually changed his theory by combining the life and sexual instincts into one group called the "life instincts" and adding a second instinct known as the "death instinct." He sought to establish psychology as an autonomous discipline, and his thinking moved away from its initial Darwinian anchoring.

## William James and the Psychology of Instincts

William James published his classic treatise, *Principles of Psychology*, in 1890, right around the time Freud was publishing a flurry of papers on psychoanalysis. At the core of James's theory was also a system of "instincts."

James defined *instincts* as "the faculty of acting in such a way as to produce certain ends, without foresight of the ends, and without previous education in the performance" (James, 1890/1962, p. 392). Instincts were not always blind, nor were they inevitably expressed. They could be modified by experience or overridden by other instincts. In fact, said James, we possess many instincts that contradict each other and so cannot always be expressed. For example, we have sexual desire but can also be coy, are curious but also timid, are aggressive but also cooperative.

Undoubtedly, the most controversial part of James's theory was his list of instincts. Most psychologists of the day believed, like Freud, that instincts were few in number. One contemporary of James, for example, argued that "instinctive acts are in man few in number, and, apart from those connected with the sexual passion, difficult to recognize after early youth is past" (cited in James, 1890/1962, p. 405). James argued, to the contrary, that human instincts are many.

James's list of instincts begins at birth: "crying on contact with the air, sneezing, snuffling, snoring, coughing, sighing, sobbing, gagging, vomiting, hiccuping, staring, moving the limbs when touched, and sucking . . . later on come biting, clasping objects, and carrying them to the mouth, sitting up, standing, creeping, and walking" (James, 1890/1962, p. 406). As each child grows, the instincts of *imitation, vocalization, emulation, pugnacity, fear of definite objects, shyness, sociability, play, curiosity,* and *acquisitiveness* blossom. Still later, adults display the instincts for *hunting, modesty, love,* and *parenting.* Subsumed by each of these instincts is more *specificity* of our innate psychological nature. The fear instinct, for example, includes specific fears of strange men, strange animals, noises, spiders, snakes, solitude, dark places such as holes and caverns, and high places such as cliffs. The key point about all these instincts is that they evolved through natural selection and were adaptations to solve specific adaptive problems.

Contrary to the common view, James believed that humans had many *more* instincts than other animals: "no other mammal, not even the monkey, shows so large a list" (James, 1890/1962, p. 406). And it was in part the length of the list that was its downfall. Many psychologists found it preposterous that humans would have such a large set of innate propensities. By 1920, these skeptics believed that they had a theory to explain why instincts in humans are few in number and highly general: the behaviorist theory of learning.

## The Rise of Behaviorism

If William James believed that much of human behavior was driven by a variety of instincts, James B. Watson believed just the opposite. Watson emphasized a single all-purpose learning mechanism called *classical conditioning*—a type of learning in which two previously unconnected events come to be associated (Pavlov, 1927; Watson, 1924). An initially neutral stimulus such as the ring of a bell, for example, can be paired with another stimulus such as food. After many such pairings, because it has been paired repeatedly with food, the sound of the bell can elicit salivation from dogs and other animals (Pavlov, 1927).

A decade after Watson's major work, a young Harvard graduate student named B. F. Skinner pioneered a new brand of environmentalism called *radical behaviorism* and a principle of operant conditioning. According to this principle, the reinforcing consequences of behavior were the critical causes of subsequent behavior. Behavior followed by reinforcement would be repeated in the future. Behavior not followed by reinforcement (or followed by punishment) would not be repeated in the future. All behavior, except random behavior, could be explained by the "contingencies" of reinforcement.

In sharp contrast to instinctivists like William James, behaviorists assumed that the innate properties of humans were few in number. What was innate, the behaviorists believed, was merely a *general ability to learn* by reinforcing consequences. Any reinforcer could follow any behavior, and learning would occur equally in all cases. Thus, any behavior could be shaped as easily as any other behavior merely by manipulating the contingencies of reinforcement.

Although not all behaviorists endorsed all of these principles, the fundamental assumptions—few innate qualities, the general ability to learn, and the power of environmental contingencies of reinforcement—dominated the field of psychology for more than half a century (Herrnstein, 1977). The nature of human nature, it was asserted, is that humans have no distinct nature.

## The Astonishing Discoveries of Cultural Variability

If humans are general learning machines, built without innate propensities or proclivities, then all of the "content" of human behavior—the emotions, passions, yearnings, desires, beliefs, attitudes, and investments—must be added during each person's life. If learning theory offered the promise of identifying the *process* by which adults were formed, cultural anthropologists offered the promise of providing the *contents* (specific thoughts, behaviors, and rituals) on which those processes could operate (Tooby & Cosmides, 1992).

Most people are interested in stories of other cultures; the stranger and more discrepant from our own, the more interesting such stories are. North Americans wear earrings and finger rings, but certain African cultures insert bones through their noses and tattoo their lips. The mainland Chinese prize virginity, whereas the Swedes think adult virgins are a bit odd (Buss, 1989a). Some Iranian women wear veils over their hair and faces; some Brazilian women wear "dental floss" bikinis and cover practically nothing.

Anthropologists coming back from their fieldwork have long celebrated the cultural diversity they found. Perhaps the most influential was Margaret Mead, who purported to have discovered cultures in which the "sex roles" were totally reversed and sexual jealousy entirely absent. Mead depicted island paradises inhabited by peaceful peoples who celebrated shared sexuality and free love and did not compete, rape, fight, or murder.

The more discrepant other cultures were from U.S. culture, the more they were celebrated, repeated in textbooks, and splashed over the news media. If tropical paradises existed in other cultures, then perhaps our own problems of jealousy, conflict, and competition were due to U.S. culture, Western values, or capitalism. The human mind had the "capacity for culture," but it was the specific culture that was the causal agent responsible for filling in the blanks.

But closer scrutiny revealed snakes in the tropical cultural paradises. Subsequent researchers found that many of the original reports of these tropical cultures were simply false. Derek Freeman (1983), for example, found that the Samoan islanders whom Mead had depicted in such utopian terms were intensely competitive and had murder and rape rates higher than those in the United States! Furthermore, the men were intensely sexually jealous, which contrasted sharply with Mead's depiction of "free love" among the Samoans.

Freeman's debunking of Margaret Mead's findings created a storm of controversy, and he was widely criticized by a social science community that had embraced what now appear to be the myths perpetrated by cultural anthropologists such as Mead. But subsequent research has confirmed the findings of Freeman and, more important, the existence of numerous human universals (Brown, 1991). Male sexual jealousy, for example, turned out to be a human universal and the leading cause of spousal homicide in the many cultures that have been surveyed so far (Daly & Wilson, 1988). Emotional expressions such as fear, rage, and joy were recognized by people in cultures that had no access to television or movies (Ekman, 1973). Even the emotion of love shows universality (Jankowiak, 1995).

Some still cling to the myths of infinite cultural variability. As noted by Melvin Konner (1990): "We have never quite outgrown the idea that, somewhere, there are people living in perfect harmony with nature and one another, and that we might do the same were it not for the corrupting influences of Western culture."

The weight of the evidence started to make the portrait painted by social scientists increasingly difficult to cling to. In addition, new movements were rumbling in other branches of science, suggesting even deeper problems with the view of humans as merely having "the capacity for culture," with all the content inserted by the social environment.

## The Garcia Effect, Prepared Fears, and the Decline of Radical Behaviorism

One rumbling of discontent came from Harry Harlow (1971), who raised a group of monkeys in isolation from other monkeys in a laboratory that housed two artificial "mothers." One mother was made of wire mesh, the other of the same wire mesh covered with a soft terry cloth

*Harry Harlow's experiments were important in establishing that so-called "primary reinforcement," which is reinforcement through food, was not the main determinant of all behavior. In this example, the baby monkey is shown clinging to the terry cloth "mother," despite the fact that it gets its milk from the wire mesh "mother," contrary to the predictions of behaviorism.*

cover. Food was dispensed to the monkeys through the wire-mesh mother, not through the terry cloth mother.

According to the principles of operant conditioning, because the monkeys were receiving their primary reinforcement of food from the wire mothers, they should have become more attached to the wire mother than to the terry cloth mother. Yet precisely the opposite occurred. The baby monkeys would climb onto the wire mothers for food but chose to spend the rest of their time with the terry cloth mothers. When frightened, the monkeys ran not to the food-reinforcing mother but to the one that gave them "contact comfort." Clearly, something was going on inside the monkeys other than a response to the primary reinforcement of food.

Another rumbling of discontent came from John Garcia at the University of California at Berkeley. In a series of studies, he gave rats some food, and then several hours later, he gave them a dose of radiation that made them sick (Garcia, Ervin, & Koelling, 1966). Although the nausea occurred several hours after they ate, the rats generally learned in a single trial never to eat that type of food—seemingly responsible for their illness—again. When Garcia paired the nausea with buzzers or light flashes, however, he could not train the rats to avoid them. In other words, rats seem to come into the world "preprogrammed" to learn some things easily, such as to avoid foods linked with nausea, but find it extraordinarily difficult to learn other things.

The proposition that organisms come into this world "prepared" by evolution to learn some things and not others was picked up by Martin Seligman. Seligman and his colleagues proposed that it was indeed quite easy to "condition" people to develop certain types of fears—a fear of snakes, for example—but extremely difficult to condition people to develop other, less natural fears such as fear of electrical outlets or cars (Seligman & Hager, 1972).

In summary, fundamental assumptions of behaviorism were being violated, which suggested two important conclusions. First, rats, monkeys, and even humans seemed predisposed to learn some things very easily and to not learn other things at all. Second, the external environment is not the sole determinant of behavior. Something goes on inside the minds and brains of organisms that must be taken into account when explaining behaviors.

## Peering into the Black Box: The Cognitive Revolution

A number of forces converged in psychology to bring back the legitimacy of looking inside the head to explore the psychology underlying behavior. One force came from the violations of the fundamental "laws" of learning. A second came from the study of language, in Noam Chomsky's powerful arguments for a universal "language organ" with an underlying structure that turned out to be invariant across languages (Chomsky, 1957; Pinker, 1994). A third force came with the rise of computers and the "information-processing metaphor." All three forces coalesced into what became known as the *cognitive revolution.*

The cognitive revolution returned to psychology the respectability of looking "inside the heads" of people rather than at just the external contingencies of reinforcement. The revolution was required, in part, simply because external contingencies alone could not successfully account for the behavior being observed. Furthermore, with the rise of the computer, psychologists began to be more explicit about the exact causal processes they were proposing.

> The cognitive revolution is more or less now equated with *information processing:* A cognitive description specifies what kinds of information the mechanism takes as input, what procedures it uses to transform that information, what kinds of data structures (representations) those procedures operate on, and what kinds of representations or behaviors it generates as output. (Tooby & Cosmides, 1992, p. 64)

For an organism to accomplish certain tasks, it must solve a number of information-processing problems. To successfully accomplish the tasks of seeing, hearing, walking bipedally, and categorizing, for example, requires a tremendous amount of information-processing machinery. Although seeing with our eyes seems to come effortlessly and naturally for most of us—we just open our eyes and look—in fact it takes thousands of specialized mechanisms to accomplish, including a lens, a retina, a cornea, a pupil, specific edge detectors, rods, cones, specific motion detectors, a specialized optic nerve, and so on. Psychologists came to realize that they needed to understand the information-processing machinery in our brains to understand the causal underpinnings of human performance. The brain's "evolved function is to extract information from the (internal and external) environment and use that information to generate behavior and regulate physiology . . . so to describe the brain's operation in a way that captures its evolved function, you need to think of it as composed of programs that process information" (Cosmides, 2006, p. 7).

Information-processing mechanisms—the cognitive machinery—require the "hardware" in which they are housed: the neurobiology of the brain. But the information-processing description of a mechanism such as the eye is not the same as the description of the underlying neurobiology. Consider as an analogy the word-processing software on a computer, which contains a program that deletes sentences, moves paragraphs, and italicizes characters. The program can run on an IBM computer, a Macintosh, or any number of clone computers. Even though the underlying hardware of the machines differs, the information-processing description of the program is the same. By analogy, in principle, one could build a robot to "see" in a manner similar to a human, but the hardware would be different from the neurobiology of the human. Thus, the cognitive level of description (i.e., input, representations, decision rules, output) is useful and necessary whether or not all the underlying brainware is understood. With the downfall of certain assumptions of behaviorism and the emergence of the cognitive revolution it became respectable to look "inside the head" of the human. No longer was it viewed as "unscientific" to posit internal mental states and processes. On the contrary, it was considered absolutely necessary.

But most cognitive psychologists carried over one unfortunate assumption from the behaviorist paradigm: the assumption of domain-generality (Barrett & Kurzban, 2006; Tooby & Cosmides, 1992). The domain-general learning processes proposed by behaviorists were simply replaced by domain-general cognitive mechanisms. Missing was the idea that there might be privileged classes of information that the cognitive mechanisms were specifically designed to process.

The image of human cognitive machinery was that of a large computer designed to process any information it was fed. Computers can be programmed to play chess, do calculus, predict the weather, manipulate symbols, or guide missiles. In this sense, the computer is a domain-general information processor. But to solve any particular problem, it must be programmed in very specific ways. Programming a computer to play chess, for example, takes millions of lines of "if. . . . then" statements of programming.

One of the main problems with the domain-general assumption about the information-processing mind is the problem of *combinatorial explosion.* With a domain-general program that lacks specialized processing rules, the number of alternative options open to it in any given situation is infinite. The evolutionary psychologists John Tooby and Leda Cosmides (1992) present the following example. Suppose that within the next minute you could perform any one of one hundred possible actions—read the next paragraph in this book, eat an apple, blink your eyes, dream about tomorrow, and so on. And within the second minute, you could also perform any one of one hundred actions. After only two minutes, there would be 10,000 possible combinations of behavioral options ($100 \times 100$). After three minutes, there would be one million behavioral sequences you could perform ($100 \times 100 \times 100$) and so on. This is a combinatorial explosion—the rapid proliferation of response options caused by combining two or more sequential possibilities.

To get a computer or a person to accomplish a specific task, special programming must sharply narrow the possibilities. So combinatorial explosion renders a computer or a person incapable of solving even the simplest tasks without special programming (Tooby & Cosmides, 2005). The computer, of course, can be programmed to perform a staggering variety of tasks, limited mainly by the imagination and wizardry of the programmer. But what about humans? How are we programmed? What special information-processing problems are we "designed" to solve with our large, 1,350 cubic centimeter brain?

The idea that there might be some information-processing problems that the human mind was specially designed to solve was missing from the cognitive revolution in psychology. Humans went from being blank slates on which contingencies of reinforcement do the writing (learning theory) to general-purpose computers on which cultures write the software (cognitive theory). It was this gap, along with accumulated empirical findings and convergence from a variety of empirical sciences, that finally set the stage for the emergence of evolutionary psychology. Evolutionary psychology furnished the missing piece of the puzzle by providing a specification of the kinds of information-processing problems the human mind was designed to solve—problems of survival and reproduction.

# ■ SUMMARY

Evolutionary biology has undergone many historical developments. Evolution—change over time in organisms—was suspected to occur long before Charles Darwin came on the scene. Missing before him, however, was a theory about a causal process that could explain how organic change could occur. The theory of natural selection was Darwin's first contribution to evolutionary biology. It has three essential ingredients: variation, inheritance, and selection. Natural selection occurs when some inherited variations lead to greater reproductive success than other inherited variations. In short, natural selection is defined as changes over time due to the differential reproductive success of inherited variations.

Natural selection provided a unifying theory for the biological sciences and solved several important mysteries. First, it provided a causal process by which change, the modification of organic structures, takes place over time. Second, it proposed a theory to account for the origin of new species. Third, it united all living forms into one grand tree of descent and simultaneously revealed the place of humans in the grand scheme of life. The fact that it has now survived a century and a half of scientific scrutiny, despite many attempts to find flaws in it, must surely qualify it as a great scientific theory (Alexander, 1979).

In addition to natural selection, sometimes referred to as "survival selection," Darwin devised a second evolutionary theory: the theory of sexual selection. Sexual selection deals with the evolution of characteristics due to success in mating rather than to success in survival. Sexual selection operates through two processes: intrasexual competition and intersexual selection. In intrasexual competition, victors in same-sex contests are more likely to reproduce owing to increased sexual access to mates. In intersexual selection, individuals with qualities that are preferred by the opposite sex are more likely to reproduce. Both processes of sexual selection result in evolution—change over time due to differences in mating success.

A major stumbling block for many biologists was that Darwin lacked a workable theory of inheritance. This theory was provided when the work of Gregor Mendel was recognized and synthesized with Darwin's theory of natural selection in a movement called the Modern Synthesis. According to this theory, inheritance does not involve blending of the two parents but rather is particulate. That is, genes, the fundamental unit of inheritance, come in discrete packets that are not blended but rather are passed on intact from parent to child. The particulate theory of inheritance provided the missing ingredient to Darwin's theory of natural selection.

Following the Modern Synthesis, two European biologists, Konrad Lorenz and Nikolaas Tinbergen, started a new movement called ethology, which sought to place animal behavior within an evolutionary context by focusing on both the origins and functions of behavior.

In 1964, the theory of natural selection itself was reformulated in a revolutionary pair of articles published by William D. Hamilton. The process by which selection operates, according to Hamilton, involves not just classical fitness (the direct production of offspring), but also inclusive fitness, which includes the effects of an individual's actions on the reproductive success of genetic relatives, weighted by the appropriate degree of genetic relatedness. The inclusive fitness reformulation provided a more precise theory of the process of natural selection by promoting a "gene's eye" view of selection.

In 1966, George Williams published the now classic *Adaptation and Natural Selection*, which had three effects. First, it led to the downfall of group selection. Second, it promoted the Hamiltonian revolution. And third, it provided rigorous criteria for identifying adaptations, such as efficiency, reliability, and precision. In the 1970s, Robert Trivers built on the work of Hamilton and Williams, offering three seminal theories that remain important today: reciprocal altruism, parental investment, and parent–offspring conflict.

In 1975, Edward O. Wilson published *Sociobiology: A New Synthesis*, which attempted to synthesize the key developments in evolutionary biology. Wilson's book created controversy, mostly because of its final chapter, which focused on humans, offering a series of hypotheses but little empirical data.

Much of the resistance to Wilson's book, as well as to using evolutionary theory to explain human behavior, may be traced to several core misunderstandings. Contrary to these misunderstandings, however, evolutionary theory does not imply that human behavior is genetically determined, nor that human behavior is unchangeable. And it does not imply optimal design.

Evidence from a variety of disciplines permits us to understand some of the critical milestones in the evolutionary process that led to modern humans. Humans are mammals, which originated more than 200 million years ago. We are part of a primate line that began 85 million years ago. Our ancestors became bipedal 4.4 million years ago, developed crude stone tools 2.5 million years ago, and might have begun to cultivate fire 1.6 million years ago. As the brains of our ancestors expanded, we developed more sophisticated tools and technology and started to colonize many parts of the world.

While changes were taking place within evolutionary biology, the field of psychology followed a different course. Sigmund Freud drew attention to the importance of survival and sexuality by proposing a theory of life-preserving and sexual instincts, paralleling Darwin's distinction between natural selection and sexual selection. In 1890, William James published *Principles of Psychology*, which proposed that humans have a number of specific instincts. In the 1920s, however, U.S. psychology turned away from evolutionary ideas and embraced a version of radical behaviorism: the idea that a few highly general principles of learning could account for the complexity of human behavior.

In the 1960s, however, empirical findings suggested important violations of the general laws of learning. Harry Harlow demonstrated that monkeys do not prefer wire-mesh "mothers," even when they receive their primary food reinforcement from those mothers. John Garcia showed that organisms could learn some things readily and rapidly. Something was going on inside the brains of organisms that could not be accounted for solely by the external contingencies of reinforcement.

The accumulation of these findings led to the cognitive revolution, reinstating the importance and respectability of looking "inside the heads" of people. The cognitive revolution was based on the information-processing metaphor—descriptions of mechanisms inside the head that take in specific forms of information as input, transform that information through decision rules, and generate behavior as output.

The idea that humans might come predisposed or specially equipped to process some kinds of information and not others set the stage for the emergence of evolutionary psychology, which represents a true synthesis of modern psychology and modern evolutionary biology.

## ■ SUGGESTED READINGS

Buss, D. M. (2009). The great struggles of life: Darwin and the emergence of evolutionary psychology. *American Psychologist, 64,* 140–148.

Confer, J. C., Easton, J. E., Fleischman, D. S., Goetz, C., Lewis, D. M., Perilloux, C., & Buss, D. M. (2010). Evolutionary psychology: Controversies, questions, prospects, and limitations. *American Psychologist, 65,* 110–126.

Darwin, C. (1859). *On the origin of species.* London: Murray.

Dawkins, R. (1989). *The selfish gene* (new edition). New York: Oxford University Press.

Williams, G. C. (1966). *Adaptation and natural selection.* Princeton, NJ: Princeton University Press.

Klein, R. G. (2008). Out of Africa and the evolution of human behavior. *Evolutionary Anthropology, 17,* 267–281.

Wilson, D. S. (2007). *Evolution for everyone: How Darwin's theory can change the way we think about our lives.* New York: Delacorte Press.

# THE NEW SCIENCE OF EVOLUTIONARY PSYCHOLOGY

# CHAPTER 2

*Evolutionary psychology is arguably one of the most important new developments in the behavioral sciences over the past 20 years.*

—Boyer & Heckhausen, 2000, p. 917

*E*volutionary psychologist Karl Grammer formed a team of researchers to study sexual signals as they occur in a seminatural context: singles bars (Grammer, 1996). He stationed one set of observers inside the bars and used specially designed rating forms to record observations of how often women were touched by men at the bar. A different member of the research team approached each woman as she left the bar and asked whether she would consent to be part of the study. Women participants were photographed and completed a brief questionnaire that requested information about their use of birth control and the current point in their menstrual cycles (e.g., time since the start of their last periods). Grammer then digitized the photographic images and used a computer program to calculate the proportion of skin each woman revealed.

For the group of women who were not taking oral contraceptives, men in the singles bar were far more likely to initiate touching with women who were at the most fertile time of their cycle—around the time of ovulation. Women who were not ovulating, in contrast, were touched less. So contrary to conventional wisdom, men *might* be able to detect subtle cues to when women are ovulating. But there is another interpretation. Ovulating women also displayed more sexual signals via their clothing: They wore tighter, more revealing blouses and shorter skirts and showed more skin. So it might not be the case that men are astutely detecting when women ovulate. Rather, ovulating women might be actively sending sexual signals—an interpretation that's supported by another study that found that ovulating women *initiate* sexual encounters more than women at other phases of the cycle (Gangestad et al., 2004).

These new lines of research highlight two features of the science of evolutionary psychology. One is discovering previously unsuspected links between features of human reproductive biology—in this case, women's ovulation—and manifest behavior. Second, thinking about *adaptive function,* such as whether men have adaptations to detect when women ovulate or whether women have adaptations to respond to their own ovulation (e.g., Bryant & Haselton, 2009), provides the critical impetus for new research.

This chapter focuses on the logic and methods of the science of evolutionary psychology, a new scientific synthesis of modern evolutionary biology and modern psychology. It utilizes theoretical advances in evolutionary biology such as inclusive fitness theory, the theory of parental investment and sexual selection, and the development of more rigorous standards for evaluating the presence or absence of adaptation. Evolutionary psychology also incorporates conceptual and empirical advances in psychology, including information-processing models, knowledge from artificial intelligence, as well as discoveries such as universal emotional expression (Ekman, 1973), universals in the ways people categorize plants and animals (Atran, 1990; Berlin, Breedlove, & Raven, 1973), and universals in human mating strategies (Lippa, 2009). The goal of this chapter is to introduce the conceptual foundations of this new synthesis. Later chapters will build on this foundation. Let's start by asking why psychology needs to be integrated with evolutionary biology.

## ■ THE ORIGINS OF HUMAN NATURE

### Three Theories of the Origins of Complex Adaptive Mechanisms

If you walk around with bare feet for a few weeks, you will develop calluses on your soles. The callus-producing mechanisms—manufacturing numerous new skin cells when repeated friction is encountered—function to protect the anatomical and physiological structures of your feet from damage. If you ride around in your car for a few weeks, however, your car tires will not get thicker. Why not?

Your feet and your car tires are both subject to the laws of physics. Friction tends to wear down physical objects, not build them up. But your feet, unlike your tires, are subject to another set of laws—the laws of natural selection. Your feet have callus-producing mechanisms because of natural selection. Evolution by selection is a creative process; the callus-producing mechanisms are the adaptive products of that creative process. They exist now because in the past those who tended, however slightly, to have genes that predisposed them to develop extra skin thickness as a result of friction had this extra element to aid in their survival, and hence lived to reproduce more than those without the beneficial predisposition. As descendants of these successful ancestors, we carry with us the adaptive mechanisms that led to our ancestors' success.

In the past century, three major theories have been proposed to account for the origins of adaptations such as callus-producing mechanisms. One theory is *creationism,* or "intelligent design," the idea that a supreme deity created all of the plants and animals, from the largest whales to the smallest plankton in the ocean, from the simple single-celled amoebas to the complex human brain. Creationism is not viewed as a "scientific theory" for three reasons.

First, it cannot be tested because specific empirical predictions do not follow from its major premise. Whatever exists does so simply because the Supreme Being has created it. Second, creationism has not guided researchers to any new scientific discoveries. Third, creationism has not proved useful as a scientific explanation for already discovered organic mechanisms. Creationism, therefore, is a matter of religion and belief, not a matter of science. It cannot be proved to be false, but it has not proven useful as a predictive or an explanatory theory (Kennair, 2003).

A second theory is *seeding theory*. According to seeding theorists, life did not originate on earth. In one version of this theory, the seeds of life arrived on earth via a meteorite. In a second version of seeding theory, extraterrestrial intelligent beings came down from other planets or galaxies and planted the seeds of life on earth. Regardless of the origins of the seeds, however, evolution by natural selection presumably took over, and the seeds eventually evolved into humans and the other life forms observed today.

Seeding theory is in principle testable. We can study meteorites for signs of life, which would lend plausibility to the theory that life originated elsewhere. We can scour the earth for signs of extraterrestrial landings. We can look for evidence of life forms that could not have originated on earth. Seeding theory, however, runs into three problems. First, there is currently no solid scientific evidence on earth that such "seedings" have taken place. Second, seeding theory has not led to any new scientific discoveries, nor has it explained any existing scientific puzzles. Most important, however, seeding theory simply pushes the causal explanation for life forms back in time. If the earth was really seeded by extraterrestrial beings, what causal processes led to the origins of these intelligent beings?

We are left with the third option: *evolution by natural selection*. Although evolution by natural selection is called a theory, its fundamental principles have been confirmed so many times—and never disconfirmed—that it is viewed by most biologists as a fact (Alcock, 2009). The components of its operation—differential reproduction due to inherited design differences—have been shown to work in both the laboratory and the wild. The differing sizes of the beaks of finches on different islands in the Galápagos, for example, have been shown to have evolved to correspond to the size of the seeds prevalent on each island (Grant, 1991). Larger beaks are needed when the seeds are large, whereas smaller beaks are better when the seeds are small. The theory of natural selection has many virtues that scientists seek in a scientific theory: (1) it explains known facts; (2) it leads to new predictions; and (3) it provides guidance to important domains of scientific inquiry.

So among the three theories—creationism, seeding theory, and natural selection—there is no real contest. Evolution by natural selection is the only known *scientific* theory that can explain the astonishing diversity of life we see around us today. And it is the only known scientific theory that has the power to account for the origins and structure of complex adaptive mechanisms—from callus-producing mechanisms to large brains—that comprise human nature.

## The Three Products of Evolution

There are three products of the evolutionary process—*adaptations, by-products* (or concomitants) of adaptation, and *random effects* (or noise), as shown in Table 2.1 (Buss et al., 1998; Tooby & Cosmides, 1990).

TABLE *2.1*   **Three Products of the Evolutionary Process**

| Product | Brief definition |
| --- | --- |
| Adaptations | Inherited and reliably developing characteristics that came into existence through natural selection because they helped to solve problems of survival or reproduction better than alternative designs existing in the population during the period of their evolution; example: umbilical cord |
| By-products | Characteristics that do not solve adaptive problems and do not have functional design; they are "carried along" with characteristics that do have functional design because they happen to be coupled with those adaptations; example: belly button |
| Noise | Random effects produced by forces such as chance mutations, sudden and unprecedented changes in the environment, or chance effects during development; example: particular shape of a person's belly button |

An adaptation may be defined as an inherited and reliably developing characteristic that came into existence through natural selection because it helped to solve a problem of survival or reproduction during the period of its evolution (after Tooby & Cosmides, 1992, pp. 61–62).

Let's break down this definition into its core elements. An adaptation must have genes "for" that adaptation. Those genes are required for the passage of the adaptation from parents to children; hence, adaptations have a genetic basis. Most adaptations, of course, cannot be traced to single genes but rather are products of many genes. The human eye, for example, is constructed by hundreds of genes. Past environments selected the genes we have today; environments during a person's lifetime are necessary for the proper development of adaptations, and current environments are responsible for activating adaptations once they have developed.

An adaptation must develop reliably among species members in all "normal" environments. That is, to qualify as an adaptation, it must emerge at the appropriate time during an organism's life in reasonably intact form and hence be characteristic of most or all of the members of a given species. There are important exceptions to this, such as mechanisms that exist in only one sex or in a specific subset of the population (Buss & Hawley, 2011), which will be covered later; but for now, it is important to stress that *most* adaptations are species-typical.

The reliably developing feature of adaptations does *not* mean that the adaptation must appear at birth. Indeed, many adaptations develop long after birth. Walking is a reliably developing characteristic of humans, but most humans do not begin to walk until a full year after birth. Breasts are reliably developing features in women but do not develop until puberty.

Adaptations are fashioned by the process of selection. Selection acts as a sieve in each generation, filtering out the many features that do not contribute to propagation and letting through those that do (Dawkins, 1996). This sieving process recurs generation after generation so that each new generation is a bit different from its parent generation. Those characteristics that make it through the filtering process in each generation do so because they contribute to the solution of an adaptive problem of either survival or reproduction better than alternative (competing) designs existing in the population. The *function* of an adaptation refers to the adaptive problem it evolved to solve, that is, precisely *how* it contributes to survival or reproduction. The function of an adaptation is typically identified and confirmed by evidence of "special design," whereby the components or "design features" all contribute in a precise manner to solve a particular adaptive problem. As was noted in Chapter 1, standards for evaluating a hypothesized function of an adaptation typically include *efficiency* (solving the problem in a proficient manner), *economy* (solving the problem in a cost-effective manner), *precision* (all the component parts specialized for achieving a particular end), and *reliability* (performing dependably in the contexts in which it is designed to operate) (see Confer et al., 2010; Tooby & Cosmides, 1992, 2005; Williams, 1966).

Each adaptation has its own period of evolution. Initially a *mutation,* a copying error in a piece of DNA, occurs in a single individual. Although most mutations hinder survival or reproduction, some, by chance alone, end up helping the organism survive and reproduce. If the mutation is helpful enough to give the organism a reproductive advantage over other members of the population, it will be passed down to the next generation in greater numbers. In the next generation, therefore, more individuals possess the characteristic that was initially a mutation in a single person. Over many generations, if it continues to be successful, the mutation will spread to the entire population, so every member of the species will have it.

The *environment of evolutionary adaptedness,* or *EEA,* refers to the statistical composite of selection pressures that occurred during an adaptation's period of evolution responsible for producing the adaptation (Tooby & Cosmides, 1992). Stated differently, the EEA for each adaptation refers to the selection forces, or adaptive problems, that were responsible for shaping it over deep evolutionary time. The EEA for the eye, for example, refers to the specific selection pressures that fashioned each of the components of the visual system over hundreds of millions of years. The EEA for bipedal locomotion involves selection pressures on a shorter timescale, going back roughly 4.4 million years. The key point is that the EEA does not refer to a specific time or place, but rather to the selection forces that are responsible for shaping adaptations. Therefore, each adaptation has its own unique EEA. The adaptation's *period of evolution* refers to the time span during which it was constructed, piece by piece, until it came to characterize the universal design of the species.

Although adaptations are the primary products of evolution, they are certainly not the only products. The evolutionary process also produces *by-products* of adaptations. By-products are

*Belly buttons are not adaptations—they are not good for catching prey or deterring predators. Rather, they are by-products of something that was an adaptation—the formerly functional umbilical cord by which a fetus obtained nutrients from its mother.*

characteristics that do not solve adaptive problems and do not have functional design. They are "carried along" with characteristics that do have functional design because they happen to be coupled with those adaptations, just as the heat from a lightbulb is a by-product of design for light.

Consider the human belly button. There is no evidence that the belly button, per se, helps humans survive or reproduce. A belly button is not good for catching food, detecting predators, avoiding snakes, finding good habitats, or choosing mates. It does not seem to be directly or indirectly involved in the solution to an adaptive problem. Rather, the belly button is a by-product of something that is an adaptation—namely, the umbilical cord that provided food to the growing fetus. The hypothesis that something is a by-product of an adaptation, therefore, requires identifying the adaptation of which it is a by-product and the reason why its existence is associated with that adaptation.

The third and final product of the evolutionary process is *noise* or *random effects*. Random effects can be produced by forces such as mutations, sudden and unprecedented changes in the environment, or accidents during development. These random effects sometimes harm the smooth functioning of an organism, such as throwing sand into a machine or spilling scalding coffee onto the hard drive of your computer will ruin its functional operation. Some random effects are neutral—they neither contribute to nor detract from adaptive functioning—and some are beneficial to an organism. The glass encasement of a lightbulb, for example, often contains perturbations from smoothness due to imperfection in the materials and the process of manufacturing that do not affect the functioning of the bulb; a bulb can function equally well with or without such perturbations. Noise is distinguished from by-products in that it is not linked to the adaptive aspects of design features but rather is independent of such features.

In summary, the evolutionary process produces three products—adaptations, by-products of adaptations, and random effects. In principle, we can analyze the component parts of a species and conduct studies to determine which are adaptations, which are by-products, and which are due merely to random effects. Evolutionary scientists differ in their estimates of the relative sizes of these three categories of products. Some believe that even uniquely human qualities, such as language, are merely incidental by-products of our large brains (Gould, 1991). Others see overwhelming evidence that human language is an adaptation (Pinker, 1994). Fortunately, we do not have to rely on the beliefs of scientists because we can test their ideas directly.

Despite scientific quibbles about the relative size of the three categories of evolutionary products, all evolutionary scientists agree on one fundamental point: *Adaptations are the primary product of evolution by selection* (Alcock, 2009; Dawkins, 1982; Dennett, 1995; Gould, 1997; Trivers, 1985; Williams, 1992). Even critics of evolutionary psychology, such as Stephen Jay Gould, "do not deny either the existence and central importance of adaptation, or the production of adaptation by natural selection. . . . I know of no other scientific mechanism other than natural selection with the proven power to build structures for such eminently workable design" (Gould, 1997, pp. 53–58).

And so the core of all animal natures, including humans, consists of a large collection of adaptations. Some of these adaptations are sense organs—eyes, ears, nose, taste buds—that provide windows to adaptively relevant information in our environment. Some of these adaptations help us to move through our environment, such as an upright skeletal posture, leg bones, and our big toes. Evolutionary psychologists tend to focus on one special subclass of the adaptations that comprise human nature—psychological adaptations.

## Levels of Evolutionary Analysis in Evolutionary Psychology

One of the essential features of any science is the formulation of hypotheses. In the case of evolutionary psychology, the nature of hypotheses centers on adaptive problems and their solutions. More specifically, it centers on the adaptive problems faced by our ancestors and on the adaptive psychological solutions to those problems. In order to see precisely how evolutionary psychologists formulate these hypotheses, we must describe a hierarchy of levels of analysis within evolutionary psychology, as shown in Figure 2.1.

***General Evolutionary Theory.*** The first level of analysis is general evolutionary theory. In its modern form, evolution by natural selection is understood from the "gene's eye" perspective—differential gene replication is the engine of the evolutionary process by which

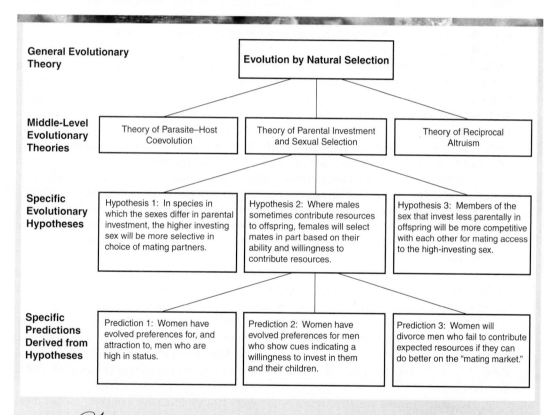

FIGURE 2.1 **Levels of Evolutionary Analysis.** The figure shows one version of the hierarchy of levels of analysis in evolutionary psychology. General evolutionary theory occupies the highest level in the hierarchy. Each middle-level theory must be consistent with general evolutionary theory, but cannot be derived from it. Specific evolutionary hypotheses about evolved psychological mechanisms or behavior patterns are derived from each middle-level theory. Each specific evolutionary hypothesis can generate a variety of specific testable predictions. Support for each hypothesis and theory is evaluated by the cumulative weight of empirical evidence.

adaptations are formed (Cronin, 2005; Dawkins, 1982, 1989; Hamilton, 1964; Williams, 1966). Evolutionary theory, of course, includes more than the process of natural selection, as described in Chapter 1. Natural selection, however, is the only known fundamental causal process capable of creating complex functional design and hence will be treated here as the most general level in the hierarchy of evolutionary theorizing.

At this general level, even though we talk about evolutionary "theory," it is widely accepted by biological scientists as fact. Most of the research in evolutionary psychology proceeds from the assumption that evolutionary theory is correct, but the research does not test that assumption directly.

There are observations that could, in principle, falsify general evolutionary theory. If scientists observed complex life forms that were created in time periods too short for natural selection to have operated (e.g., in seven days), then the theory would be proved false. If scientists discovered adaptations that functioned solely for the benefit of other species, then the theory would be proved false. If scientists discovered adaptations that functioned for the benefit of same-sex competitors, then the theory would be proved false (Darwin, 1859; Mayr, 1982; Williams, 1966). No such phenomena have ever been documented.

***Middle-Level Evolutionary Theories.***   Moving one level down (see Figure 2.1), we find middle-level theories such as Trivers's theory of parental investment and sexual selection. These middle-level theories are still fairly broad, covering entire domains of functioning. They are also fair game for scientific testing and possibly being proved false. Let's examine just one theory to illustrate this point—Trivers's theory of parental investment as the driving force behind sexual selection. This theory, which is itself an elaboration of Darwin's theory of sexual selection (1871), provided one of the key ingredients for predicting the operation of mate choice and intrasexual competition (competition between members of the same sex). Trivers argued that the sex that invests more resources in its offspring (often, but not always, the female) will evolve to be more choosy or discriminating in selecting a mate. The sex that invests fewer resources in its offspring, in contrast, will evolve to be less choosy and more competitive with members of its own sex for sexual access to the valuable, high-investing opposite sex.

The fundamental tenets of Trivers's theory have been strongly supported by empirical evidence from a variety of species (Alcock, 2009). In the many species in which females invest more heavily in offspring than males, females are in fact more likely to be choosy and discriminating. There are a few species, however, in which males invest more than females. In some species, for example, the female implants her eggs in the male, and he is the one who carries the offspring until they are born. In species such as the Mormon cricket, poison-arrow frog, and pipefish seahorse, for example, males invest more than females in this way (Jones et al., 2001, Trivers, 1985).

The male pipefish seahorse receives the eggs from the female and then carries them around in his kangaroo-like pouch. These females compete aggressively with each other for the "best" males, and males in turn are choosy about who they mate with. This so-called "sex-role reversed" species supports Trivers's theory, showing that it is not "maleness" or "femaleness" itself that causes the sex difference in choosiness; rather, it is the relative parental investment of the two sexes. So the cumulative weight of the evidence provides substantial support for Trivers's middle-level theory of parental investment as a determinant of relative choosiness and competitiveness for mates (also see Klug et al., 2010).

*Unlike many species, the female of Mormon cricket is larger, stronger, and more aggressive than the male. This is predicted by the theory of parental investment. In this species, the male does more parental investment, and so females are selected for the size and other qualities that lead to success in competition with other females.*

Look again at Figure 2.1 (page 41). You can see that Trivers's middle-level theory is compatible with general evolutionary theory; he is not proposing something that could not come about by the evolutionary process. At the same time, however, parental investment theory is not logically derivable from general evolutionary theory. There is nothing in the theory of natural selection that says anything about parental investment. Thus middle-level theories must be compatible with general evolutionary theory, but they must also stand or fall on their own merits.

***Specific Evolutionary Hypotheses.***   Let's move one level down on Figure 2.1 to examine the specific evolutionary hypotheses. One hypothesis that has been advanced for humans, for example, is that women have evolved specific preferences for men who have resources to offer (Buss, 1989a; Symons, 1979). The logic is as follows. First, because women invest heavily in children, they have evolved to be choosy when they pick mates (standard prediction from parental investment theory). Second, the *content* of women's choices should reflect whatever has historically increased the survival and reproduction of their children. Therefore, women are hypothesized to have evolved mate preferences for men who are both able and willing to contribute resources to them and their children. This is an evolutionary *psychological* hypothesis because it proposes the existence of a specific psychological mechanism—a desire—that is designed to solve a specific human adaptive problem—that of securing a man who appears highly capable of investing in children.

This specific evolutionary psychological hypothesis can be tested empirically. Scientists can study women across a wide variety of cultures and determine whether they in fact prefer men who are both able and willing to contribute resources to them and their children. To provide strong tests of the hypothesis, however, we must see what specific predictions it generates—moving to the lowest level of the hierarchy in Figure 2.1. On the basis of the hypothesis that women prefer men who have a lot of resources to offer, we could make the following predictions: (1) Women will value in men specific qualities known to be linked with the acquisition of resources such as social status, intelligence, and somewhat older age; (2) in a singles bar, women's attention, as measured by eye gaze, will be drawn more to men who appear to have resources than to men who do not; and (3) women whose husbands fail to provide economic resources will be more likely to divorce them than women whose husbands do contribute economic resources.

All of these predictions follow from the evolutionary psychological hypothesis that women have a specific evolved preference for men with resources. The value of the hypothesis rests with the scientific tests of predictions derived from it. If the predictions fail—if women are shown not to desire personality characteristics known to be linked with resource acquisition, do not gaze more at men with resources in singles bars, and are not more likely to divorce husbands who fail to provide resources—then the hypothesis will not be supported. If the predictions succeed, then the hypothesis is supported, at least for the moment.

This is highly oversimplified, of course, and several additional levels of analysis are often involved. We could perform an even more detailed analysis of the sorts of information-processing mechanisms needed to solve the adaptive problem of securing a man's investment and use as a guide an analysis of the relevant ancestral cues that would have been available to our human ancestors in those environments. Because we know that humans spent 99 percent of their evolutionary history as hunter-gatherers (Tooby & DeVore, 1987), for example, we could predict that part of women's evolved preference will include the specific qualities needed for successful hunting such as athletic prowess, good hand-eye coordination, and the physical endurance needed for long hunts.

All the conditions of standard science hold. If the predictions do not pan out empirically, then the hypotheses on which they were based are called into question. If key hypotheses are called into question by predictive failures, then the truth or value of the middle-level theory that generated the hypotheses is doubtable. Theories that are consistently supported are hailed as major middle-level theories, especially if they generate interesting and fruitful avenues of research. Theories that fail to generate such avenues or that fail empirically are abandoned.

This hierarchy of levels of analysis is useful in answering questions such as: What evidence could falsify evolutionary formulations? A particular hypothesis about a psychological mechanism could be wrong, even if the theory one level up that led to the hypothesis is entirely correct. Trivers's middle-level theory of parental investment could be correct, for example, even if it turned out that women have not evolved specific mate preferences for men with resources. Perhaps the relevant mutations for women's preferences did not arise, or perhaps women in ancestral conditions were constrained from making their own mating choices.

Similarly, even if the specific evolutionary psychology hypothesis is correct—in this case, that women have evolved specific mate preferences for men with resources—there is no guarantee that each and every prediction derived from it will be correct. It might be the case, for example, that women do desire qualities in men linked with resources but do not divorce men who fail to provide for them. Perhaps women whose husbands fail to provide are stuck with them because of laws that prohibit divorce. Or perhaps a woman perceives that she won't be able to do much better and so decides to stick it out. Any of these factors could render this specific prediction false.

The key point is that the evaluation of evolutionary formulations rests with the cumulative weight of the evidence, and not necessarily with any single prediction. Evolutionary hypotheses, when formulated precisely, are highly testable and eminently capable of being falsified when the evidence fails to support predictions derived from them (see Ketelaar & Ellis, 2000, for an excellent discussion of the issue of falsifiability).

***Two Strategies for Generating and Testing Evolutionary Hypotheses.*** The hierarchy of levels in Figure 2.1 shows one scientific strategy for generating evolutionary hypotheses and predictions. This strategy is called the top-down or theory-driven approach to hypothesis generation. One can start at the top with general evolutionary theory and derive hypotheses. For example, we could predict solely based on inclusive fitness theory that humans will help close genetic relatives more than they will distant genetic relatives. Or we could generate a hypothesis based on Trivers's middle-level theory of parental investment. Either way, the derivations flow downward in the diagram, going from the general to the specific.

The top-down strategy illustrates one of the ways in which theories can be extraordinarily useful. Theories provide both a set of working premises from which specific hypotheses can be generated and a framework for guiding researchers to important domains of inquiry such as investing in kin or children.

There is a second strategy for generating evolutionary psychological hypotheses (see Table 2.2). Instead of starting with a theory, we can start with an observation. Once the observation is made about the existence of a phenomenon, we can then proceed in a bottom-up fashion and generate a hypothesis about its function. Because humans are keen perceivers of other people, they generally notice things even without a formal theory to direct attention to

TABLE 2.2 **Two Strategies of Generating and Testing Evolutionary Hypotheses**

| Strategy 1: Theory-Driven or "Top-Down" Strategy | Strategy 2: Observation-Driven or "Bottom-Up" Strategy |
|---|---|
| *Step 1: Derive Hypothesis from Existing Theory*<br>Example: From parental investment theory, we can derive the hypothesis that because women have a greater obligatory investment in offspring than men, women will tend to be more choosy or discriminating in their selection of a mate. | *Step 1: Develop Hypothesis about Adaptive Function Based on a Known Observation*<br>Example: A. Observation: Men seem to give higher priority than women to physical appearance in the selection of a mate. B. Hypothesis: Women's physical appearance provided ancestral men with cues to fertility. |
| *Step 2: Test Predictions Based on Hypothesis*<br>Example: Conduct an experiment to test the prediction that a woman will impose a longer delay and more stringent standards before consenting to sex to evaluate a man's quality and commitment. | *Step 2: Test Predictions Based on Hypothesis*<br>Example: Conduct experiments to determine whether men's standards of attractiveness are closely based on cues to a woman's fertility. |
| *Step 3: Evaluate Whether Empirical Results Confirm Predictions*<br>Example: Women impose longer delays and impose more stringent standards than men before consenting to sex (Buss & Schmitt, 1993; Kennair et al., 2009). | *Step 3: Evaluate Whether Empirical Results Confirm Predictions*<br>Example: Men find a low waist-to-hip ratio, a known fertility correlate, attractive (Dixon et al., 2010; Singh, 1993). |

them. For example, most people don't need a theory to tell them that humans communicate through spoken language, walk upright on two legs, and sometimes wage war on other groups. There is nothing in general evolutionary theory that would have generated the hypothesis that language, bipedal locomotion, or group-on-group warfare would have evolved.

The fact that we observe many things about both ourselves and other species that were not predicted in advance by evolutionary theory does not undermine the theory. But it does raise a problem: How can we explain these phenomena? Can evolutionary thinking help us understand them?

Consider a common observation that has been documented by scientific research: A woman's physical appearance is a significant part of her desirability to men. This is something many people observe without the guidance of any scientific theory. Even your grandmother could probably have told you that most men prefer attractive women. But an evolutionary perspective probes deeper. It asks why.

The most widely advocated evolutionary hypothesis is that a woman's appearance provides a wealth of cues to her fertility (Sugiyama, 2005). What men find attractive, according to this hypothesis, should be specific physical or behavioral features that are linked with fertility. Over evolutionary time, men who were drawn to women showing these fertility cues would have outreproduced men who were drawn to women lacking fertility cues.

Psychologist Devendra Singh has proposed one such feature: the ratio of the waist to the hips, or WHR (Singh, 1993). A low WHR, indicating that the waist is smaller in circumference than the hips, is linked with fertility for two reasons. First, women in fertility clinics with low WHRs get pregnant sooner than women with higher WHRs. Second, women with higher WHRs show a higher incidence of heart disease and endocrinological problems, both of which are linked with lower fertility. So Singh proposed that men will prefer women with low WHRs and that a desire evolved in men to home in on this powerful physical cue to women's fertility.

In a series of studies across several different cultures, Singh presented men with line drawings of women with various WHRs. Some showed a WHR of .70 (waist seven-tenths the size of the hips), others a WHR of .80, and still others a WHR of .90. Men were instructed to circle the figure they found most attractive. In each culture, in samples ranging from Africa to Brazil to the United States, men of varied ages found the .70 WHR woman to be the most attractive. Eye-tracking studies that presented men with visual images of women confirm that this area of the body, along with breasts, receives the highest number of initial visual fixations, suggesting that men's assessments of the hourglass figure occurs very rapidly and automatically (Dixon et al., 2010). So although the notion that men value physical appearance in women is a common observation, specific evolutionary hypotheses can be generated and tested about *why* this phenomenon occurs.

Two conclusions about this "bottom-up" strategy of generating and testing hypotheses can be drawn. First, it is perfectly legitimate for scientists to observe phenomena and subsequently formulate hypotheses about their origins and functions. In astronomy, for example, the finding of the expanding universe was observed first, followed by theories that attempted to explain it. The bottom-up strategy provides a nice complement to the "top-down" theory-driven hypotheses about phenomena that might exist, but have yet to be documented.

Second, the value of an evolutionary hypothesis depends in part on its precision. The more precise the hypothesis, the easier it is to generate specific predictions that follow from it. These predictions are most often based on an analysis of the "design features" the hypothesized adaptation should have if the hypothesis is correct. Step by step, prediction by prediction, hypotheses that fail to yield empirically verified predictions are discarded; those that consistently yield empirically verified predictions are retained. So the entire enterprise shows a cumulative quality as the science moves closer and closer to discovering the existence, complexity, and functionality of evolved psychological mechanisms.

## ■ THE CORE OF HUMAN NATURE: FUNDAMENTALS OF EVOLVED PSYCHOLOGICAL MECHANISMS

In this section, we will address the core of human nature from an evolutionary psychological perspective. First, all species, including humans, have a nature that can be described and explained. Second we provide a definition of evolved psychological mechanisms—the core units that comprise human nature. Finally, we examine important properties of evolved psychological mechanisms.

### All Species Have a Nature

It is part of the male lion's nature to walk on four legs, grow a large furry mane, and hunt other animals for food. It is part of the butterfly's nature to enter a flightless pupa state, wrap itself in a cocoon, and emerge to soar, fluttering gracefully in search of food and mates. It is part of the porcupine's nature to defend itself with quills, the skunk's to defend itself with a spray, the stag's to defend itself with antlers, and the turtle's to defend itself with a shell. All species have a nature; that nature is different for each species. Each species has faced somewhat unique selection pressures during its evolutionary history and therefore has confronted a unique set of adaptive problems.

Humans also have a nature—qualities that define us as a unique species—and all psychological theories imply its existence. For Sigmund Freud, human nature consisted of raging sexual and aggressive impulses. For William James, human nature consisted of dozens or hundreds of instincts. Even the most ardent environmentalist theories, such as B. F. Skinner's theory of radical behaviorism, assume that humans have a nature—in this case, consisting of a few highly general learning mechanisms. All psychological theories require at their core fundamental premises about human nature.

Because evolution by selection is the only known causal process capable of producing the fundamental components of that human nature, all psychological theories are implicitly or explicitly evolutionary. If humans have a nature and evolution by selection is the causal process that produced that nature, then the next question is: What great insights into human nature can be provided by examining our evolutionary origins. Can examining the *process* of evolution tell us anything about the *products* of that process in the human case? Answers to these key questions form the core of the rest of this book.

Whereas the broader field of evolutionary biology is concerned with the evolutionary analysis of all the integrated parts of an organism, evolutionary psychology focuses more narrowly on those parts that are psychological—the analysis of the human mind as a collection of evolved mechanisms, the contexts that activate those mechanisms, and the behaviors generated by those mechanisms. And so, we turn now directly to the class of adaptations that make up the human mind: evolved psychological mechanisms.

*Each species carries its own unique nature—
unique adaptations that differ from those of
other species. The porcupine, skunk, and turtle
all defend themselves against predators, but
each uses a different means of doing so.*

## Definition of an Evolved Psychological Mechanism

An *evolved psychological mechanism* is a set of processes inside an organism with the following
properties:

**1.** *An evolved psychological mechanism exists in the form that it does because it solved
a specific problem of survival or reproduction recurrently over evolutionary history.*
This means that the form of the mechanism, its set of design features, is like a key made to
fit a particular lock. Just as the shape of the key must be coordinated to fit the internal
features of the lock, the shape of the design features of a psychological mechanism must be
coordinated with the features required to solve an adaptive problem of survival or reproduction. Failure to mesh with the adaptive problem meant failure to pass through the selective
sieve of evolution.

**2.** *An evolved psychological mechanism is designed to take in only a narrow slice of
information.* Consider the human eye. Although it seems as though we open our eyes and see
nearly everything, the eye is actually sensitive only to a narrow range of input from the broad
spectrum of electromagnetic waves—those within the visual spectrum. We do not see X-rays,
which are shorter than those in the visual spectrum. Nor do we see radio waves, which are
longer.

Even within the visual spectrum, however, our eyes are designed to process a narrower subset of information (Marr, 1982; Van der Linde et al., 2009). Human eyes have specific edge detectors that pick up contrasting reflections from objects and motion detectors that pick up movement. They also have specific cones designed to pick up certain information about the colors of objects. So the eye is not an all-purpose seeing device. It is designed to process only narrow subsets of information—waves within a particular range of frequency, edges, motion, and so on—from among the much larger domain of potential information.

Similarly, the psychological mechanism of a predisposition to learn to fear snakes is designed to take in only a narrow slice of information—slithery movements from self-propelled elongated objects. Our evolved preferences for food, landscapes, and mates are all designed to take in only a limited subset of information from among the infinite array that could potentially constitute input. The limited cues that activate each mechanism are those that recurred during the EEA or those in the modern environment that closely mimic these ancestral cues.

**3.** *The input of an evolved psychological mechanism tells an organism the particular adaptive problem it is facing.* The input of seeing a slithering snake tells you that you are confronting a particular survival problem, namely, physical damage and perhaps death if bitten. The different smells of potentially edible objects—rancid and rotting versus sweet and fragrant—tell you that you are facing an adaptive survival problem of food selection. The input, in short, lets the organism know which adaptive problem it is dealing with. This almost invariably occurs outside consciousness. Humans do not smell a pizza baking and think, "Aha! I am facing an adaptive problem of food selection!" Instead, the smell unconsciously triggers food selection mechanisms, and no awareness of the adaptive problem is necessary.

**4.** *The input of an evolved psychological mechanism is transformed through decision rules into output.* Upon seeing a snake, you can decide to attack it, run away from it, or freeze. Upon smelling a pizza just out of the oven, you can choose to devour it or walk away from it (perhaps if you are on a diet). The decision rules are a set of procedures—"if, then" statements—for channeling an organism down one path or another. When publicly confronting an angry rival, for example, humans might have "if, then" decision rules such as: "If the angry rival is larger and stronger, then avoid a physical fight; if the angry rival is smaller and weaker, then accept the public challenge and fight." In this example, inputs (a confrontation by an angry rival of a particular size) are transformed through decision rules ("if, then" procedures) into output (behavior to either fight or flee) (see Figure 2.2).

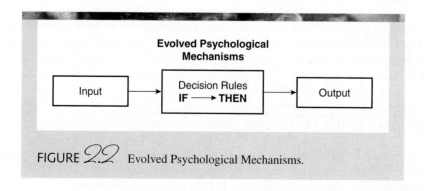

FIGURE 2.2    Evolved Psychological Mechanisms.

**5.** *The output of an evolved psychological mechanism can be physiological activity, informa- tion to other psychological mechanisms, or manifest behavior.* Upon seeing a snake, you may get physiologically aroused or frightened (physiological output); you may use this information to evaluate your behavioral options such as freezing or fleeing (information to other psychologi- cal mechanisms); or you can use this evaluation for action, such as running away (behavioral output).

Consider another example: sexual jealousy. Let's say you go to a party with your romantic partner and then leave the room to get a drink. When you return, you spot your partner talking animatedly with another person. They are standing very close to each other and looking deeply into each other's eyes, and you notice that they are lightly touching each other. These cues might trigger a reaction we can call sexual jealousy. The cues act as input to the mechanism, signaling to you an adaptive problem—the threat of losing your partner. This input is then evaluated ac- cording to a set of decision rules. One option is to ignore the two of them and feign indifference. Another option is to threaten the rival. A third option is to become enraged and hit your partner. Still another option would be to reevaluate your relationship. Thus, the output of a psychologi- cal mechanism can be physiological (arousal), behavioral (confronting, threatening, hitting), or input into other psychological mechanisms (reevaluating the status of your relationship).

**6.** *The output of an evolved psychological mechanism is directed toward the solution to a specific adaptive problem.* Just as the cues to a partner's potential infidelity signal the presence of an adaptive problem, the output of the sexual jealousy mechanism is geared toward solving that problem. The threatened rival may leave the scene, your romantic partner may be deterred from flirting with others, or your reevaluation of the relationship may cause you to cut your losses and move on. Any of these might help with the solution to your adaptive problem.

Stating that the output of a psychological mechanism leads to solutions to specific adaptive problems does not imply that the solutions will always be optimal or successful. The rival may not be deterred by your threats. Your partner may have a fling with your rival despite your display of jealousy. The main point is *not* that the output of a psychological mechanism *always* leads to a successful solution, but rather that the output of the mechanism *on average* tends to solve the adaptive problem better than competing strategies in the environments in which it evolved.

An important point to keep in mind is that a mechanism that led to a successful solution in the evolutionary past may or may not lead to a successful solution now. Our strong taste preferences for fat, for example, were clearly adaptive in our evolutionary past because fat was a valuable and scarce source of calories. Now, however, with hamburger and pizza joints on every street corner, fat is no longer a scarce resource. Thus, our strong taste for such substances now causes us to overconsume fat, which can lead to clogged arteries and heart attacks and thereby hinder our survival. The central point is that evolved mechanisms exist in the forms that they do because they led to success on average during the period in which they evolved. Whether they are currently adaptive—that is, whether they currently lead to increased survival and reproduction— is an empirical matter that must be determined on a case-by-case basis.

In summary, an evolved psychological mechanism is a set of procedures within the organism designed to take in a particular slice of information and transform that information via decision rules into output that historically has helped with the solution to an adaptive problem. The psychological mechanism exists in current organisms because it led, on average, to the successful solution of a specific adaptive problem for that organism's ancestors.

# Important Properties of Evolved Psychological Mechanisms

This section examines several important properties of evolved psychological mechanisms. They provide nonarbitrary criteria for "carving the mind at its natural joints" and tend to be problem specific, numerous, and complex. These features combine to yield the tremendous flexibility of behavior that characterizes modern humans.

### *Evolved Psychological Mechanisms Provide Nonarbitrary Criteria for "Carving the Mind at Its Joints."*   A central premise of evolutionary psychology is that the primary nonarbitrary way to identify, describe, and understand psychological mechanisms is to articulate their functions—the specific adaptive problems they were designed by selection to solve.

Consider the human body. In principle, the mechanisms of the body could be described in an infinite number of ways. Why do anatomists identify as separate mechanisms the liver, the heart, the hand, the nose, and the eyes? The answer is function. The liver is recognized as a mechanism that performs functions different from those performed by the heart or the hand. The eyes and the nose, although located close together, perform different functions and operate according to different inputs (electromagnetic waves in the visual spectrum versus odors). If an anatomist tried to lump the eyes and the nose into one category, it would seem ludicrous. Understanding the component parts of the body requires the identification of function. Function provides a nonarbitrary way to understand these component parts.

Evolutionary psychologists believe that similar principles should be used for understanding the mechanisms of the mind. Although the mind could be divided in an infinite number of ways, most of them would be arbitrary. A powerful nonarbitrary analysis of the human mind is one that rests on function. If two components of the mind perform different functions, they can be regarded as separate mechanisms (although they may interact with each other in interesting ways).

### *Evolved Psychological Mechanisms Tend to be Problem Specific.*   Imagine giving someone directions to get from New York City to a specific street address in San Francisco, California. If you gave general directions such as "head west," the person might end up as far south as Texas or as far north as Alaska. The general direction would not reliably get the person to the right state.

Now let's suppose that the person did get to the right state. The "head west" direction would be virtually useless because west of California is ocean. The general direction would not provide any guidance to get to the right city within California, let alone the right street address. To get the person to the right state, city, street, and location on that street, you would need to give more specific instructions. Furthermore, although there are many ways to get to a particular street address, some paths will be far more efficient and time-saving than others.

The search for a specific street address on the other side of the country is a good analogy for what is needed to reach a specific adaptive solution. Adaptive problems, like street addresses, are specific—don't get bitten by that snake, select a habitat with running water and places to hide, avoid eating food that is poisonous, select a mate who is fertile, and so on. There is no such thing as a "general adaptive problem" (Symons, 1992).

Because adaptive problems are specific, their solutions tend to be specific as well. Just as general instructions fail to get you to the correct location, general solutions fail to get you to the right adaptive solution. Consider two adaptive problems: selecting the right foods to eat (a survival

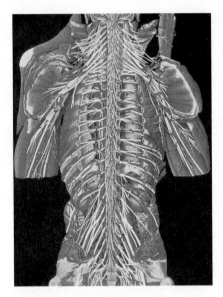

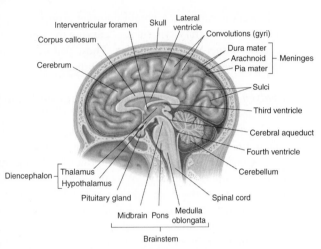

*Just as the body contains many specialized and complex physiological and anatomical mechanisms, many evolutionary psychologists believe that the mind, housed in the brain, also contains many specialized and complex mechanisms.*

problem) and selecting the right mate with whom to have children (a reproduction problem). What counts as a "successful solution" is quite different for the two problems. Successful food selection involves identifying objects that have calories and particular vitamins and minerals and do not contain poisonous substances. Successful mate selection involves, among other things, identifying a partner who is fertile and will be a good parent.

What might be a general solution to these two selection problems, and how effective would it be at solving them? One general solution would be "select the first thing that comes along." This would be disastrous because it might lead to eating poisonous plants or marrying an infertile person. If anyone had implemented such a general solution to these adaptive problems in human evolutionary history, he or she would have failed to become one of our ancestors.

To solve these selection problems in a reasonable way, one would need more specific guidance about the important qualities of foods and mates. Fruit that looks fresh and ripe, for example, will signal better nutrients than fruit that looks rotten. People who look young and healthy will be more fertile, on average, than people who look old and ill. We need *specific selection criteria*—qualities that are part of our selection mechanisms—to solve these selection problems successfully.

The specificity of mechanisms is further illustrated by errors. If you make an error in food selection, there is an array of mechanisms tailored to correcting that error. When you bite a piece of bad food, it may taste terrible, in which case you would spit it out. You may gag on it if it makes its way past your taste buds. And if it makes its way all the way down to your stomach, you may vomit—a specific mechanism designed to get rid of toxic or harmful ingested substances. But if you make an error in mate selection, you do not spit, gag, or throw up (at least not usually). You correct your error in other ways—by leaving or selecting someone else.

In summary, problem specificity of adaptive mechanisms tends to be favored over generality because (1) general solutions fail to guide the organism to the correct adaptive solutions; (2) even if they do work, general solutions lead to too many errors and thus are costly to the organism; and (3) what constitutes a "successful solution" differs from problem to problem. The adaptive solutions, in short, have dedicated procedures and content-sensitive elements to solve adaptive problems successfully.

***Humans Possess Many Evolved Psychological Mechanisms.*** Humans, like most organisms, face a large number of adaptive problems. The problems of survival alone number in the dozens or hundreds—problems of thermal regulation (being too cold or too hot), avoiding predators and parasites, ingesting life-sustaining foods, and so on. Then there are problems of mating such as selecting, attracting, and keeping a good mate and getting rid of a bad mate. There are also problems of parenting such as breastfeeding, weaning, socializing, attending to the varying needs of different children, and so on. Then there are the problems of investing in kin, such as brothers, sisters, nephews, and nieces; dealing with social conflicts; defending against aggressive groups; and grappling with the social hierarchy.

Because specific problems require specific solutions, numerous specific problems will require numerous specific solutions. Just as our bodies contain thousands of specific mechanisms—a heart to pump blood, lungs for oxygen uptake, a liver to filter out toxins—the mind, according to this analysis, must also contain hundreds or thousands of specific mechanisms. Because a large number of different adaptive problems cannot be solved with just a few mechanisms, the human mind must be made up of a large number of evolved psychological mechanisms.

***The Specificity, Complexity, and Numerousness of Evolved Psychological Mechanisms Give Humans Behavioral Flexibility.*** The definition of a psychological mechanism, including the key components of input, decision rules, and output, highlights why adaptations are not rigid "instincts" that invariably show up in behavior. Recall the example of callus-producing mechanisms that have evolved to protect the structures beneath the skin. You can design your environment so that you don't experience repeated friction. In this case, your callus-producing mechanisms will not be activated. The activation of the mechanisms depends on contextual input from the environment. In the same way, all psychological mechanisms require input for their activation.

Psychological mechanisms are not like rigid instincts for another important reason—the decision rules. Decision rules are "if, then" procedures such as "if the snake hisses, then run for your life" or "if the person I'm attracted to shows interest, then smile and decrease distance." For most mechanisms, these decision rules permit at least several possible response options. Even in the simple case of encountering a snake, you have the options of attacking it with a stick, freezing and hoping it will go away, or running away. In general, the more complex the mechanism, the greater the number of response options there will be.

Consider a carpenter's toolbox. The carpenter gains flexibility not by having one "highly general tool" that can be used to cut, poke, saw, screw, twist, wrench, plane, balance, and hammer. Instead, the carpenter gains flexibility by having a large number of highly specific tools in the toolbox. These highly specific tools can then be used in many combinations that would not be possible with one highly "flexible" tool. Indeed, it is difficult to imagine what a "general" tool would even look like, since there is no such thing as a "general carpenter's problem." In a similar fashion, humans gain their flexibility from having a large number of complex, specific, functional psychological mechanisms.

With each new mechanism that is added to the mind, an organism can perform a new task. A bird has feet that enable it to walk; adding wings enables it to fly. Adding a beak to a bird enables it to break the shells of seeds and nuts and get at their edible core. With each new specific mechanism that is added, the bird can complete a new task that it could not have done before. Having feet as well as wings gives the bird the flexibility to both walk and fly.

This leads to a conclusion contrary to human intuition, which for most of us holds that having a lot of innate mechanisms causes behavior to be inflexible. In fact, just the opposite is the case. The more mechanisms we have, the greater the range of behaviors we can perform, and hence the greater the flexibility of our behavior.

***Beyond Domain-Specific Psychological Mechanisms.***   All of the arguments presented in the preceding pages suggest that humans must possess a large number of specialized psychological mechanisms, each dedicated to solving specific adaptive problems. This conclusion is widely accepted within the field of evolutionary psychology and indeed lies at the foundation of evolutionary approaches to all species (Alcock, 2009). As one evolutionary psychologist put it, "The idea that a single generic substance can see in depth, control the hands, attract a mate, bring up children, elude predators, outsmart prey, and so on, without *some* degree of specialization, is not credible. Saying that the brain solves these problems because of its 'plasticity' is not much better than saying it solves them by magic" (Pinker, 2002, p. 75). Some evolutionary psychologists, however, have argued that *in addition* to these specific mechanisms, humans *also* have evolved several domain-general mechanisms (e.g., Chiappe & MacDonald, 2005; Figueredo, Hammond, & McKiernan, 2006; Geary & Huffman, 2002; Livingstone, 1998; Mithen, 1996; Premack, 2010). Examples of proposed general mechanisms are general intelligence, concept formation, analogical reasoning, working memory, and classical conditioning (see Chapter 1).

The proponents of domain-general mechanisms contend that although recurrent features of adaptive problems select for specialized adaptations, humans have faced many novel problems that did not recur with sufficient regularity for specific adaptations to have evolved. Furthermore, we know that humans routinely solve ancient adaptive problems in highly novel ways; for example, we can get food from a vending machine, mates from the Internet, and tools from a hardware store. Everyone recognizes that humans have been able to flourish in an environment very different from that in which we evolved, "a constantly changing world far removed from the Pleistocene" (Chiappe & MacDonald, 2005, p. 6). Chiappe and MacDonald (2005) propose that domain-general mechanisms, such as general intelligence, evolved precisely to "allow for the solution of non-recurrent problems in attaining evolutionary goals" (2005, p. 3) or to develop new solutions to old problems.

The central thrust of their argument is that in human evolutionary history, humans were forced to cope with rapidly changing environments—unpredictable changes in climate, fluctuations between cold ice ages and warm weather, rapid changes due to volcanoes and earthquakes, and so on. Similarly, Geary and Huffman (2002) contend that many information patterns over human evolutionary history were highly variable, which might favor the evolution of more general psychological mechanisms that are open to experience (see also Geary, 2009). Domain-general mechanisms, these theorists propose, would be necessary to handle novelty, unpredictability, and variability. Interestingly, Kanazawa (2003b) marshals a similar argument, but proposes that "general intelligence" is actually a domain-specific adaptation designed to solve a narrow class of problems—those that are evolutionarily novel.

Some evolutionary psychologists remain skeptical about whether truly domain-general mechanisms could evolve (e.g., Cosmides & Tooby, 2002). Just because people can perform evolutionary novel tasks such as surfing the Internet or driving a car does not necessarily mean that the adaptations that allow us to perform these tasks are themselves domain general. For that matter, just because you can train a grizzly bear to ride a bicycle or a dolphin to rock to music does not mean that the adaptations that allow these novel behaviors are domain general. At this point in the science of evolutionary psychology, it is premature to draw any firm conclusions about whether humans possess more domain-general mechanisms in addition to the specific ones. What is clear is this: The assumption of domain specificity has been used successfully to discover important mechanisms of the human mind. Subsequent chapters in this book document these scientific successes. Whether comparable empirical discoveries will be made by research programs based on the premise of domain-general mechanisms remains an open question.

What is also apparent, however, is that the human mind cannot consist solely of isolated separate mechanisms that are entirely walled off from each other. Selection favors functionally specialized mechanisms *that work well together* in various combinations and permutations. Adaptations "talk to each other," so to speak. Data gleaned from some mechanisms, for example, provide information to other mechanisms, as when information from sight, smell, and internal hunger all provide input into decision rules about the edibility of food objects. In this sense, evolutionary psychologists tend *not* to make "information encapsulation" a defining feature of evolved psychological mechanisms (Hagen, 2005), as is sometimes used when invoking the concept of "modularity" (Fodor, 1983). The property of information encapsulation means that psychological mechanisms have access only to self-contained information and cannot access information in other psychological mechanisms.

Furthermore, humans also likely have *superordinate mechanisms* that function to regulate other mechanisms. Imagine walking through the woods when you suddenly encounter a hungry lion, a bush bursting with ripe berries, and an attractive potential mate. What do you do? You might choose first to avoid the lion, even at the cost of foregoing the berries and the potential mate. If you are near starvation, you might choose instead to take a chance on grabbing some berries before fleeing the lion. Evolved psychological mechanisms clearly interact with each other in complex ways. They are turned on and off in various sequences that are not fully understood. The possibility that humans possess evolved superordinate regulatory mechanisms remains promising and awaits future research.

## Learning, Culture, and Evolved Psychological Mechanisms

A common question that arises when evolved psychological mechanisms are postulated is some variant of the following: *Aren't the human behaviors we observe caused by learning and culture, not evolution? Aren't human behaviors the product of nurture, not nature?* To answer these questions, we must carefully analyze the precise form of explanations that invoke evolved psychological mechanisms and the form of those that invoke learning and culture.

To start with, the framework of evolutionary psychology dissolves dichotomies such as "nature versus nurture," "innate versus learned," and "biological versus cultural." If you go back to the definition of evolved psychological mechanisms, you will note that (1) environments featuring recurrent selection pressure over deep time formed each mechanism; (2) environmental input during a person's development is necessary for the emergence of each mechanism; and

(3) environmental input is necessary for the activation of each mechanism. Thus, it does not make sense to ask whether a callus or jealous behavior is "evolved" or "learned." "Evolved" is not the opposite of "learned." All behavior requires evolved psychological mechanisms combined with environmental input at each stage in the causal chain.

Next, let us ask precisely what it means to say that something is learned. As typically used in psychology, invoking "learning" as an explanation is simply the weak claim that something in the organism changed as a consequence of input from the environment. Humans do learn, of course. They are affected by their environments and cultures. Learning, however, requires structures in the brain—evolved psychological mechanisms—that enable them to learn: "after all, 3-pound cauliflowers do not learn, but 3-pound brains do" (Tooby & Cosmides, 2005, p. 31). The explanatory challenge is not well met simply by slapping the label of "learning" on a behavior. We have to identify the nature of the underlying learning mechanisms that enable humans to change their behavior as a consequence of environmental input.

Now what is the nature of these learning mechanisms? Let's consider three concrete examples: (1) people learn to avoid having sex with their close genetic relatives (learned incest avoidance); (2) people learn to avoid eating foods that may contain toxins (learned food aversions); (3) people learn from their local culture what actions lead to increases in status and prestige (learned prestige criteria). There is compelling evidence that each of these forms of learning is best explained by *different evolved learning mechanisms.*

Solving the adaptive problem of incest avoidance requires learning about a class of individuals—one's close genetic relatives—with whom one should not have sex. How can people learn who these individuals are? The evolved incest avoidance learning mechanism functions by using a reliable cue to who are genetic relatives—those with whom they grow up. Duration of co-residence with a member of the opposite sex during childhood powerfully predicts lack of sexual attraction—and indeed the amount of repulsion at the idea of having sex with them (Lieberman, Tooby, & Cosmides, 2003).

Now consider learned food aversions. We learn food aversions through a mechanism that makes us feel nauseous after we consume certain foods. Those who have an intense dislike of mushrooms or liver or fish have typically experienced an earlier event in which they got sick after consuming such a food. Finally, consider how we learn which cues in our local culture are linked with status and prestige. Among hunter-gatherer societies, good hunting skills lead to prestige. In academia, individuals who have prominent publications that are cited a lot by other scholars attain high prestige. Among other local cultures, number of tattoos, size of motorcycle, or skill at guitar playing is associated with high prestige. People learn prestige criteria, in part, by scrutinizing the attention structure—those high in prestige are typically those to whom the most people pay the most attention (Chance, 1967). By attending to (and often trying to imitate) the qualities, clothing styles, and behaviors of those to whom others pay the most attention, we learn the prestige criteria of our local culture.

These three forms of learning—incest avoidance, food aversion, and prestige criteria—clearly require different evolved learning mechanisms to function. Each form operates on the basis of inputs from different set of cues—co-residence during development, nausea paired with food ingestion, and the attention structure, respectively. Each has different functional output—lack of sexual attraction to relatives, disgust at the sight and smell of certain substances, and attention to those to whom others are attending. And importantly, each form of learning solves a different adaptive problem.

There are three critical points to draw from this analysis. First, labeling something as "learned" does not provide an explanation; it is simply a description that environmental input changes the organism in some way. Second, "learned" and "evolved" are not competing explanations; rather, learning *requires* specialized evolved psychological mechanisms to occur. Third, evolved learning mechanisms are often specific in nature (see Chapter 13 for an extended discussion of the evolutionary psychology of culture).

# ■ METHODS FOR TESTING EVOLUTIONARY HYPOTHESES

Once clearly formulated hypotheses about evolved psychological mechanisms and associated predictions are specified, the next step is to test them empirically. Evolutionary psychologists have a wide array of scientific methods at their disposal (Schmitt, 2008; Simpson & Campbell, 2005). The scientific foundation of evolutionary psychology, as we will see, rests not on a single method, but rather on convergent evidence from a variety of methods and sources of data (see Table 2.3).

## Comparing Different Species

Comparing species that differ along particular dimensions provides one source of evidence for testing functional hypotheses. The comparative method involves "testing predictions about the occurrence of the trait among species other than the animals whose behavior the researcher is trying to understand" (Alcock, 1993, p. 221). As an example, consider the following sperm competition hypothesis: The function of producing large sperm volume is to displace competing males' sperm and hence increase the odds of fertilizing a female's egg.

One strategy for testing this hypothesis is to compare species that differ in the prevalence of sperm competition. In highly monogamous species, sperm competition is rare or absent.

TABLE *2.3* **Methods and Data Sources for Testing Evolutionary Hypotheses**

| Methods for Testing Evolutionary Hypotheses | Sources of Data for Testing Evolutionary Hypotheses |
| --- | --- |
| 1. Compare different species | 1. Archeological records |
| 2. Cross-cultural methods | 2. Data from hunter-gatherer societies |
| 3. Physiological and brain imaging methods | 3. Observations |
| 4. Genetic methods | 4. Self-reports |
| 5. Compare males and females | 5. Life-history data and public records |
| 6. Compare individuals within a species | 6. Human products |
| 7. Compare the same individuals in different contexts | |
| 8. Experimental methods | |

In certain species of birds (e.g., ring doves) and mammals (e.g., gibbons), males and females pair off to produce offspring and rarely have sex outside the pair-bond. In other species, such as bonobo chimpanzees, females will copulate with a number of males (de Waal, 2006). In this species, there is a great deal of sperm competition. Thus, we know that sperm competition is high in promiscuous species and low in monogamous species.

Now comes the test. We can line up species by the degree to which sperm competition is likely to be prevalent. Among primates, for example, gorillas tend to be the least promiscuous, followed by orangutans, humans, and chimpanzees, which are the most promiscuous. Next, we can obtain comparative data on the sperm volume in each of these species as indicated by testicular weight, corrected for body size. The prediction from the sperm competition hypothesis is that males in species that show a lot of sperm competition should have higher testicular weight (indicating a high volume of sperm) compared with species that show lower levels of sperm competition.

The comparative evidence yields the following findings. The testes of male gorillas account for 0.02 percent of body weight; of male orangutans, 0.05 percent of body weight; of human males, 0.08 percent of body weight; and of the highly promiscuous chimpanzees, 0.27 percent of body weight (Short, 1979; Smith, 1984). In sum, males in the species showing intense sperm competition display larger testicular volume; males in the species with the least sperm competition display the lowest testicular volume. The comparative method thus supports the sperm competition hypothesis.

The method of comparing different species, of course, is not limited to sperm competition and testicular volume. We can also compare species that are known to face a particular adaptive problem with those known not to face that problem. We can compare cliff-dwelling goats and non–cliff-dwelling goats to test the hypothesis that goats that graze on cliffs will have specialized adaptations to avoid falling, such as better spatial orientation abilities. We can compare species that have known predators with those lacking those predators to test the hypothesis that there are specific adaptations to combat those predators (e.g., specific alarm calls sounded when encountering an image of the predator). Comparing different species, in short, is a powerful method for testing hypotheses about adaptive function (Fraley, Brumbaugh, & Marks, 2005).

## Cross-Cultural Methods

Cross-cultural methods provide valuable tools for testing evolutionary psychological hypotheses (Schmitt, 2008). The most obvious method pertains to adaptations that are hypothesized to be universal, such as basic emotions (Ekman, 1973), adaptations for cooperation (Cosmides & Tooby, 2005), or sex-differentiated mating strategies (Lippa, 2009; Schmitt, 2005). Comparing different cultures can also be used to examine adaptations hypothesized to respond to differing ecologies. Mate preferences, for example, have been hypothesized to be sensitive to ecological variations in parasite prevalence, which has been confirmed in a study of thirty-seven cultures (Gangestad, Haselton, & Buss, 2006).

Cross-cultural methods can also be used to test competing theories by pitting them against each other. Lippa et al. (2010), for example, explored gender differences in a mental rotation task across fifty-three cultures. Mental rotation ability has been hypothesized to be part of a male hunting adaptation, because hunters have to anticipate the trajectories of spears and other hunting implements as they move through space to coincide with the trajectory of a moving animal. In contrast, according to social role theory, psychological gender differences are hypothesized to be a function of the roles assigned by different cultures, and hence should diminish as equality between the sexes increases. Lippa's cross-cultural study found two key findings: (1) the gender differences in mental rotation ability were universal across cultures, and (2) contrary to social role theory, the gender differences were actually somewhat *larger* in cultures with more gender quality. Cross-cultural methods, in short, are extremely valuable for testing a range of evolutionary hypotheses, as well as for pitting competing hypotheses against each other.

## Physiological and Brain Imaging Methods

Physiological methods can be used to assess phenomena such as emotional arousal, sexual arousal, and stress. These methods can be used both to identify the biological substrates of psychological adaptations as well as to test hypotheses about design features of those adaptations. Flinn, Ward, & Noone (2005) tested the hypothesis that children living with stepparents would experience higher levels of stress than children living with two biological parents. They found that indeed stepchildren had higher levels of cortisol—one of the key hormones that gets released when people experience stress—than nonstepchildren. Another study confirmed the hypothesis that testosterone, one of the key hormones involved in mate competition, would be reduced in men who were in committed romantic relationships (McIntyre et al., 2006). Yet another study found that the presence of attractive women increased men's testosterone levels (Ronay & von Hippel, 2010). In sum, physiological methods become valuable both in testing hypotheses about adaptations as well as in identifying the underlying substrates of adaptations.

Brain imaging techniques, such as functional magnetic resonance imaging (fMRI), are increasingly being used to test hypotheses about adaptations and their underlying neural basis. FMRI methods have been used to test hypotheses about adaptations for kin recognition, language, spatial cognition, romantic attraction, and jealousy (Platek, Keenan, & Shackelford, 2007). Although brain imaging techniques are limited in the range of phenomena they are able to examine, because participants in studies must remain immobile while they are exposed to stimuli, their use in testing evolutionary psychological hypotheses has increased dramatically over the past decade.

## Genetic Methods

Traditional behavioral genetic methods, such as twin studies and adoption studies, can be used to test some evolutionary hypotheses (Segal, 2011). One evolutionary hypothesis, for example, proposes a context-dependent adaptation in females to shift to early onset of sexuality and menarche (age of first menstruation) when growing up without an investing father around, compared to a delayed onset of sexuality when there is an investing father (e.g., Belsky, 1997; Ellis, 2011). Behavioral genetic methods can determine whether individual differences in onset of female sexuality is environmentally mediated, as the evolutionary hypothesis suggests, or instead is genetically mediated, which would refute the hypothesis.

Molecular genetic methods are more recent. They are designed to identify the specific genes that underlie hypothesized adaptations. Individual variations in the alleles of the DRD4 gene provide one example. The 7R allele of the DRD4 gene has been linked with novelty seeking and extraversion (Ebstein, 2006), and it occurs at dramatically different rates in different geographical regions (e.g., higher in North America than in Asia). The 7R allele has been hypothesized to be advantageous in exploiting resources in novel environments (Chen et al., 1999; Penke, Denissen, & Miller, 2007). The finding that the 7R allele is substantially more common in nomadic than in sedentary populations supports this evolutionary psychological hypothesis (Eisenberg et al., 2008).

Molecular genetic methods have also revealed fascinating findings about human evolution. First, they can be used to test between competing hypotheses about modern human origins out of Africa, as we saw in Chapter 1. Second, they can identify the genetic basis of some simple adaptations that have emerged within the past 10,000 years, such as the gene that facilitates the digestion of dairy products (Bersaglieri et al., 2004). And third, molecular genetic studies show that there has been an *acceleration* of human adaptive evolution over the past 40,000 years, and especially during the past 10,000 years (the Holocene) (Hawks et al., 2007). This astonishing finding runs contrary to the earlier view by many scientists that genetic evolution has slowed or stopped, supplanted entirely by purely cultural evolution.

## Comparing Males and Females

Sexually reproducing species usually come in two forms: male and female. Comparing the sexes provides another method for testing hypotheses about adaptation. One comparative strategy involves analyzing the different natures of the adaptive problems faced by males and females. In species with internal female fertilization, for example, males face the adaptive problem of "paternity uncertainty." They never can "know" with complete certainty whether they are the genetic father of their mate's offspring. The females, however, do not confront this adaptive problem. They "know" that their own eggs, not a rival's eggs, are fertilized because the eggs can only come from within themselves.

On the basis of this analysis, we can compare males and females to see whether males have evolved specific adaptations that have the function of increasing their chances of paternity. We will examine these adaptations in detail in Chapter 5, but one example will suffice to make the point here: male sexual jealousy. Although both sexes are equally jealous overall, studies have shown that men's jealousy, far more than women's, is activated specifically by signals of *sexual* infidelity, suggesting one solution to the problem of paternity uncertainty (Buss et al., 1992; Schützwohl, 2008). Once activated, men's jealousy motivates behavior designed to repel a rival or to dissuade a mate from an infidelity. The fact that men's jealousy is especially triggered by cues to sexual infidelity points to a facet of men's psychology that corresponds to a sex-linked adaptive problem—that of uncertainty of parenthood. In sum, comparing the sexes within one species can be a powerful method of testing evolutionary hypotheses.

## Comparing Individuals within a Species

A third method involves comparing some individuals with other individuals within one species. Consider young and older women. Teenage girls have many years of potential reproduction ahead of them; women in their late thirties have fewer fertile years left. We can use these differences to formulate and test hypotheses about adaptation.

For example, suppose you hypothesized that younger women would be more likely to abort a developing fetus than older women if there weren't an investing man around to help. The evolutionary rationale is this: Because they have many reproductive years left, younger women can "afford" to lose the chance to have a child to wait for a more opportune time to reproduce. The older woman may not get another chance to have a child. Comparing the rates of abortion, miscarriage, and infanticide in the two groups of women provides one method for testing this hypothesis.

Comparing individuals within a species is not restricted, of course, to age. We can compare individuals who are poor to those who are rich to test the hypothesis that the poor will engage in "riskier" strategies of acquiring resources; the rich might be more "conservative" to protect their wealth. We can compare women who have many strong brothers around to protect them with women who are only children to see whether women in the second group are more vulnerable to abuse at the hands of men. We can compare individuals who differ in their desirability as mates or individuals who differ in the sizes of their extended families. In short, within-species comparison also constitutes a powerful method for testing evolutionary hypotheses about adaptation.

## Comparing the Same Individuals in Different Contexts

Another approach is to compare the same individuals in different situations. Among the Siriono of eastern Bolivia, for example, one man who was a particularly unsuccessful hunter had lost several wives to men who were better hunters. He suffered a loss of status within the group, due to both his poor hunting and his loss of wives to other men. Anthropologist A. R. Holmberg took up hunting with this man, gave him game that others were later told the man had killed, and taught him the art of killing game with a shotgun. Eventually, as a result of the man's increased hunting success, he enjoyed an increase in social status, attracted several women as sex partners, and started insulting others rather than being the victim of insults (Holmberg, 1950).

Comparing the same individuals in different situations is a powerful method for revealing evolved psychological mechanisms. Hypotheses can be formulated about the adaptive problems confronted in two different situations and hence about which psychological mechanisms will be activated in each. In the case of the Siriono man who went from low to high status thanks to a change in his hunting ability, the higher status apparently caused him to be more self-confident. It also seems to have affected the psychological mechanisms of other Siriono men, who shifted from insulting the man to being more respectful.

Unfortunately, it is sometimes difficult for researchers to wait until a person moves from one context to another. People often find a niche and stay there. Furthermore, even when people do shift situations, many things tend to change at once, making it difficult for researchers to isolate the specific causal factor responsible for a change. Because of the problems of separating the specific causal factors responsible, scientists sometimes try to "control" the situation in psychological experiments.

## Experimental Methods

In experiments, one group of subjects is typically exposed to a "manipulation" and a second group serves as a "control." Let's say that we develop a hypothesis about the effect of threat on the tightness of "in-group cohesion." The hypothesis states that humans have evolved a specific psychological mechanism whose function is to react adaptively to threats from the outside, such as an invasion by a hostile group of humans. Under threat conditions, group cohesion should increase, as manifested by such tendencies as showing favoritism toward in-group members and showing an increase in prejudice toward out-group members.

In the laboratory, experimenters choose one group of subjects at random and tell them they may have to go to a smaller room because another group has first priority on the room they are in. Before they leave, the experimenter gives them $100 as payment for participating in the study, with instructions to divide the money between the two groups however they want. The control group is also charged with dividing the money between their group and another group but is not told that the other group is taking over their room. We can then compare how the control group and the experimental group decide to split up the money. If there is no difference between the experimental and control groups, we would conclude that our prediction had failed. If the threatened group allocated more money to itself but the control group allocated equally, then our prediction would be confirmed—external threat increases in-group favoritism. In sum, the experimental method—subjecting different groups to different conditions (sometimes called manipulations)—can be used to test hypotheses about adaptations.

# ■ SOURCES OF DATA FOR TESTING EVOLUTIONARY HYPOTHESES

In addition to the research methods, evolutionary psychologists have a wealth of other sources from which they can obtain data for testing hypotheses. This section briefly presents some of these sources.

## Archeological Records

Bone fragments secured from around the world reveal a paleontological record filled with interesting artifacts. Through carbon-dating methods, we can obtain rough estimates of the ages of skulls and skeletons and trace the evolution of brain size through the millennia. Bones from large game animals found at ancestral campsites can reveal how our ancestors solved the adaptive problem of securing food. Fossilized feces can provide information about other features of the ancestral diet. Analyses of bone fragments can also reveal sources of injury, disease, and death. The archeological record provides one set of clues about how we lived and evolved and the nature of the adaptive problems our ancestors confronted.

## Data from Hunter-Gatherer Societies

Current studies of traditional peoples, especially those relatively isolated from Western civilization, also provide a rich source of data for testing evolutionary hypotheses. Studies by anthropologists Kim Hill and Hillard Kaplan (1988), for example, show that successful hunters do not benefit directly from their efforts because meat is shared by the group, but they do benefit in other reproductively relevant ways. The children of successful hunters receive more care and attention from the group, resulting in their superior health. Successful hunters also are sexually attractive to women and tend to have more mistresses and more desirable wives.

Findings from contemporary hunter-gatherers, of course, are not definitive. There are many differences among the various groups of tribal societies. But this data source provides evidence that, in conjunction with other sources of data, allows us to formulate and test hypotheses about human psychology.

## Observations

Systematic observations provide a third method for testing evolutionary hypotheses. Anthropologist Mark Flinn devised a behavioral scanning technique for systematically gathering observations in Trinidad (Flinn, 1988a; Flinn, Ward, & Noone, 2005). Every day, he walked through the targeted village, visiting every household and recording each observation he made on a record sheet. He was able to confirm, for example, the hypothesis that men with fertile wives engaged in more intense "mate guarding" than men with less fertile wives (i.e., those who were pregnant or old). He determined this through behavioral scans that showed that men tended to get into more fights with other men when their wives were fertile and fewer fights when their wives were not fertile. Observational data can be collected from a variety of sources—trained observers such as Flinn, husbands or wives of the target subjects, friends and relatives, even casual acquaintances. Data from observations, like all sources of data, contain potential flaws and biases. An observer may have preconceptions about what he or she expects to observe, which could bias the recordings. Observers also may not be privy to important domains of behavior, such as sexual behavior, because people prefer to guard their privacy. Researchers must be sensitive to these sources of bias and be sure to supplement their observations with other sources of data.

## Self-Reports

Reports by the actual subjects provide an invaluable source of data. Self-report data can be secured through interviews or questionnaires. There are some psychological phenomena that can be examined only through self-report. Consider sexual fantasies. These are private experiences that leave no fossils and cannot be observed by outsiders. In one study, evolutionary psychologists Bruce Ellis and Donald Symons were able to test hypotheses about sex differences in sexual fantasy (Ellis & Symons, 1990). They found that men's sexual fantasies tended to involve more sexual partners and more partner switching and were more visually oriented. Women's sexual fantasies tended to have more mystery, romance, emotional expressions, and context. Without self-report, this sort of study could not be conducted.

Self-report has been used to test a variety of evolutionary psychological hypotheses about mate preferences (Buss, 1989a), violence against spouses (Kaighobadi & Shackelford, 2009), tactics of deception (Tooke & Camire, 1991), tactics of getting ahead in social hierarchies (Kyl-Heku & Buss, 1996), and patterns of cooperation and helping (McGuire, 1994).

Like all data sources, self-report carries with it biases and limitations. People may be reluctant to divulge behavior or thoughts they fear will be judged undesirable, such as extramarital affairs or unusual sexual fantasies. People may lie. Subjects may say things just to please the experimenter or to sabotage the study. For these reasons, evolutionary psychologists try not to rely exclusively on self-report.

## Life-History Data and Public Records

People leave traces of their lives on public documents. Marriages and divorces, births and deaths, crimes and misdemeanors, are all part of the public record. In one series of studies, the evolutionary biologist Bobbi Low was able to unearth data on marriages, divorces, and remarriages from different parishes in Sweden recorded many centuries ago. The priests of these parishes kept scrupulously accurate and detailed records of these public events. By looking at marriage and divorce rates from 400 years ago, we can see whether the patterns that occur today are long-standing and recurrent over human history or merely products of our modern times. Low was able to test a number of evolutionary hypotheses using these public records. She confirmed, for example, that wealthier men tended to marry younger (and hence more fertile) women compared with poorer men (Low, 1991).

Public records, in short, provide an invaluable source of data for testing evolutionary hypotheses. They are limited, of course, in many ways. Rarely do the public records contain all the information researchers seek to rule out potential alternative explanations. Yet public records, especially if used in conjunction with other sources of data, can be treasure troves for creative scientists.

## Human Products

The things humans make are products of their evolved minds. Modern fast-food restaurants, for example, are products of evolved taste preferences. Hamburgers, French fries, milk shakes, and pizza are filled with fat, sugar, salt, and protein. They sell well precisely because they correspond to, and exploit, evolved desires for these substances. Thus, food creations reveal evolved taste preferences.

Other sorts of human products reveal the design of our evolved minds. The pornography and romance novel industries, for example, can be viewed as creations of common fantasies. The themes common in plays, paintings, movies, music, operas, novels, soap operas, and popular songs all reveal something about our evolved psychology (Carroll, 2005). Human creations thus can serve as an additional data source for testing evolutionary hypotheses.

*We live in a modern food environment vastly different from the one in which our eating adaptations evolved. Fat and sugar, once scarce resources, are now readily available in great quantities. This changed environment may now lead to behaviors that are maladaptive in the sense that they hinder our survival.*

## Transcending the Limitations of Single Data Sources

All data sources have limitations. The fossil record is fragmentary and has large gaps. With contemporary hunter-gatherers, we do not know the degree to which current practices are contaminated by modern influences. In self-reports, people may lie or fail to know the truth. With observational reports, many important domains of behavior are hidden from prying eyes; those that are not may be distorted due to observer bias. Laboratory experiments are often contrived and artificial, rendering their generalizability to real-world contexts questionable. Life data from public records, although seemingly objective, can also be subject to systematic biases. Even human products must be interpreted through a chain of inferences that may or may not be valid.

The solution to these problems is to use multiple data sources in testing evolutionary hypotheses. Findings that emerge consistently across data sources that do not share methodological limitations are especially powerful. By using multiple data sources, researchers can transcend the limitations of any single data source and arrive at a firmer empirical foundation for evolutionary psychology.

## ■ IDENTIFYING ADAPTIVE PROBLEMS

It is clear that humans, like many species, have faced an extraordinary number of adaptive problems over human evolutionary history, giving rise to many complex adaptive mechanisms. The next critical question is: How do we know what these adaptive problems are?

No amount of conceptual work can definitively yield a complete list of all the adaptive problems humans have faced. This indeterminacy is caused by several factors. First, we cannot rewind the evolutionary clock and see all the things our ancestors confronted in the past. Second, each new adaptation creates new adaptive problems of its own, such as becoming coordinated with other adaptive mechanisms. Identifying the full set of human adaptive problems is an enormous task that will occupy scientists for decades to come. Nonetheless, several guidelines give us a start.

## Guidance from Modern Evolutionary Theory

One guideline is the structure of modern evolutionary theory itself, which tells us that the differential reproduction of genes coding for design differences, either through producing descendants or through helping genetic relatives produce descendants, is the engine of the evolutionary process. Therefore, all adaptive problems must by definition be things that are required for reproduction or that aid reproduction, however indirectly.

So to start, evolutionary theory guides us to the following broad classes of adaptive problems.

1. *Problems of survival and growth:* getting the organism to the point at which it is capable of reproduction
2. *Problems of mating:* selecting, attracting, and retaining a mate and performing the needed sexual behavior required for successful reproduction

3. *Problems of parenting:* helping offspring survive and grow to the point at which they are capable of reproduction
4. *Problems of aiding genetic relatives:* the tasks entailed in aiding the reproduction of nondescendant kin who carry copies of one's genes

These four classes of problems provide a reasonable starting point.

## Guidance from Knowledge of Universal Human Structures

A second source of guidance to identifying adaptive problems comes from the accumulated knowledge of universal human structures. All humans, aside from the occasional hermit, live in groups. Knowledge of that fact suggests a host of potential adaptive problems to which humans might have evolved solutions. One obvious problem, for example, is how to make sure that you are included in the group and are not ostracized or cast out (Baumeister & Leary, 1995; Kurzban & Neuberg, 2005). Another problem is that group living means that members of the same species live closer and hence are in more direct competition with one another for access to the resources needed to survive and reproduce.

All known human groups have social hierarchies—another structural feature of our species. The fact that hierarchies are universal suggests another class of adaptive problems (see Chapter 12). These include the problem of getting ahead (because resources increase as one rises in the hierarchy), the problem of preventing slips in status, the problem of upcoming competitors vying for your position, and the problem of being in a subordinate position. In sum, identifying universal features of human social interaction—such as group living and social hierarchies—provides a guide to identifying human adaptive problems.

## Guidance from Traditional Societies

A third source of guidance comes from traditional societies, such as hunter-gatherers. These societies more closely resemble the conditions under which we evolved than do modern societies. There is strong evidence, for example, that humans have been hunters and gatherers for 99 percent of human history—roughly the past several million years before the advent of agriculture 10,000 years ago (Tooby & DeVore, 1987). Examining hunter-gatherer societies, therefore, provides clues about the sorts of adaptive problems our ancestors faced.

It is virtually impossible to hunt large game alone, at least with the tools that were available prior to the invention of guns and other weapons. In hunter-gatherer societies, large game hunting almost invariably occurs in groups or coalitions. To be successful, these coalitions must solve an array of adaptive problems, such as how to divide the work and how to coordinate the efforts of the group, both of which require clear communication.

## Guidance from Paleoarcheology and Paleoanthropology

A fourth source of guidance comes from stones and bones. Analyses of the teeth of our human ancestors, for example, reveal information about the nature of the ancestral diet. Analyses of skeletal fractures reveal information about how our ancestors died. Bones can even give clues to what sorts of diseases plagued ancestral human populations and thereby reveal another set of adaptive problems.

## Guidance from Current Mechanisms

A fifth and highly informative source of information comes from the current psychological mechanisms characteristic of humans. The fact that the most common human phobias across cultures are snakes, spiders, heights, darkness, and strange men and not, for example, cars or electrical outlets reveals a wealth of information about ancestral survival problems. It tells us that we have evolved propensities to fear likely ancestral dangers but not modern dangers. The universality of sexual jealousy tells us that ancestral women and men were not always sexually faithful to their mates. In short, our current psychological mechanisms provide windows for viewing the nature of the adaptive problems that plagued our ancestors.

## Guidance from Task Analysis

A more formal procedure for identifying adaptive problems (and subproblems) is known as *task analysis* (Marr, 1982). Task analysis starts with an observation about a human structure (e.g., humans live in groups with status hierarchies) or a well-documented phenomenon (e.g., humans favor their genetic relatives). A task analysis poses this question: For this structure or phenomenon to occur, what cognitive and behavioral tasks must be solved?

Let's consider the observation that people tend to aid genetic relatives over nonrelatives. If you are a college student, the odds are high that your parents are helping you out in some way, with tuition, room, board, clothes, or a method of transportation. The odds are also high that your parents are not helping your neighbor's children, even if they like them a lot. Parental aid, of course, is just one limited example of the widespread tendency of people to help those who carry copies of their genes. People also tend to help close genetic relatives more than distant genetic relatives (Stewart-Williams, 2008).

A task analysis involves identifying the cognitive tasks that must be solved for it to occur using only information that would have been available in ancestral environments. For example, people need a way to identify those who carry copies of their genes—the problem of kin recognition. They must have solved this problem using only information that was available at the time, such as features of physical appearance. Furthermore, people need to solve the problem of gauging how closely related their genetic relatives are—the problem of closeness of kinship. People don't think about these things consciously most of the time; they happen automatically. A task analysis, in short, enables us to identify the adaptive problems that *must* be solved for the phenomenon we observe to occur as well as the design features of the potential adaptations that are capable of solving them.

## Organization of Adaptive Problems

This book is organized around human adaptive problems and the psychological solutions that have evolved to solve them. We begin with survival problems because without survival, there can be no reproduction. We then move directly to the problem of mating, including the issues of selecting, attracting, and retaining a desirable mate. Then we shift to the products of mating—children. Human children cannot survive and thrive without parental help, so this section covers the ways in which parents invest in their children. All of this occurs within a larger kin group, the strands of DNA that humans share with genetic relatives. The book then shifts to the larger social sphere within which we live—cooperation, aggression, conflict between the sexes, and social status. The final chapter pans back to take a broader focus. It deals with reformulating the major branches of psychology using an evolutionary perspective, considering topics such as reasoning (cognitive psychology), dominance (personality psychology), psychopathology (clinical psychology), and social relationships (social psychology).

## ■ SUMMARY

This chapter covered four topics: (1) the logic of generating hypotheses about our evolved psychological mechanisms, (2) the products of the evolutionary process, (3) the nature of evolved psychological mechanisms, and (4) the scientific procedures by which we test these hypotheses.

The logic of evolutionary hypotheses starts with an examination of the four levels of analysis, going from most general to most specific—general evolutionary theory, middle-level evolutionary theories, specific evolutionary hypotheses, and specific predictions about empirical phenomena derived from these hypotheses. One method of hypothesis generation is to start at the higher levels and move down. A middle-level theory can produce several hypotheses, each of which in turn yields several testable predictions. This can be described as the "top-down" strategy of hypothesis and prediction formation.

A second method is to start with a phenomenon known or observed to exist, such as the importance men attach to a woman's appearance. From this phenomenon, one can generate hypotheses about the possible function for which it was designed. This bottom-up method is called *reverse engineering* and is a useful supplement to the top-down method.

The evolutionary process produces three products: adaptations, by-products of adaptations, and random effects or noise. Evolutionary psychologists tend to focus on adaptations. More specifically, they focus on one special subclass of adaptations that comprises human nature: psychological mechanisms.

Psychological mechanisms are information-processing devices that exist in the form they do because they have solved specific problems of survival or reproduction recurrently over human evolutionary history. They are designed to take in only a narrow slice of information, transform that information through decision rules, and produce output in the form of physiological activity, information to other psychological mechanisms, or manifest behavior. The output of an evolved psychological mechanism is directed toward the solution to a specific adaptive problem. Evolved psychological mechanisms provide nonarbitrary criteria for "carving the mind at its joints," tend to be problem specific, and are large in number and functional in nature.

Once a hypothesis about an evolved psychological mechanism is formulated, the next step in the scientific endeavor is testing it. Testing evolutionary hypotheses relies on comparisons, finding out whether groups that are predicted to differ in a particular way actually do. This method can be used to test hypotheses by comparing different species, comparing people in different cultures, comparing people's physiological reactions and brain images, comparing people with different genes, comparing males and females within a species, comparing different individuals of each sex, and comparing the same individuals in different contexts.

Evolutionary psychology has a wealth of additional sources to draw on, including the archeological record, contemporary hunter-gatherer societies, self-report, observer-report, data evoked from subjects in laboratory experiments, life-history data from public records, and products made by people.

Every source of data has strengths, but each also has limitations. Each provides information that typically cannot be obtained in the same form through other data sources. And each has flaws and weaknesses not shared by others. Studies that test evolutionary hypotheses using two or more data sources are better than studies that rely on a single source.

The final section of this chapter outlined major classes of adaptive problems. Four classes of adaptive problems follow from modern evolutionary theory: problems of survival and growth, problems of mating, problems of parenting, and problems of genetic relatives. Additional insights into identifying adaptive problems come from knowledge of universal human structures, traditional tribal societies, paleoarcheology, task analysis, and current psychological mechanisms. Current mechanisms such as a fear of heights, a taste for fatty foods, and a preference for savanna-like landscapes provide windows for viewing the nature of past adaptive problems.

## ■ SUGGESTED READINGS

Barrett, H. C., & Kurzban, R. (2006). Modularity in cognition: Framing the debate. *Psychological Review, 113,* 628–647.

Buss, D. M. (Ed.). (2005). *The handbook of evolutionary psychology.* New York: Wiley.

Crawford, C., & Krebs, D. (Eds.) (2008). *Foundations of evolutionary psychology.* New York: Erlbaum.

Kennair, L. E. O. (2002). Evolutionary psychology: An emerging integrative perspective within the science and practice of psychology. *Human Nature Review, 2,* 17–61.

Pinker, S. (1997). *How the mind works.* New York: Norton.

Tooby, J., & Cosmides, L. (2005). Conceptual foundations of evolutionary psychology. In D.M. Buss (Ed.), *The handbook of evolutionary psychology* (pp. 5–67). New York: Wiley.

# PROBLEMS
# OF SURVIVAL

This part consists of a single chapter devoted to what is known about human adaptations to the problems of survival. Darwin coined the phrase "the hostile forces of nature" to describe the forces that impede survival. Modern humans are descendants of ancestors who succeeded in combating these hostile forces. The beginning of Chapter 3 covers the problem of food acquisition and selection and examines hypotheses about how ancestral humans acquired food—the hunting hypothesis and the gathering hypothesis, and the scavenger hypothesis. Next, human adaptations for habitat selection, the preferences that guide our decisions about places to live, are examined. Next, we explore fears, phobias, anxieties, and other adaptations designed to combat various environmental dangers ranging from snakes to diseases. Then the intriguing question of why humans die is addressed, and Chapter 3 ends with a provocative analysis of a genuine evolutionary mystery: why some people commit suicide.

# COMBATING THE HOSTILE FORCES OF NATURE

## Human Survival Problems

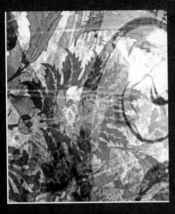

*. . . organisms aiming to survive must not only decide what to eat but also avoid being eaten themselves.*

—Todd, 2000, p. 951

*There is nothing in the body that never goes wrong.*

—Randolph Nesse and George Williams, 1994, p. 19

*D*ifferential reproduction is the "bottom line" of the evolutionary process, the engine that drives natural selection. To reproduce, organisms must survive—at least for a while. Charles Darwin summed it up best: "As more individuals are produced than can possibly survive, there must in every case be a struggle for existence, either one individual with another of the same species, or with the individuals of distinct species, or with the physical conditions of life" (1859, p. 53). So, an examination of the adaptive problems of survival is a logical starting point for human evolutionary psychology.

Living poses a number of problems. Although our current style of living protects us a great deal, everyone has at some point encountered forces that endanger survival. Darwin called these the "hostile forces of nature," and they include climate, weather, food shortages, toxins, diseases, parasites, predators, and hostile conspecifics (members of the same species).

Each of these hostile forces has created adaptive problems for humans—problems that have recurred in each generation over the long expanse of evolutionary history. The adaptive problems selected for successful survival solutions. They imposed a filter through which those who succumbed to disease, parasites, predators, harsh winters, and long dry summers failed to pass. As Darwin noted, "in the great battle of life . . . the structure of every organic being is related, in the most essential yet often hidden manner, to that of all the other organic beings, with which it comes into competition for food and residence, or from which it has to escape, or on which it preys" (1859, p. 61).

*Food shortages are one of the most important "hostile forces of nature" for many species. In humans, food sharing serves functions beyond securing fuel for the body, including courtship attraction and solidifying social bonds.*

Humans have always had to interact with the biological world in highly specialized ways. We have to know what we can eat, what might poison us, what we can capture, and what can capture us. Scientific work over the past decade has indeed shown that humans universally appear to have a fairly sophisticated "folk biology" (Atran, 1998; Berlin, 1992; Keil, 1995). The core of this *folk biology* is the intuition that living things come in discrete packets that correspond to distinct species and that each distinct species has an internal "essence" that produces its growth, bodily functions, external form, and special powers. Nettles have an internal essence that produces thorns that can sting you. Lions have an internal essence that produces canine teeth and specialized claws that can kill you.

This folk biology appears to emerge early in life and is universal across cultures (Sperber & Hirshfeld, 2004). People all over the world, for example, spontaneously divide all species into *plants* and *animals* (Atran, 1998). Children as young as preschool age show beliefs about the internal essences of species. They believe, for example, that if you remove the insides of a dog, it loses its "essence" and is no longer really a dog anymore—it can't bark or bite. But if you remove its outsides or change its external appearance so that it doesn't look like a dog, children still believe that it has retained its essential "dogness." They believe that if a piglet is raised by cows, it will oink when it grows up rather than moo. Children's folk biology even appears to contain a sense of function. Children as young as age three believe, for example, that the thorns of a rose are there because they somehow help the rose, but children do not believe that the barbs of barbed wire are there because they help the wire.

It is likely that the universal folk biology, with the core belief that different members of the same species share hidden causal essences, is an evolved cognitive adaptation (Sperber & Hirshfeld, 2004). It emerges early in life without any apparent instruction from parents

(Gelman, Coley, & Gottfried, 1994). It appears to be universal across cultures around the world (Atran, 1998). And it is likely to be central to solving many of the survival problems discussed throughout this chapter—things that are nutritious versus things that are poisonous, things that we can prey upon and things that can prey upon us.

Let us look, then, at the fascinating collection of adaptations that make up the human survival machine—the mechanisms of the body and mind that have evolved to combat the hostile forces of nature. The first problem to be faced is finding fuel for the machine.

## ■ FOOD ACQUISITION AND SELECTION

Without food and water we would all die: "Diet is the primary factor allowing or constraining the rest of a species' system of adaptations" (Tooby & DeVore, 1987, p. 234). Indeed, most animals spend more waking hours engaged in the search, capture, and intake of food than in any other activity (Rozin, 1996). Finding food is as necessary for survival as finding a mate is for reproduction. In the modern world, humans simply go to the grocery store or a restaurant. Our ancestors, roaming the grassy savanna plains, did not have it so easy. Many obstacles lay between waking up hungry and dozing off at night with a full belly.

The most pressing general problem in food selection is how to obtain adequate amounts of calories and specific nutrients such as sodium, calcium, and zinc without at the same time consuming dangerous levels of toxins that could rapidly lead to death (Rozin & Schull, 1988). This requires searching for food; recognizing, capturing, handling, and consuming it; and digesting it to absorb its nutrients. And these activities must be coordinated with an assessment of one's internal metabolic state, including whether one is suffering from a negative energy balance—burning up more calories than are being taken in—or a specific nutritional deficiency (Rozin & Schull, 1988).

The problems of food selection become especially crucial for omnivores—species that regularly eat both plants and animals—for example, rats and humans. Eating a wide range of foods—plants, nuts, seeds, fruits, meats—increases one's odds of being poisoned because toxins are widespread throughout the plant world. A profound evolutionary insight is that plant toxins themselves are adaptations that reduce the odds of the plants being eaten. Toxins thus help plants defend themselves from predators, but they hurt humans and other animals that rely on the plants for survival. In a very real sense, our ancestors were in conflict with plants.

### Social and Cultural Aspects of Food

The sharing of food is a major social activity for humans. Among some societies such as the Kwakiutl of the northwest coast of North America, rich men throw "potlatches" for the group, in which they feast on food and drink for hours and evaluate a man's status by the lavishness of the spread (Piddocke, 1965; Vayda, 1961). Other cultures such as the !Kung San of Botswana have specific words for special kinds of hunger, such as being "meat hungry" (Shostak, 1981). Sharing food is also a strategy of courtship, a sign of the closeness of relationships, and a means for reconciling after a conflict (Buss, 2003).

Fishermen tell tales about the fish they catch, farmers about the size of their vegetables, hunters about their prowess in taking down a large animal. Failure to provide food can lead a man to lose status in the group (Hill & Hurtado, 1996; Holmberg, 1950). It is not uncommon among cultures such as the Ganda and Thonga tribes in Central Africa and the Ashanti in the coastal region of Nigeria for women to seek to divorce husbands who fail to provide food

(Betzig, 1989). Even the myths and religions of cultures abound with stories of food and drink: Eve and Adam eating the apple, Jesus turning water into wine, Jesus multiplying the two small fish and five barley loaves to feed the masses, and the prohibitions against eating pork.

Food and its consumption have become frequently used metaphors. We find tall tales "hard to swallow," thick prose "difficult to digest," a stroke of good fortune "sweet," a good book "juicy," and a social disappointment "bitter" (Lakoff & Johnson, 1980). Food, in short, permeates our psychological preoccupations, verbal discourse, social interaction, and religious beliefs on a daily basis.

## Food Preferences

All over the world, people spend more money on food than practically anything else. People in Western countries such as Germany and the United States spend 21 percent of their income on food, second only to income spent on leisure activities (Rozin, 1996). In less wealthy countries such as India and China, 50 percent of all income is spent on food. Worldwide, however, food takes center stage in parent–infant interactions. There may be nothing more important for survival early in life than determining what should be ingested or avoided (Rozin, 1996).

We do not usually compare ourselves with rats, but humans and rats have some similar adaptations when it comes to eating. Both human and rat infants solve the problem of food seeking and consumption by getting all the needed calories from mother's milk. This prevents infants from consuming lethal toxins until they can begin to secure food on their own.

Do humans have evolved food preferences? Both humans and rats have evolved taste preferences for *sweet* foods, which provide rich sources of calories (Birch, 1999; Krebs, 2009). A study of food preferences among the Hadza hunter-gatherers of Tanzania found that honey was the most highly preferred food item, an item that has the highest caloric value (Berbesque & Marlow, 2009). Human newborn infants also show a strong preference for sweet liquids. Both humans and rats dislike *bitter* and *sour* foods, which tend to contain toxins (Krebs, 2009). They also adaptively adjust their eating behavior in response to deficits in water, calories, and salt (Rozin & Schull, 1988). Experiments show that rats display an immediate liking for salt the first time they experience a salt deficiency. They likewise increase their intake of sweets and water when their energy and fluids become depleted. These appear to be specific evolved mechanisms, designed to deal with the adaptive problem of food selection, and coordinate consumption patterns with physical needs (Krebs, 2009; Rozin, 1976).

Both humans and rats have an adaptation called *neophobia,* defined as a strong aversion to new foods. Rats typically sample new and unfamiliar food only in very small doses, and when they do so, they eat the new foods separately—never together. By keeping samples small and new foods separate, the rats have the opportunity to learn what makes them sick, thus avoiding a potentially deadly overconsumption of poisons. Interestingly, when a rat eats both a familiar food and a new food at the same meal and subsequently gets sick, it thereafter avoids only the new food. It seems to "assume" that the familiar food is safe and the new food is the source of the sickness. Humans typically have to be coaxed by parents or others to try new foods, indicating an important social element to human food consumption (Birch, 1999).

## Disgust: The Disease-Avoidance Hypothesis

The emotion of *disgust* is a hypothesized adaptation that serves as a defense against microbial attack, protecting people from the risk of disease (Curtis, Aunger, & Rabie, 2004; Oaten,

Stevenson, & Case, 2009). Disgust is an emotion that involves feelings of revulsion and sometimes nausea. It motivates strong withdrawal from the disgust-producing stimulus. If the emotion of disgust is an evolved defense against disease, several predictions follow. One is that disgust should be evoked most strongly by disease-carrying substances. The second is that these disgust elicitors should be universal across cultures. Empirical resource supports both predictions (Curtis & Biran, 2001). People from cultures ranging from the Netherlands to West Africa find foods potentially contaminated by parasites or unhygienic preparation to be exceptionally disgusting. Examples are rotting flesh, dirty food, bad-smelling food, food leftovers, moldy food, a dead insect in food, and witnessing food preparation by someone with dirty hands. Foods that have had contact with worms, cockroaches, or feces evoke especially strong disgust reactions.

A cross-cultural study asked Americans and Japanese to list the things they found most disgusting. Feces and other body wastes were the most frequently mentioned items, at 25 percent of the written responses (Rozin, 1996). Feces in particular are known to harbor harmful elements, including parasites and toxins, and are particularly dangerous to humans. Another study found that students refuse to drink from a glass that has been thoroughly cleaned and sterilized when told that it had once held dog feces (Rozin & Nemeroff, 1990). Other evidence of the universality of disgust comes from studies that find that the facial expression of disgust is universally recognized; it is expressed by people who are blind from birth; and it is interpreted correctly by people who are born deaf (Oaten et al., 2009).

Another prediction from the disease-avoidance hypothesis of disgust is a gender difference: Since women typically care for their infants and children, they need to protect them from disease, as well as themselves. And indeed, women find images depicting disease-carrying objects to be more disgusting than men do, and also perceive that the risk of disease is greater from those objects than men do (Curtis et al., 2004). Individuals who have especially heightened sensitivity to contamination and who were most easily disgusted have significantly fewer infections—a finding that provides direct evidence of the protective function of disgust (Stevenson, Case, & Oaten, 2009).

Contaminated food, of course, is not the only thing that evokes the emotion of disgust. Potential contact with people who have poor hygiene, who appear diseased witnessing body boundary violations such as a gaping wound, and who have certain sex practices such as anal sex—all of which are possible conduits for disease transmission—often evokes disgust (Tyber, Lieberman, & Griskevicius, 2009). Much empirical evidence, in short, supports the disease-avoidance hypothesis of disgust. It is an emotion that evolved to avoid predictable classes of disease conduits that jeopardized survival.

Interestingly, there are some situations in which it would be advantageous to turn off or suppress the disgust reaction to solve other adaptive problems, such as caring for a wounded ally or a close kin member (Case, Repacholi, & Stevenson, 2006). In an experiment in which mothers were asked to smell feces from different infants, mothers rated feces from their own infants as considerably less disgusting than feces from other infants, even when the feces samples were intentionally mislabeled (Case et al., 2006). The disgust most people experience at the thought of eating human flesh might also be turned off under dire conditions in which individuals are facing starvation. Evidence has been mounting that prehistoric humans sometimes resorted to cannibalism, possibly under conditions of famine (Stoneking, 2003). All these findings suggest that humans have the capacity to either shut off or override their disgust reaction in the service of solving other adaptive problems.

## Sickness in Pregnant Women: The Embryo Protection Hypothesis

During the first three months of pregnancy, some women develop pregnancy sickness—a heightened sensitivity and a nauseous reaction to particular foods that is commonly known as morning sickness. The percentage of women who report experiencing such reactions ranges from 75 percent (Brandes, 1967) to 89 percent (Tierson, Olsen, & Hook, 1986). Actual vomiting percentages are lower, roughly 55 percent. If food aversions are added to the definition of pregnancy sickness, then close to 100 percent of all pregnant women would report pregnancy sickness during the first trimester (Profet, 1992). Although the term "sickness" implies that something is malfunctioning, recent evidence suggests precisely the opposite. Profet (1992) hypothesizes that pregnancy sickness is an adaptation that prevents mothers from consuming and absorbing *teratogens*—toxins that might be harmful to the developing baby.

Toxins occur in a variety of plants, including many we consume regularly such as apples, bananas, potatoes, oranges, and celery. The black pepper that we use to spice our food contains safrole, which is both carcinogenic (causes cancer) and mutagenic (causes mutations). The special problem that humans face, which becomes more pronounced during pregnancy, is how to get the valuable nutrients from plants without at the same time incurring the costs of their toxins.

Plants and the predators that consume them seem to have coevolved (Profet, 1992). Plants signal their toxicity with chemicals. Vegetables such as cabbage, cauliflower, broccoli, and brussels sprouts, for example, get their strong tastes from allyl isothiocyanate. Rhubarb leaves contain oxalate (Nesse & Williams, 1994). Humans find these chemicals bitter and unpleasant—an adaptation that helps them avoid consuming toxins.

The specific foods pregnant women report finding distasteful include coffee (129 women out of the sample of 400), meat (124), alcohol (79), and vegetables (44). In contrast, only three women reported aversions to bread, and not a single woman reported an aversion to cereals (Tierson, Olsen, & Hook, 1985). Another study of one hundred women experiencing their first pregnancies found similar results (Dickens & Trethowan, 1971). Of the one hundred women, thirty-two described aversions to coffee, tea, and cocoa; eighteen cited aversions to vegetables; and sixteen cited aversions to meat and eggs. Many became nauseated when smelling fried or barbecued food, which contains carcinogens, and some nearly fainted when smelling spoiled meat, which was teeming with toxin-producing bacteria. If pregnant women do consume these foods, they are more likely to vomit. Vomiting prevents the toxins from entering the mother's bloodstream and passing through the placenta to the developing fetus (Profet, 1992).

Evidence supports Profet's hypothesis that pregnancy sickness is an adaptation to prevent the ingestion of teratogens. First, the foods pregnant women find repugnant appear to correspond to those carrying the highest doses of toxins. Meats, for example, often contain toxins due to fungal and bacterial decomposition, and pregnant women seem to have specialized meat-avoidance mechanisms during the first trimester (Fessler, 2002). Second, pregnancy sickness occurs precisely at the time when the fetus is most vulnerable to toxins, roughly two to four weeks after conception, which is when many of the fetus's major organs are being formed. Third, pregnancy sickness decreases around the eighth week and generally disappears entirely by the fourteenth week, coinciding with the end of the sensitive period for organ development.

Perhaps the clinching piece of evidence comes from the success of the pregnancy itself. Women who do *not* have pregnancy sickness during the first trimester are roughly three times more likely to experience a spontaneous abortion than women who do experience such sickness (Profet, 1992). In one study of 3,853 pregnant women, only 3.8 percent of the women who experienced pregnancy sickness had spontaneous abortions, whereas 10.4 percent of the women who had not experienced pregnancy sickness had spontaneous abortions (Yerushalmy & Milkovich, 1965).

Most adaptations are expected to be universal, so cross-cultural evidence is critical. Although pregnancy sickness has not been explored much in other cultures, the ethnographic record contains evidence of its existence among the !Kung of Botswana, the Efe Pygmies of Zaire, and the Australian Aborigines. The mother of a !Kung woman, Nisa, reported why she suspected that Nisa was pregnant: "If you are throwing up like this, it means you have a little thing inside your stomach" (Shostak, 1981, p. 187). A recent study of twenty-seven traditional societies revealed that pregnancy sickness was observed in twenty and not observed in seven. The twenty societies in which pregnancy sickness was observed were far more likely to use meat and other animal products, which typically contain pathogens and parasites at higher rates than do plants (Fessler, 2002; Flaxman & Sherman, 2000). More extensive cross-cultural research is clearly needed to test the embryo protection hypothesis (see Pike, 2000, who fails to support this hypothesis in a sample of sixty-eight pregnant Turkana women residing in Kenya, Africa).

Profet's analysis of pregnancy sickness highlights one of the benefits of adaptationist thinking. A phenomenon previously regarded as an illness appears to be an exquisitely tailored mechanism designed to combat a hostile force of nature—one that would impair the survival of a child even before it is born.

## Fire and Cooking

At least one aspect of food consumption is unique among modern humans—we build fires and cook our food. Anthropologist Richard Wrangham has advanced the hypothesis that cooking was one of the keys to the emergence of modern humans (Carmody & Wrangham, 2009; Wrangham et al., 1999). Most noncooked foods are highly fibrous and provide relatively few calories compared to the effort needed to chew and digest them. Cooking renders fibrous fruits, tubers, and raw meat much more easily digestible. It frees up energy, reduces the costs of digestion, and has the added benefit of killing off microorganisms that could be toxic to humans. According to the cooking hypothesis, the invention of fire and the ability to cook provided the key evolutionary impetus for the evolution of extraordinarily large human brains.

Evidence supporting Wrangham's cooking hypothesis includes the following: (1) cooking food provides a predictable increase in its net energy value; (2) cooking renders food more easily digestible; (3) cooking is a human universal; (4) the human brain requires a tremendous number of calories to function, and fibrous fruits and other raw foods rarely can provide enough; and (5) on exclusively raw-food diets, humans fare poorly, and among women, many lose the ability to reproduce.

The cooking hypothesis is controversial among scientists. One of the key issues hinges on when the intentional use of fire entered the human repertoire. For Wrangham's hypothesis that cooking was the key invention that led to large human brains to be correct, cooking had to be widely used 1.6 to 1.9 million years ago, when our *Homo erectus* ancestors appeared in the fossil record with substantially larger brains than their predecessors. The evidence for the controlled use of fire that long ago is thin. Many scientists believe that cooking did not occur until 500,000 years ago, and strong evidence for cooking does not appear until roughly 200,000 years ago (Gorman, 2007). Until more conclusive proof of the use of controlled fire at *Homo erectus* sites can be established, some scientists will remain skeptical of Wrangham's cooking hypothesis.

## Why Humans Like Spices: The Antimicrobial Hypothesis

Humans have to eat, but eating poses dangers to survival. Taking things from outside the body and ingesting them provides an avenue for entry of dangerous microorganisms, as well as toxins that can cause sickness or death. These hazards are present in almost everything we eat, and most of us have experienced their effects—feeling "sick to my stomach" or vomiting because of "food poisoning."

In today's environment, we can minimize these dangers. But imagine the time of our ancestors, a time before refrigerators and artificial preservatives, when food was scarce and sanitation standards were lower. One obvious solution is cooking, which kills off most microorganisms. Another potential solution is the use of spices (Billing & Sherman, 1998; Sherman & Flaxman, 2001).

Spices come from plants—flowers, roots, seeds, shrubs, and fruits. Spices emit unique smells and have specific tastes due to chemicals called "secondary compounds." These compounds usually function in plants as defense mechanisms to prevent macroorganisms (herbivores, or plant-eating animals) and microorganisms (pathogens) from attacking them. The use of spice plants among humans goes back thousands of years. Explorers such as Marco Polo and Christopher Columbus took great risks to search for lands with abundant spices. It is difficult to find in a modern book of recipes a single dish that does not contain spices. Why are humans so concerned with spices and their addition to the foods eaten?

According to the *antimicrobial hypothesis,* spices kill or inhibit the growth of microorganisms and prevent the production of toxins in the foods we eat and so help humans to solve a critical problem of survival: avoiding being made ill or poisoned by the foods we eat (Sherman & Flaxman, 2001). Several sources of evidence support this hypothesis. First, of the thirty spices for which we have solid data, all killed many of the species of food-borne bacteria on which they were tested. Would you hazard a guess about which spices are most powerful in killing bacteria? They are onion, garlic, allspice, and oregano. Second, more spices, and more potent spices, tend to be used in hotter climates, where unrefrigerated food spoils more quickly, promoting the rapid proliferation of dangerous microorganisms. In the hot climate of India, for example, the typical meat dish recipe calls for nine spices, whereas in the colder climate of Norway, fewer than two spices are used per meat dish on average. Third, more spices tend to be used in meat dishes than in vegetable dishes (Sherman & Hash, 2001). This is presumably because dangerous microorganisms proliferate more on unrefrigerated meat; dead plants, in contrast, contain their own physical and chemical defense mechanisms and so are better protected from bacterial invasion. In short, the use of spices in foods is one means that humans have used to combat the dangers carried on the foods we eat.

The authors of the antimicrobial hypothesis are not proposing that humans have a specialized evolved adaptation for the use of spices, although they do not rule out this possibility. Rather, it is more likely that eating certain spices was discovered through accident or experimentation; people discovered that they were less likely to feel sick after eating leftovers cooked with aromatic plant products. Use of those antimicrobial spices spread through cultural transmission—by imitation or verbal instruction.

## Why Humans Like to Drink Alcohol: An Evolutionary Hangover?

Primates have been eating fruit for at least 24 million years. Indeed, most primates, including chimpanzees, orangutans, and gibbons, are primarily frugivorous—fruit is the mainstay of their diet. The ripest fruits, which are greatly preferred, contain high amounts to two ingredients: sugar and ethanol. Indeed, the "ethanol plumes" emitted by fruit might provide cues to its ripeness. Primates, including humans, have been consuming low levels of ethanol for millions of years through ripe fruit.

Modern humans, however, live in a world that is far removed from this low level of ethanol consumption. The ethanol levels in fruit are typically only 0.6 percent (Dudley, 2002). On the basis of a reasonable set of assumptions, ingestion of fruit might yield a blood ethanol level of only 0.01 percent, far lower than the typical legal definition of drunk, which is 0.08 percent. Our ancestors did not have the kegs of beer, bottles of wine, or flasks of whiskey that currently contain highly concentrated amounts of alcohol. According to the *frugivory by-product hypothesis,* the human penchant for drinking alcohol is not an adaptation but rather is a by-product of adaptive fondness for ripe fruit (Dudley, 2002; Singh, 1985). "Alcohol not only has a distinct taste but it also has a unique odor and is often associated with the color and fragrance of ripe fruits. . . . Utilizing the odor and taste of alcohol enables the animal to predict the caloric value of a food" (Singh, 1985, p. 273). That is, all humans have adaptations that favor the consumption of ripe fruit, but these can go awry in the modern world of artificial drinks with high alcohol content. Indeed, alcoholism might be a currently maladaptive by-product of the overindulgence of these frugivorous mechanisms. So the next time you reach for a drink, perhaps you'll think of your primate ancestors having their version of a party—sitting around a tree eating ripe fruit.

## The Hunting Hypothesis

Ancestral methods of securing food have been linked to the rapid emergence of modern humans. The importance of hunting in human evolution, for example, has been a major source of controversy in anthropology and evolutionary psychology. One widely held view is the model of "man the hunter" (Tooby & DeVore, 1987). According to this view, the transition from mere foraging to large game hunting provided a major impetus for human evolution, with a cascading set of consequences including a rapid expansion of tool making and tool use, the development of a large human brain, and the evolution of complex language skills necessary for communication on cooperative hunts.

*Large game hunting typically requires cooperation and communication among several hunters. According to the hunting hypothesis, large game hunting provided a major driving force for human evolution, with ramifications for tool making, tool use, language, and the enlargement of the brain.*

The initial impetus for the human shift to a diet high in meat may have been spurred by an ecological change that took place in Africa associated with global cooling a few million years ago. It produced a dramatic increase in open grassland, making plant food scarce and animals increasingly attractive as a food resource (Ulijaszek, 2002).

Human groups consume far more meat than any other primate species. Among chimpanzees, for example, meat constitutes only 4 percent of the diet. Among humans, the proportion of meat in the diet ranges from 20 to 40 percent and goes as high as 90 percent during cold hunting seasons. Furthermore, it is difficult for humans to get all essential nutrients, such as cyanocobolamine, from an exclusively vegetarian diet (Tooby & DeVore, 1987), although in the modern environment a diet rich in animal meat and fat may be more dangerous than a vegetarian diet. This suggests that meat has been a central feature of the human diet for thousands of generations.

Modern tribal societies often hunt as a major method for food acquisition. For example, the Aka Pygmies, who dwell in the tropical rain forests of the Central African Republic, spend roughly 56 percent of their subsistence time hunting, 27 percent of their subsistence time gathering, and 17 percent of their subsistence time processing food (Hewlett, 1991). The !Kung of Botswana, another example, are excellent hunters and devote a lot of time to hunting. On average, hunting provides 40 percent of the calories in the !Kung diet, but this can dip below 20 percent in a lean season and can reach more than 90 percent during a successful hunting season (Lee, 1979).

Our bodies are walking archives that show a long history of meat eating (Milton, 1999). Contrast the gut of an ape with that of a human. The ape's gut consists mainly of a colon, a large, winding tube that is well designed for processing a vegetarian diet permeated with tough fiber. The human gut, in contrast, is dominated by the small intestines, distinguishing us from all other primates. The small intestines provide the place where proteins are rapidly broken down and nutrients absorbed, suggesting that humans have a long evolutionary history of eating protein-rich food such as meat.

The fossil record of the teeth of human ancestors provides another clue to diet. The thin enamel coating on human tooth fossils does not show the heavy wear and tear known to occur from a diet mainly of fibrous plants. Vitamin evidence provides a third clue. The human body cannot produce vitamins A and B12, even though these are vital for human survival. Precisely these two vitamins are found in meat. A fourth clue comes from a bounty of bones found in Olduvai Gorge in Tanzania, Africa, discovered in the summer of 1979 by three independent researchers: Richard Potts, Pat Shipman, and Henry Bunn (Leakey & Lewin, 1992). These bones were ancient, estimated to be nearly 2 million years old, and many bore cut marks, tangible evidence of ancestral butchers. All of these clues suggest a long evolutionary history in which meat was an essential part of the diet of human ancestors.

***The Provisioning Hypothesis.***   Proponents of the hunting hypothesis argue that it can explain a large number of unusual features of human evolution (Tooby & DeVore, 1987). Perhaps most important, it can explain the fact that human males are unique among primates in their heavy parental investment in children. This has been called the *provisioning hypothesis.* Because meat is an economical and concentrated food resource, it can be transported effectively back to the home base to feed the young. In contrast, it is far less efficient to transport low-calorie food over long distances. Hunting thus provides a plausible explanation for the emergence of the heavy investment and provisioning that men channel toward their children.

Although provisioning is often regarded as an adaptive explanation for the evolution of hunting, the hunting hypothesis can also explain several other aspects that characterize humans. One is the emergence of *strong male coalitions,* which appear to be characteristic of humans worldwide. Hunting provides one such plausible explanation (chimpanzees form male–male coalitions as well, but these tend to be transient and opportunistic rather than enduring; de Waal, 1982). Large game hunting requires the coordinated action of cooperators. Single individuals can rarely succeed in taking down a large animal. The primary plausible alternatives to hunting as a hypothesis for the emergence of male coalitions are group-on-group aggression and defense and in-group political alliances, activities that also could have selected for strong male coalitions (Tooby & DeVore, 1987).

Hunting can also account for the emergence in humans of *strong reciprocal altruism* and *social exchange.* Humans seem to be unique among primates in showing extensive reciprocal relationships that can last years, decades, or a lifetime (Tooby & DeVore, 1987). Meat from a large game animal comes in quantities that far exceed what a single hunter could possibly consume. Furthermore, hunting success is highly variable; a hunter who is successful one week might fail the next (Hill & Hurtado, 1996). These conditions favor food sharing from hunting. The costs to a hunter of giving away meat he cannot eat immediately are low because he cannot consume all the meat himself, and leftovers will soon spoil. The benefits can be large, however, when the recipients of his food return the favor at a later time. In essence, hunters can "store" surplus meat in the bodies of their friends and neighbors (Pinker, 1997).

Hunting also provides a plausible explanation for the *sexual division of labor.* Men's larger size, upper body strength, and ability to throw projectiles accurately over long distances make them well suited for hunting (Watson, 2001). Ancestral women, often preoccupied by pregnancy and children, were less well suited for hunting. Among modern hunter-gatherers, the division of labor is strong: Men hunt and women gather, often carrying their young with them. Indeed, even in modern environments, men and women differ sharply in their recreational activities. In a study of 3,479 Norwegians, more men than women hunt (both large game and small game) and fish; more women than men pick berries and mushrooms (Røskaft, Hagen, Hagen, & Moksnes, 2004). The sexes can exchange food—meat provided by men from the hunt and plant foods provided by women from gathering. In sum, hunting provides a plausible explanation for the strong division of labor that characterizes modern humans (Tooby & DeVore, 1987).

Finally, hunting also provides a powerful explanation for the emergence of stone tool use. Stone tools are regularly found at the same sites as bones from large animals—sites dating back 2 million years (Klein, 2000). Their main function seems to have been for killing and then separating the valuable meat from the bones and cartilage.

In summary, while the provisioning of women and children is often hypothesized to be the primary adaptive explanation for the origins of hunting, the hunting hypothesis can explain a host of other human phenomena as well. It can at least partially explain the emergence of strong coalitions among men, reciprocal alliance and social exchange among friends, the sexual division of labor, and the development of stone tools.

### The Show-Off Hypothesis: Status Competition among Men.

Hunting produces resources that are unique among the food groups in two respects. First, meat comes in large packages, sometimes more than the hunter and his immediate family can consume. Second, the packages are unpredictable. A successful streak of taking down two large animals in a week can be followed by a long period of hunting failure (Hawkes, O'Connell, & Blurton Jones, 2001a, 2001b).

These qualities establish the conditions for the sharing of meat beyond the confines of one's immediate family, and these periodic "bonanzas" would become known to everyone in the community (Hawkes, 1991).

These considerations led anthropologist Kristen Hawkes to propose the *show-off hypothesis* (Hawkes, 1991). Hawkes suggests that women would prefer to have neighbors who are show-offs—men who go for the rare but valuable bonanzas of meat—because they benefit by gaining a portion of it. If women benefit from these gifts, especially in times of shortage, then it would be to their advantage to reward men who pursue the show-off strategy. They could give such hunters favorable treatment, such as siding with them in times of dispute, providing health care to their children, and offering sexual favors.

Men pursuing the risky hunting strategy would therefore benefit in several ways. By gaining increased sexual access to women, they increase their odds of fathering more children. The favored treatment of their children from neighbors increases the survival and possible reproductive success of those children. An analysis of data from five hunter-gatherer societies—Ache of Paraguay, Hadza of the East African savanna, !Kung of Botswana and Namibia, Lamalera of the Indonesian island of Lembata, and Meriam of Australia—concluded that the better hunters typically have more mates, more desirable mates, and higher rates of offspring survival (Smith, 2004).

Evidence supporting the show-off hypothesis comes from the Ache, a native population of eastern Paraguay (Hill & Hurtado, 1996; Hill & Kaplan, 1988). Historically, the Ache have been a nomadic group and have used both hunting and gathering to secure food. Anthropologists Kim Hill and Hillard Kaplan lived with the Ache for several years, using data from foraging trips in the forest directly observed between 1980 and 1985. On the foraging trips, the Ache move in small bands, shifting to a new camp almost daily. Among the Ache, although gathered food is consumed primarily by the gatherer and immediate family, meat from the hunt is distributed widely within the group. Hawkes (1991) found that fully 84 percent of the resources acquired by men were shared outside the immediate family—that is, with people other than himself, his wife, and his children. In contrast, only 58 percent of the foods gathered by women were shared outside of the immediate family.

More recent evidence in favor of the show-off hypothesis comes from Hadza foragers, who live in the savanna woodlands in Tanzania, Africa (Hawkes et al., 2001a, 2001b). Hunting is Hadza men's work, and men spend roughly four hours each day in pursuit of game, typically large game. Meat from the kills is typically shared widely. Neither hunters nor their families get more meat than anyone else in the group, a finding that calls into question a pure form of the provisioning hypothesis. Successful Hadza hunters, however, gain great social status—prestige that can be parlayed into powerful social alliances, the deference of other men, and greater mating success.

The show-off hypothesis can be considered a rival of the provisioning hypothesis, at least in its pure form. Men hunted, Hawkes argues, not to provide for their own families, but rather to gain the status benefits of sharing their bounty with neighbors. The fact that successful Ache hunters do benefit in the currencies of increased sexual access and better survival of their children supports the show-off hypothesis. As Kristen Hawkes concluded: "men may choose risky endeavors, not in spite of, but partly because the gamble gives them the chance to claim favors they can win by showing off" (1991, p. 51). Nonetheless, the two hypotheses are not incompatible. Men may have hunted to provide for their families *and* to gain the status, sexual, and alliance benefits outside of their families. Indeed, evidence from the !Kung Bushmen of Botswana and Namibia supports the idea that successful hunters accrue *all* of these benefits (Wiessner, 2002).

## The Gathering Hypothesis

In contrast to the view that men provided the critical evolutionary impetus for the emergence of modern humans through hunting, an opposing view suggests that women provided the critical impetus, through gathering (Tanner, 1983; Tanner & Zihlman, 1976; Zihlman, 1981). According to this hypothesis, stone tools were invented and used not for hunting, but rather for digging up and gathering various plants. The gathering hypothesis would explain the transition from forests to savanna woodlands and grasslands because the use of tools made the securing of gathered food possible and more economical (Tanner, 1983). After the invention of stone tools for gathering was the invention of containers to hold the food and the elaboration of tools for hunting, skinning, and butchering animals. According to the gathering hypothesis, securing plant food through the use of stone tools provided the primary evolutionary impetus for the emergence of modern humans. According to this view, hunting came only much later and did not play a role in the emergence of modern humans.

The gathering hypothesis provides a useful corrective to the exclusive focus on male hunting in the evolution of humans and helps account for the fact that the diet of our primate relatives, and hence likely of our prehominid ancestors, consisted mainly of plant food. It also helps account for the fact that more than 35 percent of the diets of modern hunter-gatherers consist of gathered plant foods (Marlow, 2005).

A key predictor of the amount of time a woman spends foraging is how much food her husband brings back. Women with husbands who provide well spend less time foraging than women with husbands who provide little (Hurtado et al.,1992). Women seem to adjust their

*In nearly every traditional society, food secured through gathering accounts for the majority of calories consumed by all members of the group. According to the gathering hypothesis, gathering gave rise to the making and use of stone tools, providing a driving force for the evolution of modern humans.*

behavior to changing adaptive demands, increasing gathering to compensate for a poor provider and decreasing it to avoid exposing young children to environmental hazards.

## Comparing the Hunting and Gathering Hypotheses

Despite the importance of women's gathering, the gathering hypothesis has been criticized by those who don't think it can successfully explain the divergence of humans in the primate lineage (see Tooby & DeVore, 1987). Men worldwide do, in fact, hunt. If gathering were the sole or even the most productive human method of food getting, then why wouldn't men just gather and stop wasting their time hunting? The gathering hypothesis, in other words, does not account for the division of labor between the sexes observed across a wide variety of cultures, with men hunting and women gathering.

The hunting hypothesis, in contrast, can explain this division of labor. It explains why women do not hunt regularly—they are occupied with pregnancy and dependent children, which makes hunting a more onerous, more risky, and less profitable enterprise. In short, hunting is more cost effective for men than for women. In addition, the division of labor allows both types of resources—animals and plants—to be exploited.

The gathering hypothesis does not explain the high parental investment by human males. It does not account for the emergence of a powerful male coalitional psychology. And it does not account for why humans penetrated many environments that lack plant resources; the Eskimos, for example, live almost entirely on animal meat and fat. The gathering hypothesis also cannot explain why the human gut structure, including the huge size of the small intestine in comparison to that of plant-eating primates, seems designed specifically to process meat (Milton, 1999).

The gathering hypothesis has trouble explaining why humans form strong extended reciprocal alliances that can last for decades. It also has trouble explaining why women should share their food with men, who would be essentially parasites sponging off women's labor unless they gave them something in return, such as meat (see Wrangham et al., 1999, who argue that ancestral men *did* steal the food that women had gathered). An exchange of gathered food for meat, however, could explain why women would have been willing to share with men the food they collected and processed.

In summary, it is clear that over millions of years of primate and human history, ancestral females have gathered plant foods. Stone tools undoubtedly made plant gathering more efficient, and gathering likely played a key role in reciprocal exchanges between the sexes. But the gathering hypothesis falls short in accounting for several known facts about humans: the division of labor between the sexes, the emergence of high male parental investment, and the sharp differences between humans and apes.

Although the controversy has not yet been settled, there is clear agreement that human ancestors were omnivores and that both meat and gathered plants were important ingredients in their diet. The high prevalence of male hunters and female gatherers among traditional societies, although not definitive evidence, provides one more clue that both activities are part of the human pattern of procuring food.

## Adaptations to Gathering and Hunting: Sex Differences in Specific Spatial Abilities

If women have specialized in gathering and men in hunting, we would expect that women and men would have dedicated cognitive abilities that supported these activities. Irwin Silverman and his colleagues have proposed a hunter-gatherer theory of spatial abilities that has led to some remarkable empirical findings (Silverman et al., 2000; Silverman & Eals, 1992). The theory proposes that men will show superior abilities in the types of spatial tasks that would have facilitated success in hunting:

> Tracking and killing animals entail different kinds of spatial problems than does foraging for edible plants; thus, adaptation would have favored diverse spatial skills between the sexes throughout much of their evolutionary history . . . the ability to orient oneself in relation to objects and places, in view or conceptualized across large distances, and to perform mental transformations necessary to maintain accurate orientations during movement. This would enable the pursuit of prey animals across unfamiliar territory, and also accurate placement of projectiles to kill or stun the quarry. (Silverman & Eals, 1992, pp. 514–515)

Because hunting often takes the hunter far away from the home base, selection would favor hunters who could find their way home without getting lost along the way.

Locating and gathering edible nuts, berries, fruit, and tubers would require a different set of spatial skills, according to Silverman:

> . . . the recognition and recall of spatial configurations of objects; that is, the capacity to rapidly learn and remember the contents of object arrays and spatial relationships of the objects to one another. Foraging success would also be increased by peripheral perception and incidental memory for objects and their locations. (Silverman & Eals, 1992, p. 489)

In short, the theory predicts that women will be better at "spatial location memory" as a gathering adaptation; men will be better at navigational abilities, map reading, and the sort of mental rotations that hurling a spear through space to take down an animal requires.

The results of many studies now confirm these sex differences in spatial abilities. Women outperform men on spatial tasks involving location memory and object arrays such as those shown in Figure 3.1 (Silverman & Philips, 1998). Women's superiority in this ability has also been extended to memory for uncommon and unfamiliar objects that have no verbal labels (Eals & Silverman, 1994). A study designed to assess the universality of sex differences in the different types of spatial ability received strong support (Silverman, Choi, & Peters, 2007). In all forty countries and all seven ethnic groups chosen for this study, men scored higher than women on the three-dimensional mental rotations task. Women in thirty-five of forty countries and all seven of the ethnic groups scored higher than men on the object location memory task.

Studies also have used more naturalistic (ecologically valid) methods to explore object recognition and object location memory (New et al., 2007). Among large and complex arrays of plants, women located specific plants more quickly and made fewer mistakes in identifying them than did men. Women also showed a clear superiority over men in factual knowledge about plants (Laiacona, Barbarotto, & Capitani, 2006). Thus, the female superiority in object location memory and factual knowledge about plants supports the hypothesis that women have evolved specialized adaptations for gathering—adaptations that reflect a long-standing division of labor between the sexes (Silverman & Choi, 2005).

Men, in contrast, exceed women in spatial tasks that require mental rotation of objects and navigation through unfamiliar terrain. In one study, participants were led on a winding roundabout route through a wooded area and then required to stop at various places and point to their place of origin. Then they were requested to lead the experimenter back using the most direct

FIGURE 3.1 Women tend to score higher on test of spatial location memory, a sex difference hypothesized to be an adaptation to gathering.

*Source:* Silverman, I., Choi, J., & Peters, M. (2007). The hunter-gatherer theory of sex difference in spatial abilities: Data from 40 countries. *Archives of Sexual Behavior, 36*, 261–268 (Figure 1, p. 264). Reprinted with permission from Springer.

route possible. Men performed better than women on these tasks. Men also outperformed women in mental rotation tasks (Lippa, Collaer, & Peters, 2009), such as imagining what an object would look like from a different vantage point. Finally, women tend to use more concrete landmarks when giving directions, such as trees and specific objects, whereas men tend to use more abstract and Euclidian directions such as "north" and "south."

Taken together, all these findings support the conclusion that men and women have evolved somewhat different spatial specializations, one that facilitates effective gathering and one that favors effective hunting (and perhaps male–male fighting—see Ecuyer-Dab & Robert, 2004). Nonetheless, it is worth noting that effect size for the female superiority in object location memory is typically not large (Voyer et al., 2007), so further tests of the "gathering hypothesis" are needed (Elizabeth Cashdan, personal communication, July 28, 2010).

## ■ FINDING A PLACE TO LIVE: SHELTER AND LANDSCAPE PREFERENCES

Imagine you are on a camping trip. You wake up in the morning with an empty stomach and need to urinate. As you go about your business, the sun beats down on your head and thirst parches your throat, and you quickly come to appreciate the nearby stream with its cold, clean water. But it's time to head off for the day. You pack your gear and look around you. In which directions are you drawn? Some seem beautiful. They promise attractive vistas, perhaps a running stream for water and fishing, lush vegetation, and a safe place to camp. But there are also dangers that you must attend to—wild animals, steep cliffs, and the harsh heat of the sun.

Now imagine that this camping trip lasts not a few days or weeks, but your entire lifetime. This is what our ancestors faced, roaming the savanna of Africa, continuously looking for habitable places to camp. Because there are large costs to choosing a poor place to inhabit, one with meager food resources and vulnerability to hostile forces, and great benefits to choosing a good place, selection would have forged adaptations designed to make our choices wisely. This hypothesis has been the subject of testing by evolutionary psychologists (Kaplan, 1992; Orians & Heerwagen, 1992; Ruso, Renninger, & Atzwanger, 2003).

### The Savanna Hypothesis

Orians (1980, 1986) championed the *savanna hypothesis* of habitat preferences: Selection has favored preferences, motivations, and decision rules to explore and settle in environments abundant with the resources needed to sustain life while simultaneously avoiding environments lacking resources and posing risks to survival. The savanna of Africa, widely believed to be the site in which humans originated, fulfills these requirements.

The savanna houses large terrestrial animals, including many primates such as baboons and chimpanzees. It offers more game for meat than do tropical forests, more vegetation for grazing, and wide-open vistas conducive to a nomadic lifestyle (Orians & Heerwagen, 1992).

*Humans seem to prefer savanna-like environments that offer prospect (resources) and refuge (places to hide).*

Trees there protect sensitive human skin from the harsh sun and provide a refuge for escaping from danger.

Studies of landscape preferences support for the savanna hypothesis. In one study, subjects from Australia, Argentina, and the United States evaluated a series of photographs of trees taken in Kenya. Each photograph focused on a single tree, and pictures were taken under standardized conditions, in similar daylight and weather. The trees selected for inclusion varied in four qualities—canopy shape, canopy density, trunk height, and branching pattern. Participants from all three cultures showed similar judgments. All showed a strong preference for savanna-like trees— those forming a moderately dense canopy and trunks that separated in two near the ground. Participants also tended to dislike skimpy and dense canopies (Orians & Heerwagen, 1992).

A large body of evidence supports the conclusion that natural environments are consistently preferred to human-made environments (Kaplan & Kaplan, 1982). One study (Kaplan, 1992) summarizes the results from thirty different studies in which participants rated color photographs or slides on a five-point scale. The studies varied widely, including scenes from Western Australia, Egypt, Korea, British Columbia, and the United States. Participants included college students and teenagers, Koreans and Australians. The study concluded that natural environments are consistently preferred over human-made environments. And when the latter contain trees and other vegetation, they are rated more positively than similar environments that lack trees or vegetation (Ulrich, 1983). People who are placed in a stressful situation show less physiological distress when viewing slides of nature scenes (Ulrich, 1986). These results support the hypothesis that humans have evolved preferences that are consistent across cultures and that different landscapes can have profound effects on our psychology and physiology.

In a more elaborate extension of the savanna hypothesis, Orians and Heerwagen (1992) proposed three stages of habitat selection. *Stage 1* may be called *selection*. On first encounter with a habitat or landscape, the key decision is whether to explore or to leave. These initial responses tend to be highly affective or emotional. Open environments devoid of cover are abandoned. Completely closed forest canopies, which restrict viewing and movement, also are abandoned.

If the initial reaction is positive in the selection stage, people enter *stage 2*, which may be called *information gathering*. In this stage, the environment is explored for its resources and potential dangers. One study determined that people have a great fondness for mystery at this stage (Kaplan, 1992). People tend to like paths that wind around a bend until they are out of sight and hills that promise something lying beyond them. Mapping also includes an assessment of risk. The same promise of resources around the bend may contain a snake or a lion. So mapping at this stage also entails scrutiny for places for hiding, refuge to conceal oneself and one's family. Multiple places for concealment also afford evaluation from multiple perspectives and multiple routes for escape, should that prove necessary.

*Stage 3* of habitat selection may be called *exploitation,* and involves another decision about whether to stay in the habitat long enough to reap the benefits of the resources it offers. This decision involves trade-offs—the same site that provides good foraging may leave one vulnerable to predators (Orians & Heerwagen, 1992). A craggy cliff that provides good opportunities for surveillance may leave one at risk of making a precipitous fall. Thus, the final decision in this stage, to stay long enough to reap the benefits of the habitat, requires complex cognitive calculations.

Another set of calculations pertains to the time frame of decisions (Orians & Heerwagen, 1992). This temporal dimension can range from the need to assess immediate transitory states to predictions of events over the course of years. Weather patterns are crucial to immediate time frames. Thunder and lightning may signal the need for immediate cover. Humans have poor vision at night, and so have to take cover as darkness falls. The lengthening of shadows and reddening of the sun as it approaches the horizon may trigger the selection of a temporary campsite.

On a longer time frame are seasonal changes, a shift from winter to spring or fall to winter. Seasonal changes bring new information that must be freshly evaluated. Spring brings the budding of lush vegetation and the promise of ripe fruit. Fall turns vegetation brown and signals an impending winter. The savanna hypothesis predicts that people will show strong preferences for signals of harvest—the greenness of grass, the budding of trees, the appearance of fruit on bushes. Bare tree limbs and brown grass should therefore be less agreeable. As noted by Orians and Heerwagen: "It may be difficult for many of us, with the year-round supplies of a wide array of fruits and vegetables in our supermarkets, to understand the importance of the first salad greens of the season to people throughout most of human history" (1992, p. 569).

Flowers, although not commonly eaten by humans, are universally loved. They signal the onset of greens and fruits long absent during the winter months. Bringing flowers to hospital patients may have a real purpose: Studies show that the mere presence of flowers in a hospital room improves the rate of recovery of hospital patients and puts them in a more positive psychological state (Watson & Burlingame, 1960).

Selection has grooved and scored our environmental preferences. Although we live in a modern world far from the savanna plain, we modify our environments to correspond to that ancient habitat. Humans create architecture that mimics the comfortable sensation of living under a forest canopy. We love views and hate living in basements. We recover more quickly from hospital stays if we can view trees outside the hospital window (Ulrich, 1984). And we paint pictures and shoot photographs that recreate the vistas and mysteries of an ancient savanna habitat (Appleton, 1975).

## ■ COMBATING PREDATORS AND OTHER ENVIRONMENTAL DANGERS: FEARS, PHOBIAS, ANXIETIES, AND "ADAPTIVE BIASIS"

All humans experience anxiety and fear that signal danger on certain occasions. The adaptive rationale for human fears seems obvious: They cause us to deal with the source of danger, serving a survival function. This is widely recognized, as reflected in a book, *The Gift of Fear: Survival Signals that Protect Us from Violence*, a *New York Times* best seller (De Becker, 1997). The book urges readers to listen to their intuitive fears because they provide the most important guide we have for avoiding danger.

Isaac Marks (1987) phrased the evolutionary function of fear crisply:

Fear is a vital evolutionary legacy that leads an organism to avoid threat, and has obvious survival value. It is an emotion produced by the perception of present or impending danger and is normal in appropriate situations. Without fear few would survive long under natural conditions. Fear girds our loins for rapid action in the face of danger and alerts us to perform well under stress. It helps us fight the enemy, drive carefully, parachute safely, take exams, speak well to a critical audience, keep a foothold in climbing a mountain. (p. 3)

TABLE *3.1*  **Six Functional Defenses against Acute Attack**

| Defense | Definition |
|---------|-----------|
| Freeze | Stopping, becoming alert, watchful, vigilant, and on guard |
| Flight | Rapidly fleeing or running away from the threat |
| Fight | Attacking the source of the threat |
| Submit | Appease or yield to a member of one's own species to prevent attack |
| Fright | Becoming muscularly immobile, or "playing dead" |
| Faint | Losing consciousness to signal to an attacker that one is not a threat |

*Sources:* Bracha, H. S. (2004). Freeze, flight, fight, fright, faint: Adaptionist perspectives on the acute stress response spectrum. *CNS Spectrums, 9,* 679–685; Marks, I. (1987). *Fears, phobias, and rituals: Panic, anxiety, and their disorders.* New York: Oxford University Press.

*Fear* is defined as "the usually unpleasant feeling that arises as a normal response to realistic danger" (Marks, 1987, p. 5). Fears are distinguished from *phobias*, which are fears that are wildly out of proportion to the realistic danger, are typically beyond voluntary control, and lead to the avoidance of the feared situation.

Marks (1987) and Bracha (2004) outline six ways in which fear and anxiety can afford protection (Table 3.1):

**1.** *Freezing:* This response aids the vigilant assessment of the situation, helps conceal one from the predator, and sometimes inhibits an aggressive attack. If you are not sure that you've been spotted or cannot readily determine the location of the predator, freezing may be better than lashing out or fleeing.

**2.** *Fleeing:* This response distances the organism from specific threats. When you encounter a snake, for example, running away may be the easiest and safest way to avoid receiving a poisonous bite.

**3.** *Fighting:* Attacking, bashing, or hitting a threatening predator may neutralize the threat by destroying it or causing it to flee. This mode of protection entails an assessment of whether the predator can be successfully vanquished or repelled. A spider can be squashed more easily than can a hungry bear.

**4.** *Submission or appeasement:* This response typically works mainly when the threat is a member of one's own species. Among chimpanzees, performing submissive greetings to the alpha male effectively prevents a physical attack. The same might be true for humans.

**5.** *Fright:* This is a response in which the person "plays dead" by becoming immobile. The adaptive advantage of becoming immobile occurs in circumstances in which fleeing or fighting will not work—for example, if the predator is too fast or too strong. Predators are sensitive to motion by potential prey, and sometimes lose interest in a prey that remains motionless for a while (Moskowitz, 2004). By "playing dead," the predator may loosen its grip, possibly opening up an opportunity for escape.

**6.** *Faint:* Fainting is losing consciousness to signal to an attacker that one is not a threat. The hypothesized function of fainting in response to the sight of blood or a sharp weapon is that it helps warfare noncombatants, such as women and children, to "non-verbally communicate to . . . adversaries that one was not an immediate threat and could be safely ignored" (Bracha, 2004, p. 683). Thus, fainting might have increased the noncombatant's chances of surviving violent conflicts that were likely to be common over human evolutionary history. If this hypothesis is correct, it follows that women and children would be more likely than men to faint at the sight of blood, and the evidence strongly supports this prediction (Bracha, 2004).

These behavioral responses to acute threat are adaptively patterned in that they often unfold in a predictable sequence (Bracha, 2004). The first response is typically to freeze, which allows the individual to avoid detection (if lucky) and to plan the best means of escape (Moskowitz, 2004). If the predator continues to close in, the next response is to flee. If fleeing is unsuccessful and the predator pounces, the individual's next response is to fight. When there is no chance of successfully fleeing or fighting, the individual resorts to fright or immobility. Sometimes, this "playing dead" strategy causes the predator to lose interest, opening up a potential opportunity to flee. This sequence of defenses is not unique to humans, but rather occurs in most mammalian species (Bracha, 2004). Fainting, on the other hand, appears to be unique to humans, and may have evolved over the past 2 million years in response to warfare (Bracha, 2004).

In addition to these behavioral responses, fear also brings about a predictable set of *evolved physiological reactions* (Marks & Nesse, 1994). Epinephrine, for example, is produced by fear, and this hormone acts on blood receptors to aid blood clotting, should one sustain a wound. Epinephrine also acts on the liver to release glucose, making energy available to the muscles for fight or flight. Heart rate speeds up, increasing the blood flow and hence circulation. The pattern of blood flow gets diverted from the stomach to the muscles. If you are faced with a threatening lion, digestion can wait. People also start to breathe more rapidly, increasing the oxygen supply to the muscles and speeding the exhalation of carbon dioxide.

## Most Common Human Fears

Table 3.2 shows a catalog of the common subtypes of fears, along with the hypothesized adaptive problems for which they might have evolved (Nesse, 1990, p. 271). Charles Darwin succinctly described the function of fear when he declared, "May we not suspect that the . . . fears of children, which are quite independent of experience, are the inherited effects of real dangers . . . during ancient savage time?" (Darwin, 1877, pp. 285–294). Humans are far more likely to develop fears of dangers that were present in the ancestral environment than of dangers in the current environment. Snakes, for example, are hardly a problem in large urban cities, but automobiles are. Fears of cars, guns, electrical outlets, and cigarettes are virtually unheard of, since these are evolutionarily novel hazards—too recent for selection to have fashioned specific fears. The fact that more city dwellers go to psychiatrists with fears of snakes and strangers than fears of cars and electrical outlets provides a window into the hazards of our ancestral environment.

The specific fears of humans seem to emerge in development at precisely the time when the danger would have been encountered (Marks, 1987). Specialized perceptual templates for spiders suggesting an evolved spider-detection mechanism, for example, have been documented to emerge by five months of age (Rakison & Derringer, 2007). Interestingly, spider fear seems to be spider-specific. Perhaps because spiders are predators that mostly use poison to subdue their prey, and consequently are especially dangerous, spiders evoke greater fear than any other group of arthropods (Gerdes, Uhl, & Alpers, 2009). Fears of heights and strangers emerge in infants around six months of age, which coincide with the time when they start to crawl away from their

TABLE 3.2  **Specific Fears and Relevant Adaptive Problem**

| Subtype of Fear | Adaptive Problem |
|---|---|
| Fear of snakes | Receiving poisonous bite |
| Fear of spiders | Receiving poisonous bite |
| Fear of heights | Damage from falls from cliffs or trees |
| Panic | Imminent attack by predator or human |
| Agoraphobia | Crowded places from which one cannot escape |
| Small animal phobias | Dangerous small animals |
| Disease | Contamination |
| Separation anxiety | Loss of protection from attachment figure |
| Stranger anxiety | Harm from unfamiliar males |
| Social anxiety | Loss of status; ostracism from group |
| Mating anxiety | Public rejection of courtship attempt |

Information from various sources, including Fessler, Eng, & Navarrete (2005), Nesse (1990), and Rakison (2008, 2009).

mothers (Scarr & Salapatek, 1970). In a study concerning heights, 80 percent of infants who had been crawling for forty-one or more days avoided crossing over a "visual cliff" (an apparent vertical drop that was in fact covered with sturdy glass) to get to their mothers (Bertenthal, Campos, & Caplovitz, 1983). Crawling increases the risk of contact with spiders, dangerous falls, and encounters with strangers without the protective mother in close proximity, and so the emergence of these fears at this time seems to coincide with the onset of the adaptive problems. Human infants' fear of strangers has been documented in a variety of different cultures, including Guatemalans, Zambians, !Kung Bushmen, and Hopi Indians (Smith, 1979). In fact, the risk of infants being killed by strangers appears to be a common "hostile force of nature" in nonhuman primates (Hrdy, 1977; Wrangham & Peterson, 1996), as well as in humans (Daly & Wilson, 1988). Interestingly, human children are considerably more fearful of male strangers than of female strangers—fears that correspond to likelihood that male strangers historically have been more dangerous than female strangers (Heerwagen & Orians, 2002).

*Separation anxiety* is another kind of fear for which there is widespread cross-cultural documentation, peaking between nine and thirteen months of age (Kagan, Kearsley, & Zelazo, 1978). In one cross-cultural study, experimenters recorded the percentage of infants who cried after their mothers left the room. At the peak age of separation anxiety, 62 percent of Guatemalan Indians, 60 percent of Israelis, 82 percent of Antigua Guatemalans, and 100 percent of African bush infants exhibited this overt display of separation anxiety.

*Animal fears* emerge around age two, as the child begins a more expansive exploration of its environment. *Agoraphobia,* the fear of being in public places or spaces from which escape might be difficult, can emerge later, as the young leave the home base (Marks & Nesse, 1994). The developmental timing of the emergence of fears, in short, seems to correspond precisely to the onset of the adaptive problem, in this case a threat to survival. This illustrates the point that psychological mechanisms do not have to show up "at birth" to qualify as evolved adaptations. The onset of specific fears, like the onset of puberty, reflects developmentally timed adaptations.

Some fears show clear sex differences. Adult women are significantly more likely than men to develop fears and phobias of snakes and spiders. In two compelling experiments with eleven-month olds, Rakison (2009) discovered that this gender difference originates in infancy. Women report greater fear of events in which they might get injured, including assault, robbery, burglary, rape, and car accidents (Fetchenhauer & Buunk, 2005). This is especially interesting in light of the fact that, with the exception of rape, men are more likely to experience these threats to survival than women. Fetchenhauer and Buunk explain these sex differences by proposing that sexual selection has created risk-taking strategies in men (to obtain status, resources, and mating opportunities), whereas it favored more cautious strategies in women because of the need to protect their offspring. A similar hypothesis might also explain sex differences in fear of snakes—38 percent of women but only 12 percent of men listed fear of snakes as the most common object of intense fear (Agras, Sylvester, & Oliveau, 1969).

The evolutionary psychological basis of specific fears does not merely involve *emotional* reactions but extends to the ways in which we *attend to* and *perceive* the world around us. In a fascinating series of studies, one set of participants was instructed to search for fear-relevant images such as spiders and snakes that were embedded among images of nonfear stimuli such as flowers and mushrooms (Öhman, Flykt, & Esteves, 2001). In another condition, the procedure was reversed: searching for nonfear stimuli amidst images of fear-relevant stimuli. People found the snakes and spiders significantly faster than they were able to find the harmless objects. Indeed, they located the feared stimuli faster regardless of how confusing the array of images was, or how many distractors were present. It was as if the snakes and spiders "popped out" of the visual array and were automatically perceived. These "popping" effects have been documented both in adults and in young children between the ages of three and five (LoBue & DeLoache, 2008). When we look out over an open field, our information-processing mechanisms lead us to detect the "snake in the grass."

The human attention bias toward ancestral dangers occurs in another fascinating phenomenon: our perception of sounds. Evolutionary psychologist John Neuhoff has documented what he calls "an adaptive bias in the perception of looming auditory motion" (Neuhoff, 2001). He

*Humans tend to develop more fears of snakes—hazards in the environments in which we evolved—than of cars, guns, or electrical outlets, which are more hazardous in modern environments.*

found that there is a striking asymmetry in perceptions of "approaching" versus "receding" sound. Changes in approaching sounds are perceived as greater than equivalent changes in receding sounds. In addition, approaching sounds were perceived as starting and stopping closer to us than equivalent receding sounds. This "auditory bias," Neuhoff argues, is a perceptual adaptation that is designed to give us a margin of safety in avoiding dangerous approaching hazards such as predators. What we hear is adaptively biased to avoid dangers in the world. In sum, our adaptations to survival, such as our speedy visual perception of dangers and the auditory looming bias, affect what we see and how we hear the world around us. (See Box 3.1 for an adaptive bias in the domain of vision.)

## Children's Antipredator Adaptations

It is likely that predators have been a recurrent survival hazard throughout human evolutionary history. Dangerous carnivores include lions, tigers, leopards, and hyenas, as well as various reptiles such as crocodiles and pythons (Brantingham, 1998). Estimates of the severity and frequency of encounters with predators are necessarily speculative, but damage to ancient bones, such as puncture marks on hominid skulls that correspond precisely to leopard canines, suggest that predation on human ancestors occurred. In modern times, among the Ache foragers of Paraguay, a study of the causes of death revealed that 6 percent were killed by jaguars and 12 percent died of snakebites (Hill & Hurtado, 1996).

Although children's fears of animals are likely to be part of the evolved defense system, recent research has focused on the information-processing mechanisms required to avoid predators (Barrett, 2005). Barrett and his colleagues argue that children require at least three cognitive skills: (1) a category of "predator" or "dangerous animal" that forms the building block of an antipredator defense; (2) the inference that predators have motivations or "desires" to eat prey, which lead to predictions of the predator's behavior (e.g., if predator is hungry and sees prey, it will chase and try to kill prey); and (3) an understanding that death is a potential outcome of an interaction with a predator. Understanding death

BOX *3.1*

## Evolved Navigation Theory and the Descent Illusion

Imagine standing on a branch in a tall tree or at the edge of a steep cliff and looking down. A slight slip could result in sudden death. Do humans have adaptations to solve survival problem of precipitous falls from heights? One solution has already been mentioned—an evolved fear of heights. Another solution is proposed by a fascinating new theory— evolved navigation theory (ENT) (Jackson & Cormack, 2007, 2008). Navigation through vertical spaces creates different adaptive problems than navigating through horizontal spaces. Being at the

top of tall structures poses a risk of death by falling, either by getting too close to the edge of a cliff or while attempting to descend. Indeed, descending is much more hazardous, resulting in more frequent falls, than ascending. According to ENT, humans have evolved specialized adaptations, such as in the visual and locomotion systems, to solve these and other navigational problems.

A prime example is the novel discovery of the *descent illusion* (Jackson & Cormack, 2008). In a series of controlled experiments, Jackson and

*(Continued)*

BOX *3.1* Continued

The Descent Illusion. *Humans over evolutionary time have fallen much more while descending than while ascending. Jackson and Cormack (2007) predicted from this that people would overestimate heights much more while standing above than below. They found that the distance that people perceive while standing on top of a five-story building is equivalent to the actual height of a nine-story building.*

Cormack discovered that people perceive 32 percent greater vertical distance when viewing from the top compared to when viewing from the bottom. Overestimating vertical distances from the top presumably causes people to be especially wary of cliffs and other positions of height from which they must descend cautiously, thus reducing the likelihood of death due to precipitous falls.

The descent illusion illustrates the logic of a broader theory of perception and cognitive biases—error management theory (EMT). According to

EMT, when there are asymmetries in the costs of errors made under conditions of uncertainty, selection will favor "adaptive biases" to err in the direction of making the less costly error (Buss & Haselton, 2000; Haselton & Nettle, 2006). Just as we err on the side of caution when it comes to snakes and spiders, our visual perceptual adaptations are designed to err in vertical distance estimations—an adaptation to combat the dangers of heights. Our perceptual adaptations are not always designed to perceive objective accuracy. Sometimes they are designed to produce "adaptive illusions."

entails knowing that the dead prey loses the ability to act and that this loss of ability is *permanent* and *irreversible.*

Barrett (1999) demonstrated that children as young as three years of age have a sophisticated cognitive understanding of predator–prey encounters. Children from both an industrialized culture and a traditional hunter-horticulturalist culture were able to spontaneously describe the flow of events in a predator–prey encounter in an ecologically accurate way. Moreover, they understood that after a lion kills a prey, the prey is no longer alive, can no longer eat, and can no longer run and that the dead state is permanent. This sophisticated understanding of death from encounters with predators appears to be developed by age three to four.

In summary, this research on children's understanding of death, combined with the research on fears, the selective visual attention to snakes and spiders, and biases in auditory looming, suggests that humans have evolved an array of survival adaptations to cope with the many problems that jeopardized the lives of our ancestors.

## Darwinian Medicine: Combating Disease

Diseases infect humans many times during the course of life. Humans have evolved adaptations to combat diseases, but not all of these are intuitively obvious. The emerging science of Darwinian medicine is overturning conventional wisdom in how we react to common things like the fever that makes us sweat and reduces iron levels in our blood—both of which occur as a result of infectious disease (Williams & Nesse, 1991).

*Fever.*   When you go to a physician with a fever, the timeworn recommendation to take two aspirin and call in the morning might be offered. Millions of Americans each year take aspirin and other drugs to reduce fever. Recent research suggests that fever-reducing drugs may prolong disease. Fever may be a natural and useful defense against disease.

When cold-blooded lizards are infected with a disease, they commonly find a hot rock on which to bask. This raises their body temperature, which combats the disease. Lizards that cannot find a warm place on which to perch are more likely to die. A similar relationship between body temperature and disease has been observed in rabbits. When given a drug to block fever, diseased rabbits are more likely to die (Kluger, 1990).

Early in the twentieth century, a physician named Julius Wagner-Jauregg observed that syphilis was rarely seen in places where malaria was common (Nesse & Williams, 1994). At that time, syphilis killed 99 percent of those who were infected. Wagner-Jauregg intentionally infected syphilis patients with malaria, which produces a fever, and found that 30 percent of those patients survived—a huge increase in survival. The fever from malaria apparently helped to cure the fatal effects of syphilis.

One study found that children with chicken pox whose fevers were reduced by acetaminophen took nearly a day longer to recover than children whose fevers were not reduced (Doran et al., 1989). Another researcher intentionally infected subjects with a cold virus and gave half the subjects a fever-reducing drug and half a placebo (a pill containing no active substances). Those given the fever-reducing drug had more nasal stuffiness, a worse antibody response, and a slightly longer-lasting cold (Graham et al., 1990).

*Iron-Poor Blood.*   Iron is food for bacteria. They thrive on it. Humans have evolved a means of starving these bacteria. When a person gets an infection, the body produces a chemical (leukocyte endogenous mediator) that reduces blood levels of iron. At the same time, the infected person spontaneously reduces the consumption of iron-rich food such as ham and eggs, and the human body reduces the absorption of whatever iron is consumed (Nesse & Williams, 1994). These natural bodily reactions essentially starve the bacteria, paving the way to combat the infection for a quick recovery.

Although this information has been available since the 1970s, apparently few physicians and pharmacists know about it (Kluger, 1991). They continue to recommend iron supplements, which interfere with our evolved means for combating the hostile force of infections.

Among the Masai tribe, fewer than 10 percent suffered infections caused by an amoeba. When a subgroup was given iron supplements, 88 percent of them developed infections (Weinberg, 1984). Somali nomads have naturally low levels of iron in their diets. When investigators sought to correct this with iron supplements, there was a 30 percent jump in infections within a month (Weinberg, 1984). Old people and women in America are routinely given iron supplements to combat "iron-poor blood," which might paradoxically increase their rate of infections.

In sum, humans have evolved natural defense mechanisms such as fever and blood iron depletion that help combat disease. Interfering with these adaptations by artificially reducing fever or increasing blood iron seems to cause more harm than healing. Advances in Darwinian medicine are leading to novel insights into nutrition, miscarriage, hygiene, cancer, and longevity (Nesse & Sterns, 2008). They offer the hope of improving the quality of life and possibly the length of life.

# ■ WHY DO PEOPLE DIE?

Because survival is so important for reproduction, and we have so many adaptations designed to keep us alive, why do we die at all? Why couldn't selection have fashioned mechanisms that allow us to live forever? And why do some people commit suicide, an act that seems so contrary to anything that evolution would favor? This final section explores these puzzling questions.

## The Theory of Senescence

The answer to these mysteries has been partially solved by senescence theory (Williams, 1957). *Senescence* is not a specific disease, but rather *the deterioration of all bodily mechanisms as organisms grow older.* Senescence theory starts with an observation: The power of natural selection decreases dramatically with increasing age. To understand why this occurs, consider a twenty-year-old woman and a fifty-year-old woman. Selection operates far more intensely on the younger woman, since anything that happens to her could affect most of her future reproductive years. A gene activated at age twenty that weakened a woman's immune system, for example, could damage her entire reproductive capacity. If the same damaging gene became activated in the fifty-year-old instead, it would have almost no impact on the woman's reproductive capacity. Selection operates only weakly on the older woman, since most or all of her reproduction has already occurred (Nesse & Williams, 1994).

Williams (1957) took this observation as a starting point and developed a pleiotropic theory of senescence. *Pleiotropy* is the phenomenon whereby a gene can have two or more different effects. Let's say that there is a gene that boosts testosterone in men, causing them to be more successful in competing with other men for status early in life. But the elevated testosterone also has a negative effect later in life—increasing the risk of prostate cancer. This pleiotropic gene can be favored by selection—that is, it increases in frequency—because the early advantage in status gains for men outweighs the later cost in lowered survival. Through this pleiotropic process, we have evolved a number of genes that help us early in life but cause damaging effects later in life, when selection is weak or absent.

The pleiotropic theory of senescence helps to explain not only why our organs all wear out at roughly the same time late in life, but also why men die younger than women—roughly seven years earlier on average (Kruger & Nesse, 2006; Williams & Nesse, 1991). The effects of selection operate more strongly on men than on women because the reproductive variance of men is higher than that of women. Stated differently, most fertile women reproduce, and the maximum number of children they can have is sharply restricted—roughly twelve, for all practical purposes. Men, in contrast, can produce dozens of children *or* be shut out of reproduction entirely. Because men have greater variability in reproduction, selection can operate more intensely on them than on women. In particular, selection will favor genes that enable a man to compete successfully for mates early in life to be one of the few who reproduces a lot or to avoid being excluded entirely.

Selection for men's success in mate competition will be favored, even if it means that these genes have detrimental effects on survival later in life. Even though men can and sometimes do reproduce for a longer period of time than women, senescence theory explains why these later reproductive events will have a much smaller impact than events occurring earlier in life for men. Genes will be selected for early success in mate competition more strongly in men than in women, at the expense of genes that promote survival later. This strong selection for early advantage produces a higher proportion of pleiotropic genes that cause early death. As one researcher noted, "it seems likely that males suffer higher mortality than do females because in the past they have enjoyed higher *potential* reproductive success, and this has selected for traits that are positively associated with high reproductive success but at a cost of decreased survival" (Trivers, 1985, p. 314). Men, in short, are "designed" to die sooner than women, and the theory of senescence helps to solve the mystery of why.

In summary, selection is most potent early in life because any events that happen early can affect the entire span of a person's reproductive years. As people get older, the power of selection weakens. Something that happened to you in old age right before you died would likely have no effect on your reproductive capacity. This means that selection will favor adaptations that give beneficial effects early in life, even if they come with heavy costs later on. These heavy costs cumulate in old age, resulting in the deterioration of all body parts at roughly the same time. In this sense, organisms can be said to be "designed" to die.

## The Puzzle of Suicide

The senescence of organisms, eventually resulting in death, may be inevitable, but there is an even deeper puzzle for evolutionary psychology: Why would anyone intentionally take his or her own life? Survival is surely necessary for reproduction. So what could account for suicide?

Evolutionary psychologist Denys de Catanzaro (1991, 1995) has developed an evolutionary theory of suicide. His central argument is that suicide will be most likely to occur when an individual has a dramatically reduced ability to contribute to his or her own inclusive fitness. Indicators of this dramatically reduced capacity include expectations of poor future health, chronic infirmity, disgrace or failure, poor prospects for successful heterosexual mating, and perceptions of being a burden on one's genetic kin. Under these conditions, it is at least plausible that the replication of an individual's genes would have a better chance without him or her around. If a person is a burden to his or her family, for example, then the kin's reproduction, and hence the person's own fitness, might suffer as a result of his or her survival.

To test this evolutionary theory of suicide, de Catanzaro looked at *suicidal ideation:* whether a person had ever considered suicide, had recently considered suicide, intended to kill himself or herself within one year, intended to kill himself or herself ever, or had previously engaged in suicidal behavior. The dependent measure was a sum of responses to these items. Suicidal ideation is not actual suicide, of course. Many people have thoughts of suicide without actually killing themselves. Nonetheless, because suicide is usually a premeditated event, a lot of suicidal ideation will almost invariably precede an actual suicide. So suicidal ideation is a reasonable index to examine as a proxy for actual suicide.

In another part of the questionnaire, de Catanzaro asked participants a series of questions about their perceived burdensomeness to family, perceived significance of contributions to family and society, frequency of sexual activity, success with members of the opposite sex, homosexuality, number of friends, treatment by others, financial welfare, and physical health. Participants responded to each item using a seven-point scale ranging from $-3$ to $+3$. The participants varied—a large public sample, a sample of the elderly, a sample from a mental hospital, a sample of inmates at a maximum security center housing those who had committed antisocial crimes, and two samples of homosexuals.

The results supported de Catanzaro's evolutionary theory of suicide. When the measure of suicidal ideation was correlated with the other items on the questionnaire, he found the following results.[1] For men in the public sample, ages eighteen to thirty years, the following correlations were found with suicidal ideation: burden to family ($+.56$), sex in last month ($-.67$), success in heterosexual relations ($-.67$), sex ever ($-.45$), stability of heterosexual relations ($-.45$) sex last year ($-.40$), and number of children ($-.36$). For young women in the public sample, similar results were found, although they were not quite as strong: burden to family ($+.44$), sex ever ($-.37$), and contribution to family ($-.36$).

For older samples, health burdens took on increased importance and showed a strong correlation with suicidal ideation. For the public sample of men over the age of fifty, for example, the following significant correlations were found with suicidal ideation: health ($-.48$), future financial problems ($+.46$), burden to family ($+.38$), homosexuality ($+.38$), and number of friends ($-.36$). Women over the age of fifty in the public sample showed similar results: loneliness ($+.62$), burden to family ($+.47$), future financial problems ($+.45$), and health ($-.42$).

---

[1] Correlations describe the relationships between variables, and range from +1 to –1. A positive correlation means that as one variable increases, the other variable also increases. A negative correlation means that as one variable increases, the other decreases.

Findings such as these have now been reported by independent researchers. In a study of 175 American university students, Michael Brown and his colleagues tested de Catanzaro's theory of suicide (Brown et al., 1999). They found that individuals with low reproductive potential (e.g., who perceive that they are not attractive to members of the opposite sex) and high burdensomeness to kin reported more suicidal ideation, as well as more depression and hopelessness.

Interestingly, the evolved suicide adaptation hypothesis also helps to explain sex differences in the rate and the patterning of actual suicides. Although men commit suicide at higher rates than women at every age, the sex difference peaks at two points in life—during the years of the most intense mate competition (roughly ages 15 to 35) and in old age (70 and later). During the mid-20s, for example, men are more than six times as likely as women to commit suicide; after age 70, men are more than seven times as likely as women to commit suicide (Kruger & Nesse, 2006). The evolved suicide adaptation hypothesis explains this pattern. First, more men than women fail in heterosexual mating, and these failures occur during the peak years of mate competition. Second, men are more likely than women to suffer from infectious diseases, cardiovascular diseases, and liver disease, especially in the later years of life, making them more likely than women to become a burden to their families. In summary, results from independent investigators provide preliminary support for de Catanzaro's evolutionary theory of suicide.

Other evolutionary psychologists, such as Gad Saad, argue that suicide is a maladaptive response to sex-linked "defeats" in evolutionarily relevant domains (Saad, 2007a). Saad highlights the key finding that men are far more likely than women to commit suicide following the loss of occupational status. Romantic breakup, rather than loss of a job or status, in contrast, triggers suicide in some women. One argument in favor of the maladaptive by-product hypothesis is that no matter how dire someone's current circumstances are, the future often brings opportunities to better them. Mates can usually be replaced and jobs can usually be regained, so it seems maladaptive to take oneself out of the reproductive game entirely. Finally, the suicide adaptation and the maladaptive by-product hypotheses each might be partially correct. The suicide adaptation hypothesis seems most powerful in explaining suicides when a person is a burden to kin. The maladaptive by-product hypothesis, in contrast, may provide a better explanation of sex-differentiated triggers of suicide in cases in which the taking one's own life eliminates any prospect of future reproduction.

## Homicide

Humans experience death at the hands of other humans. Indeed, some have argued that humans have become the most important "hostile force of nature" (Alexander, 1987). There are different types of homicide such as infanticide, rivalry killing, mate killing, and warfare. Although wars and murders today often makes headlines, there is good evidence that modern murder rates are substantially lower than in previous times. Some argue that traditional hunter-gatherers provide evidence of murder rates that may have occurred over human evolutionary history. Among the Hiwi hunter-gatherers of Venezuela and Colombia, for example, 35 percent of all adult deaths were caused by either homicide or warfare (Hill, Hurtado, & Walker, 2007). Similar rates have been found in other South American foragers such as the Yanomamö (Chagnon, 1983) and the Gebusi of Papua New Guinea (Keeley, 1996), although rates vary dramatically across cultures. We will explore the topic homicide in greater detail in subsequent chapters—infanticide in Chapter 7 (Parenting) and one-on-one homicides and warfare in Chapter 10 (Aggression and Warfare). To foreshadow those discussions, a key issue will be whether humans have evolved psychological adaptations specifically designed to kill other humans. For now, it is important to bear in mind that there is substantial and compelling evidence from a variety of sources that death at the hands of other humans historically has indeed been an important hostile force of nature.

## ■ SUMMARY

Food shortages, toxins, predators, parasites, diseases, and extremes of climate are hostile forces of nature that recurrently plagued our ancestors. Humans have evolved adaptive mechanisms to combat these impediments to survival. One of the most important survival problems is obtaining food. In addition to the problem of food shortages, organisms face the problem of selecting which foods to consume (e.g., those that are rich in calories and nutrients), selecting which foods to avoid (e.g., those that are filled with toxins), and actually procuring edible foods. Humans evolved as omnivores, consuming a wide variety of plants and animals. Among the human adaptations are specific food preferences for calorically rich food; specific mechanisms for avoiding the consumption of toxic food, such as the emotion of disgust; and mechanisms for getting rid of toxins such as gagging, spitting, vomiting, coughing, sneezing, diarrhea, and pregnancy sickness. People also use spices that kill off food-borne bacteria, a practice that likely spreads through cultural transmission, supporting the antimicrobial hypothesis. Our taste for alcohol probably originated in the eating of ripe fruit, since ripe fruit contains low levels of ethanol. The use of fire to cook foods may have been critical in human evolution, functioning both to kill dangerous microbes and to render a wider array of potential foods more easily digestible.

One of the most controversial topics in human evolution is how human ancestors procured their food. Two basic hypotheses have been advanced: the hunting hypothesis and the gathering hypothesis. All available evidence points to an ancestral pattern characterized by male hunting, female gathering, and perhaps occasional opportunistic scavenging. Sex differences in spatial ability reflect adaptations to hunting and gathering. Women on average outperform men on tasks involving spatial location memory—a likely adaptation that facilitates efficient gathering of nuts, fruits, and tubers. Men on average outperform women on spatial tasks involving the mental rotation of objects, navigation, and map reading—the sorts of abilities that are likely to facilitate efficient hunting.

Another adaptive problem of survival involves finding a place to live. Humans have evolved preferences for landscapes rich in resources and places where one can see without being seen, mimicking the savanna habitats of our ancestors.

All habitats contain hostile forces that impede survival. Humans have evolved a variety of specific fears to avoid these dangers. The human fears of snakes, spiders, heights, and strangers, for example, appear to be present across a variety of cultures and emerge at specific times in development, suggesting adaptive patterning. Humans have at least six behavioral responses to a fear-inducing stress: Freeze, flight, fight, submit, fright, and faint. In addition to fears, humans appear to have predictable biases in their attention: They can easily pick out snakes and spiders amidst an array of nondangerous images. Humans have an auditory looming bias that gives us an extra margin of safety when we hear sounds of danger approaching. We also have the descent illusion, overestimating heights when viewed from the top compared to when viewed from the bottom—an adaptation likely designed to prevent dangerous falls from heights. Finally, children as young as age three appear to have a sophisticated understanding of death as a result of an interaction with a predator.

Diseases and parasites are ubiquitous hostile forces of nature, especially for long-lived organisms. Humans appear to have evolved a variety of adaptive mechanisms to combat diseases and parasites. Contrary to conventional medical wisdom, the human mechanism that elevates body temperature and creates a fever is a natural bodily function to combat infectious diseases. Taking aspirin or similar drugs to combat fever has the paradoxical effect of prolonging disease.

Given the importance of survival in the evolutionary scheme of things, why people die (or do not live longer) poses an interesting puzzle. The theory of senescence explains why. Basically, selection is most potent early in life because any events that happen early can affect the entire span of a person's reproductive years. As people get older, however, the power of selection weakens; in the extreme, a bad event that happened to you right before you died would have no effect on your reproduction. This means that selection will favor adaptations that give beneficial effects early in life, even if they come with heavy costs later on.

Perhaps even more puzzling is the phenomenon of suicide—when a person intentionally ends his or her own life. Suicidal ideation occurs most commonly among those with poor reproductive prospects, who experience failure at heterosexual mating, who are in poor health, who have poor financial prospects for the future, and who perceive themselves to be a large burden on their kin. Evidence points to the possibility that humans have evolved context-sensitive psychological mechanisms to evaluate future reproductive potential and net cost to genetic kin.

Homicide has been an important cause of death. Evidence from traditional hunter-gatherers suggest that mortality due to one-on-one killings and war can get as high as 35 percent. A key question is whether humans have evolved psychological adaptations to kill other humans—a topic taken up in detail in subsequent chapters.

All these evolved mechanisms help humans to survive long enough to reach adulthood. Once there, however, humans still encounter hostile forces that impede survival. But they also face a new set of adaptive challenges—those of mating, a topic to which we now turn.

## ■ SUGGESTED READINGS

Hill, K., Hurtado, K., & Walker, R. S. (2007). High adult mortality among Hiwi hunter-gatherers: Implications for human evolution. *Journal of Human Evolution, 52,* 443–454.

Jackson, R. E., & Cormack, J. K. (2007). Evolved navigation theory and the descent illusion. *Perception and Psychophysics, 69,* 353–362.

Kruger, D. J., & Nesse, R. M. (2006). An evolutionary life-history framework for understanding sex differences in human mortality rates. *Human Nature, 17,* 74–97.

Marlow, F. W. (2005). Hunter-gatherers and human evolution. *Evolutionary Anthropology, 14,* 54–67.

Oaten, M., Stevenson, R. J., & Case, T. I. (2009). Disgust as a disease-avoiding mechanism. *Psychological Bulletin, 135,* 303–321.

Öhman, A., & Mineka, S. (2003). The malicious serpent: Snakes as a prototypical stimulus for an evolved module of fear. *Current Directions in Psychological Science, 12,* 5–9.

# PART 3

# CHALLENGES OF SEX AND MATING

Because differential reproduction is the engine that drives the evolutionary process, the psychological mechanisms surrounding reproduction should be especially strong targets of selection. If selection has not sculpted psychological mechanisms designed to solve adaptive problems posed by sex and mating, then evolutionary psychology would be "out of business" before it even got off the ground. In this part we consider the problems of mating and examine the large empirical foundation that evolutionary psychology has established in this domain.

Part 3 is divided into three chapters. Chapter 4 examines how women select mates. It presents evidence from large-scale cross-cultural studies designed to test evolutionary psychological hypotheses. Women's mate preferences are complex and sophisticated because of the large number of complex adaptive problems that women have had to solve over the expanse of evolutionary history. The chapter concludes with an examination of how women's desires affect actual mating behavior.

Chapter 5 deals with men's mate preferences and how they are designed to solve a somewhat different set of adaptive problems. According to the metatheory of evolutionary psychology, men and women are predicted to differ only in domains in which they have recurrently faced different adaptive problems over human evolutionary history. In all other domains, the sexes are predicted to be similar. This chapter highlights the domains in which the adaptive problems that men have confronted are distinct—problems such as selecting a fertile partner and ensuring certainty in paternity when investing in a long-term mate.

Chapter 6 focuses on short-term sexual strategies. This chapter reviews scientific findings on sperm competition and female orgasm—physiological clues that suggest a long ancestral history of nonmonogamous mating. Because humans experience both short-term and long-term mating, they show a degree of flexibility rarely observed in other species. Which strategy an individual pursues often depends on context. The chapter ends with a review of the major contextual variables, such as individual mate value and ratio of men to women in the mating pool, that affect whether a person pursues a short-term or a long-term mating strategy.

# CHAPTER 4

# WOMEN'S LONG-TERM MATING STRATEGIES

*. . . to an extraordinary degree, the predilections of the investing sex—females—potentially determine the direction in which the species will evolve. For it is the female who is the ultimate arbiter of when she mates and how often and with whom.*

—Sarah Blaffer Hrdy, 1981

Nowhere do people have an equal desire for all members of the opposite sex. Everywhere some potential mates are preferred, others shunned. Imagine living as our ancestors did long ago—struggling to keep warm by the fire; hunting meat for our kin; gathering nuts, berries, and herbs; and avoiding dangerous animals and hostile humans. If we were to select a mate who failed to deliver the resources promised, who had affairs, who was lazy, who lacked hunting skills, or who heaped physical abuse on us, our survival would be tenuous, our reproduction at risk. In contrast, a mate who provided abundant resources, who protected us and our children, and who devoted time, energy, and effort to our family would be a great asset. As a result of the powerful survival and reproductive advantages that were reaped by those of our ancestors who chose mates wisely, many specific desires evolved. As descendants of those winners in the evolutionary lottery, modern humans have inherited a specific set of mate preferences.

Scientists have also documented evolved mate preferences in many nonhuman species. The African village weaverbird provides a vivid illustration (Collias & Collias, 1970). When a female weaverbird arrives in the vicinity of a male, he displays his recently built nest by suspending himself upside down from the bottom and vigorously flapping his wings. If the male impresses the female, she approaches the nest, enters it, and examines the nest materials, poking and pulling them for as long as ten minutes. During this inspection, the male sings to her from nearby. At any point in this sequence, she may decide that the nest does not meet her standards and depart to inspect another male's nest. A male whose nest is rejected by several females will often break it down and rebuild another from scratch. By exerting a preference for males capable of building superior nests, the female weaverbird addresses the problems of protecting and provisioning her chicks. Her preferences have evolved because they bestowed a reproductive advantage over other weaverbirds who had no preferences and who mated with any male who happened to come along.

Women, like weaverbirds, also prefer males with "nests" of various kinds. Consider one of the problems that women in evolutionary history had to face: selecting a man who would be willing to commit to a long-term relationship. A woman in our evolutionary past who chose to mate with a man who was flighty, impulsive, philandering, or unable to sustain a relationship found herself raising her children alone and without benefit of the resources, aid, and protection that a more dependable mate might have offered. A woman who preferred to mate with a reliable man who was willing to commit to her would have had children who survived, thrived, and multiplied. Over thousands of generations, a preference for men who showed signs of being willing and able to commit evolved in women, just as preferences for mates with adequate nests evolved in weaverbirds. This preference solved key reproduction problems, just as food preferences solved key survival problems.

# ■ THEORETICAL BACKGROUND FOR THE EVOLUTION OF MATE PREFERENCES

This section reviews two important theoretical issues that are key to understanding the evolution of mate preferences. The first topic deals with the definition of the two distinct types that exist in sexually reproducing species—males and females—and the related issue of the influence of parental investment on the nature of mating. The second topic pertains to mate preferences as evolved psychological mechanisms.

## Parental Investment and Sexual Selection

It is a remarkable fact that what defines biological sex is simply the size of the sex cells. Mature reproductive cells are called *gametes*. Each gamete has the potential to fuse with another gamete of the opposite sex to form a *zygote*, which is defined as a fertilized gamete. Males are the sex with the small gametes, females with the large gametes. The female gametes remain reasonably stationary and come loaded with nutrients; the male gametes are endowed with greater mobility. Along with differences in size and mobility comes a difference in quantity. Men produce millions of sperm, which are replenished at a rate of roughly 12 million per hour. Women, on the other hand, produce a fixed and unreplenishable lifetime supply of approximately 400 ova.

Women's greater initial investment per gamete does not end with the egg. Fertilization and gestation, key components of human parental investment, occur internally in women. One act of sexual intercourse, which requires minimal male investment, can produce an obligatory and energy-consuming nine-month investment by the woman. In addition, women alone engage in the activity of lactation (breastfeeding), which lasts as long as four years in some societies (Shostak, 1981).

No biological law of the animal world dictates that females must invest more than males. Indeed, in some species such as the Mormon cricket, pipefish seahorse, and Panamanian poison arrow frog, males in fact invest more (Trivers, 1985). The male Mormon cricket produces a large spermatophore that is loaded with nutrients. Females compete with each other for access to the high-investing males holding the largest spermatophores. Among these so-called sex-role reversed species, males are more discriminating than females about mating. In particular, the females that are chosen by the males for depositing their spermatophore contain 60 percent more eggs than females who are rejected (Trivers, 1985). Among all 4,000 species of mammals and the more than 200 species of primates, however, the females—not the males—undergo internal fertilization and gestation.

The great initial parental investment of females makes them a valuable reproductive resource (Trivers, 1972). Gestating, bearing, lactating, nurturing, protecting, and feeding a child are exceptionally valuable reproductive resources. Those who hold valuable resources do not give them away haphazardly. Because women in our evolutionary past risked investing enormously as a consequence of having sex, evolution favored women who were highly selective about their mates. Ancestral women suffered severe costs if they were indiscriminate: They experienced lower reproductive success, and fewer of their children survived to reproductive age.

In summary, Trivers's (1972) theory of parental investment and sexual selection makes two profound predictions: (1) The sex that invests more in offspring (typically, but not always, the female) will be more discriminating or selective about mating; and (2) the sex that invests less in offspring will be more competitive for sexual access to the high-investing sex. In the case of humans, it is clear that women have greater *obligatory* parental investment. When it comes to long-term mating or marriage, however, both men and women typically invest heavily in children, and so the theory of parental investment predicts that both sexes should be very choosy and discriminating.

## Mate Preferences as Evolved Psychological Mechanisms

Consider the case of an ancestral woman trying to decide between two men, one of whom shows great generosity to her with his resources and the other of whom is stingy. All else being equal, the generous man is more valuable to her than the stingy man. The generous man may share his meat from the hunt, aiding her survival. He may sacrifice his time, energy, and resources for the benefit of the children, aiding the woman's reproductive success. In these respects, the generous man has higher value than the stingy man as a mate. If, over evolutionary time, generosity in men provided these benefits repeatedly and the cues to a man's generosity were observable and reliable, selection would have favored the evolution of a preference for generosity in a mate.

Now consider a more complicated and realistic scenario in which men vary not just in their generosity but also in a bewildering variety of ways that are significant in the choice of a mate. Men differ in their physical prowess, athletic skill, ambition, industriousness, kindness, empathy, emotional stability, intelligence, social skills, sense of humor, kin network, and position in the status hierarchy. Men also differ in the costs they carry into a mating relationship: Some come with children, a bad temper, a selfish disposition, and promiscuous proclivities. In addition, men differ in hundreds of ways that may be irrelevant to women. From among the thousands of ways in which men differ, selection over hundreds of thousands of years focused women's preferences, laser-like, on the most adaptively valuable characteristics. Women lacking specific adaptively relevant preferences are not our ancestors; they were out-reproduced by choosier women.

The qualities people prefer, however, are not static. Because preferences change over time, mate seekers must gauge the future potential of a prospective partner. A man might lack resources now but, as a medical student, might have excellent future promise. Gauging a man's mate value requires looking beyond his current position and evaluating his future potential.

In short, evolution has favored women who prefer men possessing those attributes that confer benefits and who dislike men possessing those attributes that impose costs. Each separate attribute constitutes one component of a man's value to a woman as a mate. Each of her preferences tracks one critical component.

Preferences that give priority to particular components, however, do not completely solve the problem of choosing a mate. In selecting a mate, a woman must deal with the problem of identifying and correctly evaluating the cues that signal whether a man indeed possesses a particular resource. The assessment problem becomes especially acute in areas in which men are apt to deceive women, such as pretending greater status than they actually possess or feigning greater commitment than they are truly willing to give.

Finally, women face the problem of integrating their knowledge about a prospective mate. Suppose that one man is generous but emotionally unstable. Another man is emotionally stable but stingy. Which man should a woman choose? Selecting a mate requires psychological mechanisms that make it possible to add up the relevant attributes and give each its appropriate weight on the whole. Some attributes weigh more than others in arriving at the final decision about whether to choose or reject a particular man.

## ■ THE CONTENT OF WOMEN'S MATE PREFERENCES

With this theoretical background in mind, we turn now to the actual content of women's mate preferences (summarized in Table 4.1). As the previous discussion implies, choosing a mate is a complex task, and so we do not expect to find simple answers to what women want.

### Preference for Economic Resources

The evolution of the female preference for males offering resources may be the most ancient and pervasive basis for female choice in the animal kingdom. Consider the gray shrike, a bird living in the Negev Desert of Israel (Yosef, 1991). Just before the start of the breeding season, male shrikes begin amassing caches of edible prey such as snails and useful objects such as feathers and pieces of cloth in numbers ranging from 90 to 120. They impale these items on thorns and other pointed projections within their territories. Females scan the available males and choose to mate with those with the largest caches. When Yosef arbitrarily removed portions of some males' stock and added edible objects to the supplies of others, females still preferred to mate with the males with the larger bounties. Females entirely avoided males without resources, consigning them to bachelorhood.

Among humans, the evolution of women's preference for a long-term mate with resources would have required two preconditions. First, resources would have to be accruable, defensible, and controllable by men during human evolutionary history. Second, men would have to differ from each other in their holdings and their willingness to invest those holdings in a woman and her children.

TABLE 4.1 **Adaptive Problems in Long-Term Mating and Hypothesized Solutions**

| Adaptive Problem | Evolved Mate Preference |
|---|---|
| Selecting a mate who is able to invest | Good financial prospects<br>Social status<br>Older age<br>Ambition/industriousness<br>Size, strength, and athletic ability |
| Selecting a mate who is willing to invest | Dependability and stability<br>Love and commitment cues<br>Positive interactions with children |
| Selecting a mate who is able to physically protect her and children | Size (height)<br>Bravery<br>Athletic ability |
| Selecting a mate who will show good parenting skills | Dependability<br>Emotional stability<br>Kindness<br>Positive interactions with children |
| Selecting a mate who is compatible | Similar values<br>Similar ages<br>Similar personalities |
| Selecting a mate who is healthy | Physical attractiveness<br>Symmetry<br>Health<br>Masculinity |

Over the course of human evolutionary history, women could often garner far more resources for their children through a single spouse than through several temporary sex partners. Men invest in their wives and children with provisions to an extent unprecedented among primates. In all other primates, females must rely solely on their own efforts to acquire food because males rarely share those resources with their mates (Smuts, 1995). Men, in contrast, provide food, find shelter, defend territory, and protect children. They tutor children in sports, hunting, fighting, hierarchy negotiation, friendship, and social influence. They transfer status, aiding offspring in forming reciprocal alliances later in life. These benefits are unlikely to be secured by a woman from a temporary sex partner.

So the stage was set for the evolution of women's preferences for men with resources. But women needed cues to signal a man's possession of those resources. These cues might be indirect, such as personality characteristics that signal a man's upward mobility. They might be physical, such as a man's athletic ability or health. They might include reputation, such as the esteem in which a man is held by his peers. The possession of economic resources, however, provides the most obvious cue.

## Preference for Good Financial Prospects

Currently held mate preferences provide a window for viewing our mating past, just as our fears of snakes and heights provide a window for viewing ancestral hazards. Evidence from dozens of studies documents that modern U.S. women indeed value economic resources in mates substantially more than men do. In a study conducted in 1939, for example, U.S. men and women rated eighteen characteristics for their relative desirability in a marriage partner, ranging from irrelevant to indispensable. Women did not view good financial prospects as absolutely indispensable, but they did rate them as important, whereas men rated them as merely desirable but not very important.

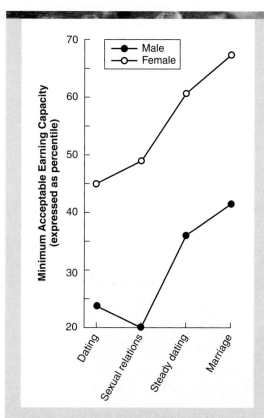

FIGURE *4.1* **Minimum Acceptable Earning Capacity at Each Level of Involvement.** Women maintain considerably higher minimum standards for financial capacity in mates, reaching peak standards in the long-term mating context (marriage).

*Source:* Kenrick, D. T., Sadalla, E. K., Groth, G., & Trost, M. R. (1990). Evolution, traits, and the stages of human courtship: Qualifying the parental investment model. *Journal of Personality, 58,* 97–116. Reprinted with permission.

Women in 1939 valued good financial prospects in a mate about twice as highly as men did, a finding that was replicated in 1956 and again in 1967 (Buss et al., 2001).

The sexual revolution of the late 1960s and early 1970s failed to change this sex difference. In an attempt to replicate the studies from earlier decades, in the mid-1980s 1,491 people in the United States were surveyed using the same questionnaire (Buss, 1989a). Women and men from Massachusetts, Michigan, Texas, and California rated eighteen personal characteristics for their value in a marriage partner. As in the previous decades, women still valued good financial prospects in a mate roughly twice as much as did men. In 1939, for example, women judged "good financial prospect" to be 1.80 in importance on a scale ranging from 0 (irrelevant) to 3 (indispensable); men in 1939 judged "good financial prospect" to be only 0.90 in importance. By 1985, women judged this quality to be 1.90 in importance, whereas men judged it to be 1.02 in importance—still roughly a twofold difference between the sexes (Buss et al., 2001).

Douglas Kenrick and his colleagues devised a useful method for revealing how much people value different attributes in a marriage partner by having men and women indicate the "minimum percentiles" of each characteristic they would find acceptable (Kenrick et al., 1990). U.S. college women indicate that their minimum acceptable percentile for a husband on earning capacity is the seventieth percentile, or above 70 percent of all other men, whereas men's minimum acceptable percentile for a wife's earning capacity is only the fortieth (see Figure 4.1).

Personal ads in newspapers and magazines confirm that women actually in the marriage market desire strong financial resources (Gustavsson & Johnsson, 2008; Wiederman, 1993). In short, sex differences in preference for resources are not limited to college students and are not bound by the method of inquiry.

Nor are these female preferences restricted to America, to Western societies, or to capitalist countries. A large cross-cultural study was conducted of thirty-seven cultures on six continents and five islands using populations ranging from coast-dwelling Australians to urban Brazilians to shantytown South African Zulus (Buss et al., 1990). Some participants came from nations that practice *polygyny* (the mating or marriage of a single man with several women), such as Nigeria and Zambia. Other participants came from nations that are more *monogamous* (the mating of one man with one woman), such as Spain and Canada. The countries included those in which living together is as common as marriage, such as Sweden and Finland, as well as countries in which living together without marriage is frowned on, such as Bulgaria and Greece. The study sampled a total of 10,047 individuals in thirty-seven cultures, as shown in Figure 4.2 (Buss, 1989a).

Male and female participants in the study rated the importance of eighteen characteristics in a potential mate or marriage partner, on a scale from unimportant to indispensable. Women across all continents, all political systems (including socialism and communism), all racial groups, all religious groups, and all systems of mating (from intense polygyny to presumptive

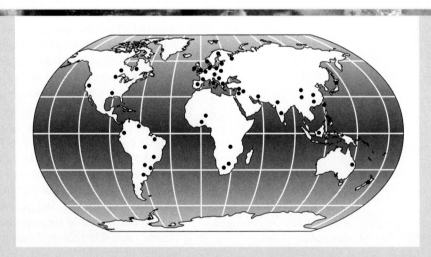

FIGURE 4.2   **Locations of Thirty-Seven Cultures Studied in an International Mate Selection Project.** Thirty-seven cultures, distributed as shown, were examined by the author in his international study of male and female mating preferences. The author and his colleagues surveyed the mating desires of 10,047 people on six continents and five islands. The results provide the largest database of human mating preferences ever accumulated.

*Source:* Buss, D. M. (1994a). The strategies of human mating. *American Scientist, 82,* 238–249. Reprinted with permission.

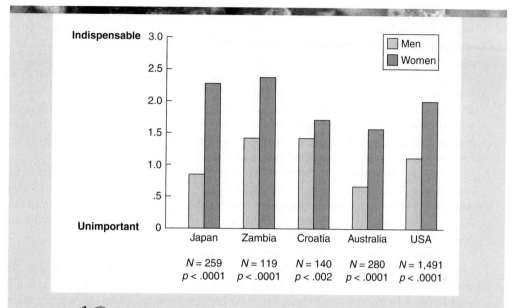

FIGURE 4.3 **Preference for Good Financial Prospect in a Marriage Partner.**
Participants in cultures rated this variable, in the context of seventeen other variables, on how desirable it would be in a potential long-term mate or marriage partner using a four-point rating scale, ranging from 0 (irrelevant or unimportant) to 3 (indispensable).

$N$ = sample size.

$p$ values less than .05 indicate that sex difference is significant.

*Source:* Buss, D. M., & Schmitt, D. P. (1993). Sexual strategies theory: An evolutionary perspective on human mating. *Psychological Review, 100,* 204–232. Copyright © 1993 by the American Psychological Association. Adapted with permission.

monogamy), placed more value than men on good financial prospects. Overall, women valued financial resources roughly twice as much as did men (see Figure 4.3). There are some cultural variations. Women from Nigeria, Zambia, India, Indonesia, Iran, Japan, Taiwan, Colombia, and Venezuela valued good financial prospects a bit higher than women from South Africa (Zulus), the Netherlands, and Finland. In Japan, for example, women valued good financial prospect roughly 150 percent more than men, whereas women from the Netherlands deem it only 36 percent more important than their male counterparts, less than women from any other country. Nonetheless, the sex difference remained invariant: Women worldwide desired financial resources in a marriage partner more than men.

These findings provided the first extensive cross-cultural evidence supporting the evolutionary basis for the psychology of human mating. Since that study, findings from other cultures continue to support the hypothesis that women have evolved preferences for men with resources. A study of mate selection in the country of Jordan found that women more than men valued economic ability, as well as qualities linked to economic ability such as status, ambition, and education (Khallad, 2005). Using a different method—analysis of folktales in forty-eight cultural areas including bands, tribes, preindustrial states, Pacific islands, and all the major continents—Jonathan Gottschall and colleagues found the same sex difference (Gottschall et al., 2003). Substantially more female than male characters in the folktales from each culture placed a primary emphasis on wealth or status in their expressed mate preferences. Gottschall found similar results in a historical analysis of European literature (Gottschall et al., 2004). A study of 500 Muslims living in the United States found that women sought financially secure, emotionally sensitive, and sincere partners, the latter likely being a signal of willingness to commit to a long-term relationship (Badahdah & Tiemann, 2005). Finally, an in-depth study of the Hadza of Tanzania, a hunter-gatherer society, found that women place a great importance on a man's foraging abilities—primarily his ability to hunt (Marlow, 2004).

This fundamental sex difference also appears prominently in modern forms of mating, such as speed dating and mail-order brides. In a study of speed dating, in which individuals engage in four-minute conversations to determine whether they are interested in meeting the other person again, women chose men who indicated that they had grown up in affluent neighborhoods (Fisman et al., 2006). Another study of a community sample of 382 speed daters, ranging in age from eighteen to fifty-four, found that women's choices, more than men's choices, were influenced by a potential date's income and education (Asendorpf, Penke, & Back, 2010). A study of the mate preferences of mail-order brides from Colombia, the Philippines, and Russia found that these women sought husbands who had status and ambition—two key correlates of resource acquisition (Minervini & McAndrew, 2006). As the authors conclude, "women willing to become MOBs [mail-order brides] do not appear to have a different agenda than other mate-seeking women; they simply have discovered a novel way to expand their pool of prospective husbands" (2006, p. 17). A study of personal advertisements in Sweden, a culture that has a high level of economic equality between the sexes, found that women sought resources three times as often as did men (Gustavsson & Johnsson, 2008). A study of 2,956 Israelis who subscribed to a computer dating service found that women, far more than men, sought mates who owned their own cars, had good economic standing, and placed a high level of importance on their careers (Bokek-Cohen, Peres, & Kanazawa, 2007). Women also place tremendous value on *intelligence* in a long-term mate (Buss et al., 1990; Prokosch et al., 2009), a quality highly predictive of income and occupational status (Buss, 1994b). Even in more traditional societies, such as the Kipsigis of Kenya, women (as well as the women's parents when choosing for them) preferentially select men who have resources such as large plots of land (Borgerhoff Mulder, 1990).

Finally, a study of the reproductive outcomes of women living in preindustrial Finland in the eighteenth and nineteenth centuries found that women married to wealthier men had higher survival rates and a larger number of children who survived to adulthood than women married to poorer men (Pettay et al., 2007).

The enormous body of empirical evidence across different methods, time periods, and cultures supports the hypothesis that women have evolved a powerful preference for long-term mates with the ability to provide resources. Today's women are the descendants of a long line of women who had these mate preferences—preferences that helped them to solve the adaptive problems of survival and reproduction.

## Preference for High Social Status

Traditional hunter-gatherer societies, which are our closest guide to what ancestral conditions were probably like, suggest that ancestral men had clearly defined status hierarchies, with resources flowing freely to those at the top and trickling slowly down to those at the bottom

(Betzig, 1986; Brown & Chia-Yun, n.d.). Cross-culturally, groups such as the Melanesians, the early Egyptians, the Sumerians, the Japanese, and the Indonesians include people described as "head men" and "big men" who wield great power and enjoy the resource privileges of prestige. Among various South Asian languages, for example, the term "big man" is found in Sanskrit, Hindi, and several Dravidian languages. In Hindi, for example, *bara asami* means "great man, person of high position or rank" (Platts, 1960, pp. 151–152). In North America, north of Mexico, "big man" and similar terms are found among groups such as the Wappo, Dakota, Miwok, Natick, Choctaw, Kiowa, and Osage. In Mexico and South America, "big man" and closely related terms are found among the Cayapa, Chatino, Mazahua, Mixe, Mixteco, Quiche, Terraba, Tzeltal, Totonaca, Tarahumara, Quechua, and Hahuatl. Linguistically, therefore, it seems that many cultures have found it important to invent words or phrases to describe men who are high in status.

Women desire men who command a high position because social status is a universal cue to the control of resources. Along with status come better food, more abundant territory, and superior health care. Greater social status bestows on children social opportunities missed by the children of lower-ranking males. For male children worldwide, access to more and better quality mates typically accompanies families of higher social status. In one study of 186 societies ranging from the Mbuti Pygmies of Africa to the Aleut Eskimos, high-status men invariably had greater wealth and more wives and provided better nourishment for their children (Betzig, 1986).

One study examined short-term and long-term mating to discover which characteristics people especially valued in potential spouses, as contrasted with potential sex partners (Buss & Schmitt, 1993). Several hundred individuals evaluated sixty-seven characteristics for their desirability or undesirability in the short or long term, rating them on a scale ranging from $-3$ (extremely undesirable) to $+3$ (extremely desirable). Women judged the likelihood of success in a profession and the possession of a promising career to be highly desirable in a spouse, giving average ratings of $+2.60$ and $+2.70$, respectively. Significantly, these cues to future status are seen by women as more desirable in spouses than in casual sex partners, with the latter ratings reaching only $+1.10$ and $+0.40$, respectively. U.S. women also place great value on education and professional degrees in mates—characteristics that are strongly linked with social status.

The importance that women grant to social status in mates is not limited to the United States or even to capitalist countries. In the vast majority of the thirty-seven cultures considered in the international study on choosing a mate, women valued social status in a prospective mate more than men in both communist and socialist countries, among Africans and Asians, among Catholics and Jews, in the southern tropics and the northern climes (Buss, 1989a). In Taiwan, for example, women valued status 63 percent more than men; in Zambia, women valued it 30 percent more; in West Germany, women valued it 38 percent more; and in Brazil, women valued it 40 percent more (see Figure 4.4).

Hierarchies are universal features among human groups, and resources tend to accumulate to those who rise in the hierarchy. Women historically appear to have solved the adaptive problem of acquiring resources in part by preferring men who are high in status. Indeed, when forced to trade off among different mate characteristics, women prioritize social status, viewing it as a "necessity" rather than a "luxury" (Li, 2007).

## Preference for Somewhat Older Men

The age of a man also provides an important clue to his access to resources. Just as young male baboons must mature before they are able to enter the upper ranks in the baboon social hierarchy, human adolescents rarely command the respect, status, or position of more mature men.

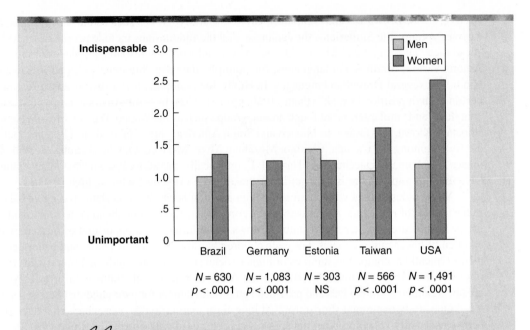

FIGURE 4.4 **Preference for Social Status in a Marriage Partner.** Participants in thirty-seven cultures rated this variable, in the context of eighteen other variables, on how desirable it would be in a potential long-term mate or marriage partner using a four-point rating scale, ranging from 0 (irrelevant or unimportant) to 3 (indispensable).

$N$ = sample size.

$p$ values less than .05 indicate that sex difference is significant.

NS indicates that sex difference is not significant.

*Source:* Buss, D. M., Abbott, M., Angleitner, A., Asherian, A., Biaggio, A. et al. (1990). International preferences in selecting mates: A study of 37 cultures. *Journal of Cross-Cultural Psychology, 21,* 5–47.

This reaches extremes among the Tiwi, an aboriginal tribe located on two islands off the coast of Northern Australia (Hart & Pilling, 1960). The Tiwi are a gerontocracy in which the very old men wield most of the power and prestige and control the mating system through their complex networks of alliances. Even in U.S. culture, status and wealth tend to accumulate with increasing age.

In all thirty-seven cultures included in the international study on mate selection, women preferred older men (see Figure 4.5). Averaged over all cultures, women prefer men who are roughly three-and-a-half years older. The preferred age difference ranges from French Canadian women, who seek husbands just a shade under two years older, to Iranian women, who seek husbands more than five years older.

To understand why women value older mates, we must consider the things that change with age. One of the most consistent changes is access to resources. In contemporary Western societies, income generally increases with age (Jencks, 1979). These status trends are not limited to the Western world. Among the Tiwi, a polygynous people, men are typically at least thirty

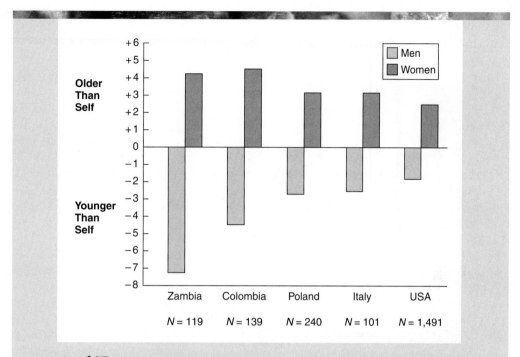

FIGURE 4.5 **Age Differences Preferred between Self and Spouse.** Participants recorded their preferred age difference, if any, between self and potential spouse. The scale shown is in years, with positive values signifying preference for older spouses and negative values signifying preference for younger spouses.

*N* = sample size.

*Source:* Buss, D. M., & Schmitt, D. P. (1993). Sexual strategies theory: An evolutionary perspective on human mating. *Psychological Review, 100,* 204–232. Copyright © 1993 by the American Psychological Association. Adapted with permission.

before they have enough social status to acquire a first wife (Hart & Pilling, 1960). Rarely does a Tiwi man under the age of forty attain enough status to acquire more than one wife. Older age, resources, and status are coupled across cultures.

In traditional societies, part of this linkage may be related to physical strength and hunting prowess. Physical strength increases in men as they get older, peaking in the late twenties and early thirties. In traditional hunter-gatherer societies such as the Tsimane Amerindians of the Bolivian Amazon and the Inuit of the Canadian Arctic, hunting skill peaks even later—roughly the mid- to late 30s (Collings, 2009; Gurven, Kaplan, & Gutierrez, 2006). A study of a small-scale Amazonian society in Ecuador found that a man's hunting ability was the strongest predictor of women's judgments of a man's attractiveness (see Figure 4.6), closely followed by a man's status and reputation as a good warrior (Escasa, Gray, & Patton, 2010). So women's preference for older men may stem from our hunter-gatherer ancestors, for whom the resources derived from hunting were critical to survival. The possession of resources, however, is not enough.

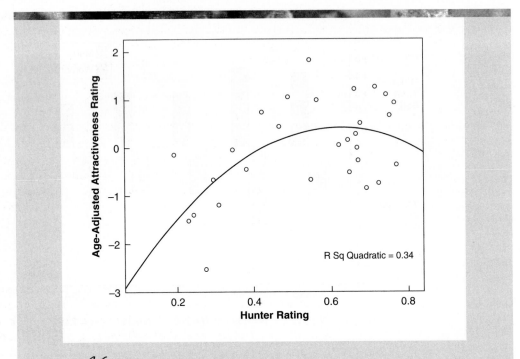

FIGURE 4.6 **Hunter Rating and Attractiveness.** Among an Amazonian population, a man's hunting skills proved to be the strongest predictor of attractiveness judgments by women.

*Source:* Escasa, M., Gray, P. B., & Patton, J. Q. (2010). Male traits associate with attractiveness in Conambo, Ecuador. *Evolution and Human Behavior, 31,* 193–299 (Figure 3, p. 197). Reprinted with permission from Elsevier.

Women also need men who possess traits that are likely to lead to the sustained acquisition of resources over time. A man's ambition is one of these traits.

## Preference for Ambition and Industriousness

How do people get ahead in everyday life? Among all the tactics, sheer hard work proves to be one of the best predictors of past and anticipated income and promotions. Those who say they work hard and whose spouses agree that they work hard achieve higher levels of education, status, and higher annual salaries, and anticipate greater salaries and promotions than those who failed to work hard. Industrious and ambitious men secure a higher occupational status than lazy, unmotivated men (Jencks, 1979; Kyl-Heku & Buss, 1996; Lund et al., 2007; Willerman, 1979).

U.S. women seem to be aware of this connection, because they indicate a desire for men who show the characteristics linked with getting ahead. In the 1950s, for example, 5,000 undergraduates were asked to list characteristics that they sought in a potential mate. Women far more than men desired mates who enjoy their work, show career orientation, demonstrate industry, and display ambition (Langhorne & Secord, 1955). The 852 single U.S. women and 100 married U.S. women in the international study on mate selection unanimously rated ambition and industriousness as important or indispensable (Buss, 1989a). Women in the study of short- and long-term mating regard men who lack ambition as extremely undesirable, whereas men view lack of ambition in a wife as neither desirable nor undesirable (Buss & Schmitt, 1993). Women across cultures are likely to discontinue a long-term relationship with a man if he loses his job, lacks career goals, or shows a lazy streak (Betzig, 1989).

In the overwhelming majority of cultures, women value ambition and industry more than men do, typically rating them as between important and indispensable. In Taiwan, for example, women rate ambition and industriousness as 26 percent more important than men do, women from Bulgaria rate it as 29 percent more important, and women from Brazil rate it as 30 percent more important. This cross-cultural and cross-historical evidence supports the key evolutionary expectation that women have evolved a preference for men possessing signs of the *ability* to acquire resources and a disdain for men lacking the ambition that often leads to resources.

## Preference for Dependability and Stability

Among the eighteen characteristics rated in the worldwide study on mate selection, the second and third most highly valued characteristics, after love, are a dependable character and emotional stability or maturity. In twenty-one of thirty-seven cultures, men and women had the same preference for dependability in a partner (Buss et al., 1990). Of the remaining sixteen cultures, women in fifteen valued dependability more than men. Averaged across all thirty-seven cultures, women rated dependable character a 2.69, where a 3 signifies indispensable; men rate it nearly as important, with an average of 2.50. In the case of emotional stability or maturity, the sexes differ more. Women in twenty-three cultures value this quality significantly more than men do; in the remaining fourteen cultures, men and women value emotional stability equally. Averaging across all cultures, women give this quality a 2.68, whereas men give it a 2.47.

These characteristics may possess great value to women worldwide for two reasons. First, they are reliable signals that resources will be provided consistently over time. Second, men who lack dependability and emotional stability provide erratically and inflict heavy emotional and other costs on their mates (Buss, 1991). They tend to be self-centered and monopolize shared resources. Furthermore, they are frequently possessive, monopolizing much of the time of their wives. They show higher-than-average sexual jealousy, becoming enraged when their wives merely talk with someone else, and are dependent, insisting that their mates provide for all of their needs. They tend to be abusive both verbally and physically. They display inconsiderateness, such as by failing to show up on time, and they are moodier than their more stable counterparts, often crying for no apparent reason. They have more affairs than average, suggesting further diversion of time and resources (Buss & Shackelford, 1997a). All these costs indicate that such men will absorb their partners' time and resources, divert their own time and resources elsewhere, and fail to channel resources consistently over time. Dependability and stability are personal qualities that signal increased likelihood that a woman's resources will not be drained by the man.

The unpredictable aspects of emotionally unstable men inflict additional costs by preventing solutions to critical adaptive problems. The erratic supply of resources can wreak havoc with accomplishing the goals required for survival and reproduction. Meat that is suddenly not available because an unpredictable, changeable, or variable mate decided at the last minute to take a nap rather than go on the hunt is sustenance counted on but not delivered. Resources that are supplied predictably can be more efficiently allocated to the many adaptive hurdles that must be overcome in everyday life. Women place a premium on dependability and emotional stability to reap the benefits that a mate can provide to them consistently over time.

## Preference for Height and Athletic Prowess

The importance of physical characteristics in the female choice of a mate is notable throughout the animal world. Male gladiator frogs are responsible for creating nests and defending the eggs. In the majority of courtships, a stationary male gladiator frog is deliberately bumped by a female who is considering him. She strikes him with great force, sometimes enough to rock him back or even scare him away. If the male moves too much or bolts from the nest, the female hastily leaves to find an alternative mate. Bumping helps a female frog assess how successful the male will be at defending her clutch. The bump test reveals the male's physical ability to protect.

Women sometimes face physical domination by larger, stronger males, which can lead to injury and sexual domination. These conditions undoubtedly occurred with some regularity dur-

*Women prefer men who are relatively tall, athletic, muscular, and display a V-shaped torso, with shoulders broader than hips—signals that indicate a man's ability to protect a woman and her children.*

ing ancestral conditions. Indeed, studies of many nonhuman primate groups reveal that male physical and sexual domination of females has been a recurrent part of our primate heritage. Primatologist Barbara Smuts lived among the baboons residing in the savanna plains of Africa and studied their mating patterns (Smuts, 1985). She found that females frequently formed enduring "special friendships" with males who offered physical protection to themselves and their infants. In return, these females granted their "friends" preferential mating access during times of estrus.

One benefit to women of long-term mating is the physical protection a man can offer. A man's size, strength, physical prowess, and athletic ability are cues that signal solutions to the problem of protection. Evidence shows that women's preferences in a mate embody these cues. Women judge short men to be undesirable for either a short-term or a long-term mate (Buss & Schmitt, 1993). In contrast, women find it very desirable for a potential marriage partner to be tall, physically strong, and athletic. A study of women from Britain and Sri Lanka found strong preferences for male physiques that were muscular and lean (Dixon et al., 2003). Women also prefer and find attractive men with "V-shaped" torso, that is broad shoulders relative to hips (Hughes & Gallup, 2003). Interestingly, women can accurately estimate a man's shoulder-to-hip ratio merely from the sound of his voice (Hughes, Harrison, & Gallup, 2009).

Tall men are consistently seen as more desirable as dates and mates than are short or average men (Courtiol et al., 2010; Ellis 1992). Two studies of personal ads revealed that, among women who mentioned height, 80 percent wanted a man to be 6 feet or taller (Cameron, Oskamp, & Sparks, 1978). Personals ads placed by taller men received more responses from women than those placed by shorter men (Lynn & Shurgot, 1984). Indeed, a study of the "hits" received by 1,168 personal advertisements in Poland found that a man's height was one of the four strongest predictors of the number of women who responded to the male ads (the others being education level, age, and resources) (Pawlowski & Koziel, 2002). Tall men are perceived as more dominant, are more likely to date, and are more likely to have attractive partners than shorter men (see Brewer & Riley, 2009, for a review). Women solve the problem of protection from other aggressive men at least in part by preferring a mate who has the size, strength, and physical prowess to protect them. These physical qualities also contribute to solutions to other adaptive problems such as resource acquisitions and genes for good health, since tallness is also linked with status, income, symmetrical features, and good health (Brewer & Riley, 2009).

Among the Mehinaku tribe of the Brazilian Amazon, anthropologist Thomas Gregor (1985) noted the importance of men's wrestling skills as an arena in which these differences become acute:

> A heavily muscled, imposingly built man is likely to accumulate many girlfriends, while a small man, deprecatingly referred to as a *peristsi,* fares badly. The mere fact of height creates a measurable advantage . . . . A powerful wrestler, say the villagers, is frightening . . . he commands fear and respect. To the women, he is "beautiful" (*awitsiri*), in demand as a paramour [lover] and husband. (p. 35)

Evolutionary psychologist Nigal Barber summarizes the evidence for women's preferences: "traits of male body structure such as height, shoulder width, and upper-body musculature are sexually attractive to women and also intimidating to other men" (Barber, 1995, p. 406).

## Preference for Good Health: Symmetry and Masculinity

Mating with someone who is unhealthy would have posed a number of adaptive risks for our ancestors. First, an unhealthy mate would have a higher risk of becoming debilitated, thus failing to deliver whatever adaptive benefits he or she might otherwise have provided such as food, protection, health care, and investment in childrearing. Second, an unhealthy mate would be at an increased risk of dying, prematurely cutting off the flow of resources and forcing a person to incur the costs of searching for a new mate. Third, an unhealthy mate might transfer communicable diseases or viruses to the chooser, impairing his or her survival and reproduction. Fourth, an unhealthy mate might infect the children of the union, imperiling their chances of surviving and reproducing. And fifth, if health is partly heritable, a person who chooses an unhealthy mate would risk passing on genes for poor health to his or her children. For all these reasons, it comes as no surprise that women and men both place a premium on the health of a potential mate. In the study of thirty-seven cultures, on a scale ranging from 0 (irrelevant) to +3 (indispensable), women and men both judged "good health" to be highly important. Averaged across the cultures, women gave it a +2.28 and men gave it a +2.31 (Buss et al., 1990).

An important physical marker of good health is the degree to which the face and body are *symmetrical* (Gangestad & Thornhill, 1997; Grammer & Thornhill, 1994; Shackelford & Larsen, 1997; Thornhill & Møeller, 1997). Environmental events and genetic stressors produce deviations from bilateral symmetry, creating lopsided faces and bodies. Some individuals are able to withstand such events and stresses better than others—that is, they show *developmental stability*. The presence of facial and bodily symmetry is an important health cue, reflecting an individual's ability to withstand environmental and genetic stressors. Therefore, women are hypothesized to have evolved a preference for men who show physical evidence of symmetry. Such symmetry would not only increase the odds of the mate being around to invest and less likely to pass on diseases to her children, it may have direct genetic benefits as well. By selecting a man with symmetrical features, a woman may be in essence selecting a superior complement of genes to be transmitted to her children.

Some evidence supports the hypothesis that symmetry is indeed a health cue and that women especially value this quality in mates (Gangestad & Thornhill, 1997; Thornhill & Møeller, 1997). First, facially symmetric individuals score higher on tests of physiological, psychological, and emotional health (Shackelford & Larsen, 1997). Second, there is a small but positive relationship between facial symmetry and judgments of physical attractiveness in both sexes. Third, facially symmetrical men, compared with their more lopsided counterparts, are judged to be more sexually attractive to women, have more sexual partners during their lifetimes, have

*Most women find men with symmetrical faces, as exemplified by the actor Denzel Washington (left), to be more attractive than men with asymmetrical faces, as illustrated by the musician and actor Lyle Lovett (right). Symmetry is hypothesized to be a health cue that signals a relative absence of parasites, genetic resistance to parasites, or a relative lack of environmental insults during development.*

more extra-pair copulations, and begin sexual intercourse earlier in life. Facial symmetry is linked to judgments of health (Jones et al., 2001). Men with more symmetrical faces experienced fewer respiratory illnesses, suggesting better disease resistance (Thornhill & Gangestad, 2006). Some researchers, however, question the quality of the studies and conclude that the evidence on the association between symmetry and health is not yet convincing (Rhodes, 2006).

Another health cue might stem from masculine features. The average faces of adult men and women differ in several fundamental respects. Men tend to have longer and broader lower jaws, stronger brow ridges, and more pronounced cheekbones, primarily as a consequence of pubertal hormones such as testosterone. Victor Johnston and his colleagues developed a sophisticated experimental tool to vary these features, in the form of a 1,200-frame QuickTime movie (Johnston et al., 2001). The computer program allows a person to search through a multidimensional space containing hundreds of faces that vary in masculinity, femininity, and other features. Participants use a slider control and single-frame buttons to move back and forth through the 1,200-frame movie to locate the frame containing the desired target, such as "most attractive for a long-term mate." The researchers tested forty-two women between the ages of eighteen and thirty-five who were not taking oral contraceptives and obtained an evaluation of the point in their menstrual cycle.

Women overall, regardless of their point in the menstrual cycle, preferred faces that were more masculine-looking than average. Although not all studies find a female preference for facial masculinity (e.g., Waynforth, Delwadia, & Camm, 2005), a meta-analysis of ten studies confirmed that masculinity is attractive in male faces, although the effect size is modest (+.35) (Rhodes, 2006). Women also find vocal masculinity to be attractive (Feinberg et al., 2008). Why would women find masculine-looking males attractive? Johnston argues that masculine features are signals of good health. The production of high levels of testosterone is known to compromise the human immune system. According to Johnston's argument, only males who are quite healthy can "afford" to produce high levels of testosterone during their development. Less healthy males must suppress testosterone production, lest they compromise their already weaker immune systems. As a result, healthy males end up producing more testosterone and developing more rugged masculine-looking faces. If Johnston's argument is correct, women's preference for masculine faces is essentially a preference for a healthy male.

One piece of evidence in support of this view came when Johnston went through the 1,200-frame QuickTime movie a second time and asked the women to pick out the face they viewed as the "healthiest." The faces women chose were indistinguishable from their judgments of "the most attractive face," supporting the theory that masculine appearance might be valued by women because it signals health (also see Boothroyd et al., 2005, for a study that failed to support the link between facial masculinity and perceived health). Another study found that men with more masculine faces had fewer respiratory diseases, suggesting that it might be a signal of disease resistance (Thornhill & Gangestad, 2006). Other researchers present evidence that women's preferences for masculine features reflect an attraction to dominance rather than health (Boothroyd et al., 2007). Future research is needed to determine which hypothesis, or both, is correct.

In summary, several sources of evidence point to the importance of health in women's mate selection: an expressed desire for health in long-term mates found in all thirty-seven cultures; an attraction to symmetry, a known health cue, in male faces and bodies; and an attraction to masculine male faces that are simultaneously judged to be healthy. Health likely achieves its importance through the multiple benefits it confers on a mate selector, both environmental and genetic: longer life, more reliable provisioning, a lower likelihood of communicable diseases, and better genes that can be passed on to children.

## Love and Commitment

Women have long faced the adaptive problem of choosing men who not only have the necessary resources but also show a *willingness to commit* those resources to them and their children. This may be more problematic than it at first seems. Although resources can often be directly observed, commitment cannot. Instead, gauging commitment requires looking for cues that signal the likelihood of future fidelity in the channeling of resources. Love may be one of the key cues to commitment.

According to conventional wisdom in the social sciences, "love" is a relatively recent invention, introduced a few hundred years ago by romantic Europeans (Jankowiak, 1995). Research suggests that this conventional wisdom is radically wrong. There is evidence that loving thoughts, emotions, and actions are experienced by people in cultures worldwide—from the Zulu in the southern tip of Africa to the Eskimos in the cold northern ice caps of Alaska. In a survey of 168 diverse cultures around the world, anthropologists William Jankowiak and Edward Fischer examined four sources of evidence for the presence of love: the singing of love songs, elopement by lovers against the wishes of parents, cultural informants reporting personal anguish and longing for a loved one, and folklore depicting romantic entanglements. Using the presence of these phenomena, they found evidence for the presence of romantic love in 88.5 percent of the cultures (Jankowiak, 1995; Jankowiak & Fischer, 1992). Clearly love is not a phenomenon limited to the United States or to Western culture.

To identify precisely what love is and how it is linked to commitment, several study examined acts of love (Buss, 1988a, 2006a; Wade, Auer, & Roth, 2009). Acts of commitment top women's and men's lists, being viewed as most central to love. Such acts include giving up romantic relations with others, talking of marriage, and expressing a desire to have children with this person. When performed by a man, these acts of love signal the intention to commit resources to one woman and her future children. Reports of experiencing love are powerfully predictive of feelings of subjective commitment—far more than are reports of sexual desire (Gonzaga et al., 2008). The hypothesis that the commitment of paternal care to children is one of the functions of love attains support from a comparative and phylogenetic analysis of different species (see Chapter 2) that looked at the links between adult attachment and paternal care (Fraley, Brumbaugh, & Marks, 2005). Species that exhibited adult attachment were more likely to be characterized by male parental investment in offspring than species that did not. Thus, one function of the female preference for love in a mate is to ensure the commitment of his parental resources to the children they produce together.

Commitment, however, has many facets that signal particular ways of sharing resources. One major component of commitment is fidelity, exemplified by the act of remaining faithful to a partner when not physically together. Fidelity signals the exclusive commitment of sexual resources to a single partner. Another aspect of commitment is the channeling of resources to the loved one, such as buying an expensive gift. Acts such as this signal a serious intention to commit to a long-term relationship. Emotional support is yet another facet of commitment, revealed by such behavior as being available in times of trouble and listening to the partner's problems. Commitment entails a channeling of time, energy, and effort to the partner's needs at the expense of fulfilling one's own personal goals. Acts of reproduction also represent a direct commitment to one's partner's reproduction. All these acts, which are viewed as essential to love, signal the commitment of sexual, economic, emotional, and genetic resources to one person.

Because love is a worldwide phenomenon, and because the primary function of acts of love is to signal commitment, women are predicted to place a premium on love in the process of choosing a long-term mate. The international study on choosing a mate confirmed the importance of love across cultures. Among eighteen possible characteristics, mutual attraction or love proved to be the most highly valued in a potential mate by both sexes, rated 2.87 by women and 2.81 by men (Buss et al., 1990). Nearly all women and men, from the tribal enclaves of South Africa to the bustling streets of Brazilian cities, gave love the top rating, indicating that it is an indispensable part of marriage. Another study of love in forty-eight nations found high levels of love in all of them, although lower levels of love in cultures marked by high levels of ecological stress (Schmitt et al., 2009).

Researchers have made progress in identifying the underlying brain mechanisms involved in love (Bartels & Zeki, 2004; Fisher, Aron, & Brown, 2005). Using functional magnetic resonance imaging (fMRI) technology, researchers scanned the brains of individuals who were intensely in love while they thought about their loved one. The specific areas of the brain that "lit up" (showed an increased blood flow, indicating changes in neural activity) centered on the caudate nucleus and the ventral tegmental areas. These areas contain cells that produce dopamine, which stimulates the reward centers of the brain, analogous to experiencing a "rush" of cocaine (Fisher, 2006). Thus, researchers are beginning to make progress in identifying the underlying brain circuits involved in the adaptation of love.

## Preference for Willingness to Invest in Children

Another adaptive problem that women face when selecting a long-term mate is gauging men's willingness to invest in children. This adaptive problem is important for two reasons: (1) Men sometimes seek sexual variety and so may channel their efforts toward other women (mating effort) rather than toward children (parental effort) (see Chapter 6); and (2) men evaluate the likelihood that they are the actual genetic father of a child and tend to withhold investment from the child when they know or suspect that the child is not their own (La Cerra, 1994).

To test the hypothesis that women have an evolved preference for men who are willing to invest in children, psychologist Peggy La Cerra constructed slide images of men in several different conditions: (1) a man standing alone; (2) a man interacting with an eighteen-month-old child, including smiling, making eye contact, and reaching for the child; (3) a man ignoring the child, who was crying; (4) a man and the child simply facing forward (neutral condition); and (5) a man vacuuming a living room rug. The same models were depicted in all conditions.

After viewing these slide images, 240 women rated each image on how attractive they found the man in each slide as a date, as a sexual partner, as a marriage partner, as a friend, and as a neighbor. The rating scale ranged from −5 (very unattractive) to +5 (very attractive). First, women found the man interacting with the child positively to be more attractive as a marriage partner (average attractiveness rating, 2.75) than the same man either standing alone (2.0) or standing neutrally next to the child (2.0). Second, women found the man who ignored the child in distress to be low in attractiveness as a marriage partner (1.25), indeed the lowest of all. Third, the effect of interacting positively with the child proved *not* to be a result of the man showing domestic proclivities in general. Women found the man vacuuming, for example, to be less attractive (1.3) than the man simply standing alone doing nothing (2.0).

*La Cerra (1994) found that women find the man interacting positively with the baby considerably more attractive, suggesting a mate preference for men who display a willingness to invest in children. Comparable photographs of women, shown either ignoring or interacting positively with a baby, produced no effect on men's judgments of women's attractiveness.*

This study suggests that women prefer men who show a willingness to invest in children as marriage partners. Is this preference unique to women? To address this issue, La Cerra conducted another study, this time using women as models and men as raters. Women were posed in conditions parallel to those of the male models in the first study. The results for men were strikingly different from those for women. Men found the woman standing alone to be just as attractive (average attractiveness rating, 2.70) as the woman interacting positively with the child (2.70). In fact, the varying contexts made little difference to men in their judgments of how attractive the woman was as a marriage partner.

In short, women appear to have a specific preference for, and attraction to, men who show a willingness to invest in children, but the reverse is not true. These findings have been replicated by Gary Brase who made several methodological improvements (Brase, 2006). On a personal note, La Cerra observed that one catalyst for her research was witnessing a poster of an attractive man holding an infant—an image that drew her attention and also proved to be a highly effective advertising technique for targeting female markets (La Cerra, 1994, p. 87).

An interesting study explored the importance of men's interest in infants on women's attraction to a man as a long-term mate (Roney et al., 2006). The experimenters gave a sample of men the "interest in infants test," which assesses the degree to which men prefer to look at infant faces—a measure that predicts men's actual levels of interaction with infants. Next, these men's faces were photographed. Then, a sample of 29 women rated each photo on a set of variables that included "likes children." A second rating sheet had the women rate each man's attractiveness as a short-term and long-term romantic partner. The results proved fascinating. First, women were able to accurately detect men's interest in infants simply from looking at the photos of their faces. It is likely that women were picking up on the positivity and happiness in the facial expressions of men who had an interest in children. Second, men who women perceived as liking infants were judged to be very attractive as long-term mates; men's perceived liking of infants, in contrast, did not boost their attractiveness in women's eyes as a short-term mate.

Taken together, these studies point to the importance of paternal qualities—a man's interest in, and willingness to invest in, children—as critical to women's selection of a long-term mate.

## Preference for Similarity

Successful long-term mating requires sustained cooperative alliances over time. Similarity leads to emotional bonding, cooperation, communication, mating happiness, lower risk of breaking up, and possibly increased survival of children (Buss, 2003). Women and men alike show strong preferences for mates who share their values, political orientations, worldviews, intellectual level, and to a lesser extent their personality characteristics. The preference for similarity translates into actual mating decisions, a phenomenon known as *homogamy*—people who are similar on these characteristics date (Wilson, Cousins, & Fink, 2006) and get married (Buss, 1985) more often than those who are dissimilar. Homogamy for physical appearance might be due to "sexual imprinting" on the opposite-sex parent during childhood (Bereczkei, Gyuris, & Weisfeld, 2004). Interestingly, daughters who received more emotional support from their fathers were more likely to choose similar-looking mates. Finally, there is strong homogamy for overall "mate value," with the "10s" mating with other "10s" and the "6s" mating with other "6s" (Buss, 2003).

## Additional Mate Preferences: Kindness, Humor, Incest Avoidance, and Voice

Women's desires are even more complex than the previous discussion indicates, and new discoveries are being made every year. A few of the more noteworthy ones are mentioned here.

Women greatly value the traits of kindness, altruism, and generosity in a long-term mate (Barclay, 2010; Phillips et al., 2008). The thirty-seven-culture study found "kind and understanding" was universally ranked as the most desirable quality in a long-term mate out of thirteen ranked qualities (Buss et al., 1990). Barclay (2010) experimentally manipulated vignettes that differed only in the presence or absence of hints of altruistic tendencies (e.g., when the phrase "I enjoy helping people" was embedded within a longer description of the potential mate). Women strongly preferred men with altruistic tendencies as long-term mates. Another study discovered that women find kindness to be especially desirable when the kind acts are directed toward themselves, their friends, and their family, but shift their preferences to lower levels of kindness in potential partners when the kind acts are directed toward other targets such as other women (Lukaszewski & Roney, 2010).

Kindness and altruistic proclivities signal the possession of abundant resources (Miller, 2007), the willingness to provide resources to a woman (Buss, 1994b), good character (Barclay, 2010), good parenting and partnering proclivities qualities (Buss & Shackelford, 2008; Tessman, 1995), and a cooperative and non-cost inflicting disposition (Buss, 2010).

Women clearly prefer long-term mates who have a good sense of humor (Buss & Barnes, 1986; Miller, 2000). Humor has many facets, two of which are humor production (making witty remarks, telling jokes) and humor appreciation (laughing when someone else produces humor). In long-term mating, women prefer men who produce humor, whereas men prefer women who are receptive to their humor (Bressler, Martin, & Balshine, 2006). Precisely why do women value humor in a mate? One theory proposes that humor is an indicator of "good genes" (a fitness indicator) signaling creativity and excellent functioning of complex cognitive skills that are not impaired by a high mutation load (Miller, 2000). Although there is some support for this theory (Bressler et al., 2006), additional studies are needed. Other research indicates that humor is used to indicate interest in initiating and maintaining social relationships (Li et al., 2009).

Another set of preferences centers on what women avoid or find intolerable in a mate. Incest avoidance is one of the most important. Reproducing with genetic relatives is known to create "inbreeding depression," offspring with more health problems and lower intelligence because of the expression of deleterious recessive genes. Evidence is mounting that humans have powerful incest-avoidance mechanisms, such as the emotion of disgust at the thought of passionately kissing or having sex with a sibling (Fessler & Navarette, 2004; Lieberman, Tooby, & Cosmides, 2003). Growing up with a sibling is a key cue that activates the inbreeding avoidance adaptation (Lieberman, 2009; Lieberman, Tooby, & Cosmides, 2007). These incest-avoidance mechanisms are stronger in women than in men, which is consistent with parental investment theory—given that women have greater obligatory parental investment in offspring, the costs of making a poor mating decision are typically higher for women than for men. Indeed, the characteristic "is my sibling" is one of the most powerful "deal breakers" for women when considering a potential mate, right up there with "beats me up," "will have sex with other people on a regular basis when he is with me," and "is addicted to drugs" (Burkett & Cosmides, 2006).

Several studies support the hypothesis that women find a deep voice especially attractive in a potential mate (Evans, Neave, & Wakelin, 2006; Feinberg et al., 2005; Puts, 2005). Hypotheses for why a deep male voice is attractive are that it signals (1) sexual maturity, (2) a larger body size, (3) good genetic quality, (4) dominance, or (5) all of the above. Evidence that voice attractiveness is important to women in mate selection is indicated by the findings that men with attractive-sounding voices have sexual intercourse earlier, have a larger number of sex partners, and are more often chosen by women as affair partners. These findings, along with direct evidence that women prefer men with a low voice pitch mainly in casual sex partners, suggest that this preference is more central to short-term than to long-term mating (Puts, 2005) (see Chapter 6).

# ■ CONTEXT EFFECTS ON WOMEN'S MATE PREFERENCES

From an evolutionary perspective, preferences are not predicted to operate blindly, oblivious to context or condition. Just as human desires for particular foods (e.g., ripe fruit) depend on context (e.g., whether one is hungry or full), women's preferences in a mate also depend in part on relevant contexts. Several contexts have been explored: the magnitude of resources a woman already has prior to her search for a mate, the presence of other women, the temporal context of mating (committed versus casual mating), and the woman's mate value.

## Effects of Women's Personal Resources on Mate Preferences

An alternative explanation to the evolutionary psychological theory has been offered for the preferences of women for men with resources—the structural powerlessness hypothesis (Buss & Barnes, 1986; Eagly & Wood, 1999). According to this view, because women are typically excluded from power and access to resources, which are largely controlled by men, women seek mates who have power, status, and earning capacity. Women try to marry upward in socioeconomic status because this provides their primary channel for gaining access to resources. Men do not value economic resources in a mate as much as women do because they already have control over these resources and because women have fewer resources anyway.

The society of Bakweri, from Cameroon in West Africa, casts doubt on this theory by illustrating what happens when women have real power (Ardener, Ardener, & Warmington, 1960). Bakweri women hold greater personal and economic power because they have more resources and are in scarcer supply than men. Women secure resources not only through their own labors on plantations but also from casual sex, which is a lucrative source of income. There are roughly 236 men for every hundred women, an imbalance that results from the continual influx of men from other areas of the country to work on the plantations. Because of the extreme imbalance in numbers of the sexes, women have considerable latitude to exercise their choice in a mate. Women thus have more money than men and more potential mates to choose from. Yet Bakweri women persist in preferring mates with resources. Wives often complain about receiving insufficient support from their husbands. Indeed, lack of sufficient economic provisioning is the reason most frequently cited by women for divorce. Bakweri women change husbands if they find a man who can offer them more money and pay a larger bride-price. When women are in a position to fulfill their evolved preference for a man with resources, they do so. Having dominant control of economic resources apparently does not negate this mate preference.

Professionally and economically successful women in the United States also value resources in men. A study of married couples identified women who were financially successful, as measured by their salary and income, and contrasted their preferences in a mate with those of women with lower salaries and income (Buss, 1989a). The financially successful women were well educated, tended to hold professional degrees, and had high self-esteem. The study showed that successful women place an even greater value than less professionally successful women on mates who have professional degrees, high social status, and greater intelligence and who are tall, independent, and self-confident. Women's personal income was positively correlated with the income they wanted in an ideal mate (+.31), the desire for a mate who is a college graduate (+.29), and the desire for a mate with a professional degree (+.35). Contrary to the structural powerlessness hypothesis, these women expressed an even stronger preference for high-earning men than did women who are less financially successful.

In a separate study, psychologists Michael Wiederman and Elizabeth Allgeier found that college women who expect to earn the most after college put more weight on the promising financial prospects of a potential husband than did women who expect to earn less. Professionally successful women, such as medical and law students, also place heavy importance on a mate's earning capacity (Wiederman & Allgeier, 1992).

Cross-cultural studies consistently find small but positive relationships between women's personal access to economic resources and preferences for mates with resources. A study of 1,670 Spanish women seeking mates through personal advertisements found that women who have more resources and status were more likely to seek men with resources and status (Gil-Burmann, Pelaez, & Sanchez, 2002). A study of 288 Jordanians found that both women and men with high socioeconomic status place more, not less, value on the mate characteristics of having a college graduate degree and being ambitious-industrious (Khallad, 2005). A study of 127 individuals from Serbia concluded as follows: "The high status of women correlated positively with their concern with a potential mate's potential socio-economic status, contrary to the prediction of the socio-structural model" (Todosijevic, Ljubinkovic, & Arancic, 2003, p. 116). An Internet study of 1,851 women, studying the effects of women's actual income, found that "wealthier women prefer good financial prospects over physical attractiveness" (Moore et al., 2006, p. 201). Other large-scale cross-cultural studies continue to falsify the structural powerlessness hypothesis, or social role theory as it is sometimes called (Lippa, 2009; Schmitt et al; 2009). Taken together, these results not only fail to support the structural powerlessness hypothesis, but they also directly contradict it.

## The Mere Presence of Attractive Others: Mate Copying

Mate choices can be influenced by the mating decisions of others. When a person's attraction to, or choice of, a potential mate is influenced by the preferences and mating decisions of others, this phenomenon is called *mate copying*. Mate copying has been documented earlier in a variety of species ranging from birds to fish (Dugatkin, 2000; Hill & Ryan, 2006). Now it has been documented in humans. Two studies found that women judged a man to be more attractive when he was surrounded by women compared to when he was standing alone (Dunn & Doria, 2010; Hill & Buss, 2008a). Two other studies discovered a mate copying effect only when the man being evaluated was paired with a physically attractive woman (Little et al., 2008; Waynforth, 2007). A fifth study replicated the effect of a man being paired with an attractive woman using videotaped interactions in a speed dating setting, and found that the mate copying effect only occurred if the woman in the videotape showed interest in the man (Place et al., 2010). Presumably, if she did not show interest in the man, women interpret this as evidence that he is lower in mate value. Taken together, these studies reveal that women use social information, in this case a man being paired with an attractive and interested woman, as an important cue to his desirability as a mate.

## Effects of Temporal Context on Women's Mate Preferences

A mating relationship can last for a lifetime, but often matings are of shorter duration. In Chapter 6, we will explore short-term mating in detail, but it is worthwhile to highlight now the findings that show that women's preferences shift as a function of temporal context. Buss and Schmitt (1993) asked undergraduate women to rate sixty-seven characteristics on their desirability in short-term and long-term mates. The rating scale ranged from $-3$ (extremely undesirable) to $+3$ (extremely desirable). Women found the following qualities to be more desirable in long-term marriage contexts than in short-term sexual contexts: "ambitious and career-oriented" (average rating, 2.45 in long term versus 1.04 in short term), "college graduate" (2.38 versus 1.05), "creative" (1.90 versus 1.29), "devoted to you" (2.80 versus 0.90), "fond of children" (2.93 versus 1.21), "kind" (2.88 versus 2.50), "understanding" (2.93 versus 2.10), "responsible" (2.75 versus 1.75), and "cooperative" (2.41 versus 1.47). These findings suggest that temporal context matters a great deal for women, causing shifts in their preferences depending on whether a marriage partner or a casual sex partner is sought (Schmitt & Buss, 1996).

In another study, Joanna Scheib (1997) constructed stimuli consisting of photographs paired with written descriptions of the personality characteristics presumed to describe the men in each photo. The written descriptions emphasized traits such as dependable, loyal, kind, mature, patient, and so on. Pairs of these photos and accompanying descriptions were shown to 160 heterosexual women. Participants were shown five pairs of the stimulus men and asked to choose one man from each pair. Women tended to select the men with good character traits such as dependable, kind, and mature when choosing a potential husband more than when choosing a short-term sex partner. In the long-term marital context, women tended to choose character over looks. Similarly, Li and Kenrick (2006) found that women valued warmth and trustworthiness highly in a long-term mate, but considerably less so in a short-term mate.

## Effects of Women's Mate Value on Mate Preferences

A woman's physical attractiveness and youth are two indicators of her mate value, or overall desirability to men (see Chapter 5). As a consequence, women who are young and more physically attractive have more numerous mating options and so can become choosier in their selections. But does a woman's mate value influence her mate preferences? To find out, evolutionary psychologist Anthony Little and his colleagues had seventy-one women rate themselves on their perceptions of their own physical attractiveness and subsequently showed them photos of men's faces that varied along the masculinity–femininity dimension (Little et al., 2002). Women's self-rated attractiveness was significantly linked to attraction to masculine faces: The two variables correlated at +.32. In a separate study, researchers found that women who view themselves as physically attractive also show a more pronounced preference for symmetrical male faces (Feinberg et al., 2006). In an important control condition, they did *not* find such a relationship between women's self-rated attractiveness and a preference for symmetrical female faces. This suggests that the preference shift found with male faces cannot be attributed to judgments of attractiveness in general; rather, it appears to be specific to mate choice.

Studies of personal ads in Canada, the United States, Croatia, and Poland have found that women who are higher in mate value—women who are younger and more physically attractive—specified a longer list of traits that they sought or required in a potential mate than did women lower in mate value (Pawlowski & Dunbar, 1999a; Waynforth & Dunbar, 1995). Nearly identical results have been found in Brazil (Campos, Otta, & Siqueira, 2002) and Japan (Oda, 2001). Furthermore, women who perceive themselves as higher in mate value tended to impose higher minimum standards in what they would require of a long-term mate on a wide variety of characteristics, notably social status, intelligence, and family orientation (Regan, 1998). A Croatian study of 885 found that women high on self-perceived physical attractiveness, compared to their less-attractive peers, preferred higher levels of education, intelligence, good health, good financial prospects, good looks, and favorable social status in a potential mate (Tadinac & Hromatko, 2007). A U.S. study had interviewers evaluate 107 women for face, body, and overall attractiveness (Buss & Shackelford, 2008). Attractive women expressed a desire for higher levels of hypothesized "good genes" indicators such as masculinity, physical attractiveness, sex appeal, and physical fitness. They also expressed a greater desire for potential income of a mate, good parenting qualities such as fondness for children, and good partner indicators such as being a loving partner. A speed dating study conducted in Germany examined actual mate choices made by women (Todd et al., 2007). Women high on self-perceived physical attractiveness actually chose men high on overall desirability, an aggregate score that included wealth and status, family orientation, physical appearance, attractiveness, and healthiness. Attractive women apparently want it all.

Taken together, these studies all point to the same general conclusion: Women who are higher in mate value both prefer and seek men who are higher in mate value as reflected in masculinity, symmetry, and the sheer number of qualities that contribute to men's desirability.

## ■ HOW WOMEN'S MATE PREFERENCES AFFECT ACTUAL MATING BEHAVIOR

For preferences to evolve, they must affect actual mating decisions because it is those decisions that have reproductive consequences. For a number of reasons, however, preferences should not show a *perfect* correspondence with actual mating behavior. People can't always get what they want for a variety of reasons. First, there are a limited number of highly desirable potential mates. Second, one's own mate value limits access to those who are highly desirable. In general, only the most desirable women are in a position to attract the most desirable men, and vice versa. Third, parents and other kin sometimes influence one's mating decisions, regardless of personal preferences. Despite these factors, women's mate preferences must have affected their actual mating decisions some of the time over the course of human evolutionary history or they would not have evolved. Following are several sources of evidence that preferences do affect mating decisions.

### Women's Responses to Men's Personal Ads

One source of evidence comes from women's responses to personal ads posted by men in newspapers. If women's preferences affected their mating decisions, then they would be predicted to respond more often to men who indicate that they are financially well off. Baize and Schroeder (1995) tested this prediction using a sample of 120 personal ads placed in two different newspapers, one from the West Coast and the other from the Midwest. The authors mailed a questionnaire to those who posted the ads, asking for information about personal status, response rate, and personality characteristics.

Several variables significantly predicted the number of letters men received in response to their ads. First, *age* was a significant predictor, with women responding more often to older men than to younger men ($r = +.43$). Second, *income* and *education* were also significant predictors, with women responding more to men with ads indicating higher salaries ($r = +.30$) and more years of education ($r = +.37$). Baize and Schroeder ended their article on a humorous note by recalling the question posed by Tim Hardin in his famous folk song: "If I were a carpenter and you were a lady, would you marry me anyway, would you have my baby?" Given the cumulative research findings, the most likely answer is: No.

Similar results have now been found in Poland in a study of response rates to ads placed by 551 men (Pawlowski & Koziel, 2002). Men with higher levels of education, men who were somewhat older, men who were taller, and men who offered more resources all received a larger number of responses from women than did men who lacked these qualities.

## Women's Marriages to Men High in Occupational Status

A study of 21,973 men from a U.S. data set gathered in the year 1910 found that the higher a man's socioeconomic status, the greater the chances that he would actually marry (Pollet & Nettle, 2007). Poor men were far more likely to remain bachelors, unable to attract women, presumably because they failed to fulfill women's desire for men with resources and status. Another study of the Kipsigis from Kenya, Africa, found that men who owned a lot of land were more likely to attract women as wives, and multiple wives if they were quite wealthy (Borgerhoff Mulder, 1990). Kipsigis women and their parents act on their mate preferences for men with resources. In fact, many studies of polygynous societies reveal that the higher a man's status and resource holdings, the more likely he is to have multiple wives (see Perusse, 1993, for a review).

Another source of findings pertains to women who are in a position to get what they want—women who have the qualities that men desire in a mate such as physical attractiveness (see Chapter 5). In three separate sociological studies, researchers discovered that physically attractive women in fact marry men who are higher in social status and financial holdings than do women who are less attractive (Elder, 1969; Taylor & Glenn, 1976; Udry & Ekland, 1984). In one study, the physical attractiveness of women was correlated with the occupational prestige of their husbands (Taylor and Glenn, 1976). For different groups, the correlations were all positive, ranging between +.23 and +.37.

A longitudinal study was conducted at the Institute of Human Development in Berkeley, California (Elder, 1969). Physical attractiveness ratings were made by staff members of then unmarried women when they were adolescents. This sample of women was then followed up in adulthood after they had married, and the occupational statuses of their husbands were assessed. The results were examined separately for working-class and middle-class women. The correlations between a woman's attractiveness in adolescence and her husband's occupational status roughly a decade later were +.46 for women with working-class backgrounds and +.35 for women of middle-class backgrounds. For the sample as a whole, a woman's physical attractiveness correlated more strongly with her husband's status (+.43) than did other women's variables such as class of origin (+.27) or IQ (+.14). In sum, attractiveness in women appears to be an important path to upward mobility; women who are most in a position to get what they want appear to select men who have the qualities that most women desire.

## Women's Marriages to Men Who Are Older

Another source of data on women's actual mate choices comes from demographic statistics on the age differences between brides and grooms at marriage. Recall that women express a desire for men who are somewhat older. Specifically, in the international study of thirty-seven cultures, on average women preferred men who were 3.42 years older (Buss, 1989a). Demographic data on actual age differences were secured from twenty-seven of these countries. From this sample, the actual age difference between brides and grooms was found to be 2.99 years. In every country, grooms were older on average than brides, ranging from a low of 2.17 years in

Ireland to a high of 4.92 years in Greece. In short, women's preferences for older husbands translate into actual marriages to older men. Actual mating decisions of women accord well with their expressed preferences.

## Effects of Women's Preferences on Men's Behavior

Another indication of the potency of women's mate preferences comes from their effects on men's behavior. The theory of sexual selection predicts that the mate preferences of one sex should establish domains of mate competition in the opposite sex. If women value resources, for example, men should compete with each other to acquire and display those resources in mate competition. Many studies document exactly that. In studies of tactics of attraction, men are more likely than women to display resources, talk about their professional successes, flash money, drive expensive cars, and brag about their accomplishments (Buss, 1988b; Schmitt & Buss, 1996). When men derogate their competitors, they use tactics such as indicating that a rival is poor, lacks ambition, and is unlikely to succeed professionally (Buss & Dedden, 1990; Schmitt & Buss, 1996). In studies of deception tactics, men are more likely than women to inflate their status, prestige, and income to potential mates (Haselton et al., 2005).

One study of 5,020 individuals using an online dating service discovered that men were more likely than women to misrepresent the magnitude of their personal assets, notably their income and education level (Hall et al., 2010). A separate study of online dating profiles examined deception about physical attributes by comparing the profile's reported height and weight with the researcher's actual measurement of these variables using a standard tape measure and weight scale (Toma, Hancock, & Ellison, 2008). It was found that men lied more about their height. Taken together, this body of research suggests that men are aware of women's preferences for resources and the qualities linked with their acquisition, as well as their preferences for tall men, and take actions in an effort to embody (or appear to embody) what women want.

Roney (2003) hypothesized that mere exposure to attractive women would activate cognitive adaptations in men designed to embody the qualities that women want in a mate. Specifically, he predicted that exposure to young attractive women would (1) increase the importance men place on their

*Mere exposure to an attractive woman activates a cascade of psychological processes in men, such that they place greater value on the qualities that women want (resources, ambition) and describe themselves as possessing those qualities (see text for a description of the studies).*

own financial success, (2) experience feeling more ambitious, and (3) produce self-descriptions that correspond to what women want. Using a cover story to disguise the purpose of the study, Roney had one group of men rate the effectiveness of advertisements containing young attractive models and another group of men rate the effectiveness of ads containing older less-attractive models. Following this exposure, the men responded to the key measures to test his hypotheses.

When asked "With respect to your job/career you would like to have, how important are the following to you?" The rating scale ranged from 1 (not important) to 7 (very important). Men exposed to young attractive women rated "having a large income" to be 5.09, whereas men exposed to older less-attractive models rated it only 3.27—an astonishing large effect size. Similar differences occurred in rating the importance of "being financially successful." A full 60 percent of the men exposed to young attractive models described themselves as "ambitious," compared to 9 percent of the men exposed to older less-attractive models. Another study found that merely having a young woman in the same room caused men to increase the importance they attach to having material wealth (Roney, 2003). Similar effects have been found by independent researchers. Men "primed" with attractive images of women display more creativity, independence, and nonconformity, causing them to stand out from other men (Griskevicius, Cialdini, & Kenrick, 2006; Griskevicius, Goldstein et al., 2006). In short, when mating motives are "primed" by exposure to young attractive women, a cascade of psychological shifts occurs in men such that they value and display precisely what women want and hence what men need to succeed in mate competition.

## ■ SUMMARY

We now have the outlines of an answer to the mystery of women's long-term mate preferences. Modern women have inherited from their successful ancestors wisdom about the men they consent to mate with. Ancestral women who mated indiscriminately were likely to have been less reproductively successful than those who exercised choice. Long-term mates bring with them a treasure trove of assets. Selecting a long-term mate who has the relevant assets is clearly an extraordinarily complex endeavor. It involves a number of distinctive preferences, each corresponding to a resource that helps women solve critical adaptive problems.

That women seek resources in a marriage partner might seem obvious. Because resources cannot always be directly discerned, women's mating preferences are keyed to other qualities that signal the likely possession, or future acquisition, of resources. Indeed, women may be less influenced by money per se than by qualities that lead to resources, such as ambition, intelligence, and older age. Women scrutinize these personal qualities carefully because they reveal a man's potential.

Potential, however, is not enough. Because many men with a rich resource potential are themselves highly discriminating and are at times content with casual sex, women are faced with the problem of commitment. Seeking love is one solution to the commitment problem. Acts of love signal that a man has in fact committed to a particular woman.

To have the love and commitment of a man who could be easily downed by other men in the physical arena, however, would have been a problematic asset for ancestral women. Women who mated with small, weak men lacking physical prowess and courage would have risked damage from other men and loss of the couple's joint resources. Tall, strong, athletic men offered ancestral women protection. In this way, their personal well-being and their children's well-being could be secured against incursion. Modern women are the descendants of successful women who selected men in part for their strength and prowess.

Finally, resources, commitment, and protection do a woman little good if her husband becomes diseased or dies or if the couple is so mismatched that the partners fail to function as an effective team. The premium that women place on a man's health ensures that husbands will be capable of providing these benefits over the long haul. And the premium that women place on similarity of interests and traits with their mate helps to ensure fidelity and stability. These multiple facets of current women's mating preferences thus correspond well to adaptive problems faced by our female ancestors thousands of years ago.

Women's preferences are not rigid or invariant but rather change in important and adaptive ways across several contexts: their personal access to resources, temporal context, personal mate value, and presence of attractive women who seem interested in a man. Preferences also shift as a function of sexual orientation (see Box 4.1). According to the structural powerlessness hypothesis, women who have a lot of personal access to resources are predicted not to value resources in a mate as much as women lacking resources. This hypothesis receives no support

---

BOX *4.1*

## What about Lesbian Sexual Orientation?

Although there have been several theories that have attempted to explain male homosexual orientation (see Chapter 5), practically no efforts have been made to explain the puzzle of primary or exclusive lesbian orientation, which occurs in 1 to 2 percent of women (Bailey et al., 1997). As many theorists, such as Mike Bailey, Frank Muscarella, and James Dabbs, have pointed out, homosexuality is not a singular phenomenon. Lesbianism and male homosexuality, for example, appear to be quite different: Male sexual orientation tends to appear early in development, whereas female sexuality appears to be far more flexible over the lifespan (Baumeister, 2000). Future theories might attend to the large individual differences within those currently classified as lesbian and gay. For example, mate preferences vary across lesbians who describe themselves as "butch" as opposed to "femme" (Bailey et al., 1997; Bassett, Pearcey, & Dabbs, 2001). Butch lesbians tend to be more masculine, dominant, and assertive, whereas femme lesbians tend to be more sensitive, cheerful, and feminine. The differences are more than merely psychological; butch lesbians, compared to their femme peers, have higher levels of circulating testosterone, more masculine waist-to-hip ratios, more permissive attitudes toward casual sex, and less desire to have children (Singh et al., 1999). Femme lesbians place greater importance than butch lesbians on financial resources in a potential romantic partner and experience sexual jealousy over rivals who are more physically attractive. Butch lesbians place less value on financial resources when seeking partners but experience greater jealousy over rival competitors who are more financially successful. The psychological, morphological, and hormonal correlates imply that *butch* and *femme* are not merely arbitrary labels but rather reflect genuine individual differences.

Despite the theoretical and empirical attention to understanding and explaining homosexual orientation and same-sex sexual behavior, their origins remain scientific mysteries. Progress might accelerate with the realization of the possibility that there may be no single theory that can fully explain both gay males and lesbians, much less one that can explain the profound individual differences among those with a same-sex sexual orientation.

One recent study discovered that lesbian women, compared to heterosexual women, were more likely to report having experienced both physical and sexual abuse at the hands of men, with the unwanted sexual contact tending to occur relatively early in life (between the ages of 6 and 15) (Harrison et al., 2008). If replicated, this finding may partly explain why some women prefer same-sex sexual partners.

from the existing empirical data, however. Indeed, women with high incomes value a potential mate's income and education more, not less, than women with lower incomes. Women also show sensitivity to the contexts of long-term versus short-term mating. Specifically, in long-term mating contexts, women especially value qualities that signal that the man will be a good provider and a good father. These qualities are considerably less important in women's desires in a short-term mate. In a phenomenon known as mate copying, women are more likely to find men desirable if they are with other women, and particularly if other women are physically attractive and seem interested in them. Women who are higher in objectively assessed and self-perceived attractiveness raise their mating standards and seek men who are relatively more masculine, symmetrical, high in status, attractive, healthy, and physically fit.

For preferences to evolve, they must have had a recurrent impact on actual mating behavior. We do not expect that women's preferences will show a one-to-one correspondence with behavior. People cannot always get what they want. Nonetheless, several lines of research support the notion that women's preferences do in fact affect actual mating behavior. Women respond more to personal ads in which men indicate good financial status. Men high in status and resources are more likely to marry. If living in a polygynous society, high-status men are more likely to attract multiple wives. Poor men are more likely to remain bachelors. Women who embody what men desire (e.g., by being physically attractive) are in the best position to get what they want, and so their mate selections are most revealing. Several studies show that physically attractive women do indeed tend to marry men with higher incomes and occupational status. Demographic statistics further show that women worldwide tend to marry older men, which directly corresponds to women's expressed preference for such men. Finally, women's preferences have strong effects on men's behavior. Men are more likely than women to display resources in their attraction tactics and to derogate their competitors using verbal slurs that indicate that their rivals are poor and lack ambition. Furthermore, when men deceive women in online dating profiles, they tend to exaggerate their income, education, and height. The mere exposure of men to young attractive women activates a psychological cascade in men, such that they increase the importance they attach to financial success and feel more ambitious. Portions of men's behavior, in short, can be predicted from what women want in a mate. On the basis of this cumulation of studies, it is reasonable to conclude that women's mate preferences have a substantial impact on their own mating behavior and on the mating strategies of men.

## ■ SUGGESTED READINGS

Buss, D. M. (2003). *The evolution of desire: Strategies of human mating* (rev. ed.). New York: Free Press.

Johnston, V. S., Hagel, R., Franklin, M., Fink, B., & Grammer, K. (2001). Male facial attractiveness: Evidence for hormone-mediated adaptive design. *Evolution and Human Behavior, 22,* 251–267.

Li, N. P., Griskevicius, V., Durante, K. M., Jonason, P. K., Pasisz, D. J., & Aumer, K. (2009). An evolutionary perspective on humor: Sexual selection or interest indication? *Personality and Social Psychology Bulletin, 35,* 923–936.

Lieberman, D. (2009). Rethinking the Taiwanese minor marriage data: Evidence the mind uses multiple kinship cues to regulate inbreeding avoidance. *Evolution and Human Behavior, 30,* 153–160.

Miller, G. (2001). *The mating mind.* New York: Anchor Books.

Place, S. S., Todd, P. M., Penke, L., & Asendorpf, J. B. (2010). Humans show mate copying after observing real mate choices. *Evolution and Human Behavior, 31,* 320–325.

Regan, P. C. (1998). Minimum mate selection standards as a function of perceived mate value, relationship context, and gender. *Journal of Psychology and Human Sexuality, 10,* 53–73.

Ronay, R., & von Hippel, W. (2010). The presence of an attractive woman elevates testosterone and physical risk taking in young men. *Social Psychological and Personality Science, 1,* 57–64.

Roney, J. R., Hanson, K. N., Durante, K. M., & Maestripieri, D. (2006). Reading men's faces: Women's mate attractiveness judgments track men's testosterone and interest in infants. *Proceedings of the Royal Society, B, 273,* 2169–2175.

Schmitt, D. P., Youn, G., Bond, B., Brooks, S., Frye, H. et al. (2009). When will I feel love? The effects of culture, personality, and gender on the psychological tendency to love. *Journal of Research in Personality, 43,* 830–846.

Trivers, R. L. (1972). Parental investment and sexual selection. In B. Campbell (Ed.), *Sexual selection and the descent of man: 1871–1971* (pp. 136–179). Chicago: Aldine.

# MEN'S LONG-TERM MATING STRATEGIES

# CHAPTER 5

*Why does a particular maiden turn our wits so upside-down?*

—William James (1890)

$\mathcal{F}$or selection to have produced psychological mechanisms in men that incline them to seek marriage and commit years and decades of investment to a woman, it is reasonable to assume that there were adaptive advantages to long-term mating under some circumstances. This chapter examines the logic and evidence of men's long-term mating strategies. We start with the theoretical background for the evolution of men's mate preferences. Then we examine the content of men's mate preferences. The final section explores the effects of context on men's long-term mating strategies.

## ■ THEORETICAL BACKGROUND FOR THE EVOLUTION OF MEN'S MATE PREFERENCES

This section covers the theoretical background for two topics. The first is why men would marry at all—what are the potential adaptive benefits that ancestral men could have gained from marriage? The second topic deals with complexities surrounding the content of men's desires, and how selection might have fashioned specific mate preferences in men.

### Why Men Might Benefit from Commitment and Marriage

One solution to the puzzle of why men would seek marriage comes from the ground rules set by women. Because it is clear that many ancestral women required reliable signs of male commitment before consenting to sex, men who failed to commit might have failed to attract any women at all.

Another benefit of marriage is an increase in the quality of the woman a man would be able to attract. Men who are willing to promise long-term resources, protection, and investment in children are appealing to women, as we saw in Chapter 4, so men who are willing to commit to the long term have a wider range of women from which to choose. Such men attract desirable women because women typically desire lasting commitment, and highly desirable women are in the best position to get what they want.

A third potential benefit would be an increase in the odds that the man is the father of the children a woman bears. Through marriage a man gains repeated sexual access—in the majority of cases, exclusive sexual access. Without this repeated or exclusive access, his certainty in paternity would be jeopardized. Thus, men who marry gain the reproductive benefit of an increase in paternity certainty.

A fourth potential benefit of marriage would have been an increase in the survival of the man's children. In human ancestral environments, it is likely that infants and young children more frequently died without the prolonged investment from two parents or related kin (Hill & Hurtado, 1996). Even today, among the Ache Indians of Paraguay, children without an investing father suffer a death rate more than 10 percent higher than children whose fathers remain alive.

Over human evolutionary history, even children who did survive without their father's investment might have suffered from the absence of his teaching and political alliances, because both of these assets help to solve mating problems later in life. Fathers in many cultures past and present have had a strong hand in arranging beneficial marriages for their sons and daughters.

Men also benefit from marriage by an increase in status. In many cultures, males are not considered to have achieved true manhood until they have married. Increased status, in turn, can bring a bounty of benefits, including better resources for his children and additional mates (see Chapter 12). By marrying, men also gain access to coalitional allies through his wife's family, which provide additional reproductively relevant benefits.

In summary, there are seven potentially powerful adaptive benefits that would have accrued to men willing to make the commitment of marriage: (1) increased odds of succeeding in attracting a mate, (2) increased ability to attract a more desirable mate, (3) increased paternity certainty, (4) increased survival of his children, (5) increased reproductive success of children accrued through paternal investment, (6) increased social status, and (7) added coalitional allies.

## The Problem of Assessing a Woman's Fertility or Reproductive Value

To be reproductively successful, ancestral men had to marry women with the capacity to bear children. A woman with the capacity to bear many children obviously would have been more beneficial in reproductive currencies than a woman capable of bearing few or none. Men cannot observe a woman's reproductive value directly, and so selection could only have fashioned preferences in men for qualities that are correlated with reproductive value.

When we compare humans with their closest primate relative, the chimpanzee, we see a startling discontinuity in the female advertisement of reproductive status. When the female chimpanzee is capable of conceiving, she goes into a phase called *estrus*—the time during which she releases her eggs and shows maximal sexual receptivity. The receptivity of estrus is usually advertised by bright red swollen genitals and scents that are highly attractive to chimpanzee males. Most, although not all, of the sexual activity among the chimpanzees takes place during the estrus phase, when the female is most likely to conceive.

Humans show a markedly different form of mating. First, women's ovulation is relatively concealed or cryptic. Unlike chimpanzee females, when women release their eggs for potential fertilization, the event is not accompanied by a pronounced genital swelling. Second, sexual activity among most humans occurs throughout the woman's ovulation cycle. Unlike the chimpanzee, sexual activity is not generally concentrated during the phase in which the female is most likely to conceive.

The transition from advertised estrus to concealed ovulation posed a poignant adaptive problem for human ancestral males. When ovulation is not advertised, how could males discern a female's reproductive status? The concealment of ovulation, in short, shifted the problem from one of detecting when a woman was ovulating to one of determining which women were likely to be *capable* of conceiving children—the problem of determining a woman's reproductive value or fertility.

*Reproductive value* refers to the number of children a person of a given age and sex is likely to have in the future. A woman who is fifteen years old, for example, has a higher reproductive value than a woman who is thirty because, on average, the younger woman is likely to bear more children in the future than is the older woman. Individual women may, of course, defy these averages. The fifteen-year-old might decide never to have children, and the thirty-year-old could have six. The key is that reproductive value refers to the *average expected* future reproduction of a person of a given age and sex (see Figure 5.1).

Reproductive value differs from *fertility*, which is defined as actual reproductive performance, measured by the number of viable offspring produced. In human populations, women in their mid-twenties tend to produce the most viable children, and so fertility among humans reaches a peak in the mid-twenties.

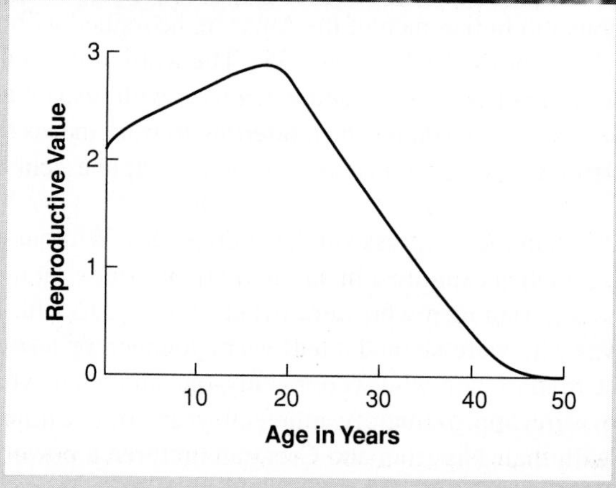

The differences between fertility and reproductive value can be illustrated by contrasting two females, ages fifteen and twenty-five. The younger female has a higher reproductive value because her *future* reproduction is expected to be higher. The twenty-five-year-old female, in contrast, would be more fertile because women in their mid-twenties produce more children, on average, than do women in their teens.

The solution to the problem of detecting fertility or reproductive value, however, is more difficult than it might at first appear. The number of children a woman is likely to bear in

FIGURE 5.1 **Typical Reproductive Value Curve for Women.** The figure shows the number of children a woman of a given age is likely to have, on average, in the future.

her lifetime is not stamped on her forehead. It is not encoded in her social reputation. Even women themselves lack direct knowledge of their reproductive value.

Ancestral men, however, could have evolved adaptations sensitive to observable qualities of a woman that are *correlated* with underlying reproductive value. Two potentially observable cues would have been a woman's youth and her health (Symons, 1979; Williams, 1975). Old or unhealthy women clearly could not reproduce as much as young, healthy women. But precisely which observable qualities of a woman might signal youth and health? And do men's desires in a marriage partner focus heavily on her reproductive capacity?

## ■ THE CONTENT OF MEN'S MATE PREFERENCES

In some ways men's mate preferences are similar to those of women. Like women, men express a desire for partners who are intelligent, kind, understanding, and healthy (Buss, 2003). Also, like women, men look for partners who share their values and are similar to them in attitudes, personality, and religious beliefs. But because ancestral men confronted a different set of adaptive mating problems than did ancestral women, their descendants are predicted to hold a somewhat different set of mate preferences as adaptive solutions. These preferences start with one of the most powerful cues to a woman's reproductive status—her age.

### Preference for Youth

Youth is a critical cue because a woman's reproductive value declines steadily as she moves past age twenty. By the age of forty, a woman's reproductive capacity is low, and by fifty, it is essentially zero. Men's preferences capitalize on this. Within the United States, men uniformly express a desire for mates who are younger than they are. Men's preference for youthful partners is not limited to Western cultures. When anthropologist Napoleon Chagnon was asked which females are most sexually attractive to Yanomamö Indian men of the Amazon, he replied without hesitation, "Females who are *moko dude*" (Symons, 1989, pp. 34–35). The word *moko,* when used with respect to fruit, means that the fruit is harvestable, and when used with respect to a woman, it means that the woman is fertile. Thus, *moko dude,* when referring to fruit, means that the fruit is perfectly ripe, and when referring to a woman, means that she is postpubescent but has not yet borne her first child.

Nigerian, Indonesian, Iranian, and Indian men express similar preferences. Without exception, in every one of the thirty-seven societies examined in an international study on mate selection, men preferred younger wives. Nigerian men who were twenty-three years old, for example, expressed a preference for wives who were six and a half years younger, or just under seventeen years old (Buss, 1989a). Croatian men who were twenty-one and a half years old expressed a desire for wives who were approximately nineteen years old. Chinese, Canadian, and Colombian men shared with their Nigerian and Croatian brethren a powerful desire for young women. On average, men from the thirty-seven cultures expressed a desire for wives approximately two and a half years younger than themselves (refer back to Figure 4.5, page 117). Interestingly, an eye-tracking study found that both male and female judges exhibited a larger number of eye fixations and longer dwell time when viewing female faces perceived to be younger—suggesting greater "attentional adhesion" to young female faces (Fink et al., 2008).

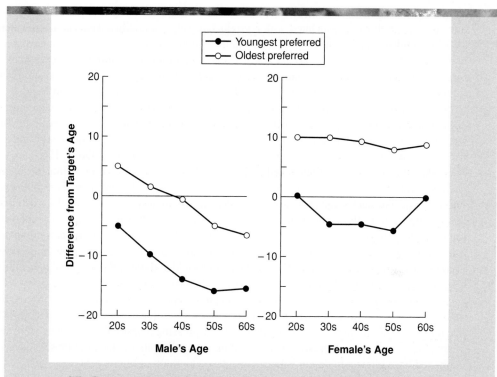

FIGURE 5.2 **Men's and Women's Age Preferences as They Get Older.** As men get older, they prefer women as mates who are increasingly younger than they are *(left)*. Women's age preferences do not show this pattern *(right)*.

*Source:* Kenrick, D. T., & Keefe, R. C. (1992). Age preferences in mates reflect sex differences in reproductive strategies. *Behavioral and Brain Sciences, 15*, 75–133. Reprinted with permission.

Although men universally prefer younger women as wives, the strength of this preference varies somewhat from culture to culture. Among Scandinavian countries such as Finland, Sweden, and Norway, men prefer their brides to be only one or two years younger. Men in Nigeria and Zambia prefer their brides to be six and a half and seven and a half years younger, respectively. In Nigeria and Zambia, which practice polygyny like many cultures worldwide, men who can afford it are legally permitted to marry more than one woman. Because men in polygynous mating systems are typically older than men in monogamous systems, by the time they have acquired sufficient resources to attract wives, the larger age difference preferred by Nigerian and Zambian men may reflect their advanced age when they acquire wives.

A comparison of the statistics offered in personal ads in newspapers reveals that a man's age has a strong effect on what he desires. As men get older, they prefer as mates women who are increasingly younger. Men in their thirties prefer women who are roughly five years younger, whereas men in their fifties prefer women who are ten to twenty years younger (Kenrick & Keefe, 1992) (see Figure 5.2).

One evolutionary model predicts that what men desire is not youth per se but rather features of women that are associated with reproductive value or fertility. This perspective leads to a counterintuitive prediction when it comes to the age preferences of adolescent males: Teenage males should prefer women who are *slightly older* than they are, contrary to the typically observed pattern of men desiring younger partners, because slightly older women have higher fertility than women their own age or women who are younger (Kenrick et al., 1996).

To test this prediction, one study (Kenrick et al., 1996) surveyed 103 teenage males and 106 females ranging in age from twelve to nineteen. The participants received the following instructions: "I'd like you to think for a second about what type of person you would find attractive. Imagine you were going on a date with someone" (Kenrick et al., 1996, p. 1505).

Each participant was then asked about his or her age limits. The experimenter began by asking, "Would you date someone who was [the subject's age]," followed by "How about someone who was [subject's age minus one]." If affirmative answers were given, the experimenter then continued until the participant stated that a particular age was too young. The experimenter then asked about the maximum acceptable age of a dating partner. Finally, participants were asked about the ideal age of a dating partner, "the most attractive person you could possibly imagine" (Kenrick et al., 1996, p. 1505). The results yielded three variables: ideal age, minimum age, and maximum age of dating partner desired. The results are shown in Figure 5.3.

Although these teenage males were willing to accept dates with females who were slightly younger, they were far more willing to accept dates with older women. The "most attractive" age mirrors these findings, with adolescent males expressing a desire for dates who were several years older on average. Interestingly, this finding occurs despite the fact that these older women expressed little interest in dating younger men (second graph in Figure 5.3).

To get an overview of the pattern of men's preferences for the age of women as a function of their own age, the data from all age groups were combined into a single graph, shown in Figure 5.4. This graph shows clearly that at the youngest ages, teenage males prefer females a few years older than themselves. But with advancing age, men prefer women who are increasingly younger than they are.

These data concerning teenagers are important in rendering several alternative explanations less plausible. One explanation for men's desire for young women, for example, is that young women are easier to control and are less dominant than older women, and men seek to mate with women they can control. If this were the *sole* reason for men's preference for young women, however, then we would expect that teenage males would also prefer younger women, but they don't.

Another explanation for men's desire for young women is based on learning theory. Because women tend to prefer men who are somewhat older, men may have received more reward or reinforcement for seeking dates with younger women. This reinforcement explanation, however, fails to account for the preferences of the teenage males, who prefer older women despite the fact that the interest is rarely mutual.

Taken together with the cross-cultural data, these findings lend strong support to an evolutionary psychological explanation: Men desire young women because over evolutionary time, youth has consistently been linked with fertility. This explanation accounts for two facts that all other theories have difficulty explaining: First, that men desire women who are increasingly younger than they are as the men themselves get older; second, that teenage males prefer women a few years older than they are despite the fact that such women rarely reward them for such interest.

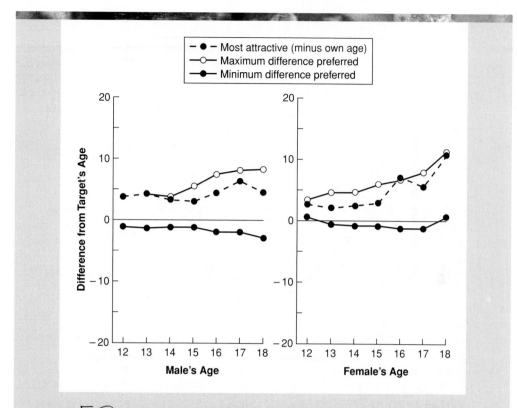

FIGURE 5.3  **Age Preferences for Mates Expressed by Teenagers.** Note that male teenagers, unlike older males, prefer women as mates who are somewhat older than they are *(left).*

*Source:* Kenrick, D. T., Keefe, R. C., Gabrielidis, C., & Cornelius, J. S. (1996). Adolescents' age preferences for dating partners: Support for an evolutionary model of life-history strategies. *Child Development, 67,* 1499–1511. Reprinted with permission.

Nonetheless, an important anomaly remains unexplained by the evolutionary hypothesis. Although men prefer women who are increasingly younger than they are as long-term mates as they get older, the actual age preferences of older men is beyond maximum fertility. Men who are fifty, for example, prefer women who are in their mid-thirties (in sharp contrast to men's age preferences for a short-term mate, which remain at the age of peak fertility—see Buunk et al., 2001). There are a few possible explanations. First, older men may have difficulty in actually attracting dramatically younger women, and their preferences may reflect a compromise between their ideal and what they can get (Buunk et al., 2001). Second, large age discrepancies may create less compatibility, greater marital conflict, and more marital instability. Indeed, the mate homicide rate rises as a function of the magnitude of the age discrepancy between partners (Daly & Wilson, 1988). Third, modern marriage likely differs from ancestral marriage. In modern marriages, couples spend a great deal of time together, socialize as a couple, and act as companions.

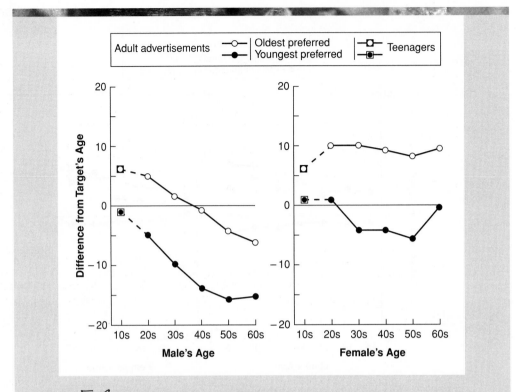

FIGURE 5.4 **Comparison of Teenage Preferences with Those Expressed in Adult Advertisements.** The figure shows that teenagers tend to prefer mates close to themselves in age. As they age, males increasingly prefer mates younger than themselves, whereas females prefer mates consistently a few years older.

*Source:* Kenrick, D. T., Keefe, R. C., Gabrielidis, C., & Cornelius, J. S. (1996). Adolescents' age preferences for dating partners: Support for an evolutionary model of life-history strategies. *Child Development, 67,* 1499–1511. Reprinted with permission.

Judging from hunter-gatherer groups, ancestral marriages were more likely to involve sharp division of labor, with women spending the bulk of their time with children and other women and men hunting and socializing with other men. Thus, the importance of similarity and compatibility for functioning in modern marriages may have created a shift in men's age preferences above the point of maximum female fertility. Which of these explanations, or which combination, turns out to be correct must await future research.

## Evolved Standards of Physical Beauty

Evolutionary logic leads to an even more powerful set of expectations for universal standards of beauty. Just as our standards for attractive landscapes embody cues such as water, game, and refuge, mimicking our ancestors' savanna habitats (Orians & Heerwagen, 1992), our standards

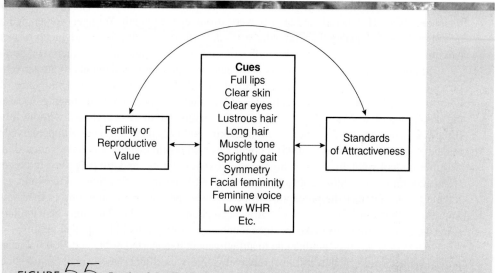

FIGURE 5.5 **Logic of the Evolution of Standards of Attractiveness.** Standards of female attractiveness are hypothesized to have evolved to embody reliably observable cues to fertility or reproductive value.

for female beauty embody cues to women's reproductive value. Beauty is in the *adaptations* of the beholder (Symons, 1995).

Our ancestors had access to two types of observable evidence of a woman's reproductive value: (1) features of *physical appearance,* such as full lips, clear skin, smooth skin, clear eyes, lustrous hair, good muscle tone, and body fat distribution; and (2) features of *behavior,* such as a bouncy youthful gait, an animated facial expression, and a high energy level. These physical cues to youth and health, and hence to fertility and reproductive value, have been hypothesized to be some of the key components of male standards of female beauty (Symons, 1979, 1995) (see Figure 5.5).

Psychologists Clelland Ford and Frank Beach discovered several universal cues that correspond with the evolutionary theory of beauty (1951). Signs of youth, such as clear, smooth skin, and signs of health, such as an absence of sores and lesions, are universally regarded as attractive. Any cues to ill health or older age are seen as less attractive. Poor complexion is always considered unattractive. Ringworm, facial disfigurement, and filthiness are universally undesirable. Freedom from disease is universally attractive.

Among the Trobriand Islanders in northwestern Melanesia, for example, anthropologist Bronislaw Malinowski reports that "sores, ulcers, and skin eruptions are naturally held to be specially repulsive from the viewpoint of erotic contact" (Malinowski, 1929, p. 244). The "essential conditions" for beauty, in contrast, are "health, strong growth of hair, sound teeth, and smooth skin." Specific features, such as bright, shining eyes and full, well-shaped lips rather than thin or pinched lips, are especially important to the islanders.

Another cue to youth and health is the *length and quality of women's hair.* One study interviewed 230 women at various public locations about their age, subjective health status, and relationship status, and obtained observer measures of hair length and hair quality (Hinsz, Matz, & Patience, 2001). Hair length and quality were strong cues to youth: Younger women had longer hair of higher-rated quality than did older women. Furthermore, observer's judgments of women's hair quality were positively correlated with women's subjective judgments of their own health.

Studies confirm that *skin quality* is especially important in judgments of attractiveness. It provides a cue to a woman's age and a partial record of her lifetime health (Sugiyama, 2005). Clear unblemished skin signals an absence of parasites, absence of skin-damaging diseases during development, and possibly "good genes" to withstand disease and heal without infection (Singh & Bronstad, 1997). Studies find that skin quality is indeed linked with perceived facial attractiveness (Fink & Neave, 2005). Female faces with skin that has a homogeneous skin color distribution, not splotchy, receive higher attractiveness ratings and are perceived to be younger (Fink, Grammer, & Matts, 2006; Fink et al., 2008). Furthermore, more skin blood color in female faces enhances the perception of healthiness, perhaps corresponding to the subjective impression that some faces seem to "glow" (Stephen et al., 2009). This may also explain why some women use rouge as makeup, since it enhances perceptions of health and vitality.

*Facial femininity* is another cue to attractiveness (Gangestad & Scheyd, 2005). Facial femininity includes cues such as full lips, relatively large eyes, thinner jaws, small chin, high cheekbones, and a relatively short distance between mouth and jaw. Female facial femininity is likely to be a marker of reproductive value for two reasons. First, as women age, their facial features become less feminine. Second, facial femininity is linked with higher levels of estrogen, the ovarian hormone that correlates with fertility (Schaefer et al., 2006). Meta-analyses reveal that facial femininity is one of the most powerful cues to women's attractiveness (Rhodes, 2006). Feminine voices—relatively high pitched—are also found to be more attractive in women (Collins & Missing, 2003; Feinberg et al., 2005).

*Facial symmetry* is another correlate of female attractiveness (Gangestad & Scheyd, 2005; Rhodes, 2006). You may recall from Chapter 4 that symmetry is hypothesized to be a cue to developmental stability, a hypothesized sign of "good genes" and the capacity to withstand environmental insult. Symmetrical female faces are indeed judged to be healthier than less symmetrical faces (Fink et al., 2006). Facial symmetry is positively correlated with judgments of attractiveness, although the link is weaker than that of facial femininity (Rhodes, 2006).

*Facial averageness* is another quality linked with attractiveness, although this may seem counterintuitive. Researchers created computer composites of the human face, superimposing faces on each other to create new faces (Langlois & Roggman, 1990). The new faces differed in the number of individual faces that made them up—four, eight, sixteen, or thirty-two. The composite faces—the averages of the individual faces—were judged more attractive than the individual faces. And the more faces that went into the composite, the more attractive the face was judged to be. Two competing hypotheses have been advanced to explain why average faces are attractive. First, people may show a generalized cognitive preference for things that are easily processed, and stimuli that match an average prototype may be easier to process. People do indeed find averaged images of fish, birds, and even cars more attractive than individual fish, birds, or cars (Rhodes, 2006). Second, averageness may be a marker of genetic or phenotypic quality (Gangestad & Scheyd, 2005). Deviations from averageness may be cues to environmental insults such as disease or genetic mutations.

*Leg length,* especially long legs relative to torso length, has been hypothesized to be a cue to health and biomechanical efficiency (Sorokowski & Pawlowski, 2008). Using silhouette stimuli that held overall height constant, but varied leg length, researchers discovered that legs roughly 5 percent longer than average are viewed as maximally attractive in women (Sorokowski & Pawlowski, 2008). Other studies confirm that both sexes view relatively longer legs as more attractive in women (Bertamini & Bennett, 2009; Swami, Einon, & Furnham, 2006). Perhaps this explains why some women wear high-heeled shoes—they make legs appear to be relatively longer. Interestingly, a study of 9,998 Chinese found that women with longer legs had more off-spring, an association especially strong in women from lower socioeconomic backgrounds (Fielding et al., 2008).

***Standards of Beauty Emerge Early in Life.***   Most traditional psychological theories of attraction have assumed that standards of attractiveness are learned gradually through cultural transmission and therefore do not emerge clearly until a child is three or four years old or even later (Berscheid & Walster, 1974; Langlois et al., 1987). However, psychologist Judith Langlois and her colleagues have overturned this conventional wisdom by studying infants' social responses to faces (Langlois, Roggman, & Reiser-Danner, 1990).

Adults evaluated color slides of White and Black female faces for their attractiveness. Then infants two to three months and six to eight months old were shown pairs of these faces that differed in degree of attractiveness. Both younger and older infants gazed longer at the more attractive faces, suggesting that standards of beauty apparently emerge quite early in life. In a second study, they found that twelve-month-old infants played significantly longer with facially attractive dolls than with unattractive dolls. This evidence challenges the commonly held view that the standards of attractiveness are learned through gradual exposure to current cultural models. No training seems necessary for these standards to emerge.

***Standards of Beauty Are Consistent across Cultures.***   The constituents of beauty are neither arbitrary nor culture bound. When psychologist Michael Cunningham asked people of different races to judge the facial attractiveness of Asian, Hispanic, Black, and White women in photographs, he found tremendous consensus about who is and who is not considered good-looking (Cunningham et al., 1995). The average correlation between racial groups in their ratings of the attractiveness of these photographs was +.93. In a second study by the same investigators, Taiwanese subjects agreed with the other groups in the average ratings of attractiveness ($r = +.91$). Degree of exposure to Western media did not affect the judgments of attractiveness in either study. In a third study, Blacks and Whites showed tremendous agreement about which women's faces were most and least attractive ($r = +.94$). Consensus has also been found among Chinese, Indian, and English subjects; between South Africans and North Americans; between Black and White Americans; and between Russians, Ache Indians, and Americans (Cross & Cross, 1971; Jackson, 1992; Jones, 1996; Morse, Gruzen, & Reis, 1976; Thakerar & Iwawaki, 1979).

***Beauty and the Brain.***   Evolutionary psychologists are beginning to use neuroscience technology to identify the links between psychological mechanisms and specific brain circuits. Exploiting the new technology of functional magnetic resonance imaging (fMRI), scientists Itzhak Aharon, Nancy Etcoff, and their colleagues sought to identify the "reward value" of different images (Aharon et al., 2001). They exposed heterosexual male participants to four sets of faces differing in attractiveness, as determined by prior ratings: attractive females, average females, attractive males, and average males. While participants viewed these images, their brains were neuroimaged in six regions. The results proved to be dramatic. When men looked at attractive female faces, the nucleus accumbens area of the brain became especially activated. The nucleus accumbens is known to be fundamental reward circuitry—that is, it is a well-documented pleasure center of the brain. This reward circuit of the brain *fails* to become activated when men look at either typical female faces or any of the male faces. Beautiful female faces, in short, are especially rewarding to men, psychologically and neurologically. This important finding takes the field a step closer to identifying the specific neurological bases of mating adaptations that have been well documented psychologically and behaviorally.

## Body Fat, Waist-to-Hip Ratio, and Body Mass Index

Facial beauty is only part of the picture. Features of the rest of the body may also provide cues to a woman's reproductive capacity. Standards for female bodily attractiveness vary somewhat from culture to culture. The most culturally variable standard of beauty seems to be in the preference for a slim versus a plump body build, and it is linked with the social status that build conveys. In cultures where food is scarce, such as among the Bushmen of Australia, plumpness signals wealth, health, and adequate nutrition during development (Rosenblatt, 1974). Indeed, there is powerful evidence that in ecologies where food shortages are common, such as in Kenya, Uganda, and certain parts of Equador, men prefer women who are heavier and possess more body fat (Sugiyama, 2005). Even within cultures, men prefer heavier women when there are economic hard times (Pettijohn & Jungeberg, 2004), when they are hungry (Pettijohn, Sacco, & Yerkes, 2009), and when they feel poor (Nelson & Morrison, 2005). In cultures where food is relatively abundant, such as the United States and many Western European countries, the relationship between plumpness and status is reversed, and the wealthy distinguish themselves by being thin (Symons, 1979). Thus, although "body-weight preference varies across cultures and time, it does so in predictable ways" (Sugiyama, 2005, p. 318), suggesting context-dependent adaptations.

One study revealed a disturbing aspect of U.S. women's and men's perceptions of the desirability of plump or thin body types (Rozin & Fallon, 1988). Men and women viewed nine female figures that varied from very thin to very plump. The women were asked to indicate their ideal for themselves, as well as their perception of what men's ideal female figure was. In both cases, women selected a figure that was slimmer than average. When men were asked to select which female figure they preferred, however, they selected the figure of exactly average body size. So U.S. women think that men want them to be thinner than is in fact the case. A study of 7,434 individuals from twenty-six cultures in ten world regions found the same pattern—men consistently prefer female bodies that are heavier in weight than women's perceptions of what men prefer (Swami et al., 2010).

Psychologist Devendra Singh has discovered one preference for body shape that may be universal: the preference for a particular ratio between the size of a woman's waist and the size of her hips (Singh, 1993; Singh & Young, 1995). Before puberty, boys and girls show similar fat distributions. At puberty, however, a dramatic change occurs. Men lose fat from their buttocks and thighs, whereas the release of estrogen in pubertal girls causes them to deposit fat in the lower trunk, primarily on their hips and upper thighs. Indeed, the volume of body fat in this region is 40 percent greater for women than for men.

The waist-to-hip ratio (WHR) is thus similar for the sexes before puberty, in the range of .85 to .95. After puberty, however, women's hip fat deposits cause their WHRs to become significantly lower than men's. Healthy, reproductively capable women have WHRs between

*Women with a low WHR* (left panel) *are judged to be more attractive than women with a higher WHR* (right panel). *A relatively low WHR signals that the woman is young, healthy, and not pregnant.* *Source:* Henss, R. (2000). Waist-to-hip ratio and female attractiveness: Evidence from photographic stimuli and methodological considerations. *Personality and Individual Differences, 28,* 501–513. Reprinted with permission from Elsevier.

.67 and .80, whereas healthy men have a ratio in the range of .85 to .95. Abundant evidence now shows that the WHR is an accurate indicator of women's reproductive status. Women with lower ratios show earlier pubertal endocrine activity. Married women with higher ratios have more difficulty becoming pregnant, and those who do get pregnant do so at a later age than women with lower ratios. The WHR is also an accurate indication of long-term health status. Diseases such as diabetes, hypertension, heart attack, stroke, and gallbladder disorders have been shown to be linked with the distribution of fat, as reflected by the ratio, rather than with the total amount of fat per se. One study found that women with a low WHR (as indicated by small waist) *and* relatively large breasts, compared to women from three groups with different combinations of body-shape variables, had 26 percent higher levels of the ovarian hormone oestradiol (E2), which is a good predictor of fertility and pregnancy success (Jasienska et al., 2004). The link between the WHR and both health and reproductive status makes it a reliable cue for ancestral men's preferences in a mate.

Singh discovered that WHR is indeed a powerful part of women's attractiveness. In a dozen studies conducted by Singh, men rated the attractiveness of female figures that varied in both WHR and total amount of fat. Again, men found the average figure to be more attractive than either a thin or a fat figure. Regardless of the total amount of fat, however, men find women with low WHRs the most attractive. Women with a WHR of 0.70 are seen as more attractive than women with a WHR of 0.80, who in turn are seen as more attractive than women with a WHR of 0.90. Studies with line drawings and with computer-generated photographic images produced the same results. The bodies of women who underwent surgery to remove fat from their stomachs and implant it on their buttocks—creating a lower WHR—were judged more attractive post-operation (Singh & Randall, 2007). Singh's analysis of *Playboy* centerfolds and winners of U.S. beauty contests over the past thirty years confirmed the invariance of this cue. Although both centerfolds and beauty contest winners got slightly thinner over that period, their WHRs remained the same, roughly 0.70.

A preference for a relatively low WHR has also been found in the United Kingdom, Australia, Germany, India, and Guinea-Brissan (Africa) and on the Azore Islands (Connolly, Mealey, & Slaughter, 2000; Furnham, Tan, & McManus, 1997; Singh, 2000).

A cross-cultural study of female "escorts" advertised online found that the average values of the stated WHRs, as calculated from reported body measurements of waist and hips, were .70, .75, .71, .76, and .69 in Europe, Oceania, Asia, North America, and Latin America, respectively (Saad, 2008). Another study found that men who were blind from birth, when assessing female body shape through touch, prefer the low WHR mannequin models, suggesting that the preference for low WHR can develop with the total absence of visual input (Karremans, Frankenhuis, & Arons, 2010). Finally, an eye-tracking study discovered that initial visual fixations occurred most often for female waists and breasts, and that men rated women with a low WHR as most attractive, regardless of breast size (Dixon et al., 2010).

Two studies have failed to replicate this effect—one in Peru (Yu & Shepard, 1998) and one among the Hadza in Tanzania (Marlow & Wetsman, 2001). In fact, among the Hadza, men were found to prefer somewhat heavier women with a higher WHR. But these apparent failures to replicate turn out not to be as straightforward as initially believed. It is becoming increasingly clear that WHR assessment is more complex than an "invariant preference" for a specific WHR such as .70. Notably, the normal range of women's WHR is higher in foraging societies than in Western populations, and the average WHR of the most fertile females is higher in foraging societies (Sugiyama, 2005). Thus, when stimuli are used that more accurately characterize the local cultural range of WHR, men tend to find attractive a WHR that is *lower than the local average* (Sugiyama, 2004a). One of the failures to replicate previously noted for the Hadza turned out differently when the stimuli included profile views of buttocks rather than frontal views (Marlow, Apicella, & Reed, 2005). As the authors concluded, "these results imply that there is less disparity between American and Hadza preferences for the actual WHR of real women" (Marlow et al., 2005, p. 458).

Individuals differ in preferences for WHR in ways that are contingent on sexual strategy pursued. Specifically, men who tend to pursue a short-term sexual strategy have a stronger preference for low WHR than men pursuing a long-term mating strategy (Schmalt, 2006). And men pursuing a short-term mating strategy are more likely than men pursuing a long-term strategy to approach women with a low WHR (Brase & Walker, 2004). Although the explanation for these findings is open to question, it is plausible that men with higher "mate value" may be initiating contact with the most physically attractive women. In sum, WHR is an important bodily cue to female attractiveness and is known to be linked to female fertility. Nonetheless, preferences for specific WHR values vary predictably with the actual values of WHR in the local culture and also with sexual strategy pursued.

Another hypothesized cue to female body attractiveness is body mass index (BMI), a measure of overall body fat as calculated from a person's weight and height. BMI and WHR are positively correlated—as WHR increases, so does BMI. One study found that BMI was a better predictor of attractiveness judgments than WHR, and that statistically controlling for BMI, WHR did not predict attractiveness judgments (Cornelissen, Tovee, & Bateson, 2009).

The authors conclude that although WHR is indeed an important predictor of attractiveness, this is largely explained by the effect of total body fat on WHR. Another study using an eye-tracking procedure reinforced this conclusion, finding that eye fixations clustered around the waist and breasts, but not on the pelvic or hip regions (Cornelissen, Hancock et al., 2009). Other research, in contrast, supports the primacy of WHR over BMI. A brain imaging study found that male brain reward centers (especially the nucleus accumbens) were activated in response to naked female bodies with a low WHR, but were not activated by those with a lower BMI (Platek & Singh, 2010). Another study found that attractiveness of ten photographs of rear-facing nude women was significantly influenced by WHR, even after controlling for BMI (Perilloux, Webster, & Gaulin, 2010). A third study found that both WHR and BMI predicted attractiveness judgments, but also found that waist circumference was a stronger predictor than either (Rilling et al., 2009). Future research is needed to resolve the controversy over the relative contributions of WHR, BMI, and waist circumference to judgments of women's body shape attractiveness.

## Sex Differences in the Importance of Physical Appearance

Because of the abundance of cues conveyed by a woman's physical appearance, and because male standards of beauty have evolved to correspond to these cues, men place a premium on physical appearance and attractiveness in their mate preferences. A cross-generational mating study spanning a fifty-seven-year period from 1939 to 1996 in the United States gauged the value men and women place on different characteristics in a mate (Buss et al., 2001). The same eighteen characteristics were measured at roughly one-decade intervals to determine how mating preferences have changed over time in the United States. In all cases, men rated physical attractiveness and good looks as more important and desirable in a potential mate than did women.

This does not mean that the importance people place on attractiveness is forever fixed. On the contrary, the importance of attractiveness has increased dramatically in the United States in the twentieth century (Buss et al., 2001). For example, the importance attached to good looks in a marriage partner on a scale of 0 to 3 increased between 1939 and 1996 from 1.50 to 2.11 for men and from 0.94 to 1.67 for women, showing that mate preferences can change. Indeed, these changes point to the importance of *cultural evolution* and the impact of input from the social environment. The sex difference so far remains invariant, however.

These sex differences are not limited to the United States or even to Western cultures. Regardless of location, habitat, marriage system, or cultural living arrangement, men in all thirty-seven cultures included in the study on choosing a mate—from Australians to Zambians—valued physical appearance in a potential mate more than women (see Figure 5.6). China typifies the average difference in importance attached to beauty, with men a 2.06 and women a 1.59. This internationally consistent sex difference persists despite variations in race, ethnicity, religion, hemisphere, political system, or mating system. Among the Hadza, more than five times as many men as women placed great importance on the fertility of a potential spouse—one who could bear many children (Marlow, 2004). When asked "How can you tell?" most Hadza men responded by saying "you can tell just by looking," suggesting that men are aware that physical appearance conveys vital information about fertility. Men's preference for physically

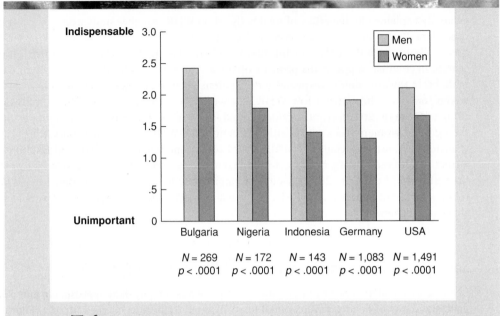

FIGURE 5.6   **Desire for Physical Attractiveness in a Long-Term Mate.**
Participants in thirty-seven cultures rated this variable, in the context of eighteen other variables, on how desirable it would be in a potential long-term mate or marriage partner using a four-point rating scale, ranging from 0 (irrelevant or unimportant) to 3 (indispensable).

$N$ = sample size.

$p$ values less than .05 indicate that sex difference is significant.

*Source:* Buss, D. M., & Schmitt, D. P. (1993). Sexual strategies theory: An evolutionary perspective on human mating. *Psychological Review, 100,* 204–232. Copyright © 1993 by the American Psychological Association. Adapted with permission.

attractive mates appears to be the product of a species-wide psychological mechanism that transcends cultural variation.

## Do Men Have a Preference for Ovulating Women?

Perhaps one of the most obvious predictions one could make about men's desires is that they should show a strong preference for women at the time women *ovulate*—when the egg is released into the woman's uterus to potentially be fertilized by a sperm. Ancestral men who were able to detect ovulating women would have several reproductive advantages over men who could not. First, they could channel their courtship, seduction, and sexual behavior toward ovulating women at that time, thus maximizing the odds of successful fertilization. Second, they could save a tremendous amount of effort by avoiding women who were not ovulating. Third, a married man could restrict his mate-guarding efforts to the period in which his spouse was ovulating.

In humans, however, ovulation is "concealed" or "cryptic"; conventional scientific wisdom is that there is no evidence that men can detect when women are ovulating (Symons, 1992, p. 144). Despite the tremendous reproductive advantages of detecting and desiring ovulating women, selection seems not to have given men these adaptations. Perhaps this conclusion is too hasty.

There are several lines of evidence that suggest that men might, in fact, be able to detect when women ovulate (Symons, 1995). First, during ovulation, women's skin becomes suffused with blood. This corresponds to the "glow" that women sometimes appear to have, a healthy reddening of the cheeks. Second, women's skin lightens slightly during ovulation as compared with other times of the menstrual cycle—a cue universally thought to be a sexual attractant (van den Berghe & Frost, 1986). A cross-cultural survey found that "of the 51 societies for which any mention of native skin preferences . . . is made, 47 state a preference for the lighter end of the locally represented spectrum, although not necessarily for the lightest possible skin color" (van den Berghe & Frost, 1986, p. 92).

Third, during ovulation, women's levels of circulating estrogen increase, which produces a corresponding decrease in women's WHR (Symons, 1995, p. 93). A lower WHR, as noted earlier, is known to be sexually attractive to men (Singh, 1993). Fourth, ovulating women are touched more often in singles bars (Grammer, 1996). Fifth, men found the body odor of women, taken from cotton pads worn under the armpit, to be more attractive and pleasant smelling during the follicular (fertile) stage of the menstrual cycle (Havlicek et al., 2005; Singh & Bronstad, 2001). Sixth, men who smelled T-shirts worn by ovulating women displayed a subsequent rise in testosterone levels compared to men who smelled shirts worn by nonovulating women or shirts with a control scent (Miller & Maner, 2010). Seventh, there are vocal cues to ovulation—women's voices rise in pitch, in the attractive feminine direction, at ovulation (Bryant & Haselton, 2009). Eighth, women's faces are judged by both sexes to be more attractive during the fertile than during the luteal phase (Roberts et al., 2004). Ninth, women report feeling more attractive and desirable, as well as an increased interest in sex, around the time of ovulation (Roder, Brewer, & Fink, 2009). And tenth, a study of professional lap dancers working in gentlemen's clubs found that ovulating women received significantly higher tips than women in the non-ovulation phases of their cycle (see Figure 5.7) (Miller, Tybur, & Jordan, 2007). So we have ten pieces of circumstantial evidence pointing to the possibility that men can detect when women ovulate.

Another study lends circumstantial support to the woman-initiated contact hypothesis. Researchers looked at a sample of married women over a period of twenty-four months (Stanislaw & Rice, 1988). Ovulation was determined by measuring basal body temperature, which rises just prior to ovulation. Over the twenty-four months, women put an "X" on a chart on those days on which they experienced "sexual desire." Women's reported desire increased steadily as ovulation approached, peaked at or just after ovulation, and then decreased steadily as they approached the infertile period of menstruation. So the fact that ovulating women are touched more at singles bars may reflect their increased sexual desire, increased exposure of skin, and perhaps other sexual signals that researchers did not examine.

In summary, definitive studies on whether men can detect when women ovulate remain to be conducted. The available evidence is sufficient to suggest that there are *potentially* observable

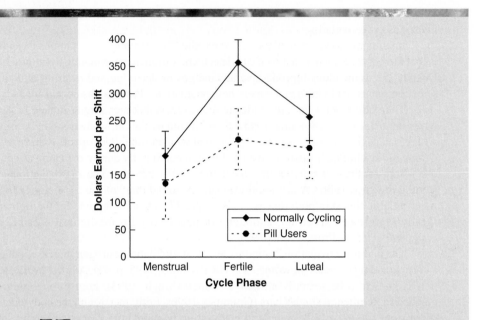

FIGURE *5.7* **Effects of ovulatory cycle phase (menstrual phase, fertile estrous phase, or luteal phase) on tip earnings per shift, for normally cycling women versus women using hormonal contraception (pill users).** Error bars represent 95 percent confidence intervals.

*Source:* Miller, G. F., Tybur, J. M., & Jordan, B. D. (2007). Ovulatory cycle effects on tip earnings by lap dancers: Economic evidence for human estrus? *Evolution and Human Behavior, 28,* 375–381. (Figure 2, p. 378). Reprinted with permission from Elsevier.

physical changes in a woman's skin and body when she ovulates—changes known to be sexually attractive to men.

## Solutions to the Problem of Paternity Uncertainty

Women are rare among primates in possessing the unusual adaptation of concealed or cryptic ovulation, although it may be less concealed than we think. Such relatively cryptic female ovulation obscures a woman's current reproductive status. Concealed ovulation dramatically changed the ground rules of human mating. Women became attractive to men not just during ovulation but throughout the ovulatory cycle. Cryptic ovulation created a special adaptive problem for men by decreasing the certainty of their paternity. Consider a primate male who prevents other males from mating with a female for the brief period during which she is in estrus. In contrast to human males, he can be fairly "confident" of his paternity. The period during which he must sequester and have sex with her is sharply constrained. Before and after her estrus, he can go about his other business without running the risk that his partner will become impregnated by another male.

Ancestral men did not have this luxury. Because mating is not the sole activity needed for humans to survive and reproduce, women could not be "guarded" around the clock. The more time a man spent guarding, the less time he had available for grappling with other adaptive problems. Ancestral men, therefore, were faced with a unique paternity problem not faced by other primate males: how to be certain of their paternity when ovulation was concealed.

Marriage potentially provided one solution (Alexander & Noonan, 1979; Strassman, 1981). Men who married would benefit reproductively relative to other men by substantially increasing their certainty of paternity. Repeated sexual contact throughout the ovulation cycle raised the odds that a woman would bear a given man's child. The social traditions of marriage function as a public joining of the couple, providing a clear signal about who is mated with whom, and thus potentially reducing conflict within male coalitions. Marriage also provides opportunities to learn intimately about one's mate's personality, making it difficult for her to hide signs of infidelity.

For an ancestral man to reap the reproductive benefits of marriage, he had to seek reasonable assurances that his wife would remain sexually faithful to him. Men who failed to recognize fidelity cues would have suffered in reproductive success because they lost the time and resources devoted to searching, courting, and competing. By failing to be sensitive to these cues, a man risked losing the benefits of the woman's parental investment in his children, which might instead be diverted to another man's children. Perhaps even more devastating in reproductive terms, failure to ensure fidelity meant that his own efforts would be channeled to another man's offspring.

Our forebears could have solved this uniquely male adaptive problem by seeking qualities in a potential mate that might increase the odds of securing their paternity. At least two preferences in a mate could solve the problem for males: (1) the desire for *premarital chastity* and (2) the quest for *postmarital sexual fidelity*. Before the use of modern contraceptives, chastity would likely have provided a clue to the future certainty of paternity. On the assumption that a woman's proclivities toward chaste behavior would be stable over time, her premarital chastity would signal her likely future fidelity. A man who didn't select a chaste mate may have risked becoming involved with a woman who would cuckold him.

Today it seems that men value virgin brides more than women value virgin grooms, at least in the United States according to a cross-generational mating study. But the value men place on virginity has declined over the past half-century, coinciding with the increasing availability of birth control (Buss et al., 2001). In the 1930s, men viewed chastity as close to indispensable, but in the past few decades, they have rated it desirable but not crucial. Among the eighteen characteristics rated in the study, chastity went from the tenth most valued in 1939 to the seventeenth most valued in the 1990s. Despite the decline in the value of chastity in the twentieth century and despite regional variations, a significant sex difference remains—men more than women emphasize chastity as being important in a potential long-term mate.

The trend for men to value chastity more than women holds up worldwide, but it varies tremendously among cultures. At one extreme, people in China, India, Indonesia, Iran, Taiwan, and the Palestinian Arab areas of Israel attach a high value to chastity in a potential mate. At the opposite extreme, people in Sweden, Norway, Finland, the Netherlands, Germany, and France believe that virginity is largely irrelevant or unimportant in a potential mate (Buss, 1989a) (see Figure 5.8).

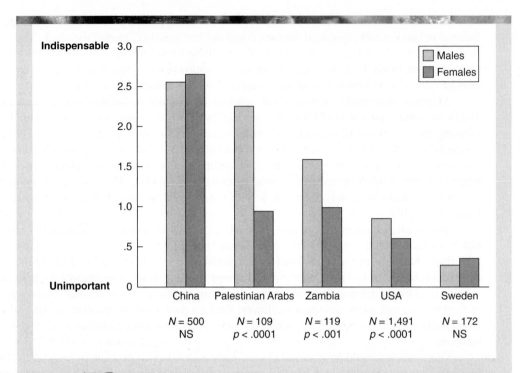

FIGURE 5.8 **Desire for Chastity, or No Previous Experience with Sexual Intercourse, in a Long-Term Mate.** Participants in thirty-seven cultures rated this variable, in the context of eighteen other variables, on how desirable it would be in a potential long-term mate or marriage partner using a four-point rating scale, ranging from 0 (irrelevant or unimportant) to 3 (indispensable).

$N$ = sample size.

$p$ values less than .05 indicate that sex difference is significant.

NS indicates that sex difference is not significant.

*Source:* Buss, D. M., & Schmitt, D. P. (1993). Sexual strategies theory: An evolutionary perspective on human mating. *Psychological Review, 100,* 204–232. Copyright © 1993 by the American Psychological Association. Adapted with permission.

In contrast to the worldwide consistency in the different preferences by sex for youth and physical attractiveness, only 62 percent of the cultures in the international study on choosing a mate placed a significantly different value by gender on chastity in a committed mateship. Where sex differences in the value of virginity are found, however, men invariably placed a greater value on it than did women. In no case did women value chastity more than men.

The cultural variability in the preference of each sex for chastity may be due to several factors: the prevailing incidence of premarital sex, the degree to which chastity can be demanded in a mate, the economic independence of women, or the reliability with which it can be evaluated. Chastity differs from other attributes, such as a woman's physical attractiveness, in that it is less directly observable. Even physical tests of female virginity are unreliable, whether from variations in the structure of the hymen, its rupture due to nonsexual causes, or its deliberate alteration (Dickemann, 1981).

Variation in the value that people place on chastity may be traceable in part to variability in the economic independence of women and in women's control of their own sexuality. In some cultures, such as Sweden, premarital sex is not discouraged and practically no one is a virgin at marriage (Posner, 1992). One reason may be that women in Sweden are far less economically reliant on men than in most other cultures. Marriage provides few benefits for Swedish women as compared with women in most other cultures (Posner, 1992). The Swedish social welfare system includes daycare for children, long paid maternity leaves, and many other material benefits. Swedish taxpayers effectively provide what husbands formerly provided, freeing women from their economic dependence on men. That independence lowers the cost to women of a free and active sex life before marriage, or as an alternative to marriage. Thus practically no Swedish women are virgins at marriage, and in fact the importance that Swedish men place on chastity has declined to a worldwide low of 0.25 on a 0-to-3 scale (Buss, 1989a).

From a man's reproductive perspective, a more important cue than virginity to paternity certainty is a reliable signal of future fidelity. If men cannot require that their mates be virgins, they can require of them sexual loyalty. A study of short- and long-term mating found that U.S. men view lack of sexual experience as desirable in a spouse (Buss & Schmitt, 1993). Furthermore, men see promiscuity as especially undesirable in a marriage partner, rating it −2.07 on a scale of −3 to +3. The actual amount of prior sexual activity in a potential mate, rather than virginity per se, would have provided an excellent guide for ancestral men to solve the problem of paternity uncertainty. Contemporary studies show that the best predictor of extramarital sex is premarital sexual permissiveness—people who have many sexual partners before marriage are more likely to be unfaithful than those who have few sexual partners before marriage (Thompson, 1983; Weiss & Slosnerick, 1981).

Modern men place a premium on fidelity. When U.S. men evaluated sixty-seven possible characteristics for their desirability in a committed mateship, faithfulness and sexual loyalty emerged as the most highly valued traits (Buss & Schmitt, 1993). Nearly all men gave these traits the highest rating possible, an average of +2.85 on a scale of −3 to +3. Cross-cultural tests remain to be conducted to see whether this is a universal male desire.

Men regard unfaithfulness as the least desirable characteristic in a wife, rating it a −2.93, reflecting the high value that men place on fidelity. Unfaithfulness proves to be more upsetting to men than any other pain a spouse could inflict on her mate—a finding for which there is excellent cross-cultural evidence (Betzig, 1989; Buss, 1989b; Daly & Wilson, 1988). Women also become extremely upset over an unfaithful mate, but several other factors, such as sexual aggressiveness, exceed infidelity in the grief they cause women.

In summary, we now have the outlines of some of the qualities that men desire in a long-term mate (but see Box 5.1 for a mystery of men's mating). In addition to the personality characteristics of kindness, dependability, and compatibility, men place a premium on youth and physical attractiveness. Standards of attractiveness correlate highly with female fertility. In essence, men's desire for physical attractiveness solves the problem of seeking women who are reproductively capable. Reproductive capability, however, is not enough. Internal female fertilization posed a second adaptive problem for men, who value sexual fidelity and perhaps cues to controllability (Brown & Lewis, 2004) in a long-term mate as solutions to the problem of paternity uncertainty.

BOX *5.1*

# Homosexual Orientation: An Evolutionary Puzzle

Heterosexual orientation is a prime example of a psychological adaptation—roughly 96 to 98 percent of men and 98 to 99 percent of women have a primary orientation toward heterosexuality. Any orientation that lowered the likelihood of successful reproduction would be ruthlessly selected against. The persistence of a small percentage of primarily or exclusively lesbian women and homosexual men poses a genuine evolutionary puzzle. Empirical studies show that sexual orientation has a small to moderate heritable component (Bailey et al., 1999) and that homosexual men have lower rates of reproduction than heterosexuals (Bobrow & Bailey, 2001; McKnight, 1997; Muscarella, 2000).

One evolutionary explanation of male homosexuality was the *kin altruism theory* (Wilson, 1975). According to this theory, genes for homosexual orientation could have evolved if they led homosexuals to invest heavily enough in their genetic relatives to offset the costs of forgoing direct reproduction. The kin altruism theory, however, received no empirical support from an American study of gay and heterosexual men. Gay men did not differ from heterosexual men in their likelihood of funneling resources toward kin (Bobrow & Bailey, 2001; Rahman & Hull, 2005). In fact, gay men reported being more estranged from their genetic relatives, contrary to the kin altruism theory.

In contrast, several studies in Samoa did find greater avuncular tendencies among male homosexuals (*fa'afafine*)—specifically, compared to their heterosexual counterparts, *fa'afafine* did invest more in nieces and nephews (Vasey & VanderLaan, 2010). They reported babysitting more for them, buying them toys, and investing money in their education. So the kin altruism theory may still be in the running as an explanation for male homosexuality, awaiting more extensive cross-cultural research.

A second evolutionary theory is called the *female fertility hypothesis*, which suggests that genes for male homosexuality can evolve if they produce an increased reproductive rate in the female relatives of male homosexuals—a reproductive advantage that has more than compensates for the lower rates of reproduction of gay males (Iemmola & Campiero Ciani, 2009). The key tests of the female fertility hypothesis involve examining the reproductive rates of female kin of homosexuals compared to the female kin of heterosexuals. Evidence has steadily been accumulating that, although male homosexuals produce about a fifth of the number of offspring as heterosexual men, the maternal female relatives of gay males (e.g., their mothers, maternal aunts) indeed produce significantly more offspring than the maternal female relatives of heterosexual men (Iemmola & Campiero Ciana, 2009). These results have been found by other researchers (e.g., Rahman et al., 2008). If future research continues to confirm the female fertility hypothesis, it would resolve (at least partially) the Darwinian paradox of male homosexuality—that genes transmitted through the maternal line simultaneously increase the likelihood of producing homosexual males while increasing the reproductive rates of females.

Another theory proposes that we should focus on the functions of homoerotic behavior per se, rather than sexual orientation (Muscarella, 2000). Evolutionary psychologist Frank Muscarella proposes a specific function for homoerotic behavior: alliance formation. According to this theory, homoerotic behavior by young men with older men provided a strategy for gaining allies, boosting themselves up the status hierarchy, and ultimately gaining greater sexual access to women. The *alliance formation theory* has several virtues, such as focusing on the functions of homosexual behavior, and an emphasis on cross-species comparative framework (same-sex sexual contact has also been documented in other primate species). Nonetheless, the theory encounters several empirical difficulties. Although it might explain practices in a minority of cultures, such as ancient Greece or certain New Guinean tribes, there is no evidence that the majority of young men in most cultures use homoerotic behavior as a strategy of alliance formation. Indeed, nonsexual same-sex alliances appear to be the norm and are commonly accomplished without sexual activity. Furthermore, there is no evidence that men who engage in homoerotic behavior succeed more than those who do not in forming alliances or ascending in status.

In sum, of the three evolutionary theories of homosexuality thus far advanced, the kin altruism theory has received mixed empirical support while the female fertility hypothesis has accrued the strongest empirical support. More extensive cross-cultural tests of these theories are needed, although scientists are now making good progress in explaining what has long been considered an evolutionary paradox.

# ■ CONTEXT EFFECTS ON MEN'S MATING BEHAVIOR

In this section, we look at the effects of context on men's mating behavior. First, we consider the fact that desires rarely show a one-to-one correspondence with actual mating behavior. Men who are high in "mate value" should have better odds of getting what they want in a mate. Second, there is a notable discrepancy between modern environments and the ancestral environments in which we evolved. Over the course of evolutionary history, humans most likely evolved in small groups containing perhaps fifty to two hundred individuals (Dunbar, 1993). In these small groups, a particular man would have encountered at most a few dozen attractive women. In modern environments, humans are bombarded with literally thousands of images of attractive models from billboards, magazines, television, Internet, and movies. This section considers the possible impact of this modern environment on human mating mechanisms.

## Men in Positions of Power

Although most men place a premium on youth and beauty in a mate, it is clear that not all men are successful in achieving their desires. Men lacking the status and resources that women want are predicted to have the most difficult time attracting such women and may have to settle for less than their ideal. Evidence for this possibility comes from men who have historically been in a position to get exactly what they prefer, such as kings and other men of unusually high status. In the 1700s and 1800s, for example, wealthier men from the Krummerhörn population of Germany married younger brides than did men lacking wealth (Voland & Engel, 1990). Similarly, high-status men from the Norwegian farmers, of 1700s to 1900s, to the Kipsigis in contemporary Kenya consistently married younger brides than did their lower-status counterparts (Borgerhoff Mulder, 1988; Røskaft, Wara, & Viken, 1992).

Kings and despots routinely stocked their harems with young, attractive, nubile women and had sex with them frequently (Betzig, 1992). The Moroccan emperor Moulay Ismail the Bloodthirsty, for example, acknowledged siring 888 children. His harem included 500 women. But when a woman reached the age of thirty, she was banished from the emperor's harem, sent to a lower-level leader's harem, and replaced by a younger woman. Roman, Babylonian, Egyptian, Incan, Indian, and Chinese emperors all shared the tastes of Emperor Ismail and enjoined their trustees to scour the land for as many young pretty women as could be found.

Marriage patterns in the United States today confirm the fact that men with resources are most able to actualize their preferences. High-status older males, such as rock stars Rod Stewart

*Men with status and resources—qualities that women desire in a long-term mate—are better able than men without status and resources to translate their preferences for young attractive women into actual mating behaviors.*

and Mick Jagger and movie stars Warren Beatty and Jack Nicholson, frequently select women two or three decades younger. Several sociological studies have examined the impact of a man's occupational status on the physical attractiveness of the woman he marries (Elder, 1969; Taylor & Glenn, 1976; Udry & Eckland, 1984). Men high in occupational status are able to marry women who are considerably more physically attractive than can men low in occupational status. Indeed, a man's occupational status seems to be the best predictor of the attractiveness of the woman he marries.

Men who enjoy high status and income are apparently aware of their ability to attract more desirable women. In a study of a computer dating service involving 1,048 German men and 1,590 German women, ethologist Karl Grammer found that as men's income goes up, they seek younger partners (Grammer, 1992). Men earning more than 10,000 DM (deutsche marks), for example, advertised for mates who were between five and fifteen years younger, whereas men earning less than 1,000 DM advertised for mates who were between zero and five years younger. Each increment in income is accompanied by a decrease in the age of the woman sought.

## Contrast Effects from Viewing Attractive Models

Advertisers exploit the universal appeal of beautiful, youthful women. Madison Avenue is sometimes charged with advancing a single arbitrary standard of beauty that everyone else must live up to. This accusation is at least partially false. The standards of beauty, as we have seen, are not arbitrary but rather embody reliable cues to fertility and reproductive value. Advertisers that more closely exploit existing mate preferences are almost sure to be more successful than those that do not. Advertisers perch a clear-skinned, regular-featured young woman on the hood of the latest car because the image exploits men's evolved psychological mechanisms and therefore sells cars.

The media images we are bombarded with daily, however, have a potentially pernicious consequence. In one study, after groups of men looked at photographs of either highly attractive women or women of average attractiveness, they were asked to evaluate their commitment to their current romantic partners (Kenrick et al., 1994). The men who had viewed pictures of attractive women thereafter judged their actual partners to be less attractive than did the men who had viewed pictures of women who were average in attractiveness. They also rated themselves as less committed to, less satisfied with, less serious about, and less close to their actual partners. Parallel results were obtained in another study in which men viewed physically attractive nude centerfolds: They rated themselves as less attracted to their partners (Kenrick, Gutierres, & Goldberg, 1989). A similar contrast effect has been documented in an experiment in which participants watched a mock videotaped interview with an opposite-sex stranger (Mishra, Clark, & Daly, 2007). Men who viewed videos of women who smiled and acted warmly, key cues to receptivity, subsequently rated their own partners as less attractive than did men watching the same women who did not smile or act warmly. No such effect was found for women viewing analogous videos of men. The authors conclude that men shift the allocation of their mating effort, not just in response to a woman's physical attractiveness, but also in response to cues to female receptivity.

The reasons for these changes are found in the unrealistic nature of the images and in the psychological mechanisms of men. The few attractive women selected for advertisements are chosen from thousands. *Playboy,* for example, is reputed to shoot roughly 6,000 pictures for each monthly magazine. From these thousands of pictures, a few are selected for publication. So what men see are the most attractive women in the most attractive pose in the most attractive airbrushed photograph. It is doubtful that in ancestral environments, men would have seen even a dozen women considered attractive by today's measure. The presence of a relative abundance of attractive women, however, might reasonably induce a man to consider switching mates, and hence he would decrease his commitment to his existing mate.

Consider modern times. We carry with us the same evaluative mechanisms that evolved in ancient times. Now, however, these mechanisms are artificially activated by the dozens of attractive women we witness daily in our advertisement-saturated culture, in magazines, on billboards, on TV, and in movies. These images do not represent real women in our actual social environment. Rather, these images exploit mechanisms designed for a different environment.

As a consequence of viewing such images men may become dissatisfied with, and less committed to, their mates. The potential damage inflicted by these images affects women as well because they create a spiraling and unhealthy competition with other women. Women find themselves competing with other women to embody the images they see daily—images they believe are desired by men. The unprecedented rates of eating disorders and cosmetic surgery may stem in part from these media images. The images work by exploiting men's existing evolved standards of beauty and women's competitive mating mechanisms on an unprecedented scale.

## Testosterone and Men's Mating Strategies

The hormone testosterone (T) plays a key role in male "mating effort," the time and energy devoted to pursuing mates and besting same-sex competitors (Ellison, 2001). Higher T levels facilitate male pursuit of females, and T levels increase after interacting with an attractive woman (Roney, Mahler, & Maestripieri, 2003). Maintaining high levels of T, though, can be costly for men. T can compromise immune functioning, and because it is linked with mating effort, it may interfere with parenting effort (it's difficult for a man to be a good parent if he's always chasing other women). Consequently, evolutionists have hypothesized that T levels should drop after a man succeeds in attracting a long-term mate, and studies have found precisely that effect (Burnham et al., 2003; Gray et al., 2004). One study found that men in committed relationships had 21 percent lower T levels than unpaired men (see Figure 5.9). Married men who had children had even lower levels of T.

There could be at least two different reasons for the link between T and relationship status. One is that T levels drop *after* becoming involved in a committed relationship. Alternatively, perhaps men with low T levels are more likely to get into committed relationships, whereas high T men prefer to remain free to pursue short-term mating. What is the evidence? First, men in the later stages of a relationship have lower T levels than men in the early stages of a relationship (Gray et al., 2004). Second, a longitudinal study found that divorced men who remarry experience a subsequent drop in T levels (Mazur & Michalek, 1998). These findings suggest that T levels drop after forming a committed relationship. Circumstantial evidence for this comes from

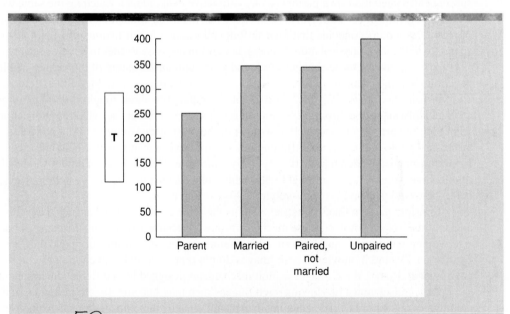

FIGURE 5.9 **Relationship between Testosterone (T) and Relationship Status.**
Men in committed relationships have lower T levels than men not in relationships. Men with children have especially low T levels.

*Source:* Adapted and modified from Burnham et al. (2003). Men in committed, romantic relationships have lower testosterone levels. *Hormones and Behavior, 44,* 120 (Figure 1).

a study that discovered that professional tennis players perform substantially worse during the year after they get married. The authors suggest that lowered levels of T as a consequence of marriage likely account for men's lowered levels of competitive prowess (Farrelly & Nettle, 2007).

Men in committed relationships, however, do not always entirely refrain from additional mating attempts. According to the mating effort hypothesis, men in relationships who pursue additional matings should have higher T levels than men who remain monogamous. That is precisely what McIntyre and colleagues discovered (McIntyre et al., 2006). They asked men in relationships: "Would you ever consider having an 'affair' (sex with someone else) behind the back of your relationship partner?" Men who said "yes" had higher T levels than men who said "no." These findings support the mating effort hypothesis. T is linked with allocating time and energy to seeking and competing for mates; T levels drop after the successful formation of a relationship and the production of children in order to facilitate pair-bonding and parental effort, but only if the man is not pursuing extra-pair sex.

Exposure to potential mates is known to trigger rapid rises in T levels in many nonhuman species, and evidence is cumulating that similar effects occur in humans. One study found that merely having a brief conversation with a young woman increased men's T levels (Roney, Simmons, & Lukaszewski, 2010). Field experiments of skateboarders found that the mere presence of an attractive woman produced an increase in risk taking by young men (including more crashes), as well as elevated T levels (Ronay & von Hippel, 2010).

*The mere presence of an attractive woman causes men to increase their level of risk-taking (skateboarding study) as well as their level of testosterone—a key hormone involved in mating effort.*

## The Necessities and Luxuries of Mate Preferences

Norman Li and colleagues have devised an important method—the budget allocation method—to determine which mate qualities are "necessities" and which are "luxuries." Imagine that you are financially poor and thus have a limited budget (Li et al., 2002). You might spend most of your money on the necessities of life, such as food. As your budget increases, however, most people would spend more on luxuries—TVs, iPods, expensive cars, or designer clothes. Li applied these economic concepts to the domain of mate preferences. What do people prefer when they have a low versus a high budget of "mating dollars," a concept that corresponds to "mate value"?

To find out, Li and colleagues gave participants varying budgets—low, medium, and high. They discovered that when given a *low* budget and asked to allocate their mating dollars across a number of mate attributes, men allocated a relatively large proportion of their budget to physical attractiveness and women allocated a relatively large proportion of their budget to resources—precisely in line with the sex differences found in all the other studies of mate preferences. As the budget increased, however, men and women spent increasing proportions of their mating dollars on "luxuries" such as kindness, creativity, and liveliness (although kindness and intelligence came close to being necessities).

The varying budgets—low, medium, and high—are likely to show some parallels to individual differences in "mate value." Those low in mate value have less choice, so they want to ensure adequate levels on the necessities of mating—for men, some minimum level of attractiveness; for women, some minimum level of resources and status. As mate value increases, people can afford to be choosier on a wider array of characteristics.

## ■ EFFECT OF MEN'S PREFERENCES ON ACTUAL MATING BEHAVIOR

In this section we examine the impact of men's long-term mate preferences on behavior. First, we explore a study of personal ads to see whether men respond more to the ads of women who indicate qualities that embody men's desires. Second, we look at age preferences and actual mating decisions. Finally, we look at the effects of men's mate preferences on women's mating strategies and examine whether women who are trying to attract men strive to embody the preferences that men express.

### Men's Responses to Women's Personal Ads

If men act on their preferences for women who are young and physically attractive, then they should respond more to women who display these qualities. In a natural experiment, two psychologists examined the responses of men to personal ads placed in two newspapers, one in the Midwest and the other on the West Coast (Baize & Schroeder, 1995). The mean age of the sample respondents was thirty-seven, with a range from twenty-six to fifty-eight.

When responses to the ads placed by men and women were compared, several striking differences emerged. First, men tended to respond to women's ads more than women responded to men's ads. Men tended to receive only 68 percent as many letters as women did. Second, younger women received more responses from men than did older women. Third, although mentioning *physical attractiveness* produced more responses from both sexes, it produced significantly more responses for women than for men. In sum, men's responses to women's personal ads provide a natural source of evidence suggesting that men act on their preferences.

## Marital Decisions and Reproductive Outcomes

Actual marriage decisions confirm the preference of men for women who are increasingly younger than they are as the men age. American grooms exceed their brides in age by roughly three years at first marriage, five years at second marriage, and eight years at third marriage (Guttentag & Secord, 1983). Men's preferences for younger women also translate into actual marriage decisions worldwide. In Sweden during the 1800s, for example, church documents reveal that men who remarried following a divorce had new brides 10.6 years younger on average (Fieder & Huber, 2007; Low, 1991). In all countries around the world, where information is available on the ages of brides and grooms, men on average exceed their brides in age, as documented in Chapter 4 (Buss, 1989a).

The age difference between spouses as a function of the age of the man is shown dramatically in Figure 5.10. This figure shows the average age difference between brides and grooms as men get increasingly older for a sample drawn from the Island of Poro over a twenty-five-year

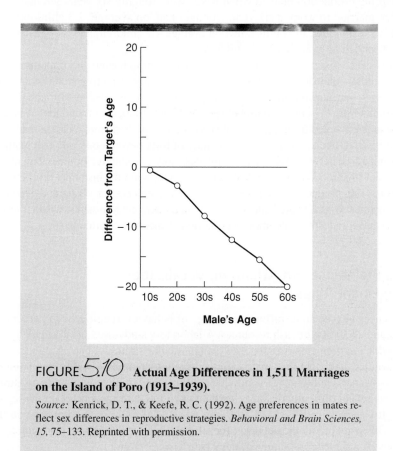

FIGURE 5.10 **Actual Age Differences in 1,511 Marriages on the Island of Poro (1913–1939).**

*Source:* Kenrick, D. T., & Keefe, R. C. (1992). Age preferences in mates reflect sex differences in reproductive strategies. *Behavioral and Brain Sciences, 15,* 75–133. Reprinted with permission.

period (Kenrick & Keefe, 1992). Men in their twenties tended to marry women just a year or two younger. Men in their thirties tended to marry women three to four years younger than themselves. Men who married in their forties, however, married women who were thirteen or fourteen years younger. These data are representative of the general trend for men to marry women who are increasingly younger as they grow older (Kenrick & Keefe, 1992). Nearly identical findings have been discovered in a modern sample from Brazil, in an analysis of 3,000 newspaper announcements of forthcoming marriages (Otta et al., 1999).

The cross-cultural data confirm the age differences between brides and grooms in actual marital decisions. The age difference ranges from about two years in Poland to roughly five years in Greece. Averaged across all countries for which we have good demographic data, grooms are three years older than their brides, roughly the same difference that is expressly desired by men worldwide (Buss, 1989a). In polygynous cultures the age difference is even larger. Among the Tiwi of Northern Australia, high-status men often have wives who are two decades younger (Hart & Pilling, 1960).

Men who marry younger women also tend to have greater reproductive output. A study of more than 10,000 post-reproductive Swedish men and women who had not changed marital partners examined offspring production as a function of parental age difference (Fieder & Huber, 2007). Offspring production peaked when wives were roughly six years younger than their husbands. Men married to women six years younger had, on average, 2.3 children; men married to women six years older, in contrast, had on average 1.7 children; and men married to women nine years older had an average of 1.2 children.

There is also evidence that physically attractive women, prior to the advent of modern birth control, had more children than less attractive women. Physically attractive Ache women of Paraguay had higher age-controlled fertility rates than less attractive women (Hill & Hurtado, 1996). A study of 1,244 women from Wisconsin, born between 1937 and 1940, also found that attractive and very attractive women, as rated from high school yearbook photos, had more children than their less attractive counterparts (Jokela, 2009). A smaller study of forty-seven modern Polish women, however, failed to find a link between female attractiveness and reproductive output (Pawlowski et al., 2008). It is possible that modern birth control technology may sever the historical link between female beauty and offspring production. Men's evolved mate preferences for young and attractive women, of course, continue to be activated and acted upon in modern environments, whether or not they currently lead to the reproductive outcomes that occurred in ancestral environments.

## Effect of Men's Preferences on Attention, Vocalization, Tips, and Engagement Rings

Men's mate preferences also seem to influence a range of behavior, ranging from perceptual attention to their actual allocation of cash resources. A laboratory study used what is called a visual cuing task in which participants first focused on a particular stimulus such as an attractive or average man or woman, and were then instructed to shift their attention to a different point on the computer screen (Maner, Gailliot, & DeWall, 2007). When the initial stimulus was an attractive woman, men had greater difficulty disengaging their attention to the new point on the screen (see Figure 5.11). It was as if men's visual attention got stuck (attentional adhesion) on the attractive woman. This perceptual bias occurred for all men, but was especially pronounced in men who tend to pursue a short-term mating strategy (see Chapter 6).

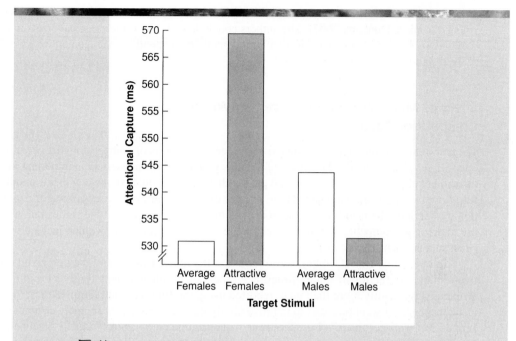

FIGURE 5.11  Initial attention was captured by images of highly attractive women, such that observers were less efficient at disengaging their attention from those images, relative to images of male targets and average-looking female targets.

*Source:* Maner, J. K., Gailliot, M. T., & DeWall, N. (2007). Adaptive attentional attunement: Evidence for mating-related perceptual bias. *Evolution and Human Behaviour, 28,* 2836 (Figure 1, p. 32). Reprinted with permission from Elsevier.

Recall that women prefer men with more masculine vocal qualities—those with lower-pitched voices. In a clever study, researchers had men make phone calls to women they believed to be real, after being shown photographs of them that were prerated as varying in physical attractiveness (Hughes, Farley, & Rhodes, 2010). Men who believed that they were speaking with an attractive woman lowered their voice pitch below their normal level, in contrast to those who believed they were speaking with an unattractive woman. When these vocal episodes were played to independent raters, the raters judged the voices to be significantly more pleasant. Furthermore, men's skin conductance increased significantly more when conversing with the attractive woman than the less attractive woman, suggesting that they were more physiologically aroused, or nervous with "mating anxiety."

Men's preferences for attractive women are also expressed in the behavioral metric of hard cash expenditures. An ecologically valid study of 374 restaurant waitresses calculated the average tips they received, recorded as a percentage of the bill (Lynn, 2009). Waitresses who were younger and had larger breasts, blond hair, and a smaller body size received more generous tips than did women lacking these attributes. And a study of 127 men who used their own funds to purchase engagement rings for the purpose of surprise proposals of marriage found that men proposing to younger women spent significantly more money if their hoped-for bride-to-be was young (Cronk & Dunham, 2007). The authors conclude that, like bride-price payments in other societies such as the Kipsigis of Kenya, the amounts men spend on engagement rings reflect evolved standards of female mate quality.

## Effect of Men's Mate Preferences on Women's Competition Tactics

The preferences of one sex are predicted to influence the forms of competition that occur in the opposite sex (Buss, 1994b). Specifically, if men's preferences have exerted an important impact on mating behavior over time, we would predict that women would compete with one another to fulfill or embody what men want. Three sources of data are relevant to examining this prediction: research on the tactics that women use to attract men, research on the tactics that women use to derogate competitors, and research on the self-descriptions that women include in their personal ads when seeking men.

In one study, Buss (1988c) examined the self-reported usage and the perceived effectiveness of 101 tactics of mate attraction. Appearance enhancement figured prominently. Women, significantly more than men, reported using the following attraction tactics: "I wore facial makeup," "I went on a diet to improve my figure," "I learned how to apply cosmetics," "I kept myself well-groomed," "I used makeup that accentuated my looks," and "I got a new and interesting hair style." The ratings of perceived effectiveness matched the self-reported performance: All acts of appearance enhancement were judged to be more effective for women in attracting men than vice versa.

William Tooke and Lori Camire (1991) looked at the usage and effectiveness of tactics of intersexual deception, or the ways in which men deceive women and women deceive men in the mating arena. They asked male and female undergraduates to report on their performances and rate the effectiveness of various tactics of deceiving the opposite sex. Women, more than men, used tactics of deception involving their physical appearance: "I sucked in my stomach when around members of the opposite sex," "I wore a hairpiece around members of the opposite sex," "I wore colored contact lenses to make my eyes appear to be a different color," "I dyed my hair," "I wore false fingernails," "I wore dark clothing to appear thinner than I really was," and "I wore padded clothing." Women's use of deceptive appearance enhancement was judged to be significantly more effective in attracting mates than men's use of such tactics. Another study found that as women get older, they tend to withhold information about their age when they place personal advertisements for mates (Pawlowski & Dunbar, 1999b). In sum, when it comes to attracting the opposite sex, women's behavior appears to be highly responsive to the preferences expressed by men.

Women also appear to be sensitive to the mate preferences of men in their interactions involving rivals (Buss & Dedden, 1990). One tactic involved derogating a rival's physical appearance using acts such as "made fun of his/her appearance," "told others that the rival was fat and ugly," and "made fun of the size and shape of the rival's body." Derogating a rival's physical appearance was judged to be more effective when women used it than when men used it. Interestingly, Maryanne Fisher found that women in the high estrogen (fertile) phase of their cycle are more likely than women in the low estrogen phase to derogate a rival's physical appearance (Fisher, 2004). She concludes: "If women compete intrasexually for 'good' mates via attractiveness, it would be advantageous to have heightened levels of competition when it matters most—during times critical for reproduction" (Fisher, 2004, p. S285).

An even larger sex difference pertained to derogation of the rival's sexual fidelity. One derogation tactic, "calling competitor promiscuous," violates men's desire for a faithful wife with acts such as "called rival a tramp," "told others that the rival had slept around a lot," and "told others that the rival was loose, and would sleep with just about anybody." Calling a competitor promiscuous was judged to be more effective for women than for men. We can conclude that women's derogation tactics are sensitive to men's long-term mate preferences, especially on the dimensions of physical appearance and desire for fidelity.

The effects of the premium men place on physical appearance may lead to negative or maladaptive outcomes for women—eating disorders. According to the *sexual competition hypothesis*, eating disorders such as anorexia (extreme thinness) and bulimia (binge eating, followed by purging through vomiting or fasting) are maladaptive by-products of a mate competition strategy of pursuing thinness (Abed, 1998). U.S. women who are engaged in especially intense intrasexual competition for mates are more prone than other women to be dissatisfied with their bodies and experience a high drive for thinness, which in turn contributes to the eating disorders of anorexia and bulimia (Faer et al., 2005). The authors argue that the combination of (1) the importance men place on physical appearance in mates, (2) media images depicting thinness in models, and (3) the high levels of health in the United States cause a kind of runaway intrasexual competition to appear youthful, with thinness being a key cue to youth (see Salmon et al., 2008).

In summary, many sources of evidence support the notion that men's preferences affect actual behavior in the mating arena. First, men respond more to personal ads advertising qualities that fulfill men's expressed preferences, such as a desire for women who are physically attractive and young. Second, men actually marry younger women, an age difference that increases with each successive marriage. And third, women's mate attraction tactics and derogation of rival tactics map closely onto the dimensions that men prefer in a long-term mate. From all this empirical evidence, we can conclude that men's mate preferences affect not only their own mating behavior, but also the mating behavior of women in their mate competition tactics.

## ■ SUMMARY

There were many potential benefits to ancestral men who married. They would have increased their chances of attracting a mate, especially a more desirable mate. By marrying, men would have increased their certainty in paternity because they gained continuous or exclusive or predominant sexual access to the woman. In the currency of fitness, men also would have benefited through the increased survival and reproductive success of their children, accrued through paternal protection and investment.

Two adaptive problems loom large in men's long-term mate selection decisions. The first is identifying women of high fertility or reproductive value—women capable of successfully bearing children. A large body of evidence suggests that men have evolved standards of attractiveness that embody cues to a woman's reproductive capacity. Signals of youth and health are central among these cues—clear skin, full lips, small lower jaw, symmetrical features, white teeth, absence of sores and lesions, facial femininity, facial symmetry, facial averageness, and a small ratio of waist to hips. Standards of beauty linked to youth, health, and fertility are consistent across cultures. Preferences for amount of body fat and WHR vary predictably across cultures depending on relative food scarcity as well as the actual WHR distributions in the local culture.

The second large adaptive problem is the problem of paternity uncertainty. Over human evolutionary history, men who were indifferent to this adaptive problem risked raising another man's children, which would have been costly in the currency of reproductive success. Men in many countries value virginity in potential brides, but this is not universal. A more likely candidate for a universal solution is to place a premium on cues to fidelity—the likelihood that the woman will have intercourse exclusively with him.

Male homosexual orientation has been called an evolutionary paradox because homosexuality is known to be linked to dramatically reduced reproductive success. Of the leading evolutionary theories, the kin altruism hypothesis has received mixed empirical support, whereas the female fertility hypothesis has received the strongest empirical support.

Many contexts affect men's long-term mating strategies. First, men who have what most women want, such as power, status, and resources, are most able to successfully attract women that most men prefer. Second, viewing attractive images of other women appears to lower men's commitment to their regular partner. Third, getting into a committed mating relationship causes a reduction in T levels in men, but only if they are monogamously oriented and do not desire extra-pair sex. Fourth, interacting with attractive women, and even their mere presence, increases men's T levels as well as their behavioral risk taking. Fifth, men's mate preferences shift as a function of their "mating budget." On limited mating budgets, men place exceptional importance on the "necessities" such as an adequate level of physical attractiveness. After these necessities are met, men pay more attention to "luxuries" such as creativity and personality traits.

Several sources of behavioral data confirm the hypothesis that men's mate preferences affect actual mating behavior. First, men who respond to personal ads show higher response rates to women who claim to be young and physically attractive. Second, men worldwide actually marry women who are younger by roughly three years; men who divorce and remarry tend to marry women who are even younger, with a five-year difference at second marriage and an eight-year difference at third marriage. Third, men married to women younger than they are have higher reproductive success. Fourth, men visually attend to attractive women more than less attractive women, and have greater difficulty disengaging that attention when instructed to do so. Fifth, men interacting with attractive women lower their vocal pitch into a more masculine range that appeals to women. Sixth, attractive waitresses, particularly those who are young, have larger breasts and blonde hair, receive more tips from men. Seventh, men spend more money on engagement rings for younger than on older brides-to-be. Eighth, women devote much more effort than do men to enhancing their physical appearance in the context of mate attraction, including wearing makeup, dieting, and using cosmetic surgery, which suggests that women are responding to the preferences that men express. And ninth, women tend to derogate their rivals by putting down their physical appearance and calling them promiscuous or "slutty"—tactics that are effective in rendering rivals less attractive to men because they violate the preferences that men hold for a long-term mate.

# ■ SUGGESTED READINGS

Bryant, G. A., & Haselton, M. G. (2009). Vocal cues of ovulation in human females. *Biology Letters, 5,* 12–15.

Cornelissen, P. L., Hancock, P. J. B., Kiviniemi, V., George, H. R., & Tovee, V. (2009). Patterns of eye movements when male and female observers judge female attractiveness, body fat, and waist-to-hip ratio. *Evolution and Human Behavior, 30,* 417–428.

Cronk, L., & Dunham, B. (2007). Amounts spent on engagement rings reflect aspects of male and female mate quality. *Human Nature, 18,* 329–333.

Dixon, B. J., Grimshaw, G. M., Linklater, W. L., & Dixon, A. F. (2010). Eye tracking of men's preferences for waist-to-hip ratio and breast size of women. *Archives of Sexual Behavior,* DOI 10.1007/s10508-009-9523-5.

Li, N. P., Bailey, J. M., Kenrick, D. T., & Linsemeier, J. A. W. (2002). The necessities and luxuries of mate preferences: Testing the tradeoffs. *Journal of Personality and Social Psychology, 82,* 947–955.

Maner, J. K., Gailliot, M. T., & DeWall, N. (2007). Adaptive attentional attunement: Evidence for mating-related perceptual bias. *Evolution and Human Behavior, 28,* 28–36.

Platek, S. M., & Singh, D. (2010). Optimal waist-to-hip ratios in women active neural reward centers in men. *PLoS ONE, 5,* 1–5.

Ronay, R., & von Hippel, W. (2010). The presence of an attractive woman elevates testosterone and physical risk taking in young men. *Social Psychological and Personality Science, 1,* 57–64.

Roney, J. R., Simmons, Z. L., & Lukaszewski, A. W. (2010). Androgen receptor genes sequence and basal cortisol concentrations predict men's hormonal responses to potential mates. *Proceedings of the Royal Society, B, 277,* 57–63.

Salmon, C., Crawford, C., Dane, L., & Zuberbier, O. (2008). Ancestral mechanisms in modern environments: Impact of competition and stressors on body image and dieting behavior. *Human Nature, 19,* 103–117.

Sugiyama, L. (2005). Physical attractiveness in adaptationist perspective. In D. M. Buss (Ed.), *The handbook of evolutionary psychology* (pp. 292–342). New York: Wiley.

Symons, D. (1979). *The evolution of human sexuality.* New York: Oxford University Press.

Tooke, W., & Camire, L. (1991). Patterns of deception in intersexual and intrasexual mating strategies. *Ethology and Sociobiology, 12,* 345–364.

Vasey, P. L., & VanderLaan, D. P. (2010). Avuncular tendencies and the evolution of male androphilia in *Fa'afafine. Archives of Sexual Behavior, 39,* 821–830.

Williams, G. C. (1975). *Sex and evolution.* Princeton, NJ: Princeton University Press.

# CHAPTER 6

# SHORT-TERM SEXUAL STRATEGIES

*[Women] not rarely run away with a favoured lover . . . . We thus see that . . . the women are not in quite so abject a state in relation to marriage as has often been supposed. They can tempt the men they prefer, and sometimes can reject those whom they dislike, either before or after marriage.*

—Charles Darwin, 1871

*The biological irony of the double standard is that males could not have been selected for promiscuity if historically females had always denied them opportunity for expression of the trait.*

—Robert Smith, 1984

𝒪magine an attractive person of the opposite sex walking up to you on a college campus and saying "Hi, I've been noticing you around town lately, and I find you very attractive. Would you have sex with me?" How would you respond? If you are like 100 percent of the women in one study, you would give an emphatic no. You would be offended, insulted, or just plain puzzled by the request. But if you are like the men in that study, the odds are good that you would say yes—as did 75 percent of those men (Clarke & Hatfield, 1989). As a man, you would most likely be flattered by the request. A subsequent study found that men report more willingness to accept sexual offers from attractive than unattractive women, whereas women report more willingness to accept sexual offers from men who are high in socioeconomic status and high in attractiveness, if the context involves some level of emotional intimacy rather than just pure sex (Greitemeyer, 2005). A third of German, Italian, and U.S. participants also found that attractiveness mattered for both sexes (Schützwohl et al., 2009). For men, 65 percent indicated some level of likelihood of having sex if the woman was slightly unattractive; 79 percent if she was moderately attractive; and 82 percent if she was extremely attractive. For women, 5 percent indicated some level of likelihood of the man was slightly unattractive; 13 percent if he was moderately attractive; and 24 percent if he was extremely attractive. The idea that men and women react differently when it comes to casual sex may not be surprising. Theories in evolutionary psychology provide a principled basis for predicting this difference and for explaining its magnitude.

## ■ THEORIES OF MEN'S SHORT-TERM MATING

 We begin by considering theories of short-term mating. First, we will look at the adaptive logic of men's short-term mating and why it would loom larger in men's than in women's psychological repertoires. Second, we examine the potential costs that men might incur from short-term mating. And third, we explore the specific adaptive problems that men must solve if they are to successfully pursue short-term mating.

### Adaptive Benefits for Men of Short-Term Mating

Trivers's (1972) theory of parental investment and sexual selection, described in Chapter 4, provides a powerful basis for expecting sex differences in the pursuit of short-term mating: Men, more than women, are predicted to have evolved a greater desire for casual sex. The same act of sex that causes a woman to invest nine months of internal gestation obligates the man to practically no investment. Over a one-year period, an ancestral man who managed to have short-term sexual encounters with dozens of fertile women would have caused many pregnancies. An ancestral woman who had sex with dozens of men in the course of the same year could produce only a single child (unless she bore twins or triplets). See Box 6.1 for a discussion of function and beneficial effects of short-term mating.

 The reproductive benefits for men who successfully pursued a short-term mating strategy would have been direct: an increase in the number of offspring produced. A married man with two children, for example, could increase his reproductive success by a full 50 percent by one short-term copulation that resulted in conception and birth. This benefit assumes, of course, that the child produced by such a brief union would have survived, which would have depended in ancestral times on a woman's ability to secure resources through other means (e.g., by herself, through kin, or through other men). Historically, men appear to have achieved increases in reproductive success mainly through increases in the number of sexual partners, not through increases in the number of children per partner (Betzig, 1986; Dawkins, 1986).

### Potential Costs of Short-Term Mating for Men

Short-term sexual strategies, however, carry potential costs for men. Over evolutionary time, men risked (1) contracting sexually transmitted diseases, a risk that increases with the number of sex partners; (2) acquiring a social reputation as a "womanizer," which could impair their chances of finding a desirable long-term mate; (3) lowering the chances that their children would survive owing to lack of paternal investment and protection; (4) suffering violence at the hands of jealous husbands or boyfriends if the women were married or mated; (5) suffering violence at the hands of the father or brothers of the women; and (6) risking retaliatory affairs by their wives and the potential for a costly divorce (Buss & Schmitt, 1993; Daly & Wilson, 1988; Freeman, 1983).

 Given the large potential adaptive advantages of short-term mating for men in the currency of increased offspring production, selection might have favored a short-term mating strategy despite these costs. We would expect selection to have favored psychological mechanisms in men to pursue short-term mating when the costs were low or could be circumvented.

BOX *6.1*

## Functions Versus Beneficial Effects of Short-Term Mating

Short-term mating may have beneficial effects that are different from the original function. For example, "securing a part as an actor or actress in a movie" may be a beneficial effect of short-term mating, but could not have been an original function of such mating. Motion pictures are a modern invention and are not part of the selective environment in which humans evolved. Of course, this does not preclude "exchange sex for position or privilege" as a more abstract function of short-term mating.

For a benefit to qualify as a function of short-term mating means (1) that there was recurrent selection pressure over human evolutionary history such that the benefit was recurrently reaped by those who engaged in short-term mating under some conditions; (2) that the costs in fitness currencies of pursuing short-term mating were less than the benefits in the contexts in which they were pursued; and (3) that selection favored the evolution of at least one psychological mechanism specifically designed to promote short-term mating in specific circumstances.

Because we cannot go back in time, we must use various standards of evidence for inferring the evolution of psychological mechanisms specifically designed to promote short-term mating. Among the

criteria we can adopt are: (1) Do people in most or all cultures engage in short-term mating under particular conditions when not physically constrained from doing so? (2) Are there specific contexts that predispose men and women to engage in short-term mating that would imply the existence of psychological mechanisms sensitive to those contexts? (3) On the basis of our knowledge of ancestral environments, is it reasonable to infer that those specific contexts would have provided recurrent opportunities to engage in short-term mating? (4) Was a potential benefit likely to be received by a woman or a man engaging in short-term mating in those contexts?

Given the prevalence of short-term mating across all known cultures, including tribal cultures such as the Ache (Hill & Hurtado, 1996), the Tiwi (Hart & Pilling, 1960), the !Kung (Shostak, 1981), the Hiwi (Hill & Hurtado, 1989), and the Yanomamö (Chagnon, 1983), the prevalence of infidelity in plays and novels dating back centuries, the evidence for human sperm competition (Baker & Bellis, 1995), and the prevalence of the desire for sexual variety, it is reasonable to infer that ancestral conditions would have permitted recurrent opportunities for women and men to benefit from short-term mating some of the time.

## Adaptive Problems Men Must Solve When Pursuing Short-Term Mating

Ancestral men who pursued a short-term sexual strategy confronted a number of specific adaptive problems—partner number or variety, sexual accessibility, identifying which women were fertile, and avoiding commitment.

*The Problem of Partner Number or Variety.* Successful pursuit of short-term mating requires an adaptation that is motivational, something that would impel men toward a variety of sex partners. One first-line solution to the problem of partner number can be expected in desire for sexual access to a large number of women (Symons, 1979). A second specialized adaptation is a relaxation of standards that men might impose for an acceptable short-term partner. A third predicted adaptation is to impose minimum time constraints—that is, to let little time elapse before seeking sexual intercourse.

*The Problem of Sexual Accessibility.*   Advantages would accrue to men who directed their mating efforts most intensely toward women who were sexually accessible. Time, energy, and courtship resources devoted to women who are unlikely to consent to sex would interfere with the successful pursuit of short-term mating. Specialized adaptations for solving the problem of sexual accessibility might occur in the form of men's short-term mate preferences. Women who show signs of being prudish, sexually inexperienced, conservative, or low in sex drive should be disfavored. Clothes signaling sexual openness or behavior signaling promiscuity might be desired by men in short-term mates because they suggest sexual accessibility.

*The Problem of Identifying Which Women Are Fertile.*   A clear evolutionary prediction is that men seeking short-term mates would prefer women who displayed cues correlated with fertility. A maximally fertile woman would have the highest probability of getting pregnant from a single act of sex. In contrast, men seeking long-term mates might be predicted to prefer younger women of higher reproductive value, because such women will be more likely to reproduce in the future (see Chapter 5 for a discussion of the distinction between fertility and reproductive value).

This distinction—fertility versus reproductive value—does not guarantee that selection will have fashioned two different standards of attraction in men, one for casual sex and another for a marriage partner. The key point is that this distinction can be used to generate a hypothesis about shifts in age preferences, which we can then test.

*The Problem of Avoiding Commitment.*   Men seeking short-term mates are predicted to avoid women who might demand serious commitments or investments before consenting to sex. The larger the investment in a particular woman, the fewer the number of sexual partners a given man can succeed in attracting. Women who require heavy investment effectively force men into a long-term mating strategy. Men seeking short-term mates, therefore, are predicted to shun women who demand commitments or heavy investments before agreeing to sex.

## ■ EVIDENCE FOR AN EVOLVED SHORT-TERM MATING PSYCHOLOGY

Casual sex typically requires the consent of both sexes. At least some ancestral women must have practiced the behavior some of the time, because if all women historically had mated monogamously for life with a single man and had no premarital sex, the opportunities for casual sex with consenting women would have vanished (Smith, 1984). The exception, of course, would occur in the context of coerced sex—a topic we will explore in Chapter 11.

### Physiological Evidence for Short-Term Mating

Existing adaptations in our psychology, anatomy, physiology, and behavior reflect the scoring of prior selection pressures. Just as the modern fear of snakes reveals an ancestral hazard, so our sexual anatomy and physiology reveal ancient short-term sexual strategies.

*Testicle Size.*   There are a number of physiological clues to the history of multiple matings. One clue comes from the size of men's testicles. Large testes typically evolve as a consequence of intense sperm competition—when the sperm from two or more males occupy the reproductive tract of one female at the same time because she has copulated with two or more males (Short, 1979; Smith, 1984). Sperm competition exerts a selection pressure on males to produce large ejaculates containing numerous sperm. In the race to the valuable egg, the larger, sperm-laden ejaculate has an advantage in displacing the ejaculate of other men inside the woman's reproductive tract.

Men's testes size, relative to their body weight, is far greater than that of gorillas and orangutans. Male testes account for .018 percent of body weight in gorillas and .048 percent in orangutans (Short, 1979; Smith, 1984). In contrast, human male testes account for .079 percent of men's body weight, or 60 percent more than that of orangutans and more than four times that of gorillas, corrected for body size. Men's relatively large testes provide one piece of evidence that women in human evolutionary history sometimes had sex with more than one man within a time span of a few days. This size of testes would have been unlikely to have evolved unless there was sperm competition. And it suggests that both sexes pursued short-term mating some of the time. But humans do not possess the largest testes of all the primates. Human testicular volume is substantially smaller than that of the highly promiscuous chimpanzee, whose testes account for .269 percent of its body weight, more than three times the percentage for men. These findings suggest that our human ancestors rarely reached the chimpanzee's extreme of relatively indiscriminate sex.

To get a concrete feel for the differences in sexuality between chimps and humans, Wrangham (1993) summarized data from a variety of studies on the estimated number of male copulation partners that females from a variety of primate species experienced per birth. The highly monogamous gorilla females averaged only one male sex partner per birth. Human females were estimated to have 1.1 male sex partners per birth, or nearly 10 percent more sex partners than gorillas. In contrast, baboon females had eight male sex partners per birth; bonobo chimp females had nine male sex partners per birth; and common chimpanzee females (*Pan troglodytes*) had thirteen male sex partners per birth. Thus, the behavior that leads to sperm competition—females having sex with a variety of males—appears to accord well with the evidence on sperm volume. Humans show higher levels of sperm competition than the monogamous gorillas but far lower levels of sperm competition than the more promiscuous chimps and bonobos.

***Variations in Sperm Insemination.***    Another clue to the evolutionary existence of casual mating comes from variations in sperm production and insemination (Baker & Bellis, 1995). In a study to determine the effect on sperm production of separating mates from each other, thirty-five couples agreed to provide ejaculates resulting from sexual intercourse, from either condoms or flowback, the gelatinous mass of seminal fluid that is spontaneously discharged by a woman after intercourse. The partners in each couple had been separated for varying intervals of time.

Men's sperm count went up dramatically with the increasing amount of time the couple had been apart since their last sexual encounter. The more time spent apart, the more sperm the husbands inseminated in their wives when they finally did have sex. When the couples spent 100 percent of their time together, men inseminated 389 million sperm per ejaculate, on average. But when the couples spent only 5 percent of their time together, men inseminated 712 million sperm per ejaculate, almost double the amount. The number of sperm inseminated increases when other men's sperm might be inside the wife's reproductive tract at the same time as a consequence of the opportunity provided for extramarital sex by the couple's separation. The increase in sperm insemination upon being reunited did not depend on the time since the man's last ejaculation. Even when the man had masturbated to orgasm while away from his wife, he still inseminated more sperm on being reunited if he had been away from her a long time.

The increase in sperm inseminated by the husband after prolonged separation ensures that his sperm will stand a greater chance in the race to the egg by crowding out or displacing a possible interloper's sperm.

## Psychological Evidence for Short-Term Mating

In this section, we consider the *psychological* evidence for short-term mating—the desire for sexual variety, the amount of time that elapses before a person seeks sexual intercourse, the lowering of standards in short-term mating, the nature and frequency of sexual fantasies, and the "closing time phenomenon."

*Desire for a Variety of Sex Partners.*    One psychological solution to the problem of securing sexual access to a variety of partners is *lust:* Men have evolved a powerful desire for sex. Men do not always act on this desire, but it is a motivating force: "Even if only one impulse in a thousand is consummated, the function of lust nonetheless is to motivate sexual intercourse" (Symons, 1979, p. 207).

To find out how many sexual partners people in fact desire, researchers asked unmarried U.S. college students to identify how many sex partners they would ideally like to have within various time periods, ranging from the following month to their entire lives (Buss & Schmitt, 1993; Kennair et al., 2009; Schmitt et al., 2003). The results from a massive cross-cultural study are shown in Figure 6.1 (Schmitt et al., 2003). In every culture in every region of the world, a substantially larger percentage of men than women desire more than one sex partner over the next month. Norwegian culture provides an especially interesting test case for these sex differences, since it is a culture with a high degree of gender equality (Kennair et al., 2009). Norwegian women desire roughly two sex partners over the next year; Norwegian men desire seven. Over the next thirty years, Norwegian women desire roughly five sex partners; men desire nearly twenty-five. Some psychologists argue that increased gender equality should result in a reduction or elimination of sex differences (Eagly & Wood, 1999). This clearly has not happened in Norway or in any other culture examined so far.

Another study analyzed forty-eight "private wishes" ranging from "to be with God when I die" to "to make a lasting contribution through creative work" (Ehrlichman & Eichenstein, 1992). The largest sex difference by far was found for one wish: "to have sex with anyone I choose." In another study that asked 676 men and women to estimate the frequency with which they experienced sexual desire, the average man estimated thirty-seven times per week, whereas the average woman estimated nine times per week (Regan & Atkins, 2006).

And in a massive cross-cultural study of 16,288 people from ten major world regions, including six continents, thirteen islands, twenty-seven languages, and fifty-two nations, the men expressed a desire for a larger number of sex partners than women did in all cases (Schmitt et al., 2003). From the small island of Fiji to the large island of Taiwan, from the north of Scandinavia to the south of Africa, in every island, continent, and culture, men expressed a substantially greater desire than did women for a variety of different sex partners.

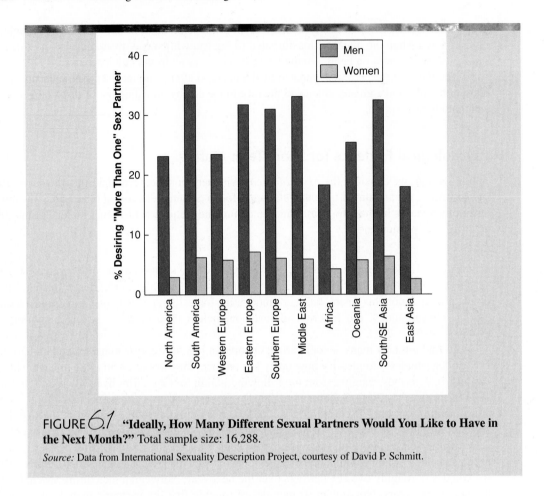

FIGURE *6.1* **"Ideally, How Many Different Sexual Partners Would You Like to Have in the Next Month?"** Total sample size: 16,288.

*Source:* Data from International Sexuality Description Project, courtesy of David P. Schmitt.

***Time Elapsed before Seeking Intercourse.*** Another psychological solution to the problem of gaining sexual access to a variety of partners is to let little time elapse between meeting the desired female and seeking sexual intercourse. College men and women rated how likely they would be to consent to sex with someone they viewed as desirable if they had known the person for only an hour, a day, a week, a month, six months, a year, two years, or five years (Buss & Schmitt, 1993). Both men and women say that they would probably have sex after knowing a desirable potential mate for five years (see Figure 6.2). At every shorter interval, however, men exceeded women in the reported likelihood of having sex.

Having known a potential mate for only one week, men are still on average positive about the possibility of consenting to sex. Women, in sharp contrast, are highly unlikely to have sex after knowing someone for just a week. Upon knowing a potential mate for merely one hour, men are slightly disinclined to consider having sex, but the disinclination is not strong. For most women, sex after just one hour is a virtual impossibility.

As with their desires, men's inclination to let little time elapse before seeking sexual intercourse offers a partial solution to the adaptive problem of gaining sexual access to a variety of

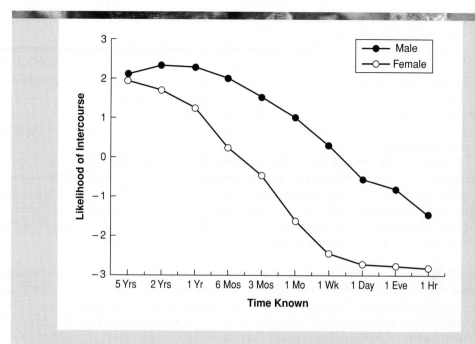

FIGURE 6.2 **Probability of Consenting to Sexual Intercourse.** Subjects rated the probability that they would consent to sexual intercourse after having known an attractive member of the opposite sex for each of a specified set of time intervals.

*Source:* Buss, D. M., & Schmitt, D. P. (1993). Sexual strategies theory: An evolutionary perspective on human mating. *Psychological Review, 100,* 204–232. Copyright © 1993 by the American Psychological Association. Reprinted with permission.

partners. Men's greater likelihood of consenting to sexual intercourse after little time has elapsed has now been extensively replicated in samples of varying ages and geographical locations within the United States (Schmitt, Shackelford, & Buss, 2001) and Norway (Kennair et al., 2009).

Evolutionary psychologists Michele Surbey and Colette Conohan found similar results when they explored "willingness to engage in casual sex" across a variety of conditions, such as a partner's level of physical attractiveness, personality, and behavioral characteristics (Surbey & Conohan, 2000). They concluded that "men reported a greater anticipated willingness to engage in sexual intercourse across all conditions compared with women" (2000, p. 367), suggesting that men lower their standards for casual sex. Furthermore, in five laboratory experiments, targets who displayed cues to "easy sexual access" were judged to be far more desirable by men than by women but only in the context of short-term mating (Schmitt, Couden, & Baker, 2001).

***The Lowering of Standards in Short-Term Mating.*** Yet another psychological solution to securing a variety of casual sex partners is a relaxation of standards imposed by men for acceptable partners. High standards for attributes such as age, intelligence, personality, and marital status function to exclude the majority of potential mates from consideration. Relaxed standards ensure more eligible players.

College students provided information about the minimum and maximum acceptable ages of a partner for temporary and permanent sexual relationships (Buss & Schmitt, 1993). College men accept an age range roughly four years wider than do women for a temporary liaison. Men at this age are willing to mate in the short run with members of the opposite sex who are as young as sixteen and as old as twenty-eight, whereas women prefer men who are at least eighteen but no older than twenty-six. This relaxation of age restrictions by men does not apply to committed mating.

Men also express significantly lower standards than the women on forty-one of the sixty-seven characteristics named as potentially desirable in a casual mate. For brief encounters, men require a lower level of such assets as charming, athletic, educated, generous, honest, independent, kind, intellectual, loyal, sense of humor, sociable, wealthy, responsible, spontaneous, co-operative, and emotionally stable. Men thus relax their standards across a range of attributes, which helps to solve the problem of gaining access to a variety of sex partners.

***Mate Preferences.*** The relaxation of standards does not mean that men have no standards. Indeed, the standards that men set for sexual affairs reveal a precise strategy to gain sexual access to a variety of partners. Compared with their long-term preferences, for casual sex, partners men dislike women who are prudish, conservative, or have a low sex drive (Buss & Schmitt, 1993). Men value sexual experience in a potential sex partner, reflecting a belief that experienced women are more sexually accessible than women who are sexually inexperienced. Promiscuity, high sex drive, and sexual experience in a woman probably signal an increased likelihood that a man can gain sexual access for the short run. Prudishness and low sex drive, in contrast, signal difficulty in gaining sexual access and thus interfere with men's short-term sexual strategy.

Evolutionary psychologists have also hypothesized that men seeking short-term sex would prioritize women's bodies, since a woman's body provides possibly the most powerful cues to her fertility (Confer et al., 2010; Currie & Little, 2009) (see Chapter 5 on WHR, BMI, and other bodily cues to fertility). In one laboratory experiment, participants viewed an image of an opposite sex individual whose face was occluded by a "face box" and whose body was occluded by a "body box" (Confer et al., 2010). Participants then were instructed to imagine themselves having either a one-night stand or a committed relationship with the person, and then asked to decide on which box they would remove to inform their decision—they could only remove one box (see Figure 6.3). Compared to the long-term mating context in which men prioritized facial information, men considering casual sex shifted significantly in the direction of prioritizing body information—a finding also discovered by Currie and Little (2009) using a different methodology. Women, in contrast, do not show this shift, and tend to prioritize a man's face in both short-term and long-term mating contexts. Although further research is needed, these findings are consistent with the hypothesis that men prioritize cues to fertility in short-term sex partners.

***Minimizing Commitment after Sex.*** Evolutionary psychologist Martie Haselton found evidence for a possible adaptation in men to facilitate the success of a short-term mating strategy: an emotional shift right after sexual intercourse (Haselton & Buss, 2001). Men with more sex partners experienced a sharp decline in how sexually attractive they found their partner immediately following intercourse, whereas neither women nor men with less sexual experience

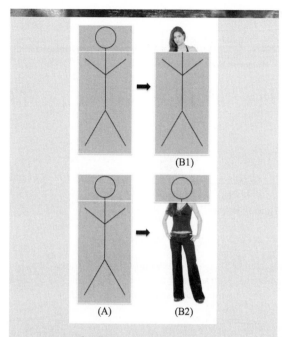

FIGURE 6.3 **Which Box Would You Remove When Seeking a Long-Term Mate versus a Short-Term Mate?** Participants could decide to remove only one box, the face box or body box, in order to inform their decision about whether they would be interested in having a short-term sexual or long-term romantic relationship with the person. Compared to the long-term mating context, men considering short-term sex were significantly more interested in finding out information about the potential mate's body—hypothesized to provide important information about a woman's fertility.

*Source:* Confer, J. C., Perilloux, C., & Buss, D. M. (2010). More than just a pretty face: Men's priority shifts toward bodily attractiveness in short-term mating contexts. *Evolution and Human Behavior, 31,* 349–353. Reprinted with permission from Elsevier.

showed this decline. One woman described her experiences in this way: "He is most passionate and all over me just as we meet; after we have sex he is content and doesn't seem to miss me that much any more." This work on the attraction-reduction effect supports the hypothesis that men have yet another psychological adaptation designed to promote the success of a casual sexual strategy, one that motivates either a hasty postcopulatory departure to minimize investment in any one woman or, alternatively, a roving eye within the context of an existing long-term mateship.

***The Closing Time Phenomenon.*** A related psychological clue to men's strategy of casual sex comes from studies that examine shifts in judgments of attractiveness over the course of an evening at singles bars (Gladue & Delaney, 1990; Nida & Koon, 1983; Pennebaker et al., 1979). In one study, 137 men and 80 women in a bar were approached at 9:00 P.M., 10:30 P.M., and 12:00 A.M. and asked to rate the attractiveness of members of the opposite sex in the bar using a ten-point scale (Gladue & Delaney, 1990). As closing time approached, men viewed women as increasingly attractive. The average judgment at 9:00 P.M. was 5.5, but by midnight it had increased to over 6.5. Women's judgments of men's attractiveness also increased over time, but women perceived the male bar patrons as less attractive overall compared with the men's perceptions of the women. Women rated the men at the bar as just below the average of 5.0 at 9:00 P.M., increasing near the midnight closing time to only 5.5 (see Figure 6.4).

Men's shift in perceptions of attractiveness near closing time occurs regardless of how much alcohol they have consumed. Whether a man consumed a single drink or six drinks had no effect on the shift in viewing women as more attractive. The often-noted "beer goggles" phenomenon, whereby women are presumed to be viewed as more attractive with men's increasing intoxication, may instead be attributable to a psychological mechanism that is sensitive to decreasing opportunities over the course of the evening for casual sex. As the evening progresses and a man has not yet been successful in picking up a woman, he views the remaining women in the bar as increasingly attractive, a shift that will presumably increase his attempts to solicit sex

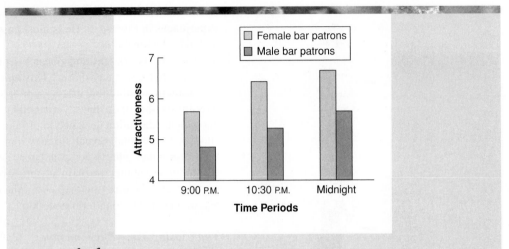

FIGURE 6.4 **The Closing Time Phenomenon.** As closing time approaches, both sexes, but especially men, find members of the opposite sex more attractive; the effect occurs even after controlling for the number of alcoholic drinks consumed. Female bar patrons were rated by men, and male bar patrons were rated by women.

*Source:* Gladue, B. A., & Delaney, J. J. (1990). Gender differences in perception of attractiveness of men and women in bars. *Personality and Social Psychology Bulletin, 16*, 378–391. Copyright © 1990 by Sage Publications, Inc. Reprinted by permission of Sage Publications, Inc.

from those women. The closing time phenomenon appears to represent a psychological solution to the problem of sexual accessibility—a context-specific lowering of standards as the likelihood of sexual accessibility starts to drop.

*Sex Differences in Sexual Fantasies and Sex Drive.* Sexual fantasies provide another psychological clue to an evolutionary history of men's proclivity to casual mating. Fantasies reveal the nature of desires that motivate men's and women's behaviors. Studies document large differences between male and female sexual fantasies. Research conducted in Japan, Great Britain, and the United States showed that men have roughly twice as many sexual fantasies as women (Ellis & Symons, 1990; Wilson, 1987). When asleep, men are more likely than women to dream about sexual events. Men's sexual fantasies more often include strangers, multiple partners, or anonymous partners. During a single fantasy episode, for example, most men report that they sometimes change sexual partners, whereas most women report that they rarely change sexual partners. Forty-three percent of women but only 12 percent of men report that they never substitute or switch sexual partners during a fantasy episode. Thirty-two percent of men but only 8 percent of women report having imagined sexual encounters with more than 1,000 different partners in their lifetime. Men are also more than four times as likely as women to have fantasies about group sex (Wilson, 1997). And 78 percent of men versus 32 percent of women answered "yes" to the question: "Would you ever engage in a threesome sexual situation?" (Hughes, Harrison, & Gallup, 2004). A sample male fantasy is "being the mayor of a small town filled with nude girls from 20 to 24. I like to take walks, and pick out the best-looking one that day, and she engages in intercourse with me. All the women have sex with me any time I want" (Barclay, 1973, p. 209). Numbers and novelty are key ingredients of men's fantasy lives.

As evolutionary psychologists Bruce Ellis and Donald Symons observed, "The most striking feature of [male fantasy] is that sex is sheer lust and physical gratification, devoid of encumbering relationships, emotional elaboration, complicated plot lines, flirtation, courtship, and extended foreplay" (Ellis & Symons, 1990, p. 544). These fantasies reveal a psychology attuned to sexual access to a variety of partners.

Women's sexual fantasies, in contrast, often contain familiar partners. Fifty-nine percent of American women but only 28 percent of American men report that their sexual fantasies typically focus on someone with whom they are already romantically and sexually involved. Emotions and personality are crucial for women. Forty-one percent of the women but only 16 percent of the men report that they focus most heavily on the personal and emotional characteristics of the fantasized partner. As one woman observed: "I usually think about the guy I am with. Sometimes I realize that the feelings will overwhelm me, envelop me, sweep me away" (Barclay, 1973, p. 211). Women tend to emphasize tenderness, romance, and personal involvement in their sexual fantasies.

Studies of sex drive reveal similar sex differences. The most massive study, involving more than 200,000 from fifty-three nations, measured sex drive with these statements: "I have a strong sex drive" and "It doesn't take me much to get sexually excited" (Lippa, 2009). In every nation, from Thailand to Croatia to Trinidad, men reported having a higher sex drive than did women. Similar findings also show up in masturbation rates and pornography consumption, both of which also show large sex differences (Petersen & Hyde, 2010). The sex difference in sex drive proved just as large in nations with high levels of gender equality such as Sweden and Denmark as it did in nations with lower levels of gender equality, such as Turkey and Saudi Arabia—a finding that contradicts the notion that these sex differences are caused by this social-structural variable.

***Sexual Regret.*** Another potential design feature of men's short-term sexual psychology centers on feelings of regret. Regret—feelings of sorrow about something in the past—is hypothesized to function to improve future decision making by motivating people to avoid prior mistakes (Poore et al., 2005). Sexual regret could operate over two classes of actions—missed sexual opportunities (sexual omission) or sexual actions taken (sexual commission). Two independent groups of researchers have documented that men more than women regret missed sexual opportunities (Poore et al., 2005; Roese et al., 2006). One study presented men and women with descriptions of regret such as "Should have tried harder to sleep with _____," "Kicked myself for missing out on a chance to have sex with _____" (Roese et al., 2006). Men regretted acts of sexual omission—failures to act on sexual opportunities—significantly more than did women. Women were more likely to have regretted action of sexual commission—wishing that they had not had sex with someone that they did have sex with (Poore et al., 2005). Another study examined whether men and women experienced terrible feelings after "hooking up" (varying forms of casual sexual behavior) (Lambert, Kahn, & Apple, 2003). A total of 46 percent of the men reported experiencing terrible feelings. Two key sources of terrible feelings were (1) that the women that they hooked up with wanted a relationship and (2) overconsumption of alcohol or drugs. Sexual regret, in short, has the hallmarks of an evolved feature in men designed to facilitate acting on future sexual opportunities and avoid entangling commitments.

## Behavioral Evidence of Short-Term Mating

Physiological and psychological evidence both point strongly to a long evolutionary history in which men sought short-term mating with a variety of women. In this section, we complete the picture by presenting behavioral evidence that men across cultures actually pursue short-term mating more than women do.

*Extramarital Affairs.* Men in most cultures pursue extramarital sex more often than do their wives. The Kinsey study, for example, estimated that 50 percent of men had extramarital affairs, whereas only 26 percent of women had them (Kinsey, Pomeroy, & Martin, 1948, 1953). Anthropologist Thomas Gregor described the sexual feelings of Amazonian Mehinaku men in this way: "Women's sexual attractiveness varies from 'flavorless' (mana) to the 'delicious' (awirintya)" (Gregor, 1985, p. 84). Gregor notes that "sad to say, sex with spouses is said to be mana, in contrast with sex with lovers, which is nearly always awirintyapa" (1985, p. 72). Kinsey summed it up best: "There seems to be no question but that the human male would be promiscuous in his choice of sexual partners throughout the whole of his life if there were no social restrictions. The human female is much less interested in a variety of partners" (Kinsey et al., 1948, p. 589).

*Prostitution.* Prostitution, the relatively indiscriminate exchange of sexual services for economic profit, is another reflection of men's greater desire for casual sex (Symons, 1979). Prostitution occurs in every society that has been thoroughly studied, from the Azande in Africa to the Zuni in North America (Burley & Symanski, 1981). Within the United States, estimates of the number of active prostitutes range from 100,000 to 500,000. Tokyo has more than 130,000 prostitutes, Poland 230,000, and Addis Ababa in Ethiopia 80,000. In Germany, there are 50,000 legally registered prostitutes and triple that number working illegally. In all cultures, men are overwhelmingly the consumers. Kinsey found that 69 percent of American men had solicited a prostitute, and for 15 percent, prostitution was a regular sexual outlet. The numbers for women were so low that they were not even reported as a percentage of the sexual outlet of women (Kinsey et al., 1948, 1953).

*Hook-Up Behavior and Friends with Benefits.* A third source of behavioral evidence comes from studies of hooking up and friends with benefits. "Hooking up" typically refers to spontaneous sexual interactions in which the participants are not in a traditional romantic relationship and there is no explicit promise of any future intimate relationship (Garcia & Reiber, 2008). "Friends with benefits" (FWB), in contrast, typically refers to a blend of traditional friendship with the "benefits" referring to having sex, but with no implied commitment to a romantic relationship (Owen & Fincham, 2010). More men than women try to initiate hooking up (Garcia & Reiber, 2008), and are more likely than women to report having at least one FWB. Although both women and men obviously engage in these forms of sexual activity, their motivation for doing so appears to differ. Men more than women report that their "ideal outcome" of hooking up is "further hookups." Women more than men report that their "ideal outcome" would be a "traditional romantic relationship." This finding might explain why more men than women report for FWB—although the means have to be identical for the sexes, men are more likely to construe a particular relationship as a FWB, whereas women may perceive it as the early stage of a romantic relationship. Women also report feelings of more regret, feelings of being "used," and depression following hook-ups or one-night stands (Campbell, 2008). Although there are

TABLE *6.1* **Clues to Ancestral Nonmonogamous Mating**

**Behavioral Clues**
Extramarital affairs
Prostitution
Hook-ups
Friends with benefits

**Physiological Clues**
Sperm volume
Variations in sperm insemination

**Psychological Clues**
Desire for sexual variety
Desire to seek sex sooner
Lowering of standards
Minimizing commitment
Sexual regret at missed opportunities
Closing time phenomenon
Sexual fantasies

important individual differences (some women just want sex; some men hope that it will lead to long-term romance), these sex differences provide another source of behavioral evidence for a fundamental difference in men's and women's sexual psychology of short-term mating.

Physiological, psychological, and behavioral evidence all point to a long evolutionary history in which short-term mating has been part of the human strategic repertoire (see Table 6.1).

# ■ WOMEN'S SHORT-TERM MATING

*I*n this section, we turn to women. First, we consider the evidence that women engage in short-term mating and likely have done so over the long course of human evolutionary history. Second, we consider hypotheses about the adaptive benefits ancestral women might have accrued from short-term mating. Third, we examine the costs of short-term mating for women. Finally, we examine the empirical evidence for the various hypotheses that have been advanced to account for women's short-term mating.

## Evidence for Women's Short-Term Mating

Evolutionary theories of human mating, as we have seen, have emphasized the tremendous reproductive benefits to men of short-term mating (e.g., Kenrick et al., 1990; Symons, 1979; Trivers, 1972). Over human evolutionary history, the reproductive benefits of short-term mating for men would have been large and direct in the form of additional children. Perhaps because of the elegance of parental investment theory and the extensive empirical support for it, many theorists have overlooked a fundamental fact about short-term mating: Mathematically, the number of short-term matings must be identical, on average, for men and women. Every time a man has a casual sexual encounter with a woman he has never met, the woman is simultaneously having a casual sexual encounter with a man she has never met.

If ancestral women never engaged in short-term mating, men could not have evolved a powerful desire for sexual variety (Smith, 1984). That desire, if matings were consensual rather than forced, required the existence of some willing women some of the time. And if ancestral women willingly and recurrently engaged in short-term mating, it would defy evolutionary logic if there were no benefits to women of doing so. In fact, there are some clues, starting with the physiology of the female orgasm, that ancestral women did engage in short-term mating.

***Orgasm in Women.***   The physiology of women's orgasm provides one clue to an evolutionary history of short-term mating. Once it was thought that a woman's orgasm functioned to make her sleepy and keep her reclined, thereby decreasing the likelihood that sperm would flow out and increasing the likelihood she would conceive. But if the function of orgasm were to keep the woman reclined so as to delay flowback, then more sperm would be retained. That is not the case. Rather, there is no link between the timing of the flowback and the number of sperm retained (Baker & Bellis, 1995).

Women discharge roughly 35 percent of sperm within thirty minutes of the time of insemination, averaged across all instances of intercourse. If the woman has an orgasm, however, she retains 70 percent of the sperm, ejecting only 30 percent. This 5 percent difference is not large, but if it occurred repeatedly, in woman after woman, generation after generation, it could add up to a large selection pressure over evolutionary time. Lack of an orgasm leads to the ejection of more sperm. This evidence is consistent with the theory that a woman's orgasm functions to draw the sperm from the vagina into the cervical canal and uterus, increasing the probability of conception.

The number of sperm a woman retains is also linked with whether she is having an affair. Women time their adulterous liaisons in a way that is reproductively detrimental to their husbands. In a nationwide sex survey of 3,679 women in Britain, all women recorded their menstrual cycles as well as the timing of their copulations with their husbands and, if they were having affairs, with their lovers. It turned out that women having affairs time their copulations, most likely unconsciously, to coincide with the point in their menstrual cycle when they were most likely to be ovulating and hence were most likely to conceive (Baker & Bellis, 1995). Furthermore, women who are having affairs are more likely to be orgasmic with their affair partner than with their regular partner (see Buss, 2003).

***Behavioral Evidence.***   The behavioral evidence also suggests that women in all but the most restrictive societies sometimes engage in extramarital sexual unions. In the United States, studies yield an affair rate ranging from 20 to 50 percent for married women (Athanasiou, Shaver, & Tavris, 1970; Buss, 1994b; Glass & Wright, 1992; Hunt, 1974; Kinsey et al., 1948, 1953). Affairs have also been documented, despite the shroud of secrecy that surrounds them, in dozens of tribal societies including the Ache of Paraguay (Hill & Hurtado, 1996), the Yanomamö of Venezuela (Chagnon, 1983), the Tiwi of Australia (Hart & Pilling, 1960), the !Kung of Botswana (Shostak, 1981), and the Mehinaku of Amazonia (Gregor, 1985). Furthermore, as noted in the previous section, studies of college women reveal that they do have sex with their opposite sex friends (26 percent according to one study), as well as attempting to initiate hook-ups (65 percent) (Garcia & Reiber, 2008). Modern cultural and tribal behavioral evidence, in short, does not suggest that women invariably pursue a monogamous long-term mating strategy all of the time.

## Hypotheses about the Adaptive Benefits to Women of Short-Term Mating

For short-term sexual psychology to evolve in women, there must have been adaptive benefits associated with casual sex in some circumstances. What might those benefits have been? Five classes of benefits have been proposed: resources, genes, mate switching, mate skill acquisition, and mate manipulation (Greiling & Buss, 2000) (Table 6.2).

***Resource Hypotheses.*** One benefit of short-term mating is resource accrual (Symons, 1979). Women could engage in short-term mating in exchange for meat, goods, or services. An ancestral

**TABLE 6.2 Hypothesized Benefits to Women: Short-Term Mating**

| Hypothesis | Author |
|---|---|
| **Resource** | |
| Investment via paternity confusion | Hrdy (1981) |
| Immediate economic resources | Symons (1979) |
| Protection through "special friendships" | Smuts (1985) |
| Status elevation | Smith (1984) |
| **Genetic Benefit** | |
| Better or "sexy son" genes | Fisher (1958) |
| Diverse genes | Smith (1984) |
| **Mate Switching** | |
| Mate expulsion | Greiling & Buss (2000) |
| Mate replacement | Symons (1979) |
| Mate insurance [backup] | Smith (1984) |
| **Short-Term for Long-Term Goal** | |
| Sex to evaluate long-term mate potential | Buss & Schmitt (1993) |
| Clarifying mate preferences | Greiling & Buss (2000) |
| Honing skills of mate attraction | Miller (personal communication, 1991) |
| **Mate Manipulation** | |
| Increasing commitment of long-term mate | Greiling (1995) |
| Revenge as deterrence | Symons (1979) |

*Source:* Greiling, H., & Buss, D. M. (2000). Women's sexual strategies: The hidden dimension of short-term extra-pair mating. *Personality and Individual Differences, 28,* 929–963.

woman might have been able to obscure the actual paternity of her offspring through several short-term matings and thus elicit resources from two or more men (Hrdy, 1981). According to this paternity confusion hypothesis, each man might be willing to offer some investment in the woman's children on the chance that they are genetically his own.

Another possible resource is protection (Smith, 1984; Smuts, 1985). Men typically provide protection to their mates and children, including defense against predators and aggressive men. Because a primary mate cannot always be around to defend and protect a woman, she might gain added protection by consorting with another man.

Finally, Smith (1984) proposed the status enhancement hypothesis of short-term mating. A woman might be able to elevate her social standing among her peers or gain access to a higher social circle by a temporary liaison with a high-status man. Clearly women might gain a variety of tangible and intangible resources through short-term mating.

**Genetic Benefit Hypotheses.** Another class of benefits can be called genetic benefits. The first is the most obvious—*enhanced fertility*. If a woman's regular mate is infertile or impotent, a short-term mate might provide a fertility backup to aid in conception.

Second, a short-term mate might provide *superior genes* compared with a woman's regular mate, especially if she has an affair with a healthy or high-status man. These genes might give her offspring better chances for survival or reproduction (Smith, 1984). One version of this is known as the sexy son hypothesis (Fisher, 1958). By mating with an especially attractive man, a woman might be able to bear a son who is especially attractive to women in the next generation. Her son thus might have increased sexual access, produce more children, and hence provide his mother with additional grandchildren.

Third, a short-term mate might provide a woman with *different genes* compared with those of her regular mate, thus enhancing the genetic diversity of her children—perhaps a hedge against environmental change (Smith, 1984).

**Mate Switching Hypotheses.** A third class of benefits pertains to mate switching. Sometimes, a woman's husband stops bringing in resources, starts abusing her, or otherwise declines in his value to her as a mate (Betzig, 1989; Fisher, 1992; Smith, 1984). Ancestral women might have benefited from short-term mating to cope with this adaptive problem.

There are several variants of this hypothesis. According to the mate expulsion hypothesis, having a short-term affair would help the woman to get rid of her long-term mate. Because men in many cultures often divorce wives who have affairs (Betzig, 1989), having an affair would be an effective means for the woman to initiate a breakup. Another variant of this hypothesis suggests that a woman might simply find a man who is far better than her husband, and so initiate a short-term encounter as a means of switching mates.

**Short-Term for Long-Term Goals Hypotheses.** Another hypothesis is that women use short-term mating as a means to assess and evaluate prospective long-term mates (Buss & Schmitt, 1993). Engaging in short-term mating allows a woman to clarify the qualities she desires in a long-term mate, evaluate her compatibility with a particular man (e.g., sexual compatibility), and reveal any hidden costs he might carry (e.g., existing children, deception). Two clear predictions follow from this hypothesis: Women will dislike in a short-term mate (1) any signals that the man is already in an existing relationship, because this would lower the odds of her successfully attracting him as a long-term mate, and (2) the attribute of promiscuity, since this would signal that he is pursuing a truly short-term rather than long-term mating strategy. Other variants of the short-term for long-term goals hypothesis are that women use short-term mating to clarify the qualities she truly desires in a long-term mate (Greiling & Buss, 2000) or to hone her skills of attraction and seduction so that she can eventually attract a more desirable long-term mate (Miller, 1991).

*Mate Manipulation Hypotheses.*  A fifth class of benefits involves manipulating her mate. By having an affair, a woman might be able to gain revenge on her husband for his infidelity, thus possibly deterring him from future infidelities (Symons, 1979). Alternatively, a woman might be able to increase the commitment of her regular mate if he saw with stark evidence that other men were seriously interested in her (Greiling & Buss, 2000).

## Costs to Women of Short-Term Mating

Women sometimes incur more severe costs than men as a consequence of short-term mating. Women risk impairing their desirability as a long-term mate if they develop reputations for promiscuousness, because men prize fidelity in potential wives. Women known to be promiscuous suffer reputational damage even in relatively promiscuous cultures, such as among the Swedes and the Ache Indians.

Lacking a long-term mate to offer physical protection, a woman who adopts an exclusively short-term sexual strategy is at greater risk of physical and sexual abuse. Although women in marriages are also subjected to battering and even rape from their husbands, the alarming statistics on the incidence of date rape, which run as high as 15 percent in studies of college women, support the contention that women not in long-term relationships are also at considerable risk (Muehlenhard & Linton, 1987). The fact that women participating in the study of short-term and long-term partners abhor lovers who are physically abusive, violent, and mentally abusive suggests that women may be aware of the risks of abuse (Buss & Schmitt, 1993). Mate preferences, if judiciously applied to avoid potentially dangerous men, can minimize these risks.

The unmarried woman in the pursuit of casual sex risks getting pregnant and bearing children without the benefit of an investing man. In ancestral times, such children would likely have been at much greater risk of disease, injury, and death. Some women commit infanticide without the presence of an investing man. In Canada, for example, single women delivered only 12 percent of the babies born between 1977 and 1983 but committed just over 50 percent of the sixty-four maternal infanticides (Daly & Wilson, 1988). The higher infanticide rates among unmarried women occur across cultures as well, such as among the Buganda of Africa. But even infanticide does not cancel the substantial costs of nine months of gestation, reputational damage, and lost mating opportunities that women incur.

An unfaithful married woman risks the withdrawal of resources by her husband. From a reproductive standpoint, she may be wasting valuable time in an extramarital liaison. Furthermore, she risks the possibility of increasing the sibling competition among her children, who may have weaker ties with each other because they were fathered by different men. Finally, women risk contracting sexually transmitted diseases from short-term mating—a risk that is greater for women than for men per act of sex (Symons, 1993).

Short-term mating thus imposes hazards for both sexes. But because there might be large benefits as well, women and men may have evolved psychological mechanisms to select contexts in which costs are minimized and benefits maximized.

## Empirical Tests of Hypothesized Benefits to Women

Several researchers have discovered that the woman who is engaged in short-term mating places a premium on the man's physical attractiveness, a finding consistent with the good genes and the sexy son hypotheses (Buss & Schmitt, 1993; Gangestad & Simpson, 1990; Kenrick et al., 1990). Women also seem to elevate the importance they place on *immediate resources* in the short-term mating context (Buss & Schmitt, 1993). Women say that they desire a short-term mate who has an extravagant lifestyle, who spends a lot of money on them early on, and who gives them gifts early in the relationship. These findings support the resource accrual hypothesis.

Several studies have found that women who have affairs are significantly less happy with their current partner, emotionally and sexually, than women who do not (Glass & Wright, 1985; Kinsey et al., 1953). This provides circumstantial support for the mate switching hypothesis.

Glass and Wright (1992) examined seventeen potential "justifications" for extramarital affairs, ranging from "for fun" to "in order to advance my career." Women rated love (e.g., falling in love with the other person) and emotional intimacy (e.g., having someone who understands your problems and feelings) as the most compelling justifications for an affair. Furthermore, 77 percent of the women viewed love as a compelling justification, compared with only 43 percent of the men. These findings provide circumstantial support for the short-term for long-term goals and mate switching hypotheses.

One study (Greiling & Buss, 2000) examined the benefits women perceive as likely to come from affairs, how beneficial these things would be if they were received, and the contexts in which women perceive that they would be likely to have an affair. The researchers also examined women who actively pursue short-term matings and asked them what benefits come from those matings. The following section summarizes the results of these studies, but several important limitations must be considered. Women's beliefs about the benefits of short-term mating do not necessarily make those benefits part of the selection pressure that led to the evolution of women's short-term mating psychology. The actual adaptive benefits that led to the evolution of women's short-term mating psychology may lie outside women's awareness. Furthermore, the benefits women actually receive in modern contexts may not mirror the adaptive benefits ancestral women received from short-term mating. With these limitations in mind, let's turn to the results.

***Hypotheses Supported: Mate Switching, Mate Expulsion, and Resources.*** One study (Greiling & Buss, 2000) examined women's perceptions of the likelihood of receiving twenty-eight specific benefits from extra-pair copulations. Women reported that engaging in an extra-pair mating made it easier for a woman to break up with her current partner (sixth most likely benefit to receive) and more likely that a woman would find a partner who she felt was more desirable than her current partner (fourth most likely benefit to receive). Interestingly, the benefit judged to be most likely to be received—sexual gratification—was not central to any of the hypotheses under investigation.

Another study examined the *contexts* that might prompt a woman to have an affair. Greiling and Buss (2000) found that the contexts most likely to promote an extra-pair mating were discovering that a partner was having an affair, having a partner who was unwilling to engage in sexual relations, and having a partner who was abusive to her—all contexts that might promote a breakup. Following closely on the heels of these contexts were feeling that she could find someone with whom she would be more compatible than her current partner, meeting someone who is willing to spend a lot of time with her, and meeting someone who is more successful and has better financial prospects than her current partner. These findings across studies support the hypothesis that mate switching is a key function of short-term mating for women.

Two of the resource hypotheses received support from two or more studies. Women were judged to be highly likely to receive resources in exchange for sex, such as free dinners, money, jewelry, or clothing (tenth most likely benefit to receive out of the list of twenty-eight). These benefits, though, were judged to be only moderately beneficial when compared with other potential benefits a woman could accrue through short-term mating. The *contexts* that were judged to promote an extra-pair encounter, however, included having a current partner who could not hold down a job and meeting someone with better financial prospects than her current partner. These contexts suggest that access to resources, or lack thereof, may be important in a woman's decision to have an extra-pair sexual liaison and imply a long-term interest in having a mate with resources rather than an exchange of sex for immediate access to resources.

### Hypothesis That Is Promising: Short-Term for Long-Term Goals.

Another hypothesis that has received empirical support is that women use short-term mating as a means to evaluate a man as a long-term mate. Women find the attribute of the man already "being in an existing relationship" moderately undesirable in a short-term mate (Buss & Schmitt, 1993). If a man is already in an existing committed relationship, it lowers the odds that a short-term sexual encounter with him will lead to a long-term relationship with him. Men seeking short-term mates, in contrast, are not bothered by the fact that the woman is already in a relationship. Women also find promiscuity to be undesirable in a short-term mate, presumably because promiscuity signals that the man is pursuing a short-term rather than a long-term mating strategy (Buss & Schmitt, 1993). A study examined nine possible reasons for having casual sex. After "I was physically attracted to the person," the second most important reason women cited was: "I actually wanted a long-term relationship with this person and thought the casual sex might lead to something more long-lasting" (Li & Kenrick, 2006). And as noted earlier, many women who engage in hook-ups or FWB hope that these short-term sexual encounters might turn into long-term romantic relationship—findings that support the short-term for long-term goals hypothesis. Although more research is clearly needed, all these findings support the hypothesis that some women use short-term mating as a means for assessing and evaluating a long-term mating prospect, or perhaps leveraging casual sex into a more committed relationship (Buss, 2003).

### Another Hypothesis That Is Promising: Good Genes.

The economics of the mating market suggest that women, in principle, can secure genes from a short-term affair partner that are superior to those of her regular partner. A highly desirable man is often willing to have a brief encounter with a less desirable woman, as long as she does not burden him with entangling commitments. The good genes hypothesis has been put to the test (Gangestad & Thornhill, 1997). The researchers measured genetic quality through the indicator of physical symmetry, as measured by calipers. Recall from Chapter 4 that symmetrical features are hypothesized to be heritable markers of health and fitness, signaling the presence of genes that facilitate resistance to diseases and other environmental insults. The researchers found that symmetrical men, compared to their more lopsided peers, tended to be more likely to have sexual relations with women who were already in relationships. That is, women appear to be choosing symmetrical men as affair partners, providing one piece of evidence that women might be going for good genes in short-term mating. Furthermore, in short-term mating, women place a great premium on physical attractiveness and "desirability to other women" (Buss & Schmitt, 1993; Gangestad & Thornhill, 1997; Li & Kenrick, 2006; Scheib, 2001). Another study found that for the context of casual sex, women prefer men who are daring, confident, strong, humorous, and successful with attractive women (Kruger, Fisher, & Jobling, 2003). In short-term mating, more than in long-term mating, women also prefer men who have a masculine facial architecture (Waynforth, Delwadia, & Camm, 2005). On the assumption that masculine features are honest signals of good genes (see Chapter 4), this preference suggests that women are seeking short-term mates for the genetic benefits they provide.

The strongest support for the good genes hypothesis of women's short-term mating comes from a raft of studies on how women's preferences shift around ovulation, the peak time of a woman's fertility (Gangestad & Thornhill, 2008; Gangestad, Thornhill, & Garver-Apgar, 2005; Garver-Apgar, Gangestad, & Thornhill, 2008). It is only during this fertile window that any genetic benefits can be reaped from short-term mating. Research has documented several shifts in women's preferences at ovulation compared to other times of their cycle: (1) an increased attraction to men with *symmetrical features*; (2) an increased preference for *facial masculinity, body masculinity, and vocal masculinity;* (3) an increased preference for men who are *tall* (Pawlowski & Jasienska, 2005); (4) an increased preference for men who display *creative intelligence* (Haselton & Miller, 2006); (5) an increased preference for men who are *physically attractive* and *muscular*; and (6) an increased preference for men who display social presence and direct intrasexual competitiveness—qualities that indicate *social dominance* (see Figure 6.5).

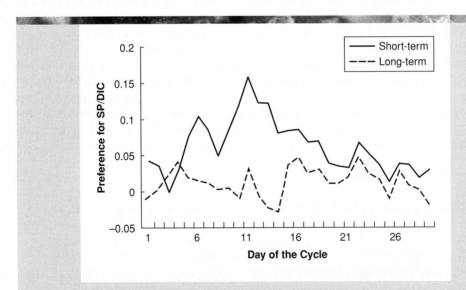

FIGURE 6.5 **Women's Preference for Men Who Display Social Presence and Direct Intrasexual Competitiveness as Short-Term Partners (solid line) and Long-Term Partners (dotted line) as a Function of Day of Their Menstrual Cycle.**

*Source:* Gangestad, S. W., Simpson, J. A., Cousins, A. J., Garver-Apgar, C. E., & Christensen, P. N. (2004). Women's preferences of male behavioral displays change across the menstrual cycle. *Psychological Science, 15,* 203–207.

Theoretically, women with existing mates could only receive genetic benefits through short-term mating if the genetic quality of their regular partner was low relative to the genetic quality of their extra-pair partner (Pillsworth, Haselton, & Buss, 2004). Indeed, women who rate their partners low on sexual attractiveness experience greater sexual desire for extra-pair partners, but only at ovulation (Pillsworth & Haselton, 2006). And women seem to choose as affair partners men who have symmetrical features, a hypothesized indicator of good genes (Gangestad et al., 2005). These findings support the hypothesis that women are going for genes that will contribute to their offspring being sexually successful. These studies all point to the viability of the good genes hypothesis as one explanation for why women have short-term extra-pair matings.

***Taking Stock of the Evolved Functions of Women's Short-Term Mating.*** Several hypotheses about the evolved functions of women's short-term mating have received some empirical support: (1) switching mates, (2) using short-term mating for long-term mating goals, (3) acquiring resources, and (4) obtaining good genes or sexy son genes. There is no requirement that women's short-term mating has one and only one function. It could have several. Women already mated to men who are low in mate value, for example, could use short-term mating to switch to a man of higher mate value. Other women might use short-term mating to assess and evaluate a man as a long-term prospect, or have sex with him for the goal of turning it into a more committed relationship. Women who live in circumstances of resource scarcity or women who are unable to attract a long-term mate might use short-term mating to acquire vital resources. And women already mated with men of low genetic quality can use short-term mating, particularly around the time of ovulation, to secure better genes.

Even these hypothesized functions might underestimate the complexity of women's short-term sexual psychology. Female sexuality, from a male perspective, is an extraordinarily valuable reproductive resource. From a female perspective, this resource is extremely *fungible,* meaning that it can be exchanged or converted into other resources (Meston & Buss, 2009). We can expect future research to explore the complexity of female short-term sexual psychology by clarifying *which women* pursue short-term mating in *which contexts* to secure *which adaptive benefits.*

## ■ CONTEXT EFFECTS ON SHORT-TERM MATING

### Individual Differences in Short-Term Mating

One window for viewing short-term mating is to contrast the subjective perceptions of costs and benefits of women who actively pursue short-term mating with those who do not. Greiling and Buss (2000) asked a sample of women to complete the Sociosexuality Orientation Inventory (SOI) (Gangestad & Simpson, 1990; see Jackson & Kirkpatrick, 2007, and Penke & Asendorpf, 2008, for more refined measurement of SOI), which assesses individual differences in whether people pursue short-term or long-term mating strategies. Women's scores on the SOI were then correlated with their perceptions of the benefits they would likely receive from short-term mating and with their perceptions of the magnitude of benefits received from short-term mating. Women who pursue short-term mating have substantially different perceptions of the benefits compared to women who tend not to pursue short-term mating. Women who tend to pursue short-term mating view three classes of benefits as more beneficial. One pertains to sexual resources. Women pursuing short-term mating view as highly beneficial having a sexual partner who is willing to experiment sexually ($r = +.51$), experiencing orgasms with the sexual partner ($r = +.47$), and experiencing great sexual pleasure because the partner was physically attractive ($r = +.39$).

Such women also see more benefits to improving their skills of attraction and seduction ($r = +.50$), supporting the mate skill acquisition hypothesis. They also view the resources from short-term mating as more beneficial, including expensive designer clothing ($r = +.45$), career advancement ($r = +.40$), jewelry ($r = +.37$), and the use of a partner's car ($r = +.35$).

Women who tend to pursue short-term mating also have different perceptions of the contexts likely to promote short-term mating. Having a regular partner who is fired ($r = +.29$), suffers a decrease in salary ($r = +.25$), or becomes terminally ill ($r = +.23$) are viewed as increasing the odds of short-term mating by such women. These results support the mate switching hypothesis—women who indicate that they have pursued short-term matings are more likely to cite problems with a partner as a rationale for an affair. Furthermore, meeting someone who is better looking than one's regular partner is perceived by such women as more likely to lead to an extra-pair mating ($r = +.25$).

Another study of individual differences using the SOI focused on shifts in "desire for commitment" from a partner (Townsend & Wasserman, 1998). Desire for commitment was measured by using items such as "I would like to know whether he/she was available for a more involved relationship (for example, not involved with anyone else at the time)" (1998, p. 183). Women who pursue short-term mating strategies, compared with their more long-term oriented peers, were considerably more willing to have sex without requiring signs of commitment from the man. Furthermore, they placed a significantly greater emphasis on the man's popularity and physical attractiveness—lending circumstantial support to the sexy son hypothesis of women's short-term mating (see also Townsend, 1998).

Two clusters of costs are viewed by short-term mating women as less likely to be incurred. The first is reputational damage. Such women view reputational damage among friends, potential partners, and high-status peer groups as significantly *less* likely to occur than do women not actively oriented toward short-term mating ($r = -.47$). Perhaps such women select contexts in which these costs are less likely to be incurred, such as a large city or when the current partner is out of town. Taken together, these findings support several of the hypothesized benefits of extra-pair mating, especially resource, mate switching, and good genes benefits.

***Can a Short-Term Sexual Strategy be Perceived by Others?*** One study videotaped twenty-four women, who differed in sexual strategy, while interacting with a male confederate (Stillman & Maner, 2009). The videotapes were then shown to a group of raters, who were asked to predict the sexual strategy of each of the women (as assessed through the women's SOI scores). Judges turned out to be reasonably accurate in estimating women's sexual strategy, with a correlation of $+.55$ between the judge's ratings and women's SOI scores. Then the researchers explored which specific cues judges used to gauge the women's SOI. Interestingly, they found some "valid" cues to SOI—eyebrow flashes and number of glances at the male confederate. The "invalid" cues, such as smiling, laughing, closeness to the confederate, and provocativeness of dress, were believed by judges to signal a short-term mating strategy in women, but in fact were not linked to women's self-reported reported sexual strategy. Sexually unrestricted women, however, do tend to show more dramatic shifts in the provocativeness of dress at ovulation compared to more sexually restricted women (Durante, Li, & Haselton, 2008). These studies suggest that women pursuing a short-term mating strategy might not dress more provocatively in general, but do dress more provocatively when they are ovulating. Another study found that women and men who have tattoos are perceived to have had a larger number of sex partners, although whether tattoos actually signal sexual strategy has not yet been determined (Wohlrab et al., 2009).

Other studies have examined *masculinity*. One found that sexually unrestricted women tended to have a more masculine facial appearance (Campbell et al., 2009). A second study found that unrestricted women tended to have higher scores on interviewer-rated physical masculinity, behavioral masculinity, as well as self-reports of childhood gender nonconformity (Mikach & Bailey, 1999). A third study found that facial masculinity was linked with a short-term mating strategy only in men, not in women (Boothroyd et al., 2008). Future research is needed to resolve this apparent discrepancy.

Other potentially observable cues to sexual strategy might reside in the mate preferences of those who pursue short-term mating. An excellent pair of studies documented that sexually unrestricted women have stronger preferences than do restricted women for men with masculine faces and bodies—preferences expressed in ratings of male photos as well as in behavioral choices in a laboratory "speed dating" study in which the women met and interacted with men who differed in masculinity (Provost et al., 2006). Men who tend to pursue a short-term mating strategy, compared to more long-term oriented men, allocate more attention to physically attractive women in laboratory studies (Duncan et al., 2007). Unrestricted men, more than restricted men, also showed a stronger preference for women with a low WHR—another finding that supports the hypothesis that men who pursue short-term mating prioritize cues to fertility.

## Other Contexts Likely to Affect Short-Term Mating

Everyone knows some men who are womanizers and others who would never stray. Everyone knows some women who enjoy casual sex and others who could not imagine sex without commitment. Individuals differ in their proclivities for casual mating. Individuals also shift their proclivities at different times and in different contexts. These variations in sexual strategy depend on a wide variety of social, cultural, and ecological conditions.

*Father Absence and Stepfather Presence.* The absence of a father while growing up has been reliably linked with the pursuit of a short-term mating strategy. Among the Mayan of Belize and the Ache of Paraguay, for example, father absence is correlated with men stating that they are unwilling to commit the time, energy, and resources needed to sustain a long-term mating relationship (Waynforth, Hurtado, & Hill, 1998). Other studies of both women and men have found that those growing up in father-absent homes are more likely to reach puberty sooner, to engage in sexual intercourse earlier, and to pursue a short-term mating strategy (e.g., Ellis et al., 1999; Surbey, 1998b). Poor or harsh parenting, especially from the father, as well as father absence is associated with daughters having an early age of reaching puberty (Tither & Ellis, 2008), having a larger number of sex partners (Alvergne, Faurie, & Raymond, 2008), as well as an increased likelihood of early reproduction (Cornwell et al., 2006; Nettle et al., 2010). One particularly harsh family environment occurs when girls are victims of sexual abuse. Childhood sexual abuse is associated with early age of puberty and early onset of sexual activity (Vigil, Geary, & Byrd-Craven, 2005).

There is currently controversy about whether these effects are solely the result of adaptations in females to shift their reproductive strategy as a function of a harsh family environment, or whether there might also be a genetic component such that fathers who are poor or absent parents pass on genes for a short-term mating strategy to their daughters (see Mendle et al., 2009; Tither & Ellis, 2008). Intriguingly, one study found that stepfather presence, even more than biological father absence, may be the critical factor promoting early sexual maturation in girls—a likely precursor to the pursuit of a short-term mating strategy (Ellis & Garber, 2000). Conversely, biological fathers may do more "daughter guarding," that is, engaging in behavior that prevents their daughters from engaging in sexual intercourse early (Surbey, 1998b). Finally, poor attachment to one's parents was linked to sexual promiscuity for both sexes (Walsh, 1995, 1999).

***Transitions across Life.*** Casual sex is also related to people's developmental stage in life. Adolescents in many cultures are more prone to temporary mating as a means of assessing their value on the mating market, experimenting with different strategies, honing their attraction skills, and clarifying their own preferences (Frayser, 1985). After they have done so, they are more ready for marriage. The fact that premarital adolescent sexual experimentation is tolerated and even encouraged in some cultures, such as the Mehinaku of Amazonia (Gregor, 1985), provides a clue that short-term mating is related to one's stage in life.

The transition points between different committed mateships offer additional opportunities for casual sex. After a divorce, for example, it is crucial to reassess one's value on the current mating market. The existence of children from the marriage generally lowers the desirability of divorced people, compared with their desirability if they had no children. The elevated status that comes with being more advanced in a career, on the other hand, may raise their desirability in comparison with the last time they were on the mating market.

***Sex Ratio.*** The abundance or deficit of eligible men relative to eligible women is another critical context that affects temporary mating. Many factors affect this sex ratio, including wars, which kill larger numbers of men than women; risk-taking activities such as physical fights, which more frequently affect men; intentional homicides, in which roughly seven times more men than women die; and different remarriage rates by age, whereby with increasing age women remarry less often than men. Men shift to brief encounters when many women are sexually available because the sex ratio is in their favor and they are therefore better able to satisfy their desire for variety (Pedersen, 1991). Among the Ache, for example, men appear to be highly promiscuous because there are 50 percent more women than men (Hill & Hurtado, 1996). When there is a surplus of men, in contrast, both sexes appear to shift toward a long-term mating strategy marked by stable marriages and fewer divorces (Pedersen, 1991). In the most comprehensive cross-cultural study of sex ratio and sexual strategies, involving 14,059 individuals in forty-eight nations, people in cultures with a surplus of women were more likely to endorse attitudes and behaviors associated with a short-term mating strategy (Schmitt, 2005).

***Mate Value, Masculinity, Body Type, and Personality.*** One context that is likely to affect short-term mating is *mate value,* one's overall desirability to members of the opposite sex. The self-perceived mating success scale (Lalumiere, Seto, & Quinsey, 1995; Landolt, Lalumiere, & Quinsey, 1995) assesses mate value. Sample items from this scale are: "members of the opposite sex notice me"; "I receive many compliments from members of the opposite sex"; "members of the opposite sex are attracted to me"; and "relative to my peer group, I can get dates with great ease."

Scores on the mate value scale were correlated with the reported sexual history of the participants, both males and females. The results were strikingly different for the sexes. High-mate-value men, relative to their lower-mate-value counterparts, tended to have sexual intercourse at an earlier age, a greater number of sex partners since puberty, a greater number of partners during the past year, a greater number of sexual invitations within the past three years, sexual intercourse a greater number of times, and no need to be attached to a person before having sex. Furthermore, high-mate-value men tended to score toward the high end of the SOI (Clark, 2006), suggesting that they are pursuing a short-term mating strategy.

Several other indicators of male mate value are linked with success at short-term mating. First, men who are high in status and resources—key indicators of men's mate value—tend to have a larger number of sex partners, indicating success at short-term mating (Kanazawa, 2003a; Perusse, 1993). Second, men high in social dominance—a predictor of future elevation in status—tend to be more unfaithful, indicating pursuit of short-term mating (Egan & Angus, 2004). Third, men with a higher shoulder-to-hip ratio (SHR)—an indicator of men's bodily attractiveness discussed in Chapter 4—have sex at an earlier age, have more sex partners and more extra-pair copulations, and are more likely to have sex with other people's mates (Hughes & Gallup, 2003). Fourth, men who compete in sports, and especially men who are successful athletic competitors, report having had a larger number of sex partners (Faurie, Pontier, & Raymond, 2004). Fifth, men who have attractive faces and masculine bodies have more short-term sex partners (Rhodes, Simmons, & Peters, 2005).

Men high in handgrip strength (Gallup, White, & Gallup, 2007) and who have high in circulating testosterone (van Anders, Hamilton, & Watson, 2007) tend to pursue a short-term mating strategy. Men with a mesomorphic (muscular) body build tend to have higher reproductive success, as gauged by offspring count (Genovese, 2008), which may reflect a short-term strategy.

The findings for a link between women's mate value and sexual strategy are more mixed. Some find no association between women's self-perceived mate value and the pursuit of a short-term mating strategy (e.g., Lalumiere et al., 1995; Landolt et al., 1995; Mikach & Bailey, 1999). On the other hand, women with a low (attractive) WHR tend to follow a more unrestricted (short-term) mating strategy and are perceived by others to be more promiscuous and less trustworthy (Brewer & Archer, 2007). One speculation is that bodily attractiveness, rather than facial or overall attractiveness, may be linked with a short-term mating strategy in women.

Personality characteristics also predict mating strategy. A study of 13,243 individuals from forty-six nations found that the traits of extraversion, low levels of agreeableness, and low levels of conscientiousness predicted an interest in short-term mating, attempts at poaching the mates of others, and succumbing to the lure of mate poaching by others (Schmitt & Shackelford, 2008). The so-called "Dark Triad" of personality—the traits of narcissism, psychopathy, and Machiavellianism—also predict exploitative short-term mating strategies, particularly in men (Jonason et al., 2009: Jonason, Li, & Buss, 2010).

## ■ SUMMARY

The scientific study of mating over the course of the twentieth century has focused nearly exclusively on marriage. Human anatomy, physiology, and psychology, however, betray an ancestral past filled with affairs and short-term mating. The obvious reproductive advantages of short-term mating to men may have blinded scientists to their benefits to women.

In this chapter, we first considered men's short-term mating. According to Trivers's theory of parental investment and sexual selection, the reproductive benefits to ancestral men as a consequence of short-term mating would have been direct—an increase in the number of children produced as a function of the number of women successfully inseminated. The empirical evidence is strong that men do have a greater desire for short-term mating than do women. Compared to women, men express a greater desire for a variety of sex partners, let less time elapse before seeking sexual intercourse, lower their standards dramatically when pursuing short-term mating, have more sexual fantasies and more fantasies involving a variety of sex partners, experience more sexual regret over missed sexual opportunities, have a larger number of extramarital affairs, and visit prostitutes more often. Although a few psychologists continue to deny these fundamental sex differences (e.g., Miller & Fishkin, 1997), the difference between men and women in the desire for sexual variety is one of the largest, most replicable, and most cross-culturally robust psychological sex differences ever documented (Schmitt et al., 2003; Petersen & Hyde, 2010).

Mathematically, however, short-term mating requires two. Except for forced copulation, men's desire for short-term sex could not have evolved without the presence of some willing women. We looked at the evidence that some women historically have engaged in short-term mating some of the time. The existence of physiological clues in men, such as testicle size and variations in sperm insemination, suggests a long evolutionary history of *sperm competition*—in which the sperm from two different men have inhabited a woman's reproductive tract at the same time. From an evolutionary perspective, it is unlikely that women would have recurrently engaged in short-term mating without reaping some adaptive benefits.

There are potentially five classes of adaptive benefits to women: economic or material resources, genetic benefits, mate switching benefits, short-term for long-term goals, and mate manipulation benefits. Based on the studies that have been conducted, the empirical evidence supports the hypothesized functions of mate switching, resource acquisition, short-term for long-term mating goals, and access to good genes or sexy son genes, and does not at all support status enhancement or mate manipulation benefits. Individuals differ in whether they tend to pursue short-term or long-term mating strategies. Interestingly, these individual differences can be detected, at least partially. Women with a short-term mating inclination show more eyebrow flashes and glances when interacting with men; dress more provocatively at ovulation; are perceived to be somewhat masculine in appearance, and are attracted to men who have especially masculine faces and bodies. Men who prioritize short-term mating tune their attention to attractive women more than their long-term oriented peers, and also show a stronger preference for women with a low WHR—a well-established cue to fertility.

The final section of this chapter examined various context effects on short-term mating. Sex ratio is one context—a surplus of women tends to promote short-term mating in both sexes. Another important context is mate value, one's desirability to members of the opposite sex. Men high in mate value, as indicated by status, dominance, high SHR, success in sports, facial attractiveness, and masculine features, are more likely to pursue short-term mating, as reflected in measures such as younger age at first intercourse and a larger number of sex partners. The link between women's mate value and preferred sexual strategy is more mixed. Some studies show no relationship between women's self-perceived mate value and sexual strategy. Others show that women with a low (attractive) WHR are slightly more inclined to pursue a short-term mating strategy; they are also *perceived* by others as somewhat more sexually unrestricted. Finally, personality characteristics predict sexual strategy. Those high on extraversion, low on agreeableness, and low on conscientiousness are more inclined to short-term mating. Those who score high on the Dark Triad—narcissism, psychopathy, and Machiavellianism—also tend to pursue an exploitative short-term mating strategy.

# ■ SUGGESTED READINGS

Campbell, A. (2008). The morning after the night before: Affective reactions to one-night stands among mated and unmated women and men. *Human Nature, 19,* 157–173.

Gangestad, S. W., Thornhill, R., & Garver-Apgar, C. E. (2005). Adaptations to ovulation. In D. M. Buss (Ed.), *The handbook of evolutionary psychology* (pp. 344–371). New York: Wiley.

Greiling, H., & Buss, D. M. (2000). Women's sexual strategies: The hidden dimension of extra-pair mating. *Personality and Individual Differences, 28,* 929–963.

Lippa, R. A. (2009). Sex differences in sex drive, sociosexuality, and height across 53 nations: Testing evolutionary and social structural theories. *Archives of Sexual Behavior, 38,* 631–651.

Schmitt, D. P., Couden, A., & Baker, M. (2001). The effects of sex and temporal context on feelings of romantic desire: An experimental evaluation of sexual strategies theory. *Personality and Social Psychology Bulletin, 27,* 833–847.

Schützwohl, A., Fuchs, A., McKibben, W. F., & Shackelford, T. K. (2009). How willing are you to accept sexual requests from slightly unattractive to exceptionally attractive imagined requestors? *Human Nature, 20,* 282–293.

Stillman, T. F., & Maner, J. K. (2009). A sharp eye for her SOI: Perception and misperception of female sociosexuality at zero acquaintance. *Evolution and Human Behavior, 30,* 124–130.

Surbey, M. K., & Conohan, C. D. (2000). Willingness to engage in casual sex: The role of parental qualities and perceived risk of aggression. *Human Nature, 11,* 367–386.

# PART 4

# CHALLENGES OF PARENTING AND KINSHIP

This part includes two chapters, one devoted to problems of parenting and one to problems of kinship. Once an organism has successfully traversed the hurdles of survival and then managed to solve the problems of mating and reproduction, the next challenge is to channel effort into the products of reproduction—the "vehicles" for parents' genes known as children (Chapter 7). This chapter starts with the puzzle of why mothers typically provide more parental care than fathers in nearly all species that provide any parental care at all. It goes on to explore the patterns of parental care, focusing on three key issues: the likely degree of genetic relatedness of the child to the parent, the child's ability to convert parental care into fitness, and tradeoffs parents face between investing in children and using their resources for other adaptive problems. The final section provides an evolutionary explanation for a phenomenon that nearly every living human has experienced: conflict between parents and children.

Chapter 8 broadens the analysis to consider extended kin, such as grandparents, grandchildren, nieces, nephews, aunts, and uncles. The theory of inclusive fitness provides a host of implications for understanding relationships between genetic relatives, including phenomena such as helping genetic relatives in life-or-death situations, leaving resources to genetic relatives in one's will, investment by grandparents in their grandchildren, and sex differences in the importance of kin relations. The chapter concludes with a broader perspective on the evolution of extended families.

# CHAPTER 7

# PROBLEMS OF PARENTING

*My mother saith he is my father. Yet for myself I know it not. For no man knoweth who hath begotten him.*

—Telemachus, son of Odysseus,
from Homer's *The Odyssey*

𝒥magine a society in which all men and women received exactly the same income. Every able-bodied adult worked. All decisions were made communally by both sexes, and all children were raised collectively by the group. How would people react when actually faced with this social arrangement? Such an experiment was in fact conducted in Israel among those living in a kibbutz. Two anthropologists— Joseph Shepher and Lionel Tiger—studied three generations living in a kibbutz, a total of 34,040 people. In their classic 1975 book *Women in the Kibbutz*, Shepher and Tiger tell that they found, astonishingly, that the division of labor by gender was actually greater in the kibbutz than in the rest of Israel (Tiger, 1996). Most striking, however, were the strong preferences exerted by women: Over time, they began to insist that their own children live with them rather than be raised collectively by other women. The men tried to veto this move, considering it a step backward, giving in to bourgeois values at the expense of the original utopian dream. The mothers and their mothers stood their ground and outvoted the men of the community. So the utopian experiment of communal child rearing reverted to the primacy of the mother–child bond—a pattern seen in every human culture.

From an evolutionary perspective, offspring are a sort of vehicle for their parents. They are the means by which their parents' genes may get transported to succeeding generations. Without children, an individual's genes may perish forever. Given the supreme importance of offspring as genetic vehicles, then, it is reasonable to expect that natural selection would favor powerful mechanisms in parents to ensure the survival and reproductive success of their children.

Aside from those of mating, perhaps no other adaptive problems are as paramount as making sure that one's offspring survive and thrive. Indeed, without the success of offspring, all the effort that an organism invested in mating would be reproductively meaningless. Evolution, in short, should produce a rich repertoire of parental mechanisms specially adapted to caring for offspring.

Given the importance of offspring, one of the astonishing facts about parental care is that many species do not engage in it at all (Alcock, 2009). Oysters, for example, simply release their sperm and eggs into the ocean, leaving their offspring adrift with not a shred of parental care. For every oyster that manages to survive under these lonely conditions, thousands die. Part of the reason for the lack of universality of parental care is that it is so costly. By investing in offspring, parents lose out on resources that could be channeled toward finding additional mates or increasing reproductive output. Parents who protect their young risk their own survival. Some become wounded or die while fending off predators that threaten their offspring. Given the costs of parental care, then, it is reasonable to expect that whenever we do observe parental care in nature, the reproductive benefits must be large enough to outweigh the costs.

The evolution of parental care has been explored in many nonhuman animal species (Clutton-Brock, 1991). Mexican free-tailed bats provide one fascinating example of the evolution of parental care. These bats live in dark caves in large colonies containing hundreds of thousands—in some cases millions—of other bats. After a female bat gives birth, she leaves the safety of the colony to forage for food. When she returns, she is faced with the problem of recognizing her own pup among the many densely packed in the cave. One square yard of the cave wall may contain several thousands pups, so the problem is not a small one. If selection operated "for the good of the species," it wouldn't matter which pup the mother bat fed, nor would there be any selection pressure to recognize and feed her own. That is not how mother bats behave, however. Eighty-three percent of the mothers actually find and feed their own pups, giving up 16 percent of their body weight in milk each day (McCracken, 1984). Each mother's evolved parental mechanisms were designed by selection to help her own genetic offspring, not the offspring of the bat species as a whole.

Another example of adaptations for parental care is found in nesting birds. Tinbergen (1963) explored the puzzle of why nesting birds would go to the trouble of removing the broken shells from their newly hatched chicks and laboriously take them, piece by piece, far away from the nest. He explored three hypotheses: (1) Eggshell removal served a sanitary function, keeping the nest free of germs and disease that might use the broken shells as a conduit; (2) eggshell removal protected the newly hatched chicks from the sharp edges that come with broken shells; and (3) eggshell removal made the nests less noticeable to predators that might be inclined to prey on the young chicks. Through a series of experiments, Tinbergen discovered that only the protection from predators hypothesis received support. The cost of parental care, in short, was outweighed by the benefits of increased survival of chicks through a decrease in predation.

Despite the paramount importance of parental care from an evolutionary perspective, such care has been a relatively neglected topic within the field of human psychology. When evolutionary psychologists Martin Daly and Margo Wilson prepared a chapter on the topic for the 1987 "Nebraska Symposium on Motivation," they scanned the thirty-four earlier volumes in the series in search of either psychological research or theories on parental motivation. Not a single one of those volumes contained even a paragraph on parental motivation (Daly & Wilson, 1995). Despite the widespread knowledge that mothers tend to love their children, the very phenomenon of powerful parental love appears to have baffled psychologists at a theoretical level. One prominent psychologist who has written several books on the topic of love noted, "The needs that lead many of us to feel unconditional love for our children also seem to be remarkably persistent, for reasons that are not at present altogether clear" (Sternberg, 1986, p. 133). From an evolutionary perspective, however, the reasons for deep parental love do seem clear. Selection has designed precisely such psychological mechanisms—parental motivation designed to ensure the survival and reproductive success of the invaluable vehicles that transport an individual's genes into the next generation. As we will see in the following sections, however, for some intriguing evolutionary reasons the love of parents is far from unconditional.

With this background in mind, let's turn to the fascinating topic of parental care and pose a question that requires us to look at humans within the broader context of species in the animal kingdom: Why do mothers in so many species, including humans, provide parental care so much more than fathers do?

## ■ WHY DO MOTHERS PROVIDE MORE PARENTAL CARE THAN FATHERS?

Evolutionary biologist John Alcock (2009) describes a fascinating film on the hunting dogs of Africa that documented the life and hostile forces encountered by one particular dog named Solo. Solo was the only surviving offspring of a female who was subordinate in her pack. Because of the mother's status, she and her offspring were vulnerable to victimization. One by one, Solo's littermates were killed by another female in the pack, a rival with whom Solo's mother had a history of antagonism. Solo's mother fought in vain to save her pups from her murderous rival. Astonishingly, while the mother risked life and limb to save her pups, the father stood by passively and did *nothing* to protect them!

Although this story is stark, it dramatically illustrates a profound truth in the evolution of life: Throughout the animal kingdom, females are far more likely than males to care for their offspring. Humans are no exception. In an amusing acknowledgment, the author of a book called *The Evolution of Parental Care* said that his "greatest debt is to my wife, . . . [who] looked after our children while I wrote about parental care" (Clutton-Brock, 1991). A tremendous volume of cross-cultural data on humans, using measures from time spent in vicinity to time spent touching to time spent teaching, shows that women indeed care for their children more intensively than men do (Bjorklund & Pellegrini, 2002; Geary, 2000, 2010). The intriguing question is why mothers more than fathers? A variety of hypotheses have been advanced to explain the predominance of female parental care. We will consider two that are most relevant to humans: (1) the paternity uncertainty hypothesis and (2) the mating opportunity costs hypothesis.

### The Paternity Uncertainty Hypothesis

Mothers throughout the animal kingdom generally are 100 percent "sure" of their genetic contribution to their offspring. It is necessary to put the "sure" in quotation marks because no conscious recognition of their certainty in parenthood is necessary. When a female gives birth or lays a fertilized egg, there is no doubt that her offspring will contain 50 percent of her genes. Males can never be "sure." The problem of *paternity uncertainty* means that from a male perspective there can always be some probability that another male has fertilized the female's eggs.

*Although we tend to take mother love for granted, a number of competing hypotheses have been proposed to explain why, in most species, mothers tend to invest more than fathers in their offspring.*

Paternity uncertainty is strongest in species with internal female fertilization, including many insects, humans, all primates, and indeed all mammals. Because of internal female fertilization, when a male comes on the scene, the female may already have mated with another male and so her eggs might already be fertilized. Or she might mate with another male at any time during their consortship, perhaps in secret. Males suffer tremendous costs by channeling their resources to other men's descendants. Resources devoted to a rival's children are resources taken away from one's own. Because of the costs that males incur as a result of misdirected parental effort, any degree of paternity uncertainty means that it will be less advantageous for males to invest their resources in parental care. Therefore, paternity uncertainty offers one explanation for the widespread occurrence of females investing more than males in parental care.

Paternity uncertainty is not enough to preclude the evolution of paternal care. But it does make it less profitable for fathers, *compared with mothers*, to invest in their offspring. Each unit of parental investment pays off more for mothers than for fathers under conditions of paternity uncertainty because some fraction of the "father's" investment will be wasted on progeny that are not his own. A full 100 percent of the mother's parental investment, in contrast, goes toward her own children. In sum, although paternity uncertainty does not preclude the evolution of male paternal care, it remains one viable cause of the widespread tendency of females to invest more in offspring than males do.

## The Mating Opportunity Cost Hypothesis

A second hypothesis stems from sex differences in mating opportunity costs. *Mating opportunity costs* are missed additional matings as a direct result of effort devoted to offspring. Females and males both suffer mating opportunity costs. While a mother is gestating or breastfeeding her child or a father is fending off predators, neither has a high probability of securing additional mates. The mating opportunity costs are higher for males than for females, however, for the reason we encountered in Chapter 6: The reproductive success of males tends to be limited primarily by the number of fertile females they can successfully inseminate. In humans, for example, males can produce more children by mating with a variety of women, but women generally cannot increase reproductive output directly by mating with a variety of men. In summary, because the mating opportunity costs of parental care will generally be higher for males than for females, males will be less likely than females to take on parental care.

According to this hypothesis, male parental care should be rare when the opportunity costs of missed matings for males are high (Alcock, 2009). When the opportunity costs males suffer from missing matings are low, however, the conditions would be more favorable for the evolution of parental care. Precisely such a condition occurs in fish species in which the males stake out and defend a specific territory (Gross & Sargent, 1985). Females then scope out the territories of various males and select one in which to lay their eggs. Males can then guard and even feed the eggs while at the same time guarding their own territory. In this case, the male's mating opportunities will not suffer as a result of parental investment. Indeed, the presence of eggs laid by other females in a given male's territory appears to make males attractive to females, prompting them to lay their eggs in territories already containing eggs. Perhaps the presence of other eggs indicates to a female that the territory is safe from predators or that another female has judged the resident male acceptable. In sum, when males do not suffer mating opportunity costs as a consequence of investing in offspring, conditions are ripe for the evolution of male parental care.

The hypothesis of mating opportunity costs may partly explain individual differences in parenting among humans. In contexts in which there is a surplus of men in the eligible mating pool, men find it difficult to pursue a short-term mating strategy. When there is a surplus of women, on the other hand, there are many more mating opportunities for men (see Chapter 6; see also Guttentag & Secord, 1983; Pedersen, 1991). Therefore, we can predict that men will be more likely to invest in children in contexts in which there is a surplus of men but will be more negligent of children when there is a surplus of women. A great deal of empirical evidence suggests that this is the case (Pedersen, 1991). In addition to sex ratio, other factors likely to explain individual differences in amount of parenting include (1) attractiveness of the male as a short-term mate (more attractive males are predicted to reduce their parental effort and increase their mating effort) (Gangestad & Thornhill, 2008) and (2) population density (large cities provide more opportunities for males to interact with females than do low-density rural areas) (Magrath & Komdeur, 2003).

In summary, two hypotheses have been advanced to explain the widespread prevalence of greater parental care in females than in males: paternity uncertainty and mating opportunity costs. These hypotheses are not intrinsically incompatible, of course, and it is likely that both account in part for the sex differences in parental care.

## ■ AN EVOLUTIONARY PERSPECTIVE ON PARENTAL CARE

At the beginning of this chapter, we noted that offspring are the vehicles fashioned by selection by which parental genes get transported into future generations, but not all offspring reproduce. Some are better at survival or have more promising mating prospects and so are better bets for successfully transporting the parents' genes. Some offspring are more likely to benefit from parental care. As a general rule, selection will favor adaptations for *parental care*—the preferential allocation of investment to one or more offspring at the expense of other forms of allocating investment—that have the effect of increasing the fitness of the parent. It follows that mechanisms of parental care will favor some offspring over others—a condition called *parental favoritism*. Stated differently, selection will favor the evolution of mechanisms in parents that favor offspring who are likely to provide a higher reproductive return on the investment (Daly & Wilson, 1995). Fathers as well as mothers should be sensitive to these conditions, as father–child bonds, although often weaker than mother–child bonds, appear to be universal across cultures (Mackey & Daly, 1995).

At the most general theoretical level, evolved mechanisms of parental care should be sensitive to three contexts (Alexander, 1979):

1. *Genetic relatedness of the offspring:* Are the children really my own?
2. *Ability of the offspring to convert parental care into fitness:* Will a given unit of my investment make a difference to the survival and reproduction of my children?
3. *Alternative uses of the resources that might be available to invest in offspring:* Will a given unit of my investment be best spent investing in children or in other activities such as investing in my sister's children or in additional mating opportunities?

## Genetic Relatedness to Offspring

In Pittsburgh, Pennsylvania, a bus driver known as Mr. G. found out after six years that his daughter, who had been calling him "Daddy" all her life, was not in fact his genetic daughter (*New York Times*, 1995). The first hint of this came when Mr. G. overheard gossip that another man in town was boasting that he was the actual father. Blood tests eventually confirmed that this was correct. Mr. G. stopped giving monthly support payments, refused to hug or kiss the girl, and stopped taking her on outings when he went to pick up his son (who was his biological child). The court ordered Mr. G. to continue child support payments. Although he had been in close contact with the girl for six years, the revelation of his lack of paternity caused an abrupt reversal of his feelings.

Daly and Wilson (1988) describe the impact of genetic relatedness on parental motivation succinctly:

> Perhaps the most obvious prediction from a Darwinian view of parental motives is this: Substitute parents will generally tend to care less profoundly for children than natural parents, with the result that children reared by people other than their natural parents will be more often exploited and otherwise at risk. Parental investment is a precious resource, and selection must favor those parental psyches that do not squander it on nonrelatives. (p. 83)

Studies of parental feelings support this prediction. In one study of stepparents conducted in Cleveland, Ohio, only 53 percent of stepfathers and 25 percent of stepmothers claimed to have any "parental feelings" at all toward their stepchildren (Duberman, 1975). Darwinian anthropologist Mark Flinn found a similar result in a Trinidadian village: Stepfathers' interactions with their stepchildren were less frequent and more aggressive than similar interactions involving genetic fathers and their children (Flinn, 1988b). Furthermore, the stepchildren apparently found these aggressive interactions unpleasant, for they left home at a younger age than genetic children.

These findings do not mean that intense feelings of parental love cannot be activated by any child other than a genetic one. Stepparents can and often do channel affection, devotion, and resources toward stepchildren. The key point is that parental love and resources are substantially *less likely* to be directed toward children by stepparents than by genetic parents. This point is recognized even in the Webster's dictionary definition of "stepmother," which includes two components: (1) the wife of one's father by a subsequent marriage and (2) one that fails to give proper care or attention (Gove, 1986).

The conflicts of interest inherent in steprelations are frequently noted in children's tales and folklore across many cultures (Daly & Wilson, 1999). One extensive cross-cultural summary of folk literature summarized these themes as follows: "Evil stepmother orders stepdaughter to be killed" and "Evil stepmother works stepdaughter to death in absence of merchant husband" (Thompson, 1955; cited in Daly & Wilson, 1988, p. 85). The theme of evil stepfathers is equally prevalent, the two major subcategories being "lustful stepfathers" (those who are inclined to abuse a stepdaughter sexually) and "cruel stepfathers" (those who are inclined to abuse stepchildren physically or emotionally). In peoples as diverse as the Irish, Indians, Aleuts, and Indonesians, folk stories depict stepparents as villains (Daly & Wilson, 1999).

Interestingly, the problems encountered in stepparent–stepchild relationships have commonly been attributed to "the myth of the cruel stepparent" or to "children's irrational fears" by the few social scientists who have observed or studied these relationships (Daly & Wilson, 1988, p. 86). But if the fears are irrational and the cruelty is indeed a myth, then it is reasonable to ask why these beliefs recur so commonly across so many diverse cultures. Do these myths, beliefs, and folklore have any substance in the reality of parent–child relationships? We will examine the evidence later within the topics of child abuse and child homicide.

In species with internal female fertilization, such as our own, maternity is 100 percent certain, but paternity is sometimes in doubt. How do men assess certainty of paternity? A man has at least two sources of information to consider the likelihood that he is the genetic father of a given child: (1) information about his partner's sexual fidelity during the period in which she conceived, and (2) perceptions of the child's resemblance to him (Daly & Wilson, 1988). It is reasonable to expect that men will have evolved psychological mechanisms sensitive to both sources of information. We also expect that a mother will attempt to influence the man's perceptions around these issues, for example by trying to convince him that she has indeed been sexually faithful or that the newborn baby is the spitting image of him.

*Father and infant: Is there a resemblance? Studies show that the mother, her relatives, and the father's relatives tend to declare that the infant looks more like the father than the mother. Is this a strategy to assure the man of paternity certainty and thereby ensure his investment in the child?*

### Who Are Newborn Babies Said to Resemble?
Daly and Wilson (1982) suggested that mothers should be motivated to promote a putative father's certainty of paternity by remarking on the newborn's similarity in appearance to him. Success in promoting the man's belief that he is the father should increase his willingness to invest in that child. To examine these efforts by mothers, Daly and Wilson secured videotapes of 111 U.S. births that

ranged in duration from five to forty-five minutes. The verbal utterances were recorded verbatim for subsequent scoring. Of the 111 videotapes, 68 contained explicit references to the baby's appearance.

By chance alone, one would expect babies to be said to resemble the mother 50 percent of the time and the father 50 percent of the time. In fact, when the baby was said to resemble either parent, the mother's remarks about the resemblance to the father were four times as frequent (80 percent) as her remarks about the baby's resemblance to her (20 percent). Sample remarks by mothers included "It looks like you" (one woman said this three times to her husband), "feels like you," "just like daddy," "he looks like you, got a head of hair like yours," and "he looks like you, honestly he does" (Daly & Wilson, 1982, p. 70).

In a second study, Daly and Wilson (1982) sent out 526 questionnaires to new parents whose names were gleaned from birth announcements in newspapers in Canada. Those who responded were asked to secure contacts with their relatives so that they also could participate in the study. Among the questions asked were "Who do you think the baby is most similar to?" The results of this second study confirmed the results of the first. Of the mothers who commented on the baby's resemblance to one of the parents, 81 percent indicated that the baby was more similar to the father, whereas only 19 percent indicated greater similarity to themselves. The mothers' relatives also showed this bias: Among those who commented on resemblance to either parent, 66 percent indicated that the baby was most similar to the putative father, whereas only 34 percent noted similarity to the mother.

The basic pattern of results—the greater the likelihood of the mother to insist on resemblance to the putative father—has been replicated in at least one other culture, Mexicans residing in the Yucatan (Regalski & Gaulin, 1993). In that study, 198 interviews were conducted with the relatives of forty-nine Mexican infants. As in the Canadian study, relatives asserted that the infant resembled the putative father substantially more than the mother. The mother and her relatives were significantly more likely than the father and his relatives to make claims about paternal resemblance. In summary, this cross-cultural replication is consistent with the hypothesis that mothers and their kin attempt to influence the putative father's perceptions of his paternity, presumably to encourage male parental investment in the child.

Another study provided insight into whether or not newborns actually resemble their fathers (McLain et al., 2000). First, mothers were more likely to point out purported resemblances between their newborns and the domestic fathers than resemblances to themselves. Second, they were more likely to comment on this resemblance when the domestic father was actually present in the room than at any other time. Third, when judges were asked to match photographs of newborns to photographs of the mothers and fathers, more accurate matches were made with the mothers. This finding suggests that the bias in mothers' remarks about resemblance to the father do not, in fact, reflect actual resemblance. Indeed, the most systematic studies to date suggest that, contrary to initial indications from one study (Christenfeld & Hill, 1995), children at ages one, three, and five do *not* resemble their fathers more than they resemble their mothers (Bredart & French, 1999).

An intriguing study suggests that perceptions of resemblance might affect men's subsequent investment in the child. Using a computerized "morphing" procedure, the experimenters created photographs of children into which either participants' faces were morphed or those of other people were morphed (Platek et al., 2002). After viewing each photograph, participants completed a questionnaire that asked about how much they would hypothetically invest in each of the children. Men found the faces into which their photo had been morphed to be the most attractive and indicated that they would spend more time with this child, invest more money in this child, and be least resentful of paying child support to this child. In contrast, women were much less affected by the child's resemblance to themselves.

Research using fMRI (functional magnetic resonance imaging) brain-scan technology has discovered that men show greater cortical activity than do women when shown images of children's faces that resemble their own (Platek, Keenan, & Mohamed, 2005). Specifically, they show higher levels of neural activation in the left front cortex, an area of the brain linked with inhibiting negative responses (Platek et al., 2004). These studies point to progress in identifying the underlying specific brain mechanisms underlying evolved psychological adaptations (Platek, Keenan, & Shackelford, 2007) (see Figure 7.1).

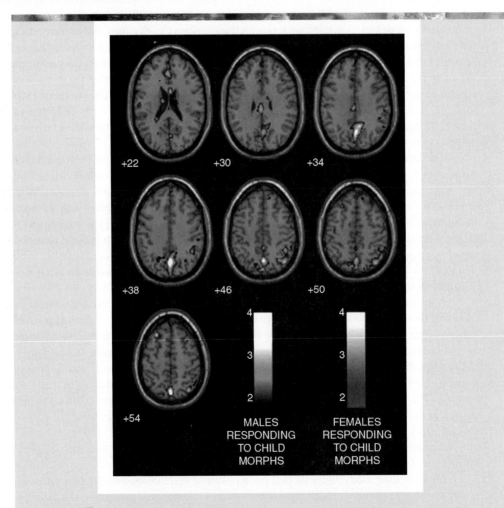

FIGURE 7.1  **Sex Difference in Activation to Self–Child Resemblance.** Bright spots indicate greater male brain activation.

*Source:* Platek, S. M., Keenan, J. P., & Mohamed, F. B. (2005). Sex differences in the neural correlates of child facial resemblance: An event-related fMRI study. *Neuro Image, 25,* 1341 (Figure 4a).

*Men who perceive that their children do not look like them inflict more abuse on their spouses.*

Another study found that fathers who perceive that their children resemble them report investing more heavily in their children—these fathers give their children more attention, spend more time with them, and get more involved in the child's schoolwork (Apicella & Marlow, 2004). Interestingly, men who perceive their wives to be trustworthy and faithful—cues to paternity certainty—invested more in their children than men who viewed their wives as untrustworthy and unfaithful.

Men's perceptions of their children's resemblance to themselves also might affect family violence. In one study, fifty-five men participating in a domestic violence treatment program evaluated the degree to which their children looked like them (Burch & Gallup, 2000). Men who judged their children to look like them reported more positive relationships with their children. But the most surprising finding was the correlation between perceptions of resemblance and the men's severity of abuse inflicted on their spouse. Men who rated their children as *not* looking like them were more likely to inflict severe physical injuries on their partners. Thus perceptions of a child's resemblance to the father might be one of the critical cues that affect both his degree of investment in the children and the magnitude of the costs he inflicts on his spouse.

***Parents' Investment in Children.*** Humans live in a modern context that is in many ways different from the ancestral contexts. Modern humans have cash economies that were nonexistent in the Pleistocene era. From a research perspective, one advantage of cash economies is that they provide concrete quantitative measures of investment.

Three evolutionary anthropologists exploited this opportunity to evaluate the effects of men's paternity uncertainty on their investment in children's college education (Anderson, Kaplan, & Lancaster, 1999). They made three predictions: (1) Men will allocate more resources to their genetic children than to their stepchildren; (2) men who are uncertain about whether children are genetically their own will invest less than men who are certain the children are their own; and (3) men will invest more in children when the child's mother is their current mate than they will in children from former mateships. This third prediction applies to both genetic children and stepchildren. Predictions 1 and 2 follow directly from the evolutionary theory of parental care and in particular from the premise of genetic relatedness. Prediction 3 is based on the hypothesis that men use parental care as a form of mating effort. That is, the transfer of resources to children by men is a means of attracting and retaining a mate.

The data for testing these predictions come from 615 men living in Albuquerque, New Mexico. These men parented 1,246 children, of whom 1,158 were genetic offspring and 88 were stepoffspring. The researchers collected data on three dependent measures: (1) whether the child received any money at all for college from the respondent (69 percent had received some money); (2) the total amount of money each child received for college from the respondent, adjusted to 1990 dollars (on average, each offspring received $13,180 from the respondent); and (3) the percentage of the child's college expenses that were paid by the respondent (on average, 44 percent of college expenses were paid by the respondents).

The results powerfully supported all three predictions. Being genetically related to the respondent rather than being a stepchild made a large difference. Compared with stepchildren, genetic children were 5.5 times more likely to receive some money for college from the respondents; they received $15,500 more for college on average and had 65 percent more of their college expenses paid for. Prediction 1—that men would allocate more investment to genetic children than to stepchildren—was strongly supported.

The second prediction pertained to the effects of men's certainty that they were actually the fathers. In the survey, the men listed every pregnancy they believed they were responsible for. Subsequently, they were asked whether they were certain that they were the fathers. A man was classified as having low confidence in paternity if he indicated that he was certain he was not the father or was unsure whether he was the father. Children of fathers with low paternity certainty were only 13 percent as likely to receive any money at all for college, and received a whopping $28,400 less for college than children whose fathers were confident that they were the genetic fathers. So prediction 2 appears to be supported.

The third prediction—that men will invest more in children of their current mates than those of their former mates, regardless of who are the genetic parents—also received strong support. A child was roughly three times as likely to receive money from the respondent if the child's mother was the respondent's mate at the time the child entered college. All else being equal, children received $14,900 more when their genetic parents were together; an additional 53 percent of the college costs of such children were paid for when the children's mothers were still mated with the respondents. The fact that men invest more in children as a function of the mating relationship with the mother, even when the children are stepchildren, supports the hypothesis that men's parental investment may function in part as "mating effort" rather than as strictly a "parental effort."

Other studies find similar effects of paternity uncertainty on male parental investment. A study of American men found that men with low paternity confidence spent less time with their putative children (while those children were in groups of other children or with other adults) and invested less in their education (Anderson, Kaplan, & Lancaster, 2007). A study of French families found that fathers of children whose faces resembled their own reported being much more "emotionally close" to them compared to those lacking resemblance (Alvergne, Faurie, & Raymond, 2010). In contrast, mother's facial resemblance to the child was unrelated to how emotionally close they felt (see Figure 7.2). And a study of Dutch men found that fathers show more affection and attachment to children whose smell they can easily recognize than toward putative children whose smell they cannot recognize (Dubas, Heikoop, & van Aken, 2009). Perhaps facial resemblance and odor recognition are two cues men use to gauge paternity.

Similar effects have been discovered in men's investment in Xhosa high school students residing in Cape Town, South Africa (Anderson, Kaplan, Lam et al., 1999). Men invested more

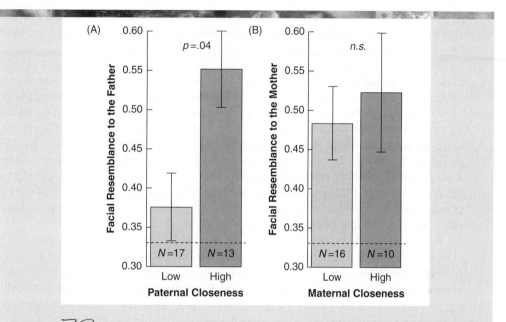

FIGURE 7.2 **Parental Investment by Fathers Is Linked to Increased Survival and Well-being of Children.** (A) Paternal closeness and resemblance to the father. (B) Maternal closeness and resemblance to the mother. Sample sizes and error bars (standard errors of the mean) are indicated. The dashed line indicates the rate of parent–child pair detection expected by chance (0.33). "High" closeness means that the child is the parent's preferred child among his/her offspring, and "low" closeness means that the child is not the parent's preferred child. Facial resemblance to the father, as assessed by external judges, predicts paternal closeness while facial resemblance to the mother is not related to maternal closeness.

$N$ = sample size.

$p$ values less than .05 indicate that sex difference is significant.

n.s. = nonsignificant.

*Source:* Alvergne, A., Faurie, C., & Raymond, M. (2010). Are parents' perceptions of offspring facial resemblance consistent with actual resemblance? Effects on parental investment. *Evolution and Human Behavior, 31,* 7–15 (Figure 2, p. 12). Reprinted with permission from Elsevier.

money, purchased more clothing, spent more time, and helped more with the homework when the high school student was a genetic offspring rather than a stepoffspring. Xhosa men did invest some amount in their stepchildren, which the researchers interpret as a form of mating effort. Evolutionary anthropologist Frank Marlow also found that among the Hadza of Tanzania, stepfathers invest less than genetic fathers do (Marlow, 1999). Indeed, Marlow found that not a single stepfather in his study engaged in direct play with a stepchild. When asked directly about their feelings, stepfathers admitted that their positive feelings were considerably weaker for their stepchildren than for their natural children.

In summary, genetic relatedness to a child is a powerful predictor of men's monetary investment. Men invest more in genetic children than in stepchildren. They also invest more when they feel certain that they are the genetic father.

***Child Abuse and Other Risks of Not Living with Both Parents.*** Parental care may be viewed as a continuum. At one end is extreme self-sacrifice, in which the parent devotes all of his or her resources to a child, perhaps even risking life and limb to save the child's life. The other end of the parental care continuum is occupied by events that inflict costs on the child, such as child abuse. At the very extreme of this continuum is infanticide, the killing of an infant, which may be regarded as a reverse assay of parental care (that is, as an assessment of the extreme opposite of parental care). Inclusive fitness theory tells us that genetic relatedness to the child would be one predictor of infanticide: The less genetically related the adult was to the child, the higher the probability of infanticide. This prediction has been tested (Daly & Wilson, 1988, 1995, 1996a, 1996b, 2007).

In the most extensive study of its kind, Daly and Wilson surveyed 841 households that included children age seventeen or younger and ninety-nine abused children from a children's aid society in Hamilton, Ontario, Canada (Daly & Wilson, 1985). Most young children live with both genetic parents, so the rates of child abuse by stepparents and genetic parents must be corrected based on these proportions to yield a common index such as "victims per 1,000 children in population." The results are shown in Figure 7.3.

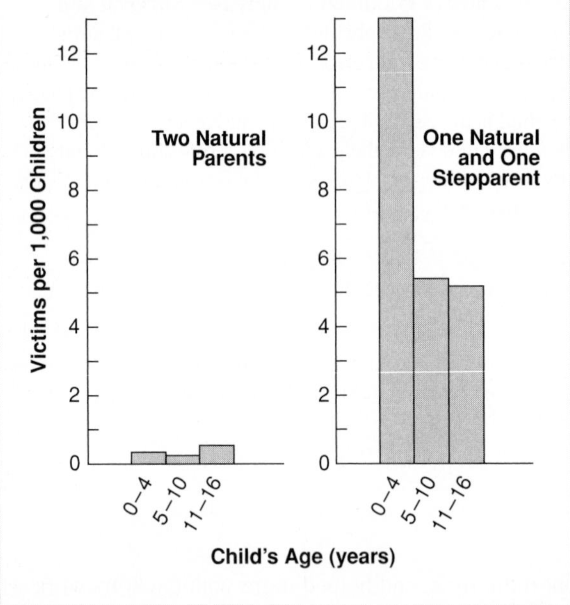

These data show that children living with one genetic parent and one stepparent are roughly *forty times* more likely to be physically abused than children living with both genetic parents. This greater risk rate occurs even when other factors such as poverty and socioeconomic status are controlled. There is indeed a higher rate of child abuse in low-income families, but it turns out that the rates in stepfamilies are roughly the same across different levels of socioeconomic status. Daly and Wilson concluded that "step-parenthood *per se* remains the single most powerful risk factor for child abuse that has yet been identified" (Daly & Wilson, 1988, pp. 87–88). Some people, of course, might claim that such findings are "obvious" or that "anyone could have predicted them." Perhaps so. But the fact remains that hundreds of previous studies of child

FIGURE 7.3 **Per Capita Rates of Child Abuse Cases Known to Children's Aid Societies and Reported to a Provincial Registry.** Hamilton, Ontario, Canada, 1983.

*Source:* Daly, M., & Wilson, M. (1988). *Homicide,* 87. New York: Aldine de Gruyter. Copyright © 1988 by Aldine de Gruyter. Reprinted with permission.

abuse failed to identify stepparents as a risk factor for child abuse until Daly and Wilson approached the problem with an evolutionary lens (Daly & Wilson, 2008).

### *Child Homicide as a Function of Genetic Relatedness to Offspring*

On February 20th, 1992, 2-year-old Scott M. died in a Montreal hospital of massive internal injuries caused by one or more abdominal blows. At the manslaughter trial of his mother's 24-year-old live-in boyfriend, doctors testified that Scott's body displayed "all the symptoms of a battered child," mainly because of "numerous bruises of varying ages." The accused, who portrayed himself as Scott's primary caretaker, admitted assaulting the mother and other adults, but [claimed that] "I don't hurt kids." According to an acquaintance, however, the accused had admitted striking the child with his elbow because Scott was "bothering him while he was trying to watch television." The trial outcome was conviction. (Daly & Wilson, 1996a, p. 77)

Events similar to this one occur every day in the United States and Canada and can be read about in every major newspaper. Daly and Wilson have explored the link between genetic relatedness and child homicide. In one study they examined 408 Canadian children who had been killed over a ten-year period by either genetic parents or stepparents. They then calculated the number of homicide victims per million coresident parent–child dyads per year. The results are shown in Figure 7.4.

The rates of child murder are clearly far higher for stepparents than for genetic parents. The risk is highest for very young children, particularly for children age two or younger. Examining a variety of different data sets of this kind, Daly and Wilson (2008) found that the risk of

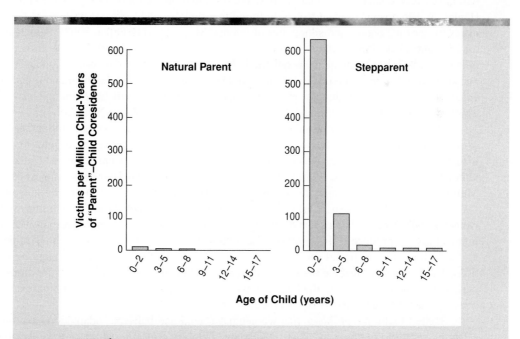

FIGURE 7.4 **The Risk of Being Killed by a Stepparent versus a Natural Parent in Relation to the Child's Age.** Canada 1974–1983.

*Source:* Daly, M., & Wilson, M. (1988). *Homicide*, 90. New York: Aldine de Gruyter. Copyright © 1988 by Aldine de Gruyter. Reprinted with permission.

a preschool-aged child being killed ranged from *forty* to *one hundred times* higher for stepchildren than for children living with two genetic parents.

Unfortunately, cross-cultural data on child abuse and homicide as a function of stepparenthood are sparse. Daly and Wilson (1988) do cite some evidence from the ethnographic record compiled in the Human Relations Area Files (HRAF), although this evidence should be evaluated with caution because it is hardly systematic and the ethnographies were assembled without specific focus on child abuse, child homicide, or stepparents. In spite of the limitations of the ethnographic record, it is worth noting that adultery, presumably resulting in some uncertainty in paternity, was mentioned as grounds for killing a child in fifteen of the thirty-nine societies in which infanticide was mentioned. In three tribal societies, men reportedly insisted that a child be killed if he or she displayed physical features that provoked suspicion that the child was not the man's own. Among the Tikopia of Oceania and the Yanomamö of Venezuela, men who married women who already had children by another man reportedly demanded that they be killed as a condition of marriage. Finally, a study of 351 deaths of Australian children under the age of five found that stepchildren had a dramatically increased risk of fatal injuries, particularly by drowning, even if their deaths were deemed to be "unintentional" (Tooley et al., 2006).

*Sex Differences in Parenting Adaptations.*   Because mothers are always 100 percent certain of their maternity, but putative fathers are not, selection should favor parental adaptations in women that differ from those in men. The "primary caretaker hypothesis" contends that women will have evolved adaptations that increase the odds that their children will survive (Babchuk, Hames, & Thompson, 1985). One study found that females had a greater preference than did males for viewing photos and silhouettes of infants (Maestripieri & Pelka, 2002). Female interest in infants peaked in childhood and adolescence: "the function of early female attraction to infants is probably to facilitate the acquisition of parenting skills through observation and hands-on experience. [F]emale interest in infants should emerge early in development and remain elevated until the first reproductive event, to ensure that females will have enough parenting experience and motivation to successfully raise their first child" (Maestripieri, 2004).

Other research has confirmed that women are better than men at recognizing infant facial expression of emotion (Babchuk et al., 1985). Women also have faster reaction times to recognizing emotional facial expressions that are both positive (e.g., happy) and negative (e.g., angry), although the sex difference is largest for the negative emotions (Hampson, van Anders, & Mullin, 2006). These findings are consistent with two hypotheses, which are variants of the "primary caretaker hypothesis." One is the "attachment promotion hypothesis," which suggests that women should be better than men at decoding *all* facial expressions of emotion—responsiveness to infants likely to produce securely attached children. The second is the "fitness threat hypothesis," which predicts a special sensitivity to dangers that might be conveyed by negative emotions. The fact that women are better than men at decoding all emotional facial expressions, but particularly adept at decoding the negative expressions, suggests that some combination of the two hypotheses is necessary to explain the findings.

Shelley Taylor has proposed that women have "tend-and-befriend" adaptations to promote offspring survival (Taylor et al., 2000). "Tending" involves protecting children from dangerous predators and other threats and calming and quieting them down to avoid detection (Taylor et al., 2000). "Befriending" involves creating and maintaining social networks that offer a social cocoon of protection. Women, for example, are more likely than men to affiliate with other people when under stress. Because it is clear that ancestral infants and children suffered from injuries and illness that would have been lethal without help from parents (Sugiyama, 2004b), we can expect future research to discover additional parenting adaptations, some of which will be sex-differentiated.

Finally, it is important to note that the existence of sex differences in parenting adaptations does not imply that men do not provide for and protect their children. Indeed, humans stand out among all primate species as being the one characterized by the highest level of paternal investment. Across all cultures, men form deep bonds with their children, provide them with food, protect them from harm, teach them skills, facilitate their social alliances, influence their mating strategies, and help to secure their position in status hierarchies (e.g., Mackey & Coney, 2000; Mackey & Immerman, 2000). Nonetheless, the greater average genetic relatedness of mothers than fathers to their children due to some level of uncertainty of paternity suggests that women will be more invested in their children, on average, than will men.

In summary, the available evidence supports the evolutionary psychological prediction that genetic relatedness is a powerful predictor of the distribution of parental benefits or the infliction of parental costs. Parental care is costly. Humans seem to have evolved psychological mechanisms that lead them to direct their care preferentially toward their genetic progeny.

## Offspring's Ability to Convert Parental Care into Reproductive Success

After considering a child's genetic relatedness (or lack thereof) to the putative parent, the next critical factor in predicting parental care is the ability of the child to utilize that care. Selection would have favored adaptations that caused parents to invest heavily in children when the children were most able to convert the parental care into fitness by an increase in their chances for survival or reproduction.

This evolutionary logic does *not* imply that parents will only care for children who are robust and healthy. In fact, under some conditions, parents are predicted to invest more in an ill child than in a healthy child, simply because the same unit of investment will benefit the former more than the latter. The key theoretical point is not whether the child is ill or healthy, but rather the child's ability to convert a given unit of parental care into fitness. Parents, of course, do not think this way, either consciously or unconsciously. No parent ever thinks, "I will invest in Sally more than in Mary because Sally can convert my investment into more gene copies." Rather, selection pressures give rise to evolved psychological mechanisms that cause shifts in investment. It is those evolved psychological mechanisms together with the current environmental events that trigger their activation and cause modern patterns of parental investment.

Evolutionary psychologist David Geary has summarized a large body of evidence suggesting that parental (and paternal) investment in children makes a substantial difference to the children's physical and social well-being (Geary, 2000). Among the Ache of Paraguay, for example, father absence before the child's fifteenth birthday is linked with a mortality rate of 45 percent, compared with a dramatically lower mortality rate of 20 percent of children whose fathers reside with them continuously through the fifteenth birthday (Hill & Hurtado, 1996). Indonesian children whose parents are divorced have a 12 percent higher mortality rate than that of children living with both parents. Similar results have been documented in Sweden, Germany, and the United States (Geary, 2000).

Parental investment also appears to affect social well-being, although the precise causal connections are difficult to establish unambiguously (Geary, 2000). Higher levels of parental investment, as indicated by parental income and amount of time spent playing with the child,

*Parental investment by fathers is linked to increased survival and well-being of children.*

are positively correlated with academic skills, social skills, and subsequent socioeconomic status. Father's investment seems to have an especially pronounced effect, accounting for four times as much variance in educational outcomes as mother's investment (this could be due to father's investment being more variable than mother's investment, which tends to be consistently high). Parents, in short, appear to make a difference to the survival and social well-being of their children. The next key question is: Which children should parents invest in most?

We cannot go back in time and identify with certainty which factors enabled a child to best use parental care. Nonetheless, Daly and Wilson (1988, 1995) have identified two reasonable candidates: (1) whether the child is born with an abnormality and (2) the age of the child. Children who are disabled in some way, other things being equal, are less likely to have future reproductive success than children who are healthy and intact. Younger children, all else being equal, are lower in reproductive value than are older children. Recall that reproductive value refers to the future probability of producing offspring. Let's examine the empirical data on these two candidates.

***Parental Neglect and Abuse of Children with Congenital Abnormalities.*** Children who have a congenital disease such as spina bifida, fibrocystic disease, cleft palate, or Down syndrome are likely to be lower in reproductive value than healthy children. Is there evidence that parents treat these children differently? One index is whether the children are abandoned either completely or partially. Studies show that indeed a large fraction of such seriously ill children are institutionalized. The 1976 U.S. census found that among those who are institutionalized, more than 16,000 children (roughly 12 percent of all institutionalized children) were never visited at all. Furthermore, roughly 30,000 (approximately 22 percent) patients were visited only once a year or less (U.S. Census Bureau, 1978). Although these findings are correlational and cannot establish causality, they are consistent with the hypothesis that parents invest less in children with abnormalities.

What about children with abnormalities who are neither institutionalized nor given up for adoption? The rates of child physical abuse and neglect in the U.S. population are estimated to be roughly 1.5 percent (Daly & Wilson, 1981). This provides a base rate against which the abuse of children with various characteristics can be compared. Daly and Wilson (1981) summarized a variety of studies, all of which suggest that children with abnormalities are abused at considerably higher rates. Across these studies, the percentage of children born with congenital physical abnormalities who are abused ranged from 7.5 percent to 60 percent—far higher than the base rate of abuse in the general population.

***Maternal Care Based on the Health of the Child.*** One direct test of the hypothesis that parents have proclivities to invest in children according to their reproductive value is offered by a study of twins, of whom one in each pair was healthier. Evolutionary psychologist Janet Mann conducted a study of fourteen infants: seven twin pairs, all of whom were born prematurely. When the infants were four months old, Mann made detailed behavioral observations of the interactions between the mothers and their infants (Mann, 1992). The interactions were observed when the fathers were not present and when both twins were awake. Among the behavioral recordings were assessments of *positive maternal behavior*, which included kissing, holding, soothing, talking to, playing with, and gazing at the infant.

Independently, the health status of each infant was assessed at birth, at discharge from the hospital, at four months of age, and at eight months of age. The health status examinations included medical, neurological, physical, cognitive, and developmental assessments.

Mann then tested the *healthy baby hypothesis:* that the health status of the child would affect the degree of positive maternal behavior. When the infants were four months old, roughly half the mothers directed more positive maternal behavior toward the healthier infants; the other half showed no preference. By the time the infants were eight months old, however, every single one of the mothers directed more positive maternal behavior toward the healthier infant, with no reversals. In sum, the results of this twin study support the healthy baby hypothesis, suggesting that mothers direct greater maternal investment toward infants who are of higher reproductive value.

A more recent study found that the level of investment mothers devote based on the health status of the child is contingent upon her own level of resources (Beaulieu & Bugental, 2008). Specifically, mothers lacking resources followed the predictable pattern—they invested less in high-risk (prematurely born) infants and invested more in low-risk (not prematurely born) infants. In contrast, mothers who have a lot of resources actually invest more in high-risk than in low-risk infants. The author argues that if parents have abundant resources, then they can afford to give abundant resources to the needier child, while still having enough resources in reserve to provide for their other children.

***Age of the Child.*** Reproductive value—expected probability of future reproduction—increases from birth to pubescence. The increase occurs because some percentage of children—especially infants—die, thereby dragging down the average reproductive value of that age class. The average fourteen-year-old, for example, will have a higher reproductive value than the average infant. On the basis of this reasoning, Daly and Wilson made a specific prediction: The younger the child, the higher the likelihood that the parents would kill it, but this age-dependent pattern of child homicide should not occur when the killer is a nonrelative because nonrelatives do not have the same interest in the child's reproductive value.

The cross-cultural evidence is sparse. In the HRAF, eleven ethnographies of diverse cultures report that a child will be killed if the birth interval is too short or the family is too large (Daly & Wilson, 1988, p. 75). In each of these eleven cases, it is the newborn that is killed; in no case does the ethnography report that the older child is put to death.

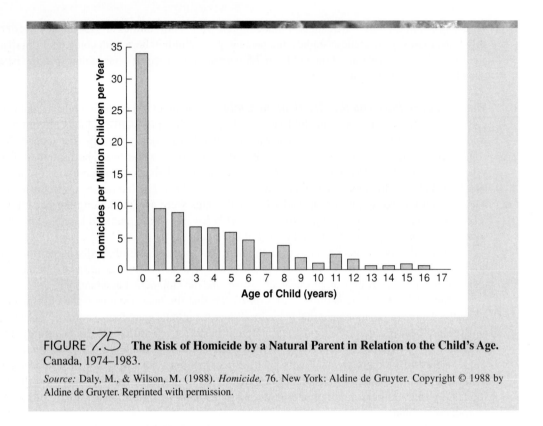

FIGURE 7.5   **The Risk of Homicide by a Natural Parent in Relation to the Child's Age.**
Canada, 1974–1983.

*Source:* Daly, M., & Wilson, M. (1988). *Homicide,* 76. New York: Aldine de Gruyter. Copyright © 1988 by Aldine de Gruyter. Reprinted with permission.

A more rigorous test of the evolutionary prediction comes from Canadian data on the risk of a child being killed by a genetic parent, depending on the child's age. These findings (Figure 7.5) show that infants are at a much higher risk of being killed by their genetic parents than any other age group of children. From that point on, the rates of child homicide decrease progressively until they reach zero at age seventeen.

One possible explanation for this decrease is simply that children become increasingly capable of defending themselves physically as they get older. But this cannot account for the data, because the risk of a child being killed at the hands of a nonrelative shows a markedly different pattern, shown in Figure 7.6. Unlike genetic parents, nonrelatives are more likely to kill one-year-old children than they are to kill infants. And also unlike genetic parents, who almost never kill their teenage children, who are most physically formidable, nonrelatives kill teenagers at a higher rate than any other age category. In short, it appears to be the increasing reproductive value of children as they age that accounts for the fact that genetic parents kill older children less often, not the increased physical formidability of those children.

In summary, two negative indicators of the child's ability to promote the parent's reproductive success—birth defects and youth—predict homicides at the hands of genetic parents. Daly and Wilson (1988) take pains to point out that they are *not* proposing that "child abuse" or "child homicide" per se are adaptations; rather, they regard child homicide as an assay or test of parental feelings. They suggest that parents will feel more favorably toward children who are

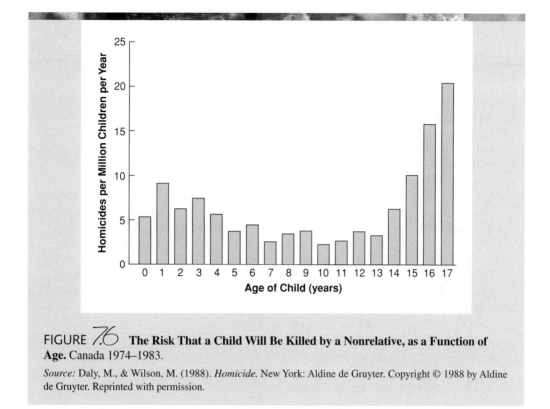

FIGURE 7.6 **The Risk That a Child Will Be Killed by a Nonrelative, as a Function of Age.** Canada 1974–1983.

*Source:* Daly, M., & Wilson, M. (1988). *Homicide.* New York: Aldine de Gruyter. Copyright © 1988 by Aldine de Gruyter. Reprinted with permission.

best able to convert parental investment into reproductive success and less favorably toward children who are less likely to be able to do so. Child homicide, according to Daly and Wilson, represents an extreme and relatively uncommon manifestation of negative parental feelings, not an adaptation in and of itself. On the other hand, there is strong evidence that parents invest more care in healthy children than in unhealthy children, suggesting that selection has favored psychological adaptations in parents sensitive to the reproductive value of their children.

***Investment in Sons versus Daughters: The Trivers-Willard Hypothesis.*** Another variable that might affect a child's ability to convert parental care into reproductive success is whether the child is a son or a daughter. On average, of course, sons and daughters have equal reproductive success, assuming an equal sex ratio in the population. But the *condition* of the son or daughter might make it more likely that one or the other would be better able to utilize parental care. This is the core insight of the *Trivers-Willard hypothesis:* Parents will produce more sons and invest more in sons when the parents are in good condition and hence have a chance of producing a son who will be highly successful in the mating game (Trivers & Willard, 1973). Conversely, if the parents either are in poor condition or have few resources to invest, then they should invest more in daughters, according to the Trivers-Willard hypothesis. Stated differently, if being in "good" condition affects male reproductive success more than female reproductive success, as we would expect in a polygynous mating system, then parents should bias investment toward sons if the parents are in good condition and toward daughters if the parents are in poor condition.

Tests of the Trivers-Willard hypothesis in humans have proved inconclusive (Keller, Nesse, & Hofferth, 2001). A few studies find a Trivers-Willard effect. In one study, for example, female infants were more likely than male infants to be killed by their parents among the higher classes (Dickemann, 1979), as would be predicted by the hypothesis (assuming that infanticide is a reverse indicator of parental investment). Similarly, among the Kipsigis of Kenya, poorer families were more likely to invest in the educations of their daughters than in their sons, whereas the reverse trend was found among richer families (Borgerhoff Mulder, 1998). Using years of education as a proxy for parental investment, Rosemary Hopcroft (2005) found that sons of high-status men attained more years of education than daughters, whereas daughters of low-status men reached higher education levels than did sons. She also found that high-status men sire more sons. Kanazawa (2005) found that tall and heavier parents had slightly more sons than daughters.

A study of 95,000 Rwandan mothers found that low-ranking polygynous wives produce more daughters than do high-ranking polygynous wives (Pollet et al., 2009). Among a sample of 3,200 U.S. children, however, researchers found no evidence that high-status parents invested more in sons than in daughters and no evidence that lower-status parents invest more in daughters than in sons (Keller et al., 2001). Quinlan, Quinlan, and Flinn (2003) found no support for the Trivers-Willard hypothesis in a rural sample from the island of Dominica. Future studies are needed to determine whether the hypothesized Trivers-Willard effects are found among different populations of humans (see Cronk, 2007, for an illuminating review).

## Alternative Uses of Resources Available for Investment in Children

Energy and effort are finite and limited. Effort allocated to one activity must necessarily take away from that allocated to others. As applied to parenting, the principle of finite effort means that the effort expended toward caring for a child cannot be allocated toward other adaptive problems such as personal survival, attracting additional mates, or investing in other kin. Selection will have fashioned in humans decision-making rules for when to invest in children and when to devote one's energy toward other adaptive problems. From a woman's perspective, two contexts that might affect these decisions are age and marital status. From a man's perspective, those with high-potential access to women might tilt their effort more toward mating than toward parenting. We consider each of these contexts in turn.

***Women's Age and Infanticide.*** Young women have many years in which to bear and invest in children, so passing up one youthful opportunity to bear and invest in a child may entail minimal cost. On the other hand, older women nearing the end of reproductive capacity who pass up an opportunity to bear and invest in children may not have another chance. As opportunities for reproduction diminish, postponing childbearing and rearing would be reproductively costly. From this perspective, we expect that natural selection would favor a decision rule that causes older women to invest immediately in children rather than postponing doing so.

Daly and Wilson (1988) examined this hypothesis using infanticide as an assay of maternal investment (or lack thereof). A specific prediction follows from the above reasoning: Younger women should be more inclined than older women to commit infanticide. This hypothesis is strongly supported in data from the Ayoreo Indians (Bugos & McCarthy, 1984). The proportion of births leading to infanticide is highest among the youngest women (ages fifteen to nineteen). Infanticide is lowest among the oldest age group of women.

The Ayoreo Indians, however, appear to have an unusually high rate of infanticide—fully 38 percent of all births—so perhaps this is an atypical sample. Is there any evidence that maternal age affects infanticide in other cultures? Daly and Wilson (1988) collected data on infanticide in Canada from 1974 through 1983 (see Figure 7.7).

As among the Ayoreo Indians, young Canadian women commit infanticide far more frequently than older Canadian women do. Teenage mothers show the highest rates of infanticide, more than three times as high as any other age group. Women in their twenties show the next highest rate of infanticide, followed by women in their thirties. Figure 7.7 shows a slight increase in infanticide among the oldest group of women, which appears to contradict the hypothesis that older women will commit infanticide less often. Daly and Wilson note that this might not prove to be a reliable finding, however, since this group consists of only three women: one aged thirty-eight and two aged forty-one.

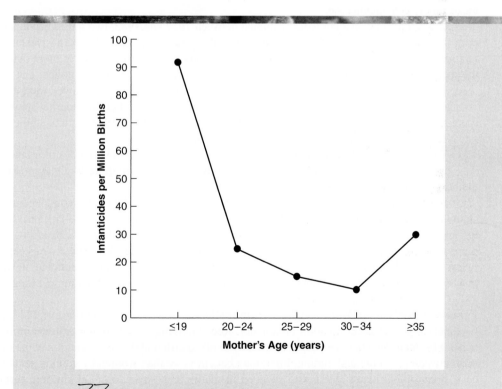

FIGURE 7.7 **The Risk of Infanticide (Homicide at the Hands of the Natural Mother within the First Year of Life) as a Function of Maternal Age.** Canada, 1974–1983.

*Source:* Daly, M., & Wilson, M. (1988). *Homicide,* 63. New York: Aldine de Gruyter. Copyright © 1988 by Aldine de Gruyter. Reprinted with permission.

So data from two cultures support the prediction that infanticide is highest among younger women, who have the most opportunities for future reproduction, and lowest among older women, who have fewer opportunities for future reproduction. Younger women presumably can use their resources for other purposes, such as stockpiling personal resources or devoting effort toward attracting investing mates. The decision rules of older women presumably tilt them toward immediate investment in children, even at the possible expense of investing in other adaptive problems.

*Women's Marital Status and Infanticide.*   An unmarried woman who gives birth faces three unsettling choices: She can try to raise the child without the help of an investing father, she can abandon the child or give it up for adoption, or she can kill the child and devote her efforts to trying to attract a husband and then have children with him. Daly and Wilson (1988) propose that a woman's marital status will affect the likelihood that she will commit infanticide.

They examined this prediction using two data sets. In the first they examined the HRAF—the most extensive ethnographic database in existence. In six cultures, infants were reportedly killed when no man would acknowledge that he was the father or accept an obligation to help raise the child. In an additional fourteen cultures, a woman's unwed marital status was declared a compelling reason for infanticide. These data are revealing, but more quantitative data would make a more convincing case.

In a sample of Canadian women studied between 1977 and 1983, two million babies were born (Daly & Wilson, 1988). Of these, unwed mothers delivered only 12 percent. Despite this relatively low percentage of unwed mothers, these women were responsible for more than half the sixty-four maternal infanticides that were reported to or discovered by the police. The astute reader might immediately think of a problem with this finding: Perhaps unwed mothers are younger, on average, than wed mothers, and so it might be youth rather than marital status that accounts for the infanticides. To address this issue, Daly and Wilson (1988) examined the separate effects of age and marital status on infanticide (Figure 7.8).

The findings are clear: Both age and marital status are correlated with rates of infanticide. At every age except the very oldest age bracket, unwed mothers are more likely than married mothers to commit infanticide.

If we evaluate all the findings together, there is substantial evidence that youth and marital status affect the likelihood that a woman will commit infanticide. Presumably, these trends reflect evolved decision rules in women concerning the ways in which they allocate effort. Older married women, whose reproductive years are quickly waning, are more likely to keep and invest in a child. Younger and unwed mothers are more likely to commit infanticide, devoting their efforts more toward other adaptive problems, such as surviving or attracting investing men.

*Parental Effort versus Mating Effort.*   Effort allocated toward parenting is effort that cannot be allocated toward securing additional mates. Recall that there are two powerful evolutionary reasons for predicting that men and women have evolved different decision rules about the trade-offs between parenting and mating. First, men benefit more than women by gaining sexual access to additional mates. Men who succeed in mating can sire additional children through increased sexual access, whereas women cannot. Second, paternity is generally less than 100 percent certain. Therefore, the same unit of investment in a child will be less likely to increase a man's reproductive success, on average, than a woman's reproductive success. These two considerations yield a prediction: Women will be more likely than men to channel energy and effort directly toward parenting rather than toward securing additional matings.

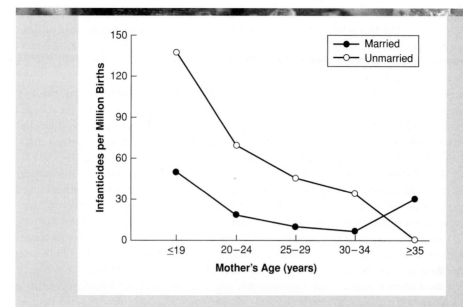

FIGURE 7.8 **The Risk of Infanticide as a Function of the Mother's Age and Marital Status.** Canada, 1974–1983.

*Source:* Daly, M., & Wilson, M. (1988). *Homicide,* 65. New York: Aldine de Gruyter. Copyright © 1988 by Aldine de Gruyter. Reprinted with permission.

Evidence from a variety of cultures supports this prediction. Among the Ye'Kwana of the Venezuelan rain forest, for example, there is a significant gender difference in time spent holding infants. Mothers hold their infants an average of 78 percent of the time, whereas fathers hold their infants only 1.4 percent of the time (Hames, 1988). The remainder of the time the infants are held by other kin, mostly females such as sisters, aunts, and grandmothers.

The Aka Pygmies of central Africa are another example (Hewlett, 1991). The Aka are known for their unusually high levels of paternal investment. Aka parents sleep in the same beds as their infants. If the child is not comforted by nursing at the mother's breast during the night, it is usually the father who cares for the infant, singing to him or her or dancing to provide comfort. The father also cleans mucus from the infant's nose and grooms the infant by cleaning off dirt, lice, or the mess from defecation. And if the mother is not around and the infant is hungry, the father will even offer the infant his own breast on which to suckle, although it obviously provides no milk.

During an average day, Aka fathers hold their infants more than fathers in any other known culture—an average of fifty-seven minutes. This unusually high level of paternal investment pales in comparison to that of Aka mothers, who hold their infants 490 minutes on an average day. So even among the Aka, a culture described as a society of "mothering men," women do the lion's share of caring for offspring.

Another cross-cultural study surveyed a variety of rural and nontechnological societies, including Mexico, Java, Quechua, Nepal, and the Philippines (reported in Barash & Lipton,

1997). The patterns of division of labor between the sexes were consistent. Fathers cared for children from 5 to 18 percent of their waking hours, the most common amount of time being 8 percent. Mothers, in contrast, spent between 39 and 88 percent of their waking hours caring for their children, the most common figure 85 percent. Women, in short, spent roughly ten times more time caring for children than did men.

Single parenting provides another telling statistic. Roughly 90 percent of single parents are women. Despite ideologies of gender equality, either men are reluctant to take a large role in direct parenting or women prefer to take a larger role. Most likely, the outcome reflects the evolved decision rules of both sexes, with men tilting their investments toward mating and women tilting their investments toward parenting.

Many other studies suggest specific parental mechanisms in mothers that appear to be weak or absent in fathers. One series of studies examined pupillary reactions of men and women in response to various pictures (Hess, 1975). When we see something that attracts us, our pupils dilate (enlarge) more than is needed to correct for the ambient degree of illumination. Thus, pupil dilation can be used as a measure of interest and attraction—a subtle measure that is reasonably immune to self-reporting biases that might affect questionnaire studies. In these studies, when women were shown slides of babies, their pupils dilated more than 17 percent; men's pupils showed no dilation at all. Furthermore, when shown slides of a mother holding a baby, women's pupils dilated roughly 24 percent, whereas men's pupils dilated only 5 percent (even this small degree of dilation may be due to men's attraction to the mother rather than the infant!).

Other studies show similar sex differences in reactions to infants. Women can identify their own newborn children within six hours of birth merely by smell, whereas fathers generally cannot (Barash & Lipton, 1997). Women also have a greater ability to recognize the facial expression of infants when pictures of them are flashed briefly on a screen; women detect emotions such as surprise, disgust, anger, fear, and distress more quickly and accurately than do men (Barash & Lipton, 1997). Interestingly, women's accuracy was not affected by the amount of previous experience with infants and children.

All these findings point to a singular conclusion: Women appear to have evolved decision rules to allocate more time to parenting and have attendant evolved mechanisms of interest and emotional mind reading that render such parenting more effective.

*When looking at an infant, women's pupils spontaneously dilate more than men's, an indication of liking for the infant.*

Presumably, men are using the effort not allocated toward parenting for other adaptive problems, such as mating. One source of evidence comes from detailed study of the Aka pygmies of central Africa. Although the Aka show heavy male parental investment compared with other cultures, there is also considerable variation among the men in how much parenting they do. When a father holds a position of high status within the tribe (*kombeti*), he devotes less than half as much effort to holding his infant as do men of lower status (Hewlett, 1991). These high-status men are usually polygynous, with two or more wives. In contrast, low-status men are fortunate to have even one wife. Low-status men appear to compensate for their standing by increasing the effort they allocate to parenting, whereas high-status men appear to be channeling extra effort into attracting additional mates (Hewlett, 1991; Smuts & Gubernick, 1992).

A questionnaire study of 170 British men who had children supports the tradeoff between mating effort and parental effort (Apicella & Marlow, 2007). Men's mate value was assessed with the items: "I believe that women find me attractive" and "I receive a lot of attention from females." Men's mating effort was assessed by the item "I spend a lot of time flirting with females." Men's parental effort was measured with the items "I believe I give my child a lot of attention" and "I spend a lot of time with my child." The researchers found that men with higher self-perceived mate value reported lower levels of parental investment and higher levels of mating effort. Interestingly, men higher in mate value, who also suspected their wives of infidelity or untrustworthiness, were especially likely to reduce their parental investment. Men with lower mate value were less likely to reduce parental investment. Although these findings need to be replicated with methods other than self-report, they support the hypothesis of a tradeoff between mating effort and parental effort.

Even when men do devote effort to parenting, it may be used as a mating tactic rather than as a means to aid the viability of the child—a hypothesis that has been developed by primatologists Barbara Smuts and David Gubernick (1992). Mark Flinn (1992), for example, studied male parental investment in a rural Trinidad village. He found that when a woman is single and has a child, men interact more with the woman's child before they are married than after, suggesting that men may be channeling effort to the child in an effort to attract the woman.

***Summary.*** We have examined three factors that affect the evolution of parenting: genetic relatedness to the child, ability of the child to convert parental care into survival and reproductive success, and alternative ways parents could use resources that might be channeled to children. Considerable evidence supports the notion that all three factors are important. Parents invest more in genetic children than in stepchildren; fathers, who are less certain of genetic relatedness, invest less in children than mothers, who are 100 percent certain of their genetic relatedness. Children who are healthy and high in reproductive value receive greater positive parental attention than children who are deformed, ill, or otherwise of low reproductive value. Men, who tend to have more opportunities than women to channel effort into mating, tend to provide less direct parental care of children. And men who are high in mate value, as indicated by their polygynous status or by self-perceptions of desirability, ramp up their mating effort and trim back on their parental effort.

# ■ THE THEORY OF PARENT–OFFSPRING CONFLICT

Evolutionary theory tells us that children are the primary vehicles for parents' reproductive success. Given the supreme importance of children to parents, you might wonder why you and your parents have ever engaged in conflict. It might come as a surprise, then, that parents and children are actually predicted to have conflicts (Trivers, 1974).

In sexually reproducing species such as humans, parents and offspring are genetically related by 50 percent. The genetic relatedness between parent and child can exert selection pressure for intense parental care, as documented above. But it also means that parents and children *differ* genetically by 50 percent. An ideal course of action for one, therefore, will rarely coincide perfectly with an ideal course of action for the other (Trivers, 1974). Specifically, parents and children will diverge in the ideal allocation of the parents' resources, the typical result being that children want more for themselves than parents want to give. Let's explore the logic of these parent–offspring conflicts.

Daly and Wilson (1988) offer a numerical example to illustrate this logic. Suppose you have one sibling who has the same reproductive value as you. Your mother comes home from a day of gathering with two food items to feed her children. As with many resources, there are *diminishing returns* associated with each increase in consumption; that is, the value of the first unit of food consumed is higher than the value of the second unit of food. The first unit of food, for example, may prevent starvation, whereas the second unit of food just makes you a little fuller and fatter. Let's say that the first item would raise your reproductive success by four units and the second item of food would raise it an additional three units. Your sibling's consumption of these food items would have the same result, with diminishing returns associated with each added food item.

Now comes the conflict. From your mother's perspective, the ideal allocation would be to give one unit of food to you and one to your sibling. This would net her eight units of increase, four for you and four for your sibling. If either you or your sibling monopolized all the food, however, the gain would only be seven (four for the first item plus three for the second). So from your mother's perspective, an equal allocation between her children would yield the best outcome.

From your perspective, however, you are twice as valuable as your sibling: You have 100 percent of your genes, whereas your sibling only has 50 percent of your genes (on average). Therefore, your mother's ideal allocation would benefit you by the four units that you receive plus only two of the units that your sibling receives (since you benefit by only 50 percent of whatever your sibling receives), for a total of six units benefit. If you manage to get all the food, however, you benefit by seven units (four for the first item plus three for the second). Therefore, from your perspective, the ideal allocation would be for you to get all the food and your sibling none. This conflicts with your mother's ideal allocation, which is to distribute equally. The general conclusion is this: The theory of parent–offspring conflict predicts that each child will generally desire a larger portion of the parents' resources than the parents want to give. Although the above example is simplified in various ways, this general conclusion applies even when siblings differ in their value to the parents and even when the parents have only a single child. If the parents were to go along with the ideal allocation of resources desired by the child, it would take away from other channels through which the parents might be reproductively successful. Interestingly, parent–child conflict over the parents' resources is predicted to occur not merely at particular times such as adolescence, but at each stage of life (Daly & Wilson, 1988).

In summary, Trivers's theory identified an important arena of *genetic conflict of interest* between parents and children—a "battleground" over the optimal allocation of resources (Godfray, 1999). Over evolutionary time, there will be an "arms race" between the genes expressed in parents and genes expressed in children. Selection is therefore predicted to fashion adaptations in children to manipulate parents toward the children's optimum resource allocation and counteradaptations in parents to tilt resource allocation toward their own optimum. As we will see, this battleground gets resolved in some strange ways.

The theory of parent–offspring conflict yields specific hypotheses that can be tested: (1) Parents and children will get into conflict about the time at which the child should be weaned, the parents generally wanting to wean the child sooner and the child wanting to continue to receive resources longer; (2) parents will encourage children to value their siblings more than children are naturally inclined to value them; and (3) parents will tend to punish conflict between siblings and reward cooperation.

There have been surprisingly few efforts to test the theory of parent–offspring conflict on humans. One notable exception is a study of suicidal behavior among adolescents by Paul Andrews (2006). In a sample of 1,601 adolescents, he found tentative support for the hypothesis that suicide attempts may be strategies by adolescents to extract extra investment from their parents—more investment than their parents would be normally inclined to give. Parent–offspring conflict, however, begins long before adolescence. It starts in the mother's womb.

## Mother–Offspring Conflict in Utero

Few relationships are believed to be as harmonious as that between mother and child. The mother is 100 percent certain of her genetic contribution, after all, so of all relationships, the genetic interests of mother and child should coincide. In an astonishing series of papers, however, biologist David Haig extended the theory of parent–offspring conflict to include conflicts that occur between the mother and her offspring in utero (Haig, 1993, 2004).

The logic of mother–fetus conflict follows directly from the theory of parent–offspring conflict described above. A mother contributes 50 percent of her genes to the fetus, but the fetus also receives 50 percent of its genes from the father. Mothers will be selected to channel resources to the child who will yield the greater reproductive benefit. This child, however, has a greater stake in itself than it has in the mother's future child. Therefore, selection will create mechanisms in the fetus to manipulate the mother to provide more nutrition than will be in the mother's best interests to provide.

The conflict begins over whether the fetus will be spontaneously aborted. As many as 78 percent of all fertilized eggs either fail to implant or are spontaneously aborted by the mother early in pregnancy (Nesse & Williams, 1994). Most of these occur because of chromosomal abnormalities in the fetus. Mothers appear to have evolved an adaptation that detects such abnormalities and aborts fetuses with them. This mechanism is highly functional, for it prevents the mother from investing in a baby that would be likely to die young. It is to the mother's advantage to cut her losses early so that she can preserve more investments for a future child who is more likely to thrive. Indeed, the vast majority of miscarriages occur before the twelfth week of pregnancy, and many occur before the woman misses her first period and so she might not even know she was pregnant (Haig, 1993). From the fetus's perspective, however, it has only one shot at life. It will do everything it can to implant itself and prevent spontaneous abortion.

One adaptation that appears to have evolved for this function is the fetal production of human chorionic gonadotropin (hCG), a hormone the fetus secretes into the mother's bloodstream. This hormone has the effect of preventing the mother from menstruating and thus allows the fetus to remain implanted. Producing a lot of hCG, therefore, appears to be an adaptation in the fetus to subvert the mother's attempts to spontaneously abort it. The female body appears to "interpret" high levels of hCG as a sign that a fetus is healthy and viable and so does not spontaneously abort.

Once implantation is successful, another conflict appears to develop over the food supply, which is provided by the mother's blood. One common side effect of pregnancy is high blood pressure. When the blood pressure is so high that it causes damage to the mother's kidneys, it is called preeclampsia. In the early stages of pregnancy, the placental cells destroy the arteriolar muscles in the mother that are responsible for adjusting the flow of blood to the fetus. Therefore anything that constricts the mother's other arteries will elevate her blood pressure, so that more blood will flow to the fetus. When the fetus "perceives" that it needs more nutrition from the mother, it releases substances into the mother's bloodstream that cause her arteries to constrict. This has the effect of raising her blood pressure and delivering more blood (and hence nutrition) to the fetus, which can damage the mother's tissues, as in preeclampsia. Clearly, the mechanism has evolved to benefit the fetus, even at the risk of inflicting damage to the mother.

Two sources of evidence support the hypothesis of an evolved mechanism in fetuses that are in conflict with the mother. First, data from thousands of pregnancies show that mothers whose blood pressure increases during pregnancy tend to have lower rates of spontaneous abortions (Haig, 1993). Second, preeclampsia is more common among pregnant women whose blood supply to the fetus is more restricted, suggesting that a fetus may secrete more hCG when the blood supply is low, thus causing the mother to develop high blood pressure.

These theories of mother–fetus conflict might seem as bizarre as science fiction. But they follow directly from Trivers's (1974) theory of parent–offspring conflict. Conflict is predicted to occur because fetuses, like children, will be selected to take a bit more of the mother's resources than mothers will be prepared to give.

## Mother–Child Conflict and Sibling Relatedness

The theory of parent–offspring conflict generates another interesting pair of predictions (Schlomer, Ellis, & Garber, 2010). First, the presence of a sibling should increase parent–child conflict, since the parent has another "vehicle" in which it can channel resources. Second, the presence of a maternal half-sibling should increase parent–child conflict even more than the presence of a full maternal sibling. The mother who produces a second child with a man who is not the father or her first child is genetically related to both children by 50 percent. The half-siblings, however, are only genetically related by 25 percent (on average).

To test these predictions, researchers studied 240 children and their mothers (Schlomer et al., 2010). They assessed the magnitude of mother–child conflict using a twenty-item questionnaire containing items such as "My mom seems to be always complaining about me" and "At least once a day we get angry with each other." The study discovered that having a younger full sibling increased mother–child conflict, compared situations with no younger siblings. Furthermore, the presence of a younger half-sibling increased the mother–child conflict even more dramatically than having a younger full sibling. These effects remained robust even after statistically controlling for other variables, such as socioeconomic status and stepfather presence. The theory of parent–offspring conflict, in short, proved especially impressive at predicting the magnitude of mother–child clashes as a function of the magnitude of genetic divergences of interest between the mother and the child.

## Parent–Offspring Conflict over Mating

Mating is one domain that is rife with potential conflicts between parents and offspring for several reasons (Apostolou, 2007, 2009; Trivers, 1974). First, specific traits in a potential mate provide asymmetric benefits to parents and their offspring. Offspring, for example, gain more from selecting a mate of superior genetic quality than do their parents because the off-spring will be genetically related to their children by a coefficient of 50 percent, whereas their parents will be related to those children (their grandchildren) by only 25 percent. Second, parents often attempt to arrange or influence the mateships of their offspring to advance their own agendas, whether or not these agendas benefit the offspring. Among the Tiwi, for example, fathers arrange the marriages of their daughters in order to establish political and social alliances that provide additional mating opportunities for the father (Hart & Pilling, 1960). Daughters in essence become "economic bargaining chips" for fathers, and an arranged mateship that benefits the father may be less than ideal from the daughter's perspective. Third, offspring may attempt to gain benefits (e.g., resources) from a short-term mating strategy, which might inflict costs on the parents by compromising family reputation. An ideal mating strategy from the perspective of the offspring may depart from an ideal mating strategy from the perspective of the parents.

Empirical tests of parent–offspring conflict over mating have centered on conflicts over mate selection and conflicts over mating strategy. First, offspring prioritize *beauty* (a possible proxy for genetic quality) in their mate preferences more than parents do for the mates of their sons and daughters (Apostolou, 2008a). Second, parents prioritize *family background* for the mates of their offspring more than their offspring do, possibly because having an in-law with a good family background favors the parent's agenda of forging social and political alliances (Apostolou, 2008b). Third, parents and offspring get into conflict over the pursuit of a short-term mating strategy (Apostolou, 2009). The rationale is that a short-term mating strategy might compromise the status and reputation of the family—a cost to the parents that would have been particularly high in preindustrial societies in which forging alliances among different kin groups through marriage is critical.

Empirical research documents that parents indeed find short-term mating to be significantly more acceptable for themselves than for their sons and daughters (Apostolou, 2009). Daughters are a particular focus of parent–offspring conflict. Parents tend to engage in "daughter guarding" (Perilloux, Fleischman, & Buss, 2008). They impose stricter curfews for their daughters than for their sons. They control the clothing choices of their daughters more than that of their sons, particularly around sexually provocative garb. And they become emotionally upset when they discover that their daughters are sexually active more than when their sons are sexually active. Because parents and offspring have a genetic commonality of interest of 50 percent, some of these forms of daughter guarding may be in the daughter's best interest—for example, to prevent them from being sexually exploited or to preserve their long-term mate value (Perilloux et al., 2008). But they may also reflect behaviors that are in the parents' best interests, such as preserving family reputation, even at the cost of depriving their daughters of the potential benefits they might reap through short-term mating (Apostolou, 2009) (see Box 7.1 for another example of parent–offspring conflict).

Theoretically, offspring should also try to influence their parent's mating or re-mating decisions. Children might try to prevent their parents from divorcing, for example, even when it is in the best interests of the parents to do so. Daughters might attempt to influence their mother's choice of a mate in order to secure an optimal stepfather—one who shows kind and generous proclivities, or one who is unlikely to sexually exploit her. Parent–offspring conflict over the parent's mating and re-mating decisions remains a topic that has yet to be explored empirically.

---

BOX *7.1*

## Killing Parents and the Asymmetry of Valuing Parents and Children

On Sunday afternoon, January 2nd, the victim (male, age 46) was killed in his home by a single shotgun blast at close range. The killer (male, 15) was the victim's son, and the circumstance was familiar to the investigating police. The home was a scene of recurring violence, in which the victim had assaulted his wife and sons, had threatened them with the same weapon he eventually died by, had even shot at his wife in the past. On the fatal Sunday, the victim was drunk, berating his wife as a "bitch" and a "whore," and beating her, when their son acted to terminate the long history of abuse. (Daly & Wilson, 1988, p. 98)

Assuming certainty in paternity, parents and children are genetically related by an *r* of .50. But it does not follow from an evolutionary perspective that they should value each other equally. Children are the vehicles for their parents' genes, but as the parents age, they become less and less valuable to their children precisely as the children become more and more valuable to their parents (i.e., as the parents' other avenues to achieving reproduction diminish). The end result is that by adulthood children are more valuable to their parents than the parents are to the children (Daly & Wilson, 1988). A clear prediction follows from this logic: Those who are less valuable will be at greater risk of being killed, so by adulthood offspring will be more likely to kill their parents than vice versa.

There is some limited empirical evidence to support this prediction, at least with fathers. In one study conducted in Detroit, of a total of eleven homicides involving parents and adult children, nine parents were killed by their adult children, whereas only two adult children were killed by their parents (Daly & Wilson, 1988). In a larger study of Canadian homicides, ninety-one fathers were killed by their adult sons (82 percent of father–son homicides), whereas only twenty adult sons were killed by their fathers (18 percent of father–son homicides). It should be noted that this sample excluded homicides involving stepfathers, a relationship that, as we saw earlier in this chapter, carries a special kind of conflict.

These homicide data are preliminary, of course, and do not reveal much about the underlying psychology of parent–offspring conflict as a consequence of the predicted asymmetry of valuation. They do suggest, however, that there are risks associated with being the less valued party in the parent–child relationship. Future research, guided by this reasoning, will undoubtedly reveal a wealth of information about the conflictual nature of this special and close genetic relationship.

---

## ■ SUMMARY

From an evolutionary perspective, offspring are the vehicles for parents' genes, so selection should favor parental mechanisms designed to ensure the survival and reproduction of offspring. Mechanisms of parental care have been documented in many nonhuman species. One of the most interesting puzzles is why mothers tend to provide more parental care than fathers. Two hypotheses have been advanced to explain this: (1) the paternity uncertainty hypothesis—males invest less than females because there is a lower probability that they have contributed genes to their putative offspring (maternity certainty being 100 percent and paternity certainty being less than 100 percent); and (2) the mating opportunity cost hypothesis—the costs to males of providing parental care are higher than for females because such investment by males curtails additional mating opportunities. Current evidence supports both the paternity uncertainty and mating opportunity cost hypotheses.

Evolved mechanisms of parental care are predicted to be sensitive to at least three contexts: (1) the genetic relatedness of offspring, (2) the ability of the offspring to convert parental care into fitness, and (3) alternative uses of the resources that might be available. Abundant empirical evidence supports the hypothesis that genetic relatedness to offspring affects human parental care. Studies show that stepparents have fewer positive parental feelings than genetic parents. Interactions between stepparents and stepchildren tend to be more conflict-ridden than those between genetic parents and children. Newborn babies are said to resemble the putative father more than the putative mother, suggesting mechanisms to influence the putative father to invest in the child. Investment in children's college education is higher with genetic children than with stepchildren and higher when paternity certainty is high. Children living with one genetic parent and one stepparent are forty times more likely to suffer physical abuse and forty to one hundred times more likely to be killed than are children living with both genetic parents. And because mothers have higher average genetic relatedness to offspring than putative fathers, due to some level of compromised paternity, we expect women to more heavily invest in children than fathers. Indeed, women more than men prefer looking at images of infants, are more skilled at recognizing infant facial expressions of emotion, and are more likely to "tend" to infants and "befriend" others as a means of protecting them. Genetic relatedness of parent to child, in short, appears to be a critical determinant of the quality of parental care.

Evolved parental mechanisms are also predicted to be sensitive to the ability of the offspring to convert parental care into reproductive success. Three lines of research support this theoretical expectation. First, children born with congenital problems such as spina bifida or Down syndrome are commonly institutionalized or given up for adoption; if they are cared for and not given up for adoption, they are far more likely to be physically abused by their parents. Second, a study of twins found that mothers tend to invest more in the healthy infants than in their less healthy twins. Third, young infants are at greater risk of abuse and homicide than are older children.

The third context predicted to affect the quality of parental care is the availability of alternative uses of resources that could be invested in a child. Effort and energy are finite, and effort allocated to one activity must necessarily take away from other activities. Several studies have examined patterns of infanticide on the assumption that such killings are reverse assays of parental care—that is, they indicate the exact opposite of parental care. Studies show that young mothers are more likely than older mothers to commit infanticide, presumably because younger women have many years ahead in which to bear and invest in offspring, whereas older women have fewer years. Unmarried women are more likely than married women to commit infanticide. These trends presumably reflect evolved decision rules in women about the ways in which they allocate effort. Finally, men, who tend to have more opportunities to channel effort into mating, tend to provide less direct parental care. Among the Aka, men who are high in status invest less in direct child care than men who are low in status. High-status Aka men channel their efforts into attracting more wives. In sum, the availability of alternative uses of resources affects decision rules about when to allocate effort to parental care.

The evolutionary theory of parent–offspring conflict suggests that the "interests" of parents and children will not coincide perfectly because they are genetically related by only 50 percent. The theory predicts that each child will generally desire a larger portion of parental resources than the parents want to give. This theory yields some predictions, such as: (1) mother–offspring conflict will sometimes occur in utero, such as over whether the fetus is spontaneously aborted; (2) parents tend to value their children more than their children value them as both get older; (3) mother–child conflict should intensify with the introduction of a younger sibling, and become especially intense with the introduction of a half-sibling; and (4) parents and their offspring will get into conflicts over mate choice and mating strategies. Empirical evidence on preeclampsia supports the first prediction—it appears that fetuses secrete large amounts of human chorionic gonadotropin (hCG) into the mother's bloodstream, which prevents the mother from menstruating and allows the fetus to remain implanted, thus subverting any attempts by the mother to spontaneously abort it. Evidence from homicide data supports the second prediction—parents, who are less valuable as they grow older, are more often killed by their older children than the reverse. On the assumption that those who are less valuable are at greater risk of being killed, adult offspring should be more likely to kill their parents than vice versa. Evidence suggests that mother–child conflict indeed intensifies with the introduction of a sibling, and increases even more with the introduction of a half-sibling to the family. Finally, parent–offspring conflict occurs around the ideal mate and preferred mating strategy. Offspring prioritize attractiveness more than parents, whereas parents prioritize family background more than offspring. Parents especially object to short-term mating in their offspring, especially their daughters, and so engage in a phenomenon known as "daughter guarding."

Parent–offspring conflict will be an important domain for future empirical studies in evolutionary psychology.

## ■ SUGGESTED READINGS

Apicella, C. L., & Marlow, F. W. (2007). Men's reproductive investment decisions. *Human Nature, 18*, 22–34.

Apostolou, M. (2009). Parent-offspring conflict over mating: The case of short-term mating strategies. *Personality and Individual Differences, 47*, 895–899.

Bjorklund, D. F., & Pellegrini, A. D. (2002). *The origins of human nature: Evolutionary developmental psychology.* Washington, DC: American Psychological Association.

Daly, M., & Wilson, M. (1988). *Homicide.* Hawthorne, NY: Aldine.

Perilloux, C., Fleischman, D. S., & Buss, D. M. (2008). The daughter-guarding hypothesis: Parental influence on, and emotional reactions to, offspring's mating behavior. *Evolutionary Psychology, 6*, 217–233.

Schlomer, G. L., Ellis, B. J., & Garber, J. (2010). Mother-child conflict and sibling relatedness: A test of hypotheses from parent-offspring conflict theory. *Journal of Research on Adolescence, 20*, 287–306.

Trivers, R. (1974). Parent–offspring conflict. *American Zoologist, 14*, 249–264.

# PROBLEMS OF KINSHIP

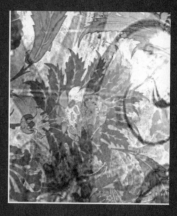

# CHAPTER 8

*Human beings, wherever we meet them, display an almost obsessional interest in matters of sex and kinship.*

—Edmund Leach, 1966

Imagine a world in which everyone loved everyone else equally. There would be no favoritism. You would be just as likely to give your food to a passing stranger as to your children. Your parents would be just as likely to pay for a neighbor's college education as they would be to pay for yours. And when forced by fate to save only one person's life when two were drowning, you would be just as likely to save a stranger as you would your brother or sister.

Such a world is hard to imagine. The evolutionary theory of inclusive fitness explains why it is so difficult to conceive. From the perspective of inclusive fitness theory, people differ in their genetic relatedness to others. As a general rule, we are related by 50 percent to our parents, children, and siblings. We are related by 25 percent to our grandparents and grandchildren, half brothers and half sisters, and uncles, aunts, nieces, and nephews. We are related by 12.5 percent, on average, to our first cousins.

From the perspective of inclusive fitness theory, an individual's relatives are all vehicles of fitness, but they differ in value. In Chapter 7, we saw that children differ in their value to their parents; in this chapter, we will explore the theory that kin differ in value to us. Theoretically, if everything else is equal, selection will favor adaptations for helping kin in proportion to their genetic relatedness. Selection will favor mechanisms for helping ourselves twice as much as we help a brother, for example. But a brother, in turn, is twice as related to us as a nephew and so would get twice the help. In life, of course, not everything is equal. Holding genetic relatedness constant, for example, one brother struggling to make it as a songwriter might benefit more from our gifts of aid than would another brother who happens to be wealthy.

Furthermore, altruism can evolve under conditions of low relatedness or even no relatedness, as we will see in Chapter 9. But if there is one straightforward prediction from inclusive fitness theory it is this: Selection will often favor the evolution of mechanisms to help close kin more than distant kin and distant kin more than strangers.

# ■ THEORY AND IMPLICATIONS OF INCLUSIVE FITNESS

*O*n this section, we first introduce Hamilton's rule—the technical formulation of inclusive fitness theory. From this perspective, we will see that the favoritism that parents show their own children can be viewed as a special case of favoritism toward the "vehicles" that contain copies of their genes. We will then explore the profound consequences of this formulation for topics such as cooperation, conflict, risk taking, and grieving.

## Hamilton's Rule

You might recall from Chapter 1 the technical concept of inclusive fitness:

> The inclusive fitness of an organism is not a property of himself, but a property of its actions or effects. Inclusive fitness is calculated from an individual's own reproductive success plus his effects on the reproductive success of his relatives, each one weighted by the appropriate coefficient of relatedness. (Dawkins, 1982, p. 186)

To understand this formulation of inclusive fitness, imagine a gene that causes an individual to behave altruistically toward another person. Altruism, as used here, is defined by two conditions: (1) incurring a cost to the self to (2) provide a benefit to the other person. The question that Hamilton (1964) posed was: Under what conditions would such an altruistic gene evolve and spread throughout the population? Under most conditions, we would expect that altruism would *not* evolve. Incurring costs to the self will hinder personal reproduction, so selection will generally operate against incurring costs for other people, many of whom are competitors. Hamilton's insight, however, was that altruism could evolve if the costs to the self were outweighed by the benefit to the recipient of the altruism, multiplied by the probability that the recipient carried a copy of that gene for altruism. Hamilton's rule, stated more formally, is that natural selection favors mechanisms for altruism when

$$c < rb$$

In this formula, $c$ is the cost to the actor, $r$ is the degree of genetic relatedness between the actor and the recipient (*genetic relatedness* can be defined as the probability of sharing a particular focal gene with another individual over and above the average population frequency of the gene; see Dawkins, 1982, and Grafen, 1991, for additional details), and $b$ is the benefit to the recipient. Both costs and benefits are measured in reproductive currencies.

This formula means that selection will favor an individual to incur costs (being "altruistic") if the benefits to a .50 kin member are more than twice the costs to the actor; if the benefits to a .25 kin member are more than four times the costs to the actor; or if the benefits to a .125 kin member are more than eight times the costs to the actor. An example will illustrate this point. Imagine that you pass by a river and notice that some of your genetic relatives are drowning in a ferocious current. You could jump in the water to save them, but you would pay with your own life. According to Hamilton's rule, selection will favor decision rules that, on average, result in your jumping into the water to save three of your brothers, but not one. You would be predicted *not* to sacrifice your own life for just one brother, because that would violate Hamilton's rule. Using the logic of Hamilton's rule, evolved decision rules should lead you to sacrifice your own life for five nieces or nephews, but you would have to save nine first cousins before you would sacrifice your own life.

The key point to remember is not that people's behavior will necessarily conform to the logic of inclusive fitness. Hamilton's rule is not a psychological theory. Instead, the key is that Hamilton's rule defines the conditions under which adaptations for aid to kin can evolve. It defines the selection pressure to which genes for altruism—indeed any genes—are subject. Any traits that happen to enter the population through mutation and violate Hamilton's rule will be ruthlessly selected against. Only those genes that code for traits that fulfill Hamilton's rule can spread throughout the population and hence evolve to become part of the species-typical repertoire. This is sometimes called an *evolvability constraint* because only genes that meet the conditions of Hamilton's rule can evolve.

Hamilton's theory of inclusive fitness is the single most important theoretical revision of Darwin's theory of natural selection in the past century. Before this theory, acts of altruism were genuinely puzzling from an evolutionary perspective because they appeared to go against the actor's personal fitness. Why might a ground squirrel give an alarm call when encountering a predator, thus making that squirrel vulnerable to the predator? Why would a woman sacrifice a kidney so that her brother might live? Hamilton's formulation of inclusive fitness solved all these puzzles in one bold stroke and showed how altruistic behavior far removed from personal reproduction could easily evolve.

## Theoretical Implications of Hamilton's Rule

> The social behaviour of a species evolves in such a way that in each distinct behaviour-evoking situation the individual will seem to value his neighbours' fitness against his own according to the coefficients of relationship appropriate to that situation. (Hamilton, 1964, p. 23)

At the most general level, the most important implication of Hamilton's theory of inclusive fitness is that psychological adaptations are expected to have evolved for different types of kin relationship. Nothing in Hamilton's theory *requires* that such kinship mechanisms necessarily evolve; after all, in some species, members don't even live with their kin, so selection could not fashion specific kin mechanisms. But the theory yields predictions about the general form of such kin mechanisms if they do evolve. In Chapter 7, we saw that there were many specific "problems of parenting," and we reviewed evidence for the evolution of parental mechanisms including the differential favoring of children according to qualities such as the probability of being the child's parent and the reproductive value of the child. The theory of inclusive fitness renders parenting as a special case of kinship, albeit an extremely important special case, because parenting represents just one way of investing in "vehicles" that contain copies of one's genes. Other specific relationships that would have recurred throughout human evolutionary history include sibships, half sibships, grandparenthood, grandchildhood, and so on. Let's consider a few of these to get a sense of the sorts of adaptive problems these kin relationships would have posed.

***Sibships.*** Brothers and sisters impose unique adaptive problems and have done so recurrently throughout human evolutionary history. First, a brother or a sister can be a major social ally—after all, your siblings are related to you by 50 percent. But sibs, perhaps more than all other relatives, are also major competitors for parental resources. As we saw in Chapter 7, parents have evolved to favor some children over others. As the theory of parent–offspring conflict suggests, what is in the best interests of the parents is not always the same as what is in the best interests of a particular child. One consequence is that siblings historically faced the recurrent adaptive problem of competing with each other for access to parental resources. Given this conflict, it is not surprising that sibling relationships are often riddled with ambivalence (Daly, Salmon, & Wilson, 1997, p. 275).

In an intriguing analysis (Sulloway, 1996, 2011), it has been proposed that the adaptive problems imposed by parents on children will create different "niches" for children, depending on their birth order. Specifically, because parents often favor the oldest child, the firstborn tends to be relatively more conservative and more likely to support the status quo. Second-borns, however, have little to gain by supporting the existing structure and everything to gain by rebelling against it. Later-borns, especially middle-borns, according to Sulloway, develop a more rebellious personality because they have the least to gain by maintaining the existing order, and a recent study of birth order and personality confirmed this prediction (Healey & Ellis, 2010). The youngest, on the other hand, might receive more parental investment than middle children, as parents often let out all the stops to invest in their final direct reproductive vehicle.

The evolutionary psychologists Catherine Salmon and Martin Daly (1998) have found some support for these speculations. They discovered that middle-borns differ from first- and last-borns in scoring lower on measures of family solidarity and identity. Middle-borns, for example, are less likely to name a genetic relative as the person to whom they feel closest. They are also less likely to assume the role of family genealogist. Middle-borns, compared to first-borns and last-borns, are less positive in attitudes toward their families and less likely to help a family member who needs help (Salmon, 2003). Interestingly, middle-borns are also less likely to cheat on their mates, although it is not known why.

These and other results (Salmon, 1999) lend some support to Sulloway's theory that birth order affects the niches a person selects, firstborns being more likely to feel solidarity with parents and perceive them as dependable, whereas middle-borns appear more likely to invest in bonds outside of the family. Interestingly, middle-born children might receive less total investment from parents even if parents treat all their children equally (Hertwig, Davis, & Sulloway, 2002). This result occurs because firstborns receive all of their parents' investments early in life before other children are born and last-borns receive all of their parents' investments after all the other children leave the house. Middle-borns, in contrast, must always share their parents' investments, because there is never a time when other siblings are not around. Thus, even when parents strive to invest equally in their children, middle-borns end up on the short end of the stick—perhaps accounting for why middle-borns are less identified with their families (Hertwig et al., 2002).

***Sibs versus Half Sibs.*** Another aspect of kinship that is theoretically critical is whether a sib is a full or a half sib. Given a common mother, for example, do you and your sibling share a father? This distinction is theoretically important because full sibs are genetically related by 50 percent on average, whereas half sibs are genetically related by only 25 percent on average. In an intriguing study of ground squirrels, Warren Holmes and Paul Sherman (1982) discovered that full sisters were far more likely than half sisters to cooperate in the mutual defense of their young.

The distinction between full and half sibs was likely a recurrent selection pr[...] the course of human evolutionary history. Mothers in contemporary tribal societies have children by different men, either from extramarital affairs or serial marriages (Hill 1996). Daly, Salmon, and Wilson (1997) speculate that it "could well be the case that in human prehistory it was a virtual toss-up whether successive children of the same woman were full or half-siblings, and the distinction between ($r = .5$) and ($r = .25$) is by no means trivial when the decision to cooperate or to compete is a close call" (Daly et al., 1997, p. 277). The conflicts that emerge in stepfamilies containing sibs of different degrees of genetic relatedness are ideal contexts for testing these speculations.

***Grandparents and Grandchildren.*** Grandparents are related to their grandchildren by an *r* of .25. The fact that modern women often live well beyond menopause has led to the hypothesis that menopause itself evolved as a means of ceasing direct reproduction to invest in children and then grandchildren, in what has become known as the "grandmother hypothesis" (Hill & Hurtado, 1991). Across cultures, postmenopausal women do contribute substantially to the welfare of their grandchildren (Lancaster & King, 1985). If grandparenting has been a recurrent feature of human evolutionary history, adaptations for allocating grandparents' investment might have evolved. As we will see later in this chapter, there is solid evidence for this hypothesis.

***Hypotheses about Universal Aspects of Kinship.*** Daly, Salmon, and Wilson (1997) outline a set of hypotheses about the universal aspects of the psychology of kinship. First, they suggest that *ego-centered kin terminology will be universal*. That is, in all societies, all kin will be classified in reference to a focal individual: "My parents are not the same people as your parents" and "My brothers are not the same as your brothers." All kin terms, in short, flow from the ego-centered focal individual.

Second, all kinship systems will make critical distinctions along the lines of *sex*. Mothers are distinguished from fathers, sisters are distinguished from brothers. This sex distinction occurs because the sex of a kin member has reproductive implications. Mothers, for example, have 100 percent certainty in their genetic relatedness to children, whereas fathers do not. Sons might become highly reproductively successful through multiple matings, whereas daughters cannot. The sex of the kin member, in short, is pivotal to the adaptive problems he or she faces, so all kin systems should make discriminations according to sex.

Third, *generation* is also critical. As we saw in Chapter 7, the relationship between parents and children is often asymmetrical. With advancing age, for example, children become increasingly valuable vehicles for their parents, whereas parents become less and less useful to their children. Therefore, we expect that all kin systems will make distinctions according to generation.

Fourth, kin relationships will be universally arrayed on a dimension of *closeness,* and closeness will be highly linked with genetic relatedness. The emotional (feeling close to someone) and cultural recognitions of "closeness," in short, are predicted to correspond to genetic closeness.

Fifth, the degree of *cooperation* and solidarity between kin will be a function of their degree of genetic relatedness. Cooperation and conflict should be predictable from the degree of genetic relatedness between kin members; people are predicted to turn to close kin rather than distant kin when it really matters; and whatever conflicts of interest exist, they will be mitigated more among close kin than among distant kin.

A sixth implication of inclusive fitness theory is that *the elder members of an extended kin family will encourage the younger members to behave more altruistically and cooperatively toward collateral kin* (i.e., kin who are not direct descendants, such as one's brothers, sisters, cousins, nephews, and nieces) than is their natural inclination. Imagine an older man who has a son, a sister, and the sister's son as relatives. From this older man's perspective, his sister's son (his nephew) is genetically related to him by .25 and so constitutes an important fitness vehicle for him. But from his own son's perspective, this person is merely a cousin and so is related to him by only .125. From his perspective, any sacrifice he makes for his cousin would have to yield eight times the cost, according to Hamilton's rule. Thus, any act of helping by the older man's son toward his sister's son (the boy's cousin) will be more beneficial to the fitness of the older man than to his son.

A seventh implication of inclusive fitness theory is that *one's position within an extended kin network will be core components of the self-concept.* Your beliefs about "who you are" will include kin linkages, such as "son of X," "daughter of Y," or "mother of Z."

An eighth implication of inclusive fitness theory is that despite differences across cultures in the exact kin terms that are employed and their putative meanings, *people everywhere will be aware who their "real" relatives are.* Consider the Yanomamö Indians of Venezuela. They use the kin term *abawa* to refer to both brothers and cousins. In English, however, we have different words, *brothers* and *cousins.* Does this terminological conflation among the Yanomamö obscure their real kin relationships? Anthropologist Napoleon Chagnon examined this issue by interviewing Yanomamö and showing them photographs of what English speakers would call their brothers and cousins. Although the Yanomamö said *"abawa"* when looking at both of the photographs, when asked "which one is your real *abawa*?" each invariably pointed to his actual blood brother and not to his cousin (Chagnon, 1981; Chagnon & Bugos, 1979). Furthermore, a "real *abawa*" is far more likely to come to a Yanomamö villager's aid in a social conflict, such as an axe fight with a rival individual or a rival group (Alvard, 2009). In short, although kin terms differ somewhat from culture to culture and some appear to blend different kinship categories, inclusive fitness theory suggests that people everywhere will be keenly aware of who their real kin are.

A final implication of inclusive fitness theory is that *kinship terms will be used to persuade and influence other people,* even when no actual kinship is involved. Consider the panhandler's request: "Hey, brother, can you spare some change?" Precisely why does the panhandler frame the request in this manner? One hypothesis is that he or she is using the kin term "brother" to activate the psychology of kinship in the target. Because we would be more likely to help a brother than a total stranger, the use of the term "brother" might in some small way trigger the psychology of kinship and hence increase the odds of our actually giving spare change. Similar forms of kin term usage are heard in college fraternities and sororities, in which members refer to each other as "brothers" and "sisters." In sum, the invocation of kinship through language is a predicted strategic implication of inclusive fitness theory.

## ■ EMPIRICAL FINDINGS THAT SUPPORT THE IMPLICATIONS OF INCLUSIVE FITNESS THEORY

The psychology of kinship has received increasing attention in the scientific literature. Several promising avenues of research have been explored in humans and in other animals. In this section, we highlight the most important of these empirical investigations.

## Alarm Calling in Ground Squirrels

When Belding's ground squirrels detect a terrestrial predator, such as a badger or a coyote, they sometimes emit a high-pitched staccato whistle that functions as an alarm call alerting other ground squirrels in the immediate vicinity to danger. The alerted squirrels then scramble to safety and avoid being picked off by the predator. The alerted squirrels clearly benefit from the alarm call because it increases their odds of survival, but the alarm caller suffers. The whistle makes the alarm caller more easily detectable, and predators are more likely to home in on the alarm caller for their meal. How can we account for this puzzling finding, which seems so contrary to individual survival?

Several hypotheses have been advanced to explain this apparent act of altruism (Alcock, 2009):

1. *The predator confusion hypothesis:* The alarm call might function to confuse the predator by creating a mad scramble, in which all the ground squirrels rush around for safety. This confusion might help the squirrels, including the alarm caller, to escape.
2. *The parental investment hypothesis:* Although the alarm caller is placed at greater risk by sounding the signal, perhaps his or her children are more likely to survive as a result. In this way, the alarm call might function as a form of parental investment.
3. *Inclusive fitness hypothesis:* Although the signaler might suffer in the currency of survival, the squirrel's aunts, uncles, brothers, sisters, father, mother, and cousins all benefit. According to this hypothesis, the signal alerts the "vehicles" that contain copies of the squirrel's genes, providing an inclusive fitness benefit.

To test these hypotheses, biologist Paul Sherman spent many summers in the California woods painstakingly marking, tracking, and studying an entire colony of Belding's ground squirrels (Sherman, 1977, 1981). The results are fascinating. Sherman was able to rule out the first hypothesis quickly. Sounding the alarm indeed puts the signaler at great risk because predators (weasels, badgers, and coyotes) stalked and killed alarm callers at a far higher rate than noncalling squirrels in the vicinity. So predators are not confused by the alarm call (hypothesis 1); instead, they home in on the alarm caller directly.

This leaves us with only two hypotheses: the parental investment hypothesis and the inclusive fitness hypothesis. When male Belding's ground squirrels mature, they leave home and join nonrelated groups. Females, on the other hand, remain with their natal group and so are surrounded by aunts, nieces, sisters, daughters, and other female relatives. It turns out that females give alarm calls far more often than males do—approximately 21 percent more often. This finding, taken alone, is consistent with both the parental investment hypothesis and the inclusive fitness hypothesis because both daughters and other genetic relatives of the alarm caller benefit from the signal.

The critical test comes with female ground squirrels who do not have daughters or other children around but do have other genetic relatives in the vicinity. Do they still emit the alarm calls when they spot a predator? The answer is yes. Females without their own children still sound the alarm, as long as they have sisters, nieces, and aunts in the area. In sum, although parental investment is likely to be one function of the alarm calls, the inclusive fitness hypothesis is also strongly supported because females sound the alarm even when they do not have offspring of their own. Sherman found further support for the inclusive fitness hypothesis in his discovery that female ground squirrels will rush to the aid of genetic relatives—their sisters as well as their daughters—to assist them in territorial conflicts with invaders, but will not help nonrelatives in such conflicts (Holmes & Sherman, 1982). These findings support the hypothesis that altruism can evolve through the process of inclusive fitness.

## Kin Recognition and Kin Classification in Humans

Providing aid to kin requires first having the ability to recognize them: "kin recognition functions in facilitating parental care, kin altruism, inbreeding avoidance, and optimal outbreeding" (Weisfeld et al., 2003). Researchers believe that early association—exposure to kin in infancy—is the key cue that primates use. Indeed, association during childhood in human populations is known to produce subsequent sexual aversion, functioning as an incest avoidance adaptation (Lieberman, Tooby, & Cosmides, 2007; Shepher, 1971).

Another kin recognition mechanism for which there is solid empirical support is based on odor: We can detect kin by smell. Mothers, fathers, grandparents, and aunts all can identify the odor of a newborn kin by smelling a shirt worn by that newborn, although women are better at it than men (Porter et al., 1986). Newborns who were breastfed prefer the odor of their mothers to other women, but do not prefer the odors of their fathers to other men (Cernoch & Porter, 1985). Finally, preadolescent children can correctly identify their full siblings by odor, but fail to correctly identify their half siblings or step siblings (Weisfeld et al., 2003).

Another method humans use to identify kin is through kin terminology. All cultures have *kin classification systems*—specific terms that describe types of kin such as mother, father, sister, brother, uncle, aunt, nephew, niece, and grandmother. Cultures differ somewhat in the particular kin included within a kin term. The English language lumps mother's sister and father's sister with the single term "aunt," for example, whereas other languages have two separate terms for these different individuals. Despite this surface variability, Doug Jones has identified a "universal grammar" governing all systems of kin classification (Jones, 2003a, 2003b). This grammar consists of three innate "primitives" of social cognition: genealogical distance, social rank, and group membership. *Genealogical distance* refers to how close (e.g., parents and siblings) or distant (second-degree or third-degree cousins) the kin are. *Social rank* refers to relative age, with the older being more highly ranked than the younger. *Group membership* distinguishes different clumps of kin, such as maternal versus paternal kin or same-sex siblings versus opposite-sex siblings. Jones argues that these three innate primitives are the cognitive building blocks used to generate terms for kin in all cultures.

The adaptive value of the genealogical distance building block is obvious based on the logic of inclusive fitness theory. It provides a means for identifying individuals of different "kinship value" to us—those from whom we are likely to receive altruism and those to whom we might channel our altruistic acts. The adaptive value of the social rank building block comes from the fact that high-ranking individuals such as parents are able to provide more help than low-ranking individuals such as children. This allows us to identify potential givers and receivers of altruism. The adaptive value of the group membership building block differs depending on the groups identified. We may wish to treat same-sex siblings differently from opposite-sex siblings, for example.

Another cue to kinship is *physical similarity* or *phenotypic resemblance*, such similarity between your face or body and the faces and bodies of others. Evidence supports the hypothesis that people do indeed use facial resemblance as a cue to kinship relatedness (Bressan & Zucchi, 2009; Park, Schaller, & Van Vugt, 2008; Platek & Kemp, 2009). Humans seem to have evolved the ability to distinguish kin from nonkin on the basis of the similarity of the other person's face to their own face. Although studies have not yet been conducted on whether people use cues of body similarity to gauge kinship, this represents another promising physical cue that might come into play.

Can humans also detect kinship among strangers or groups of other people to whom they are not related? Recent evidence suggests they can—also based on facial resemblance (Alvergne, Faurie, & Raymond, 2008; Kaminski et al., 2009). Interestingly, the upper part of the face seems to be especially important for kinship cues. When the lower half of the face was masked, performance on a kin recognition decreased by only 5 percent (Maloney & Dal Martello, 2006). When the upper half of the face was masked, however, performance on the kin recognition task declined by 65 percent. The ability to detect kinship clusters in others might be critical for solving important adaptive problems: (1) Knowing who is likely to be allied with whom if hostilities break out; (2) who not to antagonize because they have formidable kin in close proximity; and (3) who might be "exploitable" because they have few kin protectors nearby (Buss & Duntley, 2008).

In sum, humans have at least four ways of identifying kin: (1) through association; (2) through odor; (3) through kin classification generated by a universal grammar of three cognitive building blocks; and (4) through facial similarity or phenotypic resemblance. People are also skilled to detecting kinship among other people that they do not know. Kin recognition mechanisms are necessary adaptations on which many subsequent classes of behavior rely: Who will make good coalitional allies, whom to trust, whom not to have sex with (inbreeding avoidance), and whom to help in times of need. Indeed, there is now compelling evidence that kinship is a fundamental social category, much like sex and age, that people use to carve up their social world because it provides guidance to adaptive action such as altruistic and self-sacrificing behavior (Lieberman, Oum, & Kurzban, 2008).

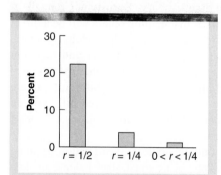

FIGURE *8.1* **Percentage of Major Helping by Closeness of Kinship.** $r$ = coefficient of relationship (e.g., $r$ of 1/2 = parents, full siblings, children; $r$ of 1/4 = half-siblings, grandparents, aunts, uncles, grandchildren, nieces, nephews; $r$ greater than zero but less than 1/4 = cousins, children of half siblings). More acts of helping are directed toward close genetic relatives than toward distant genetic relatives.

*Source:* Essock-Vitale, S. M., & McGuire, M. T. (1985). Women's lives viewed from an evolutionary perspective. II. Patterns of helping. *Ethology and Sociobiology, 6,* 143. Copyright © 1985, with permission from Elsevier Science.

## Patterns of Helping in the Lives of Los Angeles Women

In one early test of inclusive fitness theory applied to humans, two researchers studied a sample of 300 adult women from Los Angeles, ages thirty-five to forty-five. The following are reasons given by these women for receiving help:

> When I needed money to get into the union; When I broke my collarbone and he took over the house; Talking to a friend about her marital problems; Picking up a friend's kids the whole time she was sick; When my son was in trouble with the police; She kept the children when my third child was born; When her husband left her; When she had a leg amputated; Loaned us money for a house down-payment. (Essock-Vitale & McGuire, 1985, p. 141)

The women described 2,520 instances of receiving help and 2,651 instances of giving help. The predictions: (1) Among kin, helping will increase as a function of genetic relatedness; and (2) among kin, helping will increase as the recipient's reproductive value increases.

Figure 8.1 shows the percentage of instances of helping falling into three different categories of kinship: 50 percent genetic overlap, 25 percent genetic overlap, and less than 25 percent genetic overlap (e.g., first cousin). As predicted, helping exchanges were more likely to occur with close kin than with distant kin, supporting a key prediction from inclusive fitness theory. It is important to note, however, that the total percentage of instances of helping involving kin was only about a third. Many acts of helping were received from, and directed toward, close friends—a topic that we will consider in Chapter 9.

The second prediction was that helping among kin will be preferentially channeled to those of higher reproductive potential, a prediction that was also supported. Women were far more likely to help their children, nieces, and nephews than vice versa. Acts of helping flow from the older to the younger, reflecting the greater future reproductive potential of the younger recipients.

These findings are limited in a variety of ways. They are restricted to one sex (women), one city (Los Angeles), and one method of information gathering (questionnaire). As we will see, however, kinship exerts a powerful effect on helping when the sample is extended to men, to different populations, and to different methodologies. One study of 11,211 South African households, for example, discovered that the degree of genetic relatedness predicted how much money was spent on children's food, health care, and clothing (Anderson, 2005). Another study of the Pimbwe—a Tanzanian horticultural population—found that the larger the size of the maternal kin network, the healthier the children and the lower their mortality rate (Hadley, 2004).

## Life-or-Death Helping among Humans

One study explored hypotheses derived from inclusive fitness theory (Burnstein, Crandall, & Kitayama, 1994). Specifically, the researchers hypothesized that helping others will be a direct function of the recipient's ability to enhance the inclusive fitness of the helper. Helping should decrease, they reasoned, as the degree of genetic relatedness between helper and recipient decreases. Thus helping is predicted to be greater among siblings (who are genetically related by 50 percent on average) than between a person and his or her sibling's children (who are genetically related by 25 percent on average). Helping is expected to be lower still between individuals who are genetically related by only 12.5 percent, such as first cousins. No other theory in psychology predicts this precise helping gradient.

Genetic relatedness is important, but it is not the only theoretical consideration. Helping should decrease as a function of the age of the recipient, all else being equal, since helping an older relative will have less impact on one's fitness than will helping a younger relative because the latter is more likely to produce offspring that carry some of the same genes. In addition to age, genetic relatives higher in reproductive value and those who offer a better return on one's "investment" should be helped more than those of lower reproductive value and those who offer a lower return.

In studies to test these hypotheses, researchers distinguished between two types of helping: (1) helping that is substantial, such as acts that affect whether the recipient will live or die; and (2) helping that is relatively trivial, such as giving someone a little spare change. The predicted patterns of altruism should be stronger under the first type than the second.

To test these hypotheses, Burnstein and his colleagues studied two different cultures: the United States and Japan. Participants responded to questions about what they would do in a scenario in which a house was rapidly burning and they had only enough time to rescue one of the three people in the house. The researchers stressed that only the person who received help would survive—all others would perish. In the less significant form of everyday helping, subjects evaluated scenarios in which they had to indicate which persons they would help by picking up a few small items from a store. Recipients of the help varied in degree of genetic relatedness to the helper.

Helping in these hypothetical scenarios decreased steadily as the degree of genetic relatedness decreased. The .50 sibling was helped more than the .25 relatives, who in turn were helped more than those with only .125 genetic relatedness. This result proved especially strong in the life-or-death scenario.

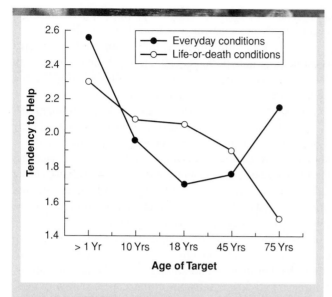

FIGURE *8.2*   **Tendency to Help as a Function of Recipient's Age under Life-or-Death versus Everyday Conditions.**

*Source:* Burnstein, E., Crandall, C., & Kitayama, S. (1994). Some neo-Darwinian decision rules for altruism: Weighing cues for inclusive fitness as a function of the biological importance of the decision. *Journal of Personality and Social Psychology, 67,* 779. Copyright © 1994 by the American Psychological Association. Reprinted with permission.

Helping in the life-or-death situation also declined steadily as the potential recipient's age increased. One-year-olds were helped more than ten-year-olds, who in turn were helped more than eighteen-year-olds. Least helped were the seventy-five-year-olds. Interestingly, the effects of age on helping were strongest in the life-or-death situation, but actually reversed in the trivial helping condition. For everyday helping such as running an errand, the seventy-five-year-olds were helped somewhat more than the forty-five-year-olds (see Figure 8.2). These findings replicated well across both Japanese and U.S. samples, providing some cross-cultural evidence.

Other studies have replicated and extended the pioneering work of Burnstein and his colleagues. Fitzgerald and Colarelli (2009) found that genetic relatedness predicted helping, but only when the altruism was extraordinary or life threatening. They also found that people help healthy kin more than those with reproductive limitations, such as having schizophrenia. Kinship predicts helping in hypothetically highly risky situations, such as fighting off attackers or defending against dangerous predators (Fitzgerald & Whitaker, 2009). Another study compared helping given to siblings, friends, and mates. Although people gave as much or more help to friends and mates as to a sibling, as the cost of the help escalated, people gave increasing amounts of help to siblings and decreasing amounts of help to mates and friends (Stewart-Williams, 2008). This finding is particularly interesting in light of the fact that participants reported feeling emotionally closer to their mates and friends than to their siblings! Yet another study of 7,265 individuals from the Netherlands found that people received more investment from their full siblings than from their half-siblings, even when the half-siblings were raised together and treated by parents as if they were full siblings (Pollet, 2007). When it really matters, kinship apparently exerts a powerful effect on acts of altruism.

## Genetic Relatedness and Emotional Closeness: Is Blood Thicker Than Water?

The Burnstein studies demonstrate clearly that genetic relatedness strongly affects helping, especially in life-or-death situations. Unexplored, however, are the underlying psychological mechanisms that motivate helping. In an effort to fill this gap, two theorists have proposed that "emotional closeness" is a psychological mediator. In one study, participants indicated how emotionally close they felt to each family member, ranging from 1 (not at all close) to 7 (extremely close) (Korchmaros & Kenny, 2001). Subsequently, they completed procedures similar to the Burnstein procedures for helping in hypothetical situations. As in the Burnstein studies, they found that genetic relatedness predicted willingness to act altruistically. But the key new findings centered on emotional closeness. Not only were individuals more likely to be emotionally close to their family members who were the most genetically related to them, but emotional closeness also statistically mediated the tendency to behave altruistically toward their family members. A larger study of 1,365 participants in Germany found similar results (Neyer & Lang, 2003), as have other studies (Korchmaros & Kenny, 2006; Kruger, 2003). Genetic relatedness proved to be a strong predictor of subjective closeness, a correlation between the two variables being a whopping +.50. These effects proved to be robust even when statistically controlling for variables such as residential proximity and frequency of contact; that is, people feel subjectively close to those who are highly genetically related even if they live far away and rarely see them.

Two other indications of emotional closeness are the frequency of contact and doing favors. Both are linked to genetic relatedness (Kurland & Gaulin, 2005). Full siblings, for example, have more frequent contact with each other than do half siblings, stepsiblings, or cousins. And the recency of doing a favor for these individuals falls out in the same order, with most favors done for full siblings and fewest favors for cousins.

Yet another indication of emotional closeness is the amount of psychological grief various relatives experience when a child dies. Parents experience more grief than relatives who are less genetically close (Littlefield & Rushton, 1986). Interestingly, the death of an elder child causes more intense grief than the death of a younger child; and the death of a healthy child causes more grief than the death of a sickly child.

In summary, emotional closeness might be one underlying psychological mechanism that prompts acts of altruism toward genetic relatives, although future research will undoubtedly uncover other underlying mechanisms. Blood, as the saying goes, might indeed be thicker than water.

## Vigilance over Kin's Romantic Relationships

As we know from the material covered in Chapters 4, 5, and 6, humans have a large array of mating adaptations because mating is so close to the engine of the evolutionary process—differential reproductive success. Because of the critical importance of success in the mating game, it would be surprising if individuals were indifferent to the mating relationships of their kin. A study tested two hypotheses: (1) Individuals will maintain greater vigilance over the mating relationships of their close than distant kin; and (2) individuals will maintain greater vigilance over the mating of their female than male kin (Faulkner & Schaller, 2007). Results supported both hypotheses using three dependent measures: awareness of the romantic partner's good and bad qualities, awareness of how the romantic relationship was progressing, and the degree to which they worried about how the romantic relationship was progressing. In sum, degree of genetic relatedness and sex of target both affect the degree to which individuals maintain vigilance over their kin's romantic relationships.

## Kinship and Stress

Stressful situations cause the release of the hormone cortisol into the blood stream. Cortisol has several functions, including releasing energy for action and affecting mental activity such as degree of alertness (Flinn, Ward, & Noone, 2005). The benefits of cortisol production in dealing with the immediate source of the stress, however, come at a cost. Cortisol tends to inhibit growth and hinder reproductive function. Thus, the cortisol produced by prolonged stress can damage bodily and reproductive functioning.

Mark Flinn and his colleagues monitored cortisol levels through saliva samples in a sample of children residing in a Caribbean village (Flinn et al., 2005). Children living in nuclear families with both parents present showed the lowest levels of cortisol. Children living only with a single mother showed elevated cortisol levels, but if other close kin were also living in the house, the children's cortisol levels were lower. Children in households with a stepfather and half sibs and households with distant relatives showed the highest levels of cortisol. The links between household composition and cortisol levels could be due to several factors (Flinn et al., 2005). Children living in difficult caretaking environments, such as those with stepfathers, half siblings, or distant relatives, could experience more frequent stressful events, such as fighting between parents, punishment by parents or stepparents, or more conflict with half siblings. Reconciliation after conflicts may be lacking. Or perhaps difficulties earlier in their lives may impair their coping abilities in dealing with the current stressors. Whatever the precise causal paths turn out to be, these results highlight the importance of close kin in creating less stressful environments and also indicate the levels of stress kids are exposed to in the absence of kin.

## Kinship and Survival

Emotional closeness and responses to hypothetical life-or-death scenarios are one thing. Actual survival is another. Is there any evidence that having kin in close proximity affects actual survival rates during real life-or-death situations? Two studies have explored this fascinating possibility. One was conducted of the survivors of the *Mayflower* pioneers in Plymouth Colony during the early years of the settling of America (McCullough & York Barton, 1990). Food was in short supply and diseases were rampant during the first cold winter of 1620–1621. Of the 103 first pioneers, a full 51 percent died. A large predictor of who lived and who died was simply the number of genetic relatives in the colony. Those who were most likely to die had the fewest relatives. Those who were most likely to live had parents and other relatives both in the colony and among the survivors. Similar results have been documented in other life-or-death situations, such as during the Donner Party disaster of 1846, in which forty out of eighty-seven people died during a bitter winter (Grayson, 1993). In studies of natural fertility populations, mothers and maternal grandmothers have an especially pronounced influence on the survival of children (Sear & Mace, 2008). A study of rural Malawi found that having older siblings of either sex is linked with higher survival rates (Sear, 2008). During evolutionary bottlenecks, when life is literally on the line, genetic relatives exert a strong influence on the odds of survival.

## Patterns of Inheritance—Who Leaves Wealth to Whom?

Another domain in which to test the theory of inclusive fitness pertains to the inheritance of wealth. When a person writes a will describing who will receive his or her wealth after he or she dies, can the pattern of distribution be predicted from inclusive fitness theory? Do people leave more money to close kin than to distant kin?

Informed by inclusive fitness theory, psychologists Smith, Kish, and Crawford (1987) tested three predictions about patterns of inheritance based on hypotheses about the evolved psychological mechanisms underlying resource allocation. (1) People will leave more of their estates to genetically related kin and spouses than to unrelated people. The inclusion of spouses in the prediction occurs not because of genetic relatedness, but rather because presumably the spouse will distribute the resources to their mutual children and grandchildren. (2) People will leave more to close kin than to distantly related kin. (3) People will leave more to offspring than to siblings, even though the average genetic relatedness is the same in these two types of relationships. The rationale for this prediction is that one's offspring, generally being younger than one's siblings, will on average have higher reproductive value. At the time in the life span when wills are typically written or go into effect, siblings are likely to be past their childbearing years, whereas children are more likely to be able to convert resources into future offspring.

To test these predictions, researchers studied the bequests of 1,000 randomly selected decedents, 552 men and 448 women, from the Vancouver region of British Columbia, Canada. Only those who left wills were included in the sample (some people do die intestate, or without a will). The researchers recorded the total dollar value of each estate, as well as the percentage of the estate that was willed to each beneficiary. The average estate was $54,000 for men and $51,200 for women. Interestingly, women tended to distribute their estates to a larger number of beneficiaries (2.8) than did men (2.0).

The first prediction was soundly confirmed. People left only 7.7 percent of their estates, on average, to nonrelatives and 92.3 percent to spouses or kin. The second prediction was also confirmed. Decedents willed more of their estates to closely related genetic kin than to more distant genetic relatives. Considering only the amount left to kin (excluding the categories of spouse and nonkin), people left 46 percent of their estates to relatives sharing 50 percent of their genes, 8 percent to relatives sharing 25 percent of their genes, and less than 1 percent to relatives sharing only 12.5 percent of their genes. These data support the hypothesis that selection has fashioned psychological mechanisms of resource allocation that favor individuals to the degree that they are genetically related. The third prediction—that people would bequeath more to offspring than to siblings—also was confirmed. Indeed, people left more than four times as much to their children (38.6 percent of the total estate) than to their siblings (7.9 percent of the estate). An analysis of 1,000 wills from British Columbia replicated these results, and also found support for all three predictions (Webster et al., 2008).

In another analysis of wills, Debra Judge (1995) replicated the finding that women tend to distribute their estates among a larger number of beneficiaries. A majority of men tended to leave their entire estates to their wives, often with expressed confidence that the wife would pass along the resources to their children. Here are a few examples of the reasons men included in their wills for channeling all of their resources to their wives:

> knowing her [wife] to be trustworthy and that she will provide for my boys . . . their education and a start in life
>> no provision for my children . . . for the reason that I know she [wife] will make adequate provision for them
>>> [wife] can handle the estate to better advantage if the same be left wholly to her and . . . [have] confidence she will provide for her said children as I would have done. (Judge, 1995, p. 306)

In sharp contrast to men who commonly expressed confidence and trust in their wives' ability to allocate resources, women who were married when they died did not express such trust. Indeed, when a husband was mentioned at all, it was often with a qualification. For example, six women intentionally excluded their husbands from their wills because they were abandoned by the husband, "for reasons sufficient [or "best known"] to me," or because of statements about the husband's "misconduct." In one case, a woman left her entire estate to her husband "as long as he lives unmarried" (Judge, 1995, p. 307).

It is difficult to draw direct inferences from this pattern of findings and quotations, but one speculation might be in order. It is known that older men are far more likely than older women to remarry (Buss, 2003). Therefore, widowers might use their previous wife's resources to attract a new mate and perhaps even start a new family. Resources will be diverted from the original wife's children and other kin to unrelated individuals. In contrast, because older women are unlikely to marry and even more unlikely to have additional children (most will be postmenopausal), the husband can be more confident that his widow will allocate the resources toward their mutual children.

A pair of studies conducted in Germany supported these interpretations (Bossong, 2001). Men and women of varying ages were asked to imagine that a doctor had told them that they were terminally ill and so had to write a will to allocate their resources across children and spouse. As with the earlier studies, women were more likely than men to allocate resources directly to their children. Men were more likely to allocate resources to their surviving spouse. However, the age of the surviving spouse mattered a lot to men. If their surviving spouse was old and postreproductive, then men were likely to allocate the lion's share to her, presumably because she would then distribute it to his children. If their surviving spouse was young, however, and hence likely to remarry and possibly have more children fathered by another man, men were far less likely to leave their money to the spouse, choosing instead to leave it directly to their children.

In summary, all three predictions received empirical support. Genetic relatives are bequeathed more than nonrelatives. Close kin receive more than distant kin. Direct descendants, primarily children, receive more than collateral kin such as sisters and brothers.

Given the fact that formal wills are relatively recent inventions, how can we interpret these findings? It is certainly not necessary to postulate a specific "will-making mechanism," because wills are too recent to have constituted a recurrent feature of our environment of evolutionary adaptedness. The most reasonable interpretation is that humans have evolved psychological mechanisms of resource allocation, that genetic relatedness is a pivotal factor in the decision rules of resource allocation, and that these evolved mechanisms operate on a relatively recent type of resources, those accumulated during one's life in the form of tangible assets that can be distributed at will.

## Investment by Grandparents

The past century has witnessed the gradual erosion of the extended family, as increased mobility has spread family members apart. Despite this departure from the extended kin contexts in which humans evolved, the relationship between grandparents and grandchildren appears to have retained a place of importance (Coall & Hertwig, 2010; Euler & Weitzel, 1996).

You might think that becoming a grandparent would be marked by great sorrow, a signal of old age and impending death. In fact, precisely the opposite is true. The arrival of grandchildren heralds a time of pride, joy, and deep fulfillment (Fisher, 1983). We have all experienced our elders proudly showing off photographs and memorabilia from the lives of their grandchildren or had to endure long-winded tales of the grandchildren's exploits and accomplishments.

There is tremendous variability, however, in how close to or distant from their grandparents grandchildren are. With some, the emotional bond is marked by warm feelings, frequent contact, and heavy investment of resources. With others, the feelings are distant, contact infrequent, and investment of resources rare. Evolutionary psychologists have turned to explaining this variability in grandparental investment.

*In humans, grandparents often invest in their grandchildren, and show relationships marked by warmth, frequent contact, and devotion. Specific patterns of grandparental investment are predictable from theories of paternity uncertainty developed by DeKay (1995) and Euler and Weitzel (1996).*

Theoretically, grandparents are genetically related by .25 to each grandchild. So on what basis could we generate predictions about differences in grandparents' investment? Recall a profound sex difference that has cropped up several times: Men face the adaptive problem of paternity uncertainty, whereas women are 100 percent certain of their maternity. This applies to grandparents as well as to parents, but there is a special twist on the theory: We are dealing with two generations of descendants, so from a grandfather's perspective, there are two opportunities for genetic kinship to be severed (DeKay, 1995). First, it is possible that he is not the genetic father of his son or daughter. Second, his son might not be the father of the putative grandchildren. This double whammy makes the blood relationships between a grandfather and his son's children the most uncertain of all grandparental relationships.

At the other end of the certainty continuum are women whose daughters have children. In this case, the grandmother is 100 percent certain that her genes are carried by her grandchildren (keep in mind that none of this need be conscious). She is undoubtedly the mother of her daughter, and her daughter is certain of her genetic contribution to her children. In sum, the theoretical prediction from the inclusive fitness theory is clear: From the grandchild's perspective, the mother's mother (MoMo) should invest the most, and the father's father (FaFa) should invest the least, all else being equal.

What about the other two types of grandparents: the mother's father (MoFa) and the father's mother (FaMo)? For each of these cases, there was one place in the line of descent where relatedness could be severed. A man whose daughter has a child might not be the actual father of his daughter. A woman with a son might not be related to her son's children if the son's wife was inseminated by another man. The investment of these two types of grandparents, therefore, is predicted to be intermediate between the most certain genetic linkage (MoMo) and the least certain genetic linkage (FaFa).

The investment that a person makes in grandchildren can take many forms, both behavioral and psychological. Behaviorally, one could examine frequency of contact, actual investment of resources, readiness to adopt, or the willing of property. Psychologically, one could examine expressed feelings of closeness, magnitude of mourning on the death of a grandchild, and willingness to make sacrifices of various sorts. The hypothesis of "discriminative grandparental investment" predicts that behavioral and psychological indicators on investment should follow the degree of certainty inherent in the different types of grandparental relationships: most for MoMo, least for FaFa, and somewhere in between these two for MoFa and FaMo.

Studies from different cultures have tested the hypothesis of discriminative grandparental solicitude. In one study conducted in the United States, evolutionary psychologist Todd DeKay (1995) studied a sample of 120 undergraduates. Each student completed a questionnaire that included information on biographical background and then evaluated each of the four grandparents on the following dimensions: grandparent's physical similarity to self, grandparent's personality similarity to self, time spent with grandparent while growing up, knowledge acquired from grandparent, gifts received from grandparent, and emotional closeness to grandparent. Figure 8.3 summarizes the results from this study.

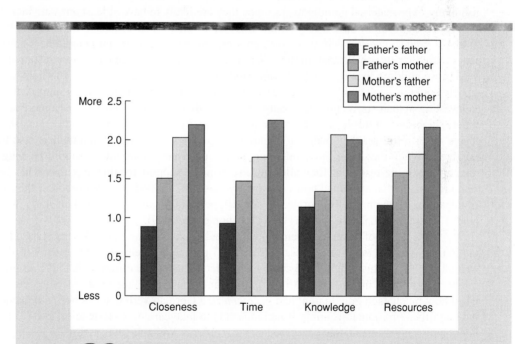

FIGURE 8.3 **Grandparental Investment in Grandchildren.** Findings show that the mother's mother is closer to, spends more time with, and invests most resources in the grandchild, whereas father's father scores lowest on these dimensions. Findings presumably reflect evolved psychological mechanisms sensitive to the degree of certainty of genetic relatedness.

*Source:* DeKay, W. T. (1995, July). Grandparental investment and the uncertainty of kinship. Paper presented to Seventh Annual Meeting of the Human Behavior and Evolution Society, Santa Barbara. Reprinted with permission.

The leftmost panel shows the rankings of subjects' emotional closeness to each of their grandparents. Participants indicated the most emotional closeness to their mother's mother and the least emotional closeness to their father's father. A similar pattern emerged for the variables of time spent with the grandparent and the resources (gifts) they received from the grandparent.

Another interesting pattern emerged for the two grandparents of intermediate relational uncertainty. In each case, for all four variables, the mother's father was ranked higher than the father's mother. How can this pattern be explained, since in each case there is one opportunity for the genetic link to be severed? DeKay (1995) had actually predicted this finding in advance by suggesting that infidelity rates were higher in the younger generation than in the older generation—a suggestion that has some empirical support (Laumann et al., 1994). Thus, the relational uncertainty would be higher for the father's mother, since the father would be in the younger generation, than for the mother's father. If this hypothesis receives further empirical support, it would suggest that grandparents might be sensitive either to prevailing rates of infidelity or to personal circumstances that might jeopardize the genetic link between them, their children, and their grandchildren.

An alternative hypothesis was suggested by Professor Bill von Hippel (personal communication, October 10, 2002). He proposed a competing explanation that centers on the presence or absence of other outlets for investing one's resources. Specifically, paternal grandmothers are also likely to be maternal grandmothers, since they are likely to have at least one daughter who has children. Thus, they have a very secure alternative outlet for investment—in their daughter's children—and so invest less in their son's children. In contrast, maternal grandfathers have no better outlet for investment than in their daughter's children and so channel more resources toward those children than do paternal grandmothers. In essence, maternal grandfathers have a reliable outlet through their daughter's children, whereas paternal grandmothers might cut back on investing in their son's children because they have their daughter's children as a more secure outlet. The beauty of this hypothesis is that it can be easily tested: Paternal grandmothers should devote fewer resources than maternal grandfathers only when paternal grandmothers also have daughters. When they have only sons, in contrast, paternal grandmothers should be roughly comparable in the resources they allocate. Preliminary support for this hypothesis has been found in a study that examined how emotionally close 767 individuals felt to each of their four grandparents (Laham, Gonsalkorale, & von Hippel, 2005), although another study with a smaller sample size failed to find this effect (Bishop et al., 2009).

Another study of the grandparental investment hypothesis was undertaken by Harald Euler and Barbara Weitzel, who studied a sample of 1,857 participants recruited in Germany (Euler & Weitzel, 1996). Of this sample, 603 cases were selected using the criterion that all four grandparents had to be living at least until the participant reached the age of seven. Subjects were asked how much each grandparent had *gekummert,* a German verb that has both a behavioral and cognitive-emotional meaning. It includes "(1) to take care of, to look after, and (2) to be emotionally and/or cognitively concerned about" (Euler & Weitzel, 1996, p. 55).

The results of the German sample showed precisely the same pattern as the first study of U.S. grandchildren. The maternal grandmother—the relationship showing no relational uncertainty—was viewed as having the most gekummert. The paternal grandfather—the most genetically uncertain of all—was viewed as having the least gekummert. As in the U.S. study, the MoFa showed more investment than the FaMo.

The latter finding is especially interesting because it rules out a potential alternative explanation: that perhaps women in general are more likely to invest than men, a sex difference that might extend to relationships with grandparents. The findings from both studies contradict this alternative. In each study, the maternal grandfathers invested more than the paternal grandmothers. In sum, the general expectation of a sex difference in investment cannot account for the fact that grandfathers, under some circumstances, invest more than grandmothers.

Essentially the same patterns of grandparental solicitude have now been replicated in Greece, France, and Germany (Euler, Hoier, & Rohde, 2001; Pashos, 2000), and in a sample of older grandparents residing in the United States (Michalski & Shackelford, 2005). When a grandchild dies, the amount of grief experienced by the grandparents also falls out in the same pattern, with maternal grandmothers grieving the most and paternal grandfathers grieving the least (Littlefield & Rushton, 1986). People generally have the best relationship with their maternal grandmother and the least good relationship with their paternal grandfather (Euler et al., 2001).

Yet another study of 831 individuals from the Netherlands found that maternal grandmothers were significantly more likely than paternal grandfathers or grandmothers to maintain frequent face-to-face contact, even as the physical distance between grandchild and grandparent increased (Pollet, Nettle, & Nelissen, 2007). The authors conclude that "maternal grandmothers do [literally] go the extra mile" (2007, p. 832).

There is some evidence that the maternal grandmother's investment makes a difference in the survival of grandchildren. A study of families living during the years of 1770 to 1861 in Cambridgeshire, England, found that maternal grandmother's survival, but not the survival of any of the other grandparents, increased the odds that the grandchildren would survive (Ragsdale, 2004). Interestingly, this effect occurred through two paths. First, the MoMo's survival increased the odds of the grandchild's survival as a result of the increased survival of the mother. Second, even controlling for the mother's survival, the MoMo's survival increased the odds of the grandchild's survival. These results support the hypothesis that maternal grandmothers invest more in grandchildren than do other grandparents—support that makes a real difference in the currency of survival.

One explanation for why grandmothers help has been called the *grandmother hypothesis*: The idea that women evolved such a long postmenopausal lifespan precisely because grandparental investment (e.g., help, care, food, wisdom) enabled women to increase their inclusive fitness (Hawkes et al., 1998; Williams, 1957). As a complement to the grandmother hypothesis, Kuhle (2007) proposed the *absent father hypothesis*—the idea that because men die at a younger age than their mates and—if they live, they sometimes leave their aging partners to mate with younger partners—it would have been beneficial for women to stop reproducing directly and instead invest existing children and grandchildren. Evidence that grandmothers do have beneficial effects on grandchildren, especially under harsh or risky circumstances, has been cumulating, although the issue of whether these effects explain why women live so long after reaching menopause remains hotly debated (see Coall & Hertwig, 2010, and associated commentaries).

Many questions remain unanswered by this research. How do prevailing rates of infidelity in each generation affect the psychology of grandparents' investment? Do grandparents monitor the likelihood that their sons might be cuckolded and shift their investment accordingly? Do grandparents scrutinize grandchildren for their perceived similarity to them as part of their decision making about investing in those grandchildren?

These questions about the evolutionary psychology of grandparental investment will likely be answered within the next decade. For now, we can conclude that findings from several different cultures support the hypothesis that grandparents' investment is sensitive to the varying probability that genetic relatedness might be severed by paternity uncertainty in each generation. (See Box 8.1 for a discussion on investment by aunts, uncles, and cousins.)

BOX *8.1*

## Investment by Aunts, Uncles, and Cousins

According to inclusive fitness theory, selection will favor mechanisms that result in investing in kin as a function of genetic relatedness. Expected relatedness is a function of two factors: (1) genealogical linkage (e.g., sisters are more closely related than uncles and nephews) and (2) paternal uncertainty caused by extra-pair copulations. In this chapter, we have looked at evidence suggesting that as paternal uncertainty increases through the paternal line, investment in grandchildren decreases. Is this effect limited to grandparents' investment, or does the logic extend to other kin relationships, such as aunts and uncles?

According to this logic, maternal aunts (sisters of the mother) should invest more than paternal aunts (sisters of the father). Similarly, maternal uncles (brothers of the mother) should invest more than paternal uncles (brothers of the father). Paternity certainty, and hence genetic relatedness, should be highest on average through the maternal line. Conversely, genetic relatedness should be lowest on average through the paternal line.

To examine this issue, a team of researchers studied 285 U.S. college students, all of whom reported that both of their biological parents were living (Gaulin, McBurney, & Brakeman-Wartell, 1997). Each participant was asked to rate a series of questions using a seven-point scale: (1) "How much concern does the maternal (paternal) uncle (aunt) show about your welfare?" (2) If you have both a maternal and a paternal uncle (aunt), which one shows more concern about your welfare?" (1997, p. 142). The researchers selected the phrase "concern about your welfare" so that participants would think broadly about the various types of benefits they might receive.

Findings support the hypothesis that maternal aunts invest more than paternal aunts and maternal uncles invest more than paternal uncles (paternity certainty and hence genetic relatedness being highest on average through the maternal line and lowest through the paternal line).

Two main effects are noteworthy. First, there is a main effect for sex: Aunts tend to invest more than uncles, regardless of whether they are maternal or paternal. Second, maternal aunts and uncles tend to invest more than paternal aunts and uncles—the predicted laterality effect.

According to the researchers, these two effects are likely to have different causes. They suggest that the sex effects (aunts invest more than uncles) occur because men tend to invest surplus resources into mating opportunities, whereas women do not.

The laterality effect, in contrast, has a different explanation, based on the probabilities of paternity uncertainty that occur through the male line. Uncertainty of paternity, and hence a lower likelihood of genetic relatedness, is the best explanation for the evolution of psychological mechanisms that lead to the investment decisions of aunts and uncles. When paternity certainty is guaranteed, as when you are a sibling of the mother of your niece or nephew, you will invest a lot. Aunts who are themselves childless are especially likely to invest in their nieces and nephews (Pollet, Kuppens, & Dunbar, 2006; Pollet et al., 2007). When paternity is uncertain, as when you are a sibling of the father of your niece or nephew, you are likely to invest less.

The same logic can be used to predict altruism toward cousins (Jeon & Buss, 2007). People should be most willing to help their mother's sister's (MoSis) children, which have the highest probability of genetic relatedness, and least willing to help their father's brother's (FaBro) children, which have the lowest probability of genetic relatedness. Helping toward father's sister's (FaSis) and mother's brother's (MoBro) children should fall in between.

A study to test these predictions asked people the following: "As you make your way throughout the city you walk past a building that is blazing with flames. You instantly realize that the building has been housing a meeting attended by your

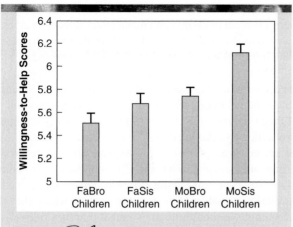

FIGURE *8.4* **Altruism toward Cousins.**
Findings show that people express a greater willingness
to help cousins with a higher likely degree of genetic
relatedness (e.g., cousins through one's mother's sister)
than cousins with a lower likely degree of genetic
relatedness (e.g., cousins through one's father's brother).

*Source:* Jeon, J., & Buss, D. M. (2007). Altruism toward cousins.
*Proceedings of the Royal Society of London* (Figure 2).

cousin ____ (fill in the initials). Your
cousin _____ in the rapidly burning
building badly needs your help, yet entering the building to save him or her
would risk injury to you" (Jeon & Buss,
2007, p. 1182). As shown in Figure 8.4,
willingness to help the different categories of cousins occurs precisely as
predicted. The results support the hypothesis that humans have adaptations sensitive to varying probabilities of genetic
relatedness; in this case, through varying
probabilities of paternity uncertainty.

In sum, genetic relatedness, as predicted by inclusive fitness theory, appears to be a major factor in investment
in relatives. When genetic relatedness is
jeopardized through paternity uncertainty, investment falls off. This effect is
robust across different sorts of relationships, including those with aunts, uncles, grandmothers, grandfathers, and
cousins (Pashos & McBurney, 2008).

## A Broader Perspective on the Evolution of the Family

What is a family? Various disciplines define this entity differently, and social scientists have not
reached a firm consensus about what constitutes a family (Emlen, 1995). Sociologists often
emphasize the childrearing function of the family, defining families as groups of adults living
together, bearing the responsibility for producing and raising children. Anthropologists, in
contrast, tend to stress kinship, defining families as groups of parents, unmarried children, and
sometimes extended kin through which lines of descent can be traced.

Evolutionary biologist Stephen Emlen defines families as "those cases where offspring
continue to interact regularly, into adulthood, with their parents" (Emlen, 1995, p. 8092). He
distinguishes two types of families: (1) *simple families,* a single parent or conjugal pair in which
only one female reproduces (e.g., a mother and her prereproductive offspring), and (2) *extended
families,* groups in which two or more relatives of the same sex may reproduce. Notice that the
presence of a breeding male is not essential to the definition of family. When the male is present,
however, the family is called *biparental* because both the mother and the father share some
responsibility for parenting. When the male is absent, the family is called *matrilineal* because
the females (or the female and her female relatives) are responsible for parenting. One defining
feature of all families is that offspring continue to live with their parents past the age at which
they are capable of reproducing on their own.

Families are so much a fact of life for humans that we take their existence for granted. The astonishing fact, however, is that a mere 3 percent of all bird and mammalian species form families (Emlen, 1995). Why are families so rare? Why do most offspring throughout the animal world leave the nest as soon as evolution has made them biologically capable of doing so, and so few remain with their parents past sexual maturity? The most likely reason is that remaining in the parental nest (or delaying departure from the nest) carries a tremendous reproductive cost. In simple families, offspring do not reproduce while living at home. In extended families, however, parents will often actively suppress the reproduction of their offspring (e.g., by interfering with mating attempts). In both cases, the offspring sacrifice reproduction by delaying departure from the family unit.

Families thus inflict two primary costs on offspring: (1) Reproduction is delayed and sometimes directly suppressed (perhaps the heaviest cost), and (2) competition for resources such as food is concentrated rather than dispersed, making life more challenging for both parents and offspring. The only way that families can evolve, in the rare instances in which they do, is when the reproductive benefits of remaining in the family are so great that they outweigh the heavy costs of forgoing early reproduction.

Two major theories have been proposed to explain the evolution of families. The first is the *ecological constraints model.* According to this theory, families emerge when there is a scarcity of reproductive vacancies that might be available to the sexually mature offspring. Under these conditions, both the cost of staying within the family and the benefits of leaving are low. The heavy cost of staying within the family—delayed reproduction—vanishes because early reproduction is not possible owing to a lack of reproductive vacancies (i.e., resource niches that provide the opportunity for reproduction).

The second theory is the *familial benefits model.* According to this theory, families form because of the bounty of benefits they provide for offspring. These benefits include (1) enhanced survival as a result of aid and protection from family members, (2) an enhanced ability to compete subsequently, perhaps by acquiring skills or greater size and maturity as a result of staying at home, (3) the possibility of inheriting or sharing the family territory or resources as a result of staying at home, and (4) inclusive fitness benefits gained by being in a position to help and be helped by genetic relatives while staying at home.

Emlen (1995) synthesizes these two theories into one unified theory of the origins of the family. His theory of family formation has three premises. First, families form when more offspring are produced than there are available reproductive vacancies to fill. This premise stems from the ecological constraints model. Second, families will form when offspring must wait for available reproductive vacancies until they are in a good position to compete for them. Third, families will form when the benefits of staying at home are large—in the form of increased survival, increased ability to develop competition skills, increased access to familial resources, and increased inclusive fitness benefits. Emlen's theory of the family is thus a synthesis of the ecological constraints and the family benefits models.

Several predictions follow from Emlen's theory. The first set of predictions involves the *family dynamics of kinship and cooperation.*

*Prediction 1: Families will form when there is a shortage of reproductive vacancies but will break up when the vacancies become available.* Families will be unstable, forming and breaking up depending on the circumstances. This prediction has been tested in several avian species (Emlen, 1995). When new breeding vacancies were created where there previously had been none, mature offspring "flew the coop" and left home to fill those vacancies, thus splitting apart an intact family. This prediction suggests that sexually mature children who are not yet in a position to compete successfully for mates or are not in a resource position to maintain a home on their own will tend to remain with their family unit.

*Prediction 2: Families that control many resources will be more stable and enduring than families that lack resources.* Among humans, the expectation would be that wealthy families will be more stable than poor families, especially when there is a chance that the children might inherit the parental resources or territory. Children coming from high-resource homes are predicted to be especially choosy about when and under what conditions they decide to leave home. By sticking around, mature children may inherit the wealth, so wealthier families should show greater stability over time than poor families. Among many species of familial birds and mammals, offspring do indeed sometimes inherit their parents' breeding place. Davis and Daly (1997) provide empirical support for this prediction by finding that high-income families are indeed more likely to maintain social ties with their extended kin than are low-income families.

*Prediction 3: Help with rearing the young will be more prevalent among families than among comparable groups lacking kin relatives.* A sister or brother, for example, might assist in raising a younger sibling, providing a key inclusive fitness benefit by living with the family. A study of the Hadza hunter-gatherers of Tanzania found support for this prediction—closely related females (sometimes called "allomothers") spent the largest percentage of time holding and caring for the children of their relatives (Crittenden & Marlowe, 2008).

Another set of predictions pertains to changes in family dynamics as a result of the loss or disruption of an existing breeder.

*Prediction 4: When a breeder is lost because of death or departure, family members will get into a conflict over who will fill the breeding vacancy.* The loss of a parent opens up a new vacancy, creating the perfect opportunity for offspring to inherit the natal resources. The higher the quality of the vacancy, the more competition and conflict there will be to fill it. Among red-cocked woodpeckers, for example, in each of twenty-three cases of the death of a father, one of the sons took over the breeding role, and the mother was forced to leave. Among humans, an analogous situation might occur if a father died and left behind a large inheritance. Children often engage in lawsuits concerning claims to an inheritance, and claims made by genetically unrelated individuals (e.g., a mistress of the father to whom he left resources) are often challenged (Smith, Kish, & Crawford, 1987).

*Prediction 5: The loss of an existing breeder and replacement by a breeder who is genetically unrelated to family members already present will increase sexual aggression.* When a mother is divorced, widowed, or abandoned and she remates with an unrelated male, the strong aversions against incest are relaxed. Stepfathers might be sexually attracted to stepdaughters, for example, thus putting mother and daughter in a kind of intrasexual rivalry. Among a variety of avian species, aggression between sons and stepfathers is common, since these unrelated males are now sexual competitors (Emlen, 1995). Among humans, having a stepfather in the home puts girls, both prepubescent and postpubescent, at a greater risk of sexual abuse (Finkelhor, 1993).

Emlen's theory, in sum, generates a rich set of testable predictions. Many of these predictions have received support from avian, mammalian, and primate species, but others remain to be tested. Especially intriguing is their applicability to human families.

***Critique of Emlen's Theory of the Family.***    Evolutionary psychologists Jennifer Davis and Martin Daly have criticized Emlen's theory, offering several useful modifications as well as empirical tests of a few key predictions (Davis & Daly, 1997). At the most general level,

Davis and Daly offer three considerations that provide a unique context for examining human families: (1) Human families might remain together because of competition from other groups, such that remaining in a large kin-based coalition is advantageous in such group-on-group competition (see Webster, 2008); (2) humans engage in extensive social exchange based on reciprocal altruism with nonkin; and (3) nonreproductive helpers, such as postmenopausal women, have little incentive to encourage their offspring to disperse, which might help to stabilize families.

These three considerations could affect the logic of Emlen's predictions. Consider prediction 1, which suggests that families will dissolve when acceptable breeding opportunities become available elsewhere. If a woman is postmenopausal and hence incapable of further reproduction, it would clearly be disadvantageous for her to abandon her family and the help she could provide when a breeding vacancy arose elsewhere. Because she is postmenopausal, she cannot exploit the breeding vacancy. Rather, it would pay to remain with her kin and continue to provide help.

Another modification pertains to the fact that humans engage in extensive social exchange. Consider prediction 3: Help with rearing the young will be more prevalent among families than among comparable groups lacking kin relatives. Women often form friendships with nonkin in which they engage in reciprocal help with childrearing (Davis & Daly, 1997). Prediction 3 could be modified to take into account that *unreciprocated* help with rearing the young will be more prevalent among families than among comparable groups lacking kin relatives. In summary, several of Emlen's predictions could be modified by considering factors that are unique to the human animal, such as extensive patterns of reciprocal alliances (see Chapter 9) and the prolonged postmenopausal period enjoyed by women.

It is clear from a cross-species comparative analysis that families are exceedingly rare. Given current social interest in "family values," evolutionary psychology has something to offer by illuminating the conditions under which families remain stable or fall apart. In the next decade, researchers will undoubtedly test these predictions and uncover a rich array of evolved psychological mechanisms—those involving cooperation as well as conflict—designed to deal with the varying adaptive problems posed by families (see Geary & Flinn, 2001).

## The Dark Side of Families

We often think of families as harmonious social enclaves that involve the benevolent transfer of resources, protection, information, and status. Indeed, even in evolution biology, the "classical" view of the family was of a harmonious unit of cooperating individuals that was designed by selection to maximize the number of surviving offspring (Parker, Royle, & Hartley, 2002). Nonetheless, well-developed evolutionary theories over the past three decades have overthrown this harmonious view and point to a darker side of family life: pervasive conflicts over resources, perhaps most centrally over the parental resources. In Chapter 7, we briefly explored two sources of conflict, based on Trivers's theory of parent–offspring conflict.

There are three fundamental sources of conflict within families (see Figure 8.5). The first is *sibling conflict.* Within the same family, siblings compete with one another for access to parental resources. Among certain bird species, siblings jostle and jockey for the best position to gain food from the parents returning to the nest. Siblings amplify their levels of begging in attempts to secure more than their fair share of resources. Occasionally, a bird will commit "siblicide" by pushing a sibling out of the nest. A review of a book on the natural history of families provides an apt summary: "[I]n spite of occasional outbreaks of harmony,

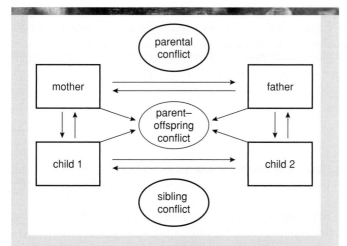

FIGURE 8.5 **Three Major Forms of Conflict within Families.** This figure shows three major types of conflict within families: sibling conflict over parental resources, parent–offspring conflict, and conflict between the mother and father.

*Source:* Modified from Parker, G. A., Royle, N. J., & Hartley, I. R. (2002). Intrafamilial conflict and parental investment: A synthesis. *Philosophical Transactions of the Royal Society of London B, 357,* 295–307.

families are shaped by conflict. In birds, parents deliberately generate much conflict within families. They screen their offspring for quality by stage-managing conflicts among them, compensate for the uncertainty of future food supplies by optimistically producing more young than they expect to rear, and generate insurance against reproductive failure by producing surplus offspring. As a result of these parental decisions, family life is filled with frequently gory and often fatal struggles between offspring" (Buckley, 2005, p. 295).

Among mammalian species, siblings sometimes compete by increasing their level of suckling, draining the maternal teats to the detriment of their littermates. These are all forms of "scramble competition," and there is every reason to assume that similar phenomena occur in human families.

Accounts of sibling conflict go far back in human recorded history, as exemplified by this quote from *Genesis* in the *King James Bible:* "Israel loved Joseph more than all his children, because he was the son of his old age: and he made him a coat of many colours. And when his brethren saw that their father loved him more than his brethren, they hated him, and they could not speak peaceably unto him."

The biblical account of Cain and Abel is also revealing, because the killing was caused, in some accounts, by conflict over a woman. Extreme forms of sibling conflict such as siblicide are rare in humans, but they do occur, and the circumstances in which they occur are revealing. Brothers, far more than sisters, sometimes become sexual competitors. Statistically, most murders of siblings are indeed brothers killing brothers. The causes are almost invariably conflicts over women or conflicts over resources that are needed to attract women (Buss, 2005b). Human siblings also compete with each other get into conflict over *grandparental* resources (Fawcett et al., 2010, p. 23). This ranges from using subtle tactics such as maintaining regular contact with grandparents to more overt tactics such as direct requests for money. And cases of siblings suing each other over inheritances when a parent or grandparent dies are so common that they only make headlines when vast sums of money are involved. There is also evidence that resource competition among siblings, such as conflict over limited land in farming communities, causes some siblings to migrate out of their natal area in order to secure resources elsewhere (Beise & Voland, 2008).

The second form of conflict is *parent–offspring conflict,* which we explored in Chapter 7. The optimal allocation of resources from the parent's perspective, for example, might be to give equal shares of resources to each offspring, although other factors such as need and ability to utilize resources obviously cause deviations from equal allocation. From the child's perspective, however, the optimal resource allocation usually involves taking more for the self at some expense to a sibling and parent. There is an old joke that illustrates this conflict. A son goes off to college and, after three months, writes a letter home pleading for more money:

> *"Dear Dad: No mon, no fun, your son."*
> *In response, the father writes back:*
> *"Dear Son: Too bad, so sad, your Dad."*

Selection can be expected to favor adaptations in children to manipulate parents to secure a larger share of resources and counteradaptations in parents not to bend solely to one child's desires.

The third fundamental type of family conflict involves conflicts between the mother and father over resource allocation, or parental conflict. Conflict between mothers and fathers centers on how much parental investment each will give to the offspring within the family. It is sometimes beneficial, for example, for one parent to withhold his or her own resources for other avenues of reproduction. Either parent might divert resources to his or her own kin and will profit if the other parent provides more resources directly to their offspring. Furthermore, either parent might use resources to obtain matings and consequently children outside of the family, who are genetically unrelated to the other parent, resulting in conflict between the parents. It would be surprising if humans had not evolved adaptations designed to deal with these forms of conflict, such as sensitivity to the other parent's diversion of resources or psychological manipulation such as guilt induction designed to extract additional resources from the other parent.

We often grow up believing that families should be harmonious sanctums within which mutual sharing yields the maximum benefit for everyone. As a consequence, when we experience turmoil, disagreement, and clashes with our parents, siblings, or children, we feel that something has gone badly awry. Entire professions, such as certain forms of psychological counseling, are designed to deal with the psychological turmoil that results from family conflict. An evolutionary perspective suggests that three fundamental sources of conflicts—between siblings, between parents and offspring, and between mothers and fathers—are likely to be pervasive. This might not help the daughter who is battling her mother, the parents who are at odds over how resources are to be allocated, or the brother and sister who cannot stand each other, but understanding the evolutionary logic of family conflict might help people to gain some perspective from the realization that they are not alone in these experiences.

# ■ SUMMARY

We started this chapter by delving deeper into Hamilton's (1964) theory of inclusive fitness, formalized by Hamilton's rule $c < rb$. For altruism to evolve, for example, the cost to the actor must be less than the benefits provided, multiplied by the genetic relatedness between the actor and the recipient. In one bold stroke, this theory offered one answer to the question of how altruism could evolve. It simultaneously extended Darwin's definition of classical fitness (personal reproductive success) to inclusive fitness (personal reproductive success plus the effects of one's actions on the fitness of genetic relatives, weighted by the degree of genetic relatedness).

Next we drew out the profound theoretical implications of inclusive fitness theory for humans. For example, (1) there will be a special evolved psychology of kinship involving psychological mechanisms dedicated to solving the differing adaptive problems confronted when dealing with siblings, half siblings, grandparents, grandchildren, aunts, and uncles; (2) sex and generation will be critical categories differentiating kin because these dimensions define important properties on one's fitness vehicles (e.g., male kin have a higher ceiling on reproduction than female kin; younger kin have higher reproductive value than older kin); (3) kin relationships will be arrayed on a dimension from close to distant, the primary predictor of closeness being genetic relatedness; (4) cooperation and kin solidarity will be a function of genetic relatedness among kin; (5) older kin members will encourage younger kin members to be more altruistic toward genetic relatives such as siblings than younger kin members will naturally be inclined to be; (6) one's position within a family will be central to one's identity; and (7) people will exploit kin terms to influence and manipulate others in nonkin contexts (e.g., "Brother, can you spare some cash?").

Empirical studies have confirmed the importance of kinship as a predictor of helping behavior. One study documented that alarm calling among ground squirrels, a potentially costly endeavor to the caller because it draws the attention of predators, occurs when close kin are likely to be nearby. Helping kin first requires the ability to recognize kin. Humans have at least four kin recognition mechanisms: (1) association; (2) odor; (3) kin classification systems based on a "universal grammar" that includes genealogical distance, social rank, and group membership resemblance; and (4) facial resemblance. A study of 300 Los Angeles women found that helping was a function of the genetic relatedness to the individual being helped. Another study showed that in hypothetical life-or-death scenarios, such as risking one's life to pull someone from a burning building, helping was highly predictable from the degree of genetic relatedness between the helper and the person being helped. In studies of inheritance, people tend to leave more to genetic relatives (and to spouses, who will presumably pass on the resources to genetic relatives) than to nonrelatives. Other studies show that the amount of grief and sorrow that individuals experience is directly related to the degree of genetic relatedness (see Segal et al., 1995, for empirical evidence and Archer, 1998, for an extended review of the psychology of grief). All of these empirical studies point to the importance of kinship as a predictor of the allocation of acts of helping.

Concern over close kin also extends to individuals maintaining vigilance over their close kin's romantic relationships, especially over female kin. Absence of close kin, on the other hand, has disadvantages. Growing up without close kin, or in stepfamilies with half siblings, can be stressful, as indicated by the higher cortisol levels of children in these families.

Grandparental investment is a special arena for testing nonintuitive predictions from inclusive fitness theory. In particular, paternity uncertainty comes into play. A paternal grandfather has double the risk of genetic relatedness being severed. First, he might not be the father of his children. Second, his son might not be the father of his own children. Grandmothers, in contrast, are 100 percent certain that they are the genetic relatives of the children of their daughters. On the basis of this logic, we should expect mothers' mothers to show the heaviest grandparental investment, on average, and fathers' fathers to show the least. The other two types of grandparents—fathers' mothers and mothers' fathers—should show investment patterns between these extremes because in each of these cases, there is one opportunity for genetic relatedness to be severed.

Empirical evidence from Germany, the United States, Greece, and France supports these predictions. Grandchildren felt closest to their maternal grandmothers and most distant from their paternal grandfathers. Furthermore, grandchildren reported that they received the most resources from their maternal grandmothers and the least from their paternal grandfathers. Although the two other types of grandparents fell in between these extremes, it is interesting to note that in both cases, the maternal grandfather invested more than the paternal grandmother. This finding rules out the idea that women invest more than men in kin across the board.

A similar logic applies to investment by aunts, uncles, and cousins. The siblings of a sister are sure that their sister is the parent of her child, so these aunts and uncles are sure that they are the genetic relatives of their nieces and nephews. The siblings of a brother, in contrast, are not certain because their brother may have been cuckolded. This leads to the prediction of differential investment by aunts and uncles, depending on whether the children are their sister's or brother's. Maternal aunts, for example, would be expected to invest more than paternal aunts.

In a study of investment by aunts and uncles, two important predictors of investment by aunts and uncles were determined. First, aunts tended to invest more than uncles, regardless of whether their nieces and nephews were the children of a brother or a sister—a sex effect. Second, the maternal aunts and uncles invested more than the paternal aunts and uncles, supporting the key prediction. Similar results were found in studies of helping cousins through maternal versus paternal lines.

The final section of this chapter examined the broader perspective on the evolution of the family. Given the fact that families are exceedingly rare in the animal world—found among roughly 3 percent of all mammals—the very existence of families requires explanation. According to Stephen Emlen, families, consisting of mature offspring continuing to reside at home, occur under two key conditions: (1) when there is a scarcity of reproductive vacancies elsewhere or (2) when there are distinct benefits of staying at home, such as enhancing survival, improving abilities to compete, and giving aid to (and receiving aid from) genetic relatives.

Several predictions follow from this theory. The theory predicts, for example, that family stability will be higher when there is more wealth, and hence greater opportunities to benefit from the family and perhaps inherit familial wealth. It predicts that the sudden death of a reproducer within the family will result in a conflict over who will fill the void (e.g., conflict over access to parental wealth). It predicts that stepfathers and stepmothers will invest less than genetic fathers and mothers and that stepfamilies will be inherently less stable and more conflicted than genetically intact families. Many of these predictions have been tested with nonhuman animals, and some with humans. Emlen's theory has been criticized on several grounds, including (1) that it fails to take into account the fact that postmenopausal women can continue to aid their families and cannot exploit available reproductive vacancies and (2) that people often engage in extensive reciprocal exchange with nonkin. These factors suggest refinements of Emlen's theory that take into account the unique aspects of the human animal.

Although early evolutionary models emphasized harmonious cooperation within members of the family, recent evolutionary models point to three important arenas of conflict: sibling conflict, parent–offspring conflict, and conflict between mother and father. Although inclusive fitness theory predicts that genetic relatedness will be an important predictor of altruism, family members almost never have identical genetic interests. As a consequence, conflict and competition within families are predicted to be pervasive.

# ■ SUGGESTED READINGS

Coall, D. A., & Hertwig, R. (2010). Grandparental investment: Past, present, and future. *Behavioral and Brain Sciences, 33,* 1–59.

Cronk, L., & Gerkey, D. (2007). Kinship and descent. In R.I.M. Dunbar & L. Barrett (Eds.), *Oxford handbook of evolutionary psychology* (pp. 463–478). New York: Oxford University Press.

Daly, M., Salmon, C., & Wilson, M. (1997). Kinship: The conceptual hole in psychological studies of social cognition and close relationships. In J. A. Simpson & D. T. Kenrick (Eds.), *Evolutionary social psychology* (pp. 265–296). Mahwah, NJ: Erlbaum.

Davis, J. N., & Daly, M. (1997). Evolutionary theory and the human family. *Quarterly Review of Biology, 72,* 407–435.

DeKay, W. T., & Shackelford, T. K. (2000). Toward an evolutionary approach to social cognition. *Evolution and Cognition, 6,* 185–195.

Faulkner, J., & Schaller, M. (2007). Nepotistic nosiness: Inclusive fitness and vigilance of kin members' romantic relationships. *Evolution and Human Behavior, 28,* 430–438.

Fawcett, T. W., van den Berg, P., Weissing, F. J., Park, J. H., & Buunk, A. P. (2010). Intergenerational conflict over parental investment. *Behavioral and Brain Sciences, 33,* 23–24.

Hamilton, W. D. (1964). The genetical evolution of social behavior. I and II. *Journal of Theoretical Biology, 7,* 1–52.

Lieberman, D., Tooby, J., & Cosmides, L. (2007). The architecture of human kin detection. *Nature, 445,* 727–731.

Mock, D. W. (2004). *More than kin and less than kind: The evolution of family conflict.* Cambridge, MA: Harvard University Press.

Platek, S. M., & Kemp, S. M. (2009). Is family special in the brain? An event-related fMRI study of familiar, familial, and self-face recognition. *Neuropsychologia, 47,* 849–858.

Pollet, T. V., Nettle, D., & Nelissen, M. (2007). Maternal grandmothers do go the extra mile: Factoring distance and lineage into differential contact with grandchildren. *Evolutionary Psychology, 5,* 832–843.

# PROBLEMS OF GROUP LIVING

Group living is a critical part of human adaptation, and evolutionary psychology suggests that the human mind contains evolved mechanisms dedicated to dealing with the problems of group living. This part contains four chapters, each devoted to a different subset of group living problems.

Chapter 9 focuses on the evolution of cooperative alliances. It introduces the theory of reciprocal altruism, which provides one theoretical solution to the evolution of cooperation. Examples of cooperation in nature, including food sharing in vampire bats and reciprocal alliances among chimpanzees, are offered next. The remainder of Chapter 9 explores research on the evolution of cooperative alliances in humans, the costs and benefits of friendship, and the evolution of cooperative coalitions.

Chapter 10 examines aggression and warfare and comes to the disturbing conclusion that our ancestors have accrued adaptive benefits by inflicting costs on other humans through violence. This chapter introduces the evolutionary logic for why men are more violently aggressive than women in all cultures around the world and provides empirical evidence for particular patterns of aggression, depending on the sex of the perpetrator and the sex of the victim. The end of this chapter explores the evolution of warfare and the controversial question of whether humans have evolved specific adaptations designed to kill other human beings.

Chapter 11 focuses on conflict between men and women. It starts by introducing the logic of strategic interference theory, which provides an overarching framework for understanding conflict between the sexes. The bulk of the chapter summarizes the empirical evidence for particular forms of such conflict, including conflict over sexual access, jealous conflict, conflicts that occur over defections from relationships, and conflict over access to resources.

Chapter 12 deals with a universal feature of human groups: the existence of status or dominance hierarchies. It presents an evolutionary rationale for the emergence of hierarchies and then focuses on more specific aspects of dominance and status in nonhumans and humans. The human evidence includes a discussion of sex differences in status striving and the behavioral manifestations of dominance and ends with a discussion of strategies of submissiveness.

CHAPTER 9

# COOPERATIVE ALLIANCES

*If thou wouldst get a friend, prove him first, and be not hasty to credit him. For some man is a friend for his own occasion, and will not abide in the day of thy trouble. . . . Again, some friend is a companion at the table, and will not continue in the day of affliction. . . . If thou be brought low, he will be against thee, and will hide from thy face. . . . A faithful friend is a strong defense: and he that hath found such a one hath found himself a treasure. Nothing doth countervail a faithful friend.*

—Sirach 6:7–15

𝒜 story is told of two friends, one of whom was accused of a robbery he had not committed. Although he was innocent, he was sentenced to four years in jail. His friend, greatly distressed by the conviction, slept on the floor each night that his friend was in jail. He did not want to enjoy the comfort of a soft bed knowing that his friend was sleeping on a single, musty mattress. Eventually, the imprisoned friend was released, and the two remained friends for life. How can we explain such puzzling behavior? Why do people form friendships and long-term cooperative alliances?

## ■ THE EVOLUTION OF COOPERATION

𝒫ersonal sacrifices made on behalf of others are not rare among friends. Every day, people help their friends in many ways large and small, from giving advice and sacrificing time to rushing to a friend's aid in a time of crisis. Acts of friendship of this sort pose a profound puzzle. Natural selection is competitive. It is selfish because it is a feedback process in which one organism's design features outreproduce those of others in an existing population. Sacrifices are costly to those who make them, yet they benefit the people for whom the sacrifices are made. How could such patterns of friendship and altruism evolve?

### The Problem of Altruism

In Chapter 8, we saw how one form of such altruism can evolve when the recipients of the aid are genetic relatives. This sort of altruism is predicted by inclusive fitness theory.

Your friends, however, are not usually your genetic relatives. So any cost you incur for a friend results in a loss to you and a gain to the friend. The great puzzle is: How could altruism among nonrelatives possibly evolve, given the selfish designs that tend to be produced by natural selection? This is the *problem of altruism.* An "altruistic" design feature aids the reproduction of other individuals, even though it causes the altruist (who has this feature) suffer a fitness cost.

The puzzle is complicated further by the findings that altruism is neither new nor unusual. First, there is evidence that social exchange—a form of cooperation—occurs across human cultures and is found frequently in hunter-gatherer cultures that are presumed to closely resemble the ancestral conditions under which humans evolved (Allen-Arave, Gurven, & Hill, 2008; Cashdan, 1989; Lee & DeVore, 1968; Weissner, 1982). Second, other species that are far removed from humans, such as vampire bats, also engage in forms of social exchange (Wilkinson, 1984). Third, other primates besides humans, such as chimpanzees, baboons, and macaques, also engage in reciprocal helping (de Waal, 1982). Taken together, this evidence suggests a long evolutionary history of altruism, going back millions of years.

## ■ A THEORY OF RECIPROCAL ALTRUISM

*A* solution to the problem of altruism has been developed, in increasingly elaborate and sophisticated ways, by the theory of *reciprocal altruism* (Axelrod, 1984; Axelrod & Hamilton, 1981; Cosmides & Tooby, 1992; Trivers, 1971; Williams, 1966). The theory of reciprocal altruism states that adaptations for providing benefits to nonrelatives can evolve as long as the delivery of such benefits is reciprocated at some point in the future.

The beauty of reciprocal altruism is that both parties benefit. Consider an example: Two hunters are friends. Their success at hunting, however, is erratic. During the course of a week, only one of the hunters will be successful. The following week, however, the other hunter might be successful. If the first hunter shares his meat with his friend, he incurs a cost of lost meat. This cost, however, might be relatively small because he may have more meat than he or his immediate family can consume before it spoils. The gain to his friend, however, might be large if he has nothing else to eat that week. The following week, the situation is reversed. Thus each of the two hunters pays a small cost in lost meat that provides a larger benefit to his friend. Both friends benefit by the reciprocal altruism more than they would if each one selfishly kept all the meat from his kill for himself. Economists call this a "gain in trade"—each party receives more in return than it costs to deliver the benefit.

In evolutionary terms, these gains in trade set the stage for the evolution of reciprocal altruism. Those who engage in reciprocal altruism will tend to outreproduce those who act selfishly, causing psychological mechanisms for reciprocal altruism to spread in succeeding generations. Reciprocal altruism, in sum, can be defined as "cooperation between two or more individuals for mutual benefit" (Cosmides & Tooby, 1992, p. 169). Approximate synonyms for reciprocal altruism include *cooperation, reciprocation,* and *social exchange.*

One of the most important adaptive problems for the reciprocal altruist is ensuring that the benefits it bestows will be returned in the future. Someone could pretend to be a reciprocal altruist, for example, but then take benefits without responding in kind later. This is called the *problem of cheating.* Later in this chapter, we will examine empirical evidence that suggests that humans have evolved specific psychological mechanisms designed to solve the adaptive problem of cheating. First, however, we will examine a fascinating computer simulation that demonstrates that reciprocal altruism can evolve and will look at a few nonhuman species to provide concrete examples of the evolution of cooperation.

## Tit for Tat

The problem of reciprocal altruism is similar to a game known as the "prisoner's dilemma." The prisoner's dilemma is a hypothetical situation in which two people have been thrown in prison for a crime they are accused of committing together and of which they are indeed guilty. The prisoners are held in separate cells so that they can't talk to each other. Police interrogate both of the prisoners, trying to get each to rat on the other. If neither one implicates the other, the police will be forced to set them both free for lack of evidence. This is the cooperative strategy, and from the prisoners' perspective, it is the strategy that would be best for both of them.

In an attempt to get each prisoner to rat on (or defect from) the other, however, the police tell each that if he confesses and implicates his partner, he will be set free and given a small reward. If both prisoners confess, however, they will both be sentenced to jail. If one confesses and the other does not, then the implicated partner will receive a stiffer sentence than he would have received if both confessed. The prisoner's dilemma is illustrated in Figure 9.1.

In this scheme, $R$ is the reward for mutual cooperation, where neither prisoner tells on the other. $P$ is the punishment each prisoner receives if both confess. $T$ is the temptation to defect—the small reward given in exchange for implicating the other. $S$ is the "sucker's payoff," the penalty one incurs if his partner defects and he does not.

|  |  | Player B | |
|---|---|---|---|
|  |  | Cooperation | Defection |
| Player A | Cooperation | $R = 3$ <br> Reward for mutual cooperation | $S = 0$ <br> Sucker's payoff |
|  | Defection | $T = 5$ <br> Temptation to defect | $P = 1$ <br> Punishment for mutual defection |

FIGURE 9.1 **The Game of Prisoner's Dilemma.** This is the payoff matrix used in the tournament run by Robert Axelrod. A game consisted of 200 match-ups between two strategies. The game is defined by $T > R > P > S$ and $R > (S + T)/2$.

*Source:* Axelrod, R., & Hamilton, W. D. (1981). The evolution of cooperation. *Science, 211,* 1390–1396. Copyright © 1981 American Association for the Advancement of Science. Reprinted with permission.

This is called the prisoner's dilemma because the rational course of action for both prisoners is to confess, but that would have a worse outcome for both than if they decided to trust each other (hence the dilemma). Consider the problem of Player A. If his partner does not confess, A will benefit by defecting—he will be set free *and* will receive a small reward for implicating his partner. On the other hand, if his partner defects, Player A would be better off defecting as well; otherwise, he risks receiving the stiffest penalty possible. In sum, the logical course of action, no matter what one's partner does, is to defect, even though cooperation would result in the best outcome for both.

This hypothetical dilemma resembles the problem of reciprocal altruism. Each person can gain from cooperating (*R*), but each is tempted to gain the benefit of a partner's altruism without reciprocating (*T*). The worst scenario for each individual is to cooperate and have a partner who defects (*S*). If the game is played only once, then the only sensible solution is to defect. Robert Axelrod and W. D. Hamilton (1981) showed that the key to cooperation occurs when the game is repeated a number of times but each player does not know when the game will end, as often happens in real life.

The winning strategy in "iterated prisoner's dilemma" games is called *tit for tat*. Axelrod and Hamilton discovered this strategy by conducting a computer tournament. Economists, mathematicians, scientists, and computer wizards from around the world were asked to submit strategies for playing 200 rounds of the prisoner's dilemma. Points were rewarded in accordance with the payoff matrix shown in Figure 9.1. The winner was whoever had the highest number of points. The strategies consisted of decision rules for interacting with other players. Fourteen strategies were submitted and were paired in competition in a round-robin computer tournament. Some strategies were highly complex, involving contingent rules for modeling the other's strategy and suddenly switching strategies midstream. The most complex had seventy-seven lines of statements in the computer language FORTRAN. The winner of the tournament, however, employed the simplest strategy of all, tit for tat, containing a mere four lines of FORTRAN statements. It had two simple rules: (1) Cooperate on the first move and (2) reciprocate on every move thereafter. In other words, start by cooperating, and continue cooperating if the other is also cooperating. If the other defects, however, then defect in kind. Trivers (1985) aptly labeled this "contingent reciprocity."

Axelrod (1984) identified three features of this strategy that represented the keys to its success: (1) *Never be the first to defect*—always start out by cooperating, and continue to cooperate as long as the other player does so; (2) *retaliate only after the other has defected*—defect immediately after the first instance of nonreciprocation; and (3) *be forgiving*—if a previously defecting player starts to cooperate, then reciprocate the cooperation and get on a mutually beneficial cycle. To summarize: "First, do unto others as you wish them to do unto you, but then do unto them as they have just done to you" (Trivers, 1985, p. 392). Strategies for encouraging cooperation that will, in turn, lead to the success of tit for tat are discussed in Box 9.1. The results of this computer tournament suggest that cooperation can evolve fairly easily in nature.

## ■ COOPERATION AMONG NONHUMANS

*E*ach species is unique in many of the adaptive problems it has confronted over the course of its evolution, but different species can arrive at similar solutions to common adaptive problems. It is instructive to examine nonhuman species to see whether they have evolved cooperation. We

BOX *9.1*

## Strategies for Promoting Cooperation

According to Axelrod's (1984) analysis of tit for tat as a key successful strategy, several practical consequences follow for the promotion of cooperation. First, *enlarge the shadow of the future.* If the other individual thinks that you will interact frequently in the extended future, he or she has a greater incentive to cooperate. If people know when the "last move" will occur and that the relationship will end soon, there is a greater incentive to defect and not cooperate. Enlarging the shadow of the future can be accomplished by making interactions more frequent and by making a commitment to the relationship, which occurs, for example, with wedding vows. Perhaps one reason that divorces are so often ugly, marred by unkind acts of mutual defection, is that both parties perceive the "last move" and a sharply truncated shadow of the future.

A second strategy that Axelrod recommends is to *teach reciprocity.* Promoting reciprocity not only helps oneself by making others more cooperative, it also makes it more difficult for exploitative strategies to thrive. The larger the number of those who follow a tit-for-tat strategy, the less successful one will be in attempting to exploit others by defecting. Essentially, the cooperators will thrive through their interactions with each other and the exploiters will suffer because of a vanishing population of those on whom to prey.

A third strategy for the promotion of cooperation is to *insist on no more than equity.* Greed is the downfall of many, perhaps best exemplified by the myth of King Midas, whose lust for gold backfired when everything he touched, even the food he wanted to eat, turned to gold. The beauty of tit for tat as a strategy is that it does not insist on getting more than it gives. By promoting equity, tit for tat elicits cooperation from others.

A fourth strategy to promote cooperation is to *respond quickly to provocation.* If your partner defects on you, a good strategy is to retaliate immediately. This sends a strong signal that you will not tolerate being exploited, which might prompt future cooperation.

A final strategy for promoting cooperation is to *cultivate a personal reputation as a reciprocator.* We live in a social world in which the beliefs others have about us—our reputations—determine whether they will befriend or avoid us. Reputations are established through one's actions, and word about one's actions spreads. Cultivating a reputation as a reciprocator will make others seek one out for mutual gain. A reputation as an exploiter will lead to social shunning. The combined effect of these strategies will create a runaway pattern of cooperation, in which those who were formerly exploiters are forced to rehabilitate their bad reputations by becoming cooperators themselves. In this way, cooperation will be promoted throughout the group.

will start with the fascinating case of vampire bats and then look at chimps, who are phylogenetically closer to humans.

## Food Sharing in Vampire Bats

Vampire bats got their name because their survival depends on the blood of other animals. They live in groups of up to a dozen adult females and associated offspring. The males leave the colony when they are capable of independence. Vampire bats hide during the day, but at night, they emerge to suck the blood of cattle and horses. Their victims, of course, are not willing donors. Indeed, the horses and cattle often flick away the bats to prevent them from feeding. The bats' ability to feed successfully increases with age and experience. One study found that 33 percent of the younger bats (under two years old) failed to get blood on any particular evening, whereas only 7 percent of the bats older than two years failed to feed (Wilkinson, 1984).

How do the bats survive failed attempts to find food? Failure at feeding, in fact, can quickly lead to death. Bats can go without blood for only three days. As shown by the statistics above, however, failure is common; all bats fail at one point or another, so the risk of death due to starvation is a constant threat. Wilkinson (1984) discovered that the bats regularly regurgitate a portion of the blood they have sucked and give it to others in the bat colony, but not randomly. Instead, they give regurgitated blood to their friends, those from whom they have received blood in the past. Wilkinson showed that the closer the association between the bats—the more often they were sighted together—the more likely they were to give blood to each other. Only bats that were sighted in close proximity at least 60 percent of the time received blood from that compatriot. Not a single bat gave blood to another bat with whom he associated for a lesser period of time.

In another part of the study, Wilkinson (1984) used a captive colony of vampire bats to explore additional aspects of reciprocal altruism. He experimentally deprived individual bats of food, and varied the length of time of the deprivation. Wilkinson discovered that the "friends" tended to regurgitate blood more often when their friends were in dire need and close to starvation (e.g., thirteen hours from death) than when they were in mild need (e.g., two days from death). He also found that the starved bats who received help from their friends were more likely to give blood to those who had helped them in their time of need. In sum, vampire bats show all the signs of having evolved reciprocal altruistic adaptations.

## Chimpanzee Politics

Among the chimpanzees at a large zoo colony in Arnhem, the Netherlands, a chimp named Yeroen reigned as the dominant adult male (de Waal, 1982). He walked in an exaggeratedly heavy manner and looked larger than he really was. Only occasionally did he need to demonstrate his dominance, raising the hair covering his body on end and running full speed at the other apes, who scattered in all directions in response to his charge. Yeroen's dominance extended to sexual activity. Although there were four adult males in the troop, Yeroen was responsible for nearly 75 percent of the matings when the females came into estrus.

As Yeroen grew older, however, things began to change. A younger male, Luit, experienced a sudden growth spurt and challenged Yeroen's status. Luit gradually stopped displaying the submissive greeting to Yeroen, brazenly showing his fearlessness. Once, Luit approached Yeroen and smacked him hard. Another time, Luit used his potentially lethal canines to draw blood. Most of the time, however, the battles were more symbolic, with threats and bluffs in the place of bloodshed. Initially, all the females sided with Yeroen, allowing him to maintain his status. Indeed, reciprocal alliances with females are essential to the maintenance of status—males defend the females against attack from other males and act as "peacemakers" in disputes; in return, the females support the males, aiding in the maintenance of their status.

One by one, however, the females gradually began to defect and sided with Luit as Luit's increasing dominance became apparent. After two months, the transition was complete. Yeroen had been dethroned and started to display the submissive greeting to Luit. The mating behavior followed suit. Whereas Luit achieved only 25 percent of the matings during Yeroen's reign of power, his copulations jumped to more than 50 percent when he took over. Yeroen's sexual access dropped to zero.

Although ousted from power and lacking sexual access, Yeroen was not ready to retire. Gradually, he formed a close alliance with an upcoming male named Nikkie. Neither Yeroen nor Nikkie dared to challenge Luit alone, but together they made a formidable alliance. Over several weeks, the alliance grew bolder in challenging Luit. Eventually, a physical fight erupted. Although all the chimpanzees involved sustained injuries, the alliance between Nikkie and Yeroen triumphed. After this victory, Nikkie secured 50 percent of the matings. And because of his alliance with Nikkie, Yeroen now secured 25 percent of the matings, up from his previous dethronement level of zero. Although Yeroen never again attained dominant status, his alliance with Nikkie was critical in avoiding total banishment from mating. Reciprocally, Nikkie's alliance with Yeroen was critical in attaining dominance over Luit.

Alliances are central features in the social lives of chimpanzees. Males regularly solicit alliances with females, grooming them and playing with their infants. Without alliances with the females, males could never attain a position of dominance in the troop. As part of the bid for alpha status, a male will bite or chase a female if she is found associating with an opponent. When she is no longer associating with the opponent, the male will be extremely friendly toward her and her infants. This is a key strategy in the formation of chimpanzee alliances: Try to sever the alliances of one's opponents and enlist the former allies. Through de Waal's fascinating study of chimpanzee politics, we catch a glimpse of the complexities of the evolution of reciprocal altruism—alliances that form not just between males, but also between the sexes.

## ■ COOPERATION AND ALTRUISM AMONG HUMANS

### Social Contract Theory

The theory of reciprocal altruism predicts that organisms can benefit by engaging in cooperative exchange. There is one problem, however: Many potential exchanges do not occur simultaneously. "If I give you a benefit now, I must trust that you will reciprocate and give me a benefit at some later time. If you fail to reciprocate, then I have incurred a net cost." In short, relationships involving reciprocal exchange are vulnerable to cheating—when people take a benefit without paying the cost of reciprocation (Cosmides & Tooby, 1992; 2005).

In nature, opportunities for simultaneous exchange sometimes occur. "I can give you a piece of fruit that I gathered in exchange for a piece of meat that you hunted." But in many contexts, there are opportunities for cooperation in which simultaneous exchange is simply not possible. "If you are being attacked by a wolf, for example, and I rush to your aid, you cannot at the same time repay me for the cost that I incurred."

Another reason that simultaneous exchange is sometimes not possible is that the needs and abilities of the interactants are rarely perfectly matched. "If I am hungry and you are the only one with an ample food supply, I cannot immediately repay you for preventing me from starving. You must trust that when you are in great need, I will rush to your side to help you." Whenever exchanges are nonsimultaneous, the window is open for defection—taking the benefit and later cheating by failing to return the favor.

Evolutionary psychologists Leda Cosmides and John Tooby have developed social contract theory to explain the evolution of cooperative exchange in humans, with special attention to how humans have solved the problem of cheating. The possibility of cheating poses an ever-present threat to the evolution of cooperation. The reason is that cheaters have an evolutionary advantage over cooperators, at least under certain conditions. "If I take the benefits that you offer but then fail to return the favor at a later time, I benefit twofold: I have gained benefits and avoided incurring the reciprocal costs." For this reason, over evolutionary time, cheaters will thrive more than cooperators until the entire population consists of noncooperators.

Reciprocal altruism can only evolve if organisms have a mechanism for detecting and avoiding cheaters. If cooperators can detect cheaters and interact only with like-minded cooperators, reciprocal altruism can gain a toehold and evolve over time. The cheaters will be at a disadvantage because they fail to benefit by entering into cooperative exchanges. What specific problems do people have to solve to evolve mechanisms that motivate forming social contracts and avoiding the ever-present threat of cheaters? Cosmides and Tooby (1992) outlined five cognitive capacities:

*Capacity 1: The ability to recognize many different individual humans.* "If you give me a benefit and I get lost in a 'sea of anonymous others' (Axelrod & Hamilton, 1981), you will be vulnerable to being cheated. You must be able to identify me and remember me as distinct from all other people." The ability to recognize many individuals might seem obvious, but this is only because humans are so good at it. One study showed that people can identify others whom they have not seen for up to thirty-four years, with a recognition rate of over 90 percent (Bahrick, Bahrick, & Wittlinger, 1975). Indeed, there is neurological evidence that this ability is located in a specific area of the brain. People with a lesion in a specific place in the right hemisphere develop a highly specific deficit: an inability to recognize faces called "prosopagnosia" (Gardner, 1974). Humans are also especially good at recognizing other individuals solely by the way they walk (Cutting, Profitt, & Kozlowski, 1978). In sum, there is good scientific evidence that humans have evolved a proficient ability to recognize many different individuals.

*Capacity 2: The ability to remember the histories of interactions with different individuals.* This capacity breaks down into several different abilities. First, one must be able to remember whether the person with whom one has interacted was previously a cooperator or a cheater. Second, one must be able to keep track of who owes what to whom. This requires some sort of "accounting system" for keeping track of the costs you have incurred and the benefits you have received from a specific individual. Failure to keep track of these histories of interaction will make a person vulnerable to being cheated. If you fail to keep track of how much you have given the other person in the past, then you have no way of knowing whether the benefit he or she returns later compensates adequately for the cost you have incurred.

*Capacity 3: The ability to communicate one's values to others.* If your friend fails to understand what you want, how can he or she provide the benefits you need? If you fail to communicate your distress to a defector, you might be vulnerable to future defections. Consider an example from de Waal's (1982) study of chimpanzees. The study concerned Puist and Luit, who had a longstanding relationship of mutual helping when one was under attack.

> This happened once after Puist had supported Luit in chasing Nikkie. When Nikkie later displayed [aggressively] at Puist she turned to Luit and held out her hand to him in search of support. Luit, however, did nothing to protect her against Nikkie's attack. Immediately Puist turned on Luit, barking furiously, chasing him across the enclosure and even hit him. (de Waal, 1982, p. 207)

Puist appears to be communicating to Luit her dissatisfaction with Luit's failure to help in a time of need. Although such chimp communications are nonverbal, among humans, language can be used to supplement emotional expressions and other nonverbal behavior as the medium of communication of desires, entitlements, and distress about an unfulfilled obligation. The phrases "you owe me," "I need this," "I am entitled to this," and "I want this" represent ways in which humans communicate their values to others.

*Capacity 4: The ability to model the values of others.* The flip side of the coin to communicating your values is the ability to understand the values of others. If you can detect *when* a person is needy and *how* he or she is needy, the benefit you provide can be tailored to that need. If I provide you with a piece of meat, failing to recognize that you are not hungry and have an ample supply of food, then the benefit I provide will not be worth much to you. By understanding the desires and needs of others, you can tailor your exchanges to maximize the benefit you provide, making the other person more indebted to you than if you had failed to model his or her values.

*Capacity 5: The ability to represent costs and benefits, independent of the particular items exchanged.* Cosmides and Tooby (1989) argue that many animals exchange a delimited set of items, such as food and sex. Humans, however, can and do exchange an astonishing array of items—knives and other tools, meat, berries, nuts, fish, shelters, protection, status, access to friends, assistance in fights, sexual access, money, blow guns, information about enemies, help on term papers, and computer programs, to name but a few. For this reason, evolved mechanisms of social exchange cannot be prewired to represent (conceptualize) and negotiate for specific items. We must be able to understand and cognitively represent the costs and benefits of a wide range of items. It is our general ability to represent costs and benefits of exchanges, not a specific ability tied to particular items, that has evolved in humans.

In sum, social contract theory proposes the evolution in humans of five cognitive capacities to solve the problem of cheaters and engage in successful social exchange. Humans must be able to recognize other individuals; remember the history of interactions with them; communicate values, desires, and needs to others; recognize them in others; and represent the costs and benefits of a variety of items of exchange.

## Evidence for Cheater-Detection Adaptations

To test social contract theory, Cosmides and Tooby conducted more than a dozen empirical studies on people's responses to logical problems. Logic refers to the inferences one can make about the truth of one statement from the truth of other statements, independent of their form. If I assert "if P, then Q," then once you find out that P is true, you logically infer that Q must also be true. This applies to all statements, such as "if I go to the grocery store, it means that I am hungry" or "if you are sexually unfaithful to me, then I will leave you."

Unfortunately, humans do not seem to be very good at solving logical problems. Imagine that in one room are a few archeologists, biologists, and chess players (Pinker, 1997, p. 334). None of the archeologists are biologists, but all of the biologists are chess players. What follows from this knowledge? More than 50 percent of college students surveyed conclude from this that none of the archeologists are chess players—clearly an invalid inference because the statement "all biologists are chess players" does not imply that no archeologists play chess. No participants in this study concluded that some chess players in the room are nonarcheologists, which is logically derivable from the premises. And roughly 20 percent claimed that no valid inferences can be drawn at all from the above premises, which is clearly wrong.

Consider one type of logic problem (Wason, 1966). Imagine that four cards are lying on a table. Each card has a letter on one side and a number on the other, but you can see only one side. Now consider this: Which cards would you need to turn over to test the following rule: "If a card has a vowel on one side, then it has an even number on the other side." Turn over only those cards you would need to turn over to test the truth value of this rule:

If you are like the majority of people in most studies, you would turn over the card with the "a," or the "a" and the "2." The "a" card is certainly correct. Because it is a vowel, if it had an odd number on the back it would mean the rule is false. The "2" card, however, yields no information relevant to testing the rule. Because the rule does *not* state that all cards with an even number on one side must have a vowel on the other, it doesn't matter whether a vowel or a consonant is on the back of the "2." In contrast, turning over the "3" card would yield a powerful test of the rule. If the back side of the "3" is a vowel, then the rule is definitively falsified. So the logically correct answer is to turn over cards "a" and "3" (the "b" card also provides no information relevant to the hypothesis, since the rule does not make any statements about what the back side of a consonant card must contain). Why are people so bad at solving problems of this sort?

According to Cosmides and Tooby (1992; 2005), the answer is that humans have not evolved to respond to abstract logical problems; they have, however, evolved to respond to problems structured as social exchanges when they are presented in terms of costs and benefits. Consider this problem: You are a bouncer at a local bar, and your job is to make sure that no one who is underage drinks alcohol. You have to test this rule: "If a person is drinking alcohol, then he or she must be twenty-one years old or older." Which of the following four people do you have to check out to do your job: someone drinking beer, someone drinking soda, a twenty-five-year-old, or a sixteen-year-old? In contrast to the abstract logic problem above, the vast majority of people correctly select the beer drinker and the sixteen-year-old. The logic of the problem is identical to the above abstract problem involving vowels and even numbers. So why are people good at solving this problem but not the abstract problem?

People reason correctly when the problem is structured as a social contract. If you drink beer but are not over twenty-one years old, then you have taken a benefit without meeting the requirement (cost) of being of age. People do well when they are "looking for cheaters," those who have taken a benefit without paying the cost.

For people to succeed at this task, it need only be structured such that they will construe the problem in terms of taking benefits and paying costs. Cosmides and Tooby were able to rule out a number of alternative hypotheses. The effect does not depend on being familiar with the content of the problem, for example. When strange and unfamiliar rules were used, such as "if you get married, you must have a tattoo on your forehead" or "if you eat mongongo nuts, you must be over six feet tall," roughly 75 percent of the subjects still answered correctly (in contrast to the fewer than 10 percent who got it right in the abstract version). According to these studies, the human mind has an evolved psychological mechanism specifically designed to detect cheaters. These findings have been replicated in other cultures, such as the Shiwiar, a foraging tribe in Ecuador (Sugiyama, Tooby, & Cosmides, 2002). Indeed, the percentage of correct answers by the Shiwiar in one condition was 86 percent, which is nearly identical to the

*If your job were to ID people to test the rule "If a person is drinking alcohol, then he or she must be at least twenty-one years old," which people would you ask for proof of age?*

performance of Harvard undergraduates, who typically get 75 to 92 percent correct. This cross-cultural evidence points to the possible universality of a cheater-detection adaptation in social exchange.

Additional evidence for a specific cheater-detection adaptation comes from work conducted with brain-damaged patients by evolutionary psychologist Valerie Stone and her colleagues (Stone et al., 2002). One patient, R. M., had sustained damage to his orbitofrontal cortex and amygdala, two regions of the brain. R. M. was able to reason correctly on some problems. For example, on problems that were structured as "precaution rules," of the form "If you engage in a hazardous activity such as X, you must take proper precautions such as Y," R. M. performed just as well as people with no brain damage. In contrast, he performed extremely poorly on social contract problems of the sort "If you take a benefit X, you must pay the cost Y." This dissociation between R. M.'s performance on the two types of reasoning tasks suggests that social-exchange reasoning might be a separate and specialized component of the human cognitive machinery. Interestingly, people with R. M.'s pattern of brain damage are susceptible to scams, exploitative relationships, and unfavorable business deals (Stone et al., 2002).

The cheater-detection mechanism appears to be highly sensitive to the perspective one adopts (Gigerenzer & Hug, 1992). Consider the following rule: "If an employee gets a pension, he has worked for ten years." What would constitute a violation of the social contract? It depends on whom you ask. When participants are instructed to take the employee's point of view, they seek out workers who have put in more than ten years but have not received a pension. This would constitute a violation of the social contract by the employer, who failed to grant the pension when it was deserved. On the other hand, when participants are instructed to take the perspective of the employer, they seek out workers who have worked for fewer than ten years but who nonetheless have taken a pension. This would constitute a violation of the social contract by the employee, who would be taking a pension without having put in the full ten years of service. Perspective, in short, appears to govern the sorts of cheaters one looks for.

## Do People Remember Cheaters?

Memory may play a special role in cheater detection. One study found that people remember the faces of known cheaters, especially low-status cheaters, better than they remember the faces of known cooperators (Mealey, Daood, & Krage, 1996). This original finding, however, has not always been replicated (Mehl & Buchner, 2008). Memory for cheaters may partly depend on their rarity in the population. One study found that cheaters were remembered best when they were rare, but worse when they were quite common (Barclay, 2008). Other studies show that people have better "source memory" for the faces of cheaters—that is, good memory for the specific cheating context in which the face was encountered (Bell & Buchner, 2009; Buchner et al., 2009). Another study found that people remember the faces of real cheaters better than those of real cooperators, even when they have no knowledge that these individuals have actually cheated or cooperated (Yamagishi et al., 2003). Oda and Nakajima (2010) discovered that people show excellent face recognition for nonaltruists in one experimental game, and behaviorally avoid interacting with them in subsequent experimental games.

Yet another study found that people show an automatic attentional bias toward the faces of people who had previously not cooperated during a prisoner's dilemma game (Vanneste et al., 2007). Perhaps those who pursue a cheating strategy might give off subtle visual cues or somehow look different from those who tend to pursue a cooperative strategy. Priming people by asking them to remember an event in their lives in which they had been cheated causes markedly better performance on the cheater-detection problem (Chang & Wilson, 2004). All these results support hypothesized cognitive capacities, both in attention and memory, in cheater detection.

Further research is clearly needed to explore social contract theory generally, and the cheater-detection mechanism in particular. Recall the basic definition of psychological mechanisms as involving "input, decision rules, and output." We know little about whether people are sensitive to certain items of input: Do men and women have special sensitivities to certain types of cheating, such as to sexual infidelity in the context of a marriage social contract or to provide physical protection in the case of friendship (Shackelford & Buss, 1996)? It seems intuitively obvious that people get mad, tell others the person has cheated, and avoid contact in the future, but we formally know little about the "output" side: What specific actions do people take when they detect a cheater and how do those actions differ depending on contexts such as status discrepancies and genetic relatedness? Nonetheless, this research is groundbreaking in showing that people do appear to have evolved psychological mechanisms designed to attend to, remember, and detect cheaters—mechanisms that are activated whenever exchanges are structured in terms of costs and benefits.

## The Detection of Prospective Altruists

Once a cheater-detection adaptation has evolved in humans, selection will favor coevolved adaptations to avoid being detected as cheaters. Cheater-detection adaptations, in turn, lead to increasingly subtle forms of cheating. These forms of cheating pose serious problems for people who seek to enter cooperative alliances. According to evolutionary psychologist William Michael Brown, humans have evolved another adaptation to solve this problem: the ability to detect the *genuineness* of altruistic acts (Brown & Moore, 2000). Consider two men giving a dollar to a homeless person. In one case, you detect that the man has genuine sympathy for the plight of the homeless person and that this sympathy motivates his desire to help. In the other case, you find out that the man doesn't care at all about the homeless person but is merely giving the person a dollar to impress his date. Which of these two men would you be more likely to seek for a cooperative venture?

Brown and Moore (2000) created a version of the Wason selection task to test whether people look for the existence of genuine emotions that might lie behind an act of altruism. The altruist-detection task had the following rule: "If X helps, then X seeks credit." Participants in the study then indicated which cards they would turn over:

| (1)<br>X helps | (2)<br>X does<br>not help | (3)<br>X does not<br>seek credit | (4)<br>X seeks<br>credit |
| --- | --- | --- | --- |

The logic behind this task is that people who help others only to receive some form of external credit for doing so are not good candidates for helping in the future and so make poor cooperative allies. Those who help others without seeking external credit, on the other hand, display genuine altruistic tendencies and so would make excellent allies. Thus the correct answer, from the perspective of altruist detection, would be to select the cards "X helps" and "X does not seek credit."

Brown and Moore (2000) found through two different experiments that the majority of people choose the pattern of cards that allowed them to detect altruists. Indeed, performance on the altruist-detection tasks was nearly as good as performance on the cheater-detection tasks, and both were far better than performance on the abstract problems. Clearly, the ability to detect genuine altruists would greatly favor the evolution of cooperation, on the assumption that the genuineness of an altruistic act is a good predictor of future acts of altruism. Research found that success of performance on the altruist-detection task was not linked with success of performance on the cheater-detection task, indicating that the two abilities are distinct (Oda, Hiraishi, & Matsumoto-Oda, 2006). Several studies reveal that altruistic dispositions in other people can be detected even from witnessing very brief video clips. In one study, judges watched 20-second silent video clips of strangers and then asked to estimate the person's generosity on a money-sharing task (Fetchenhauer, Groothuis, & Pradel, 2010). People's estimates were significantly more accurate than chance, even though the video clips were taken in a setting entirely unrelated to altruistic behavior. Another study has people complete a self-report questionnaire of their performance of altruistic acts, such as "I have donated goods or clothes to charity" and "I have 'picked up the slack' for another worker when he or she couldn't keep up the pace" (Oda et al., 2009). Those who scored either very high or very low on altruism were then videotaped in while being asked to describe their likes and dislikes. The tapes, with sound removed, were then shown to other people who did not know them. Viewers of the videotapes were able to correctly estimate the targets level of altruism. Coding of the nonverbal behavior reveals that altruists tended to display more "genuine smiles" than nonaltruists. The facial cue of genuine (spontaneous) smiles is a valid cue to altruistic and cooperative dispositions (Mehu, Grammer, & Dunbar, 2007). Although more research must be conducted to identify specific design features, current evidence points to the existence of two distinct adaptations that facilitate the evolution of cooperation: (1) *the detection of cheaters* (those who take benefits without paying costs) and (2) *the detection of altruists* (those whose motivation is genuine).

## Indirect Reciprocity Theory

Another path through which altruism can evolve is called *indirect reciprocity* (Alexander, 1987; Nowak, 2006; Nowak & Sigmund, 2005; Roberts, 2008). People who perform altruistic acts essentially advertise to others that they have a propensity for generosity and cooperation. Others in the group may glean this information either through direct observation of the altruistic actions or through word of mouth (gossip, reputation). Consequently, they become attractive to third parties as excellent cooperation partners. So the benefit to the altruist does not come directly from the person who receives the initial altruistic act, as occurs with reciprocal altruism, but rather from other people who either witnessed or heard about the person behaving generously. Indirect reciprocity may help to explain why we help strangers who are in need without expecting anything in return, and why we are especially generous when others are watching. It can also explain why people who are themselves helpful are most likely to receive help from others in the group when they are in need (Nowak, 2006).

## Costly Signaling Theory

Another path through which altruism can evolve involves *costly signaling* (Gintis, Smith, & Bowles, 2001; Grafen, 1990; McAndrew, 2002; Miller, 2007; Zahavi, 1977). The logic behind costly signaling is that individuals display acts of altruism—giving substantial gifts, donating to charity, throwing lavish dinners—to signal that they are excellent candidates for making good allies. Only those in excellent condition can afford to display these acts of altruism; those in poor condition or those who lack an abundance of resources cannot afford to display these costly signals. The lavish feasts and parties thrown by some individuals, replete with a sumptuous abundance of food and drink, might be manifestations of costly signaling. Altruistic acts that are costly to the provider yield an honest signal to others about one's quality as a coalitional ally. The key to costly signaling is that its cost ensures that it is an honest signal. Only those in excellent condition or with ample resources can afford to display the costly signal of altruistic action. Costly altruism becomes an honest cue that others then use to gauge a person's resource-holding potential, wealth, intelligence, or fitness (Miller, 2000; Millet & Dewitte, 2007).

The fitness benefits from costly signaling could come in several forms: (1) being preferentially chosen by others for cooperative relationships, (2) increased levels of cooperation within those relationships, and (3) higher status and reputation within the group, which could lead to a host of benefits, including higher quality mating opportunities (Barclay & Willer, 2007; Miller,

2000; Van Vugt & Hardy, 2009; Zahavi, 1995). One empirical test of costly signaling theory requested participants to volunteer to give assistance to one of seven different charities (Bereczkei, Birkas, & Kerekes, 2010). In one condition, participants indicated their willingness anonymously. In the other, they declared their willingness in front of a group of others. Although the volunteer time for the charities was identical (roughly four hours), the nature of the work varied in perceived costliness—from taking blood pressure (least costly) to providing assistance to mentally handicapped children (most costly). When volunteering anonymously, most chose the least taxing charity work; when volunteering publically, many more chose the costly charity work (see Figure 9.2). Those who chose the most costly altruistic investment in the public condition experienced a boost in their social reputation and popularity, as perceived by others in their group subsequently. In short, altruism through costly signaling appears to enhance a person's status and reputation, providing a plausible means by which this form of altruism can evolve.

Furthermore, altruists seem to be good at spotting each other and preferentially hanging out with each other (Fletcher & Doebeli, 2009; Pradel, Euler, & Fetchenhauer, 2009). So not only do altruists benefit by being sought after by others in general as social partners, they also benefit even more by attracting others with a high disposition toward altruism. Just as people similar in mate value tend to pair up, those who are similar in "altruist value" tend to pair up.

In sum, four powerful theories have been developed to explain the evolutionary puzzle of altruism: (1) inclusive fitness (discussed in Chapter 8), (2) reciprocal altruism, (3) indirect reciprocity, and (4) costly signaling (Johnson, Price, & Takezawa, 2008).

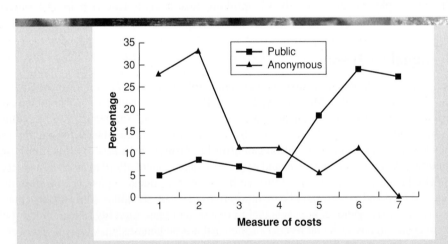

FIGURE 9.2 **Distribution of Charity Offers in Public and Anonymous Groups as a Function of the Perceived Cost of the Altruistic Action.** Costs were measured on a 7-point scale by independent raters.

*Source:* Berczkei, T., Birkas, B., & Kerekes, Z. (2010). Altruism toward strangers in need: Costly signaling in an industrial society. *Evolution and Human Behaviour, 31,* 95–103. Reprinted with permission from Elsevier.

## The Psychology of Friendship

Do these four routes to cooperation exhaust the theoretical possibilities? Tooby and Cosmides (1996) suggest another potential avenue for the evolution of cooperation and altruism in the context of friendship. They ask us to consider human intuitions—many people become angry when they hear the evolutionary explanation that their friendships are based solely on explicit reciprocity. People report feeling pleasure when they help others in need without insisting on, or expecting, any future reward. In fact, when a person insists on immediately repaying us for a favor we have performed, we interpret this as a sign of a *lack* of friendship (Shackelford & Buss, 1996). We want to help out our friends just because they are our friends and not because we will reap some later reward. Furthermore, in a marriage, which can be considered another type of cooperative relationship, an immediate reciprocal exchange orientation is typically linked with marital dissatisfaction and the expectation that the marriage might dissolve (Hatfield & Rapson, 1993; Shackelford & Buss, 1996). Are people deceiving themselves? Do we really want reciprocal rewards but fool ourselves into believing that we help our friends out of the goodness of our hearts? Tooby and Cosmides (1996) argue that we should attend to people's intuitions in these matters, for they provide a signal that friendships might in fact not be based solely on reciprocal exchange.

***Should Altruism Be Defined According to the Cost Incurred?*** According to existing evolutionary theories about the evolution of altruism, altruism is not considered to have occurred unless the individual who is the altruist incurs a cost. In kin selection, the person incurs a cost to the self that is offset by the benefit gained by a genetic relative. In reciprocal altruism, the person incurs a cost to the self that is later offset by a benefit gained when the friend returns the favor. In short, altruism has been defined by the costs the altruist incurs.

What happens when we reframe the definition? Rather than focusing on whether a person incurs costs, why not focus on the evolution of adaptations designed to deliver benefits to others? In fact, it is the existence of mechanisms designed to deliver benefits to others that we are trying to explain to begin with, regardless of whether they turn out to be costly to the altruist. Let's consider a simple example. Imagine that you are about to drive to your favorite grocery store to stock up on food for the week and a friend asks whether she can come along to pick up a few items. By letting your friend come along in your car, you incur no additional cost—you were going to the store regardless. So according to the classical theories of the evolution of altruism, this act would *not* be defined as altruism because you are not incurring a cost. Common sense, of course, tells us that you are certainly delivering a benefit to your friend, and this is true whether the act of helping your friend is beneficial to you, doesn't have any effect, or is costly.

From an evolutionary perspective, in fact, the greater the cost to a person of delivering benefits to others, the less widespread delivering such benefits will be. The less costly it is to deliver benefits to others, the more widespread they will be. Once adaptations for delivering benefits to others have evolved, further evolution will act to minimize their costs or even make it beneficial to the actor to deliver such benefits. This reasoning suggests that there is a large class of altruistic mechanisms that have gone unexplored—mechanisms that are designed to deliver benefits to others when actions stemming from them are least costly and most beneficial to the actor.

***The Banker's Paradox.*** Bankers who loan money face a dilemma: A larger number of people seek loans than any bank has money to lend. Bankers must make hard decisions about to whom they should loan money. Some people are good credit risks and demonstrate a high likelihood of paying back the money. Others are poor credit risks and might not be able to pay the money back. The "banker's paradox" (Tooby & Cosmides, 1996) is this: Those who need money most desperately are precisely the same people who are the poorest credit risks; those who need money less are far better credit risks, so the bank ends up loaning money to those who need it least while refusing to loan money to those who need it most.

This dilemma is similar to a profound adaptive problem faced by our ancestors. Each person has a limited amount of help to dispense to others. When someone most urgently needs help, however, is precisely the time when they are the worst "credit risk" and are least likely to be able to reciprocate. If one of our ancestors became injured or diseased, for example, that is precisely the time when he or she most needed help but was least likely to be a good person on whom to spend one's limited time helping. Our ancestors thus faced a dilemma similar to that of bankers: They had to make critical decisions about *to whom* to extend credit and *when* to extend credit to other individuals. Just as some people are better credit risks for banks, some people are more attractive as objects of our limited ability to assist.

What sorts of adaptations might regulate these crucial decisions? First, people should be able to evaluate whether a person to whom they extend credit will be *willing* to repay in the future. Is this person someone who commonly exploits others for their resources or someone who appreciates the help received and tries to bestow benefits on others? Second, people should be able to evaluate whether the person will be in a position to repay in the future. Is this person's fortune likely to change for the better in the future, or will the dire current circumstances continue? Third, is helping this particular person the best use of one's limited capacity to help, relative to other people who might be more attractive objects of investment?

If the recipient of the help dies, suffers a permanent loss of status within the group, or becomes severely impaired, then one's investment might be lost. If a person is in dire straits, then he or she becomes less desirable as an investment relative to individuals whose circumstances are more favorable. This might lead to adaptations that cause a person to callously abandon a friend precisely when he or she most needs help. On the other hand, if the person's trouble is temporary, such as an unusual failure at hunting, then the person might be an especially attractive object for help. Indeed, helping someone whose need is temporary might be promising because the help would be greatly appreciated by the person in need. In sum, selection should favor adaptations that motivate good decisions about when and to whom to extend one's help. Yet the problem remains: Evolution should favor psychological mechanisms that cause people to desert you precisely when you most need help. How can selection get us out of this predicament? How might we evolve to induce others to help us when we need it most?

***Becoming Irreplaceable.*** Tooby and Cosmides (1996) propose one solution to this adaptive problem: becoming irreplaceable or indispensable to others. Consider a hypothetical example. Suppose two people are in need of your assistance but you can help only one of them. Both are your friends, and both provide you with benefits that are roughly equal in value to you (e.g., one helps you with your math homework, the other helps you by providing notes from classes you miss). Both fall ill at the same time, but you can nurse only one of them back to health. Which one do you help? One factor that might influence this decision is which friend is more irreplaceable. If you know several other people who might provide you with notes from classes that you miss, for example, but you don't know anyone who is willing or able to help you with your math homework, then your math friend is more difficult to replace. A replaceable person—someone who provides benefits that are readily available from others—in short, is more vulnerable to desertion than someone who is irreplaceable, even if these two friends provide benefits to you that are equal in value. The loyalty of your friendship, according to this reasoning, should be based in part on how irreplaceable each friend has become.

How might a person act to increase the odds that he or she becomes irreplaceable and thus is an attractive object of investment for other people? Tooby and Cosmides (1996) outline several strategies. One can:

1. promote a reputation that highlights one's unique or exceptional attributes;
2. be motivated to recognize personal attributes that others value but that they have difficulty getting from other people;
3. cultivate specialized skills that increase irreplaceability;
4. preferentially seek out people or groups that value what you have to offer and what others in the group tend to lack—groups in which one's assets will be most appreciated;
5. avoid social groups in which one's unique attributes are not valued or in which one's unique attributes are easily provided by others; or
6. drive off rivals who offer benefits that you alone formerly provided.

No empirical studies have been conducted thus far to test the effectiveness of these strategies for becoming irreplaceable. However, these strategies appear to capture many aspects of what people actually do. People preferentially choose professions that make use of their unique talents, whether in the form of athletic ability, manual dexterity, spatial ability, facility with languages, or musical talent, for example. We continually split into smaller local groups—churches splinter off into denominations and sects; psychologists splinter off into different schools of thought. We do feel threatened when the "new kid in town" has talents that are similar to, or exceed, the talents that formerly we alone offered. In sum, people appear to act in many ways to cultivate a sense of individuality and uniqueness that would facilitate becoming irreplaceable—methods that encourage others to deliver benefits through thick and thin.

***Fair-Weather Friends, Deep Engagement, and the Dilemmas of Modern Living.*** It's easy to be someone's friend when times are good. It's when you are really in trouble that you find out who your true friends are. Everyone has experienced fair-weather friends who are there only when times are good. But finding a true friend, someone you know in your heart you can rely on when the going gets tough, can be a challenge.

The problem is that when times are good, fair-weather friends and true friends act pretty much alike. It's difficult to know who your true friends are when the sailing is smooth. Fair-weather friends can mimic true friends, so the adaptive problem becomes how to differentiate true friends, who are deeply engaged in your welfare, from fair-weather friends, who will disappear in your hour of deepest need (Tooby & Cosmides, 1996). Selection should fashion in humans assessment mechanisms to make these differentiations. The most reliable evidence of friendship comes from the help you receive when you are desperately in need. Receiving help during this time will be a far more reliable litmus test than help received at any other time. Intuitively, we do seem to have special recall for precisely these times. We take pains to express our appreciation, communicating that we will never forget the person who helped us when we needed it most.

Modern living creates a paradox (Tooby & Cosmides, 1996). Humans generally act to avoid episodes of treacherous personal trouble, and many of today's "hostile forces of nature" that would have put our ancestors in jeopardy have been harnessed or controlled. We have laws

*A profound adaptive problem for humans is distinguishing "true friends" who are deeply engaged in our welfare from "fair-weather friends."*

to deter robbery, assault, and murder. We have police to perform many of the functions previously performed by friends. We have medical knowledge that has eliminated or reduced many sources of disease and illness. We live in an environment that is in many ways safer and more stable than that inhabited by our ancestors. Paradoxically, therefore, we suffer from a relative scarcity of critical events that would allow us to accurately assess those who are deeply engaged in our welfare and discriminate them from our fair-weather friends. It is possible that the loneliness and sense of alienation that many feel in modern living—a lack of a feeling of deep social connectedness despite the presence of many warm and friendly interactions—might stem from the lack of critical assessment events that tell us who is deeply engaged in our welfare.

***Limited Niches for Friendships.*** According to the Tooby and Cosmides theory of the evolution of friendship, each person has a limited amount of time, energy, and effort. Just as you cannot be in two places at one time, the decision to befriend one person is simultaneously a decision not to befriend another. Each person has a limited number of *friendship niches,* so the adaptive problem is deciding who will fill these slots. The implications of this theory are different from the implications of the standard theory of reciprocal altruism, in which you bestow benefits in the expectation that they will be returned at a later time. Tooby and Cosmides (1996) suggest instead that several other factors should determine your choice of friends.

1. *Number of slots already filled.* How many friends do you already have, and are they true friends or fair-weather friends? If they are few in number, then recruit new friends, consolidate or deepen existing friendships, or make yourself more appealing to prospective friends.

2. *Evaluate who emits positive externalities.* Let's say that someone who is physically formidable lives in your neighborhood—perhaps someone who is built like Arnold Schwarzenegger. His mere existence in your neighborhood deters muggers and other criminals, so you benefit because fewer criminals prey on you and your family as a result of this person's presence. Some people provide benefits that are properly regarded as side effects of their existence or actions—benefits to you that are not really intentional acts of altruism. Economists call these beneficial side effects *positive externalities.*

    People who have special talents or abilities—such as speaking others' dialects or being better at locating berries, game, or water—might provide benefits to those with whom they associate, regardless of whether they help intentionally. Those who radiate many such positive externalities are more attractive as potential friends than are those who emit fewer, above and beyond any intentional acts of helping they perform.

3. *Select friends who are good at reading your mind.* Helping someone is easier if you can read his or her mind and anticipate needs. A friend who can read your mind and understand your desires, beliefs, and values can help you in ways that are beneficial to you, as well as less costly to him or her.

4. *Select friends who consider you to be irreplaceable.* A friend who considers you irreplaceable has a stronger stake in your well-being than does someone who considers you expendable. Filling your life with friends who consider you irreplaceable, all else being equal, should result in a greater flow of benefits. Circumstantial support for this strategy comes from research conducted to test the *alliance hypothesis* (DeScioli & Kurzban, 2009). According to the alliance hypothesis, a key function of friendship is to assemble support groups that can come to one's aid in social conflicts. A person has to know who he or she can depend on when the going gets rough, to assess the reliability of friends. And one of the best predictors of who you value as a friend is who values *you* as a friend—in other words, someone who considers you to be irreplaceable (DeScioli & Kurzban, 2009).

5. *Select friends who want the same things that you want.* Hanging around with friends who value the same things you do will have a wonderful consequence: In the process of changing their local environments to suit their own desires, they will simultaneously change your environment as you might like because the two of you desire the same things. Let's take a trivial example. Suppose you like wild parties and you have a friend who also likes wild parties. Your friend seeks out, gets invited to, and frequently attends such parties. Because you are friends with this person, you get to tag along. Your friend provides you with benefits merely because you happen to want the same things.

Because we all have a limited number of "friend slots" to fill, selection should favor psychological mechanisms that are designed to monitor the flow of benefits from each friend—benefits that are not limited to those the friend intentionally delivers but also those that flow as a result of shared values and positive externalities and the degree to which these benefits are irreplaceable. The primary risk in friendship is not being cheated, as would be the case if friendship were based solely on reciprocal exchange. Rather, the primary risk is failing to form friendships that are characterized by mutual deep engagement or being surrounded by fair-weather friends instead of true friends. The psychological mechanisms that monitor friendships, therefore, should include signals that a friend's affection might be declining, signals that another person might be better suited to filling our precious and limited friendship slots, and signals about the degree to which we are regarded as irreplaceable by our friends.

***Deep Engagement versus Reciprocal Exchange.***   The modern world is filled with social interactions involving reciprocal exchange. Every time you buy something at a store, you are exchanging money for goods. Every time you buy lunch for someone and that person reciprocates by buying you lunch the next time, you are engaging in reciprocal exchange. But these exchanges typically do not characterize true friendships. Indeed, the explicit expectation that someone will return each favor in the form of a similar favor characterizes weak friendships, which lack true genuine trust (Tooby & Cosmides, 1996).

What characterizes true friends is another constellation of emotions and expectations entirely. We feel pleasure in the company of our friends and experience pleasure rather than envy when they are successful. We derive deep satisfaction from shared values and common world views. We are moved to help our friends when they separately need our assistance, even without any explicit expectation that our efforts will be repaid immediately. Future research in evolutionary psychology will undoubtedly document the complex constellation of psychological mechanisms dedicated to the formation of deep engagement.

## Costs and Benefits of Friendship

In principle, friendships can provide a bounty of benefits linked directly or indirectly to reproduction. Friends might offer us food and shelter or take care of us when we are ill. Friends might introduce us to potential mates. Despite the potential benefits, however, friends might also become our competitors or rivals. They might inflict costs on us by revealing our personal information to our enemies, competing for access to the same valuable resources, or even competing for the same mates.

Friendships vary on a number of dimensions. One dimension is gender. Friendships may be of the same or the opposite sex; the potential benefits and costs might differ dramatically for these two types of friendship. A same-sex friendship, for example, carries the potential for intrasexual rivalry. An opposite-sex friendship usually does not. An opposite-sex friendship, however, offers a benefit that a same-sex friendship generally lacks, namely, the potential for mating. Bleske and Buss (2001) tested a number of hypotheses about the benefits and costs of friendship by gathering two sources of information from participants: (1) perceptions of *how beneficial* (or costly) various items would be if they received them from a friend and (2) reports of *how often* they received these benefits (or costs) from their friends.

The first hypothesis was that for men more than women, one function of opposite-sex friendship is to provide short-term sexual access. This hypothesis follows from the logic of the theory of parental investment (Trivers, 1972).

As predicted, men evaluated the potential for sexual access to their opposite-sex friends as significantly more beneficial than did women, as shown in Figure 9.3. Men also reported experiencing unreciprocated attraction toward their opposite-sex friends more often than did women. Women more often than men reported having an opposite-sex friendship in which their friend was

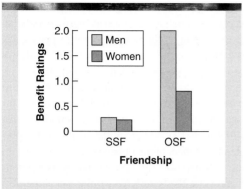

FIGURE 9.3 **Benefits of Friendship: Potential for Sexual Access.** Results show that men evaluated the potential for sexual access as significantly more beneficial than did women.

SSF = same-sex friendship; OSF = opposite-sex friendship.

*Source:* Bleske, A., & Buss, D. M. (1997, June). The evolutionary psychology of special "friendships." Paper presented at the ninth annual meeting of the Human Behavior and Evolution Society, University of Arizona, Tucson.

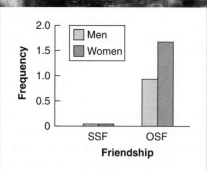

FIGURE 9.4 **Experiencing Romantic Attraction from a Friend.** Women more often than men reported having an opposite-sex friendship in which their friend felt romantically attracted to them but in which they were not romantically attracted to their friend.

SSF = same-sex friendship; OSF = opposite-sex friendship.

*Source:* Bleske, A., & Buss, D. M. (1997, June). The evolutionary psychology of special "friendships." Paper presented at the ninth annual meeting of the Human Behavior and Evolution Society, University of Arizona, Tucson.

romantically attracted to them but not vice versa (Figure 9.4). Moreover, men were denied sexual access to their opposite-sex friends more frequently than women. Another set of studies confirmed that sexual attraction is indeed a significant problem in opposite-sex friendships, and this problem leads to the termination of the friendship in roughly 38 percent of such friendships (Halatsis & Christakis, 2009). In sum, the evidence supports the hypothesis that men more than women view sexual access as a potential benefit of opposite-sex friendship.

The second hypothesis was that for women more than for men, a function of opposite-sex friendship is to provide protection. Over the course of our evolutionary history, women who were able to secure resources (e.g., food and material goods) and protection from men were more reproductively successful than were women who were unable to secure resources and protection for them and their potential offspring. Bleske and Buss (2001) hypothesized that women have an evolved preference for men who are able and willing to offer them resources and protection. In support of this hypothesis, women reported that they received protection from their opposite-sex friends. On a scale of 0 to 6, women's reports of receiving protection from their opposite-sex friends averaged 3.06, whereas men's reports averaged only 1.68—a statistically reliable difference.

A third hypothesis was that opposite-sex friendships function to provide information about the opposite sex. Given that opposite-sex friends might be more likely to have information about their own gender, men and women should perceive such information as a benefit of opposite-sex friendship more than of same-sex friendship. If gaining knowledge about what the opposite sex prefers in a short-term or a long-term mate has helped men and women solve the many adaptive problems of human mating, for example, men and women should perceive such information as highly beneficial. In support of this hypothesis, men and women did report receiving information about the opposite sex from their opposite-sex friends ($M = 2.84$) more often than from their same-sex friends ($M = 1.86$). In same-sex friendships, women received information about the opposite sex more often ($M = 2.15$) than did men ($M = 1.48$). This type of information appears to be a more characteristic benefit to women than to men of same-sex friendships. Moreover, men and women reported that receiving information about the opposite sex from an opposite-sex friend ($M = 4.15$) was more beneficial than receiving such information from a same-sex friend ($M = 3.12$). In sum, the empirical tests support the contention that friendships provide information about members of the opposite sex.

A fourth hypothesis was that men and women will perceive intrasexual rivalry as a potential cost of same-sex friendship. Same-sex friends are more likely to have similar interests, personalities, and levels of attractiveness than are two same-sex individuals taken at random (Bleske-Rechek & Lighthall, 2010). Consequently, same-sex friends might find themselves in competition with each other to attract a long-term mate. As predicted, men and women reported intrasexual rivalry over mates in their same-sex friendships ($M = 1.03$). The reported rate of competition was relatively low but significantly higher than rates of sexual rivalry in opposite-sex friendships ($M = 0.14$). Further, men and women evaluated the potential for sexual rivalry as *more costly* in a same-sex friendship ($M = 2.12$) than in an opposite-sex friendship ($M = 0.71$). These data suggest that sexual rivalry is not unique to interactions between same-sex strangers and enemies. Interestingly, men reported more frequent intrasexual rivalry in their same-sex friendships ($M = 1.35$) than did women ($M = 0.79$). It is likely that this greater sexual rivalry stems from men's greater desire for short-term casual sex—an interpretation that is supported by the finding that men view short-term sexual access as an important benefit of opposite-sex friends. In sum, the results suggest that sexual rivalry does sometimes occur in same-sex friendships, especially for men, and it is perceived to be a cost of such friendships.

Women and men also differ in their psychology of *same-sex* friendship (Vigil, 2007). Women's friendships tend to be more intimate than men's friendships. Women are more sensitive than men to the values and preferences of their friends. Women engage in more "relational maintenance," such as spending more time talking on the phone. Men more than women prefer a larger number of less intimate friendships, spend less time maintaining them, and do not share as much personal information. These differences suggest gender differences in the evolved functions of friendship. Vigil (2007) hypothesizes that, because historically women often mated exogamously (outside of their group), they faced the adaptive problem of having to rely heavily on women who were not their kin. Close intimate friendships may have helped them to obtain a safer and more secure social environment for them and their children in the absence of close kin around. In contrast to the psychological closeness and intimacy of women's friendships, men tend to use friendships to achieve some common goal, such as cooperative hunting, cooperative defense, or coalitional warfare.

## Cooperative Coalitions

Humans sometimes form *cooperative coalitions*—alliances of more than two individuals for the purpose of collective action to achieve a particular goal. Among hunter-gatherer societies, coalitions are typically formed for goals such as hunting, food sharing, launching a raid on another group, defending against attacks from another group, and building shelters. It is reasonable to hypothesize that humans have evolved specialized psychological mechanisms designed to promote cooperative coalitions.

Coalitions, however, face serious problems that can undermine their emergence: *defection* and *free-riding*. An example of defection occurs during war raids among the Yanomamö of Venezuela (Chagnon, 1983). Sometimes, while a group of Yanomamö begins to approach a neighboring group that the group seeks to raid, one or more men will claim that they have a sharp thorn in their foot or a belly ache and so must turn back and return to the home base. These defections jeopardize the success of the coalition, of course, and men who use such excuses too often will get branded as cowards.

An equally serious problem is that of free-riders—individuals who share in the rewards of the coalition but fail to contribute their fair share of work to the success of the coalition, even though they could have contributed their fair share. An example of free-riders would be people who always seem to be out of cash when the restaurant check comes, thus gaining benefits of the group outing without paying their fair share of the costs. The problems of defection and free-riding are so severe that many game theory analyses in biology and economics show that cooperative coalitions will collapse as a result. Defection often becomes the *evolutionarily stable strategy*—a strategy that, once it predominates in a population, cannot be invaded or displaced by any other strategy (Maynard Smith & Price, 1973). For cooperative coalitions to evolve, therefore, the problems of free-riders and potential defection must be solved.

Evolutionists have focused on the role of *punishment* in solving the free-rider problem (Boyd & Richardson, 1992; Gintis, 2000; Henrich & Boyd, 2001). Cooperative coalitions can evolve, in principle, as long as free-riders are punished. Experiments have shown that higher levels of cooperation occur when a system is in place to punish free-riders—to inflict costs on those who fail to contribute their fair share. But punishing free-riders raises another problem: Who will bear the costs of administering the punishment? Coalition members who punish free-riders incur a personal cost relative to those who refuse to punish free-riders. Thus, there must be some means of punishing those who refuse to punish the free-riders! Although the field has not achieved a consensus about how these problems can be solved, there is mounting evidence that humans do have adaptations to punish free-riders in the context of cooperative coalitions (Price et al., 2002). Indeed, when stringent punishments are in place for those who fail to contribute their fair share, high levels of cooperation tend to emerge (Fehr, Fischbacher, & Gächter, 2002; Kurzban et al., 2001).

One hypothesis is that "punitive sentiment" has evolved as a solution to the free-rider problem in the evolution of cooperative coalitions—a desire to harm "slackers" in the group (Price et al., 2002). This punitive sentiment could operate in at least two ways: to motivate the individual to punish free-riders *and* to encourage others in the group also to punish free-riders. In principle, the punitive sentiment could have two distinct functions: (1) to increase the chance that a reluctant member of the group will contribute and (2) to damage the free-rider's fitness relative to those who participate fully in the cooperative coalition (Price et al., 2002).

Price and colleagues (2002) examined what predicted the reported experience of punitive sentiments in a hypothetical coalitional activity, such as willingness to be drafted if the United States went to war. The single best predictor of punitive sentiments was the degree of a person's own participation in the cooperative coalition. The more a person was willing to participate (e.g., to be drafted for a war effort), the more that person wanted to punish those who could have participated but refused to do so (e.g., those who resisted being drafted for a war effort). In short, punitive sentiments might have evolved as a means of eliminating free-riders.

Cross-cultural studies, such as of the Shuar in Ecuador, support the hypothesis that the punitive sentiment may be a human universal (Price, 2005). Punishment is especially harsh toward in-group members who have failed to cooperate when they could, even more than toward out-group members (Shinada, Yamagishi, & Ohmura, 2004). One way to sum up this finding is with the phrase "false friends are worse than bitter enemies" (Shinada et al., 2004, p. 379). The underlying brain mechanisms of the punitive sentiment are being discovered; while punishing noncooperators, the brain region of the dorsal striatum becomes particularly active—a brain region linked with reward and anticipated satisfaction (de Quervain et al., 2004). People experience pleasure during the act of punishing noncooperators. Another study of brain activation found that observing an unfair game player (noncooperator) receiving physical pain also activated reward centers, especially among the male participants (Singer et al., 2006). Activation of these reward centers was especially pronounced in participants who expressed a desire for revenge. Perhaps the cliché "revenge is sweet" is true at the level of the underlying brain reward centers.

Despite the growing evidence for the evolution of a psychological mechanism of "punitive sentiment," we are still left with an intriguing problem: Those who punish free-riders incur a cost. It takes time, energy, and effort to punish someone, and punishers risk retaliation from those they punish. In this sense, punishing others could be an evolutionarily altruistic act in the sense that it provides a benefit to the whole group at a cost to the actor. Indeed, this sort of "altruistic punishment" has been documented in a study of fifteen diverse cultures, although cultures differ in the percentage of individuals who are willing to punish noncooperators (Henrich et al., 2006).

How could this form of "altruistic punishment" possibly evolve or emerge? Two competing explanations have been proposed. The first is what has been called *cultural group selection* (Boyd & Richardson, 1985; Fehr & Henrich, 2003). Cultural group selection describes a process by which certain culturally transmitted ideas, beliefs, or values spread because of the competitive advantages they provide to the social groups holding them (Henrich, personal communication, August 24, 2006). If groups competed with one another over time, and the most successful groups enforced group-altruistic norms, then cultural group selection would favor groups with the more effective norms. Through imitation or social transmission, the less successful groups could acquire the social norms of the more successful groups. Altruistic punishment that is beneficial to the group, sometimes called "strong reciprocity," could spread in this manner (also see Hagen & Hammerstein, 2006; and Tooby, Cosmides, & Price, 2006, for critiques of this explanation).

An alternative explanation is that altruistic punishers receive reputational benefits from punishing (Alexander, 1987; Barclay, 2006). A reputation as a punisher of noncooperators could benefit the punisher (1) if others are less likely to cheat known altruistic punishers (perhaps due to fear of being punished themselves) or (2) if altruistic punishers are more often sought out for cooperative relationships because they are perceived as being more trustworthy than those who fail to punish noncooperators. Barclay (2006) discovered that altruistic punishers are indeed seen as more trustworthy, more group-focused, and more worthy of respect than nonpunishers (see Figure 9.5). Another study found that in anonymous economic games, the presence of eyespots on the computer display increased prosocial behavior such as generosity, presumably because the cue of eyes triggers psychologically the feeling of being watched, which in turn activates concern with one's reputation (Haley & Fessler, 2005). The presence of an audience, even if the audience is a single witness such as the experimenter, is sufficient to increase the rates of punishing noncooperators (Kurzban, DeScioli, & O'Brian, 2007).

Mathematical models have also highlighted the key role of *shunning* or ostracizing those who do not contribute to the group (Panchanathan & Boyd, 2004). Those who shun individuals

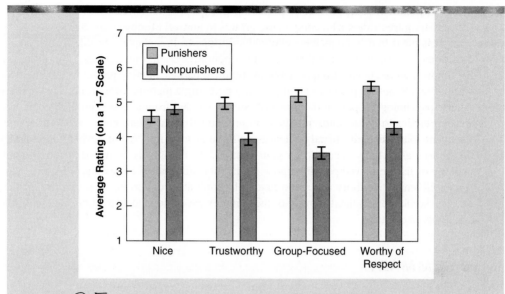

FIGURE 9.5 **Altruistic Punishment and Reputation.** Average ratings on a 7-point Likert scale of feelings toward punishers (black bars) and nonpunishers (white bars). Higher values represent more positive impressions.

*Source:* Barclay, P. (2006). Reputational benefits for altruistic punishment. *Evolution and Human Behavior, 27,* 325–344.

who either fail to help or fail to punish those who fail to help maintain a good reputation. Interestingly, those who shun free-riders may experience little or no cost to themselves. By refusing to help free-riders, shunners save the cost they would incur by helping them, so those who punish by shunning directly benefit (Fehr, 2004). The fact that people experience intense psychological and physical pain when they are shunned suggests the existence of a coevolved adaptation that motivates avoiding violating social norms that lead to ostracism (MacDonald & Leary, 2005). In sum, the punitive sentiment, with shunning as one key behavioral strategy, may have evolved as a consequence of reputational benefits and saved costs gained by those who punish noncooperators.

The study of evolved psychological mechanisms that support cooperative coalitions is very much in its infancy. Given that group living and group-against-group competition are universal features of human society, it is likely that scientists will discover additional adaptations for cooperative coalitions. Possible adaptations include gossip as a means of social bonding and controlling free-riders (Dunbar, 2004; Kniffin & Wilson, 2005), an in-group favoritism bias, prejudice against out-group members, xenophobia (hostility to strangers), adaptations to enforce group norms, ostracizing those who violate social norms (van Vugt & van Lange, 2006), and providing rewards to those who do not free ride (Kiyonari & Barclay, 2008). Cooperative coalitions cannot emerge unless the individuals involved in them can solve key adaptive problems, including (1) the problem of coordinating individuals with partially divergent interests toward a common goal, (2) the problem of imposing group obligations on members, and of course (3) punishing free-riders who could cause groups to unravel (Tooby et al., 2006).

It is clear that humans have evolved solutions to the adaptive problems of cooperative coalitions because worldwide they *do* form cooperative coalitions—gangs, fraternities, sororities, clubs, cliques, bands, troupes, factions, political parties, hunting parties, religious sects, and war parties. People experience great pleasure by being a member of a group. They experience intense psychological pain at the threat of being excluded from a valued group. People use persuasion tactics to induce individuals to align themselves to group goals. When the American President John Kennedy stirred audiences with the exhortation "Ask not what your country can do for you; ask what you can do for your country," he effectively activated the coalitional psychology of listeners. And people impose punishments on traitors, cheaters, defectors, and free-riders. Given the ubiquity and importance of cooperative coalitions in social living, the next decade should witness the discovery of the complex psychological adaptations that have allowed coalitions to evolve.

## ■ SUMMARY

We started this chapter by considering the problem of altruism: design features that aid the reproduction of other individuals, even though the altruist who has this feature incurs a cost. The puzzle is how such altruism could have evolved, given that it seems to go against Hamilton's rule. One solution came from the theory of reciprocal altruism, which states that psychological mechanisms for providing benefits to nonrelatives can evolve as long as the delivery of those benefits causes the recipient to reciprocate at some point in the future. The most important adaptive problem the reciprocal altruist faces, however, is the threat of cheaters—people who take benefits without reciprocating at a later time.

One solution to this problem emerged from a computer tournament conducted by Robert Axelrod. He discovered that tit for tat—a strategy of cooperating on the first move but reciprocating thereafter—was highly successful. It tended to promote cooperation but also helped to solve the problem of cheating by punishing defectors immediately.

Examples of reciprocal altruism occur in the animal world. Vampire bats share their blood with "friends" who were unsuccessful on any given night; at a later point, the friends reciprocate the favor, giving blood preferentially to those who have recently helped them. Among chimpanzees, reciprocal alliances form among males, among females, and among males and females.

Social contract theory proposes the evolution of five cognitive capacities in humans to solve the problem of cheaters and engage in successful social exchange. Humans must be able to recognize other individuals; remember their mutual history of interactions; communicate one's values, desires, and needs to others; recognize the values, desires, and needs of others; and represent the costs and benefits of a large variety of items of exchange. Researchers have demonstrated that people have cheater-detection mechanisms, which were revealed by showing a special ability to reason when logic problems are framed in the form of social contracts. People tend to be especially vigilant about searching for those who have taken benefits without paying the expected costs. In addition to adaptations to detect cheaters, evidence points to a specialized ability to detect those with genuinely altruistic sentiments. Choosing as allies those who are motivated to cooperate might be an important strategy in avoiding exposure to cheaters to begin with.

In addition to kin altruism and reciprocal altruism, two other evolutionary theories have been proposed to explain altruism: indirect reciprocity and costly signaling. With indirect reciprocity, altruists do not benefit by gaining a return benefit from the person they helped. Rather, *others* who witness or hear about their generosity are more likely to provide aid to the altruists. With costly signaling, acts of great helping and self-sacrifice provide an honest signal to others about one's condition and resource-holding potential because only those in excellent condition can "afford" to provide the costly signal. Costly signaling increases a person's status and reputation, which in turn benefits the costly signaler. In sum, there are at least four ways in which altruism can evolve: kin selection (altruism toward genetic relatives), reciprocal altruism, indirect reciprocity, and costly signaling.

The evolution of friendship poses a special problem that is captured by the banker's paradox: Although banks are in the business of loaning money to people who need it, the people who most need money are the worst credit risks, so banks end up loaning money to the people who need it least while denying loans to those who need it most. Similarly, when we most need help from our friends coincides with the time when we are the poorest "credit risk," unable to return benefits to those who help us. One solution to this paradox is to become irreplaceable: If we provide benefits that no one else offers, our friends have a tremendous stake in our welfare and will therefore want to help when we most need it. A key distinction is between fair-weather friends and true friends. We tend to know who our true friends are from their behavior toward us when we most need their help. It is possible that the sense of alienation many people feel stems from the fact that humans have conquered many "hostile forces of nature," and so are less likely to face life-threatening events that allow us to know who our true friends are—those who are deeply engaged in our welfare.

Some work has been conducted on the functions of friendship by exploring the perceived benefits and costs of friendships. Men and women form same-sex friendships as well as opposite-sex friendships, but the evidence points to sex differences in the functions of friendship. Men more than women perceive short-term sexual access as a benefit of opposite-sex friendships. Women more than men perceive protection as a benefit of opposite-sex friendships. Both sexes perceive information about the opposite sex to be an important benefit of opposite-sex friendship. One cost of same-sex friendship is the potential for sexual rivalry. Sexual rivalry appears to be more prevalent among male friends than among female friends, perhaps because of men's stronger desire for short-term mating, which would throw them into conflict more often.

In addition to dyadic alliances, humans also form cooperative coalitions—groups of people who use collective action to achieve a common goal. Adaptations to form these cooperative groups can evolve only if the problem of free-riding can be solved. Empirical evidence suggests that in humans, "punitive sentiments" might be part of the solution to the problem of free-riders. The anger that people feel against group members who fail to pull their weight in the group motivates punitive sentiments, which result in punishing free-riders. Scientists have identified some of the brain regions involved when people punish noncooperators, which point to reward centers; people experience pleasure when punishing or seeking revenge against violators.

Punishing others may be evolutionarily altruistic, in that the punisher incurs a personal cost not incurred by nonpunishers that benefits the entire group. If it is true that "altruistic punishers" are truly altruistic, some sort of group selection explanation, such as "cultural group selection," may be needed to explain this phenomenon. Alternatively, punishers may receive personal benefits from punishing free-riders, in which case this phenomenon can be explained by the standard theory of natural selection. Several studies point to the reputational benefits that punishers gain—they are perceived as more trustworthy, group-focused, and worthy of respect. Punishers who achieve this reputation may benefit in two ways—if their reputation deters others from attempting to free ride and if they are sought out more for inclusion in cooperative coalitions. Finally, it is worth noting that punishing free-riders may not be all that costly to the punishers, as in the simple act of shunning or ignoring the free-rider. The fact that people experience such severe psychological pain when they are shunned or ostracized points to a possible coevolved adaptation to avoid committing acts that result in ostracism.

## ■ SUGGESTED READINGS

Bereczkei, T., Birkas, B., & Kerekes, Z. (2010). Altruism toward strangers in need: Costly signaling in an industrial society. *Evolution and Human Behavior, 31*, 95–103.

Cosmides, L., & Tooby, J. (2005). Neurocognitive adaptations designed for social exchange. In D. M. Buss (Ed.), *The handbook of evolutionary psychology* (pp. 584–627). New York: Wiley.

DeScioli, P., & Kurzban, R. (2009). The alliance hypothesis for human friendship. *PLoS ONE, 4*, 1–8.

Johnson, D. D. P., Price, M. E., & Takezawa, M. (2008). Renaissance of the individual: Reciprocity, positive assortment, and the puzzle of human cooperation. In C. Crawford & D. Krebs (Eds.). *Foundations of evolutionary psychology* (pp. 331–352). New York: Erlbaum.

Maynard Smith, J. (1982). *Evolution and the theory of games.* Cambridge, UK: Cambridge University Press.

Nowak, M.A. (2006). Five rules for the evolution of cooperation. *Science, 314*, 1560–1563.

Price, M. E., Cosmides, L., & Tooby, J. (2002). Punitive sentiment as an anti-free rider psychological device. *Evolution and Human Behavior, 23*, 203–231.

Zahavi, A. (1995). Altruism as a handicap: The limitations of kin selection and reciprocity. *Journal of Avian Biology, 26*, 1–3.

# AGGRESSION AND WARFARE

CHAPTER 10

*From an evolutionary point of view, the leading cause of violence is maleness.*

—Robert Wright, 1995

$O$ne afternoon in January 1974, a group of eight chimpanzees in the Gombe National Park in Tanzania formed a fighting party and traveled south (Wrangham & Peterson, 1996). They appeared to take pains to maintain silence and stealth as they traveled toward the border of their usual home range. They crossed that border, followed by Hillali Matama, a researcher from Jane Goodall's Gombe team. A short distance away was Godi, a young male, roughly twenty-one years old, feasting peacefully on the ripe fruit of a tree. Godi usually ventured out for food with his comrades, the six other males in the Kahama chimpanzee community, but on this day, he had chosen to travel alone.

By the time Godi spotted the eight trespassers, they had already reached his feeding tree. Godi made a mad dash to elude them but they gave chase, caught up with him, and tackled him by grabbing his legs. Humphrey, one of the leading chimps in the fighting party, pinned two of Godi's limbs, holding him immobile while the others gathered around. With Godi's face pushed into the dirt, the other males attacked. In a frenzy of screaming, charging, biting, and striking, Godi's attackers looked like a human gang of adolescents beating up a lone victim who happened to be in the wrong place at the wrong time. After ten minutes, the pummeling and biting stopped, and Godi watched as his attackers left to return to their home range. Godi bled from more than a dozen wounds, his body a bruised mess from the vicious attack. The researchers never saw Godi again. Although he did not die immediately from the attack, they speculated that he almost surely died within a few days.

This attack is remarkable not for its viciousness or for the coordinated manner in which the intruders rendered their victim helpless. It is remarkable because it was the first time a scientist had witnessed chimpanzees raid a neighboring territory to assault an enemy with lethal results. It led researchers to question their long-held assumption that other primates are peaceful and harmonious and that only humans kill their own kind. It also caused researchers to question the long-held assumption that chimpanzees represented an "arcadian existence of primal innocence" or the peaceful "paradise that man had somehow lost" (Ardry, 1966, p. 222). On the contrary, leading researchers have concluded that the "male violence that surrounds and threatens chimpanzee communities is so extreme that to be in the wrong place at the wrong time from the wrong group means death" (Wrangham & Peterson, 1996, p. 21).

Humans are not chimpanzees, of course, and we must be wary of superficial comparisons between humans and other species. Evidence for extreme aggression in chimpanzees, by itself, may say nothing about aggression in humans. Wrangham and Peterson (1996), however, make a remarkable observation. Of the more than 10 million animal species that exist, including four thousand mammals, only two species have been documented to show male-initiated coordinated coalitions that raid neighboring territories and result in lethal attacks on members of their own species: chimpanzees and humans.

Humans, like chimpanzees, form aggressive male-bonded coalitions in which members support each other in a mutual quest to aggress against others. Human recorded history is filled with such rivalries: the Spartans and the Athenians, the crusades, the Hatfields and the McCoys, the Palestinians and the Israelis, the Sunnis and Shi'ites, and the Tutsis and the Hutus. In all cultures, men commonly have bonded together to attack other groups or to defend their own. Humans and chimpanzees share this unique pattern of aggression with no other known species (Wrangham & Peterson, 1996).

## ■ AGGRESSION AS A SOLUTION TO ADAPTIVE PROBLEMS

An evolutionary psychological perspective does not yield a single hypothesis about the origins of aggression. Below are leading candidates for adaptive problems for which aggression might be an evolved solution (Buss & Duntley, 2005; Buss & Shackelford, 1997b).

### Co-opt the Resources of Others

Humans, perhaps more than any other species, stockpile resources that historically have been valuable for survival and reproduction. These include fertile land and access to fresh water, food, tools, and weapons. There are many means for gaining access to the valuable resources held by others, such as engaging in social exchange, stealing, or trickery. Aggression is also a means of co-opting the resources of others.

Aggression to co-opt resources can occur at the individual or at the group level. At the individual level, one can use physical force to take resources from others. Modern-day forms include the actions of bullies at school who take lunch money, books, leather jackets, or designer sneakers from other children (Olweus, 1978). Childhood aggression is commonly about resources such as toys and territory (Campbell, 1993). Adult forms include muggings and beatings as a means to forcibly extract money or other goods from others. The *threat* of aggression might be enough to secure resources from others, as when a child gives up his lunch money to prevent a beating or

*In humans, males more than females resort to physical aggression to co-opt the resources of others. The sex difference in the use of physical aggression emerges as early as three years of age.*

a small-store owner gives mobsters money for "protection" to prevent his or her business from being ruined.

People, particularly men, often form coalitions for the purposes of forcibly co-opting the resources of others. Among the Yanomamö, for example, male coalitions raid neighboring tribes and forcibly take food and reproductive-aged women (Chagnon, 1983). Throughout recorded human history, warfare has been used to co-opt the land possessed by others, and to the victors go the spoils. The acquisition of reproductively relevant resources through aggression is one evolutionary hypothesis.

## Defend against Attack

The presence of aggressive conspecifics poses a serious adaptive problem to would-be victims: They stand to lose the valuable resources that are co-opted by their aggressors. In addition, victims might suffer injury or death, impeding both survival and reproduction. Defending against attack can also function to prevent potential harm to one's mate, children, or extended kin. Indeed, women as well as men sometimes risk their own lives in order to prevent the injury, abuse, or death of their mates or children (Buss, 2005b). Victims of aggression might also lose in the currency of status and reputation. The loss of face or honor entailed in being abused with impunity can lead to further abuse by others, who might select victims in part because of the ease with which they can be exploited or their unwillingness to retaliate.

Aggression therefore can be used to defend against attack. Aggression might be an effective solution to this adaptive problem by preventing one's resources from being taken forcibly. It can be used to cultivate a reputation that deters other would-be aggressors. And it can be used to prevent the loss of status and honor that would otherwise follow from being victimized with impunity.

## Inflict Costs on Intrasexual Rivals

A third adaptive problem is posed by same-sex rivals who are vying for the same resources. One such resource consists of access to valuable members of the opposite sex. The image of the bully kicking beach sand in the face of a weaker man and walking away with that man's girlfriend is a stereotyped notion of intrasexual competition, but the notion underlying it is powerful.

Aggression to inflict costs on rivals can range from verbal barbs to beatings and killings. Men and women both derogate their same-sex rivals, impugning their status and reputation to make them less desirable to members of the other sex (Buss & Dedden, 1990). At the other end of the spectrum, men sometimes kill their same-sex rivals in duels. Bar fights that start as trivial altercations can escalate to the point of death (Daly & Wilson, 1988). And men sometimes kill other men they find out have had sex with their wives or girlfriends (Daly & Wilson, 1988). Because evolution operates according to *differences* in designs, a cost inflicted on a rival can translate into a benefit for the perpetrator.

## Negotiate Status and Power Hierarchies

A fourth evolutionary hypothesis is that aggression functions to increase one's status or power within existing social hierarchies. Among the Ache of Paraguay and the Yanomamö of Venezuela, for example, men engage in ritual club fights with other men. Men who have survived many club fights are admired and feared and so attain status and power (Chagnon, 1983; Hill & Hurtado, 1996). Modern societies have ritualized aggression in the form of boxing matches, for example, after which the victor experiences status elevation.

Men who expose themselves to danger in warfare to kill enemies are regarded as brave and courageous and consequently experience an elevation in their status within the group (Chagnon, 1983; Hill & Hurtado, 1996). Within street gangs, men who display ferocity in their beatings of fellow or rival gang members experience status elevation (Campbell, 1993).

The hypothesis that aggression sometimes serves the adaptive function of status elevation does not imply that this strategy works in all groups. Aggression within many groups can result in a status decrement. A professor who punched another professor at a faculty meeting, for example, would almost certainly experience a decline in status. The key to the status elevation hypothesis is to specify the evolved psychological mechanisms that are sensitive to the social contexts in which aggression pays.

## Deter Rivals from Future Aggression

Cultivating a reputation as aggressive might function to deter aggression and other forms of cost infliction from others. Most people would think twice about stealing from a Mafia hit man or tangling with boxer Mike Tyson. And most would hesitate to flirt with the girlfriend of a member of the Hells Angels motorcycle gang. Aggression and the reputation for aggression thus can act as deterrents, helping to solve the adaptive problem of others attempting to co-opt one's resources and mates.

## Deter Long-Term Mates from Sexual Infidelity

A sixth hypothesis is that aggression and the threat of aggression function to deter long-term mates from sexual infidelity. Much empirical evidence suggests that male sexual jealousy is the leading cause or precipitating context of spousal battering (Daly, Wilson, & Weghorst, 1982). Studies of shelters for battered women, for example, document that in the majority of cases women cite extreme jealousy on the part of their husbands or boyfriends as the key cause of the beating (Dobash & Dobash, 1984). As repugnant as this might be, some men do beat their wives or girlfriends to deter them from consorting with other men.

## The Context-Specificity of Aggression

This account of six key adaptive problems for which aggression might be one (of several) strategic solution clearly is not exhaustive. Indeed, the next chapter explores other hypotheses about the functions of aggression in the context of mating (e.g., sexual aggression). This account does, however, suggest that aggression is not a unitary, monolithic, or context-blind strategy. Rather, aggression is likely to be highly context specific, triggered only in contexts that resemble those in which our ancestors confronted certain adaptive problems and reaped particular benefits.

Consider the use of spousal battering to solve the adaptive problem of a partner's potential infidelity. This problem is more likely to be confronted by men who are lower in relative mate value than their wives, for example, or who experience a decrement (e.g., loss of a job) in the resources that women value (Buss, 2003). Under these conditions, the probability that a woman might commit infidelity or defect from the relationship altogether is likely to be higher. Men in these conditions are predicted to be more aggressive than men whose partners are less likely to commit infidelity or to leave the relationship.

Adaptive benefits must also be evaluated within the context of *costs*. Aggression, by definition, inflicts costs on others, and those others cannot be expected to absorb the costs passively or with indifference: "Lethal retribution is an ancient and cross-culturally universal recourse for those subjected to abuse" (Daly & Wilson, 1988, p. 226). One of the most robust findings in aggression research is that aggression tends to cause retaliatory aggression (Buss, 1961). This can sometimes cause escalating cycles of aggression and counteraggression, as in the fabled family feud between the Hatfields and the McCoys (Waller, 1993).

One critical context pertains to the reputational consequences of aggression. Cultures and subcultures differ in whether aggression enhances or diminishes status. Among "cultures of honor," for example, failure to aggress when insulted can lead to status loss (Nisbett, 1993). A daughter who has brought shame on the family name by engaging in premarital sex, for example, might be killed as an "honorable" solution to the problem of restoring the status of the family (Goldstein, 2002). The failure to kill such a daughter might result in a lowering of status of the rest of her family in these cultures.

Another dimension of cost pertains to the ability and willingness of the victim to retaliate. Among schoolchildren, bullies typically select victims or "whipping boys" who cannot or will not retaliate (Olweus, 1993). Similarly, the husband of a woman with four strapping brothers and a powerful father living nearby will probably think twice before beating her for flirting with someone else. The presence of extended kin, therefore, is one context of cost that should moderate the manifestation of spousal violence. A study of domestic violence in Madrid, Spain, found that women with higher densities of genetic kin both inside and outside Madrid experienced lower levels of domestic violence (Figueredo, 1995).

In some contexts, aggressors will suffer reputational damage because of their aggression. In academic circles, for example, physical aggression is shunned, and those who engage in it can suffer ostracism. Among members of some street gangs, the failure to engage in aggression when provoked will result in an irreparable loss of status (Campbell, 1993).

The key point is that an evolutionary psychological perspective predicts that evolved mechanisms will be designed to be sensitive to context, not the rigid invariant expression of aggression depicted in earlier instinct theories. Thus, findings of variability of aggression across contexts, cultures, and individuals in no way falsify particular evolutionary hypotheses. Indeed, that very context sensitivity is a critical lever for testing evolutionary hypotheses (DeKay & Buss, 1992).

Aggression is evoked by particular adaptive problems confronted in particular cost–benefit contexts.

## ■ WHY ARE MEN MORE VIOLENTLY AGGRESSIVE THAN WOMEN?

Of homicides committed in Chicago between 1965 and 1980, 86 percent were committed by men (Daly & Wilson, 1988). Of these, 80 percent of the victims were also men. Although exact percentages vary from culture to culture, cross-cultural homicide statistics reveal strikingly similar findings. In all cultures, men are overwhelmingly more often the killers and the majority of their victims are other men. A good theory of aggression must provide an explanation for why men engage in violent forms of aggression so much more often than women do and why other men make up the majority of their victims.

An evolutionary model of intrasexual competition provides the foundation for such an explanation. It starts with the theory of parental investment and sexual selection (see Chapter 4). In species in which females invest more heavily in offspring than males do, females are a valuable limiting resource on reproduction for males. Males are constrained in their reproduction by their ability to gain sexual access to the high-investing females.

The sex difference in minimum obligatory parental investment means that males can produce more offspring than females can (see Chapter 4). Stated differently, the ceiling on reproduction is much higher for males than for females. This difference leads to differences in the *variances* in reproduction between the sexes. The differences between the haves and the have-nots are greater for males than for females.

The greater the variance in reproduction, the more selection favors riskier strategies (including intrasexual competition) within the sex that shows the higher variance. In an extreme case, such as the elephant seals off the coast of northern California, 5 percent of the males sire 85 percent of all offspring produced in a breeding season (Le Boeuf & Reiter, 1988). Species that show higher variance in the reproduction of one sex compared to the other tend to be sexually dimorphic (i.e., different in size and shape) across a variety of physical characteristics. The more intense the effective polygyny, the more dimorphic the sexes are in size and form (Trivers, 1985). Elephant seals are highly sexually dimorphic in weight, for example, with males weighing four times what females weigh (Le Boeuf & Reiter, 1988). Chimpanzees are less sexually dimorphic in weight, with males having roughly twice the weight of females. Humans are mildly dimorphic in weight, with males roughly 18 percent heavier than females. Within primate species, the greater the effective polygyny, the more pronounced the sexual dimorphism, and the greater the reproductive variance between the sexes (Alexander et al., 1979).

Effective polygyny means that some males gain more than their "fair share" of copulations while other males are shut out entirely, banished from contributing to the ancestry of future generations. This leads to more ferocious competition within the high-variance sex. In essence, polygyny selects for risky strategies, including those that lead to violent combat with rivals and those that lead to increased risk taking to acquire the resources needed to attract members of the high-investing sex.

Violence can occur at the top as well as the bottom of the hierarchy. Given an equal sex ratio, for each man who monopolizes two women, another man is consigned to bachelorhood (Daly & Wilson, 1996b). For those facing reproductive failure, a risky, aggressive strategy might

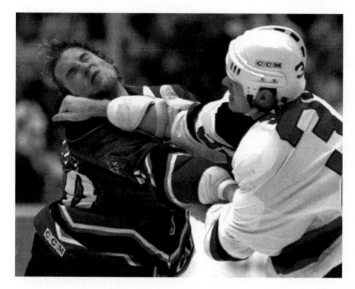

*Men across cultures are both the perpetrators and the victims of violent aggression, adaptations produced by the greater reproductive variance of men compared to women, the greater benefits to men than to women at solving adaptive problems through aggression, and the heavier costs to women than to men of using aggression.*

represent a last resort. Homicide data reveal that men who are poor and unmarried are more likely to kill compared with their more affluent and married counterparts (Wilson & Daly, 1985). In short, there are two sides to the use of aggression in competitive contexts marked by some degree of polygyny: (1) aggression by a male to "win big," thereby gaining access to multiple mates, and (2) aggression to avoid total reproductive failure.

To understand why men would take large risks in mating contexts, let's consider an analogy: foraging for food. Consider an animal who is able to secure a foraging territory that provides just enough food to stay alive but not enough food to breed. Outside this territory are risks, such as predators who might make the animal their next meal. In this situation, the only males who succeed in breeding are those willing to take risks to venture outside their secure territory to get food. Some will be killed by the predator, of course, and that's why venturing outside is risky. But others will manage to avoid the predator, secure the additional food, and thereby successfully breed. Those who fail to take the risks to venture outside their territory will fail to breed entirely. This situation selects for risk taking as a strategy for breeding. Selection in this context acts as a sieve, filtering out those who fail to take risks.

This account provides a good explanation for both facts revealed in the cross-cultural homicide record. Males are more often the perpetrators of violence because they are the products of a long history of mild but sustained effective polygyny characterized by risky strategies of intrasexual competition for access to females (see Box 10.1 for sex-differentiated patterns of anger, an emotion that motivates aggression). Men are the victims of aggression far more than women are because men are in competition primarily with other men. It is other men who form the primary sources of strategic interference, other men who impede their access to resources needed to attract women, and other men who try to block their access to women.

Women also engage in aggression, and their victims are also typically members of their own sex. In studies of verbal aggression through derogation of competitors, for example, women slander their rivals by impugning their physical appearance and hence their reproductive value (Buss & Dedden, 1990; Campbell, 1993, 1999). The forms of aggression committed by women,

BOX 10.1

## The Recalibration Theory of Anger

Because each human has fitness "interests" that differ from those of other people, social conflict is an inevitable fact of our highly social species. One source of conflict emerges when you believe that another person does not value your welfare as much as you believe that person should. A friend might not devote as much time to helping you as you think she should. A romantic partner might not meet your sexual or emotional needs at the level to which you believe you are entitled. The recalibration theory proposes that feeling and expressing anger functions to increase (recalibrate) the value that the target of your anger places on your welfare (Sell, Tooby, & Cosmides, 2009).

According to this theory, individuals with a superior ability to inflict costs and confer benefits should be more prone to anger. A man's upper body strength is a key component of his ability to inflict costs through acts of aggression. A woman's physical attractiveness is a key component of her ability to confer benefits, since it is a key component of mate value, friend value, and kin value. Therefore, the recalibration theory predicts that physically formidable men and physically attractive women should be more prone to anger, have greater success in resolving social conflicts in their favor, and experience a greater sense of entitlement than less formidable men and less attractive women.

Sell and his colleagues tested these predictions in two separate studies by measuring upper body strength on standardized weight-lifting machines, viewed as the "gold standard" for assessing strength. Physical attractiveness was measured through self-assessments with the item "I am more attractive than __% of others of my sex." The results largely supported the predictions. Stronger men (but not stronger women) reported more proneness to anger, a more frequent history of fighting, more success in prior social conflicts, a greater perceived utility of using aggression ("If I don't respond to provocation and do something to make the wrongdoers pay, they'll just do more to hurt me in the future"), and a greater sense of entitlement ("I deserve more than the average person") than physically weaker men. Conversely, attractive women and men both reported more proneness to anger, a greater utility in using personal aggression, a stronger sense of entitlement, and more success in social conflicts, although these effects were generally stronger for women than for men.

These results support predictions derived from the recalibration theory—that those who have the ability to inflict costs or confer benefits will be quicker to anger as a strategy for resolving social conflicts. Future tests of this theory will undoubtedly explore other components of the ability to inflict costs and confer benefits, such as a person's social status, coalitional strength, and kin network. Future research will also provide direct tests of the effect of anger displays on the anger-recipient's psychological shifts in valuation of the angry person, as well as behavioral changes such as acts of reparation and bestowing benefits. In the meantime, the current studies provide exciting preliminary support for the theory that the emotion of anger, a key emotion that motivates aggression, has a coherent adaptive logic.

however, are typically less violent, and hence less risky than those committed by men—facts that are accounted for by the theory of parental investment and sexual selection (see Campbell, 1995). Indeed, selection may operate *against* women who take the large physical risks entailed by aggression. Evolutionary psychologist Anne Campbell argues that women need to place a higher value on their own lives than do men on theirs, given the fact that infants depend on maternal care more than on paternal care (Campbell, 1999). Women's evolved psychology, therefore, should reflect greater fearfulness of situations that pose a physical threat of bodily injury—a prediction that is well supported by the empirical findings (Campbell, 1999).

# ■ EMPIRICAL EVIDENCE FOR DISTINCT ADAPTIVE PATTERNS OF AGGRESSION

*W*ith this theoretical background in mind, we now turn to the empirical evidence on aggression in humans. First, we consider evidence for the most straightforward prediction from the evolutionary theory of aggression: that men will be more likely than women to use violence and aggression. Then we consider in detail each of the four possible pairings of sex of perpetrator crossed with sex of victim, starting with men's aggression toward other men.

## Evidence for Sex Differences in Same-Sex Aggression

In this section, we will consider evidence for sex differences in aggression (Archer, 2009). Several sources of evidence are available: meta-analyses of sex differences in aggression, homicide statistics, studies of bullying in the classroom, and ethnographic evidence from aboriginal communities.

*A Meta-Analysis of Sex Differences in Aggression.* Psychologist Janet Hyde conducted a meta-analysis of studies of the effect sizes for sex differences in different forms of aggression (Hyde, 1986). An effect size, in this context, refers to the magnitude of the sex difference. An effect size of .80 may be considered large, .50 medium, and .20 small. The following are the effect sizes, averaged across dozens of studies, for various forms of aggression: aggressive fantasies (.84), physical aggression (.60), imitative aggression (.49), and willingness to shock others in an experimental setting (.39). All show greater male scores on aggression. Interestingly, Hyde found no evidence for a sex difference in scores on the hostility scale (.02). In summary, the results of this meta-analysis and more recent ones (Archer, 2009) support a key prediction from the previously discussed evolutionary analysis of aggression: Men use aggression more than women in a variety of forms, and the effect sizes tend to range from medium to large.

*Same-Sex Homicides.* Homicides are statistically rare, but they provide one assay for examining patterns of aggression. Daly and Wilson (1988) compiled same-sex homicide statistics from thirty-five different studies representing a broad span of cultures from downtown Detroit to the Basoga of Uganda. Although homicide rates vary widely from culture to culture, the most useful way to compare the sexes is to calculate the proportion of same-sex homicide committed by males (i.e., the percentage of same-sex homicides that are male–male homicides). A subset of these statistics is shown in Table 10.1.

In every culture for which there are data, the rate at which men kill other men far exceeds the rate at which women kill other women. As Daly and Wilson (1988) concluded, "Indeed there is no evidence that the women in *any* society have *ever* approached the level of violent conflict prevailing among men in the same society" (p. 149; emphasis in original).

*Same-Sex Bullying in Schools.* Homicides represent the most extreme form of aggression, but similar sex differences show up in milder forms of aggression, such as bullying in middle and high schools. In one study (Ahmad & Smith, 1994), researchers looked at 226 middle school (eight to eleven years old) and 1,207 high school (eleven to sixteen years old) students. Using an anonymous questionnaire, they asked each student how often he or she had been bullied, how

TABLE *10.1*  **Same-Sex Homicides in Different Cultures**

| Location | Male | Female | Proportion Male |
|---|---|---|---|
| Canada, 1974–1998 | 2,965 | 175 | .94 |
| Miami, 1925–1926 | 111 | 5 | .96 |
| Detroit, 1972 | 345 | 16 | .96 |
| Pittsburgh, 1966–1974 | 382 | 16 | .96 |
| Tzeltal Mayans, Mexico, 1938–1965 | 37 | 0 | 1.00 |
| Belo Horizonte, Brazil, 1961–1965 | 228 | 6 | .97 |
| New South Wales, Australia, 1968–1981 | 675 | 46 | .94 |
| Oxford, England, 1296–1398 | 105 | 1 | .99 |
| Scotland, 1953–1974 | 172 | 12 | .93 |
| Iceland, 1946–1970 | 10 | 0 | 1.00 |
| Denmark, 1933–1961 | 87 | 15 | .85 |
| Bison-Horn Maria, India, 1920–1941 | 69 | 2 | .97 |
| !Kung San, Botswana, 1920–1955 | 19 | 0 | 1.00 |
| Congo, 1948–1957 | 156 | 4 | .97 |
| Tiv, Nigeria, 1931–1949 | 96 | 3 | .97 |
| Basoga, Uganda, 1952–1954 | 46 | 1 | .98 |
| BaLuyia, Kenya, 1949–1954 | 88 | 5 | .95 |
| JoLuo, Kenya | 31 | 2 | .94 |

*Source:* Daly, M., & Wilson, M. (1988). *Homicide.* New York: Aldine de Gruyter. Copyright © 1988 by Aldine de Gruyter. Reprinted with permission.

often he or she had joined others in bullying others at school, and the particular forms the bullying took. The researchers found significant sex differences on all measures. In reports of bullying others, for example, 54 percent of the middle school boys reported engaging in bullying, whereas the comparable figure for same-age girls was 34 percent. In high school, 43 percent of the boys but only 30 percent of the girls reported bullying.

These sex differences, however, underestimate the rates of violent aggression. When the type of bullying is examined, a larger sex difference emerges. In the high school sample, 36 percent of the boys but only 9 percent of the girls reported being physically hurt, such as being hit or kicked, by a bully. Furthermore, 10 percent of the boys but only 6 percent of the girls reported having had their belongings taken away from them—a finding that supports the hypothesis that one function of aggression is to co-opt the resources of others. On two measures of bullying, however, girls scored higher than boys. A full 74 percent of the girls reported that others had called them nasty names, whereas only 57 percent of the boys reported this form of bullying.

The content of the verbal forms of aggression is revealing. The most frequently used nasty names and rumors spread by girls about other girls involved terms such as "bitch," "slag," "slut," and "whore." These kinds of bullying were common among high school girls but virtually absent among the middle school students, suggesting a rise in intrasexual mate competition, in which the adaptive problems of mating begin to be encountered.

Similar sex differences have been observed in other cultures. In a study conducted in Turku, Finland, 127 fifteen-year-old schoolchildren were assessed through both peer nomination techniques and self-report (Bjorkqvist, Lagerspetz, & Kaukiainen, 1992). Boys showed more than three times the rates of direct physical aggression than girls. Direct physical aggression involved tripping, taking things from another, kicking and striking, seeking revenge in games, and pushing and shoving. Indirect aggression, in contrast, was measured with items such as gossiping, shunning another person, spreading vicious rumors as revenge, breaking contact with the person, and befriending someone else as revenge. The fifteen-year-old girls showed approximately 25 percent higher rates of indirect aggression than the same-age boys.

In sum, studies of bullying support the prediction of a sex difference in the use of violent and risky forms of aggression. Males engage in these forms of aggression more frequently than females do. When females aggress—which they do—they tend to use less violent methods, such as the verbal derogation of their competitors.

***Aggression in an Australian Aboriginal Community.*** Anthropologist Victoria Burbank spent several months studying a community she calls Mangrove, a southeast Arnhem Land community of roughly 600 Australian aborigines. Burbank recorded 793 cases of aggressive behavior. Many were verbally conveyed to her by residents, often females. In roughly one-third of the cases, two or more informants conveyed information about the same aggressive episode. In 51 cases, Burbank recorded her own observations of what happened in the aggressive interactions.

Here is one sample of what Burbank (1992) recorded:

> Near here when [a man] was with two of his wives, a "brother" tried to pull them out. "You can't have them," he said. "We'll fight in camp." There the husband stabbed the young man in the side and his guts spilled out. He did this when some men had grabbed the young man but not him. He then gave him a spear and said, "Here [offering his chest] kill me and we'll die together." But everyone called out, "Not in the guts," so the dying man stabbed [the husband] in the shoulder. Then he died. (pp. 254–255)

Burbank coded the 793 aggressive episodes into categories and examined sex differences in the frequency within each category. Men overwhelmingly resorted to more dangerous aggression than women did. Of the ninety-three episodes in which a dangerous weapon was used, in twelve a gun was fired, in sixty-four a spear was thrown, and in fourteen a knife was used, all by men. In contrast, there were only two cases in which a woman used a knife and one in which a woman used a spear. In all, ninety of the aggressive episodes in which a dangerous weapon was used were committed by men and only three by women. Men, in sum, accounted for 97 percent of the aggressive episodes in which a dangerous weapon was used.

***The Young Male Syndrome.*** The evolutionary logic of same-sex aggression predicts that men will be more willing than women to engage in risky and violent tactics. Not all men, however, engage in such tactics, and this within-sex variation must also be explained. In particular, young men appear to be the most prone to engaging in risky forms of aggression—aggression that puts them at risk of injury and death. Wilson and Daly (1985) call this the "young male syndrome."

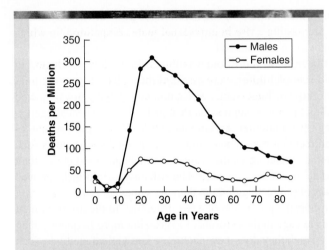

FIGURE *10.1* **Homicide Victimization Rates by Age and Sex for the United States in 1975.** The figure shows evidence for the young male syndrome, in which young men entering the mating arena show the greatest degree of risk taking and violent strategies. Data from U.S. Department of Health, Education, and Welfare (1979) and U.S. Census Bureau (1977).

*Source:* Wilson, M., & Daly, M. (1985). Competitiveness, risk-taking, and violence: The young male syndrome. *Ethology and Sociobiology, 6,* 59–73. Copyright © 1985, with permission from Elsevier Science.

An empirical illustration of the young male syndrome is shown in Figure 10.1, which gives homicide rates by age and sex of the victim for a large sample drawn from the United States in 1975 (results for other years show the same shape and distribution). Through age ten, males and females do not differ in the likelihood of becoming homicide victims. At adolescence, however, killings of males start to skyrocket, reaching a peak when they are in their mid-twenties. At that age, men are six times more likely than women to become the victims of homicide. From the mid-twenties on, men's victimization rates start to drop sharply, suggesting that men then begin to avoid physically risky tactics.

Why would young men, at the peak of their physical prowess and at the age at which death from disease is the lowest, be the most prone to place their lives at risk by engaging in violence? Daly and Wilson offer an explanation based on an evolutionary analysis of mate competition in an ancestral environment with some degree of polygyny: "Young men are both especially formidable and especially risk-prone because they constitute the demographic class upon which there was the most intense selection for confrontational competitive capabilities among our ancestors" (Daly & Wilson, 1994, p. 277). Specifically, they argue that over the course of human evolutionary history, a young man seeking a wife had to display formidable physical prowess in hunting, tribal raids, tribal defense, and the ability to defend his interests. These displays were designed to impress not only women but also other men, to deter rival men from hindering the man in his quests.

This argument, by itself, can be applied to many mammals. What makes humans unique is the importance of cultivating a *reputation*, which can have a long-lasting effect. Competitive success or failure early in life might have been a strong determinant of reputation, which could affect a man's lifetime survival and reproductive success. Demonstrations of bravery in the face of danger, for example, might have had reputational consequences that lasted a lifetime. The finding that displays of violence by young men are almost invariably performed in the presence of an audience suggests that they are designed not merely to vanquish a rival, which, after all, could be done in the dead of night or on a lonely bend in the path. The presence of an audience suggests that risky displays are also designed to impress peers and cultivate a formidable social reputation. Studies on the motives for murder attest to the importance of status and reputation. A study in Japan, for example, revealed that motives involving face, reputation, and status figured heavily in 70 percent of all murders in the 1950s and 61 percent of all murders in the 1990s, overshadowing all other motives for murder (Hiraiwa-Hasegawa, 2005).

The reputation explanation also accounts for why we bestow prestige and status on those who take risks and succeed in spite of the risks (Zahavi & Zahavi, 1996). If past success in these dangerous ventures predicts future success, and if past failure likewise predicts future failure, then it is important for people to track the outcomes of these risky ventures—information that is encoded and passed on to others in the form of one's reputation.

The young male syndrome explanation also accounts for fascinating findings from a large-scale study of episodes of violent conflicts from collective aggression (e.g., riots, gang fights) that result in death (Mesquida & Wiener, 1996). Across a variety of states and countries, they discovered that the higher the percentage of males in the age group of fifteen to twenty-nine, relative to the percentage of males thirty-years-old or older, the higher the levels of coalitional aggression. This link is so strong that the proportion of young males in a population might be the best predictor of violent aggression.

In sum, the evolutionary explanation of the "young male syndrome" can account for a host of empirical findings, including variations in collective aggression, the sudden surge in muscle strength in males from puberty through the mid-twenties, the surge in aerobic capacity in adolescence and the mid-twenties, and especially the surge in measures of quick energetic bursts that might be needed for risky forms of aggression (Daly & Wilson, 1994). All of these changes appear to be linked with the emergence of a physically risky competitive strategy.

## Contexts Triggering Men's Aggression against Men

Homicide represents the most extreme form of aggression, and homicide statistics worldwide reveal that the majority of killers are men, as are the majority of victims. Several causal contexts surround male–male homicides.

***Marital and Employment Status.*** First, killers and victims often share similar characteristics, such as being unemployed and, perhaps relatedly, unmarried. In a study of Detroit homicides in 1982, for example, although only 11 percent of the adult men in Detroit were unemployed that year, 43 percent of the victims and 41 percent of the perpetrators were unemployed (Wilson & Daly, 1985). The same study revealed that 73 percent of the male perpetrators and 69 percent of the male victims were unmarried, contrasted with only 43 percent of the same-age men in the Detroit area. Thus, lacking resources and being unable to attract a long-term mate appear to be social contexts linked with male–male homicides.

***Status and Reputation.*** One of the key motives of male–male homicide is the defense of status, reputation, and honor in the local peer group. Here is what one man said about his early gang fights: "The one giving out the most stitches got the reputation. It also made others think twice before coming near you" (Boyle, 1977, p. 67). Naively, these are often classified as "trivial altercations" in the police records. A typical case is the barroom verbal altercation that escalates out of control. The combatants, sometimes unable to back down and fearing humiliation in the eyes of their peers, break a bottle, pull a knife, or open fire. The seemingly trivial nature of the arguments sometimes puzzles police. A Dallas homicide detective noted, "Murders result from little ol' arguments over nothing at all. Tempers flare. A fight starts, and someone gets stabbed or shot. I've worked on cases where the principals had been arguing over a 10 cent record on a juke box, or over a one dollar gambling debt from a dice game" (Mulvihill, Tumin, & Curtis, 1969, p. 230).

The link between status and aggression has also been documented in laboratory experiments (Griskevicius et al., 2009). Participants were first primed with status cues. They were asked to imagine themselves graduating from college and having to compete with two other individuals for a prestigious job that comes with a luxurious corner office. After the prime, participants imagined that one of their competitors carelessly spilled a drink on them and did not apologize. Then they were asked about the likelihood that they would insult, hit, push, or get "in the face" of the rival—all measures of direct aggression. Men, but not women, reacted with greater direct aggression after their motive for status was activated.

Humans evolved in small-group living in which status and reputation were vital to a man's access to reproductively relevant resources, and particularly mating opportunities. Even in the modern environment, there is solid evidence that men who are victimized by aggression from other males during middle school and high school, which typically results in a loss of status, have significantly fewer sex partners by the time they reach college (Gallup et al., 2009). As evolutionary psychologist Frank McAndrew sums up the evidence, "the most common chain of events leading to physical aggression by human males begins with a public challenge to a man's status through direct competition with another male. . . . These threats to status provoke a biological response marked by heightened levels of testosterone, which facilitate an aggressive response if that is what is called for, or at least permitted, by the situation" (McAndrew, 2009, p.333).

One final indicator of the links between aggression and status comes from a study of two tribes in the Ecuadorian Amazon by evolutionary anthropologist John Patton (1997, 2000). Patton took photographs of every man in each of the tribes. Forty-seven informants were used, twenty-six from the Achuar coalition and twenty-one from the Quichua coalition. Each informant ranked each of thirty-three men in terms of status. In a separate task, informants judged the "warriorship" of each man: "If there was a war today, which of these men would be the best warrior?" (Patton, 1997, pp. 12–13). Warriorship scores were calculated by summing across the informants. The results are shown in Figure 10.2. Status and warriorship are highly correlated. For the Quichua men, status and warriorship are correlated at $+.90$. For the Achuar men, they are correlated at $+.77$. In short, ferocity as a warrior appears to be closely linked with one's social status within the group.

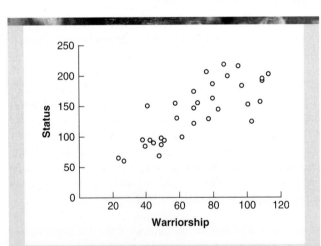

FIGURE 10.2 **Status by Warriorship.** The figure shows that men who are judged to be the best warriors are largely the same men who enjoy the highest social status.

*Source:* Patton, J. Q. (1997, June 4–8). *Are warriors altruistic? Reciprocal altruism and war in the Ecuadorian Amazon.* Paper presented at the Human Behavior and Evolution Society Meetings, University of Arizona, Tucson. Reprinted with permission.

***Sexual Jealousy and Intrasexual Rivalry.*** Sexual jealousy is another key context triggering same-sex aggression and homicide. It is predominantly men who do the killing and other men who are the victims. A summary of eight studies of same-sex killings involving "love triangles" documented that 92 percent were male–male homicides and only 8 percent were female–female homicides (Daly & Wilson, 1988, p. 185).

Rivalry and competition over women can trigger nonlethal aggression as well. In a study of mate guarding (tactics used to keep a mate and fend off rivals), for example, men more than women picked a fight with the rivals who showed interest in their mates and threatened to hit rivals who were making moves on their mates (Buss, 1988c). Thus, male aggression against rivals is manifest in a very specific context—dealing with the adaptive problem of mate retention.

## Contexts Triggering Women's Aggression against Women

If aggression is defined as inflicting costs on someone else, women's aggression can be quite potent. Evolutionary psychologist Joyce Benenson notes that a "females must compete . . . not only to initiate a long-term bond with a high status male . . . but also to maintain her mate's loyalty. She must fend off competitors for her mate's resources and protection" (Benenson, 2009, p. 269). Females tend to use *social exclusion* (*ostracism*) as a primary strategy of getting rid of their female competitors (Benenson et al., 2008). They often accomplish social ostracism through verbal aggression.

In a study of derogation of competitors, women engaged in as much verbal aggression against their rivals as did men (Buss & Dedden, 1990). The *content* of the derogation, however, was different. Women exceeded men in derogating their rivals on the basis of physical appearance and sexual promiscuity, for example. They were more likely than men to call their competitors fat and ugly, mention that the rival's thighs were heavy, make fun of the size and shape of their rival's body, and call their rival physically unattractive. Interestingly, these appearance derogations actually influence men's evaluations of the victim's physical attractiveness, and are especially effective when they are made by an attractive woman (Fisher & Cox, 2009).

In the domain of sexual conduct, women were more likely than men to say that their rivals slept around a lot, had many past boyfriends, were sexually promiscuous, and would sleep with practically anyone (Buss & Dedden, 1990). Furthermore, this derogation tactic was context dependent. When the man sought a short-term mate, derogating a competitor by implying promiscuity was not at all effective, presumably because men are relatively indifferent to this quality in a short-term mate and might even value it because it signals an increased likelihood of sexual intercourse (Schmitt & Buss, 1996). When the man sought a long-term mate, in contrast, derogating a rival on the promiscuity dimension was extremely effective, presumably because men seeking long-term mates place a premium on sexual fidelity (Buss & Schmitt, 1993).

Other studies of female aggression against females have confirmed that the functions of female aggression are primarily to inflict costs in intrasexual rivals. In a study of high school girls, for example, female aggression was found to stem from motives such as jealous rivalries, competition over boys, and the desire to be included among the "desirable" group of other women (Owens, Shute, & Slee, 2000; see also Campbell, 2002, for an extended discussion of female–female competition).

In sum, women derogate other women as often as men derogate other men in the context of competition for mates. In addition, women seem to be aware of what men desire in both short-term and long-term mating contexts, and shift their derogation tactics accordingly.

## Contexts Triggering Men's Aggression against Women

Much of men's nonsexual violence against women is directed at spouses, mates, or girlfriends, and sexual jealousy appears to be the major cause. In one study of Baltimore spousal homicides, twenty-five of thirty-six were attributed to jealousy, and the wives were victims in twenty-four of these cases (Guttmacher, 1955). In a study of battered women at safe houses or shelters, two-thirds reported that their husbands were extremely jealous (Gayford, 1975). In another study, fifty-seven of sixty battered women reported extreme jealousy and possessiveness on the part of their husbands (Hilberman & Munson, 1978). In the majority of one hundred cases of spousal violence that were investigated, the husbands reported frustration over their inability to control their wives, accusations of infidelity being the most common complaint (Whitehurst, 1971).

Sexual jealousy is also a key context for spousal homicide and apparently the most common cause across cultures (Daly & Wilson, 1988). Men who kill their wives or girlfriends typically do so under one of two key conditions: the observation or suspicion of a sexual infidelity or when the woman is terminating the relationship. The first represents cuckoldry, which places a man at risk of investing his limited resources in an offspring to whom he is not genetically related. The second represents the loss of a reproductively valuable woman to a rival—also a direct loss in the currency of fitness.

One characteristic of female victims glaringly stands out: their age. Young wives and girlfriends are far more likely to be killed than older ones (Daly & Wilson, 1988; Shackelford, Buss, & Weeks-Shackelford, 2003). Because youth is a powerful cue to a woman's reproductive value, it follows that male sexual jealousy would be especially targeted toward young mates. It is also likely that younger women are more often the objects of desire by other men, so male sexual jealousy might be triggered by the presence of rivals attempting to attract these women.

To test the hypothesis that men use violence against their mates as a means of controlling their sexuality, one study looked at 8,385 women, of whom 277 had been assaulted by their husbands over the past year (Wilson, Johnson, & Daly, 1995). Two forms of violence were assessed: "nonserious" and "serious." The assessment of nonserious violence included questions such as these: "Has your husband/partner ever threatened to hit you with his fist or anything else that could hurt you?" "Has he ever thrown anything at you that could hurt you?" "Has he ever pushed, grabbed, or shoved you?" "Has he ever slapped you?" "Has he ever kicked, bit, or hit you with his fist?" The items assessing serious violence included "Has he ever beaten you up?" "Has he ever choked you?" "Has he ever threatened to use or has he ever used a gun or knife on you?"

At a different point in the interview, the women were asked about the jealousy and controlling behaviors of their husbands with the following items: "He is jealous and doesn't want you to talk to other men"; "He tries to limit your contact with your family or friends"; "He insists on knowing who you are with and where you are at all times"; "He calls you names to put you down or make you feel bad"; "He prevents you from knowing about or having access to the family income, even if you ask."

The "autonomy-limiting" items were positively linked with violence perpetrated by husbands against their wives. In general, men who commit violence against their wives also display an inordinate amount of jealousy and controlling behavior. Even among a sample of individuals who were diagnosed as having "pathological jealousy," men were more likely than women to use extreme physical violence against their partners (Easton & Shackelford, 2009). These findings and many others lend support to the hypothesis that violence by men is used as a strategy for controlling their mates, with the goal of preventing sexual access to other men or a defection from the relationship (Kaighobadi, Shackelford, & Goetz, 2009).

## Contexts Triggering Women's Aggression against Men

It might seem that women rarely inflict violent aggression against men. In reports of spousal abuse, such as slapping, spitting, hitting, and calling nasty names, however, the percentages of male and female victims often are roughly the same (e.g., Buss, 1989b; Dobash et al., 1992).

*Defense against Attack.* Extreme aggression such as spousal homicide is less frequently perpetrated by women, but it does occur. The contexts are almost always linked with one of two factors: the woman is defending herself against a husband who is enraged over a real or suspected infidelity and after a prolonged history of physical abuse, when the woman sees no way out of the coercive grip of her husband (Daly & Wilson, 1988; Dobash et al., 1992). Male sexual jealousy, in short, appears to be at the root of women killing their husbands, as well as at the root of the more common case of men killing their wives.

## Warfare

Human recorded history, including hundreds of ethnographies of tribal cultures around the globe, reveals male coalitional warfare to be pervasive across cultures worldwide (e.g., Chagnon, 1988; Keeley, 1996; Tooby & Cosmides, 1988). Warfare is an activity pursued exclusively by men. The intended victims are most often other men, although women frequently suffer as well. Although few wars are initiated solely with the stated intent of capturing women, gaining more copulations is almost always viewed as a desired benefit of successfully vanquishing an enemy. Box 10.2 provides a description of one specific war.

*The Evolutionary Psychology of War.* In a brilliant analysis of the logic of warfare, Tooby and Cosmides (2010) drew attention to a fact that is often overlooked: War is an intensely *cooperative* venture. It could not occur without the formation of cooperative alliances among men on either side. The men must come together and function as a cooperative unit.

*Among the more than 4,000 species of mammals, only two have been observed to form coalitions that kill conspecifics: chimpanzees and humans. Human warfare is nearly exclusively a male activity. Theoretical analyses suggest that there can be profound adaptive benefits to engaging in warfare that, under certain circumstances, can outweigh the risk of dying.*

BOX 10.2

# Yanomamö Warfare

Evolutionary anthropologist Napoleon Chagnon offered a vivid description of one specific war conducted by one Yanomamö tribe against another. The conflict started with Damowa, a head man of the Monou-teri, one of the Yanomamö villages. Damowa had a habit of seducing other men's wives—an activity that led to frequent club fights within the village. When a neighboring tribe, the Patanowa-teri, raided the Monou-teri, they succeeded in capturing five women. Damowa expressed anger and convinced his tribe to declare war on the Patanowa-teri.

During the first raid, the Monou-teri surprised one of their enemies, a man named Bosibrei, who was climbing a rasha tree to get fruit. He made a fine target silhouetted against the blue sky. Damowa and his coalition sent a round of arrows at Bosibrei, killing him instantly and immediately retreated, returning home.

Aggression often provokes retaliatory aggression, and the Patanowa-teri set their sights on vengeance. They managed to catch Damowa while he was outside his garden searching for honey. He had two wives with him. Five arrows hit their mark in Damowa's stomach. Still alive, he cursed his enemies and managed to shoot one of his arrows. But a final arrow struck Damowa's neck, killing him. This time the raiders did not try to abduct more women, because they feared Damowa's comrades. So they retreated to safety, as Damowa's wives ran back to camp to alert the others. The killers escaped, and the Monou-teri themselves fled into the cover of the jungle.

With their leader dead, the Monou-teri were demoralized. But soon a new leader, Kaobawa, stepped forward and stirred the tribe into seeking revenge for Damowa's death. Failure to retaliate can lead to reputational damage: The defeated group will be perceived by others as easily exploitable, so the Monou-teri felt that they had to take action to prevent further raids.

The night before the raid, Kaobawa stirred the men into an emotional frenzy. He began to sing "I am meat hungry! I am meat hungry!" (Chagnon, 1983, p. 182). The other raiders echoed this phrase

and concluded in a high-pitched scream that sent chills down Chagnon's spine. The screaming became more and more enraged as the raiding party worked itself into a frenzy of vengeance.

At dawn the next morning, the women presented the raiders with a large cache of plantains as food for their raid. The men covered their faces and bodies in black paint. The mothers and sisters of the warriors offered parting advice, such as "Don't get yourself shot up" and "You be careful now!" (Chagnon, 1983, p. 183). The women then wept, fearful for the safety of their men.

After they had been gone for five hours, one of the raiders reappeared at the camp, complaining that a sore foot prevented him from keeping up with the others. He had enjoyed the pomp and ceremony of the previous evening, which impressed the women. But he, like many of the Yanomamö who go into battle, was deeply afraid.

The trek to reach their enemies was long and took several days. At night, the raiding party built fires to keep warm, but on the last night, this luxury had to be eliminated for fear of alerting the enemy to their presence. On the evening before the raid, several more men developed sore feet and belly aches and turned to go back to their home camp. The remaining warriors finalized their plan of attack. They decided to break into smaller groups, each consisting of four to six men. This grouping allowed them to retreat under protection: Two men from each group would lie in wait to ambush potential pursuers.

Among the raiding party was the twelve-year-old son of Damowa, who had been brought along for the chance to avenge his father's death. This was his first raid, so the older men kept him in the middle of the group to minimize his exposure to danger.

Meanwhile, back at the home camp of the Monou-teri, the women grew nervous. Unprotected women risk being kidnapped by neighboring tribes, and even allies cannot always be trusted.

The raiding party managed to shoot and kill one enemy before fleeing. They extracted their vengeance but were themselves now in great danger.

The Patanowa-teri gave chase, managing to get ahead of the Monou-teri as they retreated and ambushed them. One Monou-teri was wounded by a bamboo-tipped arrow that pierced his chest. The next morning, the Monou-teri raiding party arrived home carrying their injured comrade. Although seriously injured, he survived to go on a future raid.

When Napoleon Chagnon returned to the Yanomamö a year later, the war among the Monou-teri and Patanowa-teri was still going strong, with repeated cycles of raids and counterraids. The Monou-teri had managed to kill two Patanowa-teri and capture two of their women, and the Patanowa-teri had managed to kill one Monou-teri. At this brief juncture, then, the Monou-teri were ahead, as it were. The Patanowa-teri will not stop their raids until they have avenged the deaths of their comrades and the losses of their women. And when they do, the Monou-teri will be forced to retaliate in kind.

Yanomamö warfare highlights several key themes in the evolution of human aggression: Warfare is primarily a male activity; sexual access to women is often a central resource that flows to the victors of wars; retaliation and revenge are critical to maintaining credible reputations; and men and women are often genuinely afraid of the deadly consequences of violent tribal combat.

---

The evolution of warfare has to overcome another major obstacle: The benefits, in fitness currencies, have to be sufficiently high to overcome the devastating risks of injury and death to those who participate. War is an extremely costly venture for everyone involved. As Tooby and Cosmides noted, "It is difficult to see why any sane organism, selected to survive and genetically propagate, should seek so actively to create conditions of such remarkable personal cost and danger" (1988, p. 2). So how could evolution select for psychological mechanisms that predispose men to incur such risks? How can we account for the fact that throughout recorded human history, wars have been initiated with regularity and warriors have been prized and glorified by the members of their groups?

The evolutionary theory proposed by Tooby and Cosmides (1988) has four essential conditions that must be met for warfare adaptations to evolve.

1. *The average long-term gain in reproductive resources must be sufficiently large to outweigh the reproductive costs of engaging in warfare over evolutionary time.* What reproductive resource could be sufficiently large? An increase in sexual access to females is the most likely candidate—the resource that imposes the greatest limit on male reproduction. Women's obligatory investment in offspring makes them a valuable yet limited resource for men. This asymmetry between the sexes means that women have little to gain by going to war for increased access to men. Sperm are cheap, and there has never been a lack of men who are willing to contribute them in the quantities women need for successful fertilization. In sum, men have a great deal to gain by warfare if it results in a substantial increase in sexual access to women.

2. *Members of coalitions must believe that their group will emerge victorious.* This means not merely the belief that one's coalition will win the battle, but also the belief that the collective resources of one's coalition will be greater after the aggressive encounter than before it.

3. *The risk that each member takes and the importance of each member's contribution to the success must translate into a corresponding share of the benefits.* This is a form of the cheater-detection criterion for the evolution of cooperation that we discussed in Chapter 9. Men who do not take risks by fighting must be excluded from sharing the spoils of victory.

Men who take more risks—as leaders sometimes do when they take their men into battle—get a proportionately larger share of the spoils of war. Similarly, men whose contribution to the success of the battle is larger get a proportionately larger share.

4. *Men who go into battle must be cloaked in a "veil of ignorance" about who will live or die.* If you know that death is certain before you go into battle, you have nothing to gain by doing so. Selection would operate strongly against any psychological propensity to go into battle when death is certain. Indeed, the "battlefield panic" that causes some men to defect might reflect the operation of a psychological mechanism that propels a man out of harm's way when the likelihood of death approaches certainty. If the risk is shared with others, however, and no one knows who will survive and who will die, then selection can favor a psychological propensity to engage in coalitional warfare.

These conditions, which Tooby and Cosmides (1988) call "the risk contract of war," yield some surprising predictions. The most important pertains to the effects of some degree of mortality on evolutionary selection pressures for psychological mechanisms designed to lead men to war. Recall that natural selection operates on genes for particular design features based on their *average* reproductive consequences over evolutionary time.

Let's apply this logic to warfare. Suppose ten men form a coalition to raid a neighboring tribe. During the raid, five fertile women are captured. If all of the men survive, then the average gain in sexual access is .50 of a fertile woman per man (five women divided by ten men equals .50 average per man). Now suppose five of the men die in the battle and the same five fertile women are captured. Now the gain for each of the five surviving men is a gain in sexual access of 1.0 fertile woman (five women divided by five men equals 1.0). The *average* gain across all the men who went into battle, however, has remained unchanged at .50 (five women divided by the ten men who went into battle still equals .50). In other words, the average reproductive gain of the *decision* to go into battle is identical across the two conditions, even though in one case no men died and in the other five men died. This means that the *average* reproductive gain has not changed one bit as a consequence of half the men dying. In sum, because it operates on average reproductive effects across individuals over evolutionary time, selection can favor psychological mechanisms that lead men into war, even if those mechanisms expose men to some risk of death.

This evolutionary theory of warfare leads to some specific predictions: (1) Men, but not women, will have evolved psychological mechanisms designed for coalitional warfare; (2) sexual access to women will be the primary benefit that men gain from joining male coalitions; (3) men should have evolved psychological mechanisms that lead them to panic and defect from coalitions when death appears to be an imminent result of remaining; (4) men should be more likely to go to war when their odds of success appear high, such as when the number of men in their coalition greatly exceeds the number of men in the opposing coalition; (5) men should have evolved psychological mechanisms designed to enforce the risk contract—that is, to detect and punish cheaters, defectors, and traitors; and (6) men should have evolved psychological mechanisms designed to detect, prefer, and enlist men in the coalition who are willing and able to contribute to its success. Several lines of evidence examined in the following sections support these predictions.

***Men Engage in Warfare.*** The fact that men form coalitions for the purpose of killing men in other coalitions is observed across cultures (Alexander, 1979; Chagnon, 1988; Otterbein, 1979;

*Men have engaged in warfare for all of human recorded history, as revealed in writings, paintings, sculptures, and cave art.*

Wrangham & Peterson, 1996). In some cultures, such as the Yanomamö, tribes appear to be constantly at war. In no culture have women ever been observed forming coalitions designed to kill other human beings. These facts might seem obvious and were certainly widely known prior to the Tooby and Cosmides (1988) theory of the evolution of war. But they remain consistent with this theory and call into question alternative theories such as that war is an arbitrary social construction (van der Dennen, 1995).

***Men Are More Likely to Spontaneously Assess Their Fighting Ability.*** If men recurrently engaged in violent aggression more than women over the course of human evolutionary history, one would expect that men have evolved distinct psychological mechanisms that lead them to evaluate the conditions in which it is wise to war. One such mechanism is the self-assessment of one's fighting ability relative to other men. Evolutionary psychologist Adam Fox (1997) predicted that men have evolved mechanisms for assessing fighting ability—specifically that men will assess fighting ability more frequently than women.

To test these predictions, Fox asked a sample of college students to report how often they imagined the probable outcomes of fights involving themselves and others. The results are shown in Figure 10.3. The sex differences are dramatic. The majority of men reported imagining the probable outcomes of such fights at least once a month, the most common response being once a week. The majority of women, in contrast, reported only occasionally imagining the outcomes of fights. The most common response of women was "never." These findings support the prediction

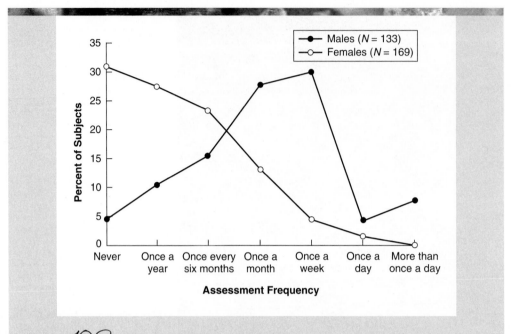

FIGURE *10.3* **Assessment of Fighting Ability.** The figure shows that men tend to spontaneously assess their own fighting ability more than women do, suggesting a possible psychological adaptation to warfare.

*Source:* Fox, A. (1997). The assessment of fighting ability in humans. Paper presented to the Ninth Annual Meeting of the Human Behavior and Evolution Society. Reprinted with permission.

that men assess their own fighting ability more often than women—a possible evolved psychological mechanism designed to gauge whether it is worthwhile to enter into combat.

There is also evidence that men have adaptations to assess the fighting ability and aggressive inclinations of other men (Sell et al., 2009, 2010). Assessment of men's upper body strength is particularly important. Studies by Aaron Sell and his colleagues show that people can accurately assess a man's strength (measured objectively through measures of weight lifting) from photos of a man's body. Even more interesting is that people can accurately estimate a man's upper-body strength from photos of just his face, with no bodily cues available! People are much less accurate at assessing women's strength. And the correlation between a man's upper body strength and judgments of his fighting ability is a whopping +.97. Accurate assessment of a man's fighting ability, compared to one's own fighting ability, provides critical information to men about decisions to engage in, or to avoid, an aggressive confrontation. These assessments are likely to have been important to ancestral men for both within-group confrontations as well as between-group confrontations that constitute war.

***Men Have Adaptations That Facilitate Success in War.*** There are many known sex differences that appear to reflect adaptations in men designed for combat (Puts, 2010). Men exceed women in upper body strength: The average man is nearly twice as strong as women in chest, shoulder, and arm strength. Men show superiority in throwing distance and throwing accuracy, which would facilitate combat involving rocks or spears. They show superiority in navigating through strange territories (see Chapter 3). Men have a strong tendency to form same-sex coalitions that explicitly exclude women. Indeed, on the night before a war raid, men often banish women from the group to minimize whatever sexual conflicts might exist among the male coalition. And one of the strongest fears of men going into combat is that they will act cowardly, thus shaming themselves in the eyes of their comrades in arms (Brown, 1991). On the flip side, men appear to experience great excitement, glory, and sense of brotherhood at the prospect of war, a phenomenon that has frequently been reported by warriors (Brown, 1991) and is also reflected in literature, such as the following prebattle speech from Shakespeare's *Henry V:*

> We few, we happy few, we band of brothers;
> For he to-day that sheds his blood with me
> Shall be my brother; be he ne'er so vile,
> This day shall gentle his condition:
> And gentlemen of England now a-bed,
> Shall think themselves accurs'd they were not here;
> And hold their manhoods cheap whiles any speaks
> That fought with us upon Saint Crispin's day.

(from Shakespeare, *Henry V,* Act IV, Scene 3)

Many other findings are consistent with the hypothesis that men have evolved adaptations that facilitate success in warfare. These include: (1) bioarchaeological evidence of mass graves from tens of thousands of years ago that contain mostly male skeletons with arrow tips and blunt force trauma, which implies a deep evolutionary history of warfare (Walker, 2001); (2) the high male mortality rate due to warfare and homicide in traditional cultures during precontact periods, which implies strong selection pressure (e.g., 36% among the Hiwi; Hill, Hurtado, & Walker, 2007); (3) laboratory studies of simulated war games find that men are substantially more likely than women to attack another country, even without provocation (Johnson et al., 2006); (4) men are more likely than women to form strong ingroup/outgroup distinctions, and to derogate outgroup members as being animalistic, diseased, or subhuman, which presumably lowers inhibitions to kill them (Van Vugt, 2009); (5) men are more likely than women to hold outgroup stereotypes, especially under conditions of threat from outgroups (Schaller, Park, & Faulkner, 2003); (6) men's groups are more rigidly hierarchical than women's groups, which may aid in responding to urgent intergroup threats that require coordinated strategies to counteract (Van Vugt, 2006); (7) men, compared to women, show a particularly strong bias against outgroups, especially toward male outgroup members (Navarrete et al., 2009, 2010); and (8) laboratory studies in which people are threatened by an outgroup member show that men, but not women, subsequently show more prejudice and discrimination toward the other group (Yuki & Yokota, 2009). Male minds, in short, seem to be designed with psychological propensities that may have facilitated success at warfare over human evolutionary history.

***Sexual Access as a Recurrent Resource That Flows to Victors.*** Two evolutionary psychologists, Craig Palmer and Christopher Tilley, tested the proposition that sexual access to women is the primary motivation for males to join gangs (Palmer & Tilley, 1995). A gang may be defined as a "self-formed association of peers, bound together by mutual interests, with identifiable leadership, well-developed lines of authority . . . who act in concert to achieve a specific purpose or purposes" (Miller, 1980, p. 121). Gang warfare is common across America, especially in large cities such as Los Angeles, and death is a common outcome. Why do males join gangs in which they risk death?

As one gang member explained, "The gang seemed to control the things I wanted. I was kind of a dork when I was in elementary school. I was really into my studies, and I didn't get involved in any stuff that the gang was doing. But then I began to see that they had the girls" (Padilla, 1992, p. 68).

Palmer and Tilley (1995) tested the prediction with empirical data, not merely individual testimonials and anecdotal evidence. They studied fifty-seven reported gang members in Colorado Springs, Colorado, and compared them with sixty-three same-age males from the same community who were not affiliated with gangs. Data on the number of sex partners during the previous thirty-day period were collected. The results: Gang members reported a significantly greater number of sex partners during the past month (average, 1.67 partners) than did nongang members for the same time period (average, 1.22). The two subjects in the study with the largest numbers of sex partners were both gang leaders, who reported eleven and ten partners within the previous ninety days. Not a single nongang member in the study reported having more than five sex partners during that same three-month interval.

Palmer and Tilley (1995) note that data from a random sample of the population found that 55 percent of men of comparable ages had only one or fewer sex partners during the previous year, and only 14 percent reported more than four sex partners during that time (Laumann et al., 1994). Some gang members have more sex partners during a single month than the average man has over the course of an entire year.

Additional empirical evidence for an increased number of sex partners among coalitional leaders comes from Chagnon's (1988) study of the Yanomamö. Among the Yanomamö, the most frequently cited explanation for going to war with another tribe is revenge for a previous killing, and the most common account of the initial cause of the fighting was "women." The Yanomamö make a social distinction between *unokais* (those who have killed) and *non-unokais* (those who have not killed). This distinction is critical to a man's reputation, and it is widely known throughout each village who are the *unokais*. The victims of the *unokai* men are primarily other men killed during raids against one of their enemies, although some of the killings took place within the group because of sexual jealousy. The number of living *unokais* in the population at the time of the study was 137. Most *unokais* have killed only once, but the few who have killed many times (the local record was sixteen killings) develop a special reputation for being *waiteri*, or fierce.

When the *unokais* were compared with the *non-unokais* of the same age, one statistical difference stood out: The *unokais* had more wives. At ages as young as twenty to twenty-four years, the *unokais* averaged 0.80 wives, almost four times as many as the *non-unokais*, who averaged only 0.13 wives. From the sample of men over the age of forty-one, the *unokais* averaged 2.09 wives and the *non-unokais* only 1.17 wives. Anecdotal evidence suggests that *unokais* also have more extramarital affairs (Chagnon, 1983). In sum, if having killed is viewed as a reasonable proxy for having participated and contributed importantly to coalitional warfare, this evidence supports the hypothesis that sexual access to women is an important reproductive resource gained through coalitional aggression.

***What Qualities Do Men and Women Seek in Coalitional Allies?*** Three researchers explored this question by asking sixty men and fifty-three women to evaluate how desirable 148 potential characteristics were in a coalition member. A coalition was defined as "a group of people with whom you identify because you pursue common goals" (DeKay, Buss, & Stone, unpublished manuscript, p. 13). Each characteristic was rated on a scale ranging from −4 (extremely undesirable in a coalition member) to +4 (extremely desirable in a coalition member).

Both men and women rated the following characteristics as highly desirable in a coalition member: being hardworking, being intelligent, being kind, being open-minded, being able to motivate people, having a wide range of knowledge, having a good sense of humor, and being considered dependable. There were notable sex differences, however, that point to the distinct functions of men's coalitions. Men more than women found the following characteristics desirable: being brave in the face of danger (2.40 vs. 1.66, men vs. women), being physically strong (1.07 vs. 0.43), being a good fighter (1.30 vs. 0.42), being able to protect others from physical harm (1.37 vs. 0.89), being able to tolerate physical pain (0.75 vs. 0.36), being able to defend oneself against physical attack (1.90 vs. 1.43), and being physically able to dominate others (0.35 vs. −0.42). Similarly, men evaluated the following qualities in a coalition member as more undesirable than did women: being poor at athletic activities (−0.68 vs. −0.23) and being physically weak (−1.08 vs. −0.55).

This is merely one study using a restricted sample of U.S. undergraduates, so no grand conclusions can be drawn. Certainly, it would be useful to replicate this study in different cultures. Nonetheless, it is interesting to note that even in the modern context of U.S. universities, seemingly so distant from the tribal warfare of human ancestral past, men seem to select coalition members in part on the basis of qualities that will help the coalition succeed in group-on-group aggression and defense.

***Summary of Warfare.*** The theory of warfare developed by Tooby and Cosmides (1988, 2010) points to an often overlooked conclusion: that warfare requires elaborate cooperation among members of one group to coordinate their aggressive actions against another group. The theory also proposes that sexual access to women would have been the key reproductive resource that selected for men to evolve a psychology of warfare. The theory leads to some surprising predictions—for example, that as long as there exists a "veil of ignorance" about who will be killed, the mortality rate will not affect the average reproductive benefits of a strategy of entering battle.

A variety of sources of empirical evidence support some of the key predictions of this theory of warfare. First, men have recurrently engaged in warfare over recorded human history, whereas there is not a single documented case of women forming same-sex coalitions to go to war. Second, men spontaneously assess their fighting ability more than women do, suggesting the existence of evolved mechanisms to evaluate the propitiousness of entering an aggressive confrontation. Third, studies of gangs and ethnographic evidence on warfare both suggest that warfare leads to increased sexual access to women. Finally, men prefer coalition members who are brave in the face of danger, are physically strong, have good fighting ability, and have the ability to protect others—qualities that make for a good comrade in battle. Although more research is needed, the available empirical evidence supports the theory that men have evolved specific psychological mechanisms for warfare.

## Do Humans Have Evolved Homicide Mechanisms?

More than 18,000 homicides are committed in the United States each year, according to FBI crime statistics (Kenrick & Sheets, 1993). Of these, more than 80 percent are committed by men (Daly & Wilson, 1988). Mainstream social scientists often explain the sex differences in homicide rates in the United States by invoking "culture-specific gender norms" (e.g., Goldstein, 1986). This theory encounters an empirical problem: The sex difference is found in *every culture* across the globe for which homicide statistics are available (Buss, 2005; Daly & Wilson, 1988). Theories that invoke local cultural norms cannot satisfactorily explain a universal human pattern.

Actual homicides are statistically rare and thus difficult to study. For every homicide that is actually committed, however, there may be dozens or hundreds of thoughts or fantasies that individuals entertain about killing. Consider this homicidal fantasy reported by a male undergraduate: "I wanted to kill my old girlfriend. She lives in (another city) and I was just wondering if I could get away with it. I thought about the (price of) airfare and how I might set up an alibi. I also thought about how I would kill her in order to make it look like a robbery. I actually thought about it for about a week and never did come up with anything" (Kenrick & Sheets, 1993, p. 15). This man did not kill his girlfriend. But the recurrence of thoughts about homicide opens up a window for investigation into the psychology of homicide.

Evolutionary psychologists Doug Kenrick and Virgil Sheets have capitalized on this opportunity, conducting two studies on a total of 760 undergraduates. Their methods were simple: They asked subjects to provide demographic information, including their age and sex, and then describe the last time they had thoughts about killing someone. They inquired about the circumstances that triggered the violent thoughts as well as the content of those thoughts: "who you wanted to kill, how you imagined doing it, etc." (Kenrick & Sheets, 1993, p. 6). They queried subjects about the frequency of fantasies, the specific relationship with the person they thought of killing, and whether the fantasy had been triggered by a physical attack, a public humiliation, or any on a list of other provocations.

First, more men (79 percent) than women (58 percent) reported experiencing at least one homicidal fantasy (see Figure 10.4). Second, 38 percent of the men, but only 18 percent of the women, reported having had several homicidal fantasies. Third, men's fantasies tended to last longer than women's fantasies. Most women (61 percent) reported that their homicidal thoughts typically lasted only a few seconds. Most men reported that their homicidal thoughts lasted a few minutes, with 18 percent reporting that their fantasies lasted a few hours or longer. These

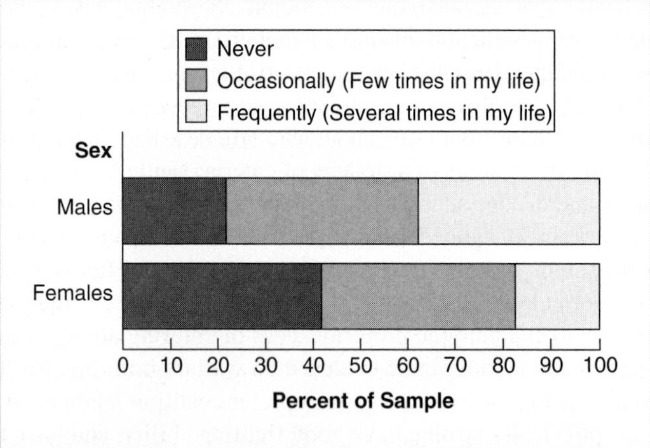

FIGURE 10.4 **The Frequency of Homicidal Fantasies.** The figure shows that a larger percentage of men than women engage in homicidal fantasies and that men also tend to have more frequent homicidal fantasies than do women.

*Source:* Kenrick, D. T., & Sheets, B. (1993). Homicidal fantasies. *Ethology and Sociobiology, 14,* 231–246. Copyright © 1993, with permission from Elsevier Science.

findings support the hypothesis that men are psychologically more disposed to homicide than women—a finding that is also supported by the actual homicide statistics.

Sex differences were also apparent in the triggers of homicidal thoughts. Men were more likely than women to have homicidal thoughts in response to a personal threat (71 percent versus 52 percent), the fact that someone stole something from them (57 percent versus 42 percent), a desire to know what it is like to kill (32 percent versus 8 percent), a conflict over money (27 percent versus 10 percent), and public humiliation (59 percent versus 45 percent).

Inclusive fitness theory predicts greater conflicts between children and their stepparents than between children and their genetic parents, and the homicidal fantasy evidence bears this out. Of those who lived with a stepparent, fully 44 percent reported fantasies about killing them. Among those who lived for longer than six years with a stepparent, 59 percent reported such homicidal fantasies. In contrast, the figures for killing a mother or a father were lower: 31 percent and 25 percent, respectively.

How can these findings be explained from an evolutionary perspective? There are two distinct possibilities. The one adopted by Kenrick and Sheets (1993) and by Daly and Wilson (1988) may be called the "slip-up hypothesis." According to this hypothesis, males have evolved a psychological propensity for violence as a means of coercive control and eliminating sources of conflict. This propensity typically results in threats of violence or sublethal violence as a behavioral output. Occasionally, however, there is a "slip," such that the violence accidentally bubbles over into a homicide: "There is brinkmanship in any such contest, and the homicides by spouses of either sex may be considered slips in this dangerous game" (Daly & Wilson, 1988). The same slip-ups may occur in other forms of homicide, such as male–male homicide.

An alternative is "homicide adaptation theory" (Buss, 2005b; Duntley, 2005a, 2005b; Duntley & Buss, 2005). According to this theory, humans have evolved specific psychological mechanisms that predispose them to kill others under certain predictable circumstances such as warfare, intrasexual rivalry, or spousal infidelity or defection. Humans have homicidal fantasies as one component of these evolved homicide mechanisms that allow a person to build and work through the homicidal scenario in his or her mind, evaluate the costs and benefits of various courses of action, and then choose to kill when the benefits outweigh the costs. In most circumstances, the costs are too great: In all societies, the person risks the wrath of kin and punishment from other interested members of the group (Daly & Wilson, 1988). These costs are weighted and deter many from killing. The proposal is *not* that men have a "killer instinct" whereby they are impelled to kill regardless of circumstances. Rather, it is that acts of killing are one part of the behavioral output of evolved homicide adaptations whose activation is triggered by particular forms of input, followed by evaluation of costs and benefits.

According to homicide adaptation theory, a number of homicide adaptations have evolved as context-sensitive solutions to an array of adaptive problems. These include protecting oneself and kin from injury or death, gaining access to scarce resources needed to survive and reproduce, eliminating rivals, removing key competitors of one's own children, and depriving rivals of access to valuable mates (Buss, 2005b; Duntley, 2005a; Duntley & Buss, 2005). Because getting killed inflicts dramatic costs on victims, however, selection has fashioned coevolved antihomicide defenses that function to prevent getting killed and to inflict costs on those who attempt to kill. The coevolution of homicide adaptations and antihomicide defenses results in offenses, defenses, tactics to counter the defenses, and tactics to counter the counters to the defenses, producing a perpetual coevolutionary arms race.

Many lines of evidence support the plausibility of homicide adaptation theory. First, the comparative evidence strongly suggests adaptations exist for killing conspecifics in many species, including chimpanzees, our closest primate relative (Wrangham, 2004). Second, the paleontological evidence—ancient bones and stones—reveals a history of human homicide going back tens of thousands of years (Larsen, 1997). Third, the cross-cultural evidence reveals that intrasexual rivalry homicides, infanticides, and warfare are universal phenomena, even in cultures previously believed to be peaceful such as the !Kung San of Africa (Ghiglieri, 1999; Keeley, 1996). Fourth, the archeological record reveals weapons such as maces, lances, tomahawks, and swords; ancient art depicting murders; and defensive structures such as moats filled with water lined with spikes on the bottom, fortresses, palisades, and other structures designed to ward off homicidal attackers. Fifth, the murder of genetic relatives is extremely rare, as predicted by inclusive fitness theory, except when those genetic relatives interfere with more successful avenues for achieving reproductive success (McCullough, Heath, & Fields, 2006). And sixth, psychological evidence reveals specialized cognitive and emotional circuits that seem well designed for killing in particular circumstances (Duntley, 2005b).

Consider as one example the circumstances that trigger homicidal thoughts, the possible targets of killing, and sex differences in how close people say they have come to killing (see Figure 10.5). Intrasexual rivals compose the largest category of homicidal ideation. Among intrasexual rivals, the most powerful triggers for men occur when a rival has sex with their mate, humiliates them in public, beats them up, or steals their money—costs that inflict some of the most severe adaptive problems on men. And men indicate a far greater likelihood than do women of coming close to killing in these circumstances, indicating a

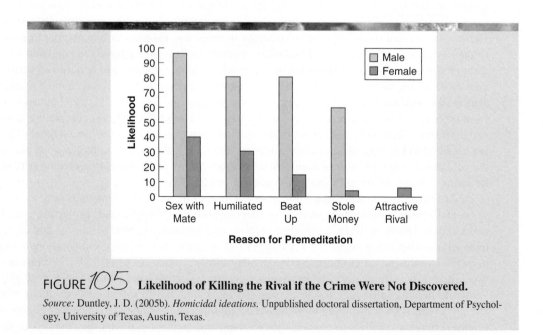

FIGURE *10.5* **Likelihood of Killing the Rival if the Crime Were Not Discovered.**

*Source:* Duntley, J. D. (2005b). *Homicidal ideations.* Unpublished doctoral dissertation, Department of Psychology, University of Texas, Austin, Texas.

close correspondence between psychological design for murder and the circumstances in which men actually do murder.

These competing evolutionary hypotheses—the slip-up hypothesis and homicide adaptation theory—have not yet been pitted against each other directly in empirical tests. The high prevalence of homicidal fantasies, the predictability of the circumstances that trigger them, the evidence of sex differences, the large fitness consequences of killing and being killed, the high prevalence of homicide in traditional hunter-gatherer societies, and the premeditated quality of many homicides, however, do not accord well with the slip-up hypothesis. Within the next decade, we can expect a resolution to the scientific debate about whether humans have evolved specific homicide adaptations.

## ■ SUMMARY

From the perspective of evolutionary psychology, aggression is not a singular or a unitary phenomenon. Rather, it represents a collection of strategies that are manifested under highly specific contextual conditions. The mechanisms underlying aggression have emerged, in this view, as solutions, albeit sometimes repugnant ones, to distinct adaptive problems such as resource procurement, intrasexual competition, hierarchy negotiation, and mate retention.

From this perspective, variability in aggression—between the sexes, among individuals, over the life span, and across cultures—is predicted. It illustrates the point that variability does not imply that biology is irrelevant. An evolutionary psychological perspective is truly interactionist: It specifies a set of causal conditions in which particular features of the perpetrator, victim, social context, and adaptive problem are likely to evoke aggression as a strategic solution.

An evolutionary perspective suggests at least six classes of benefits that would have accrued to ancestors who used an aggressive strategy: co-opting the resources of others, defending oneself and one's kin against attack, inflicting costs on intrasexual rivals, negotiating status and power hierarchies, deterring rivals from future aggression, and deterring long-term mates from infidelity or defection.

Sound evolutionary arguments predict that aggression is likely to emerge more strongly among men, with both aggressors and victims being men. Given a mating system of some degree of polygyny, sexual selection will favor risky tactics among men both to gain sexual access to more women and to avoid being excluded from mating entirely. Empirically, most physical aggression is perpetrated by men and most of the victims are men. This evidence includes same-sex homicides across cultures, the frequency of bullying in school, and ethnographic evidence of physical violence from Australian aboriginal communities.

Many contexts are linked with aggression occurring within each sex-of-perpetrator by sex-of-victim combination. Contexts triggering men's aggression against other men include being unemployed and unmarried—contexts that suggest that men are on a path to being excluded from mating, which may trigger a risky aggressive strategy. Men also aggress against other men when their status and reputation are threatened and when they observe or suspect a rival of sexually "poaching" on their mate.

Women aggress against other women primarily in the context of intrasexual competition. Women, however, are far less likely to use physical aggression, preferring instead to derogate their competitors verbally or to socially ostracize them. Two prominent derogation tactics are calling their rivals promiscuous and impugning their rival's physical appearance—both of which attain their effectiveness because they violate men's desires in a long-term mate.

Men aggress against women mainly to control their sexuality. Sexual jealousy is a key context triggering men's aggression against their mates. Presumably such aggression historically functioned to deter a mate from further infidelity or from defecting from the relationship entirely. Younger women who are higher in reproductive value are more vulnerable to aggression from their partners because ancestral men had a greater incentive to maintain exclusive sexual access to them.

Women kill men rarely, but when they do, it is typically in self-defense. The context usually involves a woman defending herself against a mate who is enraged about a real or suspected infidelity.

Warfare, defined as aggression by a cooperative coalition against another cooperative coalition, is extraordinarily rare in the animal world. Only two mammalian species have been observed to engage in coalitional aggression: chimpanzees and humans. An evolutionary perspective leads to the prediction that warfare will be practiced primarily by men, with the primary reproductive benefit being increased sexual access to women. Empirical evidence supports this theory: Men have engaged in warfare throughout human recorded history; sexual access to women appears to be a recurrent benefit that flows to victors of warfare; men more than women spontaneously assess their fighting ability relative to others; and men more than women value coalition members who are strong, are brave in the face of danger, and have good fighting abilities. And men display other phenomena that suggest evolved warfare adaptations, such as unusually high mortality rates in traditional precontact cultures; a greater proclivity to attack other countries in simulated war games; and a greater tendency to display strong ingroup/ outgroup distinctions and to derogate outgroup members as being subhuman. Although more research is needed, the available evidence supports the evolutionary theory of warfare and suggests specific psychological mechanisms designed to wage war.

The final section of the chapter considered two contrasting hypotheses designed to explain the evolution of the killing of other human beings. The first hypothesis suggests that killings are "slip-ups" or by-products that result from the use of violence and the threat of violence as a means of coercively controlling others. The second hypothesis suggests that humans, especially men, have evolved specific homicide adaptations that are designed to motivate killing other humans under specific circumstances when the benefits outweigh the costs. The high prevalence of homicidal fantasies, the predictability of the circumstances that trigger them, the evidence of gender differences, and the premeditated quality of many homicides all seem to support the homicide adaptation theory, although further research is needed to compare predictions from the two theories directly.

## ■ SUGGESTED READINGS

Buss, D. M. (2005). *The murderer next door: Why the mind is designed to kill*. New York: Penguin.

Campbell, A. (1999). Staying alive: Evolution, culture, and women's intrasexual aggression. *Behavioral and Brain Sciences, 22*, 203–252.

Chagnon, N. (1988). Life histories, blood revenge, and warfare in a tribal population. *Science, 239*, 985–992.

Daly, M., & Wilson, M. (1994). Evolutionary psychology of male violence. In J. Archer (Ed.), *Male violence* (pp. 253–288). London, UK: Routledge.

Duntley, J. D., & Shackelford, T. K. (Eds.). (2008). *Evolutionary forensic psychology.* New York: Oxford University Press.

Hill, K., Hurtado, K., & Walker, R. S. (2007). High adult mortality among Hiwi hunter-gatherers: Implications for human evolution. *Journal of Human Evolution, 52,* 443–454.

Johnson, D. D. P., McDermott, R., Barrett, E. S., Crowden, J., Wrangham, R., Mcintyre, M. H., & Rosen, S. P. (2006). Overconfidence in war games: Experimental evidence on expectations, aggression, gender, and testosterone. *Proceedings of the Royal Society B, 273,* 2513–2520.

Navarrete, C. D., Olsson, A., Ho, A. K., Mendes, W. B., Thomsen, L., & Sidanius, J. (2009). Fear extinction to an out-group face. *Psychological Science, 20,* 155–158.

Sell, A., Tooby, J., & Cosmides, L. (2009). Formidability and the logic of human anger. *Proceedings of the National Academy of Science, 106,* 15073–15078.

Van Vugt, M. (2009). Sex differences in intergroup aggression and violence: The male warrior hypothesis. *Annals of the New York Academy of Sciences, 1167,* 124–134.

Walker, P. L. (2001). A bioarchaeological perspective on the history of violence. *Annual Review of Anthropology, 30,* 573–596.

# CHAPTER 11

# CONFLICT BETWEEN THE SEXES

*There will always be a battle between the sexes because men and women want different things. Men want women and women want men.*

—George Burns

*In every age the battle of the sexes is largely a battle over sex.*

—Donald Symons, 1979

$\mathcal{M}$en and women need each other for successful reproduction. Cooperation between the sexes, therefore, is a cardinal feature of human mating. Men and women fall in love, mutually choose each other, mutually consent to have sex, and have a shared interest in their children, the shared "vehicles" of their cooperative mating venture. Despite the necessity for cooperation, conflict between the sexes pervades group living.

*Sexual conflict* may be defined as "a conflict between the evolutionary interests of individuals of the two sexes" (Parker, 2006, p. 235). "Evolutionary interests" boil down to "genetic interests." So whenever the genetic interests of a male and a female diverge, sexual conflict can ensue. A few examples help to illustrate the concept of sexual conflict: (1) Vladimir wants to have sex at the end of the first date, whereas his date, Mashenka, prefers to wait (conflict about sexual access); (2) Silvio gets Maria drunk and forces her to have sex while she is incapacitated (male rape that conflicts with female choice); (3) Yolanda deceives Cesar about the number of previous sexual partners she has had (deception about a critical cue to future fidelity); (4) Sue wants to go to a party without her husband Marc to check out whether there might be a better mate for her, whereas Marc wants to keep Sue at home to prevent her from interacting with other men (conflict between freedom of mate choice and mate guarding). In each of these cases, there is sexual conflict—a conflict between the genetic interests of the individual man and the individual woman.

This chapter explores some of the major forms of sexual conflict—conflicts over the occurrence and timing of sex, sexual aggression and defenses against sexual aggression, jealous conflicts that arise from potential "mate poachers" and signals of infidelity, mate guarding that limits a partner's mating behavior by circumventing full freedom of mate choice, and conflict over access to resources. The most poignant forms of sexual conflict center on mating conflict. As Helena Cronin observed, "Conflicts over mate choice have led males into advertising and deception, stealth and force—and females into counter-adaptations ranging from lie-detectors to anti-clamping devices" (Cronin, 2005, p. 18). We explore some of the major forms of sexual conflict within the context of strategic interference theory.

## ■ STRATEGIC INTERFERENCE THEORY

*H*uman conflict is a universal feature of social interaction, and it occurs in many forms. In Chapter 10, we examined same-sex conflict, including derogation of competitors, physical violence, and warfare. These conflicts are predictable from evolutionary accounts. Members of the same sex are often in competition with each other for precisely the same resources: members of the opposite sex and the resources needed to attract them.

Evolutionary psychologists have predicted conflict between the sexes, but not because men and women are in competition for the same reproductive resources. Rather, many sources of conflict between the sexes can be traced to evolved differences in sexual strategies. As we saw in Chapters 4, 5, and 6, both sexes have evolved short-term and long-term mating strategies. But the nature of these strategies differs for the sexes. One of the most important differences pertains to short-term mating strategies. Men, far more than women, have evolved a deeper desire for sexual variety. This desire manifests itself in many forms, including seeking sexual access sooner, more persistently, and more aggressively than women typically desire. Conversely, women have evolved to be more discriminating in short-term mating, typically delaying sexual intercourse beyond what men usually desire. Clearly, the sexes cannot simultaneously fulfill these conflicting sexual desires. This is an example of a phenomenon called *strategic interference.*

Strategic interference occurs when a person employs a particular strategy to achieve a goal and another person blocks the successful enactment of that strategy. If a woman delays sexual intercourse until she feels some emotional involvement or commitment from a man, for example, and the man persists in his sexual advances even after the woman has indicated her desire to wait, then the result is interference with the woman's sexual strategy. At the same time, however, the delays imposed by the woman interfere with the man's short-term mating strategy of seeking sex sooner. In sum, men and women come into conflict not because they are competing for the same resources, as occurs in same-sex strategic interference, but rather because the strategy of one sex can interfere with the strategy of the other.

The theory of strategic interference applies not just to conflicts about the timing of sexual intercourse. Conflict can pervade all relations between the sexes, from contact in the workplace and on the dating scene to skirmishes that occur over the course of a marriage. Sexual harassment is a form of strategic interference in the workplace. Deception on the dating scene is another form of strategic interference. A man who deceives a woman about his marital status and a woman who deceives a man about her age both violate the desires of the opposite sex and so represent forms of strategic interference. Within a marriage, sexual infidelity represents another form of strategic interference because it violates the desires of the spouse. Coercive control, threats, violence, insults, and attempts to lower a partner's self-esteem constitute other forms of strategic interference. The key point is that strategic interference—blocking the strategies and violating the desires of someone else—is predicted to pervade interactions between the sexes.

The second component of strategic interference theory postulates that the "negative" emotions such as anger, distress, and upset are psychological solutions that have evolved in part to solve the adaptive problems posed by strategic interference (Buss, 1989b). There are quotation marks around *negative* because although these emotions are generally painful to experience, they are hypothesized to be functional in solving the adaptive problems of strategic interference. First, they point out problematic events, focusing our attention on them and momentarily screening out less relevant events. Attention, after all, is a scarce resource, and must be allocated judiciously. When a person experiences anger or distress, these emotions guide his or her attention to the sources of the distress. Second, the emotions mark those events for storage in memory and easy retrieval from memory. Third, emotions lead to action, causing people to strive to eliminate the source of strategic interference or future interference.

In summary, the theory of strategic interference has two main postulates. First, strategic interference is predicted to occur whenever members of one sex violate the desires of members of the opposite sex; historically, such interference would have prevented our forebears from successfully carrying out a preferred sexual strategy and hence would have reduced their reproductive success. Second, "negative" emotions such as anger, rage, and distress represent evolved solutions to the problems of strategic interference, alerting people to the sources of interference and prompting action designed to counteract it.

We must note two important qualifiers. First, conflict per se serves no adaptive purpose. It is generally not adaptive for individuals to get into conflict with the opposite sex as an end in and of itself. Rather, conflict is more often an undesirable by-product of the fact that the sexual strategies of men and women differ in profound ways.

A second qualification is that the metaphor of the "battle between the sexes" can be misleading. The phrase implies that men as a group are united in their interests and women are likewise united in their interests and that the two groups are somehow at war with each other. Nothing could be further from the truth. An evolutionary perspective helps us to understand why. Men cannot be united with all other men as a group for the fundamental reason that men are in competition primarily with members of their own sex. The same is true for women. Therefore, a unification or a "confluence of interests" cannot occur between all members of one sex. Of course, men and women can form specific alliances with particular members of their own sex, but this in no way contradicts the fundamental principle that individuals are primarily in competition with members of their own gender.

## ■ CONFLICT ABOUT THE OCCURRENCE AND TIMING OF SEX

Disagreements about the occurrence and timing of sex might be the most common sources of conflict between men and women. In a study of 121 college students who kept daily diaries of their dating activities for four weeks, 47 percent reported one or more disagreements about their desired level of sexual intimacy (Byers & Lewis, 1988). These disagreements always show a predictable sex difference. In one study of Australian undergraduate students, for example, 53 percent of the women in the study reported that at least one man had "overestimated the level of sexual intimacy . . . desired," whereas 45 percent of the men reported that at least one woman had "underestimated the level of sexual intimacy . . . desired" (Paton & Mannison, 1995, p. 447).

Men sometimes seek sexual access with a minimum of investment. Men often guard their resources and are extraordinarily choosy about whom they invest those resources in. They are "resource coy" and often preserve their investment for long-term mates. Because women often pursue a long-term sexual strategy, they often seek to obtain investment, or signals of investment, before consenting to sex. Yet the investment that women covet is precisely the investment that men most vigorously guard. The sexual access that men seek is precisely the resource that women are so selective about giving.

## Conflict over Sexual Access

*Inferences about Sexual Intent.* A major source of conflict is that men sometimes infer sexual interest on the part of a woman when it does not exist. A series of experiments have documented this phenomenon (Abbey, 1982; Lindgren, George, & Shoda, 2007). In one study, 98 male and 102 female college students viewed a ten-minute videotape of a conversation in which a female student visits a male professor's office to ask for more time to complete a term paper. The actors in the film were a female drama student and a professor in the theater department. Neither the student nor the professor acted flirtatious or overtly sexual, although both were instructed to behave in a friendly manner. People who witnessed the tape then rated the likely intentions of the woman using a seven-point scale. Women watching the interaction were more likely to say that she was trying to be friendly, with an average rating of 6.45, and not sexy (2.00) or seductive (1.89). Men, also perceiving friendliness (6.09), were significantly more likely than women to infer seductive (3.38) and sexual intentions (3.84). A speed-dating laboratory procedure had men rate women's sexual interest in them after a brief interaction, and compared those ratings to women's self-reported sexual interest in each of the men (Perilloux et al., 2010). Again, men exhibited a sexual misperception bias, perceiving women as significantly more interested in them than women actually were. Men interpret simple friendliness and mere smiling by women as indicating more sexual interest than do women viewing exactly the same events.

Thus far, there has been only one cross-cultural test of this sex difference in perceptions of sexual intent. A sample of 196 Brazilian college students, 98 men and 98 women, evaluated four hypothetical scenarios presented in Portuguese (DeSouza et al., 1992). A parallel sample of 204 American college students evaluated the scenarios in English. In each scenario, a man and a woman spent time together at a party. The scenarios differed in whether the participants had been drinking alcohol and in whether the woman agreed to go back to the man's dorm room with him. After viewing each scenario, participants rated four questions on a seven-point scale, assessing the degree to which each character had communicated either a willingness to have sex or an expectation of having sex.

The results are shown in Figure 11.1. Brazilian college students consistently perceived more sexuality in the characters' behavior than did the American college students, with mean scores of 18.77 and 14.27, respectively. Gender differences were also highly significant, as shown in Figure 11.1. Men across both cultures perceived more sexual intent in the characters' actions than did women, with mean scores of 17.53 and 15.50, respectively.

When in doubt, men infer sexual interest. Men act on their inferences, occasionally opening up sexual opportunities. If over evolutionary history even a tiny fraction of these inferences led to

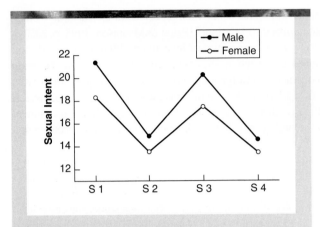

FIGURE 11.1  **Average Judgments of Sexual Intent in Brazil and the United States.** The figure shows that men tend to infer more sexual intent than women in response to the same scenario.

*Source:* DeSouza, E. R., Pierce, T., Zanelli, J. C., & Hutz, C. (1992). Perceived sexual intent in the United States and Brazil as a function of nature of encounter, subjects' nationality, and gender. *Journal of Sex Research, 29,* 251–260. Reprinted with permission.

sex, men would have evolved lower thresholds for inferring women's sexual interest. This male mechanism is susceptible to manipulation. Women sometimes use their sexuality as one such tactic. In one study of 200 university students, significantly more women than men reported using smiling and flirting as a means for eliciting special treatment from members of the opposite sex, even though they had no interest in having sex with those men (Buss, 2003).

An interesting real-world demonstration of the sexual overperception bias occurred when a supermarket chain implemented a "superior customer service" program—store employees were instructed to smile at customers and make eye contact with them. The program backfired when a number of female employees filed sexual harassment charges against the supermarket. Apparently, their friendly actions caused some of the male customers to interpret their behavior as signaling sexual interest, leading to sexual comments, overt sexual come-ons, and even stalking (Browne, 2006).

The fact that men are likely to perceive that women are interested in them sexually when they really aren't, combined with women's intentional exploitation of this psychological mechanism, creates a potentially volatile mix. The differing sexual strategies of men and women lead to conflicts over desired levels of sexual intimacy, over men's feelings that women lead them on, and over women's feelings that men are too pushy about having sex.

***Deception about Commitment.***  Another manifestation of conflict over sexual access comes from research on deception between the sexes. Men report intentionally deceiving women about emotional commitment. When 112 college men were asked whether they had ever exaggerated the depth of their feelings for a woman to have sex with her, 71 percent admitted to having done so, compared with only 39 percent of the women (Buss, 1994b; Haselton et al., 2005). In a study in which women reported on their actual experiences of deception at the hands of men, they reported the following forms of deception (percentage of women reporting them is in parentheses): "falsely implied that he had stronger feelings for me than he really had" (44%); "exaggerated how sincere, trustworthy, or kind he was" (42%); "led me to believe that we were more compatible than we really were" (36%); "led me to believe that he had stronger feelings for me in order to have sex with me" (25%) (Haselton et al., 2005).

In human courtship, the costs of being deceived about a potential mate's resources and commitment are shouldered more heavily by women. An ancestral man who made a poor choice of a sex partner risked losing only a small portion of his time, energy, and resources, although he might also have evoked the rage of a jealous husband or a protective father. An ancestral woman who made a poor choice of a casual mate, allowing herself to be deceived about the man's long-term intentions or willingness to devote resources to her, however, risked untimely pregnancy and unaided childrearing.

Because the deceived can suffer severe losses, there must have been tremendous selection pressure for the evolution of psychological vigilance to detect cues to deception and to prevent its occurrence. The modern generation is merely experiencing another cycle in the endless spiral of an evolutionary arms race between deception perpetrated by one sex and detection accomplished by the other. As the deceptive tactics grow more subtle and refined, the ability to penetrate deception becomes more acute.

Women have evolved strategies to guard against deception. When a woman seeks a committed relationship, the first line of defense is imposing courtship costs by requiring extended time, energy, and commitment before consenting to sex. More time buys the advantage of more assessment. It allows a woman greater opportunity to evaluate a man, to assess how committed he is to her, and to detect whether he is burdened by prior commitments to other women and children.

To guard against deception, women spend hours discussing with their friends the details of interactions they have had with mates or potential mates. Conversations are recounted and scrutinized. When asked whether they talk with their friends to try to figure out the real intentions of someone they have gone out with, most women admit that they do. Men, in contrast, are significantly less inclined to devote effort to this problem of assessment (Buss, 2003). Women who are not in a committed relationship are especially good at detecting men who are attempting to "fake good" (Johnson et al., 2004).

### *Cognitive Biases in Sexual Mind Reading.*

Humans live in an uncertain mating world. We must make inferences about others' intentions and emotional states. How attracted is he to her? How committed is she to him? Does that smile signal sexual interest or mere friendliness? Some psychological states, such as smoldering passions for other people, are intentionally concealed, rendering uncertainty greater and inferences more tortuous. We are forced to make inferences about intentions and concealed deeds using a collage of cues that are only probabilistically related to the deeds' occurrence. An unexplained scent on one's romantic partner, for example, could signal sexual betrayal or an innocuous aroma acquired from a casual conversation.

In reading the minds of others, there are two ways to go wrong. You can infer a psychological state that is not there, such as assuming sexual interest when it is absent. Or you can fail to infer a psychological state that is there, such as remaining oblivious to another's true romantic yearnings. According to *error management theory*, it would be exceedingly unlikely that the cost–benefit consequences of the two types of errors would be identical across their many occurrences (Haselton, 2003; Haselton & Buss, 2000, 2003; Haselton & Nettle, 2006). We intuitively understand this in the context of smoke alarms, which are typically set to be hypersensitive to any hint of smoke. The costs of occasional false alarms are minor compared to the catastrophic costs of failing to detect a real house fire. Error management theory extends this logic to cost–benefit consequences in evolutionary fitness.

According to error management theory, asymmetries in the cost–benefit consequences of mind-reading inferences, if they recur over evolutionary time, create selection pressures that produce predictable cognitive biases. Just as smoke alarms are "biased" to produce more false positives than false negatives, error management theory predicts that evolved mind-reading mechanisms will be biased to produce more of one type of inferential error than another. Two mind-reading biases have been explored in mating. The first is the sexual overperception bias, whereby men possess mind-reading biases designed to minimize the costs of missed sexual opportunities. Error management theory provides a cogent explanation for the finding that men appear to falsely infer that a woman is sexually interested in him when she merely smiles, touches his arm, or happens to stop at the local bar for a drink. Interestingly, men who view themselves as especially high in mate value are especially prone to experience the sexual overperception bias (Haselton, 2003). Men who are dispositionally inclined to pursue a short-term mating strategy also exhibit a more pronounced sexual overperception bias—a bias that would facilitate the success of a short-term mating strategy by minimizing lost opportunities (Lenton et al., 2007; Perilloux et al., 2010).

The second is the *commitment skepticism bias* in women (Haselton & Buss, 2000). According to this hypothesis, women have evolved an inferential bias designed to underestimate men's actual level of romantic commitment to her early in courtship. This bias functions to minimize the costs of being sexually deceived by men who feign commitment to pursue a strategy of casual sex. If men give flowers or gifts to women, for example, the recipients tend to *underestimate* the extent to which these offerings signal commitment in comparison with "objective" outside observers. Of course, there are good reasons for women's commitment skepticism. Men who are motivated to seek casual sex frequently attempt to deceive women about their commitment, social status, and even fondness for children (Haselton et al., 2005)—domains of deception about which women are well aware (Keenan et al., 1997).

Error management theory offers a fresh perspective on human mating problems by suggesting that certain types of errors reflect functional adaptations rather than actual flaws in the psychological machinery. It provides new insights into why men and women get into certain types of conflict—for example, men's sexual overperception bias leading to unwanted sexual come-ons. Knowledge of these biases and the evolutionary logic by which they came about might help men and women to read each others' mating minds more accurately.

**Sexual Withholding.**   Men consistently complain about women's sexual withholding, defined by such acts as being sexually teasing, saying no to intercourse, and leading a man on and then stopping him. On a seven-point scale, men judged sexual withholding to be 5.03, whereas women judged it 4.29 (Buss, 1989b). Both sexes are bothered by sexual withholding, men significantly more than women.

For women, sexual withholding fulfills several possible functions. One is to preserve their ability to choose men of high quality who are willing to commit emotionally and invest materially. Women withhold sex from certain men and selectively allocate it to others of their own choosing. Moreover, by withholding sex, women increase its value. They render it a scarce resource. Scarcity increases the price that men are willing to pay for it. If the only way men can gain sexual access is by heavy investment, then they will make that investment. Under conditions of sexual scarcity, men who fail to invest fail to secure copulations. This creates another conflict between a man and a woman: Her withholding interferes with his strategy of gaining sexual access sooner and with fewer emotional strings attached.

Another function of sexual withholding is to manipulate men's perception of a woman's value as a mate. Because highly desirable women are more sexually inaccessible to the average man by definition, women sometimes exploit men's perceptions of their desirability by withholding sexual access (Buss, 2003). A final possible function of sexual withholding, at least initially, is to encourage a man to evaluate a woman as a permanent rather than a temporary mate.

Granting sexual access early and often causes men to see a woman as a casual mate. They may perceive her as too promiscuous and too sexually available, characteristics that men avoid in committed mates.

# ■ SEXUAL AGGRESSION AND EVOLVED DEFENSES AGAINST SEXUAL AGGRESSION

This section examines sexual aggression by men and women's evolved defenses designed to prevent it. We begin with sexual harassment. Then we explore the controversy around whether men have evolved rape adaptations. Finally, we explore hypotheses and evidence for the hypothesis that women have evolved antirape adaptations.

## Sexual Harassment

Disagreements over sexual access occur not just in the context of dating and marital relationships, but also in the workplace, where people commonly seek casual and long-term mates. Sexual harassment is defined as "unwanted and unsolicited sexual attention from other individuals in the workplace" (Terpstra & Cook, 1985). Sexual harassment can range from mild forms, such as unwanted staring and sexual comments, to physical violations, such as the touching of breasts, buttocks, or crotch. Sexual harassment produces obvious conflict between the sexes and is the result of differences between men's and women's evolved psychologies (Browne, 2002, 2010).

Sexual harassment is typically motivated by the possibility that a come-on might lead to a short-term sexual encounter, although this does not exclude the possibility that it is sometimes motivated by the desire to exercise power or to seek lasting romantic relationships. The view that sexual harassment is a product of the evolved sexual strategies of men and women is supported by the profiles of typical victims, including such elements as gender, age, marital status, and physical attractiveness; their reactions to unwanted sexual advances; and the conditions under which they were harassed.

Victims of sexual harassment are typically women. In one study of complaints filed with the Illinois Department of Human Rights over a two-year period, women filed seventy-six complaints, whereas men filed only five. Another study of 10,644 federal government employees found that 42 percent of the women, but only 15 percent of the men, had experienced sexual harassment at some point (Gutek, 1985). Of the sexual harassment complaints filed in one Canadian province, ninety-three cases were filed by women and only two by men. Women are generally the victims of sexual harassment and men are generally the perpetrators. Nonetheless, given the tendency of women to *experience* greater distress to acts of sexual pushiness or aggressiveness, it is likely that women would be more upset than men by the same acts of sexual harassment (Buss, 2003; Colarelli & Haaland, 2002; Rotundo, Nguyen, & Sackett, 2001).

Although any woman may be the target of sexual harassment, the victims are disproportionately concentrated among young, physically attractive, and single women. Women over age forty-five are far less likely than younger women to experience sexual harassment (Studd & Gattiker, 1991). One study found that women between the ages of twenty and thirty-five filed 72 percent of the complaints of harassment, although they represented only 43 percent of the labor force at the time. Women over age forty-five, who represented 28 percent of the work force, filed only 5 percent of the complaints.

Reactions to sexual harassment follow the logic predicted by evolutionary psychology. When men and women were asked how they would feel if a coworker of the opposite sex asked them to have sex, 63 percent of the women said they would be insulted, whereas a minority, 17 percent of the women, said they would feel flattered. Men's reactions were just the opposite: Only 15 percent said they would be insulted, whereas 67 percent said they would feel flattered. These results support strategic interference theory.

The degree of distress that women experience after sexual advances, however, depends in part on the status of the harasser. In one study, 109 college women rated how upset they would be if a man they did not know, whose occupational status varied from low to high, persisted in asking them out on a date despite their repeated refusals (Buss, 2003). On a seven-point scale, women would be most upset by persistent advances from construction workers (4.04), garbage collectors (4.32), cleaning men (4.19), and gas station attendants (4.13) and least upset by persistent advances by premedical students (2.65), graduate students (2.80), or successful rock stars (2.71). Status and power, however, interact: Women find acts of harassment most harassing from a low-status man who has power over them (Colarelli & Haaland, 2002). The emotions in the sexually harassed that signal strategic interference on the part of the harasser apparently are sensitive to his low status.

## Sexual Aggressiveness

Sexual aggressiveness is one strategy men use to minimize the costs they incur for sexual access, although this strategy carries costs in the form of retaliation and damage to reputation. Acts of sexual aggression are exemplified by the man's demanding or forcing sexual intimacy, failing to get mutual agreement for sex, and touching a woman's body without her permission. In one study, college women were asked to evaluate 147 potentially upsetting actions that men could do to them on a scale ranging from 1 (not at all upsetting) to 7 (extremely upsetting) (Buss, 1989b). Women rated sexual aggression on average to be 6.5. No other kinds of acts that men could perform, including verbal abuse and nonsexual physical abuse, were judged by women to be as upsetting as sexual aggression—a finding independently verified in a study of Dutch individuals (ter Laak, Olthof, & Aleva, 2003). Contrary to the view held by some men, women do not want forced sex.

Men, in sharp contrast, seem considerably less bothered if a woman is sexually aggressive; they see it as relatively innocuous compared with other sources of discomfort. On the same seven-point scale, for example, men judged the group of sexually aggressive acts to be 3.02, or only slightly upsetting, when performed by a woman. A few men spontaneously wrote in the margins of the questionnaire that they would find such acts sexually arousing if a woman were to perform them. Other sources of distress, such as a mate's infidelity and verbal or physical abuse, were far more upsetting to the men—6.04 and 5.55, respectively—than sexual aggression by a woman.

One disturbing difference between men and women is that men consistently underestimate how unacceptable sexual aggression is to women. When asked to judge its negative impact on women, men rate it only 5.8 on a seven-point scale, which is significantly lower than women's own rating of 6.5. This is an alarming source of conflict between the sexes, as it implies that some men will be inclined to use sexually aggressive acts because they fail to appreciate how distressing that is to women.

## Do Men Have Evolved Rape Adaptations?

*Rape* may be defined as the use of force or the threat of force to obtain sexual intercourse. One of the most controversial issues in evolutionary psychology is whether men have evolved specialized adaptations to rape under certain circumstances or whether rape is a by-product of other evolved mechanisms. Among scorpionflies, there is evidence that males have a special anatomical clamp that functions solely in the context of raping a female (Thornhill, 1980). It is not used in other mating contexts, during which the male presents a nuptial gift as an inducement for the female to copulate. There is also evidence for specialized rape strategy in orangutans, although this might be the exception among primates, since bonobos and common chimpanzees appear to lack a distinctive rape strategy (Maggioncalda & Sapolsky, 2002). The *rape-as-adaptation theory* proposes that selection has favored ancestral males who raped in certain circumstances. Proponents of this theory advance the hypothesis that at least six specialized adaptations might have evolved in the male mind (Thornhill & Palmer, 2000):

- Assessment of the vulnerability of potential rape victims (e.g., during warfare or in non-warfare contexts in which a woman lacks the protection of husband or kin);
- A context-sensitive "switch" that motivates rape in men who lack sexual access to consenting partners (e.g., "loser" males who cannot obtain mates through regular channels of courtship);
- A preference for *fertile* rape victims;
- An increase in sperm counts of rape ejaculates compared with those occurring in consensual sex;
- Sexual arousal to the use of force or to female resistance to consensual sex;
- Marital rape in circumstances in which sperm competition might exist (e.g., when there is evidence or suspicion of female infidelity).

In contrast, the *by-product theory of rape* proposes that rape is a nondesigned and nonselected-for by-product of other evolved mechanisms, such as the male desire for sexual variety, a desire for sex without investment, a psychological sensitivity to sexual opportunities, and the general capacity to use physical aggression to achieve a variety of goals.

Unfortunately, clear-cut evidence bearing on these competing theories is lacking. Rape is a common occurrence during war, but theft, looting, property damage, and cruelty to the defeated are also common. Are there specialized adaptations for each of these behaviors, or are they by-products of other mechanisms? Definitive studies have not been conducted.

Rapists tend to target young, reproductive-aged women disproportionately. Indeed, roughly 70 percent of rape victims fall between the ages of sixteen and thirty-five (Thornhill & Thornhill, 1983). The fact that rapists tend to victimize young, fertile women, however, is not definitive evidence for or against the competing theories of rape. This result could be due to men's evolved preference for cues to fertile women in regular mating contexts (see Chapter 5), and hence rape-specific adaptations are not needed to explain this finding.

## Individual Differences in Rape Proclivity

Individual men apparently differ in their proclivity toward rape. In one study, men were asked to imagine that they had the possibility of forcing sex on a woman against her will when there was no chance of being discovered. In the study, 35 percent indicated a nonzero likelihood of rape under these conditions, although in most cases, the likelihood was slight (Malamuth, 1981; Young & Thiessen, 1992). Although these figures are alarmingly high, they do not offer clear support for the rape-adaptation theory; in fact, if the results are taken at face value, they suggest that most men are not potential rapists.

***Sexual Coercion as Part of a Life-History Strategy of Some Men.***   For a small subset of men, rape may be part of a life-history strategy marked by high levels of psychopathy, pursuit of a short-term rather than a long-term mating strategy, lack of empathy, and "hostile masculinity," particularly hostility toward women (Figueredo, Gladden, & Beck, 2010; Gladden, Sisco, & Figueredo, 2008; Lalumiere et al., 2005; Malamuth et al., 2005). Malamuth suggests that hostile masculinity might allow men to avoid feeling sympathy or empathy for the victim that might otherwise inhibit the use of sexual aggression. A majority of rapists show high levels of sexual arousal in the laboratory, as measured by penile tumescence, to stories and imagery depicting sexual violence, whereas far fewer nonrapists show such arousal (Lalumiere et al., 2005). Many rapists also have what appears to be a distinct life strategy—they have an early onset of sexual activity, have many varied sexual experiences, and tend to commit a variety of nonsexual crimes such as robbery and assault. All these findings point to the possibility that a subset of men are particularly prone not to committing just rape, but to pursuing a life strategy of antisocial and criminal activity (Lalumiere et al., 2005).

***The Mate Deprivation Hypothesis.***   According to the mate deprivation hypothesis, men who have experienced deprivation of sexual access to women will be more likely to use sexually aggressive tactics (Lalumiere et al., 1996; Quinsey & Lalumiere, 1995; Thornhill & Thornhill, 1983, 1992). Perhaps men have evolved a conditional mating strategy—when they cannot secure mates through the means of attraction, they experience deprivation, which prompts them to use sexually aggressive tactics to avoid being excluded entirely.

This hypothesis was tested on a sample of 156 heterosexual males with a mean age of twenty (Lalumiere et al., 1996). The measures of sexual coercion included both nonphysical (e.g., "Have you ever had sexual intercourse with a woman even though she didn't really want to because she felt pressured by your continual arguments?") and physical coercion (e.g., "Have you ever had sexual intercourse with a woman when she didn't want to because you used some degree of physical force?"). The measure of mating success was assessed by the self-perceived mating success scale, which included items such as "Members of the opposite sex that I like tend to like me back"; "I receive many compliments from members of the opposite sex"; "I receive sexual invitations from members of the opposite sex"; and "Members of the opposite sex are attracted to me."

The results contradicted the predictions the authors derived from the mate deprivation hypothesis of sexual aggression. Men who scored high on self-perceived mating success also tended to score high on the measures of sexual aggression, as shown in Figure 11.2. Furthermore, men who evaluated their future earning potential as high tended to use more physical coercion than did men who perceived their future earning potential as low. In summary, the results fail to support the mate deprivation hypothesis. A more recent study found a positive, but not significant, correlation between sexual coercive tactics and mating success (Camilleri, Quinsey, & Tapscott, 2009). And a third study found that men who commit sexual assault report a higher number of lifetime sex partners (Ellis, Widmayer, & Palmer, 2009).

***Partner Rapists.***   An estimated 10 to 26 percent of married women experience rape from their husbands (McKibbin et al., 2008). According to one hypothesis, this form of rape represents an

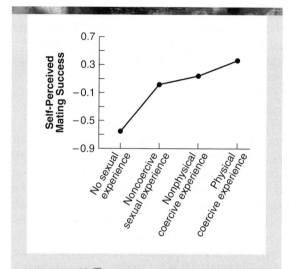

FIGURE *11.2* **Self-Perceived Mating Success and Sexual Aggression.** The figure shows that men who score high on self-perceived mating success tend to score higher on sexual coercion, contrary to mate deprivation hypothesis.

*Source:* Lalumiere, M. L., Chalmers, L. J., Quinsey, V. L., & Seto, M. C. (1996). A test of the mate deprivation hypothesis of sexual coercion. *Ethology and Sociobiology, 17,* 299–318. Copyright © 1996, with permission from Elsevier Science.

adaptation to sperm competition—men whose wives have been sexually unfaithful, or who suspect their wives of infidelity, force sex in order to combat the sperm from competing males (men presumably would not be consciously aware of this evolved function) (Goetz & Shackelford, 2009). Two empirical studies confirmed that men who knew or suspected their partners of infidelity indeed were more likely to use a variety of sexually coercive tactics, including physical force (2009). Another study also found that direct cues to a partner's infidelity were linked with a higher proclivity to use sexual coercion (Camilleri & Quinsey, 2009a).

Not all men who perceive that their partners are unfaithful, however, resort to sexual coercion. One study found that partner rapists tended to score high on psychopathy, supporting the life-history strategy theory of individual differences in rape proclivity (Camilleri & Quinsey, 2009b; Figueredo et al., 2010). Another study found that only men who perceive themselves to be equal or higher in mate value than their partner and perceive partner infidelity resort to sexually coercive tactics (Starratt, Popp, & Shackelford, 2008). In contrast, among men who perceive themselves to be lower in mate value, there is no link between perceptions of partner infidelity and the use of sexually coercive tactics. In sum, although the sperm competition hypothesis of partner rape receives some empirical support, it must be qualified by individual differences in life-history strategy (psychopathy) and relative mate value.

More than three decades ago, Donald Symons concluded, "I do not believe that available data are even close to sufficient to warrant the conclusion that rape itself is a facultative adaptation in the human male" (Symons, 1979, p. 284). The state of the evidence today suggests that this conclusion might still be apt. Nonetheless, there is good evidence for individual differences among men in rape proclivity. Psychopaths, who tend to pursue an exploitative life-history strategy seem especially prone to use sexual coercion, both with nonpartners and with partners whom they suspect might be sexually unfaithful.

## Do Women Have Evolved Antirape Adaptations?

Although the controversy over explanations of rape has centered on the motivations of men, it is also important to examine rape victims. There is one point about victim psychology that all theoretical camps agree on: Rape is abhorrent and often inflicts heavy costs on the victim. We do not need a formal theory for this insight, but it is important to examine *why* rape is experienced as extremely traumatic by victims. From an evolutionary perspective, the costs of rape begin with the interference with women's mate choice, an essential part of women's sexual strategies (see Chapter 4). A raped woman risks an unwanted and untimely pregnancy with a man she has not chosen. Furthermore, victims of rape risk being blamed or punished, resulting in damage to their reputations and their future desirability on the mating market. If they are already mated, they risk being abandoned by their regular mates. Raped women often suffer psychologically: Humiliation, anxiety, fear, rage, and depression are not uncommon in the aftermath.

Given all these large costs, *if* rape has occurred throughout human evolutionary history, it would be astonishing if selection had not favored in women the evolution of defense mechanisms designed to prevent becoming a victim. Note that this is a separate issue from that of whether men have evolved adaptations to rape. In principle, women could have evolved antirape defenses even if rape has been entirely a by-product of nonrape mechanisms in men. Although we cannot go back in time to determine with absolute certainty, historical records and anthropological ethnographies suggest strongly that rape has occurred across cultures and over time (Buss, 2003; Lalumiere et al., 2005). From the Semai of central Malaysia to the !Kung San of Botswana, there are many recorded instances of rape. Indeed, the Amazonian groups studied by Thomas Gregor have specific words for both rape (*antapai*) and gang rape (*aintyawakakinapai*) (Gregor, 1985). Evolutionary anthropologist Barbara Smuts summarizes this evidence: "Although the prevalence of male violence against women varies from place to place, cross-cultural surveys indicate that societies in which men rarely attack or rape women are the exception, not the norm" (Smuts, 1992, p. 1).

So if rape has been a recurrent hazard for women, what defenses might have evolved to lower the odds of becoming a victim? Several have been hypothesized:

- The formation of alliances with other males as "special friends" for protection (Smuts, 1992);
- Mate selection based on qualities of men such as physical size and social dominance that deter other men from sexual aggression—the "bodyguard hypothesis" (Wilson & Mesnick, 1997);
- The cultivation of female–female coalitions for protection (Smuts, 1992);
- The development of specialized fears that motivate women to avoid situations in which they might be in danger of rape (Chavanne & Gallup, 1998);
- The avoidance of risky activities during ovulation to decrease the odds of sexual assault when they are most likely to conceive (Chavanne & Gallup, 1998);
- Psychological pain from rape that motivates women to avoid rape in the future (Thornhill & Palmer, 2000).

Although research into these hypothesized defenses has barely begun, it shows great promise. Women who are not taking oral contraceptives tend to avoid risky activities, such as going to a bar alone or walking in a dimly lit area, more when they are ovulating than at other times in the cycle (Bröder & Hohmann, 2003; Chavanne & Gallup, 1998). Greater fear of rape is positively correlated with an increase in behavioral precautions, such as avoiding being alone with men they do not know well or men who come on strong sexually, suggesting an emotion that motivates behavior that lowers the odds of rape. Young women experience more fear of rape than do older women, who are more likely to fear being robbed or burgled, suggesting that fear might be tracking the statistical risks of rape (Pawson & Banks, 1993). Direct tests of the "bodyguard hypothesis" have not yet been conducted, although married women report lower rates of rape than do single women (Wilson & Mesnick, 1997).

McKibbin and colleagues (2009) have discovered four common strategies women use to avoid rape: (1) Avoiding strange or dangerous men (e.g., avoiding men with a reputation of forcing themselves on women); (2) avoiding appearing sexually receptive (e.g., not wearing revealing clothing); (3) avoiding being alone (e.g., staying in close proximity to others when going out), and (4) being prepared and showing awareness of surroundings (e.g., looking around before exiting the car). Furthermore, these researchers discovered that women who rate themselves high on physical attractiveness are significantly more likely to avoid being alone and show heightened preparedness and awareness of their surroundings (McKibbin et al., 2010). Another predictor was relationship status: Women in committed long-term relationships also avoided being alone, but also were more likely than single women to avoid appearing sexually receptive.

In sum, the modest empirical work that has been done so far suggests much promise for uncovering women's antirape defenses. Given the alarming rates of rape in modern environments, research is urgently needed on women's antirape strategies and their relative effectiveness, whether or not such strategies ultimately turn out to be specialized evolved adaptations or by-products of more general cognitive and emotional mechanisms.

## ■ JEALOUS CONFLICT

$\mathcal{M}$ates gained must be retained, at least for a time, in order to fulfill the reproductive potential inherent in the initial mate selection. Threats to mate retention come from several sources. The first is the presence of mate poachers, rivals who attempt to lure someone else's mate away either for a sexual encounter or for a long-term relationship (Schmitt & Buss, 2001). Mate poaching has been documented to be a widespread mating strategy across cultures (Schmitt et al., 2004). The second (related) threat comes from a mate's infidelity, which could be in the form of a short-term sexual infidelity or a longer-term defection from the relationship. Because both threats are likely to have been recurrent adaptive problems, it is reasonable to hypothesize that selection has favored the evolution of defenses to fend off mate poachers, to deter a mate's sexual infidelity, and to retain a mate for the long run. Evolutionary psychologists have hypothesized that the cognitive/emotional complex of jealousy and behavioral output of tactics of mate retention have evolved to deal with these adaptive problems—problems that differ in certain respects for men and women (Daly, Wilson, & Weghorst, 1982; Symons, 1979).

The potential for cuckoldry creates a serious adaptive problem for men, which is magnified in humans because of the tremendous investment that men often channel toward their children. If a man is cuckolded, he risks investing all of his resources in another man's children. Not only does he lose his own investment, but he also stands to lose the investment of his partner, who would now be investing her efforts in another man's child.

Ancestral men who failed to solve this adaptive problem not only risked suffering direct reproductive losses, but also risked losing status and reputation, which could have seriously impaired their ability to attract other mates. Consider the reaction in Greek culture to cuckoldry:

> The wife's infidelity . . . brings disgrace to the husband who is then a Keratas—the worst insult for a Greek man—a shameful epithet with connotations of weakness and inadequacy. . . . While for the wife it is socially acceptable to tolerate her unfaithful husband, it is not socially acceptable for a man to tolerate his unfaithful wife and if he does so, he is ridiculed as behaving in an unmanly manner. (Safilios-Rothschild, 1969, pp. 78–79)

Jealousy might help to solve this adaptive problem in several ways. First, it might sensitize a man to circumstances in which his partner might be unfaithful, thus promoting vigilance. Second, it might prompt actions designed to curtail his partner's contact with other men. Third, it might cause him to increase his own efforts to fulfill his partner's desires so that she would have less reason to stray. And fourth, jealousy might prompt a man to threaten or otherwise fend off rivals who show sexual interest in his partner. One clear prediction is that a man's jealousy should focus heavily on the potential *sexual* contact that his partner might have with another man.

Women also face a profound adaptive problem because of a partner's infidelity, but it is not defined by a compromise in a woman's certainty that she is the mother of her children. Rather, because men tend to channel investments and resources to women with whom they have sex, a husband might devote time, attention, energy, and effort to another woman and her children rather than to his wife and children. For these reasons, evolutionary psychologists have predicted that women's jealousy would be more likely to focus on cues to the long-term diversion of a man's commitments, such as his becoming *emotionally* involved with another woman (Buss et al., 1992).

## Sex Differences in Jealousy

Prior to studies by evolutionary psychologists, dozens of empirical studies explored the psychology of jealousy. The most common finding was that men and women do not differ in either the frequency or the magnitude of the jealousy they experience. All these studies, although informative about the equality of the sexes in experiencing jealousy, had posed the question in too global a manner. An evolutionary analysis leads to the prediction that although both sexes will experience jealousy, they will differ in the weight they give to the cues that trigger jealousy. Men are predicted to give more weight to cues to *sexual* infidelity, whereas women are predicted to give more weight to cues to a long-term diversion of investment, such as *emotional* involvement with another person (Buss et al., 1992).

In a systematic test of the hypothesized sex differences, 511 college students were asked to compare two distressing events: (a) their partner having sexual intercourse with someone else or (b) their partner becoming emotionally involved with someone else (Buss et al., 1992). Fully 83 percent of the women found their partner's emotional infidelity more upsetting, whereas only 40 percent of the men did. In contrast, 60 percent of the men experienced their partner's sexual infidelity as more distressing, whereas only 17 percent of the women did. This constitutes a huge 43 percent difference between the sexes in their responses, large by any standard in the social sciences. By posing a more precise question—not whether each sex experiences "jealousy," but rather which triggers of jealousy are more distressing—the evolutionary psychological hypothesis was able to guide researchers to discover a sex difference that had previously gone unnoticed.

To explore the generality of the findings across different scientific methods, thirty men and thirty women were brought into a psycho-physiological laboratory (Buss et al., 1992). To evaluate physiological distress from imagining the two types of infidelity, the experimenters placed electrodes on the corrugator muscle on the brow of the forehead, which contracts when people frown; on the first and third fingers of the right hand to measure electrodermal response, or sweating; and on the thumb to measure pulse or heart rate. Participants were asked to imagine either a sexual infidelity ("imagining your partner having sex with someone else . . . get the feelings and images clearly in mind") or an emotional infidelity ("imagining your partner falling in love with someone else . . . get the feelings and images clearly in mind"). Subjects pressed a button when they had the feelings and images clearly in mind, which activated the physiological recording devices for twenty seconds.

The men became more physiologically distressed by the sexual infidelity. Their heart rates accelerated by nearly five beats per minute, which is roughly the equivalent of drinking three cups of strong coffee at one time. Their skin conductance increased 1.5 units with the thought of sexual infidelity but showed almost no change from baseline in response to the thought of emotional infidelity. And their corrugator frowning increased, showing 7.75 microvolt units of contraction in response to sexual infidelity, compared with only 1.16 units in response to emotional infidelity.

Women tended to show the opposite patterns. They exhibited greater physiological distress at the thought of emotional infidelity. Women's frowning, for example, increased to 8.12 microvolt units of contraction in response to emotional infidelity, compared with only 3.03 units of contraction in response to sexual infidelity. The convergence of psychological reactions of distress with physiological patterns of distress in men and women strongly supports the hypothesis that humans have evolved mechanisms that are specific to the sex-linked adaptive problems they have recurrently faced over evolutionary history.

The evolutionary interpretation of this sex difference in jealousy has been challenged (DeSteno & Salovey, 1996). These psychologists have proposed that sexual infidelity and emotional infidelity are often correlated. People tend to get emotionally involved with those with whom they have sex and, conversely, tend to become sexually involved with those with whom they are emotionally close. But men and women might differ in their *beliefs* about the correlation. Perhaps women get more upset about a partner's emotional involvement because they think it implies that their partner will also become sexually involved. Women might believe that men can have sex, in contrast, without getting emotionally involved, and so imagining a partner's sexual involvement is less upsetting. Men's beliefs might differ. Perhaps men get more upset about a partner's sexual involvement because they think that a partner is likely to have sex only if she is also emotionally involved, whereas they think that a woman can easily become emotionally involved without having sex with a man. In sum, because men and women might hold different beliefs about the links between sexual and emotional infidelity, they might respond differently to which one is more upsetting when forced to choose.

Four empirical studies were conducted in three different cultures to test predictions from the competing hypotheses (Buss et al., 1999). The first study involved 1,122 undergraduates at a liberal arts college in the southeastern United States. The original infidelity scenarios (Buss et al., 1992) were altered to render the two types of infidelity mutually exclusive. Participants reported their relative distress in response to a partner's sexual infidelity with no emotional involvement and emotional involvement with no sexual infidelity. As shown in Figure 11.3, a notable gender difference emerged, as predicted by the evolutionary model. If the belief hypothesis were correct, then the sex difference should have disappeared. It did not.

A second study provided four additional tests of the predictions from the two models using three strategies and U.S. undergraduates. One strategy employed three different versions of rendering the two types of infidelity mutually exclusive. A second strategy involved positing that both types of infidelity had occurred and requested that participants indicate *which aspect* they found more upsetting. A third strategy used a statistical procedure to test the independent predictive value of sex and beliefs in accounting for which form of infidelity would be more distressing. The results were conclusive: Large gender differences were discovered, precisely as

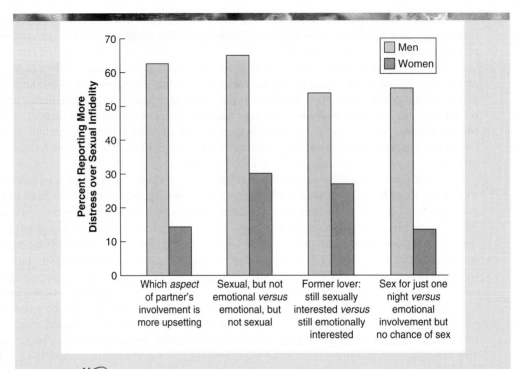

FIGURE *11.3* **Four Critical Tests of Competing Hypotheses.** The figure shows that sex differences in response to sexual versus emotional infidelity remain strong, even when subjects are requested to indicate which aspect of the infidelity was more distressing when both had occurred and when the infidelity types are rendered mutually exclusive.

*Source:* Buss, D. M., Shackelford, T. K., Kirkpatrick, L. A., Choe, J., Hasegawa, M., Hasegawa, T., & Bennett, K. (1999). Jealousy and the nature of beliefs about infidelity: Tests of competing hypotheses about sex differences in the United States, Korea, and Japan. *Personal Relationships, 6,* 125–150. Reprinted with permission of the author.

predicted by the evolutionary model (see Figure 11.3). No matter how the questions were worded, no matter which methodological strategy was employed, and no matter how stringently the conditional probabilities were controlled, the sex differences remained.

A third study replicated the six infidelity dilemmas in a non-Western sample of native Koreans. The original sex differences (Buss et al., 1992) were replicated, showing that women indicated more distress than men to emotional infidelity, whereas men more than women found sexual infidelity distressing. With two strategies to control for conditional probabilities, the gender differences again remained robust. The evolutionary hypothesis survived this empirical hurdle. A fourth study tested the predictions about jealousy and about the nature of beliefs in a non-Western Japanese sample. The results again provided support for the evolutionary hypothesis (Buss et al., 1999).

Despite the fact that the sex differences in the weighting given to the triggers of jealousy have been well documented, these findings continue to be challenged (e.g., DeSteno et al., 2002;

Harris, 2000, 2005). Some argue that real sex differences do not exist, and that domain-general social-cognitive mechanisms—the precise nature of which have not been specified—that are identical in men and women offer a better explanation of sexual and romantic jealousy than the evolutionary hypothesis (Harris, 2005). Others, such as the original authors of the double-shot hypothesis, appear to have abandoned the double-shot hypothesis entirely (DeSteno et al., 2002). Instead, they argue that the sex differences in jealousy are not real, but rather are methodological artifacts, and disappear entirely when participants respond to the jealousy scenarios under high "cognitive load," such as having participants count backwards by sevens while responding to which form of infidelity would be more distressing.

These efforts to dismiss the findings of sex differences or provide alternative explanations of them, however, have not been successful (Barrett, Frederick, & Haselton, 2006; Buss & Haselton, 2005; Sagarin, 2005; Sesardic, 2003; Ward & Voracek, 2004). First, the domain-general social-cognitive theories are founded on the premise that there are no sex-differentiated design features in the underlying psychology of jealousy—a premise that is clearly false, as indicated in this chapter. Second, the cognitive load studies are based on a fundamental misunderstanding of the logic of the evolutionary hypothesis. Nothing in the evolutionary hypothesis requires that jealousy be invariantly activated regardless of circumstances. Consider as an example a hungry woman searching for food and then suddenly imposing the "cognitive load" of a hissing poisonous snake in her path. The discovery that this woman no longer experienced hunger when faced with the "cognitive load" of being confronted by a snake would certainly not constitute evidence that humans lacked a "hunger adaptation." Similarly, showing that participant's responses change when subjected to taxing laboratory conditions does not shed light on the issue of sex differences in jealousy. As others scientists have shown, manipulations of cognitive load "cannot rule out the operation of evolved mechanisms" (Barrett et al., 2006). As an interesting historical footnote to this debate, a reanalysis of the original cognitive load study revealed that "a significant sex difference in jealousy remains among participants [even] under cognitive constraint" (Sagarin, 2005, p. 68; see also Schützwohl, 2008, for further refutation of the cognitive load experiment).

Perhaps more important than the details of any one study is evaluation by the key scientific criterion—the weight of the evidence. The sex differences in the design features of jealousy have now been discovered using an astonishingly wide array of diverse methods (see Table 11.1). The sex differences in jealousy, using the forced-choice method, are robust across cultures such as Brazil, England, Romania, Korea, Japan, the Netherlands, and Sweden, suggesting universality. The sex differences remain robust when participants are asked "which aspect" of the infidelity would be most distressing when both a sexual infidelity and an emotional infidelity have occurred. The sex differences in jealousy occur in both younger and older samples. The sex differences in physiological distress have been replicated by most, although not all, researchers (see Sagarin, 2005, for a summary). The sex differences become even more pronounced among those who have experienced an actual infidelity in their lives and when participants undergo a procedure that requires them to vividly imagine the experience of infidelity. Men, compared to women, have more difficulty forgiving a sexual than an emotional infidelity and indicate a greater likelihood of terminating a relationship following a sexual than an emotional infidelity.

Cognitively, men, compared to women, show greater memorial recall of cues to sexual than to emotional infidelity; preferentially search for cues to sexual rather than to emotional infidelity; involuntarily focus attention on cues to sexual rather than to emotional infidelity; and show faster decision times to cues to sexual than to emotional infidelity.

TABLE *11.1* **Studies Testing for the Sex Differences in Jealousy**

| Study | Sex Difference | Source |
|---|---|---|
| Sexual v. emotional: Brazil | Yes | de Souza, Verderane, Taira, & Otta, 2006 |
| Sexual v. emotional: England | Yes | Brase, Caprar, & Voracek, 2004 |
| Sexual v. emotional: Romania | Yes | Brase et al., 2004 |
| Sexual v. emotional: Korea | Yes | Buss et al., 1999 |
| Sexual v. emotional: Japan | Yes | Buss et al., 1999 |
| Sexual v. emotional: Netherlands | Yes | Buunk et al., 1996 |
| Sexual v. emotional: Sweden | Yes | Wiederman & Kendall, 1999 |
| Sexual v. emotional: older sample | Yes | Shackelford et al., 2004 |
| Sexual v. emotional: Spain | Yes | Fernandez et al., 2007 |
| Sexual v. emotional: Chile | Yes | Fernandez et al., 2006 |
| Sexual v. emotional: Ireland | Yes | Whitty & Quigley, 2008 |
| Internet infidelity: sexual v. emotional | Yes | Groothof, Dijkstra, & Barelds, 2009; Guadagno & Sagarin, in press. |
| Cognitive attention: sexual v. emotional | Yes | Thomson et al., 2007 |
| Jealousy-induced interrogations: sexual v. emotional | Yes | Kuhle, Smedley, & Schmitt, 2009 |
| Continuous measures of upset about sexual and emotional infidelity | Yes | Edlund & Sagarin, 2009 |
| Physiological distress to sexual v. emotional infidelity | Yes | Buss et al., 1992 |
| Physiological distress to sexual v. emotional infidelity | No | Harris, 2000 |
| Physiological distress to sexual v. emotional infidelity | Yes | Pietrzak et al., 2002 |
| Sexual v. emotional: sample who had experienced infidelity | Yes | Strout et al., 2005; Edlund et al., 2006 |
| Difficulty in forgiving sexual v. emotional infidelity | Yes | Shackelford, Buss, & Bennett, 2002 |
| Likelihood of terminating relationship after sexual v. emotional infidelity | Yes | Shackelford et al., 2002 |
| Memorial recall of sexual v. emotional cues to infidelity | Yes | Schützwohl & Koch, 2004 |
| Information search for cues to sexual v. emotional infidelity | Yes | Schützwohl, 2006 |
| Cognitive preoccupation with sexual v. emotional cues | Yes | Schützwohl, 2006 |
| Decision time to sexual v. emotional infidelity | Yes | Schützwohl, 2004 |
| Sibling's partner's sexual v. emotional infidelity | Yes | Michalski, Shackelford, & Salmon, 2007 |
| Child's partner's sexual v. emotional infidelity | Yes | Fenigstein & Peltz, 2002; Shackelford, Michalski, & Schmitt, 2004 |
| Different patterns of brain activation (fMRI) during imagery of sexual v. emotional infidelity | Yes | Takahashi et al., 2006 |

*Note:* See text for more details on particular studies.

A study of brain activation, using fMRI (functional magnetic resonance imaging) brain scans during imagery of sexual and emotional infidelity, found striking sex differences (Takahashi et al., 2006). Men show far greater activation than women in the amygdala and hypothalamus—brain regions involved in sexuality and aggression. Women, in contrast, showed greater activation than men in the posterior superior sulcus—a brain region involved in the process of mind reading, such as inferring a partner's future intentions. These findings are precisely what we would expect if male and female jealousy adaptations were designed to solve somewhat different adaptive problems. The authors conclude that "Our fMRI results are in favor of the notion that men and women have different neuropsychological modules to process sexual and emotional infidelity" (Takahashi et al., 2006, p. 1299). In sum, the sex differences in jealousy remain robust across cultures and across a wide range of methods, including psychological dilemmas, physiological recordings, cognitive experiments, and fMRI recordings of brain activation.

Several other sex-differentiated design features of the jealousy adaptation have been documented. First, men's jealousy is especially attuned to rivals who have status and resources; women's jealousy is especially attuned to rivals who are physically attractive (Buss et al., 2000). Interestingly, these sex differences in upset over attributes of rivals show up even in samples diagnosed as having "pathological" jealousy (Easton, Schipper, & Shackelford, 2007), as shown in Figure 11.4.

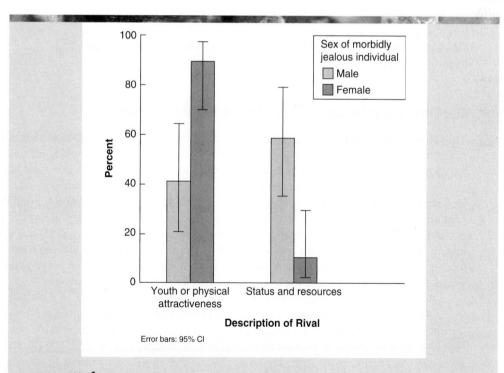

FIGURE 11.4  **Percentage of Reported Rival Description as a Function of the Sex of the Person Diagnosed with Pathological Jealousy.**

*Source:* Easton, J. A., Schipper, L. C., & Shackelford, T. K. (2007). Morbid jealousy from an evolutionary psychological perspective. *Evolution and Human Behavior, 28,* 399–402. Reprinted with permission from Elsevier.

Second, height predicts jealousy differently in men and women: Tall men in relationships tend to be somewhat less jealous than short men, presumably because they are higher in mate value (Brewer & Riley, 2009; Buunk et al., 2008). In contrast, women of average height tend to be less jealous than women who are tall or short. Third, men more than women display an "infidelity overperception bias" in overestimating their partner's likelihood of sexual infidelity (Andrews et al., 2008; Goetz & Causey, 2009). This is likely another instance of an error management bias, given that the costs of underestimating the likelihood of a partner's sexual infidelity would be worse in fitness currencies than the costs over overestimating it.

## ■ FROM VIGILANCE TO VIOLENCE: TACTICS OF MATE RETENTION

$\mathcal{P}$sychological mechanisms can evolve only if they produce behavioral output that actually solves the adaptive problem. In the case of jealousy, the behavioral output would have to (1) deter mate poachers, (2) deter a partner from committing infidelity, or (3) lower the odds that the partner will defect from the relationship. The behavioral output of jealousy in the form of mate-retention tactics ranges from vigilance to violence (Buss, 1988c).

The first step in this program of research was to secure a list of acts designed to solve the adaptive problems of infidelity and relationship defection. Table 11.2 shows a sample of these acts. Once this list of acts of mate retention was established, studies of dating and married couples tested several evolutionary psychological hypotheses about the context-specific determinants of mate retention.

### Sex Differences in the Use of Mate-Retention Tactics

The results of these studies revealed that men were more likely than women to use several tactics of mate retention. Men are more likely to conceal a partner, such as not taking her to a party where other men are present or insisting that she spend all of her free time with him. Men are also more likely to resort to threats and violence, especially against rivals, such as threatening to hit a man who was making moves on his partner or picking a fight with a man interested in her. Men are also more likely to use *resource display,* buying the partner jewelry, giving her gifts, and taking her out to expensive restaurants. Interestingly, and not predicted, was the finding that men in both dating and married couples tended to use acts of submission and self-abasement more than women. For example, more men than women reported groveling and saying that they would do anything their partner wanted to get the partner to stay in the relationship.

Women performed some acts of mate retention more than men. As predicted, women tended to enhance their appearance as a tactic of mate retention—making up their faces, wearing the latest fashions, and making themselves "extra attractive" for their mates. Women also tended to induce jealousy in their partners by flirting with other men in front of them, showing interest in other men to make their partners angry, and talking with other men to make their partners jealous. One study identified a key context in which women intentionally elicit jealousy. It examined discrepancies between a man's and a woman's admitted involvement in a relationship. These discrepancies in how involved each partner admits to being usually signal differences in the desirability of the partners; the less involved person is generally more desirable (Buss,

TABLE *11.2* **Sample Tactics and Acts of Mate Retention.** Tactics of mate retention range from vigilance to violence. These are used to keep a mate and fend off intrasexual rivals.

**Vigilance**
1. He called her at unexpected times to see who she was with.
2. He called her to make sure she was where she said she would be.

**Concealment of Mate**
1. He did not take her to the party where other men would be present.
2. He did not let her talk to other men.

**Monopolize Mate's Time**
1. He insisted that she spend all of her free time with him.
2. He would not let her go out without him.

**Jealousy Induction**
1. He talked to another woman at the party to make her jealous.
2. He showed interest in other women to make her jealous.

**Emotional Manipulation**
1. He threatened to harm himself if she ever left him.
2. He made her feel guilty about talking with other men.

**Derogation of Competitors**
1. He told her that the other guy was stupid.
2. He cut down the other guy's strength.

**Resource Display**
1. He spent a lot of money on her.
2. He bought her an expensive gift.

**Love and Care**
1. He told her that he loved her.
2. He was helpful when she really needed it.

**Submission and Self-Abasement**
1. He told her that he would change in order to please her.
2. He became a "slave" to her.

**Physical Signals of Possession**
1. He held her closer when another man walked into the room.
2. He put his arm around her in front of others.

**Intrasexual Threats**
1. He stared coldly at the other guy who was looking at her.
2. He threatened to hit the guy who was making moves on her.

**Violence toward Partner**
1. He yelled at her after she showed an interest in another man.
2. He hit her when he caught her flirting with someone else.

**Violence toward Rivals**
1. He hit the guy who made a pass at her.
2. He got his friends to beat up the guy who had made a pass at her.

*Source:* Buss, D. M. (1996, June). *Mate retention in married couples.* Paper presented to the Annual Meeting of the Human Behavior and Evolution Society. Evanston, Illinois. See Buss et al., 2008, for the short form of the mate-retention inventory.

2000a). Although women admit to inducing jealousy overall more than men, not all women use this tactic. Whereas 50 percent of the women who view themselves as more involved than their partners in the relationship intentionally provoke jealousy, only 26 percent of the women who are equally or less involved resort to provoking jealousy (White, 1980).

Women acknowledge that they are motivated to elicit jealousy to increase the closeness of their relationship, to test the strength of their relationship, to find out whether their partner still cares, and to motivate their partner to be more possessive of them. Discrepancies between partners in desirability, as indicated by differences in involvement in the relationship, cause women to provoke jealousy as a tactic to gain information about, and to increase, a partner's level of commitment. The intentional evocation of jealousy by both sexes has also been linked to obtaining reassurance about commitment and might be linked to the long-term stability of the relationship (Sheets, Fredendall, & Claypool, 1997).

In sum, men are more likely than women to conceal their mates, display resources to their mates, submit to their mates, and use violence against rivals as tactics to prevent their mates from getting involved with other men. Women are more likely than men to enhance appearance, fulfilling an evolved desire that men have for physically attractive partners. Women are also more likely to induce jealousy in their partners—perhaps as a strategy of indicating to their partners that they have other mating possibilities and thus communicating information about their desirability.

## Contexts Influencing the Intensity of Mate-Retention Tactics

Jealousy and its behavioral output in the form of mate retention are predicted to be highly sensitive to certain features of the relationship. Evolutionary psychologists have tested a series of context-specific hypotheses, including: (1) youthfulness and physical attractiveness of the wife will be positively linked with men's mate-guarding tactics; (2) men, particularly those low on good genes indicators of mate value, will increase their mate-retention efforts when their partners are ovulating; and (3) high income and status striving of the husband will be linked with higher levels of mate-retention tactics performed by women.

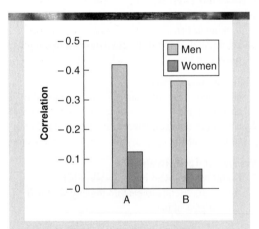

FIGURE *11.5* **Mate Retention as a Function of Age of Spouse.** The figure shows that men married to younger women devote more effort to mate retention than do men married to older women, even after controlling for men's own age and the length of the relationship. (A) shows the correlation between the intensity of mate retention and the age of spouse. (B) shows the correlation between the intensity of mate retention after controlling for own age and the length of the relationship.

*Source:* Buss & Shackelford (1997c). From vigilance to violence: Mate retention tactics in married couples. *Journal of Personality and Social Psychology, 72,* 346–361.

***Reproductive Value of the Wife: Effects of Age and Physical Attractiveness.*** As was discussed in Chapter 5, two powerful cues to a woman's reproductive value and fertility are her youth and her physical attractiveness—qualities that are known to be highly desirable to men across cultures (Buss, 1989a; Kenrick & Keefe, 1992). Men married to women of higher reproductive value—those who are younger and more physically attractive—were hypothesized to devote more effort to mate guarding than men married to women of lower reproductive value. To test this hypothesis, men's mate-retention efforts were correlated with the ages and physical attractiveness of their wives. A sample of these results is shown in Figure 11.5.

Men married to younger women reported devoting greater effort to the adaptive problem of mate retention. Further, they reported greater partner concealment, emotional manipulation, verbal signals of possession (e.g., indicating that the woman was "my wife"), possessive ornamentation (e.g., insisting that she wear his ring), intrasexual threats, and violence against rival men than did men with older wives. Graham-Kevan and Archer (2009) found similar results using a somewhat different measure of fertility—men mated to fertile women used more economic, threatening, and intimidating forms of controlling behavior, as well as isolating them from social contact with others. These results held even after statistically controlling for other variables, such as the length of the relationship and the age of the husband.

Men's mate-retention tactics were also linked with their perceptions of their partner's physical attractiveness. Men married to women they perceived to be physically attractive reported greater resource display, appearance enhancement, verbal signals of possession, and intrasexual threats than did men married to women they perceived to be less physically attractive.

***Ovulation Status of the Woman.*** A man's risk of being genetically cuckolded falls most heavily when his partner is ovulating. Consequently, evolutionary psychologists have predicted that men will increase their mate-retention efforts at precisely this time in their partner's menstrual cycle. Several studies, using women's reports of their partner's mate-retention efforts, have shown this effect (Gangestad, Thornhill, & Garver-Apgar, 2005; Haselton & Gangestad, 2006; Pillsworth & Haselton, 2006). Furthermore, women who are mated to men low on good genes indicators, such as sexual attractiveness, had partners who were especially keen on mate-retention efforts when the women were ovulating, showering them with more love and attention at this time. These findings, if confirmed by independent data sources, reveal a fundamental conflict between the sexes—men mate guard their partners most vigorously at precisely the time when the man is at the greatest risk of genetic cuckoldry and when it is in the woman's best interest to secure good genes from another man.

***Income and Status Striving of the Husband.*** Women's mate-retention tactics, in contrast to those of men, were *not* hypothesized to be a function of the husband's age or physical attractiveness, and indeed they were not. Women's efforts at mate retention, however, were hypothesized to be linked with the value of their mates on the dimensions of income and status striving—the degree to which the husband devotes his efforts to getting ahead in the status and work hierarchy (Buss & Shackelford, 1997c). These are sex-linked components of mate value that women across cultures desire in long-term mates (see Chapter 4).

To test this hypothesis, Buss and Shackelford (1997c) correlated mate-retention tactics with the partner's income and with four measures of status striving. These measures include the degree to which a person uses deception or manipulation to get ahead, industriousness and hard work, social networking, and ingratiating oneself with superiors. Six of the nineteen tactics of mate retention performed by women were significantly and positively correlated with the husband's income. Women married to men with higher incomes reported greater vigilance, violence toward partner, appearance enhancement, possessive ornamentation, and submission and self-abasement.

Women married to men who devoted more effort to status striving reported significantly more emotional manipulation, resource display, appearance enhancement, verbal signals of possession, and possessive ornamentation than women married to men who were low on status striving. These correlations remained significant even after statistically controlling for other factors, such as the ages of the spouses and the length of their relationship. A sample of these findings is shown in Figure 11.6. All of these sex differences in predictors of mate-retention effort persist at least from the newlywed year to the fourth year of marriage (Kaighobadi, Shackelford, & Buss, 2010).

Individuals within each sex also differ in the nature of their mate-retention tactics. Men who are taller, indicating higher mate value, perform fewer mate-retention tactics (Brewer & Riley, 2009). Men high in mate value (e.g., as gauged by low economic prospects) also perform

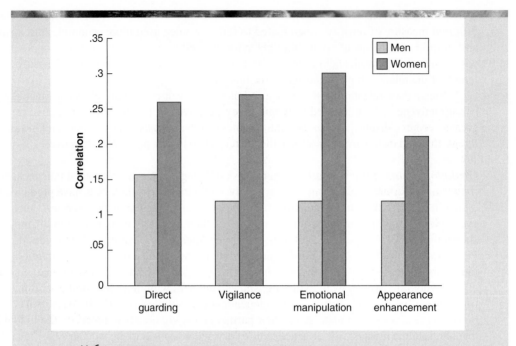

FIGURE *11.6* **Mate Retention and Spouse's Status Striving.** The figure shows that women married to men high in status striving devote more effort to mate retention than do women married to men lower in status striving. The effects of women's status striving on men's mate-retention efforts are smaller and do not reach statistical significance.

*Source:* Buss & Shackelford (1997c). From vigilance to violence: Mate retention tactics in married couples. *Journal of Personality and Social Psychology, 72,* 346–361.

more benefit-bestowing mate-retention tactics (Miner, Shackelford, & Starratt, 2009). Men lower in mate value use more cost-inflicting mate-retention tactics (e.g., insulting their partners to lower their self-esteem), perhaps because they lack the resources to bestow benefits. Those high on the "Dark Triad" of personality traits—narcissism, Machiavellianism, and psychopathy—tend to use aggressive cost-inflicting mate-retention tactics (Jonason, Li, & Buss, 2010).

## Violence toward Partners

Mate retention has an extremely destructive side: the use of violence against partners. The following is a frightening description of such violence among the Yanomamö:

> I was told about one young man in Monou-teri who shot and killed his wife in a rage of sexual jealousy, and during one of my stays in the villages a man shot his wife in the stomach with a barbed arrow. Another man chopped his wife on the arm with a machete; some tendons to her fingers were severed. A club fight involving a case of infidelity took place in one of the villages just before the end of my first field trip. The male paramour was killed, and the enraged husband cut off both of his wife's ears. (Chagnon, 1992, p. 147)

*Men sometimes use violence or threats of violence as a strategy of mate retention and infidelity prevention. Research suggests that these coercive tactics are used more often by men who are married to young and physically attractive partners.*

Why would anyone ever commit violence against a partner? Wilson and Daly (1996) provide a compelling hypothesis. Men use violence and threats as a strategy to limit a partner's autonomy, thus decreasing the odds that the partner will commit infidelity or defect from the relationship. Indeed, women who actually leave their husbands are frequently pursued, threatened, and assaulted. Wives who have left their husbands are at a substantially higher risk of being killed than are women who remain with their husbands, as shown in Figure 11.7. These spousal homicides often follow from threats to pursue and kill wives if they ever leave, and the murderers often explain their violent behavior as "a response to the intolerable stimulus of their wives' departure" (Wilson & Daly, 1996, p. 5).

Intuitively, however, this homicidal behavior seems bizarre and maladaptive. Killing a wife imposes a cost on the perpetrator as well as the victim, as the husband has essentially destroyed any access to a reproductively valuable commodity. Killing a wife, therefore, seems genuinely puzzling from an evolutionary perspective. Wilson and Daly (1996) explain this puzzle by proposing that violence is a means of deterrence:

> A threat is an effective social tool, and usually an inexpensive one, but it loses its effectiveness if the threatening party is seen to be bluffing, that is to be unwilling to pay the occasional cost of following through when the threat is ignored or defied. Such vengeful follow-through may appear counterproductive—a risky or expensive act too late to be useful—but effective threats cannot "leak" signs of bluff and may therefore have to be sincere. Although killing an estranged wife appears futile, threatening one who might otherwise leave can be self-interested, and so can pursuing her with further threats, as can advertisements of anger and ostensible obliviousness to the costs. (pp. 2–3)

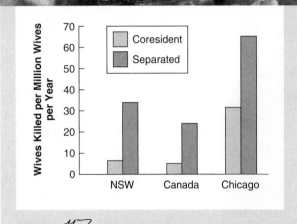

FIGURE *11.7* **Rates of Uxoricides Perpetrated by Registered-Marriage Husbands, for Coresiding versus Estranged Couples in New South Wales (NSW), Australia (1968–1986); Canada (1974–1990); and Chicago (1965–1989).**

*Source:* Wilson, M., & Daly, M. (1996). Male sexual proprietariness and violence against wives. *Current Directions in Psychological Science, 5,* 5. Reprinted with permission.

In short, the willingness to resort to extreme violence, according to this hypothesis, represents a risky strategy of deterring the wife from leaving and deterring sexual rivals—a strategy that sometimes has to be acted out to be effective.

Young and attractive women might be more vulnerable to violence from their partners. As Wilson and Daly (1993) noted, "Young wives may be more likely than older wives to terminate an unsatisfactory marriage, more likely to be approached by sexual rivals of the husband, and more likely to form new sexual relationships. Hence, we hypothesize that men will be especially jealous, proprietary and coercive toward younger wives" (Wilson & Daly, 1993, p. 285).

This hypothesis is confirmed by the spousal homicide data. The wives who are at greatest risk of being killed by their husbands are in their teenage years; the lowest rates of spousal homicide are among postmenopausal women (Daly & Wilson, 1988). Part of this finding may be attributed to the fact that young women are often married to young men, and young men are known to commit violence of all sorts more frequently than older men. The age of the man, however, cannot completely account for the findings, because young women married to older husbands are actually at greater risk of being killed than are young women married to young men (Shackelford, Buss, & Peters, 2000; Wilson & Daly, 1993).

Sexual jealousy in men predicts violence against their partners. One study of 116 couples assessed men's perceptions of their partners' interest in other men, as well as women's self-reported interest in other men (Cousins & Gangestad, 2007). Men's perceptions of their partner's interest in other men turned out to be a stronger predictor of male violence than women's actual interest in others. Another study found that men who accuse their partners of sexual infidelity are more prone to be physically violent toward them (Kaighobadi & Shackelford, 2009). A trio of studies found that men who devote a lot of effort to mate retention, particularly those who use the tactics of emotional manipulation and monopolization of the partner's time, are more likely to use physical violence to control their partner (Shackelford et al., 2005). The presence of stepchildren in the home who are genetically unrelated to the man increases the women's risk of physical violence at his hands (see Goetz et al., 2008).

Another context that may provoke violence occurs when a man lacks the resources to provide positive incentives for a mate to remain in the relationship. As we saw in Chapter 6, women whose partners lose their jobs or otherwise fail to provide economic resources indicate that they are more likely to have affairs. This leads to a specific prediction: Men who experience a relative lack of economic resources will be more likely to use violence as a mate-retention tactic than will men who have economic resources and who therefore can retain a mate with positive incentives (Wilson & Daly, 1993).

The empirical findings support this hypothesis. One study examined 1,156 women age sixteen or older who were killed in New York City over the five-year period 1990 through 1994 (Belluck, 1997). Nearly half were killed by husbands or boyfriends, either current or former. Roughly 67 percent, however, were killed in the poorest boroughs of New York: the Bronx and Brooklyn. The findings show higher rates of spousal homicide among men who are poor and unemployed—circumstances that prevent men from using positive incentives such as resource provisioning to keep a mate (Miner et al., 2009). Other factors that put women more at risk of violence from their partners include a proclivity toward short-term mating, psychopathic tendencies, and poor impulse control—components of what A. J. Figueredo conceptualizes as a "fast life history strategy" (Figueredo et al., 2010).

Several contexts might protect women from being victimized by violence from their partners. One is the presence of the woman's extended kin, who might deter a partner from committing violence against her. This is precisely what evolutionary psychologist A. J. Figueredo found in his studies of domestic violence in Spain and Mexico (Figueredo, 1995; Figueredo et al., 2001). He conducted telephone surveys of battered and nonbattered women using a measure of domestic violence that included verbal abuse, physical abuse, escalated life-threatening violence, and sexual violence. The principal hypothesis was that a woman's extended kin network would protect her against spousal abuse. Results confirmed the hypothesis: The higher the density of genetic kin both inside and outside Madrid, the lower the rates of domestic violence against women. The density of kin within Madrid had an especially strong effect, whereas having more distant kin had a weaker effect on reducing spousal abuse. Similar results were found in Mexico (Figueredo et al., 2001).

In sum, male sexual jealousy appears to be one of the central causes of violence against women within relationships. According to one hypothesis, violence is used as a coercive tactic designed to keep a mate faithful, prevent future infidelity, and prevent defection from the relationship. Not all men use violence for these goals, and not all women are equally vulnerable. Men lacking the economic resources that might otherwise keep a woman in a relationship voluntarily are more prone to using violence. Women who are young, and hence high in reproductive value and attractive to other men, appear to be especially vulnerable to violent victimization by their partners. Two factors appear to reduce a woman's risk of violence: selecting a mate who has a reliable source of economic resources and having kin living in close proximity to her.

# ■ CONFLICT OVER ACCESS TO RESOURCES

Scientists have tried for years to discover a culture in which men did not dominate women in the domains of overt political power and material resources. Although many people have heard rumors about cultures in which women dominate men, none has ever been documented in the literature. Feminist anthropologists who have spearheaded the search have concluded that such cultures do not exist (Ortner, 1974). Societies differ, of course, in the degree of social and economic inequality between the sexes.

The generalization that men tend to wield power and control resources, however, should not obscure the fact that in nearly every culture, women contribute substantially to the accrual of economic resources. In hunter-gatherer societies, for example, women sometimes contribute 60 to 80 percent of the calories through gathering food from plants (Tooby & DeVore, 1987).

Furthermore, women often exert considerable power through various means, including exerting preferential mate choice, divorcing men under certain conditions, controlling or regulating men's access to their sexuality, and influencing their sons, lovers, fathers, husbands, sisters, mothers, and grandchildren (Buss, 1994b).

It cannot be disputed that men often use resources to control or influence women. If men possess the resources that women need, then men can use those resources to control women. In the mating domain, men use their resources to attract women, as we saw in Chapter 4. Furthermore, once in relationships, women who lack resources often feel at the mercy of their partners for fear of the loss of those resources (Wilson & Daly, 1992). These key points—men's control of resources and men's use of resources to control women—appear to be issues of agreement between feminists and evolutionary psychologists (Buss, 1996a).

Feminist scholars often trace the roots of women's oppression by men to *patriarchy*, a term referring to men's dominance over women in the family specifically and in society more generally (Smuts, 1995). A reasonable scientific question pertains to the origins of the phenomena that are subsumed under this term. Although historically some feminists have offered speculation about the origins of male control and domination—for example, by tracing it to the fact that men are larger and stronger than women—no consensus has been reached on this issue (Faludi, 1991; Hooks, 1984; Jagger, 1994; Smuts, 1995). Most feminists simply take male domination and control as a starting point or a given (Smuts, 1995).

## Causes of Resource Inequality: Women's Mate Preferences and Men's Competitive Tactics

An evolutionary perspective offers insights into the origins and history of men's attempts to control women (Buss, 1996a; Smuts, 1995). First, women's preferences for men with resources, as documented in Chapter 4, are hypothesized to play a critical role in human evolution. These preferences, operating repeatedly over thousands of generations, have led women to favor as mates men who possess status and resources and to disfavor men who lack these assets. In human evolutionary history, men who failed to acquire resources were more likely to have failed to attract women as mates.

Women's desires for men with resources established the acquisition of resources as a major dimension of men's competition with each other. Modern men have inherited from their ancestors psychological mechanisms that not only give priority to resources and status, but also tend to lead men to take risks to attain resources and status (see Chapter 10). Men who failed to give the goals of status and resources high personal priority and failed to take calculated risks to best other men likewise failed to attract mates. This sort of competition carries a large price tag in male–male violence and homicide, as well as in an earlier death, on average, than women.

Women's preferences and men's strategies of intrasexual competition coevolved, as did men's preferences and women's strategies of intrasexual competition. Men might have started controlling resources to attract women, and women's preferences might have followed. Alternatively, women's preferences for successful, ambitious, and resourceful mates might have selected men for competitive strategies of risk taking, status striving, and derogation of competitors along the dimensions of status and resources. Women's preferences might have imposed selection pressure on men to form coalitions to gain resources and to engage in individual efforts aimed at besting other men to acquire the resources that women desire. Most likely, however, men's competitive strategies and women's mate preferences coevolved. The intertwining of these coevolved mechanisms created the conditions in which men could dominate in the domain of resources.

BOX *11.1*

## Are All Men United to Control Women?

Feminist writers sometimes portray all men as united for the common goal of oppressing all women (Dworkin, 1987; Faludi, 1991). Evolutionary psychological analyses suggest that this cannot be true because men and women compete mainly against members of their own sexes. Men strive to control resources at the expense of, and to the exclusion of, other men. Men deprive other men of resources, exclude other men from positions of power and status, and derogate other men to make them less desirable to women. The fact that roughly 70 percent of all homicides involve men killing other men is just the tip of the iceberg of costs that men incur as a result of their intrasexual competition (Daly & Wilson, 1988).

Women do not escape the damage inflicted by members of their own sex. Women compete with each other for access to high-status men, have sex with other women's husbands, and lure men away from their wives. Women slander and denigrate their rivals, especially those who pursue short-term mating strategies (see Chapter 10). Women and men are both victims of the sexual strategies of their own sex and so cannot be said to be united with all members of their own sex for some common goal such as oppressing the opposite sex.

The primary exception to this is when men form coalitions that function as subgroups, as we saw in Chapter 10. These coalitions are sometimes used to gain access to women's sexuality as in a brutal gang rape or a raid on a neighboring village to capture women (Smuts, 1992). Furthermore, men's coalitions can sometimes be used to exclude women from power—for example, when exclusive men's clubs in which business is transacted explicitly prevent women from joining. These same coalitions, however, are also directed against other men and their coalitions. In business, politics, and welfare, men form coalitions for their own benefit at the expense of other coalitions of men.

It must also be recognized that both men and women benefit from the strategies of the opposite sex. Men provide resources to certain women, such as their wives, mistresses, sisters, daughters, and mothers. A woman's father, brothers, and sons all can benefit from her selection of a mate with status and resources. Contrary to the view that men and women are united with members of their own sex for the purpose of oppressing the other sex, evolutionary psychology points to a different conclusion: Each individual is united in interests with some members of each sex and is in conflict with some members of each sex.

This analysis of resource inequality does not deny the existence of other contributing causes such as the sexist practice of giving women and men unequal pay for the same work. Nor does this analysis imply that men's greater control of resources is inevitable (see Smuts, 1995). It does suggest that evolutionary psychology is critical in identifying the causes of resource inequality. See Box 11.1 for further discussion of conflict and cooperation between the sexes.

## ■ SUMMARY

*Sexual conflict* is defined as genetic conflict of interest between individual males and females. Conflict between men and women pervades social living, from disagreements on dates to emotional distress within marriages. Evolutionary psychology provides several key insights into why such conflicts occur and the particular forms they take. The first insight comes from strategic interference theory, which holds that conflict results from a person blocking or impeding another person's successful enactment of a strategy designed to reach a particular goal. If a woman happens to be pursuing a strategy of long-term mating and a man is pursuing a strategy of short-term mating, each will interfere with the successful attainment of the goal of the other's strategies. Negative emotions such as anger, distress, and jealousy are hypothesized to be evolved solutions that alert individuals to strategic interference.

Conflict over sexual access is one of the largest spheres of conflict between the sexes and takes many forms. First, studies document that men consistently infer greater sexual intent than do women, especially in response to ambiguous signals such as a smile. Second, men sometimes deceive women, notably about their emotional involvement and long-term intentions, as a strategy for gaining short-term sexual access to women. Some of these conflicts stem from evolved cognitive biases, as predicted by the logic of error management theory. According to this theory, the reproductive costs of making one type of error (e.g., overinferring sexual interest when it is not present) differ from the costs of making the other type of error (e.g., failing to perceive sexual interest when it is really there). If these cost asymmetries recur over evolutionary time, selection will favor biases in social inferences. Thus, men are predicted to have a sexual overperception bias that leads them to believe that a woman is sexually interested in them in response to ambiguous cues such as a smile or going to a bar alone, a bias that functions to prevent missing sexual opportunities. Women are predicted to have a commitment skepticism bias that leads them to be wary of men's signals of commitment in order not to be deceived by men who are merely feigning emotional devotion to them.

Another manifestation of conflict occurs in the form of sexual harassment in the workplace. Men are overwhelmingly the perpetrators of sexual harassment, women overwhelmingly the victims. The victims also tend to have a particular profile: They are often young, single, and physically attractive. Women tend to get more upset about sexual harassment than do men in response to the same acts, supporting the postulate that this negative emotion serves as a signal of strategic interference. For any particular act of harassment, women's upset tends to be greater if the harasser is low in status, such as a garbage collector or a construction worker, and less if the harasser is high in status.

Sexual aggressiveness occurs outside the workplace as well. As with sexual harassment, women tend to be more upset than men by the same acts of sexual aggression, such as touching their bodies without their permission and persisting in sexual advances even if they have said no. Studies show that men tend to underestimate how upset women get about acts of sexual aggression.

One controversial issue is whether men have evolved specialized rape adaptations or whether rape is a by-product of other mechanisms such as a male desire for short-term sex combined with a generalized proclivity to use violence to achieve a variety of goals. The existing empirical findings from studies of rape do not uniquely support one hypothesis or the other. The finding that rape victims tend to be young (and hence fertile), for example, does not point to the existence of adaptations to rape, since we know on independent grounds that men have evolved mate preferences for young women in consensual mating contexts. Research is urgently needed on the underlying causes to afford paths for reducing the incidence of this abhorrent phenomenon. One promising line of research has identified a subgroup of individual men who seem especially prone to rape. Rapists, compared to nonrapists, tend to start having sex earlier, have a wider variety of sexual experiences, show penile sexual arousal to stories and images depicting rape, and tend to commit other crimes in addition to rape. Some men, in short, seem to pursue sexual coercion as part of a life-history strategy. The mate deprivation hypothesis, the notion that men who fail in mating resort to rape as a tactic, is not generally supported by the empirical findings. In contrast, men who rape their existing mating partners tend to discover or suspect their partners of infidelity, supporting the sperm competition hypothesis. Men high on psychopathy or who perceive themselves to be equal to or higher in mate value are especially prone to partner rape when they suspect infidelity.

Recent attention has focused on women's antirape defenses, such as the selection of "special friends" for protection, the choice of mates who are large and dominant, the fear of situations that place a woman at risk of rape, and the experience of psychological pain following sexual violence. Preliminary tests of hypotheses about women's antirape defenses are promising. More extensive tests are required to identify with greater precision women's strategies for defending against sexual violence.

Jealous conflict defines another large category of conflict between the sexes. Evolutionary psychologists have suggested that jealousy is an evolved solution to the problems of mate poaching and mate defection. Men's jealousy, compared to women's, will focus heavily on the sexual infidelity of a partner, since historically that would have compromised a man's paternity certainty. Women's jealousy, compared to men's, is predicted to focus more on the long-term diversion of a mate's investment and commitment. A large body of empirical evidence supports these predictions. The sex differences are robust across cultures, including Brazil, Japan, Korea, Germany, Sweden, and the Netherlands. They are reasonably robust using measures of physiological distress and highly robust using cognitive measures, such as involuntary attention, information search, decision time, and memory for cues to sexual versus emotional infidelity. And an fMRI study revealed different patterns of brain activation in the sexes, supporting the hypothesized sex differences in the evolved design features of jealousy.

The hypothesis of evolved sex differences in jealousy has been subjected to vigorous critique and controversy, which has taken two basic forms. One argument is that the sex differences do not exist at all and are merely artifacts of particular methods of measurement. This argument cannot withstand the now-sizable body of scientific findings that verify the robustness of the sex differences across methods. The second argument is that an alternative theory can explain the findings, such as the "double-shot" theory or a domain-general social-cognitive theory. The double-shot theory has been empirically refuted, and even its original proponents have apparently abandoned it.

The psychology of jealousy produces behavioral output that is designed to deter a romantic partner from leaving or committing an infidelity—behavior that ranges from vigilance to violence. Men tend to engage in intense mate-retention efforts when they are married to partners who are young and physically attractive, two known cues to a woman's reproductive value. Women tend to engage in intense mate-retention efforts when they are married to men who have higher incomes and who devote a lot of effort to status striving. Violence toward partners is an extreme and destructive mate-keeping tactic. It is used by men more than women, and tends to be used most by men who lack the economic means to keep a mate through positive incentives.

Men and women also conflict over access to resources. Evolutionary psychology sheds light on the pervasive finding that men tend to control economic resources worldwide, although there are individual and cultural differences. This is one aspect of what has been called *patriarchy*. The sex difference can be traced to the coevolution of women's preferences and men's competitive mating strategies. Women throughout evolutionary history have preferentially selected men who were able to accrue and control resources, and men have competed with one another to attract women by acquiring such resources. An evolutionary analysis also suggests that men cannot be united with all other men in their desire to keep women from gaining access to these resources. Men are in competition primarily with other men, not with women. Furthermore, men are aligned in their interests with many specific women, such as their friends, sisters, wives, lovers, nieces, and mothers.

## ■ SUGGESTED READINGS

Arnqvist, G., & Rowe, L. (2005). *Sexual conflict.* Princeton, NJ: Princeton University Press.

Buss, D. M. (2000). *The dangerous passion: Why jealousy is as necessary as love and sex.* New York: Free Press.

Edlund, J. E., Heider, J. D., Scherer, C. R, Farc, M. M., & Sagarin, B. J. (2006). Sex differences in jealousy in response to actual infidelity. *Evolutionary Psychology, 4*, 462–470.

Figueredo, A. J., & Gladden, P. R., & Beck, C. J. A. (2010). Intimate partner violence and life history strategy. In A. Goetz & T. Shackelford, (Eds.), *The Oxford handbook of sexual conflict in humans.* New York: Oxford University Press.

Goetz, A. T., Shackelford, T. K., Romero, G. A., Kaighobadi, F., & Miner, E. J. (2008). Punishment, proprietariness, and paternity: Men's violence against women from an evolutionary perspective. *Aggression and Violent Behavior, 13*, 481–489.

Haselton, M. G., & Buss, D. M. (2000). Error management theory: A new perspective on biases in cross-sex mind reading. *Journal of Personality and Social Psychology, 78*, 81–91.

Lalumiere, M. L., Harris, G. T., Quinsey, V. L., & Rice, M. E. (2005). *The causes of rape.* Washington, DC: American Psychological Association.

McKibbin, W. F., Shackelford, T. K., Goetz, A. T., & Starratt, V. G. (2008). Why do men rape? An evolutionary psychological perspective. *Review of General Psychology, 12*, 86–97.

Michalski, R. L., Shackelford, T. K., & Salmon, C. A. (2007). Upset in response to a sibling's partner's infidelities. *Human Nature, 18*, 74–84.

Platek, S. M., & Shackelford, T. K. (Eds.). (2006). *Female infidelity and paternal uncertainty: Evolutionary perspectives on male anti-cuckoldry tactics.* Cambridge, UK: Cambridge University Press.

Takahashi, H., Matsuura, M., Yahata, N., Koeda, M., Suhara, T., & Okubo, Y. (2006). Men and women show distinct brain activations during imagery of sexual and emotional infidelity. *NeuroImage, 32*, 1299–1307.

# STATUS, PRESTIGE, AND SOCIAL DOMINANCE

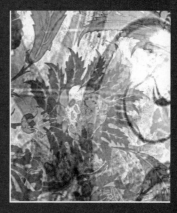

In 1996, Admiral Jeremy Boorda, chief of operations for the United States Navy, was about to be interviewed about the combat medal "V" for valor that he then displayed proudly on his chest of ribbons (Feinsilber, 1997). In fact, Admiral Boorda had never been awarded this medal. So, rather than face the shame of being exposed for the false display, he committed suicide. Rick Strandlof claimed he has received a Purple Heart for bravery when he served as a marine in the Iraq war, but the military has no record of it (Cardona, 2010). So frequent are false claims of military valor that the Stolen Valor Act of 2005 was enacted, making false claims of having won a military medal illegal. Why would people falsify their credentials and risk being exposed as frauds merely to enhance their status and reputation?

Status, prestige, esteem, honor, respect, and rank are accorded differentially to individuals in all known groups. People devote tremendous effort to avoiding disrepute, dishonor, shame, humiliation, disgrace, and loss of face. Status and dominance hierarchies form quickly. In one study of 59 three-person groups of individuals who had previously been unknown to each other, a clear hierarchy emerged within *one* minute in 50 percent and within the first *five* minutes in the other 50 percent (Fisek & Ofshe, 1970). Even more striking, group members could accurately evaluate their own future status within a new group after they had merely seen the other members and before anyone had uttered a single word (Kalma, 1991). If there were ever a reasonable candidate for a universal human motive, status striving would be at or near the top of the list (Barkow, 1989; Frank, 1985; Maslow, 1937; Symons, 1979).

# ■ THE EMERGENCE OF DOMINANCE HIERARCHIES

*C*rickets remember their history of successes and failures in fights with other crickets (Dawkins, 1989). If a cricket wins a lot of fights, it becomes more aggressive in subsequent fights. On the other hand, if it loses a lot of fights, it will become submissive, avoiding confrontations in the future. This phenomenon was documented experimentally by the evolutionary biologist Richard Alexander (1961), who introduced a "model" cricket that overpowered other crickets. After being beaten up by the model, the crickets were more likely to lose subsequent fights when battling real crickets. It is as though each cricket formed an estimate of its own fighting ability relative to others and behaved accordingly. Over time, a dominance hierarchy emerged, whereby each cricket could be assigned a rank order, with crickets lower in the hierarchy giving in to those higher up. Interestingly, male crickets who emerge victorious are more likely to seek sex from female crickets.

Similar phenomena occur throughout the animal world. The phrase "pecking order" comes from the behavior of hens. When hens first come together, they fight frequently. Over time, however, the fighting subsides because each hen learns that she is dominant to some hens but subordinate to others. This pecking order tends to be stable over time and has advantages for each individual hen. Dominant hens gain because they do not have to engage in continuous costly combat to defend rank. Subordinate hens gain because they avoid injury that would occur from challenging the dominant hens. It is important that this pecking order, or dominance hierarchy, does not have a function per se. The hierarchy is a property of the group, not of the individual. Instead, the strategies of each individual hen have a function, and in the aggregate, they produce a hierarchy. This means that we have to consider the functions of being submissive, as well as the functions of being dominant.

All-out fighting in every encounter with another individual is a foolish strategy. The loser risks injury and death and so would have been better off giving in—relinquishing its territory, food, or mate—from the start. Fighting is also costly for the victor. In addition to the risk of injury from battle, victors allocate precious energetic resources, time, and opportunities in battle. So, both losers and winners would be better off if each could determine who would win in advance and simply declare a winner without suffering the costs of fighting. By submitting, the loser is able to walk away alive and injury free. Although the loser has relinquished a resource for the moment, he or she can venture elsewhere when opportunities might be better, or the loser might lie low, waiting for a more opportune moment to challenge (Pinker, 1997).

In sum, selection will favor the evolution of assessment abilities—psychological mechanisms that include assessment of one's own fighting abilities relative to those of others. In humans, these assessment mechanisms are likely to be complex, transcending mere physical brawn to include the ability to enlist powerful friends, allies, and kin. Following assessment, strategies of dominance and submissiveness can both have functions. One function is to avoid costly confrontations. Of course, there is sometimes uncertainty about the outcome. The various bluffs and bellows and hairs-on-end might be designed to exaggerate participants' prowess and get another to back down prematurely. But selection would also favor seeing through these bluffs, since animals that submitted prematurely or needlessly would lose access to precious resources.

A *dominance hierarchy* refers to the fact that some individuals within a group reliably gain greater access than others to key resources—resources that contribute to survival or reproduction (Cummins, 1998). Those who are ranked high in the hierarchy secure greater access to these resources; those who are low ranking or subordinate have less access to these resources. In the simplest form, dominance hierarchies are *transitive*, meaning that if A is dominant over B and B is dominant over C, then A will be dominant over C.

# ■ DOMINANCE AND STATUS IN NONHUMAN ANIMALS

*M*ore than one male crayfish cannot inhabit the same territory without determining who the boss is (Barinaga, 1996). The crayfish circle each other cautiously, sizing up their rivals. They then plunge into a violent fray, trying to tear each other apart. The crayfish who emerges victorious becomes dominant, strutting around his territory. The loser slinks away to the periphery, avoiding further contact with the dominant male.

The subsequent behaviors of the winners and the losers are so different that researchers suspected that changes must occur in their nervous systems. Researchers discovered a specific neuron in crayfish that responds differently to the neurotransmitter serotonin, depending on the animal's status. In dominant crayfish, the presence of serotonin makes the neuron more likely to fire. In the losers, serotonin inhibits the neuron from firing.

One battle, however, rarely consigns an animal to a permanent position as dominant or subordinate. When researchers put two subordinate crayfish in the same territory together, one would inevitably shift from subordinate to dominant status. When the neurons were tested two weeks later, in the dominant animal, the crucial neuron was excited by serotonin rather than inhibited by it. Thus subordinate crayfish readily make the shift to dominant status when circumstances change. The same is not true of dominant crayfish, however. When researchers paired two previously dominant crayfish in the same territory, one was inevitably forced into subordinate status. But the loser, who previously had been dominant, continued to be aggressive, forcing fights with the dominant crayfish even to the point of getting itself killed. It is as if "the animals are reluctant to go from being dominant to being subordinate" (Barinaga, 1996, p. 290).

Chimpanzees also battle for dominance (de Waal, 1982). Dominant male chimps strut around, making themselves look deceptively large and heavy. The most reliable indicator of dominance status among chimps is the number of submissive greetings an animal receives from others. Submissive greetings are a short sequence of pant-grunts that are accompanied by a lowering of the body so that the submissive male is literally looking up at the dominant male. This lowering is often accomplished while making a series of quick, deep bows. Sometimes, the submissive chimp brings objects to greet the dominant chimp, such as a leaf or a stick, which he presents while kissing the feet, neck, or chest of the dominant chimp. The dominant male, in turn, reacts by stretching to full height and making his hair stand on end so that he appears even larger. An observer might conclude that the two chimps are substantially different in size, even if they are in fact the same size. One male chimp grovels while the other struts, sometimes leaping over the submissive animal. The females, in contrast, usually present their rear ends to the dominant chimp for inspection. The occasional failure to display the submissive greeting by either a male or a female is a direct challenge to the dominant chimp's status and may provoke retaliation.

Dominance status among male chimps comes with a key perk: increased sexual access to females (de Waal, 1982). The dominant chimp in a colony typically secures at least 50 percent of the copulations and sometimes as many as 75 percent, even when there are a half-dozen other males

*Chimpanzees battle for dominance; the dominant male typically gains more sexual access to females than the submissive male.*

in the colony. A survey of 700 studies concluded that middle- to high-ranking males typically have a reproductive advantage over the low-ranking males (Ellis, 1995), although there are some species, such as the rhesus macaques, in which females mate secretly with subordinate males (Manson, 1992).

Increased sexual access by dominant male chimps seems to be especially pronounced when the females enter estrus (Ellis, 1995). Three of the four studies that examined this link found that dominant males experienced greater sexual access when females entered estrus and were thus most likely to conceive. Subordinates' sexual access occurs when the females are less likely to conceive. One study using DNA fingerprinting supported this conclusion, finding that high-ranking males had indeed sired a disproportionate number of offspring. Similar results on the links between dominance, sexual access, and reproductive outcomes occur with orangutans, baboons, and macaques (Ellis, 1995; Rodriguez-Llanes, Verbeke, & Finlayson, 2009).

Two other key features of primate dominance hierarchies have been noted (Cummins, 1998, 2005). First, hierarchies are not static. Individuals continually compete for elevated position and sometimes usurp a dominant male. Ousted males sometimes regain a measure of their former dominance. Deaths and injuries of a dominant animal can result in a period of instability in which others rush to fill the void at the top of the hierarchy. Individuals continuously jockey for position in the hierarchy, rendering it a dynamic rather than static form of social organization. Second, the physical size of a primate is not the primary determinant of rank. Rising in primate hierarchies depends heavily on social skills, notably the ability to enlist allies on whom one can rely for support in contests with other individuals. For example, in one documented case, a subordinate male ended his alliance with an alpha male because the alpha had refused to support him in contests with another male over sexual access to a particular female (de Waal, 1982).

Increased sexual opportunities with females provide a powerful adaptive rationale for the evolution of dominance-striving mechanisms. It also suggests an evolutionary basis for the sex difference in the dominance-striving motive.

# ■ EVOLUTIONARY THEORIES OF DOMINANCE, PRESTIGE, AND STATUS

*An* evolutionary theory of status must specify the adaptive problems that are solved by ascending status hierarchies, as well as explain why individuals accept subordinate positions within hierarchies. Ideally, a good theory should be able to predict which tactics people will use to negotiate hierarchies. Academics, for example, jockey for position, but in different ways than might occur in an inner-city neighborhood: "Brandishing a switchblade at a scholarly conference would somehow strike the wrong note, but there is always the stinging question, the devastating riposte, the moralistic outrage, the withering invective, the indignant rebuttal, and the means of enforcement in manuscript reviews and grant panels" (Pinker, 1997, p. 498).

A good theory would also have to account for why status striving appears to be so much more prevalent among males than among females. Ideally, such a theory would also account for the behavior of those consigned to subordinate status. For example, there is compelling evidence from traditional societies that people use ridicule, ostracism, and even homicide to deter individuals whose ambitions lead them to strive for dominance over others in the group (Boehm, 1999). An ultimate theory of dominance should explain why people often strive for equality among members of the group (Boehm, 1999; Knauft, 1991). A good theory would also differentiate between *dominance hierarchies*, which determine the allocation of resources, and *production hierarchies*, which involve coordination and division of labor for the purpose of achieving a group goal (Rubin, 2000).

Finally, a good theory should identify the different paths to elevated rank or status. Several authors make a critical distinction between dominance and prestige as two distinct routes to status (elevated rank) (Henrich & Gil-White, 2001). *Dominance* involves force or the threat of force. Thus, a schoolyard bully or a mafia "made man" may attain status through an ability to inflict physical punishment on others. Individuals may defer to these dominants and relinquish resources to them in order to avoid incurring the costs of violence or the threat of force. *Prestige*, in contrast, is regarded as "freely conferred deference." Individuals may attain high prestige because they have special skills, knowledge, or social connections. Prestige hierarchies tend to be domain-specific. One person may defer to another who has superior hunting skills; another might defer to the healer who has superior medicinal skills. Among the Tsimane of Bolivia, for example, skill in food production is an excellent indicator of "respect," whereas physical size best predicts dyadic ranking of fighting ability (von Rueden, Gurven, & Kaplan, 2008). Whereas dominant individuals might instill fear in subordinates, prestigious individuals evoke admiration. Prestigious individuals may be sought for the information they can provide (Henrich & Gil-White, 2001) or for the reproductively relevant benefits they can bestow (Buss, 1995b). Thus, lower-ranking individuals seek to approach and imitate prestigious individuals, who possess valuable information that can be acquired.

***Prestige signaling, reputation, and leadership.*** In Chapter 9, we explored the role of costly signaling in the evolution of cooperation and altruism. Costly signaling also plays a key role in the acquisition of prestige (Bliege Bird & Smith, 2005; Boone, 1998; Plourde, 2008). In traditional hunter-gatherer societies, signaling comes in forms such as throwing lavish feasts for the group, providing meat from difficult-to-capture prey animals, or displaying knowledge that is valuable to the group. In modern social groups, individuals acquire prestige by displaying high levels of competence on tasks that groups value, displaying generosity by giving more than taking, and making personal sacrifices that signal commitment to the group (Anderson & Kilduff, 2009). In the path to prestige, it is better to give than to receive.

One of the keys to prestige signaling is that others have to be aware of the signals in order to accord prestige to an individual. In one experiment, participants were given an opportunity to contribute to a charity to help needy people either anonymously or in the presence of others in their group (Bereczkei, Birkas, & Kerekes, 2007). Subsequently, changes in social reputation (e.g., how much others respected the individual) were examined as a function of whether the individual offered or did not offer charity, and whether the behavior was observed by others or anonymous (see Figure 12.1). Those who chose to contribute to the charity subsequently experienced a dramatic boost in prestige in the eyes of others, only if the contributions were made publicly.

Displays that benefit others in the group or that indicate deep knowledge that is beneficial to the group is one of the keys to the evolution of *leadership* (King, Johnson, & Van Vugt, 2009; Van Vugt, Hogan, & Kaiser, 2008). Leading and following can be viewed as evolved strategies for solving adaptive problems that involve group coordination such as coalitional hunting and coalitional defense, as well as for resolving conflicts that arise within the group. Leaders usually emerge from consensus among group members about who possesses the qualities that are effective at solving these problems of coordination and conflict—those who possess knowledge and competence relevant to the task, are high in intelligence; and signal high levels of generosity by making costly sacrifices for the group (Van Vugt, 2006).

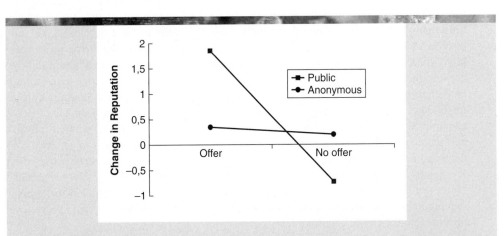

FIGURE 12.1 **The Effect of Charity Offer on the Reputation of Altruists in Public and Anonymous Groups.**

*Source:* Bereczkei, T., Birkas, B., & Kerekes, Z. (2007). Public charity offer as a proximate factor of evolved reputation-building strategy: An experimental analysis of a real-life situation. *Evaluation and Human Behavior, 28,* 277–284. Reprinted with permission from Elsevier.

## An Evolutionary Theory of Sex Differences in Status Striving

As discussed in earlier chapters, human males and females differ dramatically in the extent to which their reproductive outputs can vary. Because sperm are relatively abundant and males are not obligated to invest heavily in their offspring, the ceiling for male reproduction is much higher than that for female reproduction. Stated differently, male reproductive success is typically much more *variable* than female reproductive success. Nearly all fertile females will succeed in reproducing, regardless of their social status, but the same cannot be said of all fertile males. For each man who gains reproductive access to a disproportionate share of women, other men are consigned to matelessness. The more polygynous the mating system—that is, the more variance there is in male sexual access to women—the stronger the selection pressure on males to become one of the few who succeed in reproduction. Furthermore, selection will favor strategies directed at not being excluded from reproducing entirely.

Elevated dominance and status can give males greater sexual access along two paths. First, dominant men might be preferred as mates by women. High-status men can offer women greater protection and increased access to resources that can be used to help support them and their children, and perhaps even better health care (Buss, 1994b; Hill & Hurtado, 1996). Women in polygynous societies often prefer to share with other cowives a bounty of resources that a high-ranking man can provide rather than have all of the smaller share of resources held by a lower-ranking man (Betzig, 1986). So one potential benefit of being a high-ranking man is preferential selection by women as a mate.

A second path through which dominant men gain increased access to women is through intrasexual domination (Puts, 2010). Dominant men might simply take the mates of subordinate men, leaving these low-ranking men helpless to retaliate. As Daly and Wilson noted, "Men are known by their fellows as 'the sort who can be pushed around' and 'the sort who won't take any shit,' as people whose word means action or people who are full of hot air, as guys whose girlfriends you can chat up with impunity or guys you don't want to mess with" (1988, p. 128). Napoleon Chagnon reported this example of an interaction between two Yanomamö brothers. The higher-status brother (Rerebawa) had an affair with the wife of his lower-status brother. When the cuckolded brother found out, he attacked Rerebawa but received a sound thrashing with the blunt side of an ax. When Rerebawa gave Chagnon a tour of the village, he made it a point to introduce him to his lower-status brother by grabbing him by the wrist and dragging him to the ground, announcing, "This is the brother whose wife I screwed when he wasn't around!" (Chagnon, 1983, p. 29). This was a deadly insult that might otherwise have provoked a bloody club fight if the two Yanomamö men were of equal status. However, the subordinate brother just slunk away in shame, relieved not to have to battle his brother.

***Status and Sexual Opportunity.*** Is there evidence that elevated status in men actually leads to more sexual opportunities with women? Kings, emperors, and despots throughout recorded history have routinely collected women in harems, choosing the young, the fertile, and the attractive. The Moroccan emperor Moulay Ismail the Bloodthirsty, for example, had a harem of 500 women with whom he sired 888 children. Evolutionary anthropologist Laura Betzig assembled systematic data from the first six civilizations: Mesopotamia, Egypt, Aztec Mexico, Incan Peru, imperial India, and imperial China (Betzig, 1993). These civilizations spanned four continents and roughly 4,000 years, beginning in about 4,000 B.C.

All six civilizations show a remarkably consistent pattern. In India, Bhupinder Singh, Maharaja of Patiala in the early nineteenth century, housed 332 women in his harem. These included ten high-ranking Maharanis, fifty middle-ranking Ranis, and other assorted mistresses and servants without rank: "All of them were at the beck and call of the Maharaja. He could satisfy his lust with any of them at any time of day or night" (Dass, 1970, p. 78). This extravagant sexual access to women was restricted to those high in status and power. Many men could afford only a single wife, and some were so poor that they could not afford even one. The rich nobles, on the other hand, could easily afford harems, and until very recently, in India, many did (Betzig, 1993).

In imperial China, a similar story unfolded. In the the Chou dynasty in 771 B.C., kings kept "one queen (*hou*), three consorts (*fu-jen*), nine wives of the second rank (*pin*), twenty-seven wives of the third rank (*shih-fu*), and eighty-one concubines (*yu-chi*)" (van Gulik, 1974, p. 17). Palace agents were required to scour the land for young, beautiful, and accomplished women, who were then transported back to the palace. The least attractive were given menial work at the palace, while the most attractive were chosen for the imperial harem. The number of women corresponded closely to the status of the man. The emperor Huang-ti was said to have had intercourse with 1,200 women. The deposed emperor Fei-ti kept six palaces stocked with more than 10,000 women. Great princes were restricted to hundreds of women, great generals had thirty or more, upper-class men housed six to twelve, and middle-class men kept only three or four (Betzig, 1993).

Across the globe, in Incan Peru, there were "houses of virgins" with 1,500 women, although no upper limit was set on the number. The women waited in these houses until receiving a summons from the king, at which point they were brought to wherever the king happened to be. As in China, the number of women kept depended on the status and rank of the man. The emperors kept the most women, numbering in the thousands. Inca lords kept a minimum of 700 "for the service of his house and on whom to take his pleasure" (Cieza de Leon, 1959, p. 41). Status and rank, it appears, afforded men great sexual access to women in each of the six first recorded human civilizations.

Genetic analyses have confirmed the effects of status, power, and position on reproductive outcomes. Blood samples from sixteen populations from around the former Mongolian empire revealed that 8 percent of the men bore a chromosomal "signature" characteristic of the Mongol rulers (Zerjal et al., 2003). The most prominent ruler, Genghis Khan, established large territories for his sons who had many wives and large harems. An astonishing 16 million men in that region are likely descendants of the ruler Genghis Khan, warranting the label "Genghis Khan effect." Similar genetic results have been discovered in Ireland, where roughly one out of every five males in northwestern Ireland is likely to be a descendant of a single ruler (Moore et al., 2006b).

This linkage appears to hold in modern times as well, although not to the same extent. Legally enforced monogamy in modern Western cultures restricts the number of women a man can marry. The elimination of harems coincided with the end of the prevalence of despots and kings. Nonetheless, men who are high in status indeed gain greater sexual access to a larger number of women (Perusse, 1993). Because this access occurs in the context of legally enforced monogamy, the increased sexual access of high-status men comes from short-term sex partners and extramarital affairs. Men scoring high on social dominance, for example, admit having more affairs (Egan & Angus, 2004). And modern men who have high incomes and are high in status tend to have more frequent sex and a larger number of children (Hopcroft, 2006; Weeden et al., 2006). A study conducted in Austria revealed that even within universities, male academics in high-status positions had more children than other employees (Fieder et al., 2005). Men who are high in status marry women who are more physically attractive than men lower in status (Elder,

*Alex Joseph, surrounded by his nine wives, living in a small town in Arizona. Historically and cross-culturally, high-status men often become effectively polygynous, gaining sexual access to multiple women in the form of wives, mistresses, or concubines.*

1969; Taylor & Glenn, 1976; Udry & Eckland, 1984). High-status men also seek out women who are younger and hence more fertile (Grammer, 1992). Although the structure of modern civilization has changed considerably from that typifying the earliest civilizations, the link between a man's status and sexual access to young, attractive women has remained more or less the same.

In sum, empirical evidence supports the evolutionary rationale for predicting a sex difference in the strength of the motivation to achieve high status. All available evidence suggests that high status in men leads directly to increased sexual access to a larger number of women. Elevated status in women, of course, also could confer many reproductive advantages. But the direct increase in sexual access afforded men high in status suggests a more powerful selective rationale for a status-striving motive in men.

### Are Men Higher in Status Striving?

Is there any direct evidence that men are higher than women in dominance or status striving? Surprisingly, few studies have been devoted to this question, but there are some hints. In one six-culture study, Whiting and Edwards (1988) discovered that boys were more likely than girls to engage in rough-and-tumble play, assaults and other aggressive actions, displays of "egoistic" dominance, and acts of seeking attention. Boys in all six cultures were more likely than girls to issue dominance challenges to same-age peers. Girls, in contrast, tended to display nurturance and pleasing sociability more than boys.

Psychologist Elenor Maccoby (1990) has reviewed, perhaps more than any other psychologist, the evidence for sex differences in children across thousands of studies. She described two of the most robust sex differences in the preschool years:

> The first is the rough-and-tumble play style characteristic of boys and their orientation toward the issues of competition and dominance. . . . A second factor of importance is that girls find it difficult to influence boys. . . . Among boys, speech serves largely egoistic functions and is used to establish and protect an individual's turf. Among girls, conversation is a more socially binding process. (Maccoby, 1990, p. 516)

A sex difference in dominance motivation appears to emerge at an early age. Browne (1998, 2002) argues that temperamental sex differences, including men's higher aggressiveness, competitive striving, desire for status, and greater inclination to take risks are linked with sex differences in status and income in the workplace as adults.

Another source of evidence about sex differences comes from research on social dominance orientation (SDO) (Pratto, Sidanius, & Stallworth, 1993). Those who are high on this orientation endorse an ideology involving the legitimacy of one group's domination over another, the deservingness of discrimination and subordination of one group by another, and the allocation of more perks to one group than another. Some of the items on the SDO scale are "To get ahead in life, it is sometimes necessary to step on others"; "Rich people have their money because they are simply better people"; "Some people are just inferior to others"; "Some groups are simply not the equals of others"; "Only the best people [for example, the smartest, richest, most educated, and so on] should get ahead in this world"; "Winning is more important than how the game is played"; "[It is OK to get] ahead in life by almost any means necessary" (Pratto, 1996, p. 187).

SDO should be higher in men than in women because such an orientation led ancestral men to greater control of, and access to, women. Furthermore, women would have been selected to choose men high in SDO, since this would have led to a greater bounty of benefits for themselves and their children. Taken together, both rationales suggest an evolutionary basis for predicting a sex difference in SDO. Indeed, men consistently score higher than women on SDO scales. In one study of 1,000 Los Angeles adults, men scored higher on SDO—a sex difference that proved to be consistent across culture of origin, income, education, and political ideology (Pratto, 1996). The sex difference in SDO has also been documented in other cultures, most notably in Sweden, which is one of the most egalitarian cultures on earth. In sum, men appear to score higher on attitudes endorsing getting ahead, including those that justify one person's higher status than another and one group's dominance over another. These findings support the evolutionary theory of a sex difference in motivation to gain dominance or status.

***Men and Women Express Their Dominance through Different Actions.*** Another source of evidence for a sex difference in dominance comes from the acts through which men and women express their dominance. In one study, 100 acts previously mentioned as dominant were listed (Buss, 1981). Examples are "I took command of the situation after the accident," "I talked a great deal at the meeting," "I demanded a back rub," "I decided which programs the group would watch on TV," and "I hung up the phone on my lover." The first study asked men and women to rate each act for its social desirability, or how worthwhile it was in their eyes. Profound sex differences emerged. Women more than men tended to rate *prosocial dominant acts* as more socially desirable, including "Taking charge of things at the committee meeting," "Taking a stand on an important issue without waiting to find out what others thought," "Soliciting funds for an important cause," and "Being active in many community and campus activities."

In sharp contrast, men more than women tended to rate *egoistic dominant acts* as more socially desirable, including "Managing to get one's own way," "Flattering to get one's own way," "Complaining about having to do a favor for someone," and "Blaming others when things went wrong." Men appear to regard more selfish dominant acts as more desirable, or less undesirable, than do women.

Do these sex differences emerge in the actual behaviors of men and women? Dominant men, but not dominant women, reported performing the following acts: "I told others to perform menial tasks rather than doing them myself," "I managed to get my own way," "I told him which of two jobs he should take," "I managed to control the outcome of the meeting without the others being aware of it," and "I demanded that someone else run the errand." Dominant men, in other words, appear to perform a relatively high frequency of egoistic dominant acts, in which others are influenced for the direct personal benefit of the dominant individual. Dominant women, in contrast, tended to perform a higher frequency of prosocial dominant acts, such as "I settled a dispute among the members of the group," "I took the lead in organizing a project," and "I introduced a speaker at the meeting." Dominant women appear to express their dominance primarily through actions that facilitate the functioning and well-being of the group.

This sex difference in the expression of dominance has also been revealed through a subtle psychological experiment by Edwin Megargee (1969). Megargee wanted to devise a laboratory test situation in which he could examine the effect of dominance on leadership. He first administered a dominance scale to a large group of men and women who might serve as potential subjects. He then selected only those men and women who scored either high or low on dominance. On completion of this selection procedure, Megargee (1969) brought pairs of individuals into the laboratory, in each case pairing a high-dominant subject with a low-dominant subject. He created four conditions: (1) a high-dominant man with a low-dominant man, (2) a high-dominant woman with a low-dominant woman, (3) a high-dominant man with a low-dominant woman, and (4) a high-dominant woman with a low-dominant man.

Megargee presented each of these pairs a large box containing many red, yellow, and green nuts, bolts, and levers. Subjects were told that the purpose of the study was to explore the relationship between personality and leadership under stress. Each pair of subjects was to work as a team of troubleshooters and repair the box as quickly as possible by removing nuts and bolts of certain colors and replacing them with other colors. However, one person from the team had to be the leader, a position that entailed giving instructions to his or her partner. The second person was to be the follower and had to carry out the menial tasks requested by the leader. The experimenter then told the subjects that it was up to them to decide who would take the leading role.

The important question for Megargee was who would become the leader and who would become the follower. He simply recorded the percentage of high-dominant subjects within each condition who became leaders. He found that 75 percent of the high-dominant men and 70 percent of the high-dominant women took the leadership role in the same-sex pairs. When high-dominant men were paired with low-dominant women, however, 90 percent of the men became leaders. The most startling result occurred when the woman was high and the man low in dominance. Under these conditions, only 20 percent of the high-dominant women assumed the leadership role.

From these laboratory findings alone, one might conclude that the women in this condition were suppressing their dominance or that the men, despite being low in dominance, felt compelled to assume a standard sex role by taking charge. It turns out, however, that neither conclusion is warranted. Megargee had recorded the conversations between each pair of subjects while they were deciding who would be the leader. When he analyzed these tapes, he made a startling finding: The high-dominant women were *appointing* their low-dominant partners to the leadership position. In fact, the high-dominant women actually made the final decision about the roles 91 percent of the time! This finding suggests that women express their dominance in a different manner than the men in the mixed-sex condition. This basic sex difference in the expression of dominance has been found repeatedly by subsequent investigators (e.g., Carbonell, 1984; Davis & Gilbert, 1989; Nyquist & Spence, 1986).

Megargee's study highlights a key sex difference: Men tend to express their dominance through acts of personal ascension whereby they elevate themselves to positions of power and status. Women tend to be less oriented toward personal striving for status over others, opting instead to express their dominance for group-oriented goals. These studies, taken together, support the hypothesis that the sexes differ in status striving.

These sex differences show up in many spheres of activity. Men's personal diaries, for example, contain more references to same-sex competition (Cashdan, 1998). And in the workplace, men on average tend to take greater risks, express a greater desire for status, and are more willing to sacrifice other qualities of life such as flexible hours to get ahead (Browne, 1998, 2002).

Another possible sex difference stems from a theory that proposes that men engage in riskier resource-related behavior when they are being observed by others who are *similar* in status, but not when interacting with those who are demonstrably higher or lower in status (Ermer, Cosmides, & Tooby, 2008). The logic stems from the notion that in stable, well-established status hierarchies, it is wise to cede resources to the more formidable competitor without taking risk. Among competitors of roughly equal status, the outcomes are uncertain, and so selection should favor riskier decision making about resources. In a series of laboratory experiments to test this idea, Elsa Ermer and her colleagues had participants make decisions such as the following:

> Imagine that you bought $60 worth of stock from a company that has just filed a claim for bankruptcy. The company now provides you with two alternatives to recover some of your money. If you choose Alternative A, you will save $20 of your money. If you choose Alternative B, you will take part in a random drawing procedure with exactly a one-third probability of saving all of your money and a two-thirds probability of saving none of your money. Which of the two alternatives would you favor? (Ermer et al., 2008, p. 110).

Participants were led to believe that they were being observed and evaluated by other students who were from a higher-status college, a college of equal status, or a college of lower status. The results are shown in Figure 12.2. Men tended to choose the riskier resource decision (Alternative B) primarily when they thought they were being observed and evaluated by men of equal social status, but less so when observed by higher-status or lower-status people. Interestingly, these effects occurred only for men, not for women; and only for risky decisions involving resources, not for risky decisions about other things such as medical procedures. These results support the idea that status competitions among men tend to be most intense when they involve men of equal status, and that men shift to riskier strategies when observed by potential competitors of roughly equal status.

## Dominance Theory

Evolutionary psychologist Denise Cummins (1998, 2005) proposed a dominance theory as a framework to account for many human cognitive capacities that are otherwise puzzling. She started with the proposal that the struggle for survival in human (and chimpanzee) groups was often characterized by conflicts between those who were dominant and those who were trying to outwit those who were dominant: "The evolution of mind emerges from this scene as a strategic arms race in which the weaponry is ever-increasing mental capacity to represent and manipulate internal representations of the minds of others" (Cummins, 1998, p. 37). Selection will favor strategies that cause one to rise in dominance but also will favor the evolution of subordinate strategies to subvert the access of the dominant individual to key resources. These strategies include deception,

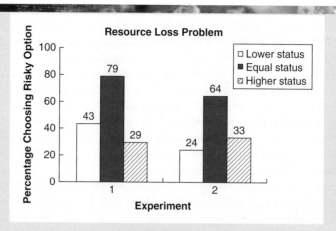

FIGURE 12.2   **Across Both Experiments, Men Chose the Risky Option on the Resource Loss Decision Problem More Often When They Were Equal in Social Status Than When They Were Relatively Lower or Higher in Status.**

*Source:* Ermer, E., Cosmides, L., & Tooby, J. (2008). Relative status regulates risky decision making about resources in men: Evidence for the co-evolution of motivation and cognition. *Evolution and Human Behavior, 29,* 106–118. (Figure 1, p. 111). Reprinted with permission from Elsevier.

guile, false subordination, friendship, and manipulation to gain access to the resources needed for survival and reproduction. Among chimpanzees, for example, subordinate males attempt to conceal their erections when their "illicit" sexual activity with a female is discovered by a dominant male, suggesting a subordinate's capacity for "reading" and deceiving a dominant male (de Waal, 1988). Cummins proposed that these cognitive capacities to reason about the minds of others have evolved in primates, including humans, to thwart the primary or exclusive access to resources by those high in dominance.

Dominance theory has two key propositions. First, humans have evolved domain-specific strategies for reasoning about social norms involving dominance hierarchies. These include understanding aspects such as permissions (e.g., who is allowed to mate with whom), obligations (e.g., who must support whom in a social contest), and prohibitions (e.g., who is forbidden to mate with whom). Second, dominance theory proposes that these cognitive strategies will emerge prior to, and separate from, other types of reasoning strategies.

Cummins marshals several forms of evidence to support the dominance theory. The first pertains to the early emergence in a child's life of reasoning about rights and obligations, called *deontic reasoning.* Deontic reasoning is reasoning about what a person is permitted, obligated, or forbidden to do (e.g., Am I old enough to be allowed to drink alcoholic beverages?). This form of reasoning contrasts with *indicative reasoning,* which is reasoning about what is true or false (e.g., Is there really a tiger hiding behind that tree?). A number of studies find that when humans reason about deontic rules, they spontaneously adopt a strategy of seeking rule violators. For example, when evaluating the deontic rule "all those who drink alcohol must be twenty-one years old or older," people spontaneously look for others with alcoholic drinks in their hands who might be underage. In marked contrast, when people evaluate indicative rules, they spontaneously look for confirming instances of the rule. For example, when evaluating the indicative rule "all polar bears have white fur," people spontaneously look for instances of white-furred polar bears rather than instances of bears that might not have white fur. In short, people adopt two different reasoning strategies, depending on whether they are evaluating a deontic or an indicative rule. For deontic rules, people seek out rule violations; for indicative rules, people seek out instances that conform to the rule. These distinct forms of reasoning have been documented in children as young as three, suggesting that reasoning emerges reliably early in life (Cummins, 1998). Perhaps not coincidentally, at age three, children organize themselves into transitive dominance hierarchies. Moreover, young children also can reason about transitive dominance hierarchies earlier in life than they can reason transitively about other stimuli (Cummins, 1998).

Dominance theory predicts that human reasoning will be strongly influenced by rank, and there is some empirical support for this proposition. Evolutionary psychologist Linda Mealey showed study participants pictures of men along with biographical information that revealed each man's social status (high versus low) and character (history of cheating, irrelevant information, or history of trustworthiness) (Mealey, Daood, & Krage, 1996). A week later, participants returned to the lab and were asked to report which of the photographs they remembered from the previous week. Several important results emerged. First, the "cheaters" were remembered far more frequently than the noncheaters. Second, memory for cheaters was especially enhanced if the cheaters were low in status, whereas the memory bias for cheaters was diminished if the cheaters were high in status. Third, the memory bias for cheaters was stronger for men than for women participants. These results support the proposal that humans have evolved selective attention and memory storage mechanisms designed for processing important social information—mechanisms that are especially sensitive to who has cheated and the status of those who have cheated. These results also support Cummins's dominance theory, which proposes that human social reasoning will be strongly affected by rank.

When people are angered or frustrated, they experience an increase in blood pressure. If they are given a chance to aggress against the person who caused their anger, their blood pressure returns to normal, but only if the "target" of their aggression is lower in status. When the target is higher in status, blood pressure remains high (Hokanson, 1961).

In the most direct test of the effects of status on social reasoning, Cummins had subjects test for the rule "if someone was assigned to lead a study session, that person was required to tape record the session" (Cummins, 1998, p. 41). The reasoner's task was to test for compliance with the rule by selecting which study session records to inspect. Here was the crucial manipulation: Half the participants were told to adopt the perspective of the high-ranking individual, in this case a dormitory resident assistant, and to check on the students under their care. The other half were told to adopt the perspective of a student (low ranking) and to check on possible violations by the dormitory resident assistant. The results showed a compelling link between status and social reasoning: 65 percent looked for potential rule violations when they were checking on people lower in status than themselves, whereas only 20 percent looked for potential rule violations when they were checking on people of equal status or higher status than themselves.

These studies all provide support for dominance theory. Deontic reasoning strategies appear to emerge early in life. People are especially sensitive to social information about what is permitted, obligatory, or forbidden. People spontaneously check for violations of deontic rules and do so more for people lower in status than those higher in status. Cummins concludes, "If one were to guess at which problems cognition evolved to solve, one would be hard pressed to come up with a better candidate than dominance" (Cummins, 1998, p. 46).

## Social Attention-Holding Theory

Whereas Cummins stresses the information-processing strategies that follow from the recurrent adaptive problems posed by dominance hierarchies, another theory developed by evolutionary psychologist Paul Gilbert (1990, 2000a) emphasizes the emotional components of dominance. Gilbert bases his theory in part on the concept of *resource-holding potential* (RHP) stemming from work conducted on nonhuman animals (Archer, 1988; Parker, 1974; Price & Sloman, 1987). RHP refers to an evaluation that animals make about themselves relative to other animals regarding their relative strengths and weaknesses. Losers of contests and those who determine before contests that they are inferior have low RHP. Winners of contests and those who determine that they are likely to win contests are superior in RHP. The behaviors that follow from these relative assessments give rise to dominance hierarchies.

After evaluations of RHP are made, three types of behavior follow. First, the animal might *attack* the other, especially if it perceives itself to be superior in RHP. Second, the animal might *flee*, especially if it perceives itself to be inferior in RHP. Third, the animal might *submit*—relinquishing critical resources to those higher in RHP. In this analysis, dominance is not a property of an individual per se but rather is a description of the relationship between two or more individuals.

According to Gilbert (1990), humans have coopted RHP for another mode: *social attention-holding potential* (SAHP). SAHP refers to the quality and quantity of attention others pay to a particular person. According to this view, humans compete with each other to be attended to, and valued by, others in the group. When group members bestow a lot of high-quality attention on an individual, that individual rises in status. Ignored individuals are banished to low status. Differences in rank, according to this theory, stem not from differences in threat or coercion, but from differences in attention conferred by others.

Why would anyone bestow status on one person and ignore another? Gilbert suggests that humans bestow attention on those who perform a function that is valued by the bestowers. A doctor who helps aid someone when he is sick, for example, receives high-quality attention from the sick person. People compete to bestow benefits on others, in this view, to rise in SAHP. Those who fail to bestow benefits are shunned and cut off from attention and resources.

The most novel theoretical contribution of Gilbert's (1990, 2000b) theory comes from hypotheses about the role of mood or emotion as a consequence of changes in rank. Going up in rank produces two hypothesized consequences—*elation* and an increase in *helping*. Winning competitive encounters tends to produce an elevated mood, or "winner's elation." Those who witness the faces of the winners and losers after an athletic contest can easily identify differences in elation. Presumably, a positive mood increases the likelihood of seeking out future competitions, along with an increased assessment of one's probabilities of winning. The second and related change is an increase in helping. Psychologists have documented that those who experience a rise in status are more likely to behave in a friendly and helpful manner (Eisenberg, 1986). Interestingly, some people avoid seeking help from others because they believe that doing so will reduce their perceived status (Fisher, Nadler, & Whitcher-Alagna, 1982). Perhaps that is why men are so often reluctant to ask for directions—an unconscious concern about status loss. Furthermore, there is evidence that higher-status individuals help more than lower-status individuals at hospital emergency wards (Brewin, 1988). In sum, elevations in rank appear to be linked with elevations in mood and helpful behavior.

Plummeting in status has a different set of consequences for mood and emotion, according to SAHP theory—the onset of social anxiety, shame, rage, envy, and depression. In public

*According to one theory, winning results in an elevated mood, producing an increase in helping behavior and an increase in the probability of winning future competitions (left). Losing can produce depression, social anxiety, and envy (right).*

speaking, the greater the potential consequences for status, the greater the *social anxiety*. Giving a talk to a group of undergraduates, for example, is generally not as anxiety provoking for professors as is giving a talk at an international conference of experts. Social anxiety presumably functions to motivate efforts to avoid status loss. *Shame* is a related emotion. Shame typically comes about when a public appraisal results in one's being the object of scorn or disdain, with the attendant decrease in perceived status. A shamed individual perceives himself or herself to be small, inferior, or contemptible. Body movements coincide with this self-evaluation, including avoiding eye contact with others, lowering one's chin, and hunching one's body posture (Wicker, Payne, & Morgan, 1983). Shame presumably motivates an individual to avoid being the object of scorn, either at present or in the future.

*Rage* is another hypothesized reaction to the loss of status. Rage may function to motivate an individual to seek revenge on the person who caused the status loss. The often-quoted remark "no one makes me look stupid and gets away with it" might represent an example of the rage and consequent revenge that follow the loss of status and might be used to justify retaliatory aggression (Gilbert, 1990).

*Envy* is one of the least studied emotions in psychology but might be extraordinarily important, according to SAHP theory. Envy is linked with rank in that people experience envy when someone else has resources, houses, mates, or prestige that they want but fail to possess. Envy may function to motivate us to imitate those who have what we want. Hero worship and the idealization of others may reflect positive manifestations of the emotion of envy (Hill & Buss, 2008b). On the negative side, envy may prompt actions designed to tear down those who have more than we do, such as derogating their achievements. An illustrative example comes from the rock singer Rod Stewart, describing why he has never won a particular music award: "It's astounding I've never won one. They tend not to give it to the British unless you're Sting [a rock musician who has won]. The sun shines out of his arse—a pure jazz musician, Mr. Serious who helps the Indians" (*Newsweek*, November 10, 2003, p. 23). Envy might prompt a husband to belittle his wife's achievements to maintain his superior rank in the marriage (Horung, McCullough, & Sugimoto, 1981). Women tend to experience more envy of rivals who are more physically attractive than they are, whereas men tend to experience more envy of rivals who have more sexual experience and more attractive mates (Hill & Buss, 2006). Envy can be extremely destructive in organizations, as when a manager undermines the efforts of his or her workers to prevent them from outshining him or her (Maner & Mead, 2010).

*Depression* is the final hypothesized emotional reaction to the loss of status, although depression can arise from many other factors as well, including the loss of attachment bonds (Gilbert, 1990). Depression from the loss of rank can occur when a person loses his or her looks, is fired from a job, perceives himself or herself to be a burden on others, or fails in some socially visible manner. There is empirical evidence that depression prompts submissive behavior designed to appease others and to prevent the onslaught or continuation of aggression from them (Forrest & Hokanson, 1975). People bounce back from depression when they find employment again or otherwise discover a way to bestow value on others and hence increase their SAHP (Andrews & Thomson, 2009).

In summary, SAHP theory proposes that many aspects of human emotional life, from elation to depression, are evolved features of psychological mechanisms designed to deal with the adaptive problems of status hierarchies. Little research has tested hypotheses about the specific functions of emotions, but the theory shows promise.

## Determinants of Dominance

A variety of verbal and nonverbal characteristics signal high dominance and status. These range from time spent talking to testosterone (T). This section summarizes the most important correlates of dominance and status. In many cases, causation cannot be inferred from the correlational data. If T is correlated with dominance, for example, does it mean that high T leads to high dominance, or does high dominance lead to high T, or both? If high-status people tend to stand taller than low-status people, does standing tall lead to status, or does status lead to standing tall, or both? We cannot answer these causal questions in most cases. Nonetheless, the correlates of dominance and status provide a fascinating portrait of what goes along with relative rank.

***Verbal and Nonverbal Indicators of Dominance.***   In summarizing this literature, Argyle (1994) concluded that dominant individuals tend to stand at full height, often facing the group, with hands on hips and an expanded chest; they gaze a lot, looking at others while talking; they do not smile much; they touch others; they speak in a loud and low-pitched voice; and they gesture by pointing to others. Not only do people infer physical and social dominance when they hear a man with a low-pitched voice, men also lower their voices when they believe that they are addressing another man who is lower than they are in dominance (Puts, Gaulin, & Verdolini, 2006). In laboratory experiments, people show selective attention—visual fixations measured through an eye-tracking device—to socially dominant men, but not to socially dominant women (Maner, DeWall, & Gailliot, 2008). The behaviors of low-ranking or submissive individuals are typically the opposite: Their body posture is often bent rather than straight; they smile a lot; they speak softly, listen while the other is speaking, and give many deferential head nods; they speak less than those who are higher in status; they don't interrupt others who are speaking; and they address the high-status persons in the group rather than the group as whole.

What about walking tall? Walking fast? Schmitt and Atzwanger (1995) predicted that a link between pace and status would occur for men but not for women. Their reasoning: Males over the course of human evolutionary history have competed for females by impressing them with signs of their hunting skills, including locomotory speed and perseverance. In a busy location in Vienna, Austria, one observer measured the pace of pedestrians. Later, a second observer interviewed each individual about his or her age, body height, and socioeconomic status. The results are shown in Figure 12.3.

Significant positive correlations were found between walking speed and socioeconomic status for men. For women, in contrast, there were no significant positive correlations. The results support the author's hypothesis that walking speed is a sex-linked status display for men but not for women.

During adolescence, socially dominant males and females tend to use both prosocial strategies (e.g., "I influence others by doing something for them in return") as well as coercive strategies (e.g., "I often bully or push others to do what I want to do") (Hawley, Little, & Card, 2008). These are what evolutionary psychologist Patricia Hawley terms "bi-strategic controllers." Although some favor one strategy over another, the bi-strategic controllers retain their dominant status and popularity, in spite of the fact that they sometimes use coercive and aggressive strategies to get what they want. Perhaps not coincidentally, socially dominant male adolescents have greater

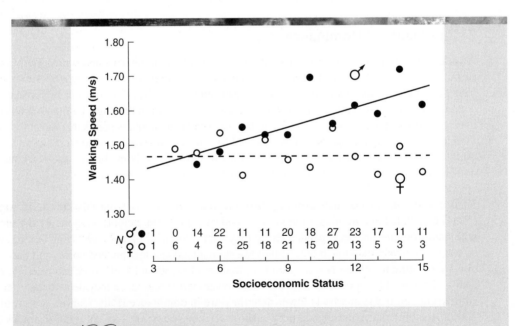

FIGURE 12.3 **Association between Walking Speed and Socioeconomic Status (SES, high numbers indicate high SES) of Pedestrians.** Men ($N = 167$) walk faster in accordance with their SES, whereas the pace of women ($N = 159$) is independent of their SES.

*Source:* Schmitt, A., & Atzwanger, K. (1995). Walking fast—ranking high: A sociobiological perspective on pace. *Ethology and Sociobiology, 16,* 451–462. Copyright © 1995, with permission from Elsevier Science.

handgrip strength, which enables them to more effectively pursue a coercive strategy (Gallup, White, & Gallup, 2007).

***Size and Dominance.*** Given the complexity of human status hierarchies and the many paths to gaining attention from others, it comes as a surprise that sheer size still counts. Indeed, the term "big man" has a dual meaning in most cultures, referring to both a man of large physical stature and a man of importance, influence, power, and authority (Brown & Chia-Yun, n.d.). In some cultures, the word for "leader" literally means "big man." Many status metaphors refer to physical stature, such as "being on *top*" and "being *under* someone's control," "walking *tall*," and "being *crestfallen*." Indeed, in reviewing the ethnographic evidence from a variety of cultures, Brown and Chia-Yun conclude that " 'big man' is a reflection or recognition in culture of a pervasive feature of nature: the tendency among humans (and other animals) for rank or social stature to correlate with physical stature" (Brown & Chia-Yun, n.d., p. 10). The preference that people express for leaders who are tall is found among cultures as diverse as the Aka Pygmies in Africa and the Mehinaku in the Amazon rainforests of Brazil. In contemporary America, people prefer their leaders to be tall; and men who are tall believe themselves to be more qualified to be leaders and demonstrate a greater interest in pursuing leadership positions than shorter men (Murray & Schmitz, in press).

The link between physical and social stature has been explored experimentally (Wilson, 1968). In one study, the same man was introduced to different audiences but was identified to each audience as having a different rank—professor, graduate student, and so on. The audiences were subsequently asked to estimate the height of the man. Audiences to whom the man was described as being high in status recalled him as being taller than audiences to whom the man was described as being lower in status. Even with people we know personally, our mental image of their height is exaggerated if we know them to be high in social status (Dannenmaier & Thumin, 1964).

In studies in the United States, it is found that tall men have an advantage in being hired, promoted, paid, and elected (Gillis, 1982). Tall men earn higher salaries. In presidential elections in the twentieth century, the taller of the two candidates won 83 percent of the time. Although humans might have the most complex and elaborate prestige hierarchies, size remains an important factor.

***Testosterone and Dominance.*** T is an androgen, perhaps the most important class of hormones that contributes to developing and maintaining "masculine" features in a variety of animals (Mazur, 2005). Castrated male chicks, for example, typically fail to develop the red comb and wattles that signal the rooster's reproductive competence, fail to crow and court hens, and avoid confrontations with other cocks. Among humans, sex differences in T are striking. Men average one hundred-thousandth of a gram of T per liter of blood, seven times the average for women (Mazur & Booth, 1998). Although T is produced in the adrenal cortex, as well as in the ovaries in women, the Leydig cells of men's testes produce a much larger amount, accounting for the large sex difference. T can be measured through blood or saliva samples.

At puberty, the male testes dramatically increase their production of T, resulting in a tenfold increase over prepubescent levels. This surge in T brings about the changes we associate with puberty: penis growth, deepening of the voice, increased muscle mass, facial and bodily hair, and an increased interest in sex (see Box 12.1 for a brief look at the effects of facial dominance on status and sexuality).

BOX 12.1

## Facial Dominance

A dominant-looking face may be another signal of status. Facial dominance is indicated by qualities such as a prominent chin, heavy brow ridges, and a muscular face; low dominance is indicated by the opposite qualities: a weak chin, slight brow ridges, and a fleshy face. Evolutionary psychologists Ulrich Mueller and Allan Mazur (1996) rated the facial dominance of 434 West Point cadets and then followed them through their military careers. They discovered that those with dominant-looking faces obtained higher ranks at the military academy. Facial dominance was also positively linked with their ranks at midcareer, as well as with promotions in late career, more than twenty years after the initial photographs were taken.

In another study, the facial dominances of fifty-eight high school boys were rated along with physical attractiveness and pubertal development (Mazur, Halpern, & Udry, 1994). Subsequently, these boys completed questionnaires that requested information about their sexual experiences. All three predictors—facial dominance, physical attractiveness, and pubertal development—were positively correlated with having experienced sexual intercourse and with the total number of sex partners. After statistically controlling for attractiveness and pubertal development, however, facial dominance still significantly predicted sexual experience. The authors concluded that a dominant facial appearance leads to increased sexual access among males.

Scientists have long suspected that T is closely connected with dominance and status in a variety of animal species. In one study, for example, low-ranking cows were treated with T (Bouissou, 1978). Subsequently, the treated cows rose in rank among the other cows. When T was withdrawn, they sank to their previous low ranks. A similar effect was documented for low-ranking roosters who were injected with T: Their comb sizes increased, and they rose in the status hierarchy, sometimes to the top position (Allee, Collias, & Lutherman, 1939).

The causal effects of T on rise in status among humans are more difficult to document, in part because ethical issues make it more difficult to experimentally manipulate T levels in humans. Higher T levels have been correlated with a variety of dominating behaviors among both prisoners and nonprisoners. High T levels are also correlated with a diverse array of rebellious and antisocial acts, especially among young males (Mazur, 2005). Higher T levels in MBA students are linked with willingness to take risks in a new business venture (White, Thornhill, & Hampson, 2006).

The "mismatch hypothesis" posits that placing high-T individuals in low-status conditions or low-T individuals in high-status conditions would create stress and impair cognitive performance (Josephs et al., 2006). The experimenters rigged a laboratory competition that placed high- and low-T individuals in either a high- or low-status condition. They found that low-T individuals thrust into the high-status condition experienced stress, as indicated by elevated heart rate, more focused attention on their personal status, and poor performance on a cognitive test. Similar results were found for high-T individuals placed in low-status conditions. To the extent that T reflects a stable individual difference indexing dominance or status, these results suggest that individuals may develop successful strategies based on their preferred level in the status hierarchy, and that thrusting them into an unaccustomed level actually interferes with the strategies that they have developed—a speculation that awaits future research.

One of the most well-documented effects with humans is that changes in status result in changes in T (Mazur, 2005). The T levels of athletes rise just prior to their matches, perhaps making individuals more willing to take risks. Perhaps more important, winners of the matches show a rise in T for up to two hours after the match, whereas the losers show a decline in T. Mood changes accompany T changes, as the high-T winners display an elevated mood relative to the low-T losers. These effects are most pronounced when the athletes regard the match as important.

Similar effects have been documented away from the athletic arena in competitions involving games of chess (Mazur, Booth, & Dabbs, 1992), reaction time "contests" in the laboratory (Gladue, Boechler, & McCaul, 1989), and symbolic challenges via verbal insults (Nisbett, 1993). Winners show elevated T levels; losers show depressed T levels. The effects of winning and losing extend even to sports fans who do not participate in the competition. When Brazil beat Italy in the 1994 World Cup in soccer, the Brazilian fans who watched the match on TV showed a rise in T, whereas the Italian fans who watched the match showed a decline (Fielden, Lutter & Dabbs, 1994).

The evolutionary function of these changes in T is not known, but one speculation is that winners are soon likely to face other challengers, so the elevated levels of T may prepare them for further contests. The decrease in T among losers may function to prevent injury by discouraging them from further confrontations until a more opportune time (Mazur & Booth, 1998). Alternatively, the elevated T levels of winners may function to elevate self-confidence, fostering the assumption of a higher-status role, perhaps even fostering an increase in sexual access to women.

A more indirect link between T and dominance implicates the waist-to-hip ratio (WHR) of men. WHR is a secondary sexual characteristic that appears to be dependent on T (Campbell et al., 2002). Men with a higher WHR, in addition to having higher T levels, are generally healthier and have fewer health problems such as diabetes, heart disease, strokes, and certain types of cancer (Singh, 2000). In two separate experiments, men with higher WHRs rated themselves as more assertive and were judged by others as being more leader-like and dominant (Campbell et al., 2002). This work might again indicate a link between T and dominance in men.

Recent research has become more nuanced in understanding the links between T and dominance. One study explored the links between T and the two components of status described earlier—dominance (e.g., "I demand respect from members of my group") and prestige (e.g., "Others recognize me from my contributions to my social group") (Johnson, Burk, & Kirkpatrick, 2007). Interestingly, T was positively correlated with dominance, but not with prestige, providing further evidence that these two components of status should be examined separately. Another study examined dominance as a function of two hormones—T and cortisol, which has been called "the stress hormone") (Mehta & Josephs, 2010). T was most strongly linked with dominance among men who also had low cortisol levels; apparently, high levels of the stress hormone block the effects of T on dominance.

Much less research has been conducted on the links between T and dominance and status among women. The scant research there is, however, has failed to uncover the same links that are found in men. A few studies report a positive correlation between T in women and levels of unprovoked violence in prisoners, but other studies have failed to confirm this link (Mazur & Booth, 1998). In one study, researchers found that status, as assessed through peer judgments, was lower among the women with high T levels, suggesting the opposite effect from that observed with men (Cashdan, 1995). Interestingly, women with high T levels tended to overestimate their own status. Thus high T levels in these women were linked with high self-assessments of status but with low peer assessments of status. Further research is needed to clarify the links between T and status in women (Grant, 2005).

The overall conclusion from this research must be confined to men, and it points to a reciprocal model of causation (Dabbs & Ruback, 1988; Mazur, 2005). High T levels in men might lead to dominating behaviors that lead to high status in some subcultures, but reciprocally, elevations in status appear to lead to rises in T levels (Bernhardt, 1997).

***Serotonin and Dominance.*** The neurotransmitter serotonin also has been explored in relation to dominance (Cowley & Underwood, 1997). Prozac, a drug that is commonly used in fighting depression and anxiety, works by increasing serotonin in the brain.

Evolutionary scientists Michael McGuire and Michael Raleigh conducted experiments on vervet monkeys and found that males with high social rank had almost twice as much serotonin in their blood as did the low-ranking monkeys (McGuire & Troisi, 1998). As with T, however, the causal paths can run in both directions. When alpha males were overthrown, their serotonin levels plummeted. When a lower-ranking male ascended to power, his serotonin levels swelled. McGuire and Raleigh discovered that they could dramatically reduce the serotonin levels of an alpha male simply by keeping him behind a one-way mirror so that the other monkeys could not see him and thus failed to perform the submissive displays. Apparently, the alpha males interpreted the failure of others to submit as a sign of lost status, so their serotonin levels plummeted.

In another study, McGuire and Raleigh studied forty-eight students in a university fraternity, including officers and regular members. They discovered that the officers' serotonin levels were 25 percent higher than those of the regular members. In an amusing small-sample test, the researchers then analyzed their own serotonin levels and found that McGuire (the lab director) had 50 percent more serotonin than Raleigh (the research assistant). In sum, the neurotransmitter serotonin joins T as one of the brain chemicals responsible for mediating one's position in the status hierarchy.

***Needed: A Theory of the Determinants of Dominance.*** The previous brief review covers merely a few of the qualities that are correlated with dominance and social status. Other correlates of dominance across cultures include athleticism, intelligence, physical attractiveness, humorousness, and good grooming (Weisfeld, 1997b). Lacking is a comprehensive theory that can explain precisely what people value in others, why they value those things, and precisely why humans hold some people in esteem and awe while others remain ignored or are humiliated. Are the qualities that lead to high status the same in men and women? Are they the same for children as for adolescents and adults? How culturally variable are prestige criteria? Which psychological mechanisms have evolved to grapple with getting ahead? Are there universals in prestige criteria, and can they be predicted in advance from an evolutionary psychological analysis? These and other key questions are being answered by cross-cultural research on prestige, status, and reputation (Buss, 1995b).

## Self-Esteem as a Status-Tracking Mechanism

Evolutionary psychologists have increasingly become interested in emotional and self-evaluative psychological mechanisms that track adaptively significant dimensions of social contexts (e.g., Barkow, 1989; Frank, 1988; Kirkpatrick & Ellis, 2001; Tooby & Cosmides, 1990). Barkow

(1989), for example, argues that self-esteem tracks dimensions of prestige, power, and status within one's referent group: "the evaluation that results in self-esteem is symbolic in nature, involving the application of criteria for the allocation of prestige" (Barkow, 1989, p. 190).

Psychologist Mark Leary and his colleagues (Baumeister & Leary, 1995; Leary et al., 1998) have formalized this idea in proposing the *sociometer theory*. The basic premise of the theory is that self-esteem functions as a subjective indicator or gauge of other people's evaluations. An increase in self-esteem signals an increase in the degree to which one is socially included and accepted by others. A loss of self-esteem follows from a downward shift in the degree to which one is included and accepted by others.

Leary anchors the rationale for sociometer theory in evolutionary logic. Humans evolved in groups and needed others to survive and reproduce. This prompted the evolution of motivations to seek the company of others, form social bonds, and curry the favor of others in the group. Failure to be accepted by others would have resulted in isolation and premature death if one were forced to live without the protective covering of the group. Given that social acceptance would have been critical to survival, selection would have favored a mechanism that enabled an individual to track the degree of acceptance by others. That mechanism, according to sociometer theory, is self-esteem. Blows to self-esteem presumably would motivate an individual to solicit favor with members of the group, to improve existing social relationships, or to seek new social relationships.

A number of empirical studies support the sociometer theory. In one study, for example, participants described a previous social encounter and provided two ratings of that encounter: (1) how included or excluded they felt by others in that encounter and (2) their self-esteem at the time (Leary & Downs, 1995). Results confirmed the prediction that higher perceived inclusion by others was linked with higher self-esteem. Lower perceived inclusion was linked with lower self-esteem. Another study found that people who have high-quality social relationships, which imply social inclusion, enjoy higher self-esteem (Denissen et al., 2008).

It requires only a small step to expand this theory to suggest that self-esteem tracks prestige, status, and reputation, as Barkow (1989) proposes. According to this extension, self-esteem would constitute a psychological mechanism that is responsible for tracking the esteem and respect in which one is held by others. Increases in status in the eyes of others should be accompanied by increases in self-esteem. Decreases in status in the eyes of others should be accompanied by decreases in self-esteem.

According to this expanded version of the sociometer theory, self-esteem would serve several evolutionary functions. First, it could serve as a motivational mechanism but not merely one to improve relations with others when their respect wanes. It could also motivate individuals to repeat or increase the frequency of actions that lead to a rise in the respect they receive from others. Accurate tracking of the regard in which one is held and of the events that cause increases in that regard can motivate an individual to maintain or increase actual status and reputation.

A second function of self-esteem would be to guide decisions about whom to challenge and to whom to submit. Knowing where one is in the pecking order provides crucial information about whom one can abuse with impunity and whom one should "not mess with." Errors in self-evaluation would have led to injury, banishment, or death. Self-esteem, by providing accurate self-assessments of one's place in the social hierarchy, aids in making decisions about challenging and submitting to others.

A third possible function of self-esteem pertains to the tracking of one's desirability in the mating market (Kirkpatrick & Ellis, 2001). In a study to test this hypothesized function, men and women were exposed to a series of models that varied along two dimensions: attractive versus nonattractive and dominant versus nondominant (Gutierres, Kenrick, & Partch, 1994). Participants were exposed to descriptive profiles and photographs of same-sex others under the guise of helping researchers evaluate possible formats for a dating service. The profiles described the individuals as either high or low in dominance, and the attached photograph was either high or low in physical attractiveness.

Women who were exposed to the physically attractive photographs of others evaluated themselves as less desirable as a marriage partner than did women who were exposed to the photographs of others who were low in physical attractiveness. Whether the other women were high or low in dominance had no impact on women's self-evaluations. The findings for the men were precisely the opposite. Men who were exposed to the photographs of same-sex others described as highly dominant rated themselves as lower in desirability as a mating partner than did men who were exposed to photographs of men described as low in dominance. The physical attractiveness of the other men had no impact on the participant's self-evaluations. This study supports the hypothesis that self-evaluations, in part, track one's perceived desirability in the mating market.

Recent work has found only partial support for the hypothesis that self-esteem tracks mate value (Penke & Denissen, 2008). Specifically, the link between mate value and self-esteem seems to apply to men, not to women. And being in a committed romantic relationship reduces the impact of mate value self-perceptions on self-esteem. On the other hand, self-esteem appears to influence mating aspirations—acceptance or rejection by members by potential mates influences self-esteem, which in turn influences the quality of mate to which one aspires (Kavanagh, Robins, & Ellis, 2010).

One interesting avenue for future research in testing the functions of self-esteem pertains to attempts to manipulate the perceptions of others. A person who acts confident of his or her ability to physically defeat a rival is sometimes given wide berth, even when obvious physical evidence is lacking. Animals often take each other at their word, so to speak (Tiger & Fox, 1971). We tend to assume at least some truthfulness in self-presentations of one's status and esteem.

But this is not always the case. *Arrogant, conceited, haughty, vain, affected, pretentious, inflated,* and *presumptuous* are personal descriptors that connote self-presentations that others believe are erroneously inflated. They may also be words that are applied to derogate competitors to convey to potential mates that a rival lacks the resources he purports to have or that a rival is deceitful in her self-presentation of status.

## Strategies of Submissiveness

We have spent most of this chapter exploring the high end of dominance and status: the signals of status, the sexual access that high-status men attain, and the fact that high-status people walk tall and fast. Perhaps our attention is naturally drawn to those high in status (Maner & Mead, 2010). But there is another side that requires exploration: the adaptive problems posed by being low in status.

***Sex Differences in Submissive Strategies.*** Submissive strategies have received astonishingly little research attention. One exception is a naturalistic study that examined sex differences in negotiating with doormen at exclusive nightclubs—powerful men who determine who is admitted and who is turned away (Salter, Grammer, & Rikowski, 2005). The researchers videotaped the males and females approaching the doormen and subsequently coded behavior. Females were far more likely than males to use appeasement and courtship gestures toward the doormen, including smiling, parading, showing their necks, touching their faces, and stroking their hair. A full 46 percent of the women smiled, for example, compared with only 18 percent of the men. The results suggest sex differences in tactics used to negotiate with powerful men, with tactics triggering sexual motivation in powerful men being one means available to women. Future research is needed to explore the tactics women and men use when negotiating with powerful women.

**Deceiving Down.**    Evolutionary biologist John Hartung asks us to consider people who are stuck in a position that they might otherwise perceive as unfair or beneath their station (Hartung, 1987). Consider a man who holds a job that he knows does not take full advantage of his talents or a wife who knows that she is more intelligent than her husband. Acting as though your job or your spouse is beneath you could put your employment or your marriage in jeopardy. Your boss might fire you for insubordination. Your spouse might seek someone with whom he or she feels more comfortable and less threatened. The adaptive solution that Hartung proposes is called *deceiving down*. Deceiving down is not "playing dumb" or pretending to be less than you are. Instead, it involves an actual reduction in self-confidence to facilitate acting in a submissive, subordinate manner.

The evolutionary logic is that situations have commonly existed in which it was adaptive to convincingly portray oneself as subordinate and hence nonthreatening. Those who are real threats risk incurring the wrath of the dominant, who might seek to vanquish anyone who is perceived as a rival. By truly acting subordinate, one avoids incurring this wrath, continuing to occupy a position within the group. It also permits one to bide one's time until a more opportune moment arises in which to seek dominant status. Whether this hypothesis pans out empirically, such that people who are forced to occupy positions beneath them actually reduce their self-esteem so that they can more convincingly display subordination, remains a question for future research.

**The Downfall of "Tall Poppies."**    The *Oxford English Dictionary* defines *tall poppy* as "an especially well-paid, privileged, or distinguished person" (Simpson & Weiner, 1989). The *Australian National Dictionary* defines *tall poppy* as "a person who is conspicuously successful" and "one whose distinction, rank, or wealth attracts envious notice or hostility" (Ramson, 1988). Psychologist Norman Feather (1994) has explored people's reactions to the fall of tall poppies, finding that they depend on a variety of factors. One common reaction is captured by the German word *Schadenfreude*, which means "experiencing pleasure in another's misfortunes." Although there is no strict equivalent word in English, when English speakers hear the definition for the first time, "their reaction is not, 'Let me see . . . Pleasure in another's misfortunes. . . . What could that possibly be? I cannot grasp the concept; my language and culture have not provided me with such a category.' Their reaction is, 'You mean there's a *word* for it? Cool!' " (Pinker, 1997, p. 367).

Occupying a subordinate position carries costs. Because high-status individuals are known to gain preferential access to key resources that enhance survival and reproduction, subordinate individuals are often left with the scraps. A study of subordinate behavior illustrates the potential strategies of subordinates (Salovey & Rodin, 1984). The researchers provided participants with feedback that their standing on a self-relevant characteristic was worse than that of a successful peer on the exact same characteristic. After receiving this feedback, participants were found to verbally derogate the successful other, were less likely to seek friendship with that person, and reported feeling more anxious and depressed about interacting with this successful other. Disparaging a more successful competitor might lead to outcomes, such as reputational damage to the competitor or the redirection of one's efforts toward a different arena, both of which could qualify as proper evolutionary functions.

Feather (1994) had participants read scenarios about the falls of tall poppies. An academic superstar, for example, might plunge in performance on a critical final exam. Feather varied features of the scenarios: whether the person's initial success was deserved, whether the fall was large or small, and whether the fall was due to some mistake made by the tall poppy. He tested participants in Japan and Australia to assess the cross-cultural generality of reactions. One of the dependent measures was the tall poppy scale, which contains items such as "It's good to see very successful people fail occasionally," "Very successful people often get too big for their boots," "Very successful people who fall from the top usually deserve their fall from grace," "Those who are very successful ought to come off their pedestals and be like other people," "People who are 'tall poppies' should be cut down to size," "Very successful people sometimes need to be brought back a peg or two, even if they have done nothing wrong" (Feather, 1994, p. 41).

Feather discovered several important conditions under which people take pleasure in the fall of a tall poppy. First, when the high status of a tall poppy was made salient, participants reported more happiness with the fall from grace. Second, when the success of a tall poppy was not perceived to be deserved, participants reported more pleasure with his or her fall than when it was perceived as deserved. Third, *envy* was the most common emotional experience participants felt toward a tall poppy, especially if the other person's success was in a domain that was important to the participant, such as academic achievement among students. Fourth, Japanese subjects reacted more favorably to the fall of tall poppies than did Australian subjects, suggesting some cultural variation in *Schadenfreude*. Fifth, subjects with low self-esteem reported more delight with the fall of tall poppies than did subjects with high self-esteem.

The available evidence suggests that one submissive strategy is to facilitate the fall of those with greater status and to take delight in their fall. The pleasure that people feel in a rival's misfortunes might act as a motivational mechanism to promote those misfortunes. Because evolution by selection always occurs on a relative basis—one's success relative to others—we expect two general strategies of getting ahead in status and dominance hierarchies. One is self-enhancement, or attempting to achieve something relative to one's competitors. The second is to promote the downfall of others. It appears from the research that humans use both strategies.

Much more research is needed to explore submissive strategies and their various functions (Price et al., 2007; Sloman & Gilbert, 2000). Evolutionary psychologist Lynn O'Connor and her colleagues, for example, have discovered at least two distinct motivational states linked to submissive behavior: a fear of harm to self and a fear of harm to another person (guilt-based submissive acts) (O'Connor et al., 2000). Social comparison, to evaluate whether one should submit, appears to be essential in activating submissive strategies (Buunk & Brenninkmeyer, 2000). Furthermore, humans have an astonishing array of submissive strategies, including creating greater distance from the dominant individual, hiding, escaping, remaining passive, signaling defeat, eliciting help from others, and signaling agreeable and cooperative proclivities (Fournier, Moskowitz, & Zuroff, 2002; Gilbert, 2000a, 2000b). And because being stigmatized within a group or ostracized from a group results in a plummeting of prestige and consequent loss of access to the resources linked with elevated position, we expect selection to have fashioned adaptations to avoid being stigmatized and ostracized, such as an increase in conformity (Kurzban & Leary, 2001; Williams, Cheung, & Choi, 2000).

# ■ SUMMARY

This chapter explored the evolutionary psychology of status and social dominance, phenomena that are observed widely throughout the animal world from crayfish to humans. A *dominance hierarchy* refers to the fact that some individuals within a group reliably gain greater access to key resources—resources that contribute to survival or reproduction. The existence of such hierarchies poses adaptive problems to which animals have evolved solutions, including motivation to get ahead and strategies to cope with subordination. Size is an important determinant of dominance in some species, but in primate species such as chimpanzees and humans, competence knowledge, generous displays, and social skills at enlisting allies become critical to attaining high status. High-ranking animals often, although not always, gain preferential access to key resources needed for survival and reproduction.

Selection has likely favored the evolution of greater motivation for status striving in men than in women. The more polygynous the mating system, the more it has paid in reproductive success for men compared to women to take risks to ascend the status hierarchy. Ascent in these systems is linked with increases in the number of wives historically and the number of sex partners currently. Across cultures and over human recorded history, high-status men consistently have acquired sexual opportunities with a large number of wives, mistresses, and sex partners. Across cultures, males form hierarchies as early as age three. Empirical evidence supports the hypothesis that men are higher in SDO—the belief that it is justified that some people or some groups are superior to others. Women tend to be more egalitarian, men more hierarchical. Men and women also differ in the actions through which they express dominance. Whereas women tend to express dominance through prosocial actions (e.g., settling disputes among others in the group), men tend more often to express dominance for personal gain and ascension (e.g., getting others to do menial tasks rather than doing them themselves). When given a choice of roles to take, dominant women tend to appoint men as leaders, whereas dominant men take the leadership role for themselves.

Denise Cummins proposed dominance theory to explain the cognitive mechanisms that might have evolved to negotiate dominance hierarchies. Dominance theory has two key propositions. First, humans have evolved domain-specific strategies for reasoning about social norms involving dominance hierarchies. These include understanding aspects such as *permissions* (e.g., who is allowed to mate with whom), *obligations* (e.g., who must support whom in a social contest), and *prohibitions* (e.g., who cannot join the ceremonial war dance). Second, these cognitive strategies are predicted to emerge prior to, and separately from, other types of reasoning strategies. Empirical evidence supporting this theory includes: (1) Children as young as age three appear to reason about dominance hierarchies, including the property of transitivity; (2) people tend to remember the faces of cheaters more if the cheaters are lower in status than if they are higher in status; and (3) people tend to look for violations of rules among lower-status individuals when they are asked to assume the perspective of a higher-status individual.

Whereas dominance theory emphasizes the reasoning mechanisms that underlie dominance, SAHP theory proposes a variety of emotional mechanisms designed to solve the adaptive problems posed by living in social hierarchies. These include *elation* after a rise in status, *social anxiety* in contexts in which status could be gained or lost, *shame* and *rage* as a consequence of

status loss, *envy* to motivate the acquisition of what others have, and *depression* to facilitate submissive posturing to avoid further attacks from superiors.

Dominance is determined and indicated by a variety of factors, including upright posture,
low resonant voice, direct eye contact, a fast-paced stride, facial features such as a strong jaw,
and physical size. The hormone T and the neurotransmitter serotonin have both been linked with
dominance, although the direction of causality is uncertain in both cases. There is some evidence
that T increases after winning and decreases after losing. In chimps, serotonin plummets following a loss of status, as when others fail to give a submissive greeting. The precise evolutionary
functions of T and serotonin remain to be clarified, but increases might play a role in maintaining dominance and decreases might help animals to avoid dangerous challenges.

Several theorists have proposed that self-esteem functions in part as a status-tracking device. The esteem in which we hold ourselves could function in at least three ways: (1) to motivate us to curry favor or repair social relations when respect from others wanes, (2) to guide us
to making appropriate decisions about whom to challenge and to whom to submit, and (3) to
track our desirability in the mating market.

Although most of this chapter focused on the high end of dominance, it is important not to
neglect the low end. Ancestral humans recurrently confronted situations in which they were subordinate, so it would be surprising if selection had not favored adaptations designed to deal with
the problems posed by subordination. Two hypothesized submissive strategies are *deceiving
down* (lowering one's self-esteem to avoid confrontation and to better carry out the subordinate
role without incurring wrath from the dominant) and *derogating tall poppies*. Cross-cultural
research is needed to provide a firmer foundation for a more complete evolutionary theory of
status, prestige, and social dominance and submissive strategies.

## ■ SUGGESTED READINGS

Anderson, C., & Kilduff, G. J. (2009). The pursuit of status in social groups. *Current Directions in Psychological Science, 18*, 295–289.

de Waal, F. (1982). *Chimpanzee politics: Sex and power among apes.* Baltimore, MD: Johns Hopkins
University Press.

Frank, R. H. (1985). *Choosing the right pond: Human behavior and the quest for status.* New York: Oxford
University Press.

Henrich, J., & Gil-White, F. (2001). The evolution of prestige: Freely conferred deference as a mechanism
for enhancing the benefits of cultural transmission. *Evolution and Human Behavior, 22*, 165–196.

King, A. J., Johnson, D. D. P., & Van Vugt, M. (2009). The origins and evolution of leadership. *Current
Biology, 19*, R911–R916.

Maner, J. K., & Mead, N. L. (in press). The essential tension between leadership and power: When leaders
sacrifice group goals for the sake of self-interest. *Journal of Personality and Social Psychology.*

Mazur, A. (2005). *Biosociology of dominance and deference.* Lanham, MD: Bowman & Littlefield
Publishers, Inc.

Sloman, L., & Gilbert, P. (Eds.). (2000). *Subordination and defeat: An evolutionary approach to mood
disorders and their therapy.* Mahwah, NJ: Erlbaum.

# PART 6

# AN INTEGRATED PSYCHOLOGICAL SCIENCE

This concluding part reviews the entire field of psychology from an evolutionary perspective. Chapter 13 reveals how an evolutionary perspective can provide key insights into each of the major branches of psychology, including cognitive, social, developmental, personality, clinical, and cultural. This chapter concludes that these current disciplinary boundaries within psychology may be somewhat artificial. Evolutionary psychology cuts across these boundaries and suggests that the field of psychology would be better organized around the adaptive problems that humans have faced over the long expanse of evolutionary history and their evolved psychological solutions.

# TOWARD A UNIFIED EVOLUTIONARY PSYCHOLOGY

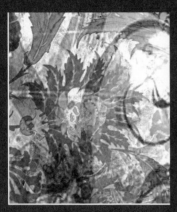

*The most exciting aspect of evolutionary psychology is that it promises a framework to integrate evidence and explanations from biology, anthropology, psychology, and other behavioral sciences in a unified description of human behavior.*

—Boyer & Heckhausen, 2000, p. 924

*Evolutionary psychology has the potential to unify our understanding of psychological phenomena under one theoretical umbrella and faces little competition for that role.*

—Ethan Remmel, 2006

$\mathcal{I}$magine that you are a Martian visiting earth to study the most commonly encountered large mammal—human beings. You discover that there exists a scientific discipline devoted to studying humans called *psychology,* so you visit a university to spy on some psychologists to see what they have discovered. The first thing you notice is that there are many different types of psychologists who go by different names. Some call themselves "cognitive psychologists" and study how the mind processes information. Some call themselves "social psychologists" and study interpersonal interactions and relationships. Some call themselves "developmental psychologists" and study how humans change psychologically throughout their life spans. Some call themselves "personality psychologists" and focus mainly on the differences between people, although some of them study human nature. Some call themselves "cultural psychologists" and highlight some astonishing differences between individualistic cultures such as the United States and collective cultures such as Japan. And some call themselves "clinical psychologists" and study ways the mind malfunctions.

As a Martian, you might find these disciplinary divisions rather odd. Social behavior, for example, certainly requires the processing of information, so why is social psychology separate from cognitive psychology? Individual differences, another example, certainly develop over time, and many of the most important individual differences are social in nature, so why is personality psychology separate from developmental and social psychology? Understanding the malfunctioning of the mind certainly requires an understanding of how the mind is supposed to function, so why is clinical psychology separate from the rest of psychology?

Despite this strange division of labor among psychologists, when you examine what they have discovered, you might come away at least somewhat impressed. Cognitive psychologists, for example, have documented a fascinating array of cognitive biases and heuristics that suggest that the human mind fails to function according to formal rules of logic (Tversky & Kahneman, 1974). Social psychologists have discovered an array of fascinating phenomena—the facts that people tend to loaf by failing to pull their fair share of the load when the group they are in gets large (Latané, 1981), that people tend to take credit for successful outcomes but blame others for unsuccessful outcomes (Nisbett & Ross, 1980), and that people tend to obey an authority figure even if it means delivering harmful electric shocks to other people (Milgram, 1974). Developmental psychologists have discovered that children develop an understanding at age three that other people have desires, don't understand until age four that other people have beliefs, and don't understand until puberty that people have sexual desires. Personality psychologists have documented some fascinating individual differences: Some people are consistently more Machiavellian or manipulative than others. And clinical psychology has uncovered an array of disorders and some of their properties—for example, twice as many women as men suffer from depression, schizophrenia shows substantial heritability and is nearly impossible to cure, and common phobias of heights and snakes can be easily cured through systematic desensitization treatment.

You want to convey to your Martian colleagues an integrated understanding of this strange species called *Homo sapiens.* You want to retain all the important insights the psychologists have discovered, but you don't want to cling to the disciplinary divisions that strike you as somewhat arbitrary. Because evolution by selection is the only known process that is capable of generating complex functional organic design, evolutionary psychology appears to be the only viable metatheory that is powerful enough to integrate all these subdisciplines. This is the metatheory that seeks to present a unified understanding of the mechanisms of the mind that characterize this strange species of bipedal primates.

This chapter is devoted to panning back from the details and getting a larger, more macroscopic view of human psychology. The first section examines each of the subdisciplines of psychology and illustrates some ways in which evolutionary psychology can inform them. The second section presents an argument that the future of an integrated psychology rests with dissolving traditional disciplinary boundaries.

# ■ EVOLUTIONARY COGNITIVE PSYCHOLOGY

All psychological mechanisms entail, by definition, information-processing devices that are tailored to solving adaptive problems. Because many of the adaptive problems that humans have confronted over the course of evolutionary history are intrinsically social, cognitive psychology must deal with the ways in which we process information about other people. The entire cognitive system, according to an evolutionary psychological perspective, is a complex collection of interrelated information-processing devices, functionally specialized for solving specific classes of adaptive problems.

Traditional cognitive psychology is anchored by several core assumptions that evolutionary psychology challenges (Cosmides & Tooby, 1994). First, mainstream cognitive psychologists tend to assume that cognitive architecture is general purpose and content free. This means that the information-processing devices that are responsible for food selection are assumed to be the same as those for mate and habitat selection. These general-purpose mechanisms include the abilities to reason, learn, imitate, calculate means–ends relationships, compute similarity, form concepts, and remember things. Evolutionary psychologists, as documented throughout this book, make precisely the opposite assumption: that the mind is likely to consist of a large number of specialized mechanisms, each tailored to solving a different adaptive problem.

One consequence of the mainstream cognitive assumption of a general-purpose information-processing device is that little attention has been given to the sorts of stimuli that are used in cognitive experiments. Cognitive psychologists tend to select stimuli on the basis of ease of presentation and experimental manipulability. This leads to categorization studies that use triangles, squares, and circles rather than anything corresponding to natural categories such as kin, mates, enemies, or edible objects. Indeed, many cognitive psychologists have intentionally used artificial stimuli precisely because they want to get rid of the messy "content" with which subjects might have had prior experience. Literally, hundreds of experiments were conducted using "nonsense syllables" to study memory processes because researchers believed that actual words with understandable content would "contaminate" the results. The use of artificial content-free stimuli makes sense if the mind is indeed a general-purpose information processor. It makes less sense if cognitive mechanisms are specialized to process information about particular tasks.

As was discussed in Chapter 2, there are at least two major problems with the assumption of general processing mechanisms: (1) What constitutes a successful adaptive solution differs from domain to domain—the qualities needed for successful food selection, for example, differ from those needed for successful mate selection; and (2) the number of possible behaviors generated by unconstrained general mechanisms approaches infinity, so the organism would have no way of distinguishing successful adaptive solutions from the blizzard of unsuccessful ones (the problem of combinatorial explosion discussed in Chapter 2).

A second core assumption of traditional cognitive psychology is *functional agnosticism*—the view that information-processing mechanisms can be studied without understanding the adaptive problems they were designed to solve. Evolutionary psychology, in contrast, infuses the study of human cognition with functional analysis. Just as we cannot understand the human liver without knowing what it is designed to do (e.g., filter toxins), evolutionary psychologists contend that we cannot understand how humans categorize, reason, make judgments, and store and retrieve specific things from memory without understanding the functions of the cognitive mechanisms on which these activities are based.

In sum, evolutionary psychologists replace the core assumptions of mainstream cognitive psychology—general-purpose and content-free mechanisms along with functional agnosticism—with a different set of assumptions that permits integration with the rest of life science (Tooby & Cosmides, 1992):

1. The human mind consists of a set of evolved information-processing mechanisms embedded in the human nervous system.
2. These mechanisms and the developmental programs that produce them are adaptations produced by natural selection over evolutionary time in ancestral environments.
3. Many of these mechanisms are functionally specialized to produce behavior that solves particular adaptive problems, such as mate selection, language acquisition, and cooperation.
4. To be functionally specialized, many of these mechanisms must be richly structured in content-specific ways.

On the basis of the work of David Ma[...]
cognitive psychology should be anchored in [...]
specifies what that problem is and why the[...]
an information processing device" (p. 44[...]
arguments:

(1) Information-processing devices are [...]
(2) They solve problems by virtue of th[...]
(3) Hence, to explain the structure of a [...]
    (a) *what* problem it was designed [...]
    (b) *why* it was designed to solve t[...]

By itself, computational theory [...]
goes about actually solving an adapti[...]
have many potential solutions. Warm-[...]
mal regulation, for example. But dogs do it through [...]
whereas humans do it through hundreds of thousands of sweat glands [...]
Computational theories don't provide a shortcut to conducting the scientific experiments to [...]
hypotheses about how organisms actually solve problems. They do, however, constrain the
search space by describing what counts as a successful solution. Computational theories are
therefore able to exclude from consideration the thousands of possibilities that fail, in principle, to solve an adaptive problem. One such constraint in humans, for example, is that the relevant information for solving the adaptive problem must have been a recurrent feature of human
ancestral environments.

Several programs of cognitive research have been based on these new assumptions about
the nature of human cognition that promise to revolutionize thinking about entire domains of
cognitive functioning. We discuss a few examples in the following sections.

## Attention and Memory

The world provides an infinite array of things that might capture human attention. Attention,
however, is an inherently limited capacity. Even if we could attend to everything in our worlds,
from the movement of each blade of grass to the nuances of the tone of each word of each conversation occurring around us, we would be overwhelmed by information irrelevant to survival
and reproduction. The same applies to memory. If we remembered everything we experienced,
we would have tremendous difficulty retrieving quickly those memories most relevant to direct-
ing adaptive action. A reasonable evolution-based prediction, therefore, is that human attention
and memory are extremely selective, designed to notice, store, and retrieve information that has
the most importance for solving adaptive problems (Klein et al., 2002).

A fascinating study of 736 front-page newspaper stories from eight countries over a 300-
year time period (1700 to 2001) revealed remarkable uniformity of content (Davis & McLeod,
2003). Here is an example from the *Boston Evening Post* in 1735: "On Sunday morning an odd
Affair happen'd where a young Man and Woman (Country People and very well drefs'd) came to
be marry'd; but before the Minifter had half perform'd the Ceremony the Woman was deliver'd
of a Daughter" (cited in Davis & McLeod, 2003, p. 211). The content across time and cultures

key themes: death (accidental or natural), murder or physical assault, ism or altruism, suicide, marital problems such as infidelity, harm or andoned or destitute family, taking a stand or fighting back, and rape or fact that these historically and cross-culturally recurrent themes correspond pics covered throughout this textbook provides naturalistic evidence that human ecially targeted toward information content of maximal relevance for solving blems that have recurred for humans over deep time.

study of human memory is also being illuminated by posing questions about evolved ns (Todd, Hertwig, & Hoffrage, 2005). Evolutionary psychologist James Nairne and his agues hypothesized that evolved memory systems should be at least somewhat domain spe- ic, sensitive to certain kinds of content or information (Nairne & Pandeirada, 2008; Nairne, Pandeirada, & Thompson, 2008; Nairne et al., 2009). They hypothesized that human memory should be especially sensitive to content relevant to evolutionary fitness, such as survival (e.g. food, predators, and shelter) and reproduction (e.g., mating). Using a standard memory para- digm involving a scenario priming task and a surprise recall task, they found that words previ- ously rated for survival-relevance in scenarios were subsequently remembered at significantly higher rates than those rated for relevance in a variety of control scenario conditions. Further- more, Nairne and his colleagues conducted experiments that pitted survival processing against well-documented powerful encoding techniques, such as ease of generating a visual image, ease of generating an autobiographical memory, and intentional learning in which subjects were instructed to remember the words for a later test. Interestingly, rating the item's relevance in the survival scenario produced better recall performance than *any* other well-known memory- enhancing techniques. The researchers conclude that "survival processing is one of the best encod- ing procedures yet identified in human memory research" (Nairne & Pandeirada, 2008, p.242).

Another study had participants who were in committed romantic relationships come into the lab for one session, during which they were asked to imagine encountering cues to their part- ner's infidelity (Schützwohl & Koch, 2004). Some of the cues were more diagnostic of sexual infidelity such as "He suddenly refuses to have sex with you" and "You notice that she seems bored when the two of you have sex." Other cues were more diagnostic of emotional infidelity, such as "He starts looking for reasons to start fights with you" and "She doesn't respond any more when you tell her that you love her." These cues were interspersed with other neutral cues. A week later, participants came back to the lab, and were given a surprise memory recall test. They were asked to write down all the cues to infidelity that they could remember. The results are shown in Table 13.1. As predicted, women more than men remembered cues to emotional

TABLE 13.1 **Spontaneous Recall of Cues**

|  | Men | Women |
| --- | --- | --- |
| Emotional | 24% | 40% |
| Sexual | 42% | 29% |

*Source:* Schützwohl, A., & Koch, S. (2004). Sex differences in jealousy: The recall of cues to sexual and emotional infidelity in personally more and less threatening conditions. *Evolution and Human Behavior, 25,* 249–257.

infidelity, whereas men more than women remembered cues to sexual infidelity. These results support the hypothesis that the content of what we remember corresponds closely to the adaptive problems we need to solve; in this case, the sex-linked adaptive problems of sexual versus emotional infidelity (see Chapter 11). In short, attention and memory are highly selective—humans are designed to notice and retrieve information that is most relevant to solving the specific adaptive problems they face.

## Problem Solving: Heuristics, Biases, and Judgment under Uncertainty

Much of so-called higher cognition concerns problem solving and judgment under conditions of uncertainty. According to many modern judgment researchers, humans are prone to errors when solving problems and making decisions under conditions of uncertainty (e.g., Nisbett & Ross, 1980; Tversky & Kahneman, 1974). Indeed, a major cottage industry has sprung up in cognitive psychology to document the various errors and biases to which humans are predisposed. Following are two examples:

1. *Base-rate fallacy:* People tend to ignore base-rate information when presented with compelling individuating information. Base rates refer to the overall proportion of something in a sample or population. Consider this example. Imagine that there is a roomful of people, 70 percent of whom are lawyers and 30 percent of whom are engineers. One is a man named George who dislikes novels, likes to do carpentry on weekends, and wears a pocket protector in his shirt pocket to carry his pens. His own writing is dull and rather mechanical, and he has a great need for order and neatness. What is the probability that George is (A) a lawyer or (B) an engineer? Most people tend to ignore the base-rate information, which suggests that it is more likely that George is a lawyer (70 percent of the people in the room are lawyers). Instead, they give too much weight to the individual information, which is highly salient, and declare that George is likely to be an engineer. This error, called the base-rate fallacy because people tend to ignore the actual mathematical proportion (of lawyers, in this sample), violates mathematical formulas by which base rate and individuating information should be combined appropriately.

2. *The conjunction fallacy:* If I tell you that Linda wears tie-dyed shirts and buttons asserting that "men are slime," and frequently tries to organize the women in her workplace, is it more likely that (A) Linda is a bank teller or (B) Linda is a feminist bank teller? A majority of people believe that (B) is more likely, despite the fact that this violates the canons of logic (see Figure 13.1): B (feminist bank tellers) is a subset of A (bank tellers), so the likelihood of A must be greater than B. Stated differently, the *conjunction* of "feminist" and "bank teller" must be lower in likelihood than bank teller alone, because conjunctive events can never exceed the likelihood of their individual elements. Because the description of Linda seems so representative of a feminist, however, most people ignore logic and go with what seems obvious.

The extensive literature showing how foolish people are is, of course, great fun. But is the model of the mind it portrays accurate? Is human cognition riddled with biases and errors, simply because humans use crude and error-prone shortcuts to make judgments under uncertainty? An evolutionary perspective would give one pause before accepting this conclusion, if only

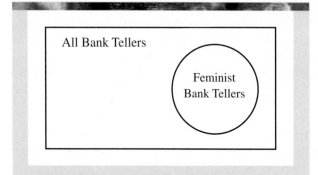

FIGURE *13.1* **Venn Diagram of Bank Tellers and Feminist Bank Tellers.** Feminist bank tellers are logically a subset of all bank tellers; therefore, the likelihood of someone being a feminist bank teller cannot be higher than the likelihood of someone being a bank teller. Yet, most participants in a study say that it is more likely that "Linda" is a feminist bank teller.

because human ancestors had to do some pretty impressive problem solving to deal with the hundreds of adaptive problems involved in surviving and reproducing.

Tooby and Cosmides (1998) argue that an evolutionary perspective presents something of a paradox when contrasted with the view of humans as riddled with cognitive biases. Humans routinely solve complex natural tasks, many of which have defied attempts to be modeled in artificial intelligence systems. In vision, object recognition, grammar induction, and speech perception, people easily surpass the performance of all artificial systems, even though scientists are equipped with all the tools of modern logic and formal statistical decision theories (Tooby & Cosmides, 1998). The paradox is this: If humans are so riddled with cognitive mechanisms that commonly cause errors and biases, how can they routinely solve complex problems that surpass any system that can be developed artificially?

Tooby and Cosmides argue for an evolutionary theory of cognitive mechanisms called *ecological rationality.* Over evolutionary time, the human environment has had certain statistical regularities: Rain often followed thunder, violence sometimes followed angry shouts, sex sometimes followed prolonged eye contact, dangerous bites often followed getting too close to a snake, and so on. These statistical regularities are called *ecological structure.* Ecological rationality consists of evolved mechanisms containing design features that utilize ecological structure to facilitate adaptive problem solving.

The shape and form of cognitive mechanisms, in other words, coordinate with the recurring statistical regularities of the ancestral environments in which humans evolved. We fear snakes and not electrical outlets, for example, because of a recurrent statistical regularity between snakes and debilitating or lethal consequences; electrical outlets are too recent an invention to have recurrently produced debilitating or lethal outcomes. Problem-solving strategies, in short, might be exquisitely designed for solving one set of problems—those that recurred over evolutionary time—but very poor at solving artificial or novel problems. When there is a mismatch between the problem presented and the problem the mechanism was designed to solve, errors will result.

Tooby and Cosmides (1998) take the argument further. Theories of formal logic that are content independent—theories that the researchers of cognitive biases claim humans should use—are exceptionally poor at solving real adaptive problems. The world is full of logically arbitrary relationships: Dung happens to be potentially dangerous to humans, for example, but provides a hospitable home for dung flies. So applying formal logic cannot in principle solve the adaptive problem of avoiding dung. The only thing that can solve it is a content-specific mechanism, one that has been built over evolutionary time to capitalize on the recurring statistical regularities associated with dung as it interacted with our hominid ancestors.

Human adaptive problem solving—which our ancestors must have done reasonably well or else they would have failed to become our ancestors—always depends on three ingredients: (1) the specific *goal* being sought (the problem that must be solved), (2) the *materials* at hand, and (3) the *context* in which the problem is embedded. Finding a single "rational" method for solving all problems independent of content is impossible. The criterion by which the "correctness" of solutions is evaluated is evolutionary: The decisions made by the cognitive mechanism led, on average, to better survival and enhanced reproduction in ancestral environments relative to alternative designs that were present at the time. What matters in the eyes of selection is not truth, validity, or logical consistency, but simply what works in the currency of reproductive success.

Before we conclude that human cognitive mechanisms are riddled with biases and errors of judgment, we need to ask which adaptive problems human cognitive mechanisms evolved to solve and what would compose "sound judgment" or "successful reasoning" from an evolutionary perspective. If humans have trouble locating their cars by color at night in parking lots illuminated with sodium vapor lamps, we would not conclude that our visual system is riddled with errors. Our eyes were designed to perceive the color of objects under natural, not artificial, light (Shepard, 1992).

Many of the research programs that have documented "biases" in judgment, it turns out, have used artificial, evolutionarily unprecedented experimental stimuli that are analogous to sodium vapor lamps. Many, for example, require subjects to make probability judgments based on a single event (Gigerenzer, 1991, 1998). "Reliable numerical statements about the probability of a single event were rare or nonexistent in the Pleistocene—a conclusion reinforced by the relative poverty of number terms in modern band level societies" (Tooby & Cosmides, 1998 p. 40). A specific woman cannot have a 35 percent chance of being pregnant; she either is pregnant or is not, so probabilities hardly make sense when applied to a single case.

The human mind, however, may have been well designed to record the *frequencies* of events: I went to the valley eight times; how many times did I find berries? The last three times I put my arm around a potential mate, how many times was I rebuffed? If some mechanisms of the human mind are designed to record event frequencies rather than single-event probabilities, then experiments that require subjects to calculate probabilities from single events may be presenting artificial and evolutionarily novel stimuli, analogous to testing vision under the illumination of sodium vapor lamps.

***Frequency Representations and Judgment under Uncertainty.*** Is there evidence that human cognitive mechanisms are designed to record event frequencies? Cosmides and Tooby (1996) advance the *frequentist hypothesis:* the proposition that some human reasoning mechanisms are designed to take as input frequency information and produce as output frequency information. Some advantages of operating on frequentist representations are that (1) they allow a person to preserve the number of events on which the judgment was based (e.g., How many times did I go to the valley to search for berries over the past two months?), (2) they allow a person to update his or her database when new events and information are encountered (e.g., adding information from a third month of trips to the valley to search for berries), and (3) they allow a person to construct new reference classes after the events have been encountered and remembered, and to reorganize the database as needed (e.g., remembering that the frequency of encountering berries differed depending on whether the trips to the valley were made in the spring or in the fall). Frequency representations can provide crucial input into problem-solving and decision-making mechanisms.

Consider the medical diagnosis problem: "If a test to detect a disease whose prevalence is 1/1000 has a false positive rate of 5% [that is, the test indicates that 5% of those tested have the disease, even though they do not], what is the chance that a person found to have a positive result actually has the disease, assuming that you know nothing about the person's symptoms or signs? _____%" (Cosmides & Tooby, 1996, p. 21). Of a sample of experts at Harvard Medical School, only 18 percent answered 2 percent, which is the "correct" answer according to most interpretations of the problem. A whopping 45 percent of the experts answered 95 percent, which suggests that they ignored the base-rate information about false positives.

But what if the same problem is presented using frequency information? That is precisely what Cosmides and Tooby (1996) did:

> 1 out of every 1000 Americans has disease X. A test has been developed to detect when a person has disease X. Every time the test is given to a person who has the disease, the test comes out positive (i.e., the "true positive" rate is 100%). But sometimes the test also comes out positive when it is given to a person who is completely healthy. Specifically, out of every 1000 people who are perfectly healthy, 50 of them test positive for the disease (i.e., the "false positive" rate is 5%).
>
> Imagine that we have assembled a random sample of 1000 Americans. They were selected by a lottery. Those who conducted the lottery had no information about the health status of any of these people. Given the information above: On average, how many people who test positive for the disease will actually have the disease? ____ out of _____. (p. 24)

The correct answer is roughly 2 percent.

In sharp contrast to the original medical diagnosis problem, 76 percent of the subjects (Stanford undergraduates) gave the correct answer, as opposed to only 12 percent who got the answer right when the problem was presented in its original format. When the information is presented in a format using frequencies, performance improves dramatically. Performance improves even more when the information is presented pictorially in a visual format (see Figure 13.2). In summary, presenting the information in frequentist terms verbally allows three-quarters of the subjects to get it right, but adding a visual frequentist representation allows almost all the subjects to get it right (see Brase, 2009, for additional experimental evidence).

These results suggest that people do *not* ignore base-rate information in making judgments, as long as the base-rate information is presented in a manner that maps more closely onto the sorts of input that humans would have been likely to process in ancestral times. The domains that are most likely to require processing about event frequency are those in which information changes rapidly over a person's life span or across generations—domains such as the locations of game animals, the distribution of edible plants, and the locations of predators. Local sampling of events during a person's life is necessary in these domains because local frequencies provide the most reliable basis for making predictions.

In sum, these results offer a challenge to the mainstream cognitive view that the problem-solving abilities of humans are riddled with errors and biases (Cummins & Allen, 1998). Evolutionary psychological analysis is helpful in identifying the sorts of adaptive problems the human mind was designed to solve. This includes an understanding of the format of the information humans are designed to process. Conducting experiments that more closely mimic the formats of the information that humans were designed to process provides a different picture of the cognitive capabilities of humans when engaged in making judgments under uncertainty (see also Wang, 1996).

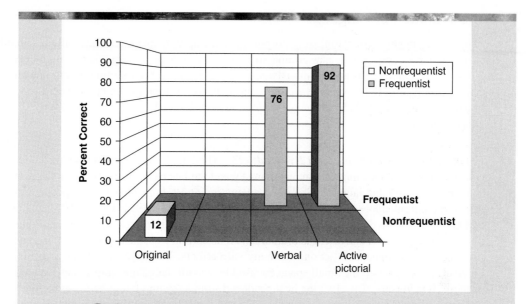

FIGURE 13.2 **Comparing the Percentage of Correct Answers for the Original, Nonfrequentist Version to the Percentage Correct for the Two Frequentist Versions.** In the active pictorial condition, which elicited the highest levels of performance, subjects were required to form a frequentist representation.

*Source:* Cosmides, L., & Tooby, J. (1996). Are humans good intuitive statisticians after all? Rethinking some conclusions from the literature on judgment under uncertainty. *Cognition, 58*, 1–73. Copyright © 1996, with permission from Elsevier Science.

The portrait of human cognitive mechanisms afforded by this line of thinking offers a marked contrast to the mainstream portrait of general mechanisms and crude heuristics. Rather than a single general intelligence, humans possess multiple intelligences. Rather than a general ability to reason, humans have many specialized abilities to reason, depending on the nature of the adaptive problems they were designed by selection to solve. Rather than general abilities to learn, imitate, calculate means–ends relationships, compute similarity, form concepts, remember things, and compute representativeness, evolutionary psychology suggests that the human mind is filled with complex and problem-specific cognitive mechanisms, each designed to solve different adaptive problems.

This view does not imply that the human mind lacks cognitive biases. Rather, many of the cognitive heuristics it contains are "adaptively biased" (Haselton et al., 2009). Thus, the "descent illusion" and "auditory looming bias" discussed in Chapter 3 are perceptual biases that solve problems of survival. Women's "commitment skepticism bias" (Chapter 11) is designed to solve the problem of mating. Men's out-group discrimination bias (Chapter 10), although possibly irrational in the modern environment, was adaptive in an ancestral environment filled with group-against-group conflict. Humans may not be rational according to standards of formal logic or domain-free statistical models of rational decision making. But they are "adaptively rational" (Kenrick et al., 2009).

## The Evolution of Language

Language is an ability of astonishing proportions: "Simply by making noises with our mouths, we can reliably cause precise new combinations of ideas to arise in each other's minds" (Pinker, 1994, p. 15). Language is an enormously complex topic, and a brief section within one chapter cannot do it justice. In this section, we limit our focus to two topics of central concern for evolutionary psychology: (1) Is language an adaptation? (2) What adaptive problems, if any, did language evolve to solve?

*Is Language an Adaptation or a By-Product?* There have been two sides to this debate. On one side are the famous linguist Noam Chomsky and the late paleontologist Stephen Jay Gould. They have argued that language is not an adaptation at all, but rather is a by-product or side effect of the tremendous growth of the human brain (Chomsky, 1991; Gould, 1987). Chomsky and Gould acknowledge that the growth of the human brain itself resulted from natural selection. Their argument is that after the brain attained its current size and complexity, language simply emerged spontaneously as one of many side effects. When you put billions of neurons together, packaged into the small space encased by a skull, language simply materializes, they propose. It is in some ways like the heat produced from a reading lamp; you cannot construct a lamp that is designed to shed light without producing as a by-product some amount of heat (see Chapter 2). Language is to the large human brain as heat is to the reading lamp—an emergent product but not central to its function or purpose. If this explanation seems clear in the case of the lamp but a bit mysterious in the case of language, it is because the physical laws by which heat by-products occur are well known but the physical laws by which language is presumed to emerge from the close proximity of tightly packed neurons have not been articulated. Indeed, some find the Chomsky–Gould argument a bit mystical. More recently, Chomsky and his colleagues appear to have softened this position to allow for the possibility that language is an evolved adaptation, suggesting that human language "may have been guided by particular selective pressures, unique to our evolutionary past, or a consequence (byproduct) of other kinds of neural organization" (Hauser, Chomsky, & Fitch, 2002).

The opposite end of the conceptual spectrum is spearheaded by evolutionary psychologist Steven Pinker. He proposes that language is an adaptation *par excellence*—produced by natural selection for the communication of information (Pinker, 1994; Pinker & Bloom, 1990). The deep structure of grammar is too well designed for the function of communication, Pinker argues, for it to be merely an incidental by-product of big brains. It includes elements that are universal across all languages: major lexical categories such as nouns, verbs, adjectives, and prepositions. It includes rules that govern the structure of phrases. It includes rules of linear order that determine which words must come before and after within a sentence in order to convey the correct meaning (e.g., in English, "Dog bites man" is distinguished from "Man bites dog"). All languages contain verb affixes that signal the temporal distribution of the event (in the past, present, or future) and many other essential and universal components.

Pinker points out that children become fluent speakers of complex grammatical sentences early in life, usually by age three, without any formal teaching or instruction. They obey quite subtle rules of grammar that are not apparent in their environments. Furthermore, language is linked to specific regions of the brain—Wernicke's area and Broca's area—and damage to these regions results in language impairment. The vocal tract of humans, in contrast to that of other primates, seems specially designed for producing the multitudes of sounds needed for language—for example, a larynx located low in the throat. Finally, auditory perception, our mechanism for hearing sounds, shows precise complementary specializations that allow us to decode the speech sounds produced by other humans. When all these points are added up, Pinker proposes, they strongly suggest that language is an adaptation, much like echolocation in bats, antennae in insects, or stereoscopic vision in monkeys. Language shows *universal complexities of design* for the communication of information, and the only known explanation for the origins of complex organic structures is evolution by natural selection (Pinker & Bloom, 1990). Pinker contends that language is an "instinct" in the sense that "people know how to talk in more or less the same sense that spiders know how to spin webs . . . language is a biological adaptation to communicate information" (Pinker, 1994, pp. 18–19).

***What Adaptive Problems Did Language Evolve to Solve?***   The dominant theory of the function of language is that it evolved to facilitate communication—the exchange of information between individuals (Pinker, 1994). Information exchange could help with an almost limitless variety of tasks: warning friends and family of danger; informing allies about the location of ripe berries; coordinating a coalition for hunting or warfare; providing instruction for the construction of shelters, tools, or weapons; and many others.

Three competing theories of the function of language have been proposed, all involving social functions. The first is the *social gossip hypothesis* (Dunbar, 1996). According to this hypothesis, language evolved to facilitate bonding among large groups of humans. Evolutionist Robin Dunbar argues that language evolved to keep tabs on complex networks of social relationships: who is having sex with whom, who has cheated whom, who can be trusted with a secret, who will make a good friend or coalitional partner, which alliances show signs of rupture, and who has a reputation for doing what to whom. Dunbar argues that language is a form of "social grooming." As the group size increased, it became impossible physically to devote the necessary time to physically grooming one's allies, as occurs among chimpanzees. Language evolved to promote social cohesion among large groups through gossip in the broadest sense—exchanging information about who is doing what to whom. The social gossip hypothesis, as a complete theory for language evolution, has been criticized on the grounds that people use language for far more than gossip or social grooming (Scott-Phillips, 2007).

The *social contract hypothesis* is another idea for the origins and function of language (Deacon, 1997). According to this hypothesis, problems of mating became more problematic when large game hunting emerged. Men had to leave their mates alone while out on the hunt, risking infidelity and vulnerability to exploitation. Language evolved, according to this idea, to facilitate explicit marriage contracts. Men and women could vow publicly their mating commitments, signaling to each other and to everyone else in the group that one's mate is off limits to others. This hypothesis encounters serious difficulties: It fails to explain how cohesive large groups form to begin with, why other species appear to solve these mating problems without resorting to language, and why marriage contracts so frequently fail (Barrett, Dunbar, & Lycett, 2002).

A third hypothesis has been termed the *Scheherazade hypothesis,* after the main character in *The Arabian Nights* (Miller, 2000). To prevent being killed, Scheherazade regaled the king with such entertaining tales that each morning he decided against killing her. The argument is that the large human brain is essentially like the peacock's tail—a sexually selected organ that evolved to signal superior fitness to potential mates. By dazzling potential mates with humor, wit, exotic tales, and word magic, those with superior language skills had a mating advantage over their mumbling, fumbling competitors. As Pinker and Bloom (1990) note, "That tribal chiefs are often both gifted orators and highly polygynous is a splendid prod to any imagination that cannot conceive of how linguistic skills could make a Darwinian difference" (p. 725). There are two potential problems with the sexual selection hypothesis of the origin of language. Sexually selected adaptations typically show striking sexual differentiation, whereas men and women have roughly equal language abilities. Sexually selected adaptations typically emerge at puberty, at the point when individuals enter mate competition, but language emerges quite early in life, becoming highly sophisticated by age three (Fitch, 2005). On the other hand, language does not reach truly mature levels of proficiency until the end of adolescence—a finding that actually supports Miller's sexual selection hypothesis (Scott-Phillips, 2007).

Although these hypotheses are sometimes discussed as though they were competing or contradictory, it is entirely possible that language has evolved over time to solve several different sorts of adaptive problems, whatever the initial impetus was for its emergence. Language is indeed used and seems well designed for exchanging information about the physical, as well as the social, world (Cartwright, 2000), so the dominant theory of information communication cannot be dismissed (Pinker & Jackendoff, 2005). Once language evolved, however, there is no reason to believe that selection would have to limit language use to its original function. It could evolve further, being used for social bonding, policing cheaters, courting mates, forming marriage contracts, and establishing peace treaties with neighboring groups. It could also evolve to influence and manipulate others—what has been called "Machiavellian intelligence" (Byrne & Whiten, 1988). It has been empirically documented, for example, that people routinely use language and gossip to manipulate social reputations, such as derogating their competitors, in the service of mate competition (McAndrew, 2008; McAndrew & Milenkovic, 2002; Schmitt & Buss, 1996).

In sum, although early formulations stressed communication or information exchange as the evolved function of language, it is likely that language subsequently evolved further, or was coopted, to solve a variety of social adaptive problems. This nicely illustrates a key theme of this chapter: Although language historically has been considered within the province of the subdiscipline of cognitive psychology, it cannot logically be divorced from the subdiscipline of social psychology.

## The Evolution of Extraordinary Human Intelligence

The brain is a metabolically expensive organ to operate. Although the human brain makes up only 2 to 3 percent of the average human's body weight, it consumes roughly 20 to 25 percent of the body's calories (Leonard & Robertson, 1994). Primates generally have large brains. Humans stand out even among primates—our brains are larger, relative to body size, than any other primate. Over the past several million years, the human brain has nearly tripled in size. Our large brains house sophisticated information-processing devices, forms of intelligence not present in our smaller-brained ancestors or current primate cousins. These include the unprecedented capacities for abstract thinking, reasoning, learning, and scenario-building. Clearly, something happened over the course of human evolution to propel us to have such large brains containing formidable forms of intelligence.

Why humans evolved these cognitive capacities has been the subject of great debate. One explanation is the *ecological dominance/social competition* (EDSC) hypothesis (Alexander, 1989; Flinn, Geary, & Ward, 2005). According to the EDSC hypothesis, human ancestors were able to subdue many of the traditional "hostile forces of nature" that previously impeded survival. These hostile forces include the "Four Horsemen of the Apocalypse," which are starvation (due to food shortages), warfare, pestilence, and extreme weather. We can grow abundant food, so rarely starve. We've developed shelters, clothing, and fire, and so rarely die from extremes of weather. According to the EDSC hypothesis, human dominance over the ecology opened the door to a new set of selective forces—competition from other humans.

The EDSC hypothesis invokes the complexities of living in large multifaceted social groups, which require solving adaptive problems such as forming coalitions, punishing cheaters, detecting deception, and negotiating complex and changing social hierarchies. Living in complex social groups imposes risks of "theft, cannibalism, cuckoldry, infanticide, extortion, and other treachery" (Pinker, 1997, p. 193). The size of ancestral human groups, in the range of 50 to 150 individuals, adds to the complexities of social adaptive problems, selecting for larger brains and greater levels of social intelligence. These new forms of intelligence are hypothesized to include consciousness, language, self-awareness, and theory of mind (ability to understand the beliefs and desires of other people). They also included "scenario building," which allowed people "to construct and rehearse potential responses to changing social situations" (Flinn et al., 2005, p. 32).

Successful social competition likely included adaptations to form coalitions for hunting, especially large game hunting, a means of acquiring vital sources of protein and precious amino acids (Tooby & Devore, 1987). Forming cooperative hunting coalitions, in turn, requires formidable communication abilities, psychological adaptations for cooperation (including the ability to detect and punish cheaters), and rules governing meat distribution. The large bounty of meat gained from hunting allowed humans to store excess food in the bodies of friends and allies, with the expectation of reciprocal returns.

It does not take a large leap to go from coalitional hunting to coalitional warfare, turning handheld weapons and cooperative coalitions toward the purpose of vanquishing other groups of humans to expropriate their resources (Alexander, 1989; Buss, 2005b; Duntley & Buss, 2005). Coevolutionary arms races between adaptations dedicated for warfare and adaptations dedicated to defending against groups of attackers, in turn, would have led to yet more forms of intelligence. It is plausible that all of these related forces—the complexities posed by intense group living and bipedalism that freed the human hand for tool invention and use, hunting, and warfare—led to many of the high levels of intelligence displayed by humans today.

One empirical prediction from the EDSC hypothesis is that as population density increases, selection pressure for greater intelligence should increase due to the more taxing demands of social competition. In the first empirical test of this prediction, Bailey and Geary (2009) gathered relevant data from 175 hominid crania dating from 10,000 to 1.9 million years ago. Using proxies for population density for the locations of the skulls, they found that indeed cranial capacity was higher in locations of higher population density. The authors conclude that although multiple pressures drove the evolution of human intelligence, "the core selective force was social competition" (Bailey & Geary, 2009).

Linda Gottfredson challenges the EDSC hypothesis for the evolution of human intelligence (Gottfredson, 2007). She argues that general intelligence (as measured by IQ tests) is not highly correlated with "social intelligence," as predicted by the EDSC hypothesis. She points out that the technological feats of humans that have raised the average survival rates of humans have not eliminated individual differences in survival—differences that would have selected for higher levels of general intelligence. Gottfredson presents compelling evidence that individual differences in survival, even today, are linked with individual differences in intelligence.

Indeed, the very technologies that humans have invented to aid in their survival—fire, tools, weapons, canoes—have created novel hazards for humans. Although fire enabled ancestral humans to expand the array of foods they could eat, fire created new hazards leading to injury or death. Although weapons enabled ancestral humans to hunt more effectively, they also created new sources of injury or death. Among the !Kung of Botswana, for example, "the most serious cause of hunting accidents, in the sense of injuries leading to death, is not the animals themselves, but the weapons [with poisoned shafts] that the !Kung use to kill those animals" (Howell, 2000, p. 55). Although canoes allowed humans to exploit new territory and food resources, they also created an increased risk of drowning. In short, although it is true that humans have attained an astonishing level of dominance over their ecologies and some historical hostile forces that impeded survival, novel technological innovations have created new hazards that result in the injury or death of *some* individuals—those who are less intelligent.

Gottfredson's *deadly innovations hypothesis* proposes that human innovation has created and even amplified the relative risk of injury and premature death, creating selection pressure for the evolution of general intelligence. Preventing accidents from novel innovations requires formidable cognitive capabilities—the ability to scenario-build or think about many different "what-if" possibilities, anticipate complex contingencies, and take precautions that lower the risks.

According to the deadly innovations hypothesis, several forces occurring over the past half-million years would have widened the survival differences between individuals of higher and lower general intelligence (Gottfredson, 2007). The first is *double-jeopardy:* Not only do the less intelligent become injured and die at higher rates, their children also suffer greater mortality as a consequence of the parents not being able to protect and provide for them. The second is *spiraling complexity:* As technologies become increasingly complex, they amplify the importance of general intelligence for avoiding the new hazards they bring. A third force is the *migration ratchet:* As humans migrated out of Africa and into the new and previously unexploited territories of Europe, Asia, the Americas, and even the Arctic, these new environments created pressure for even more innovative technologies to harness them, creating even more novel hazards.

Empirical support for the deadly innovations hypothesis comes from several sources. First, intelligence is indeed correlated with how long individuals live. One study found that each additional IQ point, such as 107 versus 106, was linked with a 1 percent reduction in the relative risk of death (O'Toole & Stankov, 1992). This means that having an IQ 15 points above average (115 as opposed to 100) would decrease your mortality risk by 15 percent. Second, IQ is also linked with sublethal injuries, which themselves hurt an individual's inclusive fitness. In the modern world, those with lower IQs are more likely to drown; get into bicycle, motorcycle, and car accidents; become injured through explosions, falling objects, and knives; and even be hit by lightning (Gottfredson, 2007). Although no individual cause, considered alone, is strongly linked with IQ, when you add them all up, they cumulate to an increased risk of injury and death.

Although the deadly innovation hypothesis for the evolutionary origins of general intelligence is consistent with evidence from modern populations, Gottfredson concedes that it remains to be pitted against competing hypotheses, such as the EDSC hypothesis. It is also possible that both are correct, because they are not necessarily contradictory. Interestingly, both theories propose adaptive functions for general intelligence—abstract thought, scenario-building, reasoning abilities, and capacity to learn from experience. They both suggest that humans have evolved these domain-general cognitive abilities, in addition to the specialized domain-specific cognitive abilities that have been documented by evolutionary psychologists.

# ■ EVOLUTIONARY SOCIAL PSYCHOLOGY

 $\mathcal{M}$ any of the most important adaptive problems humans have faced over the past several million years are inherently social in nature: negotiating social hierarchies, forming long-term social exchange relationships, using language to communicate and influence others, forming short-term and long-term mateships, managing social reputations amidst a landscape of shifting allies and rivals, and dealing with kin of varying and uncertain degrees of genetic relatedness. Because so many adaptive problems are likely to have been social, the human mind should be heavily populated with psychological mechanisms dedicated to social solutions. Much of evolutionary psychology, therefore, will be evolutionary social psychology (Buss & Kenrick, 1998; Schaller, Simpson, & Kenrick, 2006).

Evolutionary social psychology offers the promise of answering some of the most profound questions about the human animal. Why do people live in groups? Why do people form relationships—mateships, friendships, coalitions, and kin ties—that endure over years and decades? Why do we select mates and friends preferentially, and what selection criteria do we use? Why do people cooperate with some yet compete with others? Why are social relationships sometimes riddled with conflict and strife but other times characterized by love and cooperation? Because most human social interaction has taken place within the context of enduring relationships, questions about the psychology of relationships should form the core of the field of social psychology.

This focus on relationships is in sharp contrast to much mainstream social psychology, which tends to be "phenomenon" oriented. Typically, some interesting, counterintuitive, or anomalous observation is noticed and empirically documented. Examples are (1) *the correspondence bias,* the tendency to explain a person's behavior by invoking enduring dispositions, even when it can be shown that situational causes are responsible (Gilbert & Malone, 1995; Ross, 1981); (2) *the social loafing effect,* the tendency for individuals to perform less work toward a joint outcome as group size increases (Latané, 1981); (3) *self-handicapping,* the tendency to present publicly a purported weakness about oneself to provide an excuse in the event one fails at a task (Leary & Shepperd, 1986); (4) *the self-serving bias,* the tendency to make attributions that make oneself look better than others in the group (Nisbett & Ross, 1980); (5) *the confirmation bias,* the tendency to selectively seek out information that affirms (rather than falsifies) an already-held hypothesis (Hansen, 1980); and many others.

Social psychology has thus amassed a number of interesting descriptions of empirical phenomena of considerable importance. But it has not yet developed a theory powerful enough to explain the origins of these phenomena nor shown how they fit within a larger understanding of human psychology. Evolutionary psychology provides the missing framework to theoretically anchor the empirical discoveries of social psychologists.

## Capitalizing on Evolutionary Theories about Social Phenomena

Most of the major theoretical advances in evolutionary biology have been about social phenomena, yet these important theories have been almost entirely ignored by mainstream social psychologists. The first is *inclusive fitness theory* (Hamilton, 1964). A direct implication of inclusive fitness theory is that altruistic acts should be heavily directed toward other organisms that (1) are likely to have copies of the helper's genes and (2) have the ability to convert such help into increased survival or reproduction. The theory of inclusive fitness has profound consequences for the social psychology of the family, altruism, helping, coalitions, and even aggression.

The second important evolutionary theory for social psychology is *sexual selection*—the theory that evolution can occur through mating advantage accrued through (1) besting intrasexual competitors and (2) being preferentially chosen as a mate by members of the opposite sex (Darwin, 1871). This theory has already proved invaluable to discovering key psychological mechanisms in same-sex competition, homicide and other forms of violence, risk taking, mate choice, conflict between the sexes, sex differences in status striving, and even sex differences in the risk of dying. Indeed, the theory of sexual selection provides the most promising theory for understanding many of the sex differences found in humans and other primates.

The third important theory is *parental investment theory,* which provided a theoretical prediction about the operation of the two components of sexual selection (Trivers, 1972). Specifically, the sex that invests more in offspring is predicted to be more choosy in mate selection. The sex that invests less in offspring is predicted to be less choosy in mate selection and more competitive with its own sex for sexual access to the high-investing sex. This theory has led to many important discoveries about strategies of human mating and promises many more discoveries.

The theory of *reciprocal altruism* provides a fourth theoretical anchor for social psychology (Axelrod & Hamilton, 1981; Trivers, 1971; Williams, 1966). This theory offers an evolutionary explanation for many important social phenomena, such as friendship, cooperation, helping, altruism, and social exchange. It also provides a source of insights for the analysis of close relationships, including friendships and cooperative coalitions. Social exchange has been an enduring topic within mainstream social psychology. Evolutionary theories of reciprocal altruism and related theories offer an evolutionary explanation for its importance and further predictions about its form (e.g., Cosmides & Tooby, 2005).

Fifth, the theory of *parent–offspring conflict* provides another conceptual anchor for social psychology (Trivers, 1974). This theory furnishes precise predictions about family dynamics. Whereas conflict within families is often viewed as a symptom of malfunctioning, the theory of parent–offspring conflict predicts that such conflicts will be common in most families. It supplies an explanation for sibling rivalry. It accounts for the more frequent incidence of child abuse in stepfamilies. It predicts conflict between mother and child over the timing of weaning. "The theory of parent–offspring conflict also predicts conflict between children and their parents over activities such as extramarital involvement, which may be beneficial to the parent but costly for the child" (Friedman & Duntley, 1998).

Sixth, the theory of *sexual conflict* (Parker, 2006) provides a powerful guide to the ways in which men and women get into conflict. Patterns of male and female deception on the mating market, sexual aggression, women's defenses against sexual aggression, and jealous conflict within mating relationships are all illuminated by the theory that what is in the best fitness interests of a woman and a man often conflict with one another.

In sum, theoretical advances in evolutionary biology offer social psychology a powerful set of tools for anchoring and integrating social phenomena. They also provide a guide to important domains of inquiry.

## The Evolution of Moral Emotions

Consider this hypothetical dilemma: A building is burning. You can run through the left door and save a number of children who are all unrelated to you, *or* you can run through the right door and save your own child (Pinker, 2002). If you are a parent, how many children would it take for you to pick the left door and let your own child burn to death? Is there any number that would cause you to let your child incinerate in flames? Human intuitions dovetail with evolutionary theory in telling us that our standards of morality are likely to be biased in favor of genetic relatives. But isn't human moral reasoning supposed to make us rise above genetic self-interest? Does accepting evolutionary psychology doom us to a human nature of amoral egoists? This section considers the evolution of moral emotions and why they lead us to some surprising attitudes.

Most people feel that crimes such as murder, rape, incest, and child abuse are morally wrong. But what causes us to have these moral views? Historical approaches to morality have been dominated by "rationalist" theories, whereby people arrive at a moral judgment through moral reasoning (Haidt, 2001). By logic and rationality, we are presumed to weigh the issues of right and wrong, harm and misdeed, justice and fairness, and arrive at the morally correct answer. Psychologist Jon Haidt has challenged this view, arguing instead that humans have evolved *moral emotions* that produce quick automatic evaluations. Only subsequently, when we are forced to explain or rationalize our moral stances, do we grasp for the straws of reasoning that we hope will support a judgment we've already come to. Consider the following moral dilemma:

> Julie and Mark are brother and sister. They are traveling together in France on summer vacation from college. One night they are staying alone in a cabin near the beach. They decide that it would be interesting and fun if they tried making love. At the very least it would be a new experience for each of them. Julie was already taking birth control pills, but Mark uses a condom too, just to be safe. They both enjoy making love, but they decide not to do it again. They keep that night as a special secret, which makes them feel even closer to each other. What do you think about that? Was it OK for them to make love? (Haidt, 2001, p. 814)

Most people immediately say that it was wrong for Julie and Mark to commit incest. But when asked for reasons, they have difficulty. Some invoke the genetic hazards of inbreeding but then recall that double birth control was used. Some search for possible psychological damage, although it is clear from the story that neither Julie nor Mark was harmed. When pressed, participants eventually say things like "I don't know, I can't explain it, I just know it's wrong" (Haidt, 2001, p. 814).

Haidt found similar reactions to a number of other scenarios that people find disagreeable but without a clear victim. A plausible explanation is that humans have evolved moral emotions. The *repulsion of incest* evolved to prevent inbreeding and is invoked in reaction to sex between Julie and Mark (Lieberman, Tooby, & Cosmides, 2003).

Similar functional logic can be applied to other moral emotions. *Anger* toward cheaters likely evolved to punish those who violate social contracts. Anger toward cheaters motivates revenge, which in turn might deter others from cheating in the future. And revenge might be an emotion that is sweetly savored. In an interesting series of studies, participants rated a variety of different endings to Hollywood film clips that portrayed a serious injustice (Haidt & Sabini, 2000). Participants were displeased by endings in which the victim of an injustice accepted the loss, forgave the transgressor, and found growth and fulfillment. They were most satisfied by endings in which the perpetrator of the injustice suffered greatly, knew that the suffering was retribution for the transgression, and experienced public humiliation in the process. In short, the moral outrage that people experience at cheating and violations of social contracts might have evolved to serve a policing function, holding others to their commitments and obligations.

*Embarrassment* might have evolved to promote appeasement and submission. It is most clearly evoked when one is in the presence of people of higher status and is almost never experienced around people of lower status (Haidt, 2003). It occurs when one violates social conventions. *Shame* is a similar moral emotion, cutting deeper than embarrassment, being activated when a failure to measure up to standards of morality is made public. Both shame and embarrassment motivate the desire to hide and withdraw, reducing one's social presence. Displays of shame might minimize attack or punishment from dominant others, lowering the costs to the violator of the moral code.

*Guilt* is often regarded as a prototypical emotion. Whereas shame is linked to hierarchical interactions, guilt stems from violations of communal relationships (Haidt, 2003). It is likely to have evolved to signal to the harmed party that you know that you have inflicted a harm: It motivates confession and apologies. It also signals that you are motivated to repair the harm. By promoting reparation after harming a communal ally, thereby making up for the transgression, guilt functions to prevent the dissolution of valued relationships.

Evolutionary hypotheses have also been advanced for other moral emotions such as *contempt* (evoked with moral violations of disrespect, duty, or hierarchy), *sympathy* (moving people to help others who are suffering), *gratitude* (motivating people to act more prosocially to one's benefactors), and many others.

Two other examples highlight the centrality of morality to social adaptive problems. One centers on the in-group versus out-group distinction, which often provides the boundaries for determining who deserves moral treatment and who does not. Even moral injunctions such as "thou shall not kill" often refer to members of one's in-group, and not to despised out-group enemies. Evolutionary research has begun to identify the underlying design features of the psychology of in-groups and out-groups. Carlos Navarrete and his colleagues have found that conditioned fear responses to in-group members can be easily extinguished, but fear toward out-group members is stubbornly difficult to extinguish (Navarrete et al., 2009). Interestingly, it is fear of *male* out-group members that proves especially difficult to extinguish. Navarrete argues that prejudice toward male out-group specifically may have helped human ancestors to solve adaptive problems of defense against physical aggression for men, and defense against sexual coercion for women (Navarrete et al., 2010). If correct, this suggests that our understanding of morality, and attempts to extend it to wider circles of people by eliminating prejudice will require deep knowledge of our in-group and out-group evolved psychology.

Sexual selection provides another link between morality and social adaptive problems. Miller (2007) proposes that many things we consider to be morally virtuous are precisely the qualities we find attractive in a mate. Virtues such as kindness, fidelity, sacrifice for others, and magnanimity are desirable in mates because they advertise good parenting and good partner qualities, and possibly good genetic quality, and so may have been sexually selected over many thousands of generations of human evolution.

In sum, moral emotions might serve as "commitment devices" that promote prosocial deeds, reparation of harm, and punishment of cheaters, all while signaling to others that one is a good coalitional ally and can be relied on in the future. Each moral emotion seems tailored to a specific kind of conduct. The adaptive problems they solve can be grouped into three major classes: (1) *respect for authority*—restraining one's selfish urges by deferring to those in a dominant position and obeying laws, rules, and commandments from higher authority; (2) *a thirst for justice*—the adaptive value of cooperation and reciprocity, including the punishment of cheaters to avoid the collapse of beneficial mutualism; and (3) *the evolution of care*—the adaptive value of devotion, sympathy, giving toward allies, mates, and kin (Krebs, 1998, 2009). Although morality is sometimes viewed as being within the province of cognitive psychology, it clearly cannot be divorced from the social adaptive problems it evolved to solve. Additionally, morality is not a topic walled off within the cognitive realm of reasoning, but instead is intimately connected with social adaptive problems such as mating and between-group aggression.

## The Return of Group Selection as Multilevel Selection Theory

In Chapter 1, we discussed the demise of the theory of group selection, the idea that there are group-level adaptations that evolved through the differential reproduction and extinction of groups. After the publication of George Williams's (1966) critique of group selection, nearly all evolutionary biologists relinquished adherence to that idea. They did so not because group selection was theoretically impossible. In fact, Williams showed that group selection *is* theoretically possible, and may indeed have occurred for some species such as honeybees. The conclusion, rather, was that the conditions that make group selection likely—such as (a) a high degree of "shared fate" of members within the group, (b) low levels of reproductive competition within the group, and (c) recurrent patterns of differential reproduction and extinction of groups—are rarely seen in nature, and unlikely to have been a strong force for most species.

Evolutionary biologist David Wilson and evolutionary philosopher Elliot Sober have argued that group selection is far more viable than most biologists had concluded (Sober & Wilson, 1998; Wilson & Sober, 1994). The argument centers on the issue of whether groups can have functional organization in the same way that individuals have functional organization. Just as individuals can be "vehicles" of selection, so groups too can be "vehicles" of selection. They suggest, for example, that humans do many things to reduce reproductive differences within the group, such as passing laws that restrict men and women to one spouse. Groups whose members cooperate with each other better, to take another example, might have outreproduced groups composed of more selfish individuals. This resurrection of group selection is sometimes called *multilevel selection theory* to acknowledge that selection can operate on many levels, including individuals, groups within species, and even larger entities such as multispecies ecosystems.

If multiselection theory has any merit, it will have profound implications for evolutionary social psychology in pointing to group-level adaptations that may have been entirely missed by those focusing on adaptations at the level of the individual organism (e.g., altruism for self-sacrifice for the group, even when the group members are not kin). Many biologists and evolutionary psychologists remain skeptical of this new group selection (e.g., Cronk, 1994; Dawkins, 1994; Dennett, 1994; West, Griffin, & Gardner, 2007). They argue that the conditions required to make group selection a powerful force are rarely met, especially with humans. Given that humans within groups compete heavily with each other and groups often show high fluidity, with members defecting from one group to another and forming new groups with new combinations, individuals rarely have the high levels of "shared fate" within the group that would facilitate group selection.

Whether Wilson and Sober or their critics are right about the power and importance of group selection is ultimately an empirical issue. At a minimum, posing questions about group selection might indeed lead to new discoveries in human social psychology (O'Gorman, Sheldon, & Wilson, 2008), even if in the long run, group selection turns out to be the "weak force" that George Williams envisioned.

# ■ EVOLUTIONARY DEVELOPMENTAL PSYCHOLOGY

Developmental psychology is not a branch of psychology with a particular content attached to it. Rather, it is an approach to any psychological phenomena viewed from a temporal, life-span, or ontogenetic perspective. One can study personality development, social development, moral development, perceptual development, cognitive development, or developmental psychopathology. Thus developmental psychology cuts across the other traditional branches of psychology and is defined by its temporal perspective rather than by its psychological content. Because few psychological mechanisms emerge at birth fully developed, a developmental perspective will necessarily be an essential part of the proper description and understanding of nearly every psychological mechanism (Bjorklund & Pellegrini, 2002; Ellis & Bjorklund, 2005).

Evolutionary developmental psychologists (e.g., Grotuss, Bjorklund, & Csinady, 2007; King, Schlomer, & Ellis, in press) tend to stress the importance of the following conceptual issues: (1) Natural selection occurs throughout the life span, but selection tends to be especially strong early in life—if an individual fails to survive infancy and childhood, it cannot reproduce; (2) adaptations in infancy and childhood can solve adaptive problems at a particular time during development (e.g., the suckling reflex of the infant functions to obtain breast milk), or prepare the individual for an adaptive problem that it will face later (e.g., rough and tumble play in boys might prepare them for physical contests when they enter reproductive competition); (3) the extended childhood characteristics of humans prepare them for the complexities of social living later in life; (4) children have *conditional adaptations*, which allow them to respond flexibly to features of the childhood environment with strategies that are effective in coping with environments that those features statistically predict (Boyce & Ellis, 2005); and (5) gene-environment interactions occur throughout development.

One key insight currently missing from mainstream developmental psychology is this: *Human beings face predictably different adaptive problems at various points in their lives.* Infants face the problem of survival, but not the problem of mating. Problems of mating are faced predictably before problems of parenting. Problems of parenting are faced predictably before problems of grandparenting. To the degree that these adaptive problems have a specieswide temporal sequence, evolutionary psychologists will be able to formulate a developmental theory of human nature. This section provides a few examples of the heuristic value of developmental psychology (see Bjorklund & Pellegrini, 2002; Burgess & MacDonald, 2005; Ellis & Bjorklund, 2005; Segal, Weisfeld, & Weisfeld, 1997; and Surbey, 1998a, for more comprehensive treatments).

## Theory of Mind Mechanisms

The work by psychologists Allen Leslie (1991), Henry Wellman (1990), and others has documented that at roughly three years of age, children develop a "theory of mind." This entails inferences about the beliefs and desires of other individuals inhabiting each child's social world. Combining inferences about beliefs and desires enables people to predict the behavior of others. When asked to "explain" why James went to the school cafeteria, for example, a child will invoke the notion that James had a desire (hunger) and a belief (that food can be obtained in the cafeteria). Prior to the age of three (two in some studies), children do not make inferences that others have beliefs and desires. The ability to better predict other people's behavior from knowledge of their beliefs and desires helps solve adaptive problems such as anticipating hostile attacks, enlisting aid, pacifying conflicting parents, making threats more credible, and forming coalitions. A deep understanding of the beliefs, desires, and motivations of others is also central to such critical human activities as intentionally communicating with others, repairing misunderstandings in communication, teaching others, persuading others, and even intentionally deceiving others (Baron-Cohen, 1999). For all these reasons, theory of mind does not simply "click in" early in development, but continues to get increasingly sophisticated with age (Paal & Bereczkei, 2007; Wellman, Cross, & Watson, 2001). Furthermore, even in adulthood, there are stable individual differences in the ability to accurately read other people's minds—individual differences that are highly correlated with the personality trait of agreeableness (Nettle & Liddle, 2008).

The inferential procedures by which theory of mind mechanisms operate are different from those by which inferences about physical entities operate. Studies support the emergence of theory of mind at roughly the same age in different cultures (Avis & Harris, 1991). Evidence from cognitive neuroscience suggests localization of this mechanism, as indicated by the fact that it can be selectively damaged.

Work on theory of mind has focused on sex differences in the emergence of another capacity—empathizing (Baron-Cohen, 2005). *Empathizing* allows a person to both predict and to care about how others feel. Without empathizing, understanding the beliefs and desires of others enables a person to read facial expressions and writhing body movements to understand that "I can see that you are in pain." Empathizing allows a person to express the notion that "I am upset that you are in pain."

According to Baron-Cohen (2005), small but consistent sex differences emerge early in life suggesting a female superiority in empathizing. Girls show more concern for fairness than boys, do more turn-taking in conversations, respond empathically to other people's distress, are more sensitive to reading people's facial expressions, and talk more about emotions and feelings. Baron-Cohen theorizes that these sex differences originated from the different reproductive strategies of women and men—specifically, capacities important for childrearing and for negotiating the more subtle alliances and dominance hierarchies of girls and women.

The developmental story in a theory of mind mechanism might turn out to be even more complex than this. Some have hypothesized that theory of mind mechanisms are far more content saturated than has yet been proposed or discovered (Buss, 1996b). This speculation is based on the idea that theories of mind must solve very different sorts of social adaptive problems. Women, for example, might have a "theory of men's minds" that differs from their "theory of women's minds" because the sorts of adaptive problems confronting women differ depending on whether they are interacting with a man or with a woman (e.g., inferences about the other's sexual desires; Haselton & Buss, 2000).

## Life-History Strategies

Individuals who share a common evolved psychology can experience different early environmental events that channel them into alternative strategies. According to this notion, each person comes equipped with two or more potential strategies in his or her repertoire. From this species-typical menu, one strategy may be selected based on early environmental experiences. These early experiences, in essence.

***An Evolutionary Theory of Socialization.*** Psychologists Belsky, Steinberg, and Draper (1991) propose that a father's presence or absence early in a child's life can calibrate the kind of sexual strategy he or she adopts later in life. Individuals growing up in fatherless homes during the first five to seven years of life, according to this theory, develop the expectations that parental resources will not be reliably or predictably provided and that adult pair bonds will not be enduring. Accordingly, such individuals cultivate a sexual strategy marked by early sexual maturation, early sexual initiation, and frequent partner switching—a strategy that is designed to produce a large number of offspring, with low levels of investment in each. Extraverted and impulsive personality traits might accompany this strategy. Other individuals are perceived as untrustworthy, relationships as transitory. Resources sought from brief sexual liaisons are opportunistically attained and immediately extracted.

Individuals who have a reliably investing father during their first five to seven years of life, according to this theory, develop a different set of expectations about the nature and trustworthiness of others. People are seen as reliable and trustworthy, and relationships are expected to be enduring. These early environmental experiences channel individuals toward a long-term mating strategy marked by delay of sexual maturation, later onset of sexual activity, search for securely attached long-term adult relationships, and heavy investment in a small number of children.

***Attachment and Life-History Theory.*** Evolutionary scholars James Chisholm (1996) and Jay Belsky (1997) both propose an integration of life-history theory (Levins, 1968) and attachment theory (Bowlby, 1969) that suggests that these individual differences are adaptively patterned and likely to reflect the high variability of ancestral childrearing environments. Chisholm's argument starts with life-history theory, the insight that life cycles constitute evolved adaptive strategies. A core principle of life-history theory is effort allocation (Levins, 1968). Individuals have finite time and resources, and decisions must be made about their allocation to different components of fitness. The components of reproductive success such as survival, growth, mating, and parenting are often in conflict. Effort allocated to one component often precludes effort allocated to the other—there are necessary trade-offs. The effort that is used to court additional mates, for example, conflicts with the time and energy invested in parenting. According to this theory, natural selection has fashioned decision rules for changing the allocation of effort to these different components, depending on specific features of context. Strategies are thus "suites of functionally integrated anatomical, physiological, psychological, and developmental mechanisms for optimizing the tradeoffs among the components of fitness throughout the life cycle" (Chisholm, 1996; see also Charnov, 1993; Hill, 1993; Kaplan & Gangestad, 2005; Stearns, 1992).

One of the most important trade-offs is between current and future reproduction. Increased immediate reproduction occurs at the expense of future reproduction. According to Chisholm, when resources are limited or unpredictable, it might pay to increase fertility and decrease investment in any particular offspring. Chisholm further argues that the psychology of attachment constitutes an evolved set of mechanisms for making these allocation decisions.

The ancestral environments in which these mechanisms evolved, according to Chisholm, were neither as rosy nor as secure as many attachment theorists have suggested. Risk and uncertainty historically came from many sources: unpredictable food supplies, vagaries of climate and weather, diseases, parasites, predators, and, perhaps most important, other humans such as one's parents. Chisholm argues that the parents' sexual strategy, including the quantity and quality of their investment in offspring, might have provided the most adaptively significant dimension of children's environments.

Variations from *secure attachment,* in this view, represent early experiential calibrations to recurrent threats to the child's survival and growth—the parent's inability or unwillingness to invest heavily in offspring. *Avoidant attachment* (the child shows indifference to the parent) represents an adaptation to parental *unwillingness* to invest, as when the parent is pursuing a short-term mating strategy rather than investing heavily in his or her offspring. *Anxious/ambivalent attachment* (in which the child shows nervousness, fearfulness, and insecurity), in contrast, represents an adaptation to parental *inability* to invest—as when the mother herself is irritable, preoccupied, fearful, hungry, or exhausted. According to Belsky (1997), the secure attachment functioned to promote a strategy of high-investment parenting, the avoidant attachment functioned to promote an opportunistic interpersonal style marked by low-investment parenting, and anxious/ambivalent attachment evolved to foster a "helpers at the nest" style, whereby children remained at home to aid the rearing of their parents' other children.

Do attachment styles represent early environmental calibration, or do they reflect heritable individual differences, as suggested by some research (Bailey et al., 2000; Goldsmith & Harman, 1994)? Are individual differences in attachment stable over the life course? Do the underlying psychological mechanisms of attachment coordinate with the specific features of adaptive problems posed by each alternative strategy? These questions await further conceptual and empirical work. Nonetheless, studies have demonstrated that early age of menarche is indeed linked with parental marital unhappiness and more rejection from the father, as well as with an earlier age of dating men, suggesting much promise for the theory of early attachment in promoting different adult sexual strategies (Kim, Smith, & Palermiti, 1997), although it is not inconsistent with a pure heritability interpretation (see Ellis, 2005, for a discussion). Recent empirical work supports the theory that a low quality childhood environment, especially one marked by an absent father, a psychologically dysfunctional father, and family disruption, does indeed predict an early age of menarche, which can lead to early onset of sexual activity and a short-term mating strategy (Neberich et al., 2010; Tither & Ellis, 2008).

In summary, life-history theory, of mind, parental socialization, attachment styles, and paternal dysfunction, represents a few of the ways evolutionary developmental psychologists approach changes over time in the human life course. Others include the role of prolonged immaturity and play in human development (Bjorklund, 1997), children's motivations to join peer groups (MacDonald, 1996), the development of inhibitory mechanisms such as the delay of gratification and sexual restraint (Bjorklund & Kipp, 1996), the evolutionary aspects of adolescence such as mate competition and puberty rites (Surbey, 1998b; Weisfeld, 1997a; Weisfeld & Billings, 1988), sex-linked socialization practices (Low, 1989), and attachment styles as they affect adult romantic relationships (Kirkpatrick, 1998). Ultimately, a comprehensive evolutionary developmental psychology will include an account of the species-typical, sex-differentiated, and individually differentiated transformations over the life span of the adaptive problems faced and the psychological mechanisms activated.

## ■ EVOLUTIONARY PERSONALITY PSYCHOLOGY

𝒫ersonality psychology might be the broadest and the most encompassing branch of psychology. Historically, all "grand" theories of personality have hypotheses about the contents of human nature at their core, such as motives for sex and aggression (Sigmund Freud), self-actualization (Abraham Maslow), striving for superiority (Adler), or striving for status and intimacy (David McClelland, Henry Murray, & Jerry Wiggins). Hypothesized psychological features of human nature have provided much of the "core" around which these grand theories of personality have been constructed.

On the other hand, personality psychology has also been centrally concerned with the following questions: What are the most important ways individuals differ? What are the origins of individual differences? What are the psychological and physiological correlates of individual differences? What are the consequences of individual differences for social interaction, psychopathology, well-being, and the life course?

Most research and theory in evolutionary psychology have focused on species-typical psychological mechanisms, as discussed throughout this book. Individual differences, in contrast, have been relatively neglected and pose a greater challenge for evolutionary psychologists (Buss & Greiling, 1999; MacDonald, 1995; Nettle, 2006; Nettle & Penke, 2010; Tooby & Cosmides, 1990; Wilson, 1994). Evolutionary biologists have tended to focus on species-typical adaptations, ignoring individual differences except in their role of providing the raw materials on which natural selection operates. Individual differences, particularly those that are heritable, are often relegated to secondary status because they are thought to originate primarily through nonselection forces such as random mutation (Tooby & Cosmides, 1990; Wilson, 1994). Genetic differences are sometimes viewed as "noise" or "genetic junk" maintained within a population precisely because they are presumed to be *unrelated* to the core of the evolutionary process: adaptation and natural selection (Thiessen, 1972). Heritable individual differences are to species-typical adaptations, in this view, as differences in the colors of the wires in a car engine are to the engine's functional working components: One can vary the coloring of the wires without affecting the functioning of the engine (Tooby & Cosmides, 1990).

If unity of science is taken to be a reasonable goal (Wilson, E. O., 1998), these different conceptualizations are difficult to reconcile. Because natural selection tends to reduce genetic variability within populations by favoring some genes and weeding out others, why do behavioral genetic studies consistently find moderate heritability for personality dispositions (Plomin, DeFries, & McClearn, 1997)? If individual differences really are independent of adaptation and natural selection, why are individual differences reliably linked to activities closely connected with reproductive success, such as survival and sexuality? Individual differences in extraversion, for example, are linked with differences in sexual access to partners (Eysenck, 1976). Conscientiousness is known to be correlated with work and status attainment (Kyl-Heku & Buss, 1996; Lund et al., 2006). Impulsivity is linked with extramarital affairs (Buss & Shackelford, 1997a) and higher mortality rates (Friedman et al., 1995). If the individual differences studied by personality psychologists are reliably linked with reproductively relevant phenomena such as status, sexuality, and survival, perhaps they play a more important role in human evolutionary psychology than previously assumed (Buss & Hawley, 2011).

Evolutionary psychology is now grappling with ways to incorporate individual differences and species-typical psychological mechanisms within a unified conceptual framework (e.g., Bailey, 1998; Buss & Greiling, 1999; Gangestad & Simpson, 1990; MacDonald, 1995; Nettle & Penke, in press; Wilson, 1994). Several avenues look promising.

## Alternative Niche Picking or Strategic Specialization

From an evolutionary perspective, competition is keenest among those pursuing the same strategy. As one niche becomes more and more crowded with competitors, success of those in the niche can suffer compared with those seeking alternative niches (Maynard Smith, 1982; Wilson, 1994). Selection favors mechanisms that cause individuals to seek niches in which the competition is less intense.

Mating provides some clear examples. If most women pursue the man with the highest status or greatest resources, then some women would achieve more success by courting males outside the arenas in which competition is keenest. In a mating system in which both polygyny and monogamy are possible, for example, a woman might be better off securing all of the resources of a lower-status monogamous man rather than settling for a fraction of the resources of a high-status polygynous man.

The ability to exploit a niche will depend on the resources and personal characteristics an individual brings to the situation. Consider a person's birth order. It is possible that firstborns and later-borns have faced, on average, recurrently different adaptive problems over human evolutionary history. Frank Sulloway (1996), for example, argues that firstborns occupy a niche characterized by strong identification with parents and other existing authority figures. Later-borns, in contrast, have less to gain from authority identification, and more to gain by overthrowing the existing order. According to Sulloway, birth order influences niche specialization. Later-borns develop a different personality marked by greater rebelliousness, lower levels of conscientiousness, and higher levels of openness to new experiences (Sulloway, 2010). Birth order differences show up strongly among scientists: Later-borns tend to be strong advocates of scientific revolutions; firstborns tend to strenuously resist such revolutions (Sulloway, 1996).

Whether the details of Sulloway's arguments turn out to be correct, the example illustrates strategic niche specialization. Individual differences are adaptively patterned, but they are *not* based on heritable individual differences. Rather, birth order, a nonheritable individual difference, provides input (presumably through interactions with family members) into a species-typical mechanism that shapes strategic niche specialization.

## Adaptive Assessment of Heritable Qualities

Suppose that all men have an evolved decision rule of this form: Pursue an aggressive strategy when aggression can be successfully implemented to achieve goals, but pursue a cooperative strategy when aggression cannot be successfully implemented (modified from Tooby & Cosmides, 1990, p. 58). Evolved decision rules are undoubtedly more complex than this. Given this simplified rule, however, those who happen to be mesomorphic (muscular) in body build can carry out an aggressive strategy more successfully than can those who are ectomorphic (skinny) or endomorphic (rotund). Heritable individual differences in body build provide input into the decision rule, thereby producing stable individual differences in aggression and cooperativeness. In this example, the proclivity toward aggression is not directly heritable but rather would be "reactively heritable" in the sense that it is a secondary consequence of heritable body build that provides input into species-typical mechanisms of self-assessment and decision making.

Tooby and Cosmides (1990) coined the term "reactive heritability" to describe evolved psychological mechanisms designed to take as input heritable qualities as a guide to strategic solutions. According to this view, selection will favor the evolution of assessment mechanisms if such appraisals help a person choose wise strategies. Evolved mechanisms, in this view, are not only attuned to recurrent features of the external world, such as the reliability of parental provisioning, but can also be attuned to the evaluation of the self.

Assessment of heritable qualities may also aid in the choice of mating strategies. One study examined the physical appearances of teenage boys on two dimensions: the degree to which their faces looked dominant or submissive and how physically attractive others found them to be (Mazur, Halpern, & Udry, 1994). Photographs were used for the judgments of these features, a dominant person being defined as someone who "tells other people what to do, is respected, influential, and often a leader" (1994, p. 90). The teenagers who were judged to be more facially dominant and physically attractive were discovered to have had more experience with sexual intercourse. Furthermore, dominant facial appearance predicted cumulative coital experience, even after statistically controlling for facial attractiveness and pubertal development.

If facial features involved in appearing dominant and attractive are partially heritable, one can speculate that males have an evolved psychological mechanism designed to appraise the degree to which they appear dominant and attractive: "If high on these dimensions, pursue a short-term sexual strategy; if low, pursue a long-term sexual strategy." In this example, of course, one cannot rule out other variables, such as testosterone, which might simultaneously produce a more dominant-looking face and a higher sex drive. According to the conception of evolved assessment mechanisms designed to appraise one's heritable qualities, stable individual differences in the pursuit of short-term and long-term sexual strategies are not directly heritable. Instead, they represent adaptive individual differences based on the assessment of heritable information. Another example of reactive heritability centers on the trait of extraversion, which is highly correlated with both physical strength and physical attractiveness (Lukaszewski & Roney, 2010b). Strength and attractiveness apparently facilitate the success of extraverted social strategies, which involve initiating multiple social relationships, broadcasting desired qualities to others, ascending the status hierarchy, and pursuing multiple sex partners.

## Frequency-Dependent Adaptive Strategies

In general, the process of directional selection tends to use up heritable variation. Heritable variants that are more successful tend to replace those that are less successful, eventually resulting in species-typical adaptations that show little or no heritable variation in the presence or absence of basic functional components (Williams, 1966, 1975).

There is a major exception to this trend: frequency-dependent selection. In some contexts, two or more heritable variants can be sustained in equilibrium. The most obvious example is biological sex. In sexually reproducing species, the two sexes represent frequency-dependent suites of covarying adaptive complexes. If one sex becomes rare relative to the other, success increases for the rare sex, and hence selection favors parents who produce offspring of the less common sex. Typically, the sexes are maintained in an approximately equal ratio through the process of frequency-dependent selection. Frequency-dependent selection requires that the payoff of each strategy decreases as its frequency increases, relative to other strategies in the population (see Maynard Smith, 1982, and D. S. Wilson, 1998, for extensive treatments in the context of game theory).

Alternative adaptive strategies can also be maintained *within the sexes* by frequency-dependent selection. Among bluegill sunfish, for example, three different male mating strategies are observed: a "parental" strategy that defends the nest, a "sneak" strategy that matures to only a small body size, and a "mimic" strategy that resembles the female form (Gross, 1982). The sneakers gain sexual access to the female eggs by avoiding detection because of their small size, and the mimics gain access by resembling females and thus avoiding aggression from the parental males. As the mimic strategists increase in frequency, however, their success decreases because their existence depends on the parentals who guard the nest from predation. Parentals become rarer as the mimics and sneakers become more common, rendering these parasitic strategies more difficult to pursue. Thus heritable alternative strategies within the sexes are maintained by the process of frequency-dependent selection.

Linda Mealey (1995) proposed a theory of psychopathy based on frequency-dependent selection. Psychopathy (sometimes called sociopathy or antisocial personality disorder) represents a cluster of traits marked by irresponsible and unreliable behavior, egocentrism, impulsivity, inability to form lasting relationships, superficial social charm, and deficit of social emotions such as love, shame, guilt, and empathy (Cleckley, 1982). Psychopaths pursue a deceptive or "cheating" strategy in their social interactions. Psychopathy is more common among men (4%) than women (1%) (Mealey, 1995).

Psychopaths pursue a social strategy characterized by exploiting the reciprocity mechanisms of others. After feigning cooperation, psychopaths typically defect. This cheating strategy might be pursued by men who are unlikely to outcompete other men in a more traditional or mainstream status hierarchy (Mealey, 1995). A psychopathic strategy can be maintained by frequency-dependent selection. As the number of cheaters increases, and hence the average cost to the cooperative hosts increases, adaptations evolve to detect cheating and inflict costs on cheaters. As the prevalence of psychopaths increases, therefore, the average payoff of the psychopath strategy decreases. As long as the frequency of psychopaths is not too large, it can be maintained amidst a population composed primarily of cooperators (Mealey, 1995).

There is some evidence—albeit indirect—that is at least consistent with Mealey's theory of psychopathy. First, behavioral genetic studies suggest that psychopathy might be moderately heritable (Willerman, Loehlin, & Horn, 1992). Second, psychopaths appear to pursue an exploitative short-term sexual strategy, which could be the primary route through which genes for psychopathy increase or are maintained (Rowe, 1995). Psychopathic men tend to be more sexually precocious, have sex with a larger number of people, have more illegitimate children, and are more likely to separate from their wives than are nonpsychopathic men (Rowe, 1995). Psychopaths are more likely to use sexual coercion and rape to obtain sexual access to women (Lalumiere et al., 2005), as well as using physical aggression to obtain other reproductively relevant resources (Book & Quinsey, 2004; Pitchford, 2001). Interestingly, psychopaths seem to have a special talent for identifying "exploitable" victims (Buss & Duntley, 2008). Specifically, they seem to have what has been called "predatory memory" for vulnerable, sad, and helpful females (Book, Quinsey, & Langford, 2007; Camilleri, Kuhlmeier, & Chu, 2010; Wilson, Demetrioff, & Porter, 2008). This short-term, opportunistic, exploitative sexual strategy would be expected to increase in populations marked by high mobility, in which the reputational costs associated with such a strategy would be low (Wilson, 1995).

Mealey's theory of psychopathy nicely illustrates the possibility that heritable alternative strategies can be maintained by frequency-dependent selection. Frequency-dependent selection offers a potential explanation for integrating the results from behavioral genetic studies and the findings on the sexual strategies pursued by psychopaths with an evolutionary analysis of adaptive individual differences.

Another effort to identify adaptive individual differences through frequency-dependent selection comes from evolutionary psychologist A. J. Figueredo and his colleagues (Figueredo et al., 2006, 2010). They propose that individual differences cluster around a single large dimension called the K-factor (see Rushton, 1985, for an earlier version of this theory). Those high on the K-factor show early attachment to their biological father, a long-term mating strategy, high cooperativeness, and low risk taking. The low end of the K-factor is marked by low levels of attachment, high Machiavellianism, high risk taking, high impulsivity, defection from cooperative relationships, and the pursuit of a short-term mating strategy. Individual differences in the K-factor are hypothesized to be maintained by frequency-dependent selection, much like psychopathy is maintained by frequency-dependent selection. Indeed, there appears to be considerable overlap between psychopathy and scoring low on the K-factor.

An effort to explore personality differences using the logic of frequency-dependence centers on examining the benefits and costs of scoring high or low on major personality dimensions such as extraversion, conscientiousness, and agreeableness (Nettle, 2006). The benefits of extraversion include high short-term mating success, establishment of more social allies, and proclivity to explore one's environment. The costs of extraversion, however, include increased physical risks and family instability such as higher divorce rates. Similarly, high conscientiousness provides benefits in status attainment, higher life expectancy, and family stability. Its costs include delaying gratification and foregoing short-term sexual opportunities. In short, there are both benefits and costs to various personality traits, and selection can favor and maintain genetic diversity within the population.

In summary, evolutionary psychology offers a framework for considering a variety of individual differences. Differences can arise from early environmental experiences, such as father's presence or absence, which can channel an individual's development toward different adaptive strategies. Differences can arise from the occupancy of different environments in adulthood, which recurrently activate a particular mechanism. Differences can arise from alternative niche picking. And differences can arise through frequency-dependent selection. Keep in mind that not all individual differences must be adaptively patterned. Some variation could be random genetic variation unconnected with adaptation. And some personality variation may reflect individual differences in exposure to environmental insults or number of mutations, both of which might impair proper personality functioning (see Buss, 2006b; Keller & Miller, 2006). All of these sources of individual differences hold the promise of providing a truly integrative personality theory that includes both core premises about human nature and the major ways in which individuals differ (Bernard, 2009; Buss & Hawley, 2011; Denissen & Penke, 2008; Nettle & Penke, 2010).

# ■ EVOLUTIONARY CLINICAL PSYCHOLOGY

The concept of mental disorder occupies a central place in the field of clinical psychology. Clearly articulated conceptual criteria for identifying mental disorder provide a framework for determining whether individuals are functioning well or poorly and what can be done to successfully treat them.

Psychologists often invoke terms such as *adjusted* and *maladjusted, adaptive* and *maladaptive,* and *normal* and *abnormal* to identify mental disorder. However, these terms often lack clear definitional criteria. Many authors implicitly appeal to intuitions, presumably shared by readers, about what is good or bad, desirable or undesirable. The *DSM-IV_TR* (American Psychiatric Association, 2000) offers simple heuristic rules, such as notions of subjective distress, bizarreness, social harmfulness, and inefficiency.

Evolutionary psychology offers the potential for escaping intuitive appeals by providing a more rigorous set of explicit principles for identifying the presence of disorder (see Buss et al., 1997; Wakefield, 1992). Once an evolved psychological mechanism is described and its proper function is identified, a clear criterion exists for determining dysfunction: *Dysfunction occurs when the mechanism is not performing as it was designed to perform in the contexts in which it was designed to function.* A dysfunction of evolved mechanisms would be indicated, for example, if one's blood failed to clot after one's skin was cut, if one failed to sweat in response to external heat, or if one's larynx failed to rise to close off the passage to the lungs when food is swallowed.

According to this definition of dysfunction, evolved mechanisms can fail in three distinct ways: (1) The mechanism fails to become activated when the relevant adaptive problem is confronted (e.g., one confronts a dangerous snake that is threatening to strike but fails to become afraid or take evasive action); (2) the mechanism becomes activated in contexts in which it was not designed to become activated (e.g., sexually attracted to inappropriate persons, such as close genetic relatives); and (3) the mechanism fails to coordinate as it was designed to coordinate with other mechanisms (e.g., self-assessments of mate value fail to guide the sorts of people to whom one devotes mating effort).

## Causes of Mechanism Failure

Each of the three types of mechanism failure—activation failure, context failure, and coordination failure—can arise as a result of genetic factors (e.g., chance genetic variation or genetic mutations) or developmental insults (e.g., brain injury), or a combination of these causes. Brain-injured aphasics, for example, experience failures of the evolved mechanisms underlying speech production and comprehension. They appear to understand language, but are unable to speak fluently. Language input is received and processed appropriately but the mechanisms underlying speech production are not properly coordinated with the speech comprehension mechanisms. Alternatively, there might exist activation or processing failures within the speech-production mechanisms themselves (Pinker, 1994).

Chance genetic variation might underlie some mechanism failures. Although natural selection tends to produce species-typical evolved mechanisms, heritable variation might remain in the surface features of a mechanism. Nearly all humans possess functionally similar eyes, hearts, and lungs, but there are heritable individual differences in the structural forms assumed by these mechanisms (e.g., there may be slight individual differences in lung shape). This variation is largely selectively neutral. There might be cases, however, in which genetic variants co-occur to produce mechanism failures. These variants are not harmful when they exist singularly, but in rare combinations, they are dysfunctional. Some researchers have speculated that rare gene couplings might underlie certain types of schizophrenia (Gottesman, 1991).

Another source of variation is mutations. Although mutations provide the variation necessary for natural selection to occur, isolated mutations rarely enhance functioning and can be deleterious, leading to mechanism failures (Tooby & Cosmides, 1990, 1992). Humans have roughly 25,000 genes, and mutations can occur on each. All of us have some mutations, but some have more than others. Keller and Miller (2006) propose that many common mental disorders, such as autism, bipolar disorder, schizophrenia, and mild mental retardation, occur in individuals with a heavy "mutation load" (individuals who have a large number of mutations). Heavy mutation load can cause brain abnormalities, disrupting the normal operation of evolved psychological mechanisms.

## Evolutionary Insights into Problems Erroneously Thought to Be Dysfunctions

Some psychological phenomena appear to be disordered, maladaptive, maladjusted, costly, or subjectively distressful, but they are not dysfunctions. They are not caused by the failure of evolved mechanisms to function as they were designed to function. These apparently disordered behaviors and experiences fall into several major classes.

First, there can be a *discrepancy between ancestral and modern environments* (Glantz & Pearce, 1989). Our modern environment differs in many ways, sometimes radically, from the environments that were present over most of human evolutionary history. An evolved mechanism could be functioning precisely as it was designed to function, but because the environment has changed, the outcome might appear maladaptive.

At a psychological level, humans might have evolved mechanisms designed to assess their mate value relative to the individuals in their environment. Ancestral environments were probably populated with relatively small groups of people containing around 50 to 150 individuals. Assessments of relative mate value were probably fairly accurate. One result of these accurate assessments might have been to focus individuals' attraction tactics on potential mates within their own mate value range. In our current environment, however, the population is substantially larger, and the images to which individuals are exposed through television and the Internet might present an unprecedented comparison standard. Fashion models and actresses, for example, are often highly physically attractive. Extremely attractive women are a tiny fraction of the population, yet images of these women are presented at a misleadingly high frequency. This might have the effect of artificially lowering women's judgments of their value as a potential mate relative to competitors in the *local* pool of potential mates. This, in turn, might escalate intrasexual competition between women or cause them to take drastic measures to try to increase their attractiveness. In extreme cases, women might develop body image disorders, eating disorders such as anorexia and bulimia, or depression (Faer et al., 2005).

A second source of problems can arise from *normal mistakes accompanying the "on average" functioning of a mechanism.* All mechanisms work because, on average, the benefits outweighed the costs across a sample space of instances in ancestral environments, not because they work in all instances. Because evolved mechanisms are selected on the basis of their "average" effects, a properly functioning mechanism can produce many mistakes, but these mistakes do not necessarily signify dysfunction (Schlager, 1995). Perceiving a dangerous animal behind a tree when one is not there and inferring sexual intent when none is there are mistakes but might not be dysfunctional because, on average, the threshold for perceiving these phenomena led to greater inclusive fitness than did alternative thresholds. These normal mistakes must be distinguished from instances of true dysfunction. In sum, what might at first appear to be a disorder could simply be the proper functioning of an evolved mechanism that produces mistakes because it is designed to solve adaptive problems "on average" rather than successfully all of the time.

A third source of problems sometimes erroneously believed to represent disorders is *subjective distress produced by the normal operation of functional mechanisms.* Many of our evolved psychological mechanisms lead to outcomes that are subjectively distressful (Buss, 2000b). Depression, for example, is experienced by an estimated 10 percent of young adults in the United States. Because of its prevalence and close relation to sadness, depressed mood has been proposed as a reliable effect of the experience of loss (of money, mate, reputation, etc.; Nesse, 2000; Nesse & Williams, 1994; Price & Sloman, 1987). Although the experience of depression can be incredibly frustrating for those so afflicted, this emotional pain might have adaptive functions. First, a depressed mood helps us to disengage from a hopeless enterprise that might be causing losses and motivate new paths to solving adaptive problems (Andrews & Thompson, 2009). Second, it deflates our "blind" human optimism, thus allowing us to more objectively reassess our goals (Nesse & Williams, 1994; Stevens & Price, 1996). Third, depression might function to send a needy signal to family, friends, or romantic partners that elicits investment, care, and helping from others—a "cry for help" (Hagen, 1999; Watson & Andrews,

2002). There is even some evidence that there are subtypes of low mood, with different functional symptoms (Keller & Nesse, 2005). The symptom of sadness, for example, motivates avoiding future losses in a manner analogous to physical pain leading to the avoidance of future tissue damage. The symptom of crying, on the other hand, is an emotional signal to others designed to solicit help.

Anxiety, too, involves subjective distress but is produced by the normal operation of a functional mechanism that, in the face of a threat, alters our thinking, behavior, and physiology in advantageous ways (Nesse & Williams, 1994). It keeps us cautious and attentive to the possibility of physical or social harm. Although useful, the stress response is costly (excessive calorie use, tissue damage); therefore, there must be a reason why anxious responses occur so frequently. From an evolutionary perspective, the answer is clear: Of one hundred potentially dangerous situations, one death is more costly than responding to ninety-nine false alarms (Nesse & Williams, 1994).

Panic attacks might represent a functional component of the anxiety system that protects against the specific threat of attack. The cues that elicit panic are well suited to its evolved function to protect in the face of potential attack: being in wide-open spaces, being unaccompanied and far from home, and being in places where intense fear has occurred before. Panic is a normal defense against some threats; *faulty regulation* of panic results in panic disorder (Nesse, 1990).

A fourth source of problems stems from *socially undesirable behavior produced by the normal operation of functional mechanisms.* Some of our evolved mechanisms lead to outcomes that are socially undesirable. Psychopathy is one example. Void of medical incapacitations, psychopaths are identified as abnormal because of their disregard for societal norms regulating cooperative reciprocity. However, psychopaths might in fact display behavior that is produced by the normal function of mechanisms designed to promote cheating in specific ancestral contexts. For example, when sustained social interactions were not expected to occur, successful cheaters would have been able to reap the benefits of a few skewed interactions within a certain group before having to pay a cost (e.g., moving on to a new group) once their cheating behaviors were detected (Harpending & Sobus, 1987). Psychopaths do appear to display several behaviors and traits that might be the effects of an evolved cheater mechanism. These traits and behaviors include sudden changes in plans, charm, high mobility, promiscuity, and use of aliases (Harpending & Sobus, 1987; Lykken, 1995). It is not surprising that evolutionary psychology helps us understand why psychopathic behaviors are judged undesirable: They jeopardize others' fitness interests.

Child abuse and neglect, including infanticide, might be undesirable behaviors produced by the normal operation of mechanisms that function to reduce the investment of resources in nonrelatives (Daly & Wilson, 1988). To illustrate, stepparenthood is the single best predictor of child abuse. In England, Scott (1973) reported that more than half of twenty battered baby cases involved a stepfather, although only 1 percent of babies in the general population were living with a stepfather at that time. In other words, infants and children living with a stepparent are more than forty times more likely to experience child abuse than those living with two genetic parents. According to Daly and Wilson (1988), the ambiguity of the stepparent's situation resides not in a lack of knowledge about the stepparent role but rather in genuine conflicts of interest within the stepfamily that may, unfortunately, result in the abuse or neglect of an unrelated child.

The implications of evolutionizing clinical psychology are profound (Brune, 2008; McGuire & Troisi, 1998; Stevens & Price, 2000). Properly understanding the design of something greatly improves the chances of fixing the system when it breaks down. That is why you take your car to a mechanic—you know how to drive it, but the mechanic knows more about precisely how it was designed and how its mechanisms are meant to function. An evolutionary perspective also gives guidance about when to intervene. In some cases, we might be treating only the symptom, such as anxiety or depression, rather than the source (Nesse, 1990, 1991; Nesse & Williams, 1994). If we mask these symptoms, we might thwart an otherwise natural healing process. This is analogous to treating a fever or a cough: These are mechanisms designed to help fix an infection or extrude foreign matter from the respiratory system, for example. If you medicate the fever or cough, it is possible to interfere with their functions. Similarly, treating depression or anxiety (e.g., through drugs such as Prozac) might fail to get at the underlying causes of depression and anxiety (Andrews & Thompson, 2009). Alarmingly, many current drug treatments for depression such as Prozac, Paxil, Zoloft, and Celexa may also interfere with sexual desire, arousal, and orgasm, and consequently may interfere with the functions of these mechanisms, disrupting romantic relationships and commitment in pair-bonds (Fisher & Thompson, 2006). In sum, evolutionary psychology offers much promise of new and profound insights into clinical psychology.

# ■ EVOLUTIONARY CULTURAL PSYCHOLOGY

Some psychologists perpetuate the false dichotomy between "culture" and "biology" as though the two were somehow in causal competition. Statements to the effect that "culture overrides biology" and "animals have instincts, humans have culture" reflect this false dualism. Evolutionary psychology provides a true interactionist position that shows why these dichotomies are false. As we will see in this section, "culture" cannot be viewed as a separate cause because it rests on a foundation of evolved psychological mechanisms.

Social scientists who grapple with culture typically start with the observation that groups of people in one place differ in some ways from groups of people in other places. The Yanomamö Indians of Venezuela shave their heads to proudly reveal the scars they get in club fights. In other cultures, men and women put bones through their noses, tattoo their lips, pierce their ears, or put safety pins through their cheeks. Psychologists note these differences and attribute them to "culture." They presume that "biology" refers to what is invariant across humans and "culture" refers to what is variable, so it seems self-evident that "culture" accounts for the variability (Tooby & Cosmides, 1992).

Evolutionary psychology provides a different perspective. To begin with, patterns of local within-group similarity and between-group differences are best regarded as phenomena that require explanation. Transforming these differences into an autonomous causal entity called "culture" confuses the phenomena that require explanation with a proper explanation of the phenomena. Attributing such phenomena to culture provides no more explanatory power than attributing them to God, consciousness, learning, socialization, or even evolution, unless the causal processes that are subsumed by these labels are properly described. Labels for phenomena are not proper causal explanations for them.

Once we have identified the phenomena we are interested in explaining—ideas, practices, rituals, artifacts, beliefs, representations, music, and art that are shared within some groups but not others—the next step is to outline the potential causal explanations for them. A start along these lines makes a distinction between evoked and transmitted culture (Gangestad, Haselton, & Buss, 2006; Tooby & Cosmides, 1992).

## Evoked Culture

All evolved mechanisms are responsive to environmental conditions; the pupils of eyes, sweat glands, sexual arousal, and jealousy are a few obvious examples. *Evoked culture* refers to phenomena that are triggered in some groups more than in others because of differing environmental conditions. The deeper tans among Californians than among Oregonians, for example, reflect the differing levels of exposure to sunlight. Such "cultural differences" are explained simply by invoking a universal shared evolved mechanism combined with local between-group differences in input into that mechanism.

A concrete example of evoked culture is found in the patterns of cooperative food sharing among different bands of hunter-gatherers (Cosmides & Tooby, 1992). Different classes of food have different variances in their distribution. Among the Ache tribe of Paraguay, for example, meat from hunting is a high-variance food resource. On any given day, the odds that a hunter will come back with meat are only 60 percent. Gathering food, on the other hand, is a lower-variance food resource.

One variable triggering communal food sharing appears to be high variance in the food resource. Under high-variance conditions, there are tremendous benefits to sharing. You share your meat today with an unlucky friend who failed, but next week, you might be the beneficiary of reciprocity when you come back empty-handed. Under low-variance conditions, on the other hand, the benefits of food sharing are far less. Because gathered food depends on individual effort, sharing merely entails giving by those who work hard to those who are lazy.

Within the Ache, meat is shared communally. Hunters deposit their kill with a "distributor," who then allocates portions to different families, largely on the basis of family size. In the same tribe, however, gathered food is not shared outside the kin group. Halfway around the world, in the Kalahari Desert, evolutionist Elizabeth Cashdan (1989) found that some San groups are more egalitarian than others and that these cultural differences are closely linked with the variance in the food supply. The !Kung San's food supply is highly variable, and they show much food sharing. To be called a *stinge* (stingy) is one of the worst insults, and costly reputational damage is incurred for failing to share food. Among the Gana San, in contrast, food variance is low, and they tend to hoard their food more and rarely share it outside their extended families. These examples show that environmental conditions that differ from place to place can trigger the activation of different psychological mechanisms across groups. Cultural differences of this sort are examples of evoked culture. They are explained by understanding how universal evolved mechanisms are differentially activated across groups—in this case, by differences in the variability of food sources.

Another example of evoked culture comes from an analysis of cultural differences in the importance attached to physical attractiveness. Because parasites are known to degrade physical appearance, people living in ecologies with a high prevalence of parasites should place a greater value on physical attractiveness in a mate than people living in ecologies with a low prevalence of parasites (Gangestad & Buss, 1993). To test this hypothesis, the prevalence of parasites in twenty-nine cultures was correlated with the importance that the people in those cultures attached to physical attractiveness in a marriage partner. The results confirmed the hypothesis: The greater the parasite prevalence, the more important was physical attractiveness (see Figure 13.3). Although these findings can be interpreted in a variety of ways, they are at least consistent with the idea of evoked culture—cultural differences that are explained by a universal psychological mechanism that is differentially activated across groups.

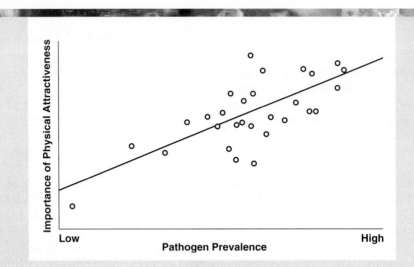

FIGURE 13.3 **Parasite Prevalence and Importance of Attractiveness.** The prevalence of parasites in the local ecology strongly predicts the importance people in the culture place on physical attractiveness in a long-term mate. Each circle in the graph represents one culture. This study illustrates that evolutionary psychology, in principle, can account for variability across cultures, in addition to human universals.

*Source:* Gangestad, S. W., & Buss, D. M. (1993). Pathogen prevalence and human mate preferences. *Ethology and Sociobiology, 14*, 89–96.

Evidence has been accumulated that ecological variables such as parasite prevalence have a profound effect on evoked cultural patterns (Nettle, 2009). Although causality is often difficult to determine unambiguously, ecological variable such as parasite prevalence has been linked to the cultural patterns—smaller ethnic groups, higher rates of polygyny, lower levels of parental care, and even greater cultural levels of "collectivism" (Nettle, 2009). In short, empirical evidence is cumulating for the idea that some cultural differences are adaptive patterns of evoked culture.

## Transmitted Culture

Transmitted culture represents another class of phenomena that requires a different sort of explanation. It refers to representations or ideas that originally exist in at least one mind and are transferred to other minds through observation or interaction (Tooby & Cosmides, 1992). The hula hoop craze, changes in clothing style or fashion, beliefs about alien beings, and jokes that are passed from one person to another are examples of transmitted culture.

These phenomena require the existence of specialized inference mechanisms in the "recipients" that recreate the representations in their minds. Because "information" emanating from other individuals in one's social group is limitless, ideas compete for the limited attention spans of humans. Evolved psychological mechanisms in the receivers must sift through this barrage of ideas, selecting only a small subset for psychological reconstruction. The subset that is selectively adopted and internally reconstructed in individuals depends on a foundation of evolved psychological mechanisms. Thus, transmitted culture, like evoked culture, rests on a foundation of evolved psychological mechanisms.

At present, we do not know what these mechanisms are, but we do know what some of their properties must be. They must include procedures for *selectively attending* to some ideas and ignoring others; *selectively encoding* some in memory and forgetting others; and *selectively transmitting* some to other people while failing to transmit others (McAndrew, Bell, & Garcia, 2007). Presumably, these mechanisms are highly saturated with content that determines relevance to the person—relevance on dimensions that would have affected survival and reproduction in ancestral environments.

Consider the tendency of humans to imitate the clothing styles of high-status members of their local social groups or the groups to which they aspire to belong. These cultural phenomena are examples of transmitted culture. But these phenomena rest on a foundation of evolved psychological mechanisms that cause people to attend to high-status people more than low-status people, encode in memory their clothing styles, and access such memories when shopping for clothes.

A full account of transmitted culture ultimately will rest not just on the psychological mechanisms of those who "receive" the cultural representations of others. It will also rest on understanding mechanisms of those who *actively transmit* cultural representations. As Allport and Postman pointed out long ago, "Rumor is set in motion and continues to travel by its appeal to the strong personal interests of individuals involved in the transmission" (1947, p. 314). The intentional spread of rumors is a perfect example of transmitted culture, and understanding a rumor will require knowing the motivations and interests of those responsible for doing the spreading (e.g., derogating a rival to lower his or her perceived mate value) (McAndrew & Milenkovic, 2002).

Theoretical analyses and empirical findings highlight several likely candidates for "biased" transmission of culture (Henrich, 2009). One is a *conformity bias*, whereby people tend to adopt cultural trends or positions held by the majority of people. Another has already been alluded to—*the prestige of the transmitter*. The effect of prestige on cultural transmission, as powerful as it appears to be, must be qualified. When prestigious people advocate ideas that appear to coincide with their self-interest, receivers tend to discount it. When prestigious people engage in costly signaling, it enhances the spread of their cultural messages. Costly signaling enhances the "credibility" of the messages (Henrich, 2009). Consider two rappers rapping about gangs and violence. One rapper turns out to have been pampered in middle-class schools and has never experienced gangs of violence. The other, say rap artist 50 Cent, has seven bullets wounds to prove his experience with violence. Who has more "street cred" when it comes to the cultural transmission of their messages?

This account of cultural phenomena is, of course, incomplete and simplified. But it is sufficient to draw the following conclusions: (1) "Culture" is not an autonomous causal agent in competition with "biology" for explanatory power; (2) cultural diversities—local within-group similarities and between-group differences—are phenomena to be explained, but do not, by themselves, provide an explanation for cultural phenomena; (3) cultural phenomena can be usefully divided into types, such as evoked culture and transmitted culture; (4) explanations for evoked culture require a foundation of evolved psychological mechanisms, without which the differently activated cultural diversity could not occur; and (5) transmitted culture also rests on a foundation of evolved psychological mechanisms that influence which ideas are attended to, encoded, retrieved from memory, and transmitted to other individuals. As Pete Richardson and Rob Boyd conclude, "nothing about culture makes sense except in light of evolution" (2005, p. 237).

## The Evolution of Art, Fiction, Movies, and Music

Why do people engage in so many activities that seem to have nothing whatsoever to do with survival and reproduction? Why do people spend hours, days, months, and years creating and consuming art, literature, music, and sporting events? These seemingly "trivial pursuits" dominate some people's entire lives. These patterns require explanation.

Evolutionary psychologists have taken two basic approaches to answering these puzzles. The first approach might be called the *display hypothesis*. According to this hypothesis, culture is "an emergent phenomenon arising from sexual competition among vast numbers of individuals pursuing different mating strategies in different mating arenas" (Miller, 1998, p. 118). Men in particular tend to create and display art and music as a strategy for broadcasting courtship displays to a wide variety of women: "As every teenager knows and most psychologists forget, cultural displays by males increase sexual access" (Miller, 1998, p. 119).

The display hypothesis can account for several known facts about the patterning of cultural displays. First, it can account for the sex differences in the production of cultural products. Men historically have produced more art, music, and literature than women across a wide variety of cultures. Women had less to gain by cultural displays, according to this argument, simply because increased short-term sexual access was rarely a goal for them (see Chapter 6). The display hypothesis can also account for the age distribution of cultural displays. Many major works of art and music are created by men in young adulthood—the time when men are most intensely engaged in intrasexual mate competition (see Figure 13.4). In short, the display hypothesis appears to account for the age and sex distribution of culture production.

The display hypothesis, however, cannot explain several other facts about art, music, and literature. First, it cannot explain the *content* of these cultural products. Why do people find some songs moving but show indifference to others? Why are Shakespeare's plays mesmerizing to some, and those of many other playwrights seem boring? Why do some movies draw millions of viewers, whereas others fade into obscurity? A complete theory of culture must explain the contents of cultural products, not just their age and sex distribution. Second, the display hypothesis cannot account for the fact that some people spend inordinate amounts of time in the *solitary* enjoyment of art, music, and literature, in contexts in which no display is evident.

In a second approach to explaining culture, Pinker suggests a general answer to these puzzles, albeit a speculative one. He argues that the answer lies *not* in specific adaptations for art, music, and literature, but rather in the evolved mechanisms of the mind for other purposes that "let people take pleasure in shapes and colors and sounds and jokes and stories and myths" (Pinker, 1997, p. 523). A mechanism of color vision designed for locating ripe fruits, for example, can be pleasurably activated by creating paintings that mimic these patterns. Psychological preferences for cues to fertile females can be exploited by paintings, photographs, movies, and Internet sites to pleasurably mimic the patterns the mechanisms were originally designed to attend to and seek out. Just as artificial drugs can be created to "juice" our pleasure centers, art, music, and literature can be created to "juice" a variety of evolved psychological mechanisms. Humans have learned to artificially activate existing mechanisms by inventing cultural products

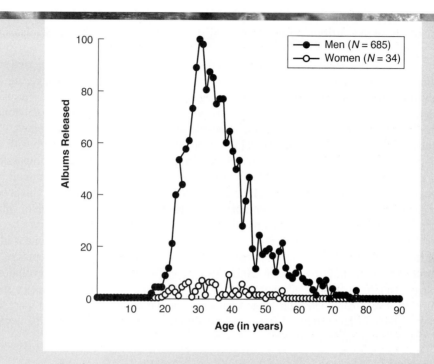

FIGURE 13.4  **Jazz Music: 1,892 Albums by 719 Musicians.** These findings support Geoffrey Miller's display hypothesis, which suggests that music, art, and literature are produced more by men than by women as a display tactic in attracting mates. In addition to the large sex difference, the age distribution roughly corresponds to the ages in which men engage in the heaviest mating effort.

*N* refers to the sample size.

Data from Carr, I., Fairweather, D., & Priestly, B., *The Essential Jazz Companion* (1988).

*Source:* Miller, G. F. (1999). Sexual selection for cultural displays, in R. Dunbar, C. Knight, & C. Power (Eds.), *The evolution of culture*, Edinburgh: University of Edinburgh Press. Reprinted with permission.

that mimic the stimuli for which the mechanisms were originally designed. These cultural activities, in short, are not adaptations but rather are nonadaptive by-products.

Pinker makes a similar argument for music: "I suspect that music is auditory cheesecake, an exquisite confection crafted to tickle the sensitive spots of at least six of our mental faculties" (1997, p. 534). These mental faculties include *language* (e.g., lyrics from songs), *auditory scene analysis* (e.g., we must segregate sounds coming from different sources, such as an animal call in a noisy forest), *emotional calls* (e.g., whining, crying, moaning, baying, and cheering are used as metaphors to describe musical passages), *habitat selection* (e.g., thunder, rushing water, growls, and other sounds might signal safe or unsafe environments), and *motor control* (e.g., rhythm, a universal component of music, mimics the motor control needed for a variety of tasks, including running and chopping, and signals qualities such as urgency, laziness, and confidence). The patterns of music we find pleasurable, according to this hypothesis, are those that artificially mimic natural stimuli that our evolved mechanisms were designed to process.

A similar argument can be made for fiction and movies. Words, plot lines, and stories depicting comedies and tragedies can activate pleasurable sensations by triggering a host of evolved mechanisms. It is probably no coincidence that the most successful novels and movies, such as *Avatar, Titanic*, and *Gone with the Wind,* contain patterns of intrasexual competition, mate choice, romance, and life-threatening hostile forces of nature. As Pinker noted, "When we are absorbed in a book or movie, we get to see breathtaking landscapes, hobnob with important people, fall in love with ravishing men and women, protect loved ones, attain impossible goals, and defeat wicked enemies" (1997, p. 539). One analysis of thirty-six common plot lines showed most were defined by one of four themes: love, sex, personal threat, or threat to the protagonist's kin (Carroll, 2005). The patterns of culture that we create and consume, although not adaptations in themselves, reveal human evolutionary psychology.

The evolutionary psychological analysis of the arts, literature, and film has blossomed over the past decade, so much so that entire books are now devoted to these topics (e.g., Boyd, Carroll, & Gottschall, 2010; Dutton, 2009). Penetrating analyses suggest that evolutionary psychology can inform artistic endeavors as diverse as the nuances of film to the poetry and politics of British novels. Although offering no final words on these cultural manifestations, shining an evolutionary lens has produced fresh insights into domains long thought to be devoid of the mechanisms of mind that define human nature.

## ■ TOWARD A UNIFIED PSYCHOLOGY

In this chapter, we have considered how evolutionary psychology approaches the major branches of psychology including cognitive, social, developmental, personality, clinical, and cultural psychology. Evolutionary psychology has also proved informative for other subbranches of psychology, such as organizational and industrial psychology (Colarelli, 1998; Nicholson, 1997), consumer and marketing psychology (Miller, 2009; Saad, 2007b), educational psychology (Geary, 2002), and environmental psychology (Kaplan, 1992). Evolutionary psychology has extended its reach and is beginning to transform other disciplines as well—such as the evolutionary analysis of the law (Jones, 1999, 2005), religion (Kirkpatrick, 1999; Pinker, 1997), arts (Boyd et al., 2010), economics (Kurzban et al., 2001; Saad & Gill, 2001; Wang, 2001), study of mathematical reasoning (Brase, 2002), psychiatry (Brune, 2008), and sociology (Hopcroft, 2002; Kanazawa, 2001), as well as hybrid disciplines such as social cognition (Andrews, 2001; DeKay & Shackelford, 2000) and cognitive neuroscience (Barkley, 2001; Platek, Keenan, & Shackelford, 2007).

Ultimately, however, evolutionary psychology can be expected to dissolve these traditional disciplinary boundaries. Human beings cannot be neatly partitioned into discrete elements such as personality, social, developmental, and cognitive. Stable individual differences traditionally have been relegated to the personality branch, but they often involve social orientations, have particular developmental antecedents, and are anchored in particular cognitive mechanisms. Social exchange and reciprocity have traditionally been regarded as belonging to social psychology. The mechanisms that underlie them, however, are information-processing devices that have developmental trajectories. The rapid changes occurring at puberty have been the traditional province of developmental psychologists. Individuals differ in the onset of puberty, however, and many of the most important changes at puberty are social. From the perspective of evolutionary psychology, many traditional disciplinary boundaries are not merely arbitrary but are misleading and detrimental to scientific progress. They imply boundaries that cleave mechanisms in arbitrary and unnatural ways. Studying human psychology via adaptive problems and their solutions—the organizing principle of this book—provides a more natural means of "cleaving nature at its joints" and hence crossing current disciplinary boundaries.

A critical task in this new psychological science will be the identification of the key adaptive problems that humans have confronted repeatedly over human evolutionary history. Evolutionary psychologists have barely scratched the surface by identifying some of the problems most obviously and plausibly linked with survival and reproduction. Many adaptive problems remain unexplored, and many psychological solutions undiscovered. It is not unreasonable to expect that the first scientists to explore these uncharted territories will come away with a great bounty.

Evolutionary psychology provides the conceptual tools for emerging from the fragmented state of current psychological science and linking psychology with the rest of the life sciences in a larger scientific integration. Evolutionary psychology provides some of the most important tools for unlocking the mysteries of where we came from, how we arrived at our current state, and the mechanisms of mind that define what it means to be human.

## ■ SUGGESTED READINGS

Boyd, B., Carroll, J., & Gottschall, J. (Eds.). (2010). *Evolution, literature, and film: A reader*. New York: Columbia University Press.

Hagen, E. H., & Hammerstein, P. (2005). Evolutionary biology and the strategic view of ontogeny: Genetic strategies provide robustness and flexibility in the life course. *Research in Human Development, 2*, 87–101.

Haselton, M. G., Bryant, G. A., Wilke, A., Frederick, D. A., Galperin, A., Franenhuis, W. E., & Moore, T. (2009). Adaptive rationality: An evolutionary perspective on cognitive bias. *Social Cognition, 27*, 733–763.

Henrich, J. (2009). The evolution of costly displays, cooperation, and religion: Credibility enhancing displays and their implications for cultural evolution. *Evolution and Human Behavior, 30*, 244–260.

MacDonald, K. (2008). Effortful control, explicit processing, and the regulation of human evolved predispositions. *Psychological Review, 115*, 1012–1031.

Neberich, W., Penke, L., Lehnart, J., & Asendorpf, J. B. (2010). Family of origin, age of menarche, and reproductive strategies: A test of four evolutionary-developmental models. *European Journal of Developmental Psychology, 7*, 153–177.

Nesse, R. M., & Ellsworth, P. C. (2009). Evolution, emotions, and emotional disorders. *American Psychologist, 64*, 129–139.

Pinker, S. (2002). *The blank slate: The modern denial of human nature*. New York: Viking.

Platek, S. M., Keenan, J. P., & Shackelford, T. K. (Eds.). (2007). *Evolutionary cognitive neuroscience*. Cambridge, MA: MIT Press.

Schaller, M., Simpson, J. A., & Kenrick, D. J. (Eds.). (2006). *Evolution and social psychology*. New York: Psychology Press.

# BIBLIOGRAPHY

Abbey, A. (1982). Sex differences in attributions for friendly behavior: Do males misperceive females' friendliness? *Journal of Personality and Social Psychology, 32,* 830–838.

Abed, R. T. (1998). The sexual competition hypothesis for eating disorders. *British Journal of Medical Psychology, 71,* 525–547.

Agras, S., Sylvester, D., & Oliveau, D. (1969). The epidemiology of common fears and phobias. *Comprehensive Psychiatry, 10,* 151–156.

Aharon, I., Etcoff, N., Ariely, D., Chabris, C. F., O'Connor, E., & Breiter, H. C. (2001). Beautiful faces have variable reward value: FMRI and behavioral evidence. *Neuron, 32,* 537–551.

Ahmad, Y., & Smith, P. K. (1994). Bullying in schools and the issue of sex differences. In J. Archer (Ed.), *Male violence* (pp. 70–83). London: Routledge.

Alcock, J. (1989). *Animal behavior: An evolutionary approach* (4th ed.). Sunderland, MA: Sinauer.

Alcock, J. (1993). *Animal behavior: An evolutionary approach* (5th ed.). Sunderland, MA: Sinauer.

Alcock, J. (2009). *Animal behavior: An evolutionary approach* (9th ed.). Sunderland, MA: Sinauer.

Alexander, R. D. (1979). *Darwinism and human affairs.* Seattle: University of Washington Press.

Alexander, R. D. (1987). *The biology of moral systems.* Hawthorne, NY: Aldine DeGruyter.

Alexander, R. D. (1989). Evolution of the human psyche. In P. Mellars & C. Stringer (Eds.), *The human revolution: Behavioral and biological perspectives on the origins of modern humans* (pp. 455–513). Princeton, NJ: Princeton University Press.

Alexander, R. D., Hoodland, J. L., Howard, R. D., Noonan, K. M., & Sherman, P. W. (1979). Sexual dimorphisms and breeding systems in pinnipeds, ungulates, primates, and humans. In N. A. Chagnon & W. Irons (Eds.), *Evolutionary biology and human social behavior.* North Scituate, MA: Duxbury Press.

Alexander, R. D., & Noonan, K. M. (1979). Concealment of ovulation, parental care, and human social evolution. In N. A. Chagnon & W. Irons (Eds.), *Evolutionary biology and human social behavior* (pp. 402–435). North Scituate, MA: Duxbury Press.

Allee, W. N., Collias, N., & Lutherman, C. (1939). Modification of the social order in flocks of hens by the injection of testosterone propionate. *Physiological Zoology, 12,* 412–440.

Allen-Arave, W., Gurven, M., & Hill, K. (2008). Reciprocal altruism, rather than kin selection, maintains nepotistic food transfers on an Ache reservation. *Evolution and Human Behavior, 29,* 305–318.

Allport, G. W., & Postman, L. (1947). *The psychology of rumor.* New York: Holt.

Alvard, M. (2009). Kinship and cooperation: The axe fight revisited. *Human Nature, 20,* 394–416.

Alvergne, A., Faurie, C., & Raymond, M. (2008). Developmental plasticity of human reproductive development: Effects of early family environment in modern-day France. *Physiology and Behavior, 95,* 625–632.

Alvergne, A., Faurie, C., & Raymond, M. (2010). Are parents' perceptions of offspring facial resemblance consistent with actual resemblance? Effects on parental investment. *Evolution and Human Behavior, 31,* 7–15.

Alvergne, A., Oda, R., Faurie, C., Matsumoto-Oda, A., Durand, V., & Raymond, M. (2008). Cross-cultural perceptions of facial resemblance between kin. *Journal of Vision, 9,* 1–10.

American Psychiatric Association. (2000). *Diagnostic and statistical manual of mental disorders* (4th ed.). Washington, DC: Author.

Anderson, C., & Kilduff, G. J. (2009). The pursuit of status in social groups. *Current Directions in Psychological Science, 18,* 295–289.

Anderson, K. G. (2005). Relatedness and investment in children in South Africa. *Human Nature, 16,* 1–31.

Anderson, K. G., Kaplan, H., Lam, D., & Lancaster, J. (1999). Paternal care by genetic fathers and stepfathers II: Reports by Xhosa high school students. *Evolution and Human Behavior, 20,* 433–451.

Anderson, K. G., Kaplan, H., & Lancaster, J. (1999). Paternal care by genetic fathers and stepfathers. I: Reports from Albuquerque men. *Evolution and Human Behavior, 20,* 405–431.

Anderson, K. G., Kaplan, H., & Lancaster, J. B. (2007). Confidence of paternity, divorce, and investment in children by Albuquerque men. *Evolution and Human Behavior, 28,* 1–10.

Andrews, P. A., Gangestad, S. W., Miller, G. F., Haselton, M. G., Thornhill, R., & Neale, M. C. (2008). Sex differences in detecting sexual infidelity: Results of a maximum likelihood method for analyzing the sensitivity to sex differences to underreporting. *Human Nature, 19,* 347–373.

Andrews, P. W. (2001). The psychology of social chess and the evolution of attribution mechanisms: Explaining the fundamental attribution error. *Evolution and Human Behavior, 22,* 11–29.

Andrews, P. W. (2006). Parent–offspring conflict and cost-benefit analysis in adolescent suicidal behavior. *Human Nature, 17,* 190–211.

Andrews, P. W., & Thomson, Jr., J. A. (2009). The bright side of being blue: Depression as an adaptation for analyzing complex problems. *Psychological Review, 116,* 620–654.

Apicella, C. L., & Marlow, F. W. (2004). Perceived mate fidelity and paternal resemblance predict men's investment in children. *Evolution and Human Behavior, 25,* 371–378.

Apicella, C. L., & Marlow, F. W. (2007). Men's reproductive investment decisions. *Human Nature, 18,* 22–34.

Apostolou, M. (2007). Sexual selection under parental choice: The role of parents in the evolution of human mating. *Evolution and Human Behavior, 28,* 403–409.

Apostolou, M. (2008a). Parent–offspring conflict over mating: The case of beauty. *Evolutionary Psychology, 6,* 303–315.

Apostolou, M. (2008b). Parent–offspring conflict over mating: The case of family background. *Evolutionary Psychology, 6,* 456–468.

Apostolou, M. (2009). Parent–offspring conflict over mating: The case of short-term mating strategies. *Personality and Individual Differences, 47,* 895–899.

Appleton, J. (1975). *The experience of landscape.* New York: Wiley.

Archer, J. (1988). *The behavioural biology of aggression.* Cambridge, UK: Cambridge University Press.

Archer, J. (1998). *The nature of grief.* London: Routledge.

Archer, J. (2009). Does sexual selection explain human sex differences in aggression. *Behavioral and Brain Sciences, 32,* 249–311.

Ardener, E. W., Ardener, S. G., & Warmington, W. A. (1960). *Plantation and village in the Cameroons.* London: Oxford University Press.

Ardry, R. (1966). *The territorial imperative.* New York: Atheneum.

Argyle, M. (1994). *The psychology of social class.* New York: Routledge.

Asendorpf, J. B., Penke, L., & Back, M. D. (2010). From dating to mating and relating: Predictors of initial and long-term outcomes of speed dating in a community sample. *European Journal of Personality,* doi:10.1002/per.768.

Athanasiou, R., Shaver, P., & Tavris, C. (1970, July). Sex. *Psychology Today,* pp. 37–52.

Atran, S. (1990). *The cognitive foundations of natural history.* New York: Cambridge University Press.

Atran, S. (1998). Folk biology and the anthropology of science: Cognitive universals and cultural particulars. *Behavioral and Brain Sciences, 21,* 547–609.

Avis, J., & Harris, P. L. (1991). Belief-desire reasoning among Baka children: Evidence for a universal conception of mind. *Child Development, 62,* 460–467.

Axelrod, R. (1984). *The evolution of cooperation.* New York: Basic Books.

Axelrod, R., & Hamilton, W. D. (1981). The evolution of cooperation. *Science, 211,* 1390–1396.

Babchuk, W. A., Hames, R. B., & Thompson, R. A. (1985). Sex differences in the recognition of infant facial expressions of emotion: the primary caretaker hypothesis. *Ethology & Sociobiology, 6,* 89–101.

Badahdah, A. M., & Tiemann, K. A. (2005). Mate selection criteria among Muslims living in America. *Evolution and Human Behavior, 26,* 432–440.

Bahrick, H. P., Bahrick, P. O., & Wittlinger, R. P. (1975). Fifty years of memory for names and faces: A cross-sectional approach. *Journal of Experimental Psychology, 104,* 54–75.

Bailey, D. H., & Geary, D. C. (2009). Hominid brain evolution: Testing climatic, ecological, and social competition models. *Human Nature, 20,* 67–79.

Bailey, J. M. (1998). Can behavior genetics contribute to evolutionary behavioral science? In C. Crawford & D. L. Krebs (Eds.), *Handbook of evolutionary psychology* (pp. 221–234). Mahwah, NJ: Erlbaum.

Bailey, J. M., Kim, P. Y., Hills, A., & Linsenmeier, J. A. W. (1997). Butch, femme, or straight acting? Partner preferences of gay men and lesbians. *Journal of Personality and Social Psychology, 73,* 960–973.

Bailey, J. M., Kirk, K. M., Zhu, G., Dunne, M. P., & Martin, N. G. (2000). Do individual differences in sociosexuality represent genetic or environmentally contingent strategies? Evidence from the Australian Twin Registry. *Journal of Personality and Social Psychology, 78,* 537–545.

Bailey, J. M., Pillard, R. C., Dawood, K., Miller, M. B., Farrer, L. A., Trivedi, S., & Murphy, R. L. (1999). A family history study of sexual orientation using three independent samples. *Behavior Genetics, 29,* 79–86.

Baize, H. R., & Schroeder, J. E. (1995). Personality and mate selection in personal ads: Evolutionary preferences in a public mate selection process. *Journal of Social Behavior and Personality, 10,* 517–536.

Baker, R. R., & Bellis, M. A. (1995). *Human sperm competition.* London: Chapman & Hall.

Barash, D. P., & Lipton, J. E. (1997). *Making sense of sex.* Washington, DC: Island Press/Shearwater Brooks.

Barber, N. (1995). The evolutionary psychology of physical attractiveness: Sexual selection and human morphology. *Ethology and Sociobiology, 16,* 395–424.

Barclay, A. M. (1973). Sexual fantasies in men and women. *Medical Aspects of Human Sexuality, 7,* 205–216.

Barclay, P. (2006). Reputational benefits for altruistic punishment. *Evolution and Human Behavior, 27,* 325–344.

Barclay, P. (2008). Enhanced recognition of defectors depends on their rarity. *Cognition, 107,* 817–828.

Barclay, P. (2010). Altruism as a courtship display: Some effects of third-party generosity on audience perceptions. *British Journal of Psychology, 101,* 123–135.

Barclay, P., & Willer, R. (2007). Partner choice creates competitive altruism in humans. *Proceedings of the Royal Society, B, 274,* 749–753.

Barinaga, M. (1996). Social status sculpts activity of crayfish neurons. *Science, 271,* 290–291.

Barkley, R. A. (2001). The executive functions of selfregulation: An evolutionary neuropsychological perspective. *Neuropsychology Review, 11,* 1–29.

Barkow, J. (1989). *Darwin, sex, and status: Biological approaches to mind and culture.* Toronto: University of Toronto Press.

Baron-Cohen, S. (1999). Evolution of a theory of mind? In M. Corballis & S. Lea (Eds.). *The descent of mind: Psychological perspectives on hominid evolution.* Oxford, UK: Oxford University Press.

Baron-Cohen, S. (2005). The empathizing system: A revision of the 1994 mode of the mindreading system. In B. J. Ellis & D. F. Bjorklund (Eds.), *The origins of the social mind: Evolutionary psychology and child development* (pp. 468–492). New York: Guilford.

Barrett, H. C. (1999). *Human cognitive adaptations to predators and prey.* Ph.D. Dissertation, University of California at Santa Barbara.

Barrett, H. C. (2005). Adaptations to predators and prey. In D. M. Buss (Ed.), *The handbook of evolutionary psychology* (pp. 200–223). New York: Wiley.

Barrett, H. C., Frederick, D. A., & Haselton, M. G. (2006). Can manipulations of cognitive load be used to test evolutionary hypotheses? *Journal of Personality and Social Psychology, 91,* 513–518.

Barrett, H. C., & Kurzban, R. (2006). Modularity in cognition: Framing the debate. *Psychological Review, 113,* 628–647.

Barrett, L., Dunbar, R. I. M., & Lycett, J. (2002). *Human evolutionary psychology.* Princeton, NJ: Princeton University Press.

Bartels, A., & Zeki, S. (2004). The neural correlates of maternal and romantic love. *NeuroImage, 21,* 1155–1166.

Bassett, J., Pearcey, S., & Dabbs, J. M., Jr. (2001). Jealousy and partner preference among butch and femme lesbians. *Psychology, Evolution, and Gender, 3*(2), 155–165.

Baumeister, R. F. (2000). Gender differences in erotic plasticity: The female sex drive as socially flexible and responsive. *Psychological Bulletin, 126,* 347–374.

Baumeister, R. F., & Leary, M. R. (1995). The need to belong: Desire for interpersonal attachments as a fundamental human motivation. *Psychological Bulletin, 117,* 497–529.

Beaulieu, D. A., & Bugental, D. (2008). Contingent parental investment: An evolutionary framework for understanding early interaction between mothers and children. *Evolution and Human Behavior, 29,* 249–255.

Beise, J., & Voland, E. (2008). Intrafamilial resource competition and mate completion shaped social-group-specific natal dispersal in the 18th and 19th century Krummhörn population. *American Journal of Human Biology, 20,* 325–336.

Bell, R., & Buchner, A. (2008). Enhanced memory for names of cheaters. *Evolutionary Psychology, 7,* 317–330.

Belluck, P. (1997). A woman's killer is likely to be her partner, a study finds. *New York Times.*

Belsky, J. (1997). Attachment, mating, and parenting: An evolutionary interpretation. *Human Nature, 8,* 361–381.

Belsky, J., Steinberg, L., & Draper, P. (1991). Childhood experience, interpersonal development, and reproductive strategy: An evolutionary theory of socialization. *Child Development, 62,* 647–670.

Benenson, J. F. (2009). Dominating versus eliminating the competition: Sex differences in human intrasexual aggression. *Behavioral and Brain Sciences, 32,* 268–269.

Benenson, J. F., Hodgdson, L., Heath, S., & Welch, P. J. (2008). Human sexual differences in the use of social ostracism as a competitive tactic. *International Journal of Primatology, 29,* 1019–1035.

Berbesque, J. C., & Marlow, F. W. (2009). Sex differences in food preferences of Hadza hunter-gatherers. *Evolutionary Psychology, 7,* 601–616.

Bereczkei, T., Birkas, B., & Kerekes, Z. (2007). Public charity offer as a proximate factor of evolved reputation-building strategy: An experimental analysis of a real-life situation. *Evolution and Human Behavior, 28,* 277–284.

Bereczkei, T., Birkas, B., & Kerekes, Z. (2010). Altruism toward strangers in need: Costly signaling in an industrial society. *Evolution and Human Behavior, 31,* 95–103.

Bereczkei, T., Gyuris, P., & Weisfeld, G. E. (2004). Sexual imprinting in human mate choice. *Proceedings of the Royal Society of London, B, 271,* 1129–1134.

Berlin, B. (1992). *Ethnobiological classification.* Princeton, NJ: Princeton University Press.

Berlin, B., Breedlove, D., & Raven, P. (1973). General principles of classification and nomenclature in field biology. *American Anthropologist, 75,* 214–242.

Bernard, L. C. (2009). Consensual and behavioral validity of a measure of adaptive individual differences dimensions in human motivation. *Motivation and Emotion, 34,* 303–319.

Bernhardt, P. C. (1997). Influences of serotonin and testosterone in aggression and dominance: Convergence with social psychology. *Current Directions in Psychological Science, 6,* 44–53.

Bersaglieri, T., Sabeti, P. C., Patterson, N., Vanderploeg, T, Schaffner, S. F., Drake J. A., Rhodes, M., Reich, D. E., & Hirchhorn, J. N. (2004). Genetic signatures of strong recent positive selection at the lactase gene. *American Journal of Human Genetics, 74,* 1111–1120.

Berscheid, E., & Walster, E. (1974). Physical attractiveness. In L. Berkowitz (Ed.), *Advances in experimental social psychology* (pp. 157–215). New York: Academic Press.

Bertamini, M., & Bennett, K. M. (2009). The effect of leg length on perceived attractiveness of simplified stimuli. *Journal of social, Evolutionary, and Cultural Psychology, 3,* 233–250.

Bertenthal, B. I., Campos, J. J., & Caplovitz, K. S. (1983). Self-produced locomotion: An organizer of emotional, cognitive, and social development in infancy. In R. N. Emde & R. Harmon (Eds.), *Continuities and discontinuities in development.* New York: Plenum.

Betzig, L. (1989). Causes of conjugal dissolution. *Current Anthropology, 30,* 654–676.

Betzig, L. (1992). Roman polygyny. *Ethology and Sociobiology, 13,* 309–349.

Betzig, L. (1993). Sex, succession, and stratification in the first six civilizations. In L. Ellis (Ed.), *Social stratification and socioeconomic inequality* (pp. 37–74). Westport, CT: Praeger.

Betzig, L. L. (1986). *Despotism and differential reproduction: A Darwinian view of history.* Hawthorne, NY: Aldine.

Billing, J., & Sherman, P. W. (1998). Antimicrobial functions of spices: Why some like it hot. *Quarterly Review of Biology, 73,* 3–49.

Birch, L. L. (1999). Development of food preferences. *Annual Review of Nutrition, 19,* 41–62.

Bishop, D. I., Meyer, B. C., Schmidt, T. M., & Gray, B. R. (2009). Differential investment behavior between grandparents and grandchildren: The role of paternity uncertainty. *Evolutionary Psychology, 7,* 66–77.

Bjorklund, D. F. (1997). The role of immaturity in human development. *Psychological Bulletin, 122,* 153–169.

Bjorklund, D. F., & Kipp, K. (1996). Parental investment theory and gender differences in the evolution of inhibition mechanisms. *Psychological Bulletin, 120,* 163–188.

Bjorklund, D. F., & Pellegrini, A. D. (2002). *The origins of human nature: Evolutionary developmental psychology.* Washington, DC: American Psychological Association.

Bjorkqvist, K., Lagerspetz, K. M. J., & Kaukiainen, A. (1992). Do girls manipulate and boys fight? Developmental trends in regard to direct and indirect aggression. *Aggressive Behavior, 18,* 117–127.

Bleske, A., & Buss, D. M. (1997, June). *The evolutionary psychology of special "friendships."* Paper presented at the ninth annual meeting of the Human Behavior and Evolution Society, University of Arizona, Tucson.

Bleske, A. L., & Buss, D. M. (2001). Opposite sex friendship: Sex differences and similarities in initiation, selection, and dissolution. *Personality and Social Psychology Bulletin, 27*, 1310–1323.

Bleske-Rechek, A., & Lighthall, M. (2010). Attractiveness and rivalry in women's friendships with women. *Human Nature, 21*, 82–97.

Bliege Bird, R., & Smith, E. A. (2005). Signaling theory, strategic interaction, and symbolic capital. *Current Anthropology, 46*, 221–248.

Bobrow, D., & Bailey, J. M. (2001). Is male homosexuality maintained via kin selection? *Evolution and Human Behavior, 22*, 361–368.

Boehm, C. (1999). *Hierarchy in the forest: The evolution of egalitarian behavior.* Cambridge, MA: Harvard University Press.

Bokek-Cohen, Y., Peres, Y., & Kanazawa, S. (2007). Rational choice and evolutionary psychology as explanations for mate selectivity. *Journal of Social, Evolutionary, and Cultural Psychology, 2*, 42–55.

Book, A. S., & Quinsey, V. L. (2004). Psychopaths: Cheaters or warrior-hawks? *Personality and Individual Differences, 36*, 35–45.

Book, A. S., Quinsey, V. L., & Langford, D. (2007). Psychopathy and the perception of affect and vulnerability. *Criminal Justice and Behavior, 31*, 531–544.

Boone, J. L. (1998). The evolution of magnanimity: When is it better to give than to receive? *Human Nature, 9*, 1–21.

Boothroyd, L. G., Jones, B. C., Burt, D. M., Cornwell, R. E., Little, A. C., Tiddeman, B. P., & Perrett, D. I. (2005). Facial masculinity is related to perceived age but not perceived health. *Evolution and Human Behavior, 26*, 417–431.

Boothroyd, L. G., Jones, B. C., Burt, D. M., DeBruine, L. M., & Perrett, D. I. (2008). Facial correlates of sociosexuality. *Evolution and Human Behavior, 29*, 211–218.

Boothroyd, L. G., Jones, B. C., Burt, D. M., & Perrett, D. I. (2007). Partner characteristics associated with masculinity, health and maturity in male faces. *Personality and Individual Differences, 43*, 1161–1173.

Borgerhoff Mulder, M. (1988). Kipsigis bridewealth payments. In L. L. Betzig, M. Borgerhoff Mulder, & P. Turke (Eds.), *Human reproductive behavior* (pp. 65–82). New York: Cambridge University Press.

Borgerhoff Mulder, M. (1990). Kipsigis women's preferences for wealthy men: Evidence for female choice in mammals? *Behavioral Ecology and Sociobiology, 27*, 255–264.

Borgerhoff Mulder, M. (1998). Brothers and sisters: How sibling interactions affect optimal parental allocations. *Human Nature, 9*, 119–162.

Bossong, B. (2001). Gender and age differences in inheritance patterns. Why men leave more to their spouses and women more to their children: An experimental analysis. *Human Nature, 12*, 107–122.

Bouissou, M. F. (1978). Effects of injections of testosterone propionate on dominance relationships in a group of cows. *Hormones and Behavior, 11*, 388–400.

Bowlby, J. (1969). *Attachment and loss: Vol. 1.* New York: Basic Books.

Boyce, W. T., & Ellis, B. J. (2005). Biological sensitivity to context: I. An evolutionary-developmental theory of the origins and functions of stress reactivity. *Development and Psychopathology, 17*, 271–301.

Boyd, B., Carroll, J., & Gottschall, J. (Eds.). (2010). *Evolution, literature, and film:* A reader. New York: Columbia University Press.

Boyd, R., & Richardson, P. (1985). *Culture and the evolutionary process.* Chicago: University of Chicago Press.

Boyd, R., & Richardson, P. J. (1992). Punishment allows the evolution of cooperation (or anything else) in sizable groups. *Ethology and Sociobiology, 13*, 171–195.

Boyle, J. (1977). *A sense of freedom.* London: Pan Books.

Bracha, H. S. (2004). Freeze, flight, fight, fright, faint: Adaptationist perspectives on the acute stress response spectrum. *CNS Spectrums, 9*, 679–685.

Brandes, J. (1967). First trimester nausea and vomiting as related to outcome of pregnancy. *Obstetrics and Gynecology, 30*, 427–431.

Brantingham, P. J. (1998). Hominid-carnivore coevolution and invasion of the predatory guild. *Journal of Anthropological Archeology, 17*, 327–353.

Brase, G. L. (2002). "Bugs" built into the system: How privileged representations influence mathematical reasoning across the lifespan. *Learning and Individual Differences, 12*, 391–409.

Brase, G. L. (2006). Cues of parental investment as a factor in attractiveness. *Evolution and Human Behavior, 27*, 145–157.

Brase, G. L. (2009). Pictorial representations in statistical reasoning. *Applied Cognitive Psychology, 23*, 369–381.

Brase, G. L., Caprar, D. V., & Voracek, M. (2004). Sex differences in response to relationship threats in England and Romania. *Journal of Social and Personal Relationships, 21*, 763–778.

Brase, G. L., & Walker, G. (2004). Male sexual strategies modify ratings of female models with specific waist-to-hip ratios. *Human Nature, 15*, 209–224.

Bredart, S., & French, R. M. (1999). Do babies resemble their fathers more than their mothers? A failure to replicate Christenfeld and Hill (1995). *Evolution and Human Behavior, 20*, 129–135.

Bressan, P., & Zucchi, G. (2009). Human kin recognition is self- rather than family-referential. *Biology Letters, 5*, 336–338.

Bressler, E. R., Martin, R. A., & Balshine, S. (2006). Production and appreciation of humor as sexually selected traits. *Evolution and Human Behavior, 27*, 121–130.

Brewer, G., & Archer, J. (2007). What do people infer from facial attractiveness? *Journal of Evolutionary Psychology, 5*, 1–9.

Brewer, G., & Riley, C. (2009). Height, relationship satisfaction, jealousy, and mate retention. *Evolutionary Psychology, 7*, 477–489.

Brewin, C. R. (1988). *Cognitive foundations of clinical psychology.* London: Erlbaum.

Bröder, A., & Hohmann, N. (2003). Variations in risk taking behavior over the menstrual cycle: An improved replication. *Evolution and Human Behavior, 24*, 391–398.

Brown, D. E. (1991). *Human universals.* New York: McGraw-Hill.

Brown, D. E., & Chia-Yun, Y. (n.d.). *"Big man" as a statistical universal.* Department of Anthropology, University of California, Santa Barbara.

Brown, R. M., Dahlen, E., Mills, C., Rick, J., & Biblarz, A. (1999). Evaluation of an evolutionary model of self-reservation and self-destruction. *Suicide and Life Threatening Behavior, 29,* 58–71.

Brown, S. L., & Lewis, B. P. (2004). Relational dominance and mate-selection criteria: Evidence that males attend to female dominance. *Evolution and Human Behavior, 25,* 406–415.

Brown, W. M., & Moore, C. (2000). Is prospective altruist-detection an evolved solution to the adaptive problem of subtle cheating in cooperative ventures? Supportive evidence using the Wason selection task. *Evolution and Human Behavior, 21,* 25–37.

Browne, K. R. (1998). An evolutionary account of women's workplace status. *Managerial and Decision Economics, 19,* 427–440.

Browne, K. R. (2002). *Biology at work: Rethinking sexual equality.* New Brunswick, NJ: Rutgers University Press.

Browne, K. R. (2006). Sex, power, and dominance: The evolutionary psychology of sexual harassment. *Managerial and Decision Economics, 27,* 145–158.

Browne, K. R. (2010). The evolutionary psychology of sexual harassment. In J. D. Duntley & T. K. Shackelford (Eds.), *Evolutionary forensic psychology* (pp. 81–100). New York: Oxford University Press.

Brune, M. (2008). *Textbook of evolutionary psychiatry: Origins of psychopathology.* New York: Oxford University Press.

Bryant, G. A., & Haselton, M. G. (2009). Vocal cues of ovulation in human females. *Biology Letters, 5,* 12–15.

Buchner, A., Bell, R., Mehl, B., & Musch, J. (2009). No enhanced recognition memory, but better source memory for the faces of cheaters. *Evolution and Human Behavior, 30,* 212–224.

Buckley, N. J. (2005). Not so happy families. *TRENDS in Ecology and Evolution, 20,* 295.

Bugos, P. E., & McCarthy, L. M. (1984). Ayoreo infanticide: A case study. In G. Hausfater & S. B. Hrdy (Eds.), *Infanticide: Comparative and evolutionary perspectives* (pp. 503–520). New York: Aldine de Gruyter.

Burbank, V. K. (1992). Sex, gender, and difference: Dimensions of aggression in an Australian aboriginal community. *Human Nature, 3,* 251–278.

Burch, R. L., & Gallup, G. G., Jr. (2000). Perceptions of paternal resemblance predict family violence. *Evolution and Human Behavior, 21,* 429–435.

Burgess, R. L. & MacDonald (Eds.). (2005). *Evolutionary perspectives on human development* (2nd ed.). Thousand Oaks, CA: Sage Publications.

Burkett, B. N., & Cosmides, L. (2006, June). *What is intolerable in a mate?* Paper presented at the Annual Meeting of the Human Behavior and Evolution Society, Philadelphia, PA.

Burley, N., & Symanski, R. (1981). Women without: An evolutionary and cross-cultural perspective on prostitution. In R. Symanski, *The Immoral Landscape: Female Prostitution in Western Societies* (pp. 239–274). Toronto: Butterworths.

Burnham, T. C., Chapman, J. F., Gray, P. B., McIntyre, M. H., Lipson, S. F., & Ellison, P. T. (2003). Men in committed, romantic relationships have lower testosterone. *Hormones and Behavior, 44,* 119–122.

Burnstein, E., Crandall, C., & Kitayama, S. (1994). Some neo-Darwinian decision rules for altruism: Weighing cues for inclusive fitness as a function of the biological importance of the decision. *Journal of Personality and Social Psychology, 67,* 773–789.

Buss, A. H. (1961). *The psychology of aggression.* New York: Wiley.

Buss, D. M. (1981). Sex differences in the evaluation and performance of dominant acts. *Journal of Personality and Social Psychology, 40,* 147–154.

Buss, D. M. (1985). Human mate selection. *American Scientist, 73,* 47–51.

Buss, D. M. (1988a). Love acts: The evolutionary biology of love. In R. J. Sternberg & M. L. Barnes (Eds.), *The psychology of love* (pp. 100–118). New Haven, CT: Yale University Press.

Buss, D. M. (1988b). The evolution of human intrasexual competition: Tactics of mate attraction. *Journal of Personality and Social Psychology, 54,* 616–628.

Buss, D. M. (1988c). From vigilance to violence: Tactics of mate retention. *Ethology and Sociobiology, 9,* 291–317.

Buss, D. M. (1989a). Sex differences in human mate preferences: Evolutionary hypotheses testing in 37 cultures. *Behavioral and Brain Sciences, 12,* 1–49.

Buss, D. M. (1989b). Conflict between the sexes: Strategic interference and the evocation of anger and upset. *Journal of Personality and Social Psychology, 56,* 735–747.

Buss, D. M. (1991). Conflict in married couples: Personality predictors of anger and upset. *Journal of Personality, 59,* 663–688.

Buss, D. M. (1994a). The strategies of human mating. *American Scientist, 82,* 238–249.

Buss, D. M. (1994b). *The evolution of desire: Strategies of human mating.* New York: Basic Books.

Buss, D. M. (1995, June). *Human prestige criteria.* Paper presented to the Human Behavior and Evolution Society Annual Meeting, University of California, Santa Barbara, CA.

Buss, D. M. (1996a). Sexual conflict: Evolutionary insights into feminist and the "battle of the sexes." In D. M. Buss & N. M. Malamuth (Eds.), *Sex, power, conflict: Evolutionary and feminist perspectives* (pp. 296–318). New York: Oxford University Press.

Buss, D. M. (1996b). The evolutionary psychology of human social strategies. In E. T. Higgins & A. W. Kruglanski (Eds.), *Social psychology: Handbook of basic principles* (pp. 3–38). New York: Guilford.

Buss, D. M. (2000a). *The dangerous passion: Why jealousy is as necessary as love and sex.* New York: Free Press.

Buss, D. M. (2000b). The evolution of happiness. *American Psychologist, 55,* 15–23.

Buss, D. M. (2003). *The evolution of desire: Strategies of human mating (Revised Edition).* New York: Free Press.

Buss, D. M. (2005). *The murderer next door: Why the mind is designed to kill.* New York: Penguin.

Buss, D. M. (2006a). The evolution of love. In R. J. Sternberg & K. Weis (Eds.), *The psychology of love* (pp. 65–86). New Haven: Yale University Press.

Buss, D. M. (2006b). The evolutionary genetics of personality: Does mutation load signals relationship load? *Behavioral and Brain Science, 29,* 409.

Buss, D. M. (2009a). The great struggles of life: Darwin and the emergence of evolutionary psychology. *American Psychologist, 64,* 140–148.

Buss, D. M. (2009b). How can evolutionary psychology successfully explain personality and individual differences? *Perspectives on Psychological Science, 4,* 359–366.

Buss, D. M. (2011). Personality and the adaptive landscape: The role of individual differences in creating and solving social adaptive problems. In D. M. Buss & P. Hawley (Eds.), *The evolution of personality and individual differences.* New York: Oxford University Press.

Buss, D. M., Abbott, M., Angleitner, A., Asherian, A., Biaggio, A., & 45 other co-authors. (1990). International preferences in selecting mates: A study of 37 cultures. *Journal of Cross-Cultural Psychology, 21,* 5–47.

Buss, D. M., & Barnes, M. F. (1986). Preferences in human mate selection. *Journal of Personality and Social Psychology, 50,* 559–570.

Buss, D. M., & Dedden, L. A. (1990). Derogation of competitors. *Journal of Social and Personal Relationships, 7,* 395–422.

Buss, D. M., & Duntley, J. (1998). *Evolved homicide modules.* Paper presented to the Annual Meeting of the Human Behavior and Evolution Society, Davis, California, July 10.

Buss, D. M., & Duntley, J. D. (2008). Adaptations for exploitation. *Group Dynamics, 12,* 53–62.

Buss, D. M., & Greiling, H. (1999). Adaptive individual differences. *Journal of Personality, 67,* 209–243.

Buss, D. M., & Haselton, M. G. (2005). The evolution of jealousy. *Trends in Cognitive Science, 9,* 506–507.

Buss, D. M., Haselton, M. G., Shackelford, T. K., Bleske, A., & Wakefield, J. C. (1998). Adaptations, exaptations, and spandrels. *American Psychologist, 53,* 533–548.

Buss, D. M., & Hawley, P. (2011). *The evolution of personality and individual differences.* New York: Oxford University Press.

Buss, D. M., & Kenrick, D. T. (1998). Evolutionary social psychology. In D. Gilbert, S. Fiske, & G. Lindzey (Eds.), *Handbook of Social Psychology.* New York: Random House.

Buss, D. M., Larsen, R., Westen, D., & Semmelroth, J. (1992). Sex differences in jealousy: Evolution, physiology, and psychology. *Psychological Science, 3,* 251–255.

Buss, D. M., & Schmitt, D. P. (1993). Sexual strategies theory: An evolutionary perspective on human mating. *Psychological Review, 100,* 204–232.

Buss, D. M., & Shackelford, T. K. (1997a). Susceptibility to infidelity in the first year of marriage. *Journal of Research in Personality, 31,* 1–29.

Buss, D. M., & Shackelford, T. K. (1997b). Human aggression in evolutionary psychological perspective. *Clinical Psychology Review, 17,* 605–619.

Buss, D. M., & Shackelford, T. K. (1997c). From vigilance to violence: Mate retention tactics in married couples. *Journal of Personality and Social Psychology, 72,* 346–361.

Buss, D. M., & Shackelford, T. K. (2008). Attractive women want it all: Good genes, economic investment, parenting proclivities, and emotional commitment. *Evolutionary Psychology, 6,* 134–146.

Buss, D. M., Shackelford, T. K., Choe, J., Buunk, B. P., & Dijkstra, P. (2000). Distress about mating rivals. *Personal Relationships, 7,* 235–243.

Buss, D. M., Shackelford, T. K., Haselton, M. G., & Bleske, A. (1997). *The evolutionary psychology of mental disorder.* Unpublished manuscript, Department of Psychology, University of Texas, Austin.

Buss, D. M., Shackelford, T. K., Kirkpatrick, L. A., Choe, J., Hasegawa, M., Hasegawa, T., & Bennett, K. (1999). Jealousy and the nature of beliefs about infidelity: Tests of competing hypotheses about sex differences in the United States, Korea, and Japan. *Personal Relationships, 6,* 125–150.

Buss, D. M., Shackelford, T. K., Kirkpatrick, L. A., & Larsen, R. J. (2001). A half century of American mate preferences. *Journal of Marriage and the Family, 63,* 491–503.

Buunk, A. P., Park, J. H., Zurriaga, R., Klavina, L., & Massar, K. (2008). Height predicts jealousy differently for men and women. *Evolution and Human Behavior, 29,* 133–139.

Buunk, B. P., Angleitner, A., Oubaid, V., & Buss, D. M. (1996). Sex differences in jealousy in evolutionary and cultural perspective: Tests from the Netherlands, Germany, and the United States. *Psychological Science, 7,* 359–363.

Buunk, B. P., & Brenninkmeyer, V. (2000). Social comparison processes among depressed individuals: Evidence for the evolutionary perspective on involuntary subordinate strategies? In L. Sloman & P. Gilbert (Eds.), *Subordination and defeat: An evolutionary approach to mood disorders and their therapy* (pp. 147–164). Mahwah, NJ: Erlbaum.

Buunk, B. P., Dijkstra, P., Kenrick, D. T., & Warntjes, A. (2001). Age preferences for mates related to gender, own age, and involvement level. *Evolution and Human Behavior, 22,* 241–250.

Byers, E. S., & Lewis, K. (1988). Dating couples' disagreements over desired level of sexual intimacy. *Journal of Sex Research, 24,* 15–29.

Byrne, R. W., & Whiten, A. (1988). *Machiavellian intelligence: social expertise and the evolution of intellect in monkeys, apes and humans.* Oxford, England: Clarendon Press.

Cameron, C., Oskamp, S., & Sparks, W. (1978). Courtship American style: Newspaper advertisements. *Family Coordinator, 26,* 27–30.

Camilleri, J. A., Kuhlmeier, V. A., & Chu, J. Y. Y. (2010). Remembering helpers and hinderers depends on behavioral intentions of the agent and psychopathic characteristics of the observer. *Evolutionary Psychology, 8,* 303–316.

Camilleri, J. A., & Quinsey, V. L. (2009a). Testing the cuckoldry risk hypothesis of partner sexual coercion in community and forensic samples. *Evolutionary Psychology, 7,* 164–178.

Camilleri, J. A., & Quinsey, V. L. (2009b). Individual differences in the propensity for partner sexual coercion. *Sexual Abuse, 21,* 111–129.

Camilleri, J. A., Quinsey, V. L., & Tapscott, J. L. (2009). Assessing the propensity for sexual coaxing and coercion in relationships: Factor structure, reliability, and validity of the tactics to obtain sex scale. *Archives of Sexual Behavior, 38,* 959–973.

Campbell, A. (1993). *Men, women, and aggression.* New York: Basic Books.

Campbell, A. (1995). A few good men: Evolutionary psychology and female adolescent aggression. *Ethology and Sociobiology, 16,* 99–123.

Campbell, A. (1999). Staying alive: Evolution, culture, and women's intrasexual aggression. *Behavioral and Brain Sciences, 22,* 203–252.

Campbell, A. (2002). *A mind of her own: The evolutionary psychology of women.* Oxford, England: Oxford University Press.

Campbell, A. (2008). The morning after the night before: Affective reactions to one-night stands among mated and unmated women and men. *Human Nature, 19,* 157–173.

Campbell, L., Cronk, L., Simpson, J. A., Milroy, A., Wilson, C. L., & Dunham, B. (2009). The association between men's ratings of women as desirable long-term mates and individual differences in women's sexual attitudes and behaviors. *Personality and Individual Differences, 46,* 509–513.

Campbell, L., Simpson, J. A., Stewart, M., & Manning, J. G. (2002). The formation of status hierarchies in leaderless groups: The role of male waist-to-hip ratio. *Human Nature, 13,* 345–362.

Campos, L. de S., Otta, E., & Siqueira, J. de O. (2002). Sex differences in mate selection strategies: Content analyses and responses to personal advertisements in Brazil. *Evolution and Human Behavior, 23,* 395–406.

Carbonell, J. L. (1984). Sex roles and leadership revisited. *Journal of Applied Psychology, 69,* 44–49.

Cardona, F. (2010, July 12). Law against fake war heroes unconstitutional, judge rules. *Austin American Statesman,* A6.

Carmody, R. N., & Wrangham, R. W. (2009). The energetic significance of cooking. *Journal of Human Evolution, 57,* 379–391.

Carroll, J. (2005). Literature and evolutionary psychology. In D. M. Buss (Ed.), *The handbook of evolutionary psychology* (pp. 931–952). New York: Wiley.

Cartwright, J. (2000). *Evolution and human behavior.* Cambridge, MA: MIT Press.

Case, T. I., Repacholi, B. M., & Stevenson, R. J. (2006). My baby doesn't smell as bad as yours: The plasticity of disgust. *Evolution and Human Behavior, 27,* 357–365.

Cashdan, E. (1989). Hunters and gatherers: Economic behavior in bands. In S. Plattner (Ed.), *Economic Anthropology* (pp. 21–48). Stanford, CA: Stanford University Press.

Cashdan, E. (1995). Hormones, sex, and status in women. *Hormones and Behavior, 29,* 354–366.

Cashdan, E. (1998). Are men more competitive than women? *British Journal of Social Psychology, 37,* 213–229.

Cernoch, J. M., & Porter, R. H. (1985). Recognition of maternal axillary odors by infants. *Child Development, 56,* 1593–1598.

Chagnon, N. A. (1981). Terminological kinship, genealogical relatedness and village fissioning among the Yanomamö Indians. In R. D. Alexander & D. W. Tinkle (Eds.), *Natural selection and social behavior* (pp. 490–508). New York: Chiron Press.

Chagnon, N. A. (1983). *Yanomamö: The fierce people* (3rd ed.). New York: Holt, Rinehart, & Winston.

Chagnon, N. A. (1988). Life histories, blood revenge, and warfare in a tribal population. *Science, 239,* 985–992.

Chagnon, N. A. (1992). *Yanomamö: The last days of Eden.* San Diego, CA: Harcourt Brace Jovanovich.

Chagnon, N. A., & Bugos, P. E. (1979). Kin selection and conflict: An analysis of a Yanomamö ax fight. In N. A. Chagnon & W. Irons (Eds.), *Evolutionary biology and human social behavior: An anthropological perspective* (pp. 213–249). North Scituate, MA: Duxbury Press.

Chance, M. R. A. (1967). Attention Structure as the Basis of Primate Rank Orders. *Man, 2,* 503–518.

Chang, A., & Wilson, M. (2004). Recalling emotional experiences affects performance on reasoning problems. *Evolution and Human Behavior, 25,* 267–276.

Charnov, E. (1993). *Life history invariants.* Oxford: Oxford University Press.

Chavanne, T. J., & Gallup, G. G., Jr. (1998). Variation in risk taking behavior among female college students as a function of the menstrual cycle. *Evolution and Human Behavior, 19,* 27–32.

Chen, C., Burton, M., Greenberger, E., & Dmitrieva, J. (1999). Population migration and the variation of dopamine D4 receptor (DRD4) allele frequencies around the globe. *Evolution and Human Behavior, 20,* 309–324.

Chiappe, D., & MacDonald, K. (2005). The evolution of domain-general mechanisms in intelligence and learning. *Journal of General Psychology, 132,* 5–40.

Chisholm, J. S. (1996). The evolutionary ecology of attachment organization. *Human Nature, 7,* 1–38.

Chomsky, N. (1957). *Syntactic structures.* The Hague: Mouton & Co.

Chomsky, N. (1991). Linguistics and cognitive science: Problems and mysteries. In A. Kasher (Ed.), *The Chomskyan turn* (pp. 26–53). Cambridge, MA: Basil Blackwell.

Christenfeld, N. J. S., & Hill, E. A. (1995). Whose baby are you? *Nature, 378,* 669.

Cieza de Leon, P. (1959). *The Incas.* Norman: University of Oklahoma Press.

Clark, A. P. (2006). Are the correlates of sociosexuality different for men and women? *Personality and Individual Differences, 41,* 1321–1327.

Clarke, R. D., & Hatfield, E. (1989). Gender differences in receptivity to sexual offers. *Journal of Psychology and Human Sexuality, 2,* 39–55.

Cleckley, H. (1982). *The mask of sanity.* New York: New American Library.

Clutton-Brock, T. H. (1991). *The evolution of parental care.* Princeton, NJ: Princeton University Press.

Coall, D. A., Hertwig, R. (2010). Grandparental investment: Past, present, and future. *Behavioral and Brain Sciences, 33,* 1–59.

Colarelli, S. M. (1998). Psychological interventions in organizations: An evolutionary perspective. *American Psychologist, 53,* 1044–1056.

Colarelli, S. M., & Haaland, S. (2002). Perceptions of sexual harassment: An evolutionary perspective. *Psychology, Evolution, and Gender, 4,* 243–264.

Collias, N. W.,& Collias, E. C. (1970). The behavior of the West African village weaverbird. *Ibis, 112,* 457–480.

Collings, P. (2009). Birth order age, and hunting success in the Canadian Arctic. *Human Nature, 20,* 354–374.

Collins, S. A., & Missing, C. (2003). Vocal and visual attractiveness are related in women. *Animal Behavior, 65,* 997–1004.

Confer, J. C., Easton, J. E., Fleischman, D. S., Goetz, C., Lewis, D. M., Perilloux, C., & Buss, D. M. (2010). Evolutionary psychology: Controversies, questions, prospects, and limitations. *American Psychologist, 65,* 110–126.

Confer, J. C., Perilloux, C., & Buss, D. M. (2010). More than just a pretty face: Men's priority shifts toward bodily attractiveness in short-term mating contexts. *Evolution and Human Behavior, 31,* 349–353.

Connolly, J. M., Mealey, L., & Slaughter, V. (2000). The development of waist-to-hip ratio preferences. *Perspectives in Human Biology, 5,* 19–29.

Cornelissen, P. L., Hancock, P. J. B., Kiviniemi, V., George, H. R., & Tovee, V. (2009). Patterns of eye movements when male and female observers judge female attractiveness, body fat and waist-to-hip ratio. *Evolution and Human Behavior, 30,* 417–428.

Cornelissen, P. L., Tovee, M. J., & Bateson, M. (2009). Patterns of subcutaneous fat deposition and the relationship between body mass index and waist-to-hip ratio: Implications for models of physical attractiveness. *Journal of Theoretical Biology, 256,* 343–350.

Cornwell, R. E., Smith, M. J. L., Boothroyd, L. G., Moore, F. R., Davis, H. P., et al. (2006). Reproductive strategy, sexual development and attraction to facial characteristics. *Philosophical Transactions of the Royal Society B, 361,* 2143–2154.

Cosmides, L. (2006). The cognitive revolution: The next wave. *APS Observer, 19,* 7–23.

Cosmides, L., & Tooby, J. (1989). Evolutionary psychology and the generation of culture. Part II. Case study: A computational theory of social exchange. *Ethology and Sociobiology, 10,* 51–97.

Cosmides, L., & Tooby, J. (1992). Cognitive adaptations for social exchange. In J. Barkow, L. Cosmides, & J. Tooby (Eds.), *The adapted mind* (pp. 163–228). New York: Oxford University Press.

Cosmides, L., & Tooby, J. (1994). Beyond intuition and instinct blindness: Toward an evolutionarily rigorous cognitive science. *Cognition, 50,* 41–77.

Cosmides, L., & Tooby, J. (1996). Are humans good intuitive statisticians after all? Rethinking some conclusions from the literature on judgment under uncertainty. *Cognition, 58,* 1–73.

Cosmides, L., & Tooby, J. (2002). Unraveling the enigma of human intelligence: Evolutionary psychology and the multimodular mind. In R. J. Sternberg & J. C. Kaufman (Eds.), *The evolution of intelligence* (pp. 145–198). Mahwah, NJ: Erlbaum.

Cosmides, L., & Tooby, J. (2005). Neurocognitive adaptations designed for social exchange. In D. M. Buss (Ed.), *The handbook of evolutionary psychology* (pp. 584–627). New York: Wiley.

Courtiol, A., Ramond, M., Godelle, B., & Ferdy, J. (2010). Mate choice and human stature: Homogamy as a unified framework for understanding mate preferences. *Evolution, 64(8),* 2189–203.

Cousins, A. J., & Gangestad, S. W. (2007). Perceived threats of female infidelity, male proprietariness, and violence in

college dating couples. *Violence and Victims, 22,* 651–668.

Cowley, G., & Underwood, A. (1997, December 29). A little help from serotonin. *Newsweek,* pp. 78–81.

Crittenden, A. N., & Marlowe, F. W. (2008). Allomaternal care among the Hadza of Tanzania. *Human Nature, 19,* 249–262.

Cronin, H. (1991). *The ant and the peacock.* Cambridge, UK: Cambridge University Press.

Cronin, H. (2005). Adaptation: "A critique of some current evolutionary thought." *The Quarterly Review of Biology, 80,* 19–27.

Cronk, L. (1994). Group selection's new clothes. *Behavioral and Brain Sciences, 17,* 615–617.

Cronk, L. (2007). Boy or girl: Gender preferences from a Darwinian point of view. *Ethics, Bioscience and Life, 2,* 23–32.

Cronk, L., & Dunham, B. (2007). Amounts spent on engagement rings reflect aspects of male and female mate quality. *Human Nature, 18,* 329–333.

Cross, J. F., & Cross, J. (1971). Age, sex, race, and the perception of facial beauty. *Developmental Psychology, 5,* 433–439.

Cummins, D. (2005). Dominance, status, and social hierarchies. In D. M. Buss (Ed.), *The handbook of evolutionary psychology* (pp. 676–697). New York: Wiley.

Cummins, D. D. (1998). Social norms and other minds: The evolutionary roots of higher cognition. In D. D. Cummins & C. Allen (Eds.), *The evolution of mind* (pp. 30–50). New York: Oxford University Press.

Cummins, D. D., & Allen, C. (Eds.). (1998). *The evolution of mind.* New York: Oxford University Press.

Cunningham, M. R., Roberts, A. R., Wu, C. H., Barbee, A. P., & Druen, P. B. (1995). "Their ideas of beauty are, on the whole, the same as ours": Consistency and variability in the cross-cultural perception of female attractiveness. *Journal of Personality and Social Psychology, 68,* 261–279.

Currie, T. E., & Little, A. C. (2009). The relative importance of the face and body in judgments of human attractiveness. *Evolution and Human Behavior, 30,* 409–416.

Curtis, V., Aunger, R., & Rabie, T. (2004). Evidence that disgust evolved to protect from risk of disease. *Proceedings of the Royal Society of London, B, 271,* S131–S133.

Curtis, V., & Biran, A. (2001). Dirt, disgust, and disease: Is hygiene in our genes? *Perspectives in Biology and Medicine, 44,* 17–31.

Cutting, J. E., Profitt, D. R., & Kozlowski, L. T. (1978). A biomechanical invariant for gait perception. *Journal of Experimental Psychology, 4,* 357–372.

Dabbs, J. M., & Ruback, R. B. (1988). Saliva testosterone and personality of male college students. *Bulletin of the Psychonomic Society, 26,* 244–247.

Daly, M., Salmon, C., & Wilson, M. (1997). Kinship: The conceptual hole in psychological studies of social cognition and close relationships. In J. A. Simpson & D. T. Kenrick (Eds.), *Evolutionary social psychology* (pp. 265–296). Mahwah, NJ: Erlbaum.

Daly, M., & Wilson, M. (1981). Abuse and neglect of children in evolutionary perspective. In R. D. Alexander &

D. W. Tinkle (Eds.), *Natural selection and social behavior* (pp. 405–416). New York: Chiron.

Daly, M., & Wilson, M. (1982). Whom are newborn babies said to resemble? *Ethology and Sociobiology, 3,* 69–78.

Daly, M., & Wilson, M. (1983). *Sex, evolution, and behavior* (2nd ed.). Boston: Willard Grant.

Daly, M., & Wilson, M. (1985). Child abuse and other risks of not living with both parents. *Ethology and Sociobiology, 6,* 197–210.

Daly, M., & Wilson, M. (1988). *Homicide.* Hawthorne, NY: Aldine.

Daly, M., & Wilson, M. (1994). Evolutionary psychology of male violence. In J. Archer (Ed.), *Male violence* (pp. 253–288). London: Routledge.

Daly, M., & Wilson, M. (1995). Discriminative parental solicitude and the relevance of evolutionary models to the analysis of motivational systems. In M. S. Gazzaniga (Ed.), *The cognitive neurosciences* (pp. 1269–1286). Cambridge, MA: MIT Press.

Daly, M., & Wilson, M. (1996a). Violence against stepchildren. *Current Directions in Psychological Science, 5,* 77–81.

Daly, M., & Wilson, M. (1996b). Evolutionary psychology and marital conflict: The relevance of stepchildren. In D. M. Buss & N. Malamuth (Eds.), *Sex, power, conflict: Evolutionary and feminist perspectives* (pp. 9–28). New York: Oxford University Press.

Daly, M., & Wilson, M. (1999). *The truth about Cinderella: A Darwinian view of parental love.* New Haven, CT: Yale University Press.

Daly M., Wilson, M. (2007). Is the "Cinderella effect" controversial? A case study of evolution-minded research and critiques thereof. In C. Crawford & D. Krebs (Eds.), *Foundations of evolutionary psychology.* Mahwah, NJ: Erlbaum.

Daly, M., & Wilson, M. (2008). Is the "Cinderella Effect" controversial?: A case study of evolution-minded research and critiques thereof. In C. Crawford & D. Krebs (Eds.), *Foundations of evolutionary psychology* (pp. 383–400). New York: Erlbaum.

Daly, M., Wilson, M., & Weghorst, S. J. (1982). Male sexual jealousy. *Ethology and Sociobiology, 3,* 11–27.

Dannenmaier, W. D., & Thumin, F. J. (1964). Authority status as a factor in perceptual distortion of size. *Journal of Social Psychology, 63,* 361–365.

Darwin, C. (1859). *On the origin of species.* London: Murray.

Darwin, C. (1871). *The descent of man and selection in relation to sex.* London: Murray.

Darwin, C. (1877). A biographical sketch of an infant. *Mind, 2,* 285–294.

Dass, J. (1970). *Maharaja.* Delhi: Hind.

Davis, B. M., & Gilbert, L. A. (1989). Effects of dispositional and situational influences on women's dominance expression in mixed-sex dyads. *Journal of Personality and Social Psychology, 57,* 294–300.

Davis, H., & McLeod, L. (2003). Why humans value sensational news: An evolutionary perspective. *Evolution and Human Behavior, 24,* 208–216.

Davis, J. N., & Daly, M. (1997). Evolutionary theory and the human family. The *Quarterly Review of Biology, 72,* 407–435.

Dawkins, R. (1982). *The extended phenotype.* Oxford: W. H. Freeman & Co.

Dawkins, R. (1986). *The blind watchmaker.* New York: Norton.

Dawkins, R. (1989). *The selfish gene* (new ed.). New York: Oxford University Press.

Dawkins, R. (1994). Burying the vehicle. *Behavioral and Brain Sciences, 17,* 617.

Dawkins, R. (1996). *Climbing mount improbable.* New York: Norton.

De Becker, G. (1997). *The gift of fear: Survival signals that protect us from violence.* Boston: Little, Brown.

de Catanzaro, D. (1991). Evolutionary limits to self-preservation. *Ethology and Sociobiology, 12,* 13–28.

de Catanzaro, D. (1995). Reproductive status, family interactions, and suicidal ideation: Surveys of the general public and high-risk group. *Ethology and Sociobiology, 16,* 385–394.

De Quervain, D. J.-F., Fischbacher, U., Treyer, V., Schellhammer, M., Schnyder, U., Buck, A., & Fehr, E. (2004). The neural basis of altruistic punishment. *Science, 305,* 1254–1258.

de Souza, A. A. L., Verderane, M. P., Taira, J. T.,& Otta, E. (2006). Emotional and sexual jealousy as a function of sexual orientation in a Brazilian sample. *Psychological Reports, 98,* 529–535.

de Waal, F. (1982). *Chimpanzee politics: Sex and power among apes.* Baltimore, MD: Johns Hopkins University Press.

de Waal, F. (1988). Chimpanzee politics. In R. W. Byrne & A. Whiten (Eds.), *Machiavellian intelligence* (pp. 122– 131). Oxford: Oxford University Press.

de Waal, F. (2006). *Our inner ape.* New York: Riverhead Books.

Deacon, T. (1997). *The symbolic species: The coevolution of language and the human brain.* Hammondsworth, England: Allen Lane.

DeKay, W. T. (1995, July). *Grandparental investment and the uncertainty of kinship.* Paper presented to the Seventh Annual Meeting of the Human Behavior and Evolution Society, Santa Barbara, CA.

DeKay, W. T.,& Buss, D. M. (1992). Human nature, individual differences, and the importance of context: Perspectives from evolutionary psychology. *Current Directions in Psychological Science, 1,* 184–189.

DeKay, W. T., Buss, D. M., & Stone, V. (unpublished manuscript). *Coalitions, mates, and friends: Toward an evolutionary psychology of relationship preferences.* Unpublished manuscript, Department of Psychology, University of Texas, Austin.

DeKay, W. T., & Shackelford, T. K. (2000). Toward an evolutionary approach to social cognition. *Evolution and Cognition, 6,* 185–195.

Dennett, D. C. (1994). E pluribus unum? *Behavioral and Brain Sciences, 17,* 617–618.

Dennett, D. C. (1995). *Darwin's dangerous idea.* New York: Simon & Schuster.

Denissen, J. J. A., & Penke, L. (2008). Motivational individual reaction norms underlying the five-factor model of personality: First steps towards a theory-based conceptual framework. *Journal of Personality, 42,* 1285–1302.

Denissen, J. J. A., Penke, L., Schmitt, D. P., & van Aken, M. A. G. (2008). Self-esteem reactions to social interactions: Evidence for sociometer mechanisms across days, people, and nations. *Journal of Personality and Social Psychology, 95,* 181–196.

DeScioli, P., & Kurzban, R. (2009). The alliance hypothesis for human friendship. *PLoS ONE, 4,* 1–8.

DeSouza, E. R., Pierce, T., Zanelli, J. C., & Hutz, C. (1992). Perceived sexual intent in the U.S. and Brazil as a function of nature of encounter, subjects' nationality, and gender. *Journal of Sex Research, 29,* 251–260.

DeSteno, D., Barlett, M. Y., Braverman, J., & Salovey, P. (2002). Sex differences in jealousy: Evolutionary mechanism or artifact of measurement? *Journal of Personality and Social Psychology, 83,* 1103–1116.

DeSteno, D. A.,& Salovey, P. (1996). Evolutionary origins of sex differences in jealousy: Questioning the "fitness" of the model. *Psychological Science, 7,* 367–372.

Dickemann, M. (1979). Female infanticide, reproductive strategies and social stratification: A preliminary model. In N. A. Chagnon & W. Irons (Eds.), *Evolutionary biology and human social behavior* (pp. 312–367). North Scituate, MA: Duxbury Press.

Dickemann, M. (1981). Paternal confidence and dowry competition: A biocultural analysis of purdah. In R. D. Alexander & D. W. Tinkle (Eds.), *Natural selection and social behavior: Recent research and new theory* (pp. 417–438). New York: Chiron Press.

Dickens, G., & Trethowan, W. H. (1971). Cravings and aversions during pregnancy. *Journal of Psychosomatic Research, 15,* 259–268.

Dixon, B. J., Grimshaw, G. M., Linklater, W. L., & Dixon, A. F. (2010). Eye tracking of men's preferences for waist-to-hip ratio and breast size of women. *Archives of Sexual Behavior,* doi:10.1007/s10508-010-9601-8.

Dixon, A. F., Halliwell, G., East, R., Wignarajah, P., & Anderson, M. J. (2003). Masculine somatotype and hirsuteness as determinants of sexual attractiveness to women. *Archives of Sexual Behavior, 32,* 29–39.

Dobash, R. E., & Dobash, R. P. (1984). The nature and antecedents of violent events. *British Journal of Criminology, 24,* 269–288.

Dobash, R. P., Dobash, R. E., Wilson, M., & Daly, M. (1992). The myth of sexual symmetry in marital violence. *Social Problems, 39,* 71–91.

Dobzhansky, T. (1937). *Genetics and the origins of species.* New York: Columbia University Press.

Doran, T. F., DeAngelis, G., Baumgardner, R. A., & Mellits, E. D. (1989). Acetaminophen: More harm than good for chickenpox? *Journal of Pediatrics, 114,* 1045–1048.

Dubas, J. S., Heikoop, M., & van Aken, M. A. G. (2009). A preliminary investigation of parent-progeny olfactory recognition and parental investment. *Human Nature, 20,* 80–92.

Duberman, L. (1975). *The reconstituted family: A study of remarried couples and their children.* Chicago, IL: Nelson-Hall.

Dudley, R. (2002). Fermenting fruit and the historical ecology of ethanol ingestion: Is alcoholism in modern humans an evolutionary hangover? *Addiction, 97,* 381–388.

Dugatkin, L. A. (2000). *The imitation factor: Evolution beyond the gene.* New York: Free Press.

Dunbar, R. I. M. (1993). Coevolution of neocortical size, group size, and language in humans. *Behavioral and Brain Sciences, 16,* 681–735.

Dunbar, R. I. M. (1996). *Grooming, gossip, and the evolution of language.* London: Faber & Faber.

Dunbar, R. I. M. (2004). Gossip in evolutionary perspective. *Review of General Psychology, 8,* 100–110.

Duncan, L. A., Park, J. H., Faulner, J., Schaller, M., Neuberg, S. L., & Kenrick, D. T. (2007). Adaptive allocation of attention: Effects of sex and sociosexuality on visual attention to attractive opposite-sex faces. *Evolution and Human Behavior, 28,* 359–364.

Dunn, M. J., & Doria, M. V. (2010). Stimulated attraction increases sex attractiveness ratings in females but not males. *Journal of Social, Evolutionary, and Cultural Psychology, 4,* 1–17.

Duntley, J. D. (2005a). Adaptations to dangers from humans. In D. M. Buss (Ed.), *The handbook of evolutionary psychology* (pp. 224–249). New York: Wiley.

Duntley, J. D. (2005b). *Homicidal ideations.* Unpublished doctoral dissertation, Department of Psychology, University of Texas, Austin, Texas.

Duntley, J. D., & Buss, D. M. (2005). The plausibility of adaptations for homicide. In P. Caruthers, S. Laurence, & S. Stich (Eds.), *The innate mind: Structure and contents* (pp. 291–304). New York: Oxford University Press.

Durante, K. M., Li, N. P., & Haselton, M. G. (2008). Changes in women's choice of dress across the ovulatory cycle: Naturalistic and laboratory task-based evidence. *Personality and Social Psychology Bulletin, 34,* 1451–1460.

Dutton, D. (2009). *The art instinct: Beauty, pleasure, and human evolution.* London, UK: Bloomsbury.

Dworkin, A. (1987). *Intercourse.* New York: Free Press.

Eagly, A. H., & Wood, W. (1999). The origins of sex differences in human behavior: Evolved dispositions or social roles? *American Psychologist, 54,* 408–423.

Eals, M., & Silverman, I. (1994). The hunger-gatherer theory of spatial sex differences: Proximate factors mediating the female advantage in recall of object arrays. *Ethology and Sociobiology, 15,* 95–105.

Easton, J. A., Schipper, L. C., & Shackelford, T. K. (2007). Morbid jealousy from an evolutionary psychological perspective. *Evolution and Human Behavior, 28,* 399–402.

Easton, J. A., & Shackelford, T. K. (2009). Morbid jealousy and sex differences in partner-directed violence. *Human Nature, 20,* 342–350.

Ebstein, R. (2006). The molecular genetic architecture of human personality: Beyond self-report questionnaires. *Molecular Psychiatry, 11,* 427–445.

Ecuyer-Dab, I., & Robert, M. (2004). Have sex differences in spatial ability evolved from male competition for mating and female concern for survival? *Cognition, 91,* 221–257.

Edlund, J. E., Heider, J. D., Scherer, C. R., Farc, M-M., & Sagarin, B. J. (2006). Sex differences in jealousy in response to actual infidelity. *Evolutionary Psychology, 4,* 462–470.

Edlund, J. E., & Sagarin, B. J. (2009). Sex differences in jealousy: Misinterpretation of nonsignificant results as refuting the theory. *Personal Relationships, 16,* 67–78.

Egan, V., & Angus, S. (2004). Is social dominance a sex-specific strategy for infidelity? *Personality and Individual Differences, 36,* 575–586.

Ehrlichman, H., & Eichenstein, R. (1992). Private wishes: Gender similarities and differences. *Sex Roles, 26,* 399–422.

Eibl-Eibesfeldt, I. (1989). *Human ethology.* New York: Aldine de Gruyter.

Eisenberg, D. T. A., Campbell, B., Gray, P. B., & Soronson, M. D. (2008). Dopamine receptor genetic polymorphisms and body composition in undernourished pastoralists: An exploration of nutrition indices among nomadic and recently settled Ariaal men of northern Kenya. *BMC Evolutionary Biology, 8,* 173.

Eisenberg, N. (1986). *Altruistic emotion, cognition, and behavior.* Hillsdale, NJ: Erlbaum.

Ekman, P. (1973). Cross-cultural studies of facial expression. In P. Ekman (Ed.), *Darwin and facial expression: A century of research in review* (pp. 169–222). New York: Academic Press.

Elder, G. H., Jr. (1969). Appearance and education in marriage mobility. *American Sociological Review, 34,* 519–533.

Ellis, B. J. (1992). The evolution of sexual attraction: Evaluative mechanisms in women. In J. Barkow, L. Cosmides, & J. Tooby (Eds.), *The adapted mind* (pp. 267–288). New York: Oxford.

Ellis, B. J. (2005). Determinants of pubertal timing: An evolutionary developmental approach. In B. J. Ellis & D. F. Bjorklund (Eds.), *Origins of the social mind: Evolutionary psychology and child development* (pp. 164–188). New York: Guilford.

Ellis, B. J. (2011). Toward an evolutionary-developmental explanation of alternative reproductive strategies: The central role of switch-controlled modular systems. In D. M. Buss & P. H. Hawley (Eds.), *The evolution of personality and individual differences.* New York: Oxford University Press.

Ellis, B. J., & Bjorklund, D. F. (2005). *Origins of the social mind: Evolutionary psychology and child development.* New York: Guilford.

Ellis, B. J., & Garber, J. (2000). Psychosocial antecedents of variation in girls' pubertal timing: Maternal depression, stepfather presence, and marital and family stress. *Child Development, 71,* 485–501.

Ellis, B. J., McFadyen-Ketchum, S., Dodge, K. A., Pettit, G. S., & Bates, J. E. (1999). Quality of early family relationships and individual differences in the timing of pubertal maturation in girls: A longitudinal test of an evolutionary model. *Journal of Personality and Social Psychology, 77,* 387–401.

Ellis, B. J., & Symons, D. (1990). Sex differences in fantasy: An evolutionary psychological approach. *Journal of Sex Research, 27,* 527–556.

Ellis, L. (1995). Dominance and reproductive success among nonhuman animals: A cross-species comparison. *Ethology and Sociobiology, 16,* 257–333.

Ellis, L., Widmayer, A., & Palmer, C. T. (2009). Perpetrators of sexual assault continuing to have sex with their victims following the initial assault: Evidence for evolved reproductive strategies. *International Journal of Offender Therapy and Comparative Criminology, 53,* 454–463.

Ellison, P. T. (2001). *On fertile ground: A natural history of reproduction.* Cambridge, MA: Harvard University Press.

Emlen, S. T. (1995). An evolutionary theory of the family. *Proceedings of the National Academy of Science, 92,* 8092–8099.

Ermer, E., Cosmides, L., & Tooby, J. (2008). Relative status regulates risky decision making about resources in men: Evidence for the co-evolution of motivation and cognition. *Evolution and Human Behavior, 29,* 106–118.

Escasa, M., Gray, P. B., & Patton, J. Q. (2010). Male traits associated with attractiveness in Conambo, Ecuador. *Evolution and Human Behavior, 31,* 193–200.

Essock-Vitale, S. M., & McGuire, M. T. (1985). Women's lives viewed from an evolutionary perspective. II. Patterns of helping. *Ethology and Sociobiology, 6,* 155–173.

Eswaran, V., Harpending, H., & Rogers, A. R. (2005). Genomics refutes an exclusively African origin of humans. *Journal of Human Evolution, 49,* 1–18.

Euler, H. A., Hoier, S., & Rohde, P. A. (2001). Relationship-specific closeness of intergenerational family ties. *Journal of Cross-Cultural Psychology, 32,* 147–149.

Euler, H. A., & Weitzel, B. (1996). Discriminative grandparental solicitude as reproductive strategy. *Human Nature, 7,* 39–59.

Evans, S., Neave, N., & Wakelin, D. (2006). Relationships between vocal characteristics and body size and shape in human males: An evolutionary explanation for a deep male voice. *Biological Psychology, 72,* 160–163.

Eysenck, H. J. (1976). *Sex and personality.* Austin, TX: University of Texas Press.

Faer, L. M., Hendriks, A., Abed, R. T., & Figueredo, A. J. (2005). The evolutionary psychology of eating disorders: Female competition for mates or for status? *Psychology and Psychotherapy: Theory, Research and Practice, 78,* 397–417.

Faludi, S. (1991). *Backlash: The undeclared war against American women.* New York: Crown.

Farrelly, D., & Nettle, D. (2007). Marriage affects competitive performance in male tennis players. *Journal of Cultural and Evolutionary Psychology, 5,* 41–48.

Faulkner, J., & Schaller, M. (2007). Nepotistic nosiness: Inclusive fitness and vigilance of kin members' romantic relationships. *Evolution and Human Behavior, 28,* 430–438.

Faurie, C., Pontier, D., & Raymond, M. (2004). Student athlete claim to have more sexual partners than other students. *Evolution and Human Behavior, 25,* 1–8.

Fawcett, T. W., van den Berg, P., Weissing, F. J., Park, J. H., & Buunk, A. P. (2010). Intergenerational conflict over parental investment. *Behavioral and Brain Sciences, 33,* 23–24.

Feather, N. T. (1994). Attitudes toward achievers and reactions to their fall: Theory and research concerning tall poppies. *Advances in Experimental Social Psychology, 26,* 1–73.

Fehr, E. (2004). Don't lose your reputation. *Nature, 432,* 449–450.

Fehr, E., Fischbacher, U., & Gachter, S. (2002). Strong reciprocity, human cooperation, and the enforcement of social norms. *Human Nature, 13,* 1–25.

Fehr, E., & Henrich, J. (2003). Is strong reciprocity a maladaptation? On the evolutionary foundations of altruism. In P. Hammerstein (Ed.), *Genetic and cultural evolution of cooperation* (pp. 55–82). New York: MIT Press.

Feinberg, D. R., DeBruine, L. M., Jones, B. C., & Little, A. C. (2008). Correlated preferences for men's facial and vocal masculinity. *Evolution and Human Behavior, 29,* 233–241.

Feinberg, D. R., Jones, B. C., DeBruine, L. M., Moore, F. R., Smith, M. J. L. et al. (2005a). The voice and face of woman: One ornament that signals quality. *Evolution and Human Behavior, 26,* 398–408.

Feinberg, D. R., Jones, B. C., Little, A. C., Burt, D. M., & Perrett, D. I. (2005b). Manipulations of fundamental and formant frequencies influence attractiveness of human male voices. *Animal Behavior, 69,* 561–568.

Feinberg, D. R., Jones, B. C., Smith, M. J. L., Moore, F. R., DeBruine, L. M., Cronwell, R. E., Hillier, S. G., & Perrett, D. I. (2006). Menstrual cycle, trait estrogen level, and masculinity preferences in the human voice. *Hormones and Behavior, 49,* 215–222.

Feinsilber, M. (1997, December 6). Inflating personal histories irresistible to some. *Austin American Statesman,* p. A1.

Fenigstein, A., & Peltz, R. (2002). Distress over the infidelity of a child's spouse: A crucial test of evolutionary and socialization hypotheses. *Personal Relationships, 9,* 301–312.

Fernandez, A. M., Sierra, J. C., Zubeidat, I., & Vera-Villarroel, P. (2006). Sex differences in response to sexual and emotional infidelity among Spanish and Chilean students. *Journal of Cross-Cultural Psychology, 37,* 359–365.

Fernandez, A. M., Vera-Villarroel, P., Sierra, J. C., & Zubeidat, I. (2007). Distress in response to emotional and sexual infidelity: Evidence of evolved gender differences in Spanish students. *Journal of Psychology, 14,* 17–34.

Fessler, D. M. T. (2002). Reproductive immunosupression and diet. *Current Anthropology, 43,* 19–38.

Fessler, D. M. T., Eng, S. J., & Navarrete, C. D. (2005). Elevated disgust sensitivity in the first trimester of pregnancy: Evidence supporting the compensatory prophylaxis hypothesis. *Evolution and Human Behavior, 26,* 344–351.

Fessler, D. M. T., & Navarrete, C. D. (2004). Thirdparty attitudes toward sibling incest: Evidence for Westermarck's hypothesis. *Evolution and Human Behavior, 25,* 277–294.

Fetchenhauer, D., & Buunk, B. (2005). How to explain gender differences in fear of crime: Towards an evolutionary approach. *Sexualities, Evolution, and Gender, 7,* 95–113.

Fetchenhauer, D., Groothuis, T., & Pradel, J. (2010). Not only states but traits—Humans can identify permanent altruistic dispositions in 20 s. *Evolution and Human Behavior, 31,* 80–86.

Fieder, M., & Huber, S. (2007). Parental age difference and offspring count in humans. *Biology Letters, 3,* 689–691.

Fieder, M., Huber, S., Bookstein, F. L., Iber, K., Schafer, K., Winckler, G., & Wallner, B. (2005). Status and reproduction in humans: New evidence for the validity of evolutionary explanations on basis of a university sample. *Ethology, 111,* 940–950.

Fielden, J., Lutter, C., & Dabbs, J. (1994). *Basking in glory: Testosterone changes in World Cup soccer fans.* Unpublished manuscript, Psychology Department, Georgia State University.

Fielding, R., Scholling, C. M., Adab, P., Cheng, K. K., Lao, X. Q., et al. (2008). Are longer legs associated with enhanced fertility in Chinese women? *Evolution and Human Behavior, 29,* 434–443.

Figueredo, A. J. (1995). *Preliminary report: Family deterrence of domestic violence in Spain.* Department of Psychology, University of Arizona.

Figueredo, A. J., Corral-Vedugo, V., Frias-Armenta, M., Bachar, K. J., White, J., McNeill, P. L., Kirsner, B. R., & Castell-Ruiz, I. del P. (2001). Blood, solidarity, status, and honor: The sexual balance of power and spousal abuse in Sonora, Mexico. *Evolution and Human Behavior, 22,* 295–328.

Figueredo, A. J., & Gladden, P. R., & Beck, C. J. A. (2010). Intimate partner violence and life history strategy. In A. Goetz & T. Shackelford (Eds.), *The Oxford Handbook of Sexual Conflict In Humans.* New York: Oxford University Press.

Figueredo, A. J., Hammond, K. R., & McKiernan, E. C. (2006). A Brunswikian evolutionary developmental theory of preparedness and plasticity. *Intelligence, 34,* 211–227.

Figueredo, A. J., Vasquez, G., Brumbach, B. H., Schneider, S. M. R., Sefcek, J. A., Tal, I. R., Hill, D., Wenner, C. J., & Jacobs, W. J. (2006). Consilience and life history theory: From genes to brain to reproductive strategy. *Developmental Review, 26,* 243–275.

Figueredo, A. J., Wolf, P. S. A., Gladden, P. R., Olderbak, S. G., Andrzejczak, D. J., & Jacobs, W. J. (2011). Ecological approaches to personality. In Buss, D. M., & Hawley, P. H., (Eds.), *The Evolution of Personality and Individual Differences.* New York: Oxford University Press.

Fink, B., Grammer, K., & Matts, P. J. (2006). Visible skin color distribution plays a role in the perception of age, attractiveness, and health in female faces. *Evolution and Human Behavior, 27,* 433–442.

Fink, B., Matts, P. J., Klingenberg, H., Kuntze, S., Weege, B., & Grammer, K. (2008). Visual attention to variation in female facial skin color distribution. *Journal of Cosmetic Dermatology, 7,* 155–161.

Fink, B., & Neave, N. (2005). The biology of facial beauty. *International Journal of Cosmetic Science, 27,* 317–325.

Fink, B., Neave, N., Manning, J. T., & Grammer, K. (2006). Facial symmetry and judgments of attractiveness, health and personality. *Personality and Individual Differences, 41,* 1253–1262.

Finkelhor, D. (1993). Epidemiological factors in the clinical identification of child sexual abuse. *Child Abuse and Neglect, 17,* 67–70.

Fisek, M. H., & Ofshe, R. (1970). The process of status evolution. *Sociometry, 33,* 327–346.

Fisher, H. (2006). The drive to love: The neural mechanism for mate choice. In R. J. Sternberg & K. Weis (Eds.), *The psychology of love* (2nd ed., pp. 87–115). New Haven, CT: Yale University Press.

Fisher, H., Aron, A., & Brown, L. L. (2005). Romantic love: An fMRI study of the neural mechanism for mate choice. *The Journal of Comparative Neurology, 493,* 58–62.

Fisher, M., & Cox, A. (2009). The influence of female attractiveness on competitor derogation. *Journal of Evolutionary Psychology, 7,* 141–155.

Fisher, H., & Thompson, A. (2006). "Lust, romance, attachment: Do the sexual side effects of serotoninenhancing antidepressants jeopardize romantic love, marriage, and fertility?" In S. Platek, J. P. Keenan, & T. K. Shackelford (Eds.), *Evolutionary Cognitive Neuroscience.* Cambridge, MA: MIT Press.

Fisher, H. E. (1992). *Anatomy of Love.* New York: Norton.

Fisher, J. D., Nadler, A., & Whitcher-Alagna, S. (1982). Recipient reactions to aid. *Psychological Bulletin, 91,* 27–54.

Fisher, M. (2004). Female intrasexual competition decreases female facial attractiveness. *Proceedings of the Royal Society of London, B, 271,* S283–S285.

Fisher, R. A. (1958). *The genetical theory of natural selection* (2nd ed.). New York: Dover.

Fisher, R. R. (1983). Transition to grandmotherhood. *International Journal of Aging and Human Development, 16,* 67–78.

Fisman, R., Iyengar, S. S., Kamenica, E., & Simonson, I. (2006, May). Gender differences in mate selection: Evidence from a speed dating experiment. *The Quarterly Journal of Economics, 121,* 673–697.

Fitch, W. T. (2005). The evolution of language: A comparative view. *Biology and Philosophy, 20,* 193–230.

Fitzgerald, C. J., & Colarelli, S. M. (2009). Altruism and reproductive limitations. *Evolutionary Psychology, 7,* 234–252.

Fitzgerald, C. J., & Whitaker, M. B. (2009). Sex differences in violent versus non-violent life-threatening altruism. *Evolutionary Psychology, 7,* 467–476.

Flaxman, S. M., & Sherman, P. W. (2000). Morning sickness: A mechanism for protecting mother and embryo. *Quarterly Review of Biology, 75,* 113–147.

Fletcher, J. A., & Doebeli, M. (2009). A simple and general explanation for the evolution of altruism. *Proceedings of the Royal Society, B, 276,* 13–19.

Flinn, M. (1988a). Mate guarding in a Caribbean village. *Ethology and Sociobiology, 9,* 1–28.

Flinn, M. (1988b). Parent–offspring interactions in a Caribbean village: Daughter guarding. In L. Betzig, M. Borgerhoff Mulder, & P. Turke (Eds.), *Human reproductive behavior: A Darwinian perspective* (pp. 189– 200). Cambridge, UK: Cambridge University Press.

Flinn, M. V. (1992). Parental care in a Caribbean village. In B. Hewlett (Ed.), *Father-child relations: Cultural and biosocial contexts* (pp. 57–84). Chicago: Aldine.

Flinn, M. V., Geary, D. C., & Ward, C. V. (2005). Ecological dominance, social competition, and coalitionary arms races: Why humans evolved extraordinary intelligence. *Evolution and Human Behavior, 26,* 10–36.

Flinn, M. V., Ward, C. V., & Noone, R. J. (2005). Hormones and the human family. In D. M. Buss (Ed.), *The handbook of evolutionary psychology* (pp. 552–580). New York: Wiley.

Fodor, J. A. (1983). *The modularity of mind.* Cambridge, MA: MIT Press.

Ford, C. S., & Beach, F. A. (1951). *Patterns of sexual behavior.* New York: Harper & Row.

Forrest, M. S., & Hokanson, J. E. (1975). Depression and autonomic arousal reduction accompanying self-punitive behavior. *Journal of Abnormal Psychology, 84,* 346–357.

Fournier, M. A., Moskowitz, D. S., & Zuroff, D.C. (2002). Social rank strategies in hierarchical relationships. *Journal of Personality and Social Psychology, 83,* 425–433.

Fox, A. (1997, June). *The assessment of fighting ability in humans.* Paper presented to the Ninth Annual Meeting of the Human Behavior and Evolution Society, University of Arizona, Tucson, AZ.

Fraley, R. C., Brumbaugh, C. C., & Marks, M. J. (2005). The evolution and function of adult attachment: A comparative and phylogenetic analysis. *Journal of Personality and Social Psychology, 89,* 731–746.

Fraley, R. C., Brumbaugh, C. C., & Marks, M. J. (2005). The evolution and function of adult attachment: A comparative and phylogenetic analysis. *Journal of Personality and Social Psychology, 89,* 731–746.

Frank, R. (1988). *Passions within reason.* New York: Norton.

Frank, R. H. (1985). *Choosing the right pond: Human behavior and the quest for status.* New York: Oxford University Press.

Frayser, S. (1985). *Varieties of sexual experience: An anthropological perspective.* New Haven, CT: HRAF Press.

Freeman, D. (1983). *Margaret Mead and Samoa: The making and unmaking of an anthropological myth.* Cambridge, MA: Harvard University Press.

Friedman, B., & Duntley, J. D. (1998, July 12). *Parentguarding: Offspring reactions to parental infidelity.* Paper presented to the Tenth Annual Meeting of the Human Behavior and Evolution Society, Davis, CA.

Friedman, H. S., Tucker, J. S., Schwartz, J. E., Tomlinson-Keasey, C., Martin, L. R., Wingard, D. L., & Criqui, M. H. (1995). Psychosocial and behavioral predictors of longevity: The aging and death of the "Termites." *American Psychologist, 50,* 69–78.

Furnham, A., Tan, T., & McManus, C. (1997). Waist-to-hip ratio and preferences for body shape: A replication and extension. *Personality and Individual Differences, 22,* 539–549.

Gallup, A. C., O'Brien, D., White, D. D., & Wilson, D. S. (2009). Peer victimization in adolescence has different effects on the sexual behavior of male and female college students. *Personality and Individual Differences, 46,* 611–615.

Gallup, A. C., White, D. D., & Gallup, G. G., Jr. (2007). Handgrip strength predicts sexual behavior, body morphology, and aggression in male college students. *Evolution and Human Behavior, 28,* 423–429.

Gangestad, S. W., & Buss, D. M. (1993). Pathogen prevalence and human mate preferences. *Ethology and Sociobiology, 14,* 89–96.

Gangestad, S. W., Haselton, M. G., & Buss, D. M. (2006). Evolutionary foundations of cultural variation: Evoked culture and mate preferences. *Psychological Inquiry, 17,* 75–95.

Gangestad, S. W., & Scheyd, G. J. (2005). The evolution of human physical attractiveness. *Annual Review of Anthropology, 34,* 523–548.

Gangestad, S. W., & Simpson, J. A. (1990). Toward an evolutionary history of female sociosexual variation. *Journal of Personality, 58,* 69–96.

Gangestad, S. W., Simpson, J. A., Cousins, A. J., Garver-Apgar, C. E., & Christensen, N. (2004). Women's preferences for male behavioral displays change across the menstrual cycle. *Psychological Science, 15,* 203–207.

Gangestad, S. W., & Thornhill, R. (1997). Human sexual selection and developmental stability. In J. A. Simpson & D. T. Kenrick (Eds.), *Evolutionary social psychology* (pp. 169–195). Mahwah, NJ: Erlbaum.

Gangestad, S. W., & Thornhill, R. (2008). Human oestrus. *Proceedings of the Royal Society of London, B, 275,* 991–1000.

Gangestad, S. W., Thornhill, R., & Garver-Apgar, C. E. (2005). Adaptations to ovulation. In D. M. Buss (Ed.), *The handbook of evolutionary psychology* (pp. 344–371). New York: Wiley.

Garcia, J., Ervin, F. R., & Koelling, R. A. (1966). Learning with prolonged delay of reinforcement. *Psychonomic Science, 5,* 121–122.

Garcia, J. R., & Reiber, C. (2008). Hook-up behavior: A biopsychosocial perspective. *Journal of Social, Evolutionary, and Cultural Psychology, 2,* 192–208.

Gardner, H. (1974). *The shattered mind.* New York: Random House.

Garver-Apgar, C. E., Gangestad, S. W., & Thornhill, R. (2008). Hormonal correlates of women's mid-cycle preference for the scent of symmetry. *Evolution and Human Behavior, 29,* 223–232.

Gaulin, S. J. C., McBurney, D. H., & Brakeman-Wartell, S. L. (1997). Matrilateral biases in the investment of aunts and uncles. *Human Nature, 8,* 139–151.

Gayford, J. J. (1975). *Wife battering: A preliminary survey of 100 cases.* London: British Medical Journal.

Geary, D. C. (2000). Evolution and proximate expression of human paternal investment. *Psychological Bulletin, 126,* 55–77.

Geary, D. C. (2002). Principles of evolutionary educational psychology. *Learning and Individual Differences, 12,* 317–345.

Geary, D. C. (2009). Evolution of general fluid intelligence. In S. M. Platek & T. K. Shackelford (Eds.), *Foundations in evolutionary cognitive neuroscience* (pp. 22–56). Cambridge, MA: MIT Press.

Geary, D. C. (2010). Male, female: *The evolution of human sex differences* (2nd ed.). Washington, DC: American Psychological Association.

Geary, D. C., & Flinn, M. V. (2001). Evolution of human parental behavior and the human family. *Parenting: Science and Practice, 1,* 5–61.

Geary, D. C., & Huffman, K. J. (2002). Brain and cognitive evolution: Forms of modularity and functions of mind. *Psychological Bulletin, 128,* 667–698.

Gelman, S., Coley, J., & Gottfried, G. (1994). Essentialist beliefs in children. In L. Hirshfeld & S. Gelman (Eds.), *Mapping the mind.* New York: Cambridge University Press.

Genovese, J. E. C. (2008). Physique correlates with reproductive success in an archival sample of delinquent youth. *Evolutionary Psychology, 6,* 369–385.

Gerdes, A. B. M., Uhl, G., & Alpers, G. W. (2009). Spiders are special: Fear and disgust evoked by pictures of arthropods. *Evolution and Human Behavior, 30,* 66–73.

Ghiglieri, M. P. (1999). *The dark side of man: Tracing the origins of violence.* Reading, MA: Perseus Books.

Gigerenzer, G. (1991). How to make cognitive illusions disappear: Beyond "heuristics and biases." In W. Stoebe & M. Hewstone (Eds.), *European Review of Social Psychology,* Vol. 2 (pp. 83–115). Chichester, England: Wiley.

Gigerenzer, G. (1998). Ecological intelligence: An adaptation for frequencies. In D. D. Cummins & C. Allen (Eds.), *The evolution of mind* (pp. 9–29). New York: Oxford University Press.

Gigerenzer, G., & Hug, K. (1992). Domain specific reasoning: Social contracts, cheating and perspective change. *Cognition, 43,* 127–171.

Gilbert, D. T., & Malone, P. S. (1995). The correspondence bias. *Psychological Bulletin, 117,* 21–49.

Gilbert, P. (1989). *Human nature and suffering.* Hillsdale, NJ: Erlbaum.

Gilbert, P. (1990). Changes: Rank, status and mood. In S. Fischer & C. L. Cooper (Eds.), *On the move: The psychology of change and transition* (pp. 33–52). New York: Wiley.

Gilbert, P. (2000a). The relationship of shame, social anxiety and depression: The role of the evaluation of social rank. *Clinical Psychology and Psychotherapy, 7,* 174–189.

Gilbert, P. (2000b). Varieties of submissive behavior as forms of social defense: Their evolution and role in depression. In L. Sloman & P. Gilbert (Eds.), *Subordination and defeat: An evolutionary approach to mood disorders and their therapy* (pp. 3–46). Mahwah, NJ: Erlbaum.

Gil-Burmann, C., Pelaez, F., & Sanchez, S. (2002). Mate choice differences according to sex and age: An analysis of personal advertisements in Spanish newspapers. *Human Nature, 13,* 493–508.

Gillis, J. S. (1982). *Too tall, too small.* Champaign, IL: Institute for Personality and Ability Testing.

Gintis, H. (2000). Strong reciprocity in human sociality. *Journal of Theoretical Biology, 206,* 169–179.

Gintis, H., Smith, E., & Bowles, S. (2001). Costly signaling and cooperation. *Journal of Theoretical Biology, 213,* 103–119.

Gladden, P. R., Sisco, M., & Figueredo, A. J. (2008). Sexual coercion and life-history strategy. *Evolution and Human Behavior, 29,* 319–326.

Gladue, B. A., Boechler, M., & McCaul, K. (1989). Hormonal response to competition in human males. *Aggressive Behavior, 15,* 409–422.

Gladue, B. A., & Delaney, J. J. (1990). Gender differences in perception of attractiveness of men and women in bars. *Personality and Social Psychology Bulletin, 16,* 378–391.

Glantz, K., & Pearce, J. (1989). *Exiles from Eden: Psychotherapy from an evolutionary perspective.* New York: Norton.

Glass, B., Temekin, O., & Straus, W., Jr. (Eds.). (1959). *Forerunners of Darwin.* Baltimore, MD: Johns Hopkins University Press.

Glass, S. P., & Wright, T. L. (1985). Sex differences in type of extramarital involvement and marital dissatisfaction. *Sex Roles, 12,* 1101–1120.

Glass, S. P., & Wright, T. L. (1992). Justifications for extramarital relationships: The association between attitudes, behaviors, and gender. *Journal of Sex Research, 29,* 361–387.

Godfray, H. C. J. (1999). Parent–offspring conflict. In L. Keller (Ed.), *Levels of selection in evolution* (pp. 100–120). Princeton, NJ: Princeton University Press.

Goldsmith, H. H., & Harman, C. (1994). Temperament and attachment: Individuals and relationships. *Current Directions in Psychological Science, 3,* 53–57.

Goldstein, J. H. (1986). *Aggression and crimes of violence* (2nd ed.). New York: Oxford University Press.

Goetz, A. T., & Causey, K. (2009). Sex differences in perceptions of infidelity: Men often assume the worst. *Evolutionary Psychology, 7,* 253–263.

Goetz, A. T., & Shackelford, T. K. (2009). Sexual coercion in intimate relationships: A comparative analysis of the effects of women's infidelity and men's dominance and control. *Archives of Sexual Behavior, 38,* 226–234.

Goetz, A. T., Shackelford, T. K., Romero, G. A., Kaighobadi, F., & Miner, E. J. (2008). Punishment, proprietariness, and paternity: Men's violence against women from an evolutionary perspective. *Aggression and Violent Behavior, 13,* 481–489.

Goldstein, M. A. (2002). The biological roots of heat-of-passion crimes and honor killings. *Politics and the Life Sciences, 21,* 28–37.

Gonzaga, G. C., Haselton, M. G., Smurda, J., Davies, M., & Poore, J. C. (2008). Love, desire, and the suppression of thoughts of romantic alternatives. *Evolution and Human Behavior, 29,* 119–126.

Gorman, R. M. (2007). Cooking up bigger brains. *Scientific American* (January), 102–105.

Gottesman, I. L. (1991). *Schizophrenia genesis.* New York: W. H. Freeman.

Gottfredson, L. S. (2007). Innovation, fatal accidents, and the evolution of general intelligence. In M. J. Roberts (Ed.), *Integrating the mind.* Hove, UK: Psychology Press.

Gottschall, J., Berkey, R., Cawson, M., Drown, C., Fleischner, M. et al. (2003). Patterns of characterization in folktales across geographic regions and levels of cultural complexity: Literature as a neglected source of quantitative data. *Human Nature, 14,* 365–382.

Gottschall, J., Martin, J., Quish, H., & Rea, J. (2004). Sex differences in mate choice criteria are reflected in folktales from around the world and in historical European literature. *Evolution and Human Behavior, 25,* 102–112.

Gould, S. J. (1987). *The limits of adaptation: Is language a spandrel of the human brain?* Paper presented to the Cognitive Science Seminar, Center for Cognitive Science, MIT, Cambridge, MA.

Gould, S. J. (1991). Exaptation: A crucial tool for evolutionary psychology. *Journal of Social Issues, 47,* 43–58.

Gould, S. J. (1997, October 9). Evolutionary psychology: An exchange. *New York Review of Books, XLIV,* 53–58.

Gould, S. J., & Eldredge, N. (1977). Punctuated equilibria: The tempo and mode of evolution reconsidered. *Paleobiology, 3,* 115–151.

Gove, P. B. (Ed.). (1986). *Webster's third new international dictionary of the English language unabridged.* Springfield, MA: Merriam-Webster.

Grafen, A. (1990). Biological signals as handicaps. *Journal of Theoretical Biology, 144,* 517–546.

Grafen, A. (1991). Modelling in behavioural ecology. In J. R. Krebs & N. B. Davies (Eds.), *Behavioural ecology,* 3rd ed. (pp. 5–31). Oxford, England: Blackwell.

Graham, N. M., Burrell, C. J., Douglas, R. M., Debelle, P., & Davies, L. (1990). Adverse effects of aspirin, acetaminophen, and ibuprophen on immune function, viral shedding, and clinical status of rhinovirus-infected volunteers. *Journal of Infectious Diseases, 162,* 1277–1282.

Graham-Kevan, N., & Archer, J. (2009). Control tactics and partner violence in heterosexual relationship. *Evolution and Human Behavior, 30,* 445–452.

Grammer, K. (1992). Variations on a theme: Age dependent mate selection in humans. *Behavioral and Brain Sciences, 15,* 100–102.

Grammer, K. (1996, June). *The human mating game: The battle of the sexes and the war of signals.* Paper presented to the Human Behavior and Evolution Society Annual Meeting, Northwestern University, Evanston, IL.

Grammer, K., & Thornhill, R. (1994). Human facial attractiveness and sexual selection: The roles of averageness and symmetry. *Journal of Comparative Psychology, 108,* 233–242.

Grant, P. R. (1991, October). Natural selection and Darwin's finches. *Scientific American, 265,* 82–87.

Grant, V. J. (2005). *Dominance, testosterone and psychological sex differences* (pp. 1–28). New York: Nova Science Publications.

Gray, P. B., Chapman, J. F., Burnham, T. C., McIntyre, M. H., Lipson, S. F., & Ellison, P. T. (2004). Human male pair bonding and testosterone. *Human Nature, 15,* 119–131.

Grayson, D. K. (1993). Differential mortality and the Donner Party disaster. *Evolutionary Anthropology, 2,* 151–159.

Green, R. E., Krause, J., Briggs, A. W., Maricic, T., Stenzel, U., et al. (2010). A draft sequence of Neandertal genome. *Science, 328,* 710–722.

Gregor, T. (1985). *Anxious pleasures: The sexual lives of an Amazonian people.* Chicago: University of Chicago Press.

Greiling, H. (1995, July) *Women's mate preferences across contexts.* Paper presented to the Annual Bibliography Meeting of the Human Behavior and Evolution Society, University of California, Santa Barbara.

Greiling, H., & Buss, D. M. (2000). Women's sexual strategies: The hidden dimension of short-term extra-pair mating. *Personality and Individual Differences, 28,* 929–963.

Greitemeyer, T. (2005). Receptivity to sexual offers as a function of sex, socioeconomic status, physical attractiveness, and intimacy of the offer. *Personal Relationships, 12,* 373–386.

Griskevicius, V., Cialdini, R. B., & Kenrick, D. T. (2006). Peacocks, Picasso, and parental investment: The effects of romantic motives on creativity. *Journal of Personality and Social Psychology, 91,* 63–76.

Griskevicius, V., Goldstein, N. J., Mortensen, C. R., Cialdini, R. B., & Kenrick, D. T. (2006). Going along versus going alone: When fundamental motives facilitate strategic (non)conformity. *Journal of Personality and Social Psychology, 91,* 281–294.

Griskevicius, V., Tybur, J. M., Gangestad, S. W., Perea, E. F., Shapiro, J. R., & Kenrick, D. T. (2009). Aggress to impress: Hostility as an evolved context-dependent strategy. *Journal of Personality and Social Psychology, 96*, 980–994.

Groothof, H. A. K., Dijkstra, P., & Barelds, D. P. H. (2009). Sex differences in jealousy: The case of internet infidelity. *Journal of Social and Personal Relationships, 26*, 1119–1129.

Gross, M. R. (1982). Sneakers, satellites and parentals: Polymorphic mating strategies in North American sunfishes. *Zeitschrift für Tierpsychologie, 60*, 1–26.

Gross, M. R., & Sargent, R. C. (1985). The evolution of male and female parental care in fishes. *American Zoologist, 25*, 807–822.

Grotuss, J., Bjorklund, D. F., & Csinady, A. (2007). Evolutionary developmental psychology: Developing human nature. *Acta Psychologica Sinica, 39*, 439–453.

Guadagno, R. E., & Sagarin, B. J. (in press). Sex differences in jealousy: An evolutionary perspective on online infidelity. *Journal of Applied Social Psychology.*

Gurven, M., Kaplan, H., & Gutierrex, M. (2006). How long does it take to become a proficient hunter? Implications for the evolution of extended development and long live span. *Journal of Human Evolution, 51*, 454–470.

Gustavsson, L., & Johnsson, J. I. (2008). Mixed support for sexual selection theories of mate preferences in the Swedish population. *Evolutionary Psychology, 6*, 575–585.

Gutek, B. A. (1985). *Sex and the workplace: The impact of sexual behavior and harassment on women, men, and the organization.* San Francisco: Jossey-Bass.

Gutierres, S. E., Kenrick, D. T., & Partch, J. (1994). *Effects of others' dominance and attractiveness on self-ratings.* Unpublished manuscript, Department of Psychology, Arizona State University, Tempe.

Guttentag, M., & Secord, P. (1983). *Too many women?* Beverly Hills, CA: Sage.

Guttmacher, M. S. (1955). Criminal responsibility in certain homicide cases involving family members. In P. H. Hoch & J. Zubin (Eds.), *Psychiatry and the law.* New York: Grune and Stratton.

Hadley, C. (2004). The costs and benefits of kin: Kin networks and children's health among the Pimbwe of Tanzania. *Human Nature, 15*, 377–395.

Hagen, E. H. (1999). The functions of post-partum depression. *Evolution and Human Behavior, 20*, 325–359.

Hagen, E. H. (2005). Controversial issues in evolutionary psychology. In D. M. Buss (Ed.), *The handbook of evolutionary psychology* (pp. 145–173). New York: Wiley.

Hagen, E. H., & Hammerstein, P. (2005). Evolutionary biology and the strategic view of ontogeny: Genetic strategies provide robustness and flexibility in the life course. *Research in Human Development, 2*, 87–101.

Hagen, E. H., & Hammerstein, P. (2006). Game theory and human evolution: A critique of some recent interpretations of experimental games. *Theoretical Population Biology, 69*, 339–348.

Haidt, J. (2001). The emotional dog and its rational tail: A social intuitionist approach to moral judgment. *Psychological Review, 108*, 814–834.

Haidt, J. (2003). The moral emotions. In R. J. Davidson, K. Scherer, & H. H. Goldsmith (Eds.), *Handbook of affective sciences* (pp. 852–870). New York: Oxford University Press.

Haidt, J., & Sabini, J. (2000). *What exactly makes revenge sweet?* Unpublished manuscript, University of Virginia.

Haig, D. (1993). Genetic conflicts in human pregnancy. *The Quarterly Review of Biology, 68*, 495–532.

Haig, D. (2004). Evolutionary conflicts in pregnancy and calcium metabolism—A review. *Placenta, 25, Supplement A, Trophoblast Research, Vol. 18*, S10–S15.

Halatsis, P., & Christakis, N. (2009). The challenge of sexual attraction within heterosexuals' cross-sex friendship. *Journal of Social and Personal Relationships, 26*, 919–937.

Haley, K. J., & Fessler, D. M. T. (2005). Nobody's watching? Subtle cues affect generosity in an anonymous economic game. *Evolution and Human Behavior, 26*, 245–256.

Hall, J. A., Park, N., Song, H., & Cody, M. J. (2010). Strategic misrepresentation in online dating: The effects of gender, self-monitoring, and personality traits. *Journal of social and Personal Relationships, 27*, 117–135.

Hames, R. B. (1988). The allocation of parental care among the Ye'kwana. In L. Betzig, M. Borgerhoff Mulder, & P. Turke (Eds.), *Human reproductive behavior: A Darwinian perspective* (pp. 237–252). Cambridge, UK: Cambridge University Press.

Hamilton, W. D. (1964). The genetical evolution of social behavior. I and II. *Journal of Theoretical Biology, 7*, 1–52.

Hampson, E., van Anders, S. M., & Mullin, L. I. (2006). A female advantage in the recognition of emotional facial expressions: Test of an evolutionary hypothesis. *Evolution and Human Behavior, 27*, 401–416.

Hansen, R. D. (1980). Commonsense attribution. *Journal of Personality and Social Psychology, 39*, 996–1009.

Harlow, H. F. (1971). *Learning to love.* San Francisco: Albion.

Harpending, H. C., & Sobus, J. (1987). Sociopathy as an adaptation. *Ethology and Sociobiology, 8*, 63S–72S.

Harris, C. L. (1992). *Concepts in zoology.* New York: HarperCollins.

Harris, C. R. (2000). Psychophysiological responses to imagined infidelity: The specific innate modular view of jealousy reconsidered. *Journal of Personality and Social Psychology, 78*, 1082–1091.

Harris, C. R. (2005). Male and female jealousy, still more similar than different: Reply to Sagarin (2005). *Personality and Social Psychology Review, 9*, 76–86.

Harrison, M. A., Hughes, S. M.., Burch, R. L., & Gallup, G. G., Jr. (2008). The impact of prior heterosexual experiences on homosexuality in women. *Evolutionary Psychology, 6*, 316–327.

Hart, C. W., & Pilling, A. R. (1960). *The Tiwi of North Australia.* New York: Hart, Rinehart, & Winston.

Hartung, J. (1987). Deceiving down: Conjectures on the management of subordinate status. In J. Lockart & D. L. Paulhus (Eds.), *Self-deception: An adaptive mechanism?* (pp. 170–185). Englewood Cliffs, NJ: Prentice-Hall.

Haselton, M., Buss, D. M., Oubaid, V., & Angleitner, A. (2005). Sex, lies, and strategic interference: The psychology of deception between the sexes. *Personality and Social Psychology Bulletin, 31*, 3–23.

Haselton, M. G. (2003). The sexual overperception bias: Evidence of a systematic bias in men from a survey of naturally occurring events. *Journal of Research in Personality, 37,* 34–47.

Haselton, M. G., Bryant, G. A., Wilke, A., Frederick, D. A., Galperin, A., Franenhuis, W. E., & Moore, T. (2009). Adaptive rationality: An evolutionary perspective on cognitive bias. *Social Cognition, 27,* 733–763.

Haselton, M. G., & Buss, D. M. (2000). Error Management Theory: A new perspective on biases in crosssex mind reading. *Journal of Personality and Social Psychology, 78,* 81–91.

Haselton, M. G., & Buss, D. M. (2001). The affective shift hypothesis: The functions of emotional changes following sexual intercourse. *Personal Relationships, 8,* 357–369.

Haselton, M. G., & Buss, D. M. (2003). Biases in social judgment: Design flaws or design features? In J. Forgas, W. von Hippel, & K. Williams (Eds.), *Responding to the Social World: Explicit and Implicit Processes in Social Judgments and Decisions* (pp. 23–43). Cambridge, UK: Cambridge University Press.

Haselton, M. G., & Gangestad, S. G. (2006). Conditional expression of women's desires and men's mate guarding across the ovulation cycle. *Hormones and Behavior, 49,* 509–518.

Haselton, M. G., & Miller, G. F. (2006). Women's fertility across the cycle increases the short-term attractiveness of creative intelligence. *Human Nature, 17,* 50–73.

Haselton, M. G., & Nettle, D. (2006). The paranoid optimist: An integrative evolutionary model of cognitive biases. *Personality and Social Psychology Review, 10,* 47–66.

Hatfield, E., & Rapson, R. L. (1993). *Love, sex, and intimacy.* New York: HarperCollins.

Hauser, M. D., Chomsky, N., & Fitch, T. (2002). The faculty of language: What is it, who has it, and how did it evolve? *Science, 298,* 1569–1579.

Havlicek, J., Dvorakova, R., Bartos, L., & Flegr, J. (2005). Non-advertised does not mean concealed: Body odour changes across the human menstrual cycle. *Ethology, 111,* 1–15.

Hawkes, K. (1991). Showing off: Tests of another hypothesis about men's foraging goals. *Ethology and Sociobiology, 11,* 29–54.

Hawkes, K., O'Connell, J. F., & Blurton Jones, N. G. (2001a). Hunting and nuclear families. *Current Anthropology, 42,* 681–709.

Hawkes, K., O'Connell, J. F., & Blurton Jones, N. G. (2001b). Hadza meat sharing. *Evolution and Human Behavior, 22,* 113–142.

Hawkes, K., O'Connell, J. F., Blurton Jones, N. G., Alverez, H., & Charnov, E. L. (1998). Grandmothering, menopause, and the evolution of life histories. *Proceedings of the National Academy of Science, 95,* 1336–1339.

Hawks, J., Wang, E. T., Cochran, G. M., Harpending, H. C., & Moyzis, R. K. (2007). Recent acceleration of human adaptive evolution. *PNAS, 104,* 20753–20758.

Hawks, J. D., & Wolpoff, M. H. (2001). The four faces of Eve: Hypothesis compatibility and human origins. *Quaternary International, 75,* 41–50.

Hawley, P. H., Little, T. D., & Card, N. A. (2008). The myth of the alpha male: A new look at dominance-related beliefs and behaviors among adolescent males and females. *International Journal of Behavioral Development, 32,* 76–88.

Healey, M. D., & Ellis, B. J. (2007). Birth order, conscientiousness, and openness to experience: Tests of the family-niche model of personality using a within-family methodology. *Evolution and Human Behavior, 28,* 55–59.

Heerwagen, J. H., & Orians, G. H. (2002). The ecological world of children. In P. H. Kahn, Jr., & S. R. Kellert (Eds.), *Children and nature: Psychological, sociocultural, and evolutionary investigations* (pp. 29–64). Cambridge, MA: MIT Press.

Henrich, J. (2009). The evolution of costly displays, cooperation, and religion: Credibility enhancing displays and their implications for cultural evolution. *Evolution and Human Behavior, 30,* 244–260.

Henrich, J., & Boyd, R. (2001). Why people punish defectors: Weak conformist transmission can stabilize costly enforcement of norms in cooperative dilemmas. *Journal of Theoretical Biology, 208,* 79–89.

Henrich, J., & Gil-White, F. (2001). The evolution of prestige: Freely conferred deference as a mechanism for enhancing the benefits of cultural transmission. *Evolution and Human Behavior, 22,* 165–196.

Henrich, J., McElreath, R., Bar, A., Ensminger, J., Barrett, C. et al. (2006). Costly punishment across human societies. *Science, 312,* 1767–1770.

Herrnstein, R. J. (1977). The evolution of behaviorism. *American Psychologist, 32,* 593–603.

Hertwig, R., Davis, J. N., & Sulloway, F. J. (2002). Parental investment: How an equity motive can produce inequality. *Psychological Bulletin, 128,* 728–745.

Hess, E. H. (1975). *The tell-tale eye.* New York: Van Nostrand Reinhold.

Hewlett, B. S. (1991). *Intimate fathers: The nature and context of Aka pygmy paternal infant care.* Ann Arbor: University of Michigan Press.

Hilberman, E., & Munson, K. (1978). Sixty battered women. *Victimology, 2,* 460–470.

Hill, K. (1993). Life history theory and evolutionary anthropology. *Evolutionary Anthropology, 2,* 78–88.

Hill, K., & Hurtado, A. M. (1989). Ecological studies among some South American foragers. *American Scientist, 77,* 436–443.

Hill, K., & Hurtado, A. M. (1991). The evolution of premature reproductive senescence and menopause in human females. *Human Nature, 2,* 313–350.

Hill, K., & Hurtado, A. M. (1996). *Ache life history.* New York: Aldine De Gruyter.

Hill, K., Hurtado, K., & Walker, R. S. (2007). High adult mortality among Hiwi hunter-gatherers: Implications for human evolution. *Journal of Human Evolution, 52,* 443–454.

Hill, K., & Kaplan, H. (1988). Tradeoffs in male and female reproductive strategies among the Ache. In L. Betzig, M. Borgerhoff Mulder, & P. Turke (Eds.), *Human reproductive behavior* (pp. 277–306). New York: Cambridge University Press.

Hill, S. E., & Buss, D. M. (2006). Envy and positional bias in the evolutionary psychology of management. *Managerial and Decision Economics, 27,* 131–143.

Hill, S. E., & Buss, D. M. (2008a). The mere presence of opposite-sex others on judgments of sexual and romantic desirability: Opposite effects for men and women. *Personality and Social Psychology Bulletin, 34,* 635–647.

Hill, S. E., & Buss, D. M. (2008b). The evolutionary psychology of envy. In R. Smith (Ed.), *The psychology of envy* (pp. 60–70). New York: Guilford.

Hill, S. E., & Ryan, M. (2006). The role of model female quality in the mate choice copying behavior of sailfin mollies. *Biology Letters, 2,* 203–205.

Hinsz, V. B., Matz, D. C., & Patience, R. A. (2001). Does women's hair signal reproductive potential? *Journal of Experimental Social Psychology, 37,* 166–172.

Hiraiwa-Hasegawa, M. (2005). Homicide by men in Japan, and its relationship to age, resources and risk taking. *Evolution and Human Behavior, 26,* 332–343.

Hokanson, J. E. (1961). The effect of frustration and anxiety on overt aggression. *Journal of Abnormal and Social Psychology, 62,* 346–351.

Holmberg, A. R. (1950). *Nomads of the long bow: The Siriono of Eastern Bolivia.* Washington, DC: U.S. Government Printing Office.

Holmes, W. G., & Sherman, P. W. (1982). The ontogeny of kin recognition in two species of ground squirrels. *American Zoologist, 22,* 491–517.

hooks, b. (1984). *Feminist theory: From margin to center.* Boston: South End Press.

Hopcroft, R. L. (2002). The evolution of sex discrimination. *Psychology, Evolution, and Gender, 4,* 43–67.

Hopcroft, R. L. (2005). Parental status and differential investment in sons and daughters: Trivers-Willard revisited. *Social Forces, 83,* 1111–1136.

Hopcroft, R. L. (2006). Sex, status, and reproductive success in contemporary United States. *Evolution and Human Behavior, 27,* 104–120.

Horung, C. A., McCullough, C. B., & Sugimoto, T. (1981). Status relationships in marriage: Risk factors in spouse abuse. *Journal of Marriage and the Family,* 675–692.

Howell, N. (2000). *Demography of the Dobe !Kung* (2nd ed.). Hawthorn, NY: Aldine de Gruyter.

Hrdy, S. B. (1977). Infanticide as a primate reproductive strategy. *American Scientist, 65,* 40–49.

Hrdy, S. B. (1981). *The woman that never evolved.* Cambridge, MA: Harvard University Press.

Hughes, S. M., Farley, S. D., & Rhodes, R. C. (2010). Vocal and physiological changes in response to the physical attractiveness of conversational partners. *Journal of Nonvebal Behavior.* doi:10.1007/s10919-010-0087-9.

Hughes, S. M., & Gallup, G. G. (2003). Sex differences in morphological predictors of sexual behavior: Shoulder to hip and waist to hip ratios. *Evolution and Human Behavior, 24,* 173–178.

Hughes, S. M., Harrison, M. A., & Gallup, G. G. Jr. (2004). Sex differences in mating strategies: Mate guarding, infidelity and multiple concurrent sex partners. *Sexualities, Evolution, and Gender, 6,* 3–13.

Hughes, S., Harrison, M. A., & Gallup, G. G., Jr. (2009). Sex-specific body configurations can be estimates from voice samples. *Journal of Social, Evolutionary, and Cultural Psychology, 3,* 343–355.

Hunt, M. (1974). *Sexual behavior in the 70's.* Chicago: Playboy Press.

Hurtado, A. M., Hill, K., Kaplan, H., & Hurtado, I. (1992). Trade-offs between female food acquisition and child care among Hiwi and Ache foragers. *Human Nature, 3,* 185–216.

Huxley, J. S. (1942). *Evolution: The modern synthesis.* London: Allen & Unwin.

Hyde, J. S. (1986). Gender differences in aggression. In J. S. Hyde & M. C. Linn (Eds.), *The psychology of gender: Advances through meta-analysis.* Baltimore, MD: Johns Hopkins University Press.

Iemmola, F., & Camperio Ciani, A. (2009). New evidence of genetic factors influencing sexual orientation in men: Female fecundity increase in the maternal line. *Archives of Sexual Behavior, 38,* 393–399.

Jackson, L. A. (1992). *Physical appearance and gender: Sociobiological and sociocultural perspectives.* Albany, NY: State University of New York Press.

Jackson, J. J., & Kirkpatrick, L. A. (2007). The structure and measurement of human mating strategies: Toward a multidimensional model of sociosexuality. *Evolution and Human Behavior, 28,* 382–391.

Jackson, R. E., & Cormack, J. K. (2007). Evolved navigation theory and the descent illusion. *Perception and Psychophysics, 69,* 353–362.

Jackson, R. E., & Cormack, J. K. (2008). Evolved navigation theory and the environmental vertical illusion. *Evolution and Human Behavior, 29,* 299–304.

Jagger, A. (1994). *Living with contradictions: Controversies in feminist social ethics.* Boulder, CO: Westview Press.

James, W. (1962). *Principles of psychology.* New York: Dover. (Original work published 1890)

Jankowiak, W. (Ed.). (1995). *Romantic passion: A universal experience?* New York: Columbia University Press.

Jankowiak, W., & Fischer, R. (1992). A cross-cultural perspective on romantic love. *Ethnology, 31,* 149–155.

Jasienska, G., Ziomkiewicz, A., Ellison, P. T., Lipson, S. F., & Thune, I. (2004). Large breasts and narrow waists indicate high reproductive potential in women. *Proceedings of the Royal Society of London, B, 271,* 1213–1217.

Jencks, C. (1979). *Who gets ahead? The determinants of economic success in America.* New York: Basic Books.

Jeon, J., & Buss, D. M. (2007). Altruism toward cousins. *Proceedings of the Royal Society of London B, 274,* 1181–1187.

Johanson, D. (2001). Origins of modern humans: Multiregional or out of Africa? www.actionbiosciences.org.

Johanson, J., & Edgar, B. (1996). *From Lucy to language.* New York: Simon & Schuster.

Johnson, A. K., Barnaxz, A., Constantino, P., Triano, J., Shackelford, T. K., & Keenan, J. P. (2004). Female deception detection as a function of commitment and self-awareness. *Personality and Individual Differences, 37,* 1417–1424.

Johnson, D. D. P., McDermott, R., Barrett, E. S., Crowden, J., Wrangham, R., Mcintyre, M. H., & Rosen, S. P. (2006). Overconfidence in war games: Experimental evidence on expectations, aggression, gender, and testosterone. *Proceedings of the Royal Society B, 273,* 2513–2520.

Johnson, D. D. P., Price, M. E., & Takezawa, M. (2008). Renaissance of the individual: Reciprocity, positive assortment, and the puzzle of human cooperation. In C. Crawford & D. Krebs (Eds.). *Foundations of evolutionary psychology* (pp. 331–352). New York: Erlbaum.

Johnson, R. T., Burk, J., & Kirkpatrick, L. A. (2007). Dominance and prestige as differential predictors of aggression and testosterone levels in men. *Evolution and Human Behavior, 28,* 345–351.

Johnston, V. S., Hagel, R., Franklin, M., Fink, B., & Grammer, K. (2001). Male facial attractiveness: Evidence for hormone-mediated adaptive design. *Evolution and Human Behavior, 22,* 251–267.

Jokela, M. (2009). Physical attractiveness and reproductive success in humans: Evidence from the late 20th century United States. *Evolution and Human Behavior, 30,* 342–350.

Jonason, P. K., Li, N. P., & Buss, D. M. (2010). The costs and benefits of the Dark Triad: Implications for mate poaching and mate retention tactics. *Personality and Individual Differences, 48,* 373–378.

Jonason, P. K., Li, N. P., Webster, G. D., & Schmitt, D. P. (2009). The Dark Triad: Facilitating a short-term mating strategy in men. *European Journal of Personality, 23,* 5–18.

Jones, B. C., Little, A. C., Penton-Voak, I. S., Tiddeman, B. P., Burt, D. M., & Perrett, D. I. (2001). Facial symmetry and judgments of apparent health: Support for a "good genes" explanation of the attractiveness-symmetry relationship. *Evolution and Human Behavior, 22,* 417–429.

Jones, D. (1996). *Physical attractiveness and the theory of sexual selection.* Ann Arbor: University of Michigan Press.

Jones, D. (2003a). The generative psychology of kinship: Part 1. Cognitive universals and evolutionary psychology. *Evolution and Human Behavior, 24,* 303–319.

Jones, D. (2003b). The generative psychology of kinship: Part 2. Generating variation from universal building blocks with Optimality Theory. *Evolution and Human Behavior, 24,* 320–350.

Jones, O. D. (1999). Sex, culture, and the biology of rape: Toward explanation and prevention. *California Law Review, 87,* 827–941.

Jones, O. D. (2005). Evolutionary psychology and the law. In D. M. Buss (Ed.), *The handbook of evolutionary psychology* (pp. 953–974). Hoboken, NJ: Wiley.

Josephs, R. A., Sellers, J. G., Newman, M. L., & Mehta, P. H. (2006). The mismatch effect: When testosterone and status are at odds. *Journal of Personality and Social Psychology, 90,* 999–1013.

Judge, D. S. (1995). American legacies and the variable life histories of women and men. *Human Nature, 6,* 291–323.

Jurmain, R., Bartelink, E. J., Leventhal, A., Bellifemine, V., Nechayev, I., Atwood, M., & DiGiuseppe, D. (2009). Paleopidemiological patterns of interpersonal aggression in a prehistoric central California population from CA-ALA-329. *American Journal of Physical Anthropology, 139,* 462–473.

Kagan, J., Kearsley, R. B., & Zelazo, P. R. (1978). *Infancy: Its place in human development.* Cambridge, MA: Harvard University Press.

Kaighobadi, F., & Shackelford, T. K. (2009). Suspicions of female infidelity predict men's partner-directed violence. *Behavioral and Brain Sciences, 32,* 281–282.

Kaighobadi, F., Shackelford, T. K., & Buss, D. M. (2010). Spousal mate retention in the newlywed year and three years later. *Personality and Individual Differences, 48,* 414–418.

Kaighobadi, F., Shackelford, T. K., & Goetz, A. T. (2009). From mate retention to murder: Evolutionary psychological perspectives on partner-directed violence. *Review of General Psychology, 13,* 327–334.

Kalma, A. (1991). Hierarchisation and dominance assessment at first glance. *European Journal of Social Psychology, 21,* 165–181.

Kaminski, G., Dridi, S., Graff, C., & Gentaz, E. (2009). Human ability to detect kinship in strangers' faces: Effects of the degree of relatedness. *Proceedings of the Royal Society, B., 276,* 3193–3200.

Kanazawa, S. (2001). Why we love our children. *American Journal of Sociology, 106,* 1761–1776.

Kanazawa, S. (2003a). Can evolutionary psychology explain reproductive behavior in contemporary United States? *The Sociological Quarterly, 44,* 291–302.

Kanazawa, S. (2003b). General intelligence as a domain-specific adaptation. *Psychological Review, 111,* 512–523.

Kanazawa, S. (2005). Big and tall parents have more sons: Further generalizations of the Trivers-Willard Bibliography hypothesis. *Journal of Theoretical Biology, 235,* 583–590.

Kaplan, H. S., & Gangestad, S. W. (2005). Life history theory and evolutionary psychology. In D. M. Buss (Ed.), *The Handbook of Evolutionary Psychology* (pp. 68–96). New York: Wiley.

Kaplan, S. (1992). Environmental preference in a knowledge-seeking, knowledge-using organism. In J. Barkow, L. Cosmides, & J. Tooby (Eds.), *The adapted mind* (pp. 581–598). New York: Oxford University Press.

Kaplan, S., & Kaplan, R. (1982). *Cognition and environment: Functioning in an uncertain world.* New York: Praeger.

Karremans, J. C., Frankenhuis, W. E., & Arons, S. (2010). Blind men prefer a low waist-to-hip ratio. *Evolution and Human Behavior, 31,* 182–186.

Kavanagh, P. S., Robins, S. C., & Ellis, B. J. (2010). The mating sociometer: A regulatory mechanism for mating aspirations. *Journal of Personality and Social Psychology, 99,* 120–132.

Keeley, L. H. (1996). *War before civilization.* New York: Oxford University Press.

Keenan, J. P., Gallup, G. G., Jr., Goulet, N., & Kulkarni, M. (1997). Attributions of deception in human mating strategies. *Journal of Social Behavior and Personality, 12,* 45–52.

Keil, F. (1995). The growth of understandings of natural kinds. In D. Sperber, D. Premack, & A. Premack (Eds.), *Causal cognition.* Oxford, UK: Clarendon Press.

Keller, M. C., & Miller, G. (2006). Resolving the paradox of common, harmful, heritable mental disorders: Which evolutionary genetics models work best? *Behavioral and Brain Sciences, 29,* 385–404.

Keller, M. C., & Nesse, R. M. (2005). Is low mood an adaptation? Evidence for subtypes with symptoms that match precipitants. *Journal of Affective Disorders, 86,* 27–35.

Keller, M. C., Nesse, R. M., & Hofferth, S. (2001). The Trivers-Willard hypothesis of parental investment: No effect in contemporary United States. *Evolution and Human Behavior, 22,* 343–360.

Kennair, L. E. O. (2003). Challenging design: How best to account for the world as it really is. *Zygon, 38,* 543–558.

Kennair, L. E. O., Schmitt, D. P., Fjeldavli, Y. L., & Harlem, S. K. (2009). Sex differences in sexual desires and attitudes in Norwegian samples. *Interpersona, 3* (Supplement 1), 1–32.

Kenrick, D. T., Griskevicius, V., Sundie, J. M., Li, N. P., Li, Y. J., & Neuberg, S. L. (2009). Deep rationality: The evolutionary economics of decision making. *Social Cognition, 27,* 764–785.

Kenrick, D. T., Gutierres, S. E., & Goldberg, L. L. (1989). Influence of popular erotica on judgments of strangers and mates. *Journal of Experimental Social Psychology, 25,* 159–167.

Kenrick, D. T., & Keefe, R. C. (1992). Age preferences in mates reflect sex differences in reproductive strategies. *Behavioral and Brain Sciences, 15,* 75–133.

Kenrick, D. T., Keefe, R. C., Gabrielidis, C., & Cornelius, J. S. (1996). Adolescents' age preferences for dating partners: Support for an evolutionary model of life-history strategies. *Child Development, 67,* 1499–1511.

Kenrick, D. T., Neuberg, S. L., Zierk, K. L., & Krones, J. M. (1994). Evolution and social cognition: Contrast effects as a function of sex, dominance, and physical attractiveness. *Personality and Social Psychology Bulletin, 20,* 210–217.

Kenrick, D. T., Sadalla, E. K., Groth, G., & Trost, M. R. (1990). Evolution, traits, and the stages of human courtship: Qualifying the parental investment model. *Journal of Personality, 58,* 97–116.

Kenrick, D. T., & Sheets, V. (1993). Homicidal fantasies. *Ethology and Sociobiology, 14,* 231–246.

Ketelaar, T., & Ellis, B. J. (2000). Are evolutionary explanations unfalsifiable? Evolutionary psychology and the Lakatosian philosophy of science. *Psychological Inquiry, 11,* 1–21.

Khallad, Y. (2005). Mate selection in Jordan: Effects of sex, socio-economic status, and culture. *Journal of Social and Personal Relationships, 22,* 155–168.

Kim, K., Smith, P. K., & Palermiti, A. (1997). Conflict in childhood and reproductive development. *Evolution and Human Behavior, 18,* 109–142.

King, A. C., Schlomer, G. L., & Ellis, B. J. (in press). Evolutionary developmental psychology. V.S. Ramachandran (Ed.), *Encyclopedia of human behavior, 2.*

King, A. J., Johnson, D. D. P., & Van Vugt, M. (2009). The origins and evolution of leadership. *Current Biology, 19,* R911–R916.

Kinsey, A. C., Pomeroy, W. B., & Martin, C. E. (1948). *Sexual behavior in the human male.* Philadelphia: Saunders.

Kinsey, A. C., Pomeroy, W. B., & Martin, C. E. (1953). *Sexual behavior in the human female.* Philadelphia: Saunders.

Kirkpatrick, L. A. (1998). Evolution, pair-bonding, and reproductive strategies: A reconceptualization of adult attachment. In J. A. Simpson & W. S. Rholes (Eds.), *Attachment theory and close relationships.* New York: Guilford.

Kirkpatrick, L. A. (1999). Toward an evolutionary psychology of religion and personality. *Journal of Personality, 67,* 921–952.

Kirkpatrick, L., & Ellis, B. J. (2001). An evolutionarypsychological approach to self-esteem: Multiple domains and multiple functions. In M. Clark & G. Fletcher (Eds.), *The Blackwell handbook in social psychology, Vol. 2: Interpersonal processes* (pp. 411–436). Oxford, England: Blackwell Publishers.

Kiyonari, T., & Barclay, P. (2008). Cooperation in social dilemmas: Free riding may be thwarted by second-order reward rather than punishment. *Journal of Personality and Social Psychology, 95,* 826–842.

Klein, R. G. (2000). Archeology and the evolution of human behavior. *Evolutionary Anthropology, 9,* 17–36.

Klein, R. G., (2008). Out of Africa and the evolution of human behavior. *Evolutionary Anthropology, 17,* 267–281.

Klein, S., Cosmides, L., Tooby, J., & Chance, S. (2002). Decisions and the evolution of memory: Multiple systems, multiple functions. *Psychological Review 109,* 306–329.

Klug, H., Heuschele, J., Jennions, M. D., & Kokko, H. (2010). The mismeasurement of sexual selection. *Journal of Evolutionary Biology, 23*:447–462.

Kluger, M. J. (1990). In P. A. MacKowiac (Ed.), *Fever: Basic measurement and management.* New York: Raven Press.

Kluger, M. J. (1991). The adaptive value of fever. In P. A. MacKowiac (Ed.), *Fever: Basic measurement and management* (pp. 105–124). New York: Raven Press.

Knauft, B. (1991). Violence and sociality in human evolution. *Current Anthropology, 32,* 391–428.

Kniffin, K. M., & Wilson, D. S. (2005). Utilities of gossip across organizational levels: Multilevel selection, free-riders, and teams. *Human Nature, 16,* 278–292.

Konner, M. (1990). *Why the reckless survive.* New York: Viking.

Korchmaros, J. D., & Kenny, D. A. (2001). Emotional closeness as a mediator of the effect of genetic relatedness on altruism. *Psychological Science, 12,* 262–265.

Korchmaros, J. D., & Kenny, D. A. (2006). An evolutionary and close relationship model of helping. *Journal of Social and Personal Relationships, 23,* 21–43.

Krebs, D. (1998). The evolution of moral behaviors. In C. Crawford & D. L. Krebs (Eds.), *Handbook of evolutionary psychology: Ideas, issues, and applications* (pp. 337–368). Mahwah, NJ: Erlbaum.

Krebs, D. L. (2009). *Sources of Morality: An Evolutionary Framework.* New York: Guilford Publishing Co.

Krebs, J. R. (2009). The gourmet ape: Evolution and human food preferences. *American Journal of Clinical Nutrition, 90,* 707S–711S.

Kruger, D. J. (2003). Evolution and altruism: Combining psychological mediators with naturally selected tendencies. *Evolution and Human Behavior, 24,* 118–125.

Kruger, D. J., Fisher, M., & Jobling, I. (2003). Proper and dark heroes as dads and cads: Alternative mating strategies in British romantic literature. *Human Nature, 14,* 305–317.

Kruger, D. J., & Nesse, R. M. (2006). An evolutionary life-history framework for understanding sex differences in mortality rates. *Human Nature, 17,* 74–97.

Kuhle, B. X. (2007). An evolutionary perspective on the ontogeny of menopause. *Maturitas, 57,* 329–337.

Kuhle, B. X., Smedley, K. D., & Schmitt, D. P. (2009). Sex differences in the motivation and mitigation of jealousy-induced interrogations. *Personality and Individual Differences, 46,* 499–502.

Kurland, J. A., & Gaulin, S. J. C. (2005). Cooperation and conflict among kin. In D. M. Buss (Ed.), *The handbook of evolutionary psychology* (pp. 447–482). New York: Wiley.

Kurzban, R., DeScioli, P., & O'Brian, E. (2007). Audience effects on moralistic punishment. *Evolution and Human Behavior, 28,* 75–84.

Kurzban, R., & Leary, M. R. (2001). Evolutionary origins of stigmatization: The functions of social exclusion. *Psychological Bulletin, 127,* 187–208.

Kurzban, R., McCabe, K., Smith, V., & Wilson, B. (2001). Incremental commitment in a real-time public goods game. *Personality and Social Psychology Bulletin, 27,* 1662–1672.

Kurzban, R., & Neuberg, S. (2005). Managing ingroup and outgroup relationships. In D. M. Buss (Ed.), *The handbook of evolutionary psychology* (pp. 653–675). New York: Wiley.

Kyl-Heku, L. M., & Buss, D. M. (1996). Tactics as units of analysis in personality psychology: An illustration using tactics of hierarchy negotiation. *Personality and Individual Differences, 21,* 497–517.

La Cerra, M. M. (1994). *Evolved mate preferences in women: Psychological adaptations for assessing a man's willingness to invest in offspring.* Unpublished doctoral dissertation, Department of Psychology, University of California, Santa Barbara.

Laham, S. M., Gonsalkorale, K., & von Hippel, W. (2005). Darwinian grandparenting: Preferential investment in more certain kin. *Personality and Social Psychology Bulletin, 31,* 63–72.

Laiacona, M., Barbarotto, R., & Capitani, E. (2006). Human evolution and the brain representation of semantic knowledge: Is there a role for sex differences? *Evolution and Human Behavior, 27,* 158–168.

Lakoff, G., & Johnson, M. (1980). *Metaphors we live by.* Chicago: University of Chicago Press.

Lalumiere, M. L., Chalmers, L. J., Quinsey, V. L., & Seto, M. C. (1996). A test of the mate deprivation hypothesis of sexual coercion. *Ethology and Sociobiology, 17,* 299–318.

Lalumiere, M. L., Harris, G. T., Quinsey, V. L., & Rice, M. E. (2005). *The causes of rape.* Washington, DC: American Psychological Association.

Lalumiere, M. L., Seto, M. C., & Quinsey, V. L. (1995). *Self-perceived mating success and the mating choices of human males and females.* Unpublished manuscript.

Lambert, T. A., Kahn, A. S., & Apple, K. J. (2003). Pluralistic ignorance and hooking up. *Journal of Sex Research, 40,* 129–133.

Lancaster, J. B., & King, B. J. (1985). An evolutionary perspective on menopause. In J. K. Brown & V. Kern (Eds.),

*In her prime: A new view of middle-aged women* (pp. 13–20). Boston: Bergin & Carvey.

Landolt, M. A., Lalumiere, M. L., & Quinsey, V. L. (1995). Sex differences in intra-sex variations in human mating tactics: An evolutionary approach. *Ethology and Sociobiology, 16,* 3–23.

Langlois, J. H., & Roggman, L. A. (1990). Attractive faces are only average. *Psychological Science, 1,* 115–121.

Langhorne, M. C., & Secord, P. F. (1955). Variations in marital needs with age, sex, marital status, and regional location. *Journal of Social Psychology, 41,* 19–37.

Langlois, J. H., Roggman, L. A., Casey, R. J., Ritter, J. M., Rieser-Danner, L. A., & Jenkins, V. Y. (1987). Infant preferences for attractive faces: Rudiments of a stereotype. *Developmental Psychology, 23,* 363–369.

Langlois, J. H., Roggman, L. A., & Reiser-Danner, L. A. (1990). Infants' differential social responses to attractive and unattractive faces. *Developmental Psychology, 26,* 153–159.

Larsen, C. L. (1997). *Bioarcheology: Interpreting behavior from the human skeleton.* Cambridge, UK: Cambridge University Press.

Latané, B. (1981). The psychology of social impact. *American Psychologist, 36,* 343–356.

Laumann, E. O., Gagnon, J. H., Michael, R. T., & Michaels, S. (1994). *The social organization of sexuality: Sexual practices in the United States.* Chicago: University of Chicago Press.

Le Boeuf, B. J., & Reiter, J. (1988). Lifetime reproductive success in northern elephant seals. In T. H. Clutton-Brock (Ed.), *Reproductive success* (pp. 344–362). Chicago: University of Chicago Press.

Leakey, R., & Lewin, R. (1992). *Origins reconsidered: In search of what makes us human.* New York: Doubleday.

Leary, M. R., & Downs, D. L. (1995). Interpersonal functions of the self-esteem motive: The self-esteem system as a sociometer. In M. H. Kernis (Ed.), *Efficacy, agency, and self-esteem* (pp. 123–144). New York: Plenum.

Leary, M. R., Haupt, A. L., Strausser, K. S., & Chokel, J. T. (1998). Calibrating the sociometer: The relationship between interpersonal appraisals and state self-esteem. *Journal of Personality and Social Psychology, 74,* 1290–1299.

Leary, M. R., & Shepperd, J. A. (1986). Behavioral self-handicaps versus self-reported handicaps: A conceptual note. *Journal of Personality and Social Psychology, 51,* 1265–1268.

Lee, R. B. (1979). *The !Kung San: Men, women, and working in a foraging society.* New York: Cambridge University Press.

Lee, R., & DeVore, I. (Eds.). (1968). *Man the hunter.* Chicago: Aldine.

Lenton, A. P., Bryan, A., Hastie, R., & Fischer, O. (2007). We want the same thing: Projection in judgments of sexual intent. *Personality and Social Psychology Bulletin, 33,* 975–988.

Leonard, W. R., & Robertson, M. L. (1994). Evolutionary perspectives on human nutrition: the influence of brain and body size on diet and metabolism. *American Journal of Human Biology, 6,* 77–88.

Leslie, A. M. (1991). The theory of mind impairment in autism: Evidence for modular mechanisms of development? In A. Whiten (Ed.), *The emergence of mind reading.* Oxford, UK: Blackwell.

Levins, R. (1968). *Evolution in changing environments.* Princeton, NJ: Princeton University Press.

Lewin, R. (1993). *The origin of modern humans.* New York: Scientific American Library.

Li, N. P. (2007). Mate preference necessities in long- and short-term mating: People prioritize in themselves what their mates prioritize in them. *Acta Psychologica Sinica, 39,* 528–535.

Li, N. P., Bailey, J. M., Kenrick, D. T., & Linsemeier, J. A. W. (2002). The necessities and luxuries of mate preferences: Testing the tradeoffs. *Journal of Personality and Social Psychology, 82,* 947–955.

Li, N. P., Griskevicius, V., Durante, K. M., Jonason, P. K., Pasisz, D. J., & Aumer, K. (2009). An evolutionary perspective on humor: Sexual selection or interest indication? *Personality and Social Psychology Bulletin, 35,* 923–936.

Li, N. P., & Kenrick, D. T. (2006). Sex similarities and differences in preferences for short-term mates: What, whether, and why. *Journal of Personality and Social Psychology, 90,* 468–489.

Lieberman, D. (2009). Rethinking the Taiwanese minor marriage data: Evidence the mind uses multiple kinship cues to regulate inbreeding avoidance. *Evolution and Human Behavior, 30,* 153–160.

Lieberman, D., Oum, R., & Kurzban, R. (2008). The family of fundamental social categories includes kinship: Evidence from the memory confusion paradigm. *European Journal of Social Psychology, 38,* 998–1012.

Lieberman, D., Tooby, J., & Cosmides, L. (2003). Does morality have a biological basis? An empirical test of the factors governing moral sentiments relating to incest. *Proceedings of the Royal Society of London, B, 270,* 819–826.

Lieberman, D., Tooby, J., & Cosmides, L. (2007). The architecture of human kin detection. *Nature, 445,* 727–731.

Lindgren, K. P., George, W. H., & Shoda, Y. (2007). Sexual intent perceptions: The role of perceiver experience and the real-person reduction. *Journal of Applied Social Psychology, 37,* 346–369.

Lippa, R. A. (2009). Sex differences in sex drive, sociosexuality, and height across 53 nations: Testing evolutionary and social structural theories. *Archives of Sexual Behavior, 38,* 631–651.

Lippa, R. A., Collaer, M. L., & Peters, M. (2010). Sex differences in mental rotation and line angle judgments are positively associated with gender equality and economic development across 53 nations. *Archives of Sexual Behavior, 39,* 990–997.

Little, A. C., Burriss, R. P., Jones, C., DeBruine, L. M., & Caldwell, C. A. (2008). Social influence in human face preference: Men and women are influenced more for long-term than short-term attractiveness decisions. *Evolution and Human Behavior, 29,* 140–146.

Little, A. C., Penton-Voak, I. S., Burt, D. M., & Perrett, D. I. (2002). Evolution and individual differences in the perception of attractiveness: How cyclic hormonal changes and self-perceived attractiveness influence female preferences for male faces. In G. Rhodes & L. A. Zebrowitz (Eds.), *Facial attractiveness: Evolutionary, cognitive, and social perspectives* (pp. 59–90). Westport, CT: Ablex.

Littlefield, C. H., & Rushton, J. P. (1986). When a child dies: The sociobiology of bereavement. *Journal of Personality and Social Psychology, 51,* 797–802.

Livingstone, K. (1998). The case for general mechanisms in concept formation. *Behavioral and Brain Sciences, 21,* 581–582.

LoBue, V., & DeLoache, J. S. (2008). Detecting the snake in the grass: Attention to fear-relevant stimuli by adults and young children. *Psychological Science, 19,* 284–289.

Lorenz, K. (1941). Vergleichende Bewegungsstudien an Anatiden. *Journal of Ornithology, 89,* 194–294.

Lorenz, K. Z. (1965). *Evolution and the modification of behavior.* Chicago: University of Chicago Press.

Low, B. S. (1989). Cross-cultural patterns in the training of children: An evolutionary perspective. *Journal of Comparative Psychology, 103,* 313–319.

Low, B. S. (1991). Reproductive life in nineteenth century Sweden: An evolutionary perspective. *Ethology and Sociobiology, 12,* 411–448.

Lukaszewski, A.W., & Roney, J. R. (2009). Estimated hormones predict women's mate preferences for dominant personality traits. *Personality and Individual Differences, 47,* 191–196.

Lukaszewski, A. W., & Roney, J. R. (2010a). Kind toward whom? Mate preferences for personality traits are target specific. *Evolution and Human Behavior, 31,* 29–38.

Lukaszewski, A. W., & Roney, J. R. (2010b, June 17). The origins of extraversion: Joint effects of facultative calibration and genetic polymorphism. Paper presented to the Annual Meeting of the Human Behavior and Evolution Society, Eugene, Oregon.

Lund, O. C. H., Tamnes, C. K., Moestue, C., Buss, D. M., & Vollrath, M. (2007). Tactics of hierarchy negotiation. *Journal of Research in Personality, 41,* 25–44.

Lykken, D. (1995). *The antisocial personalities.* Hillsdale, NJ: Erlbaum.

Lynn, M. (2009). Determinants and consequences of female attractiveness and sexiness: Realistic tests with restaurant waitresses. *Archives of Sexual Behavior, 38,* 737–745.

Lynn, M., & Shurgot, B. A. (1984). Responses to lonely hearts advertisements: Effects of reported physical attractiveness, physique, and coloration. *Personality and Social Psychology Bulletin, 10,* 349–357.

Maccoby, E. E. (1990). Gender and relationships: A developmental account. *American Psychologist, 45,* 513–520.

MacDonald, G., & Leary, M. R. (2005). Why does social exclusion hurt? The relationship between social and physical pain. *Psychological Bulletin, 131,* 202–223.

MacDonald, K. (1995). Evolution, the five-factor model, and levels of personality. *Journal of Personality, 63,* 525–568.

MacDonald, K. (1996). What do children want? A conceptualization of evolutionary influences on children's motivation in the peer group. *International Journal of Behavioral Development, 19,* 53–73.

Mackey, W. C., & Coney, N. S. (2000). The enigma of father presence in relationship to sons' violence and daughters' mating strategies: Empiricism in search of a theory. *The Journal of Men's Studies, 8,* 349–373.

Mackey, W. C., & Daly, R. D. (1995). A test of the manchild bond: The predictive potency of the teeter-totter effect. *Genetic, Social, and General Psychology Monographs, 121,* 424–444.

Mackey, W. C., & Immerman, R. S. (2000). Sexually transmitted diseases, pair bonding, fathering, and alliance formation: Disease avoidance behaviors as a proposed element in human evolution. *Psychology of Men and Masculinity, 1,* 49–61.

Maestripieri, D. (2004). Developmental and evolutionary aspects of female attraction to babies. *Psychological Science Agenda, 18*(1).

Maestripieri, D., & Pelka, S. (2002). Sex differences in interest in infants across the lifespan: A biological adaptation for parenting? *Human Nature, 13,* 327–344.

Maggioncalda, A. N., & Sapolsky, R. M. (2002). Disturbing behaviors of the orangutan. *Scientific American, 286,* 60–65.

Magrath, M. J. L., & Komdeur, J. (2003). Is male care compromised by additional mating opportunity? *TRENDS in Ecology and Evolution, 18,* 424–430.

Malamuth, N. M. (1981). Rape proclivity among males. *Journal of Social Issues, 37,* 138–157.

Malinowski, B. (1929). *The sexual life of savages in North-Western Melanesia.* London: Routledge.

Maloney, L. T., & Dal Martello, M. F. (2006). Kin recognition and the perceived facial similarity of children. *Journal of Vision, 6,* 1047–1056.

Malthus, T. R. (1798). *An essay on the principle of population.* London: J. Johnson.

Maner, J. K., DeWall, C. N., & Gailliot, M. T. (2008). Selective attention to signs of success: Social dominance and early stage interpersonal perception. *Personality and Social Psychology Bulletin, 34,* 488–501.

Maner, J. K., Gailliot, M. T., & DeWall, N. (2007). Adaptive attentional attunement: Evidence for mating-related perceptual bias. *Evolution and Human Behavior, 28,* 28–36.

Maner, J. K., & Mead, N. L. (2010). The essential tension between leadership and power: When leaders sacrifice group goals for the sake of self-interest. *Journal of Personality and Social Psychology, 99*(3), 482–497.

Mann, J. (1992). Nurturance or negligence: Maternal psychology and behavioral preference among preterm twins. In J. Barkow, L. Cosmides, & J. Tooby (Eds.), *The adapted mind* (pp. 367–390). New York: Oxford University Press.

Manson, J. H. (1992). Measuring female mate choice in Cayo Santiago rhesus macaques. *Animal Behavior, 44,* 405–416.

Marks, I. (1987). *Fears, phobias, and rituals: Panic, anxiety, and their disorders.* New York: Oxford University Press.

Marks, I. M., & Nesse, R. M. (1994). Fear and fitness: An evolutionary analysis of anxiety disorders. *Ethology and Sociobiology, 15,* 247–261.

Marlow, F. (1999). Showoffs or providers? The parenting effort of Hadza men. *Evolution and Human Behavior, 20,* 391–404.

Marlow, F., Apicella, C., & Reed, D. (2005). Men's preferences for women's profile waist-to-hip ratio in two societies. *Evolution and Human Behavior, 26,* 458–468.

Marlow, F., & Wetsman, A. (2001). Preferred waist-to-hip ratio and ecology. *Personality and Individual Differences, 30,* 481–489.

Marlow, F. W. (2004). Mate preferences among Hadza hunter-gatherers. *Human Nature, 4,* 365–376.

Marlow, F. W. (2005). Hunter-gatherers and human evolution. *Evolutionary Anthropology, 14,* 54–67.

Marr, D. (1982). *Vision: A computational investigation into the human representation and processing of visual information.* San Francisco: Freeman.

Marth, G., Schuler, G., Yeh, R., Davenport, R., Agarwala, R., Church, D., Wheelan, S., Baker, J., Ward, M., Kholodov, M., Phan, L., Czbarka, E., Murvia, J., Cutler, D., Wooding, S., Rogers, A., Chakravarti, A., Harpending, H. C., Kwok, P.-Y., & Sherry, S. T. (2003). Sequence variations in the public human genome data reflect a bottlenecked population history. *Proceedings of the National Academy of Sciences, 100,* 376–381.

Maslow, A. H. (1937). Dominance-feeling, behavior, and status. *Psychological Review, 44,* 404–429.

Maynard Smith, J. (1982). *Evolution and the theory of games.* Cambridge, UK: Cambridge University Press.

Maynard Smith, J., & Price, G. (1973). The logic of animal conflict. *Nature, 246,* 15–18.

Mayr, E. (1942). *Systematics and the origin of species.* New York: Columbia University Press.

Mayr, E. (1982). *The growth of biological thought.* Cambridge, MA: Harvard University Press.

Mazur, A. (2005). *Biosociology of dominance and deference.* Lanham, MD: Bowman & Littlefield Publishers, Inc.

Mazur, A., & Booth, A. (1998). Testosterone and dominance in men. *Behavioral and Brain Science, 21,* 353–363.

Mazur, A., Booth, A., & Dabbs, J. (1992). Testosterone and chess competition. *Social Psychology Quarterly, 55,* 70–77.

Mazur, A., Halpern, C., & Udry, J. R. (1994). Dominant looking male teenagers copulate earlier. *Ethology and Sociobiology, 15,* 87–94.

Mazur, A., & Michalek, J. (1998). Marriage, divorce, and male testosterone. *Social Forces, 77,* 315–330.

McAndrew, F. T. (2002). New evolutionary perspectives on altruism: Multilevel-selection and costly-signaling theories. *Current Directions in Psychological Science, 11,* 79–82.

McAndrew, F. T. (2008). Can gossip be good? *Scientific American Mind Magazine,* October/November, 26–33.

McAndrew, F.T. (2009). The interacting roles of testosterone and challenges to status in human male aggression. *Aggression and Violent Behavior, 14,* 330–335.

McAndrew, F. T., Bell, E. K., & Garcia, C. M. (2007). Who do we tell, and whom do we tell on? Gossip as a strategy for status enhancement. *Journal of Applied Social Psychology, 37,* 1562–1577.

McAndrew, F. T., & Milenkovic, M. A. (2002). Of tabloids and family secrets: The evolutionary psychology of gossip. *Journal of Applied Social Psychology, 32,* 1–20.

McCracken, G. F. (1984). Communal nursing in Mexican free-tailed bat maternity colonies. *Science, 223,* 1090–1091.

McCullough, J. M., Heath, K. M., & Fields, J. D. (2006). Culling cousins: Kingship, kinship, and competition in mid-millennial England. *History of the Family, 11,* 59–66.

McCullough, J. M., & York Barton, E. (1990). Relatedness and mortality risk during a crisis year: Plymouth colony, 1620–1621. *Ethology and Sociobiology, 12,* 195–209.

McGuire, A. M. (1994). Helping behaviors in the natural environment: Dimensions and correlates of helping. *Personality and Social Psychology Bulletin, 20,* 45–56.

McGuire, M. T., & Troisi, A. (1998). *Darwinian psychiatry.* New York: Oxford University Press.

McIntyre, M. H., Gangestad, S. W., Gray, P. B., Chapman, J. F., Burnham, T. C., O'Rourke, M. T., & Thornhill, R. (2006). Romantic involvement often reduces men's testosterone levels—but not always: The moderating effects of extra-pair sexual interest. *Journal of Personality and Social Psychology, 91,* 642–651.

McKibbin, W. F., Shackelford, T. K., Goetz, A. T., Bates, V. M., & Starrett, V. G. (2009). Developmental and initial psychometric assessment of the rape avoidance inventory. *Personality and Individual Differences, 46,* 336–340.

McKibbin, W. F., Shackelford, T. K., Goetz, A. T., & Starratt, V. G. (2008). Why do men rape? An evolutionary psychological perspective. *Review of General Psychology, 12,* 86–97.

McKibbin, W. F., Shackelford, T. K., Miner, E. J., Bates, V. M., & Liddle, J. R. (2010). Individual differences in women's rape avoidance behaviors. *Archives of Sexual Behavior.*

McKnight, J. (1997). *Straight science: Homosexuality, evolution and adaptation.* New York: Routledge.

McLain, D. K., Setters, D., Moulton, M. P., & Pratt, A. E. (2000). Ascription of resemblance of newborns by parents of nonrelatives. *Evolution and Human Behavior, 21,* 11–23.

Mealey, L. (1995). The sociobiology of sociopathy: An integrated evolutionary model. *Behavioral and Brain Sciences, 18,* 523–599.

Mealey, L., Daood, C., & Krage, M. (1996). Enhanced memory for faces of cheaters. *Ethology and Sociobiology, 17,* 119–128.

Megargee, E. I. (1969). Influence of sex roles on the manifestation of leadership. *Journal of Applied Psychology, 53,* 377–382.

Mehl, B., & Buchner, A. (2008). No enhanced memory for faces of cheaters. *Evolution and Human Behavior, 29,* 35–41.

Mehta, P., & Josephs, R. (2010). Testosterone and cortisol jointly regulate dominance: Evidence for a dual-hormone hypothesis. *Hormones and Behavior, 58,* 898–906.

Mehu, M., Grammer, K., & Dunbar, R. I. M. (2007). Smiles when sharing. *Evolution and Human Behavior, 28,* 415–422.

Mendle, J., Harden, K. P., Turkheimer, E., Van Hulle, C. A., D'Onofrio, B. M., Brooks-Gunn, J., Rodgers, J. L., Emery, R. E., & Lahey, B. B. (2009). Associations between father absence and age of first sexual intercourse. *Child Development, 80,* 1463–1480.

Mesquida, C. G., & Wiener, N. I. (1996). Human collective aggression: A behavioral ecology perspective. *Ethology and Sociobiology, 17,* 247–262.

Meston, C., & Buss, D. M. (2009). Why humans have sex. *Archives of Sexual Behavior, 36,* 477–507.

Meston, C. M., & Buss, D. M. (2009). *Why women have sex.* New York: Holt.

Michalski, R. L., & Shackelford, T. K. (2005). Grandparental investment as a function of relational uncertainty and emotional closeness with parents. *Human Nature, 16,* 293–305.

Michalski, R. L., Shackelford, T. K., & Salmon, C. A. (2007). Upset in response to sibling's partner's infidelities. *Human Nature, 18,* 74–84.

Mikach, S. M., & Bailey, J. M. (1999). What distinguishes women with unusually high numbers of sex partners? *Evolution and Human Behavior, 20,* 141–150.

Milgram, S. (1974). *Obedience to authority.* New York: Harper & Row.

Miller, G. (2000). *The mating mind.* New York: Doubleday.

Miller, G. F. (1998). How mate choice shaped human nature: A review of sexual selection and human evolution. In C. Crawford & D. Krebs (Eds.), *Handbook of Evolutionary Psychology* (pp. 87–129). Mahwah, NJ: Erlbaum.

Miller, G. F. (1999). Sexual selection for cultural displays. In R. Dunbar, C. Knight, & C. Power (Eds.), *The Evolution of culture.* Edinburgh: Edinburgh University Press.

Miller, G. F. (2007). Sexual selection for moral virtues. *Quarterly Review of Biology, 82,* 97–125.

Miller, G. F. (2009). *Spent: Sex, Evolution, and Consumer Behavior.* New York: Viking.

Miller, G. F., Tybur, J. M., & Jordan, B. D. (2007). Ovulatory cycle effects on tip earnings by lap dancers: Economic evidence for human estrus? *Evolution and Human Behavior, 28,* 375–381.

Miller, L. C., & Fishkin, S. A. (1997). On the dynamics of human bonding and reproductive success: Seeking "windows" on the "adapted for" human environmental interface. In J. A. Simpson & D. T. Kenrick (Eds.), *Evolutionary social psychology* (pp. 197–235). Mahwah, NJ: Erlbaum.

Miller, S. L., & Maner, J. K. (2010). Scent of a woman: Men's testosterone responses to olfactory ovulation cues. *Psychological Science, 21,* 276–283.

Miller, W. B. (1980). Gangs, groups and serious youth crime. In D. Shichor & D. H. Kelly (Eds.), *Critical issues in juvenile delinquency* (pp. 115–138). Lexington, MA: Lexington Books.

Millet, K., & Dewitte, S. (2007). Altruistic behavior as a costly signal of general intelligence. *Journal of Research in Personality, 41,* 316–326.

Milton, K. (1999). A hypothesis to explain the role of meat-eating in human evolution. *Evolutionary Anthropology, 8,* 1–21.

Miner, E. J., Shackelford, T. K., & Starratt, V. G. (2009). Mate value of romantic partners predicts men's partner-directed verbal insults. *Personality and Individual Differences, 46,* 135–139.

Miner, E. J., Starratt, V. G., & Shackelford, T. K. (2009). It's not all about her: Men's mate value and mate retention. *Personality and Individual Differences, 47,* 214–218.

Minervini, B. P., & McAndrew, F. T. (2006). The mating strategies and mate preferences of mail order brides. *Cross-Cultural Research, 37,* 1–20.

Mishra, S., Clark, A., & Daly, M. (2007). One woman's behavior affects the attractiveness of others. *Evolution and Human Behavior, 28,* 145–149.

Mithen, S. (1996). *The prehistory of the mind.* London: Thames & Hudson.

Moore, F. R., Cassidy, C., Smith, M. J. L., & Perrett, D. I. (2006a). The effects of female control of resources on sex-differentiated mate preferences. *Evolution and Human Behavior, 27,* 193–205.

Moore, L. T., McEvoy, B., Cape, E., Simms, K., & Bradley, D. G. (2006b). A Y-chromosome signature of hegemony in Gaelic Ireland. *The American Journal of Human Genetics, 78,* 334–338.

Morse, S. T., Gruzen, J., & Reis, H. (1976). The "eye of the beholder": A neglected variable in the study of physical attractiveness. *Journal of Personality, 44,* 209–225.

Moskowitz, A. K. (2004). "Scared stiff": Catatonia as an evolutionary-based fear response. *Psychological Review, 111,* 984–1002.

Muehlenhard, C. L., & Linton, M. A. (1987). Date rape and sexual aggression in dating situations: Incidence and risk factors. *Journal of Counseling Psychology, 2,* 186–196.

Mueller, U., & Mazur, A. (1996). Facial dominance of West Point cadets as a predictor of later military rank. *Social Forces, 74,* 823–850.

Mulvihill, D. J., Tumin, M. M., & Curtis, L. A. (1969). *Crimes of violence* (Vol. 11). Washington, DC: U.S. Government Printing Office.

Murray, G. R., & Schmitz, J. D. (in press). Caveman politics: Leadership preferences and physical stature. *Social Science Quarterly.*

Muscarella, F. (2000). The evolution of homoerotic behavior in humans. *Journal of Homosexuality, 40,* 51–77.

Nairne, J. S., & Pandeirada, J. N. S. (2008). Adaptive memory: Remembering with a stone-age brain. *Current Directions in Psychological Science, 17,* 239–243.

Nairne, J. S., Pandeirada, J. N. S., & Thompson, S. R. (2008). Adaptive memory: The comparative value of survival processing. *Psychological Science, 19,* 176–180.

Nairne, J. S., Pandeirada, J. N. S., Gregory, K. J., & Van Arsdall, J. E. (2009). Adaptive memory: Fitness relevance and the hunter-gatherer mind. *Psychological Science, 20,* 740–746.

Navarrete, C. D., Mcdonald, M. N., Molina, L. E., & Sidanius, J. (2010). Prejudice at the nexus of race and gender: An outgroup male target hypothesis. *Journal of Personality and Social Psychology, 98,* 933–945.

Navarrete, C. D., Olsson, A., Ho, A. K., Mendes, W. B., Thomsen, L., & Sidanius, J. (2009). Fear extinction to an out-group face. *Psychological Science, 20,* 155–158.

Neberich, W., Penke, L., Lehnart, J., & Asendorpf, J. B. (2010). Family of origin, age of menarche, and reproductive strategies: A test of four evolutionary-developmental models. *European Journal of Developmental Psychology, 7,* 153–177.

Nelson, L. D., & Morrison, E. L. (2005). The symptoms of resource scarcity: Judgments of food and finances influence preferences for potential partners. *Psychological Science, 16,* 167–173.

Nesse, R. M. (1990). Evolutionary explanations of emotions. *Human Nature, 1,* 261–289.

Nesse, R. M. (1991, November/December). What good is feeling bad?: The evolutionary benefits of psychic pain. *The Sciences,* 30–37.

Nesse, R. M. (2000). Is depression an adaptation? *Archives of General Psychiatry, 57,* 14–20.

Nesse, R. M., & Stearns, S. C. (2008). The great opportunity: Evolutionary applications to medicine and public health. *Evolutionary Applications, 1,* 28–48.

Nesse, R. M., & Williams, G. C. (1994). *Why we get sick.* New York: Times Books Random House.

Nettle, D. (2006). The evolution of personality variation in humans and other animals. *American Psychologist, 61,* 622–631.

Nettle, D. (2009). Ecological influences on human behavioural diversity: A review of recent findings. *Trends in Ecology and Evolution, 24,* 618–24.

Nettle, D., & Liddle, B. (2008). Agreeableness is related to social-cognitive, but not social-perceptual, theory of mind. *European Journal of Personality, 22,* 323–335.

Nettle, D., & Penke, L. (2010). Personality: Bridging the literatures from human psychology and behavioural ecology. *Philosophical Transactions of the Royal Society B, 365,* 4035–4050.

Neuhoff, J. G. (2001). An adaptive bias in the perception of looming auditory motion. *Ecological Psychology, 13,* 87–110.

New, J., Krasnow, M. M., Truxaw, D., & Gaulin, S. J. C. (2007). Spatial adaptations for plant foragaing: Women excel and calories count. *Proceedings of the Royal Society, B, 274,* 2679–2684.

*New York Times* (December 4, 1995). Man ordered to support child who isn't his. p. A13.

*Newsweek* (November 10, 2003). [Rod Stewart quote]. p. 23.

Neyer, F. J., & Lang, F. R. (2003). Blood is thicker than water: Kinship orientation across adulthood. *Journal of Personality and Social Psychology, 84,* 310–321.

Nicholson, N. (1997). Evolutionary psychology: Toward a new view of human nature and organizational society. *Human Relations, 50,* 1053–1078.

Nida, S. A., & Koon, J. (1983). They get better looking at closing time around here, too. *Psychological Reports, 52,* 657–658.

Nisbett, R. E. (1993). Violence and U.S. regional culture. *American Psychologist, 48,* 441–449.

Nisbett, R. E., & Ross, L. (1980). *Human inference: Strategies and shortcomings of social judgment.* Englewood Cliffs, NJ: Prentice-Hall.

Nowak, M. A. (2006). Five rules for the evolution of cooperation. *Science, 314,* 1560–1563.

Nowak, M. A., & Sigmund, K. (2005). Evolution and indirect reciprocity. *Nature, 437,* 1291–1298.

Nyquist, L. V., & Spence, J. T. (1986). Effects of dispositional dominance and sex role expectations on leadership behaviors. *Journal of Personality and Social Psychology, 50,* 97–98.

Oaten, M., Stevenson, R. J., & Case, T. I. (2009). Disgust as a disease-avoidance mechanism. *Psychological Bulletin, 135*, 303–321.

O'Connor, L. E., Berry, J. W., Weiss, J., Schweitzer, D., & Sevier, M. (2000). Survivor guilt, submissive behaviour and evolutionary theory: The down-side of winning in social competition. *British Journal of Medical Psychology, 73*, 519–530.

Oda, R. (2001). Sexually dimorphic mate preference in Japan. *Human Nature, 12,* 191–206.

Oda, R., Hiraishi, K., & Matsumoto-Oda, A. (2006). Does an altruist-detection cognitive mechanism function independently of a cheater-detection cognitive mechanism? Studies using Wason selection tasks. *Evolution and Human Behavior, 27*, 366–388.

Oda, R., & Nakajima, S. (2010). Biased face recognition in the Faith Game. *Evolution and Human Behavior, 31,* 118–122.

Oda, R., Yamagata, N., Yabiku, Y., & Matsumoto-Oda, A. (2009). Altruism can be assessed correctly based on impression. *Human Nature, 20,* 331–341.

O'Gorman, R., Sheldon, K. M., & Wilson, D. S. (2008). For the good of the group? Exploring group-level evolutionary adaptations using multilevel selection theory. *Group Dynamics, 12,* 17–26.

Öhman, A., Flykt, A., & Esteves, F. (2001). Emotion drives attention: Detecting the snake in the grass. *Journal of Experimental Psychology: General, 130,* 466–478.

Olweus, D. (1978). *Aggression in schools.* New York: Wiley.

Olweus, D. (1993). *Bullying at school.* Oxford, UK: Blackwell Publishers.

Orians, G. (1980). Habitat selection: General theory and applications to human behavior. In J. S. Lockard (Ed.), *The evolution of human social behavior* (pp. 49–66). Chicago: Elsevier.

Orians, G. (1986). An ecological and evolutionary approach to landscape aesthetics. In E. C. Penning- Rowsell & D. Lowenthal (Eds.), *Landscape meaning and values* (pp. 3–25). London: Allen & Unwin.

Orians, G. H., & Heerwagen, J. H. (1992). Evolved responses to landscapes. In J. Barkow, L. Cosmides, & J. Tooby (Eds.), *The adapted mind* (pp. 555–579). New York: Oxford University Press.

Ortner, S. B. (1974). Is female to male as nature is to nurture? In M. Z. Rosaldo & L. Lamphere (Eds.), *Women, culture, and society* (pp. 67–88). Stanford, CA: Stanford University Press.

Otta, E., Queiroz, R. da S., Campos, L. de S., da Silva, M. W. D., & Silveira, M. T. (1999). Age differences between spouses in a Brazilian marriage sample. *Evolution and Human Behavior, 20,* 99–103.

Otterbein, K. (1979). *The evolution of war.* New Haven, CT: HRAF Press.

O'Toole, B. I., & Stankov, L. (1992). Ultimate validity of psychological tests. *Personality and Individual Differences, 13,* 699–716.

Owen, J., & Finchham, F. D. (2010). Effects of gender and psychosocial factors on "friends with benefits" relationship among young adults. *Archives of Sexual Behavior.* doi:10.1007/s10508-010-9691-3.

Owens, L., Shute, R., & Slee, P. (2000). "I'm in and you're out . . ." Explanations for teenage girls' indirect aggression. *Psychology, Evolution, and Gender, 2,* 19–46.

Paal, T., & Bereczkei, T. (2007). Adult theory of mind, cooperation, and Machiavellianism: the effect of mindreading on social relations. *Personality and Individual Differences, 43,* 541–551.

Padilla, F. M. (1992). *The gang as an American enterprise.* New Brunswick, NJ: Rutgers University Press.

Palmer, C. T., & Tilley, C. F. (1995). Sexual access to females as a motivation for joining gangs: An evolutionary approach. *The Journal of Sex Research, 32,* 213–217.

Panchanathan, K., & Boyd, R. (2004). Indirect reciprocity can stabilize cooperation without the secondorder free rider problem. *Nature, 432,* 499–502.

Park, J. H., Schaller, M., & Van Vugt, M. (2008). Psychology of human kin recognition: Heuristic cues, erroneous inferences, and their implications. *Review of General Psychology, 12,* 215–235.

Parker, G. A. (1974). Assessment strategy and the evolution of fighting behaviour. *Journal of Theoretical Biology, 47,* 223–243.

Parker, G. A. (2006). Sexual selection over mating and fertilization: An overview. *Philosophical Transactions of the Royal Society, B, 361,* 235–259.

Parker, G. A., Royle, N. J., & Hartley, I. R. (2002). Intrafamilial conflict and parental investment: A synthesis. *Philosophical Transactions of the Royal Society of London B, 357,* 295–307.

Pashos, A. (2000). Does paternal uncertainty explain discriminative grandparental solicitude? A crosscultural study in Greece and Germany. *Evolution and Human Behavior, 21,* 97–109.

Pashos, A., & McBurney, D. H. (2008). Kin relationships and caregiver biases of grandparents, aunts, and uncles. *Human Nature, 19,* 311–330.

Paton, W., & Mannison, M. (1995). Sexual coercion in high school dating. *Sex Roles, 33,* 447–457.

Patton, J. Q. (1997, June). *Are warriors altruistic? Reciprocal altruism and war in the Ecuadorian Amazon.* Paper presented at the Human Behavior and Evolution Society Meetings, University of Arizona, Tucson.

Patton, J. Q. (2000). Reciprocal altruism and warfare: A case from the Ecuadorian Amazon. In L. Cronk, N. A. Chagnon, & W. Irons (Eds.), *Adaptation and human behavior: An anthropological perspective* (pp. 417–436). New York: Aldine de Gruyter.

Pavlov, I. P. (1927). *Conditioned reflexes,* trans. G. V. Anrep. London: Oxford University Press.

Pawlowski, B., & Dunbar, R. I. M. (1999a). Impact of market value on human mate choice decisions. *Proceedings of the Royal Society of London B, 266,* 281–285.

Pawlowski, B., & Dunbar, R. I. M. (1999b). Withholding age as putative deception in mate search tactics. *Evolution and Human Behavior, 20,* 53–69.

Pawlowski, B., Goothroyd, L. G., Perrett, D. I., & Kluska, S. (2008). Is female attractiveness related to final reproductive success? *Coll. Antropol., 32,* 315–319.

Pawlowski, B., & Jasienska, G. (2005). Women's preferences for sexual dimorphism in height depend on menstrual cycle phase and expected duration of relationship. *Biological Psychology, 70,* 38–43.

Pawlowski, B., & Koziel, S. (2002). The impact of traits offered in personal advertisements on response rates. *Evolution and Human Behavior, 23,* 139–149.

Pawson, E., & Banks, G. (1993). Rape and fear in a New Zealand city. *Area, 25,* 55–63.

Pedersen, F. A. (1991). Secular trends in human sex ratios: Their influence on individual and family behavior. *Human Nature, 2,* 271–291.

Penke, L., & Asendorpf, J. B. (2008). Beyond global sociosexual orientations: A more differentiated look at sociosexuality and its effects on courtship and romantic relationships. *Journal of Personality and Social Psychology, 95,* 1113–1135.

Penke, L., & Denissen, J. J. A. (2008). Sex differences and lifestyle-dependent shifts in the attunement of self-esteem to self-perceived mate value: Hints to an adaptive mechanism. *Journal of Research in Personality, 42,* 1123–1129.

Penke, L., Denissen, J. J. A., & Miller, G. F. (2007). The evolutionary genetics of personality. *European Journal of Personality, 21,* 549–587.

Pennebaker, J. W., Dyer, M. A., Caulkins, R. S., Litowixz, D. L., Ackerman, P. L., & Anderson, D. B. (1979). Don't the girls get prettier at closing time: A country and western application to psychology. *Personality and Social Psychology Bulletin, 5,* 122–125.

Perilloux, C., Easton, J. A., Fleischman, D. S., & Buss, D. M. (2010, June 18). *The who and whom of sexual misperception.* Paper presented at the annual meeting of the Human Behavior and Evolution Society, University of Oregon, Eugene, Oregon.

Perilloux, C., Fleischman, D. S. & Buss, D. M. (2008). The daughter-guarding hypothesis: Parental influence on, and emotional reactions to, offspring's mating behavior. *Evolutionary Psychology, 6,* 217–233.

Perilloux, H. K., Webster, G. D., & Gaulin, S. J. C. (2010). Signals of genetic quality and maternal investment capacity: The dynamic effects of fluctuating asymmetry and waist-to-hip ratio on men's ratings of women's attractiveness. *Social Psychological and Personality Science, 1,* 34–42.

Perusse, D. (1993). Cultural and reproductive success in industrial societies: Testing the relationship at proximate and ultimate levels. *Behavioral and Brain Sciences, 16,* 267–322.

Petersen, J. L., & Hyde, J. S. (2010). A meta-analytic review of research on gender differences in sexuality, 1993–2007. *Psychological Bulletin, 136,* 21–38.

Pettay, J. E., Helle, S., Jokela, J., & Lummaa, V. (2007). Natural selection on female life-history traits in relation to socio-economic class in pre-industrial human populations. *Plos ONE,* July, 1–9.

Pettijohn, R. F., & Jungeberg, B. J. (2004). *Playboy* playmate curves: Changes in facial and body feature preferences across social and economic conditions. *Personality and Social Psychology Bulletin, 30,* 1186–1197.

Pettijohn, T. F., II., Sacco, D. F., Jr., & Yerkes, M. J. (2009). Hungry people prefer more mature mates: A field test of the environmental security hypothesis. *Journal of Social, Evolutionary, and Cultural Psychology, 3,* 216–232.

Phillips, T., Barnard, C., Ferguson, E., & Reader, T. (2008). Do humans prefer altruistic mates? Testing a link between sexual selection and altruism toward nonrelatives. *British Journal of Psychology, 99,* 555–572.

Piddocke, S. (1965). The potlatch system of the southern Kwakiutl: A new perspective. *Southwestern Journal of Anthropology, 21,* 244–264.

Pietrzak, R., Laird, J. D., Stevens, D. A., & Thompson, N. S. (2002). Sex differences in human jealousy: A coordinated study of forced-choice, continuous rating-scale, and physiological responses on the same subjects. *Evolution and Human Behavior, 23,* 83–94.

Pike, I. L. (2000). The nutritional consequences of pregnancy sickness: A critique of a hypothesis. *Human Nature, 11,* 207–232.

Pillsworth, E. G., & Haselton, M. G. (2006). Male sexual attractiveness predicts differential ovulatory shifts in female extra-pair attraction and male mate retention. *Evolution and Human Behavior, 27,* 247–258.

Pillsworth, E. G., Haselton, M. G., & Buss, D. M. (2004). Ovulatory shifts in female sexual desire. *Journal of Sex Research, 41,* 55–65.

Pinker, S. (1994). *The language instinct.* New York: Morrow.

Pinker, S. (1997). *How the mind works.* New York: Norton.

Pinker, S. (2002). *The blank slate: The modern denial of human nature.* New York: Viking.

Pinker, S., & Bloom, P. (1990). Natural language and natural selection. *Behavioral and Brain Sciences, 13,* 707–784.

Pinker, S., & Jackendoff, R. (2005). The faculty of language: What's special about it? *Cognition, 95,* 201–236.

Pitchford, I. (2001) The origins of violence: Is psychopathy an adaptation? *Human Nature Review, 1,* 28–36.

Place, S. S., Todd, P. M., Penke, L., & Asendorpf, J. B. (2010). Humans show mate copying after observing real mate choices. *Evolution and Human Behavior, 31,* 320–325.

Platek, S. M., Burch, R. L., Panyavin, I. S., Wasserman, B. H., & Gallup, G. G., Jr. (2002). Reactions to children's faces: Resemblance affects males more than females. *Evolution and Human Behavior, 23,* 159–166.

Platek, S. M., Keenan, J. P., & Mohamed, F. B. (2005). Sex differences in the neural correlates of child facial resemblance: An event-related fMRI study. *NeuroImage, 25,* 1336–1344.

Platek, S. M., Keenan, J. P., & Shackelford, T. K. (2007). *Evolutionary cognitive neuroscience.* Cambridge, MA: MIT Press.

Platek, S. M., & Kemp, S. M. (2009). Is family special in the brain? An event-related fMRI study of familiar, familial, and self-face recognition. *Neuropsychologia, 47,* 849–858.

Platek, S. M., Raines, D. M., Gallup, G. G., Jr., Mohamed, F. B., Thompson, J. W. et al. (2004). Reactions to children's faces: Males are more affected by resemblance than females are, and so are their brains. *Evolution and Human Behavior, 25,* 394–405.

Platek, S. M., & Singh, D. (2010). Optimal waist-to-hip ratios in women active neural reward centers in men. *PLoS ONE, 5,* 1–5.

Platts, J. T. (1960). *A dictionary of Urdu, Classical Hindi, and English.* Oxford: Oxford University Press.

Plomin, R., DeFries, J. C., & McClearn, G. E. (1997). *Behavioral genetics: A primer* (3rd ed.). New York: Freeman.

Plourde, A. M. (2008). The origins of prestige goods as honest signals of skill and knowledge. *Human Nature, 19,* 374–388.

Pollet, T. V. (2007). Genetic relatedness and sibling relationship characteristics in a modern society. *Evolution and Human Behavior, 28,* 176–185.

Pollet, T. V., Fawcett, T. W., Buunk, A., & Nettle, D. (2009). Sex-ratio biasing toward daughters among lower-ranking co-wives in Rwanda. *Biology Letters, 5,* 765–768.

Pollet, T. V., Kuppens, T., & Dunbar, R. I. M. (2006). When nieces and nephews become important: Differences between childless women and mothers in relationships with nieces and nephews. *Journal of Cultural and Evolutionary Psychology, 4,* 83–94.

Pollet, T. V., & Nettle, D. (2007). Driving a hard bargain: Sex ratio and male marriage success in a historical US population. *Biology Letters.* doi:10. 1098/rsbl.2007.0543.

Pollet, T. V., Nettle, D., & Nelissen, M. (2007). Maternal grandmothers do go the extra mile: Factoring distance and lineage into differential contact with grandchildren. *Evolutionary Psychology, 5,* 832–843.

Poore, J. C., Haselton, M. G., von Hippel, W., & Buss, D. M. (2005). *Sexual regret.* Paper presented to the Annual Meeting of the Society of Personality and Social Psychologists. New Orleans, January.

Porter, R. H., Balogh, R. D., Cernoch, J. M., & Franchi, C. (1986). Recognition of kin through characteristic body odors. *Chemical Senses, 11,* 389–395.

Posner, R. A. (1992). *Sex and reason.* Cambridge, MA: Harvard University Press.

Pradel, J., Euler, H. A., & Fetchenhauer, D. (2009). Spotting altruistic dictator game players and mingling with them: The elective assortation of classmates. *Evolution and Human Behavior, 30,* 103–113.

Pratto, F. (1996). Sexual politics: The gender gap in the bedroom, the cupboard, and the cabinet. In D. M. Buss & N. M. Malamuth (Eds.), *Sex, power, conflict: Evolutionary and feminist perspectives* (pp. 179–230). New York: Oxford University Press.

Pratto, F., Sidanius, J.,& Stallworth, L. M. (1993). Sexual selection and the sexual and ethnic basis of social hierarchy. In L. Ellis (Ed.), *Social stratification and socioeconomic inequality* (pp. 111–137). Westport, CT: Praeger.

Premack, D. (2010). Why humans are unique: Three theories. *Perspectives on Psychological Science, 5,* 22–32.

Price, J. S., Gardner, R., Jr., Wilson, D. R., Sloman, L., Rohde, P., & Erikson, M. (2007). Territory, rank and mental health: The history of an idea. *Evolutionary Psychology, 5,* 531–534.

Price, J. S., & Sloman, L. (1987). Depression as yielding behavior: An animal model based on Schjelderup-Ebb's pecking order. *Ethology and Sociobiology, 8,* 85–98.

Price, M. E. (2005). Punitive sentiment among the Shuar and in industrialized societies: Cross-cultural similarities. *Evolution and Human Behavior, 26,* 279–287.

Price, M. E., Cosmides, L., & Tooby, J. (2002). Punitive sentiment as an anti-free rider psychological device. *Evolution and Human Behavior, 23,* 203–231.

Profet, M. (1992). Pregnancy sickness as adaptation: A deterrent to maternal ingestion of teratogens. In J. Barkow, L. Cosmides, & J. Tooby (Eds.), *The adapted mind* (pp. 327–366). New York: Oxford University Press.

Prokosch, M. D., Coss, R. G., Scheib, J. E., & Blozis, S. A. (2009). Intelligence and mate choice: Intelligent men are always appealing. *Evolution and Human Behavior, 30,* 11–20.

Provost, M. P., Kormos, C, Kosakoski, G., & Quinsey, V. L. (2006). Sociosexuality in women and preference for masculinization and somatotype in men. *Archives of Sexual Behavior, 35,* 305–312.

Puts, D. A. (2005). Mating context and menstrual phase affect women's preferences for male voice pitch. *Evolution and Human Behavior, 26,* 388–397.

Puts, D. A. (2010). Beauty and the beast: Mechanisms of sexual selection in humans. *Evolution and Human Behavior, 31,* 157–175.

Puts, D. A., Gaulin, S. J. C., & Verdolini, K. (2006). Dominance and the evolution of sexual dimorphism in human voice pitch. *Evolution and Human Behavior, 27,* 283–296.

Quinlan, R. J., Quinlan, M. B., & Flinn, M. V. (2003). Parental investment and age at weaning in a Caribbean village. *Evolution and Human Behavior, 24,* 1–16.

Quinsey, V. L., & Lalumiere, M. L. (1995). Evolutionary perspectives on sexual offending. *Sexual Abuse: A Journal of Research and Treatment, 7,* 301–315.

Ragsdale, G. (2004). Grandmothering in Cambridgeshire, 1770–1861. *Human Nature, 15,* 301–317.

Rahman, Q., Collins, A., Morrison, M., Orrells, J. C., Cadinouche, K., Greenfield, S., & Begum, S. (2008). Maternal inheritance and familial fecundity factors in male homosexuality. *Archives of Sexual Behavior, 37,* 962–969.

Rahman, Q., & Hull, M. S. (2005). An empirical test of the kin selection hypothesis of male homosexuality. *Archives of Sexual Behavior, 34,* 461–467.

Rakison, D. H. (2009). Does women's greater fear of snakes and spiders originate in infancy? *Evolution and Human Behavior, 30,* 438–444.

Rakison, D. H., & Derringer, J. (2007). *Do infants possess an evolved spider-detection mechanism?* Department of Psychology, Carnegie Mellon University, Pittsburgh, PA.

Ramson, W. S. (1988). *Australian national dictionary.* Melbourne: Oxford University Press.

Regalski, J. M., & Gaulin, S. J. C. (1993). Whom are Mexican infants said to resemble? Monitoring and fostering paternal confidence in the Yucatan. *Ethology and Sociobiology, 14,* 97–113.

Regan, P. C. (1998). Minimum mate selection standards as a function of perceived mate value, relationship context, and gender. *Journal of Psychology and Human Sexuality, 10,* 53–73.

Regan, P. C., & Atkins, L. (2006). Sex differences and similarities in frequency and intensity of sexual desire. *Social Behavior and Personality, 34,* 95–102.

Relethford, J. H. (1998). Genetics of modern human origins and diversity. *Annual Review of Anthropology, 27,* 1–23.

Rhodes, G. (2006). The evolutionary psychology of facial beauty. *Annual Review of Psychology, 57,* 199–226.

Rhodes, G., Simmons, L. W., & Peters, M. (2005). Attractiveness and sexual behavior: Does attractiveness enhance mating success? *Evolution and Human Behavior, 26,* 186–201.

Richardson, P. J., & Boyd, R. (2005). *Not by genes alone: How culture transformed human evolution.* Chicago: University of Chicago Press.

Ridley, M. (1996). *Evolution* (2nd ed.). Cambridge, MA: Blackwell Science.

Rilling, J. K., Kaufman, T. L., Smith, E. O., Patel, R., & Worthman, C. M. (2009). Abdominal depth and waist circumference as individual determinants of human female attractiveness. *Evolution and Human Behavior, 30,* 21–31.

Roberts, G. (2008). Language and the free-rider problem: An experimental paradigm. *Biological Theory, 3,* 174–183.

Roberts, S. C., Havlicek, J., Flegr, J., Hruskova, M., Little, A. C., Jones, B. C., Perrett, D. I., & Petrie, M. (2004). Female facial attractiveness increases during the fertile phase of the menstrual cycle. *Proceedings of the Royal Society of London, B* (Supplement), S1–S3.

Roder, S., Brewer, G., & Fink, B. (2009). Menstrual cycle shifts in women's self-perception and motivation: A daily report method. *Personality and Individual Differences, 47,* 616–619.

Rodriguez-Llanes, J. M., Verbeke, G., & Finlayson, C. (2009). Reproductive benefits of high social status in male macaques (*Macaca*). *Animal Behaviour, 78,* 643–649.

Roese, N. J., Pennington, G. L., Coleman, J., Janicki, M., Li, N. P., & Kenrick, D. T. (2006). Sex differences in regret: All for love or some for lust? *Personality and Social Psychology Bulletin, 32,* 770–780.

Ronay, R., & von Hippel, W. (2010). The presence of an attractive woman elevates testosterone and physical risk taking in young men. *Social Psychological and Personality Science, 1,* 57–64.

Roney, J. R. (2003). Effects of visual exposure to the opposite sex: Cognitive aspects of mate attraction in human males. *Personality and Social Psychology Bulletin, 29,* 393–404.

Roney, J. R., Hanson, K. N., Durante, K. M., & Maestripieri, D. (2006). Reading men's faces: Women's mate attractiveness judgments track men's testosterone and interest in infants. *Proceedings of the Royal Society, B, 273,* 2169–2175.

Roney, J. R., Mahler, S. V., & Maestripieri, D. (2003). Behavioral and hormonal responses of men to brief interactions with women. *Evolution and Human Behavior, 24,* 365–375.

Roney, J. R., Simmons, Z. L., & Lukaszewski, A. W. (2010). Androgen receptor genes sequence and basal cortisol concentrations predict men's hormonal responses to potential mates. *Proceedings of the Royal Society, B, 277,* 57–63.

Rosenblatt, P. C. (1974). Cross-cultural perspectives on attractiveness. In T. L. Huston (Ed.), *Foundations of interpersonal attraction* (pp. 79–95). New York: Academic Press.

Røskaft, E., Hagen, M. L., Hagen, T. L., & Moksnes, A. (2004). Patterns of outdoor recreation activities among Norwegians: An evolutionary approach. *Ann. Zool. Fennici, 41,* 609–618.

Røskaft, E., Wara, A., & Viken, A. (1992). Reproductive success in relation to resource-access and parental age in a small Norwegian farming parish during the period 1700–1900. *Ethology and Sociobiology, 13,* 443–461.

Ross, L. (1981). The "intuitive scientist" formulation and its developmental implications. In J. H. Flavell & L. Ross (Eds.),*Social cognitive development* (pp. 1–41). Cambridge, UK: Cambridge University Press.

Rotundo, M., Nguyen, D.-H., & Sackett, P. R. (2001). A meta-analytic review of gender differences in perceptions of harassment. *Journal of Applied Psychology, 86,* 914–922.

Rowe, D. C. (1995). Evolution, mating effort, and crime. *Behavioral and Brain Sciences, 18,* 573–574.

Rozin, P. (1976). The selection of food by rats, humans and other animals. In J. Rosenblatt, R. A. Hinde, & E. Shaw (Eds.), *Advances in the study of behavior: Vol. 6* (pp. 21–76). New York: Academic Press.

Rozin, P. (1996). Towards a psychology of food and eating: From motivation to module to model to marker, morality, meaning and metaphor. *Current Directions in Psychological Science, 5,* 18–24.

Rozin, P., & Fallon, A. (1988). Body image, attitudes to weight, and misperceptions of figure preferences of the opposite sex: A comparison of men and women in two generations. *Journal of Abnormal Psychology, 97,* 342–345.

Rozin, P., & Nemeroff, C. (1990). The laws of sympathetic magic. In J. Stigler, R. Shweder, & G. Herdt (Eds.), *Cultural psychology* (pp. 205–232). Cambridge, UK: Cambridge University Press.

Rozin, P., & Schull, J. (1988). The adaptive-evolutionary point of view in experimental psychology. In R. C. Atkinson, R. J. Herrnstein, G. Lindzey, & R. D. Luce (Eds.), *Stevens'handbook of experimental psychology: Vol. 1. Perception and motivation* (2nd ed., pp. 503–546). New York: Wiley.

Rubin, P. H. (2000). Hierarchy. *Human Nature, 11,* 259–279.

Ruso, B., Renninger, L., & Atzwanger, K. (2003). Human habitat preferences: A generative territory for evolutionary aesthetics research. In E. Voland & K. Grammer (Eds.), *Evolutionary aesthetics* (pp. 279–294). Berlin: Springer Verlag.

Rushton, J. P. (1985). Differential K theory: The sociobiology of individual and group differences. *Personality and Individual Differences, 6,* 441–452.

Saad, G. (2007a). Suicide triggers as sex-specific threats in domains of evolutionary import. *Medical Hypotheses, 68,* 692–696.

Saad, G. (2007b). *The evolutionary bases of consumption.* Mahwah, NJ: Erlbaum.

Saad, G. (2008). Advertised waist-to-hip ratios of online female escorts: An evolutionary perspective. *International Journal of e-Collaboration, 4,* 40–50.

Saad, G., & Gill, T. (2001). Sex differences in the ultimatum game: An evolutionary psychological perspective. *Journal of Bioeconomics, 3,* 171–194.

Safilios-Rothschild, C. (1969). Attitudes of Greek spouses toward marital infidelity. In G. Neubeck (Ed.), *Extramarital relations* (pp. 78–79). Englewood Cliffs, NJ: Prentice-Hall.

Sagarin, B. J. (2005). Reconsidering evolved sex differences in jealousy: Comment on Harris (2003). *Personality and Social Psychology Review, 9,* 62–75.

Salmon, C. (2003). Birth order and relationships: Family, friends, and sexual partners. *Human Nature, 14,* 73–88.

Salmon, C., Crawford, C., Dane, L., & Zuberbier, O. (2008). Ancestral mechanisms in modern environments: Impact of competition and stressors on body image and dieting behavior. *Human Nature, 19,* 103–117.

Salmon, C. A. (1999). On the impact of sex and birth order on contact with kin. *Human Nature, 10,* 183–197.

Salmon, C. A., & Daly, M. (1998). Birth order and familial sentiment: Middleborns are different. *Evolution and Human Behavior, 19,* 299–312.

Salovey, P., & Rodin, J. (1984). Some antecedents and consequences of social-comparison jealousy. *Journal of Personality and Social Psychology, 47,* 780–792.

Salter, F., Grammer, K., & Rikowski, A. (2005). Sex differences in negotiating with powerful males. *Human Nature, 16,* 306–321.

Scarr, S., & Salapatek, P. (1970). Patterns of fear development during infancy. *Merrill-Palmer Quarterly, 16,* 53–90.

Schaefer, K., Fink, B., Grammer, K., Mitteroecker, P., Gunz, P., & Bookstein, F. L. (2006). Female appearance: Facial and bodily attractiveness as shape. *Psychology Science, 48,* 187–205.

Schaller, M., Park, J. H., & Faulkner, J. (2003). Prehistoric dangers and contemporary prejudices. *European Review of Social Psychology, 14,* 105–137.

Schaller, M., Simpson, J. A., & Kenrick, D. T. (2006). *Evolution and social psychology.* New York: Psychology Press.

Scheib, J. E. (1997, June). *Context-specific mate choice criteria: Women's trade-offs in the contexts of long-term and extra-pair mateships.* Paper presented to the Annual Meeting of the Human Behavior and Evolution Society, University of Arizona, Tucson, AZ.

Scheib, J. E. (2001). Context-specific mate choice criteria: Women's trade-offs in the contexts of long-term and extra-pair mateships. *Personal Relationships, 8,* 371–389.

Schlager, D. (1995). Evolutionary perspectives on paranoid disorder. *The Psychiatric Clinics of North America, 18,* 263–279.

Schlomer, G. L., Ellis, B. J., & Garber, J. (2010). Mother-child conflict and sibling relatedness: A test of hypotheses from parent-offspring conflict theory. *Journal of Research on Adolescence, 20,* 287–306.

Schmalt, H. D. (2006). Waist-to-hip ratio and female physical attractiveness: The moderating role of power motivation and the mating context. *Personality and Individual Differences, 41,* 455–465.

Schmitt, A., & Atzwanger, K. (1995). Walking fast—ranking high: A sociobiological perspective on pace. *Evolution and Human Behavior, 16,* 451–462.

Schmitt, D. P. (2005). Sociosexuality from Argentina to Zimbabwe: A 48-nation study of sex, culture, and strategies of human mating. *Behavioral and Brain Sciences, 28,* 247–311.

Schmitt, D. P. (2008). Research methods in evolutionary psychology. In C. Crawford & D. Krebs (Eds.), *Foundations of evolutionary psychology: Ideas, issues, and applications (pp. 213–235).* Mahwah, NJ: Lawrence Erlbaum.

Schmitt, D. P. and 118 members of the International Sexuality Description Project. (2003). Universal sex differences in the desire for sexual variety: Tests from 52 nations, 6 continents, and 13 islands. *Journal of Personality and Social Psychology, 85,* 85–104.

Schmitt, D. P. and 121 members of the International Sexuality Description Project. (2004). Patterns and universals of mate poaching across 53 nations: The effects of sex, culture, and personality on romantically attracting another person's partner. *Journal of Personality and Social Psychology, 86,* 560–584.

Schmitt, D. P., & Buss, D. M. (1996). Strategic self-promotion and competitor derogation: Sex and context effects on perceived effectiveness of mate attraction tactics. *Journal of Personality and Social Psychology, 70,* 1185–1204.

Schmitt, D. P., & Buss, D. M. (2001). Human mate poaching: Tactics and temptations for infiltrating existing relationships. *Journal of Personality and Social Psychology, 80,* 894–917.

Schmitt, D. P., Couden, A., & Baker, M. (2001). The effects of sex and temporal context on feelings of romantic desire: An experimental evaluation of sexual strategies theory. *Personality and Social Psychology Bulletin, 27,* 833–847.

Schmitt, D. P., & Shackelford, T. K. (2008). Big five traits related to short-term mating: From personality to promiscuity across 46 nations. *Evolutionary Psychology, 6,* 246–282.

Schmitt, D. P., Shackelford, T. K., & Buss, D. M. (2001). Are men really more "oriented" toward short-term mating than women? *Psychology, Evolution, & Gender, 3,* 211–239.

Schmitt, D. P., Youn, G., Bond, B., Brooks, S., Frye, H., et al. (2009). When will I feel love? The effects of culture, personality, and gender on the psychological tendency to love. *Journal of Research in Personality, 43,* 830–846.

Schützwohl, A. (2004). Which infidelity type makes you more jealous? Decision strategies in a forced-choice between sexual and emotional infidelity. *Evolutionary Psychology, 2,* 121–128.

Schützwohl, A. (2006). Sex differences in jealousy: Information search and cognitive preoccupation. *Personality and Individual Differences, 40,* 285–292.

Schützwohl, A. (2008). Relief over the disconfirmation of the prospect of sexual and emotional infidelity. *Personality and Individual Differences, 44,* 666–676.

Schützwohl, A., Fuchs, A., McKibben, W. F., & Shackelford, T. K. (2009). How willing are you to accept sexual requests from slightly unattractive to exceptionally attractive imagined requestors? *Human Nature, 20,* 282–293.

Schützwohl, A., & Koch, S. (2004). Sex differences in jealousy: The recall of cues to sexual and emotional infidelity in personally more and less threatening conditions. *Evolution and Human Behavior, 25,* 249–257.

Scott, P. D. (1973). Fatal battered baby cases. *Medicine, Science, and the Law, 13,* 120–126.

Scott-Phillips, T. C. (2007). The social evolution of language, and the language of social evolution. *Evolutionary Psychology, 5,* 740–753.

Sear, R. (2008). Kin and child survival in rural Malawi: Are matrilineal kin always beneficial in a matrilineal society? *Human Nature, 19,* 277–293.

Sear, R., & Mace, R. (2008). Who keeps children alive? A review of the effects of kin on child survival. *Evolution and Human Behavior, 29,* 1–18.

Segal, N. (2011). Twin, adoption, and family methods as approached to the evolution of individual differences. In D. M. Buss & P. Hawley (Eds.), *The evolution of personality and individual differences.* New York: Oxford University Press.

Segal, N. L., Weisfeld, G. E., & Weisfeld, C. C. (1997). *Uniting psychology and biology: Integrative perspectives on human development.* Washington, DC: American Psychological Association.

Segal, N. L., Wilson, S. M., Bouchard, T. J., & Gitlin, D. G. (1995). Comparative grief experiences of bereaved twins and other bereaved relatives. *Personality and Individual Differences, 18,* 511–524.

Seligman, M., & Hager, J. (1972). *Biological boundaries of learning.* New York: Appleton-Century-Crofts.

Sesardic, N. (2003). Evolution of human jealousy: A just-so story or a just-so criticism? *Philosophy of the Social Sciences, 33,* 427–443.

Sell, A., Bryant, G. A., Cosmides, L., Tooby, J., Sznycer, D., von Rueden, C., Krauss, A., & Gurven, M. (2010). Adaptations in humans for assessing physical strength from the voice. *Proceedings of the Royal Society B.* doi:10.1098/rspb.2010.0769

Sell, A., Cosmides, L., Tooby, J., Sznycer, D., von Rueden, C., & Gurven, M. (2009). Human adaptations for the visual assessment of strength and fighting ability from the body and face. *Proceedings of the Royal Society B, 276,* 575–584.

Sell, A., Tooby, J., & Cosmides, L. (2009). Formidability and the logic of human anger. *Proceedings of the National Academy of Science, 106,* 15073–15078.

Shackelford, T. K., & Buss, D. M. (1996). Betrayal in mateships, friendships, and coalitions. *Personality and Social Psychology Bulletin, 22,* 1151–1164.

Shackelford, T. K., Buss, D. M., & Bennett, K. (2002). Forgiveness or breakup: Sex differences in responses to a partner's infidelity. *Cognition and Emotion, 16,* 299–307.

Shackelford, T. K., Buss, D. M., & Peters, J. (2000). Wife killing: Risk to women as a function of age. *Violence and Victims, 15,* 273–282.

Shackelford, T. K., Buss, D. M., & Weeks-Shackelford, V. (2003). Wife-killings committed in the context of a "lovers triangle." *Journal of Basic and Applied Social Psychology, 25,* 137–143.

Shackelford, T. K., Goetz, A. T., Buss, D. M., Euler, H. A., & Hoier, S. (2005). When we hurt the ones we love: Predicting violence against women from men's mate retention. *Personal Relationships, 12,* 447–463.

Shackelford, T. K., & Larsen, R. J. (1997). Facial asymmetry as indicator of psychological, emotional, and physiological distress. *Journal of Personality and Social Psychology, 72,* 456–466.

Shackelford, T. K., Michalski, R. L., & Schmitt, D. P. (2004). Upset in response to a child's partner's infidelities. *European Journal of Social Psychology, 34,* 489–497.

Shackelford, T. K., Voracek, M., Schmitt, D. P., Buss, D. M., Weekes-Shackelford, V. A., & Michalski, R. L. (2004). Romantic jealousy in early adulthood and later life. *Human Nature, 15,* 283–300.

Sheets, V. L., Fredendall, L. L., & Claypool, H. M. (1997). Jealousy evocation, partner reassurance, and relationship stability: An exploration of potential benefits of jealousy. *Evolution and Human Behavior, 18,* 387–402.

Shepard, R. N. (1992). The perceptual organization of colors: An adaptation to regularities of the terrestrial world? In J. Barkow, L. Cosmides, & J. Tooby (Eds.), *The adapted mind* (pp. 495–532). New York: Oxford University Press.

Shepher, J. (1971). Mate selection among second generation kibbutz adolescents and adults: Incest avoidance and negative imprinting. *Archives of Sexual Behavior, 1,* 293–307.

Sherman, P. W. (1977). Nepotism and the evolution of alarm calls. *Science, 197,* 1246–1253.

Sherman, P. W. (1981). Kinship, demography and Belding's ground squirrel nepotism. *Behavioral Ecology and Sociobiology, 8,* 251–259.

Sherman, P. W., & Flaxman, S. M. (2001). Protecting ourselves from food. *American Scientist, 89,* 142–151.

Sherman, P. W., & Hash, G. A. (2001). Why vegetable recipes are not very spicy. *Evolution and Human Behavior, 22,* 147–164.

Shinada, M., Yamagishi, T.,& Ohmura, Y. (2004). False friends are worse than bitter enemies: "Altruistic" punishment of in-group members. *Evolution and Human Behavior, 25,* 379–393.

Short, R. V. (1979). Sexual selection and its component parts, somatic and genital selection, as illustrated by man and great apes.*Advances in the Study of Behavior, 9,* 131–158.

Shostak, M. (1981). *Nisa: The life and words of a !Kung woman.* Cambridge, MA: Harvard University Press.

Silverman, I., & Choi, J. (2005). Locating places. In D. M. Buss (Ed.), *The handbook of evolutionary psychology* (pp. 177–199). New York: Wiley.

Silverman, I., Choi, J., Mackewn, A., Fisher, M., Moro, J., & Olshansky, E. (2000). Evolved mechanisms underlying wayfinding: Further studies on the hunter-gatherer theory of spatial sex differences. *Evolution and Human Behavior, 21,* 201–213.

Silverman, I., Choi, J., & Peters, M. (2007). On the universality of sex-related spatial competencies. *Archives of Human Sexuality, 36,* 261–268.

Silverman, I., & Eals, M. (1992). Sex differences in spatial abilities: Evolutionary theory and data. In J. H. Barkow, L. Cosmides, & J. Tooby (Eds.), *The adapted mind* (pp. 533–549). New York: Oxford University Press.

Silverman, I., & Phillips, K. (1998). The evolutionary psychology of spatial sex differences. In C. Crawford &

D. L. Krebs (Eds.), *Handbook of evolutionary psychology* (pp. 595–612). Mahwah, NJ: Erlbaum.

Simpson, G. G. (1944). *Tempo and mode in evolution.* New York: Columbia University Press.

Simpson, J. A., & Campbell, L. (2005). Methods of evolutionary sciences. In D. M. Buss (Ed.), *The handbook of evolutionary psychology* (pp. 119–144). New York: Wiley.

Simpson, J. A., & Weiner, W. S. C. (1989). *The Oxford English Dictionary* (2nd ed.). Oxford, UK: Clarendon Press.

Singer, T., Seymour, B., O'Doherty, J., Stephan, K. E., Dolan, R. J., & Frith, C. D. (2006). Empathic neural responses are modulated by the perceived fairness of others. *Nature, 439,* 466–469.

Singh, D. (1985). Evolutionary origins of the preference for alcohol. *Proceedings of the 34th International Congress on Alcoholism and Drug Dependence,* 273–276.

Singh, D. (1993). Adaptive significance of waist-to-hip ratio and female physical attractiveness. *Journal of Personality and Social Psychology, 65,* 293–307.

Singh, D. (2000). Waist-to-hip ratio: An indicator of female mate value. *International Research Center for Japanese Studies, International Symposium 16,* 79–99.

Singh, D., & Bronstad, P. M. (1997). Sex differences in the anatomical locations of human body scarification and tattooing as a function of pathogen prevalence. *Evolution and Human Behavior, 18,* 403–416.

Singh, D., & Bronstad, P. M. (2001). Female body odor is a potential cue to ovulation. *Proceedings of the Royal Academy of London, B, 268,* 797–801.

Singh, D., & Randall, P. K. (2007). Beauty is in the eye of the plastic surgeon: Waist-to-hip ratio (WHR) and women's attractiveness. *Personality and Individual Differences.*

Singh, D., & Young, R. K. (1995). Body weight, waist-to-hip ratio, breasts, and hips: Role in judgments of female attractiveness and desirability for relationships. *Ethology and Sociobiology, 16,* 483–507.

Singh, D., Vidaurri, M., Zambarano, R. J., & Dabbs, J. M. (1999). Lesbian erotic role identification: Behavioral, morphological, and hormonal correlates. *Journal of Personality and Social Psychology, 76,* 1035–1049.

Sloman, L., & Gilbert, P. (Eds.), (2000). *Subordination and defeat: An evolutionary approach to mood disorders and their therapy.* Mahwah, NJ: Erlbaum.

Smith, E. A. (2004). Why do good hunters have higher reproductive success? *Human Nature, 15,* 343–364.

Smith, M. S., Kish, B. J., & Crawford, C. B. (1987). Inheritance of wealth as human kin investment. *Ethology and Sociobiology, 8,* 171–182.

Smith, P. K. (1979). The ontogeny of fear in children. In W. Sluckin (Ed.), *Fear in animals and man* (pp. 164–168). London: Van Nostrand.

Smith, R. L. (1984). Human sperm competition. In R. L. Smith (Ed.), *Sperm competition and the evolution of mating systems* (pp. 601–659). New York: Academic Press.

Smuts, B. B. (1985). *Sex and friendship in baboons.* New York: Aldine de Gruyter.

Smuts, B. B. (1992). Men's aggression against women. *Human Nature, 6,* 1–32.

Smuts, B. B. (1995). The evolutionary origins of patriarchy. *Human Nature, 6,* 1–32.

Smuts, B. B., & Gubernick, D. J. (1992). Male-infant relationships in nonhuman primates: Paternal investment or mating effort? In B. S. Hewlett (Ed.), *Father–child relations: Cultural and bio-social contexts* (pp. 1–30). Hawthorne, NY: Aldine de Gruyter.

Sober, E., & Wilson, D. S. (1998). *Unto others: The evolution and psychology of unselfish behavior.* Cambridge, MA: Harvard University Press.

Sorokowski, P., & Pawlowski, B. (2008). Adaptive preferences for leg length in a potential partner. *Evolution and Human Behavior, 29,* 86–91.

Sperber, D., & Hirshfeld, L. (2004). The cognitive foundations of cultural stability and diversity. *Trends in Cognitive Science, 8,* 40–46.

Stanislaw, H., & Rice, F. J. (1988). Correlation between sexual desire and menstrual cycle characteristics. *Archives of Sexual Behavior, 17,* 499–508.

Starratt, V. G., Popp, D., & Shackelford, T. K. (2008). Not all men are sexually coercive: A preliminary investigation of the moderating effect of mate desirability on the relationship between female infidelity and male sexual coercion. *Personality and Individual Differences, 45,* 10–14.

Stearns, S. (1992). *The evolution of life histories.* New York: Oxford University Press.

Stephen, I. D. Coetzee, V., Smith, M. L., & Perrett, D. I. (2009). Skin blood perfusion and oxygenation colour affect perceived human health. *PLoS ONE, 4,* 1–7.

Sternberg, R. (1986). A triangular theory of love. *Psychological Review, 93,* 119–135.

Stevens, A., & Price, J. (1996). *Evolutionary Psychiatry.* London: Routledge.

Stevens, A., & Price, J. (2000). *Evolutionary psychiatry* (2nd ed.). London: Routledge.

Stevenson, R. J., Case, T. I., & Oaten, M. J. (2009). Frequency and recency of infection and their relationship with disgust and contamination sensitivity. *Evolution and Human Behavior, 30,* 363–368.

Stewart-Williams, S. (2008). Human beings as evolved nepotists: Exceptions to the rule and effects of costs of help. *Human Nature, 19,* 414–425.

Stillman, T. F., & Maner, J. K. (2009). A sharp eye for her SOI: Perception and misperception of female sociosexuality at zero acquaintance. *Evolution and Human Behavior, 30,* 124–130.

Stillman, T. F., Maner, J. K., & Baumeister, R. F. (2010). A thin slice of violence: Distinguishing violent from nonviolent sex offenders at a glance. *Evolution and Human Behavior, 31,* 298–303.

Stone, V. E., Cosmides, L., Tooby, J., Kroll, N., & Knight, R. T. (2002). Selective impairment of reasoning about social exchange in a patient with bilateral limbic system damage. *Proceedings of the National Academy of Sciences, 99,* 11531–11536.

Stoneking, M. (2003). Widespread prehistoric human cannibalism: Easier to swallow? *TRENDS in Ecology and Evolution, 18,* 489–490.

Strait, D. S., Grine, F. E., & Moniz, M. A. (1997). A reappraisal of early hominid phylogeny. *Journal of Human Evolution, 32,* 17–82.

Strassman, B. I. (1981). Sexual selection, parental care, and concealed ovulation in humans. *Ethology and Sociobiology, 2,* 31–40.

Stringer, C. (2002). *The evolution of modern humans: Where are we now?* London: The Natural History Museum.

Stringer, C., & McKie, R. (1996). *African exodus: The origins of modern humanity.* New York: Henry Holt.

Strout, S. L., Laird, J. D., Shafer, A., & Thompson, N. S. (2005). The effect of vividness of experience on sex differences in jealousy. *Evolutionary Psychology, 3,* 263–274.

Studd, M. V., & Gattiker, U. E. (1991). The evolutionary psychology of sexual harassment in organizations. *Ethology and Sociobiology, 12,* 249–290.

Sugiyama, L. (2004a). Is beauty in the context-sensitive adaptations of the beholder? Shiwiar use of waist-to-hip ratio in assessments of female mate value. *Evolution and Human Behavior, 25,* 51–62.

Sugiyama, L. (2004b). Does the occurrence and duration of health insults among Shiwiar foragerhorticulturalists indicate that health care provisioning reduces juvenile mortality? *Socioeconomic Aspects of Human Behavioral Ecology: Research in Economic Anthropology, 23,* 377–400.

Sugiyama, L. (2005). Physical attractiveness in adaptationist perspective. In D. M. Buss (Ed.), *The handbook of evolutionary psychology* (pp. 292–342). New York: Wiley.

Sugiyama, L. S., Tooby, J., & Cosmides, L. (2002). Cross-cultural evidence of cognitive adaptations for social exchange among the Shiwiar of Equadorian Amazonia. *Proceedings of the National Academy of Sciences, 99,* 11537–11542.

Sulloway, F. (1996). *Born to rebel.* New York: Pantheon.

Sulloway, F. (2011). Why siblings are like Darwin's finches: Birth order, sibling competition, and adaptive divergence within the family. In D. M. Buss & P. H. Hawley (Eds.), *The evolution of personality and individual differences.* New York: Oxford University Press.

Surbey, M. K. (1998a). Developmental psychology and modern Darwinism. In C. Crawford & D. Krebs (Eds.), *Handbook of evolutionary psychology* (pp. 369–403). Mahwah, NJ: Erlbaum.

Surbey, M. K. (1998b). Parent and offspring strategies in the transition to adolescence. *Human Nature, 9,* 67–94.

Surbey, M. K., & Conohan, C. D. (2000). Willingness to engage in casual sex: The role of parental qualities and perceived risk of aggression. *Human Nature, 11,* 367–386.

Swami, V., Einon, D., & Furnham, A. (2006). The leg-to-body ratio as a human aesthetic criterion. *Body Image, 3,* 317–323.

Swami, V., Frederick, D. A., Aavik, T., Alcalay, L., Allik, J., et al. (2010). The attractive female body weight and female body dissatisfaction in 26 countries across 10 world regions: Results of the International Body Project I. *Personality and Social Psychology Bulletin, 36,* 309–325.

Swami, V., Miller, R., Furnham, A., Penke, L., & Tovee, M. J. (2008). *Personality and Individual Differences, 44,* 98–107.

Symons, D. (1979). *The evolution of human sexuality.* New York: Oxford.

Symons, D. (1989). The psychology of human mate preferences. *Behavioral and Brain Sciences, 12,* 34–45.

Symons, D. (1992). On the use and misuse of Darwinism in the study of human behavior. In J. Barkow, L. Cosmides, & J. Tooby (Eds.), *The adapted mind* (pp. 137–159). New York: Oxford University Press.

Symons, D. (1993). How risky is sex? *The Journal of Sex Research, 30,* 344–346.

Symons, D. (1995). Beauty is in the adaptations of the beholder: The evolutionary psychology of human female sexual attractiveness. In P. R. Abramson & S. D. Pinkerton (Eds.), *Sexual nature, sexual culture* (pp. 80–118). Chicago: University of Chicago Press.

Tadinac, M., & Hromatko, I. (2007). Own mate value and relative importance of a potential mate's qualities. *Studia Psychologica, 49,* 251–263.

Takahashi, H., Matsuura, M., Yahata, N., Koeda, M., Suhara, T., & Okubo, Y. (2006). Men and women show distinct brain activations during imagery of sexual and emotional infidelity. *NeuroImage, 32,* 1299–1307.

Tanner, N. M. (1983). Hunters, gatherers, and sex roles in space and time. *American Anthropologist, 85,* 335–341.

Tanner, N. M., & Zihlman, A. (1976). Women in evolution part 1: Innovation and selection in human origins. *Signs: Women, Culture, and Society, 1,* 585–608.

Tattersall, I. (2000). Paleoanthropology: The last halfcentury. *Evolutionary Anthropology, 9,* 2–16.

Taylor, P. A., & Glenn, N. D. (1976). The utility of education and attractiveness for females' status attainment through marriage. *American Sociological Review, 41,* 484–498.

Taylor, S. E., Klein, L. C., Lewis, B. P., Gruenewald, T. L., Gurung, R. A. R., & Updegraff, J. A. (2000). Biobehavioral responses to stress in females: Tend-and-befriend, not fight-or-flight. *Psychological Review, 107,* 411–429.

Templeton, A. R. (2005). Haplotype trees and modern human origins. *Yearbook of Physical Anthropology, 48,* 33–59.

Templeton, A. R. (2007). Genetics and recent human evolution. *Evolution, 61*(7), 1507–1519.

ter Laak, J. J. F., Olthof, T., & Aleva, E. (2003). Sources of annoyance in close relationships: Sex-related differences in annoyance with partner behaviors. *The Journal of Psychology, 137,* 545–559.

Terpstra, D. E., & Cook, S. E. (1985). Complainant characteristics and reported behaviors and consequences associated with formal sexual harassment charges. *Personnel Psychology, 38,* 559–574.

Tessman, I. (1995). Human altruism as a courtship display. *Oikos, 74,* 157–158.

Thakerar, J. N., & Iwawaki, S. (1979). Cross-cultural comparisons in interpersonal attraction of females toward males. *Journal of Social Psychology, 108,* 121–122.

Thiessen, D. D. (1972). A move toward species-specific analysis in behavior genetics. *Behavior Genetics, 2,* 115–126.

Thompson, A. P. (1983). Extramarital sex: A review of the research literature. *Journal of Sex Research, 19,* 1–22.

Thompson, S. (1955). *Motif-index of folk-literature.* Vols. 1–6. Bloomington, IN: Indiana University Press.

Thomson, J. W., Patel, S., Platek, S. M., & Shackelford, T. K. (2007). Sex differences in implicit association and attentional demands for information about infidelity. *Evolutionary Psychology, 5,* 569–583.

Thornhill, R. (1980). Rape in *Panorpa* scorpionflies and a general rape hypothesis. *Animal Behavior, 28,* 52–59.

Thornhill, R., & Gangestad, S. W. (2006). Facial sexual dimorphism, developmental stability, and susceptibility to disease in men and women. *Evolution and Human Behavior, 27,* 131–144.

Thornhill, R., & Møeller, A. P. (1997). Developmental stability, disease, and medicine. *Biological Review, 72,* 497–548.

Thornhill, R., & Palmer, C. (2000). *A natural history of rape: Biological bases of sexual coercion.* Cambridge, MA: MIT Press.

Thornhill, R., & Thornhill, N. (1983). Human rape: An evolutionary perspective. *Ethology and Sociobiology, 4,* 137–173.

Thornhill, R., & Thornhill, N. (1992). The evolutionary psychology of men's coercive sexuality. *Behavioral and Brain Sciences, 15,* 363–421.

Tierson, F. D., Olsen, C. L., & Hook, E. B. (1985). Influence of cravings and aversions on diet in pregnancy. *Ecology of Food and Nutrition, 17,* 117–129.

Tierson, F. D., Olsen, C. L., & Hook, E. B. (1986). Nausea and vomiting of pregnancy and association with pregnancy outcome. *American Journal of Obstetrics and Gynecology, 155,* 1017–1022.

Tiger, L. (1975). *Women in the Kibbutz.* New York: Harcourt, Brace, Janovich.

Tiger, L. (1996). My life in the human nature wars. *The Wilson Quarterly, 20,* 14–25.

Tiger, L., & Fox, R. (1971). *The imperial animal.* New York: Holt, Rinehart, & Winston.

Tinbergen, N. (1951). *The study of instinct.* New York: Oxford University Press.

Tinbergen, N. (1963). The shell menace. *Natural History, 72,* 28–35.

Tither, J. M., & Ellis, B. J. (2008). Impact of fathers on daughters' age of menarche: A genetically and environmentally controlled sibling study. *Developmental Psychology, 44,* 1409–1420.

Todd, P. M., Hertwig, R., & Hoffrage, U. (2005). Evolutionary cognitive psychology. In D. M. Buss (Ed.), *The handbook of evolutionary psychology* (pp. 776–802). New York: Wiley.

Todd, P. M., Penke, L., Fasolo, B., & Lenton, A. P. (2007). Different cognitive processes underlie human mate choice and mate preferences. *PNAS, 104,* 15011–15016.

Todosijevic, B., Ljubinkovic, S., & Arancic, A. (2003). Mate selection criteria: A trait desirability assessment study of sex differences in Serbia. *Evolutionary Psychology, 1,* 116–126.

Toma, C. L., Hancock, J. T., & Ellison, N. B. (2008). Separating fact from fiction: An examination of deceptive self-presentation in online dating profiles. *Personality and Social Psychology Bulletin, 34,* 1023–1036.

Tooby, J., & Cosmides, L. (1988). *The evolution of war and its cognitive foundations.* Institute for Evolutionary Studies, Technical Report #88-1.

Tooby, J., & Cosmides, L. (1990). On the universality of human nature and the uniqueness of the individual: The role of genetics and adaptation. *Journal of Personality, 58,* 17–68.

Tooby, J., & Cosmides, L. (1992). Psychological foundations of culture. In J. Barkow, L. Cosmides, & J. Tooby (Eds.), *The adapted mind* (pp. 19–136). New York: Oxford University Press.

Tooby, J., & Cosmides, L. (1996). Friendship and the banker's paradox: Other pathways to the evolution of adaptations for altruism. *Proceedings of the British Academy, 88,* 119–143.

Tooby, J., & Cosmides, L. (1998). *Ecological rationality and the multimodular mind: Grounding normative theories in adaptive problems.* Unpublished manuscript, University of California, Santa Barbara.

Tooby, J., & Cosmides, L. (2005). Conceptual foundations of evolutionary psychology. In D. M. Buss (Ed.), *The handbook of evolutionary psychology* (pp. 5–67). New York: Wiley.

Tooby, J., and Cosmides, L. (2010). Groups in mind: The coalitional roots of war and morality. In H. Høgh-Olesen (Ed.), *Human morality and sociality: Evolutionary and comparative perspectives.* New York: Palgrave MacMillan.

Tooby, J., Cosmides, L., & Price, M. E. (2006). Cognitive adaptations for n-person exchange: The evolutionary roots of organizational behavior. *Managerial and Decision Economics, 27,* 103–129.

Tooby, J., & DeVore, I. (1987). The reconstruction of hominid behavioral evolution through strategic modeling. In W. G. Kinzey (Ed.), *The evolution of human behavior* (pp. 183–237). New York: State University of New York Press.

Tooke, W., & Camire, L. (1991). Patterns of deception in intersexual and intrasexual mating strategies. *Ethology and Sociobiology, 12,* 345–364.

Tooley, G. A., Karakis, M., Stokes, M., & Ozanne-Smith, J. (2006). Generalising the Cinderella effect to unintentional childhood fatalities. *Evolution and Human Behavior, 27,* 224–230.

Townsend, J. M. (1998). *What women want—what men want: Why the sexes still see love and commitment so differently.* New York: Oxford University Press.

Townsend, J. M., & Wasserman, T. (1998). Sexual attractiveness: Sex differences in assessment criteria. *Evolution and Human Behavior, 19,* 171–191.

Trinkaus, E., & Zimmerman, M. R. (1982). Trauma among the Shanidar Neandertals. *American Journal of Physical Anthropology, 57,* 61–76.

Trivers, R. (1974). Parent–offspring conflict. *American Zoologist, 14,* 249–264.

Trivers, R. (1985). *Social evolution.* Menlo Park, CA: Benjamin/Cummings.

Trivers, R. L. (1971). The evolution of reciprocal altruism. *Quarterly Review of Biology, 46,* 35–57.

Trivers, R. L. (1972). Parental investment and sexual selection. In B. Campbell (Ed.), *Sexual selection and the descent of man: 1871–1971* (pp. 136–179). Chicago: Aldine.

Trivers, R. L., & Willard, D. E. (1973). Natural selection of parental ability to vary the sex ratio of offspring. *Science, 179,* 90–92.

Tversky, A., & Kahneman, D. (1974). Judgment under uncertainty: Heuristics and biases. *Science, 185,* 1124–1131.

Tyber, J. M., Lieberman, D., & Griskevicius, V. (2009). Microbes, mating, and morality: Individual differences in three functional domains of disgust. *Journal of Personality and Social Psychology, 97,* 103–122.

U.S. Census Bureau. (1978). 1976 survey of institutionalized persons: A study of persons receiving long-term care. *Current population reports.* (Special Studies Series P-23, No. 69). Washington, DC: U.S. Government Printing Office.

Udry, J. R., & Eckland, B. K. (1984). Benefits of being attractive: Differential payoffs for men and women. *Psychological Reports, 54,* 47–56.

Ulijaszek, S. J. (2002). Human eating behaviour in an evolutionary ecological context. *Proceedings of the Nutrition Society, 61,* 517–526.

Ulrich, R. (1983). Aesthetic and affective response to natural environment. In I. Altman & J. F. Wohlwill (Eds.), *Behavior and the natural environment* (pp. 85–125). New York: Plenum.

Ulrich, R. (1984). View through a window may influence recovery from surgery. *Science, 224,* 420–421.

Ulrich, R. (1986). Human response to vegetation and landscapes. *Landscape and Urban Planning, 13,* 29–44.

Van Anders, S. M., Hamilton, L. D., & Watson, N. V. (2007). Multiple partners are associated with higher testosterone in North American men and women. *Hormones and Behavior, 51,* 454–459.

van den Berghe,, Q., , P. L., & Frost, P. (1986). Skin color preference, sexual dimorphism and sexual selection: A case of gene culture coevolution. *Ethnic and Racial Studies, 9,* 87–113.

van der Dennen, J. M. G. (1995). *The origin of war* (Vols. 1 & 2). Groningen, The Netherlands: Origin Press.

van der Linde, I., Rajashekar, U., Bovik, A. C., & Cormack, L. K. (2009). Visual memory for fixated regions of natural scenes dissociates attraction and recognition. *Perception, 38,* 1152–1171.

van Gulik, R. H. (1974). *Sexual life in ancient China.* London: E. J. Brill.

van Vugt, M., & van Lange, P. A. M. (2006). The altruism puzzle: Psychological adaptations for prosocial behavior. In M. Schaller, J. A. Simpson, & D. T. Kenrick (Eds.), *Evolution and social psychology* (pp. 237–262). New York: Psychology Press.

van Vugt, M. (2006). The evolutionary origins of leadership and followership. *Personality and Social Psychology Review, 10,* 354–372.

van Vugt, M. (2009). Sex differences in intergroup aggression and violence: The male warrior hypothesis. *Annals of the New York Academy of Sciences, 1167,* 124–134.

van Vugt, M., & Hardy, C. L. (2009). Cooperation through competition: Conspicuous contributions as costly signals in public goods. *Group Processes & Intergroup Relations,* 1–11.

van Vugt, M., Hogan, R., & Kaiser, R. B. (2008). Leadership, followership, and evolution: Some lessons from the past. *American Psychologist, 63,* 182–196.

Vanneste, S., Verplaetse, J., Van Hiel, A., & Braeckman, J. (2007). Attention bias toward noncooperative people: A dot probe classification study in cheating detection. *Evolution and Human Behavior, 28,* 272–276.

Vasey, P. L., & VanderLaan, D. P. (2010). Avuncular tendencies and the evolution of male androphilia in *Fa'afafine. Archives of Sexual Behavior, 39,* 821–830.

Vayda, A. P. (1961). A re-examination of Northwest Coast economic systems. *Transactions of the New York Academy of Sciences, (Series 2), 23,* 618–624.

Vigil, J. M. (2007). Asymmetries in the friendship preferences and social styles of men and women. *Human Nature, 18,* 143–161.

Vigil, J. M., Geary, D. C., & Byrd-Craven, J. (2005). A life history assessment of early childhood sexual abuse in women. *Developmental Psychology, 41,* 553–561.

Voland, E., & Engel, C. (1990). Female choice in humans: A conditional mate selection strategy of the Krummerhörn women (Germany 1720–1874). *Ethology, 84,* 144–154.

von Rueden, C., Gurven, M., & Kaplan, H. (2008). The multiple dimensions of male social status in an Amazonian society. *Evolution and Human Behavior, 29,* 402–415.

Voyer, B., Postma, A., Brake, B., & Imperato-McGinley, J. (2007). Gender differences in object location memory: A meta-analysis. *Psychonomic Bulletin & Review, 14,* 23–38.

Wade, N. (1997, June 24). Dainty worm tells secrets on the human genetic code. *New York Times,* p. B9.

Wade, T. J., Auer, G., & Roth, T. M. (2009). What is love: Further investigation of love acts. *Journal of Social, Evolutionary, and Cultural Psychology, 3,* 290–304.

Wakefield, J. C. (1992). The concept of mental disorder: On the boundary between biological facts and social values. *American Psychologist, 47,* 373–388.

Walker, P. (1995). *Documenting patterns of violence in earlier societies: The problems and promise of using bioarchaeological data for testing evolutionary theories.* Paper presented at the Annual Conference of the Human Behavior and Evolution Society, Santa Barbara, CA: July 2.

Walker, P. L. (2001). A bioarcheological perspective on the history of violence. *Annual Review of Anthropology, 30,* 573–596.

Wallace, A. R. (1858). On the tendency of varieties to depart indefinitely from the original type. *Journal of the Proceedings of the Linnean Society (Zoology), 3,* 53–62.

Waller, A. L. (1993). The Hatfield-McCoy feud. In W. Graebner (Ed.), *True stories from the American past* (pp. 35–54). New York: McGraw-Hill.

Walsh, A. (1995). Parental attachment, drug use, and facultative sexual strategies. *Social Biology, 42,* 95–107.

Walsh, A. (1999). Life history theory and female readers of pornography. *Personality and Individual Differences, 27,* 779–787.

Wang, X. T. (1996). Evoltuionary hypotheses of risk-sensitive choice: Age differences and perspective change. *Ethology and Sociobiology, 17,* 1–15.

Ward, J., & Voracek, M. (2004). Evolutionary and social cognitive explanations of sex differences in romantic jealousy. *Australian Journal of Psychology, 56,* 165–171.

Wason, P. (1966). Reasoning. In B. M. Foss (Ed.), *New horizons in psychology.* London: Penguin.

Watson, D., & Burlingame, A. W. (1960). *Therapy through horticulture.* New York: Macmillan.

Watson, J. B. (1924). *Behaviorism.* New York: Norton.

Watson, N. V. (2001). Sex differences in throwing: Monkeys having a fling. *Trends in Cognitive Science, 5,* 98–99.

Watson, P. J., & Andrews, P. W. (2002). Toward a revised evolutionary adaptationist analysis of depression: The social navigation hypothesis. *Journal of Affective Disorders, 72,* 1–14.

Waynforth, D. (2007). Mate choice copying in humans. *Human Nature, 18,* 264–271.

Waynforth, D., Delwadia, S., & Camm, M. (2005). The influence of women's mating strategies on preference for masculine facial architecture. *Evolution and Human Behavior, 26,* 409–416.

Waynforth, D., & Dunbar, R. I. M. (1995). Conditional mate choice strategies in humans: Evidence from "lonely hearts" advertisements. *Behaviour, 132,* 755–779.

Waynforth, D., Hurtado, A. M., & Hill, K. (1998). Environmentally contingent reproductive strategies in Mayan and Ache males. *Evolution and Human Behavior, 19,* 369–385.

Webster, G. D. (2008). The kinship, acceptance, and rejection model of altruism and aggression (KARMAA): Implications for interpersonal and intergroup aggression. *Group Dynamics, 12,* 27–38.

Webster, G. D., Bryan, A., Crawford, C. B., McCarthy, L., & Cohen, B. H. (2008). Lineage, sex, and wealth as moderators of kin investment. *Human Nature, 19,* 189–210.

Weeden, J., Abrams, M. J. K., Green, M. C., & Sabini, J. (2006). Do high status people really have fewer children? Education, income, and fertility in contemporary U.S. *Human Nature, 17,* 277–392.

Weinberg, E. D. (1984). Iron withholding: A defense against infection and neoplasia. *Physiological Review, 64,* 65–102.

Weisfeld, G. E (1997a). Puberty rites as clues to the nature of human adolescence. *Cross-Cultural Research, 31,* 27–54.

Weisfeld, G. E. (1997b). Discrete emotions theory with specific reference to pride and shame. In N. L. Segal, G. E. Weisfeld, & C. C. Weisfeld (Eds.), *Uniting psychology and biology* (pp. 419–443). Washington, DC: American Psychological Association.

Weisfeld, G. E., & Billings, R. (1988). Observations on adolescence. In K. B. MacDonald (Ed.), *Sociobiological perspectives on human development* (pp. 207–233). New York: Springer-Verlag.

Weisfeld, G. E., Czilli, T., Phillips, K. A., Gall, J. A., & Lichtman, C. M. (2003). Possible olfaction-based mechanisms in human kin recognition and inbreeding avoidance. *Journal of Experimental Child Psychology, 85,* 279–295.

Weiss, D. L., & Slosnerick, M. (1981). Attitudes toward sexual and nonsexual extramarital involvements among a sample of college students. *Journal of Marriage and the Family, 43,* 349–358.

Weissner, P. (1982). Risk, reciprocity and social influences on !Kung San economics. In E. Leacock & R. B. Lee (Eds.), *Politics and history in band societies.* Cambridge, UK: Cambridge University Press.

Wellman, H. (1990). *The child's theory of mind.* Cambridge, MA: MIT Press.

Wellman, H. H., Cross, D., & Watson, J. (2001). Meta-analysis of theory-of-mind development: The truth about false belief. *Child Development, 72,* 655–684.

West, S. A., Griffin, A. S., & Gardner, A. (2007). Social semantics: Altruism, cooperation, mutualism, strong reciprocity, and group selection. *European Society for Evolutionary Biology, 20,* 415–432.

White, G. L. (1980). Inducing jealousy: A power perspective. *Personality and Social Psychology Bulletin, 6,* 222–227.

White, R. E., Thornhill, S., & Hampson, E. (2006). Entrepreneurs and evolutionary biology: The relationship between testosterone and new venture creation. *Organization Behavior and Human Decision Processes, 100,* 21–34.

Whitehurst, R. N. (1971). Violence potential in extramarital sexual responses. *Journal of Marriage and the Family, 33,* 683–691.

Whiting, B., & Edwards, C. P. (1988). *Children of different worlds.* Cambridge, MA: Harvard University Press.

Whitty, M. T., & Quigley, L. -L. (2008). Emotional and sexual infidelity offline and in cyberspace. *Journal of Marriage and the Family, 34,* 461–468.

Wicker, F. W., Payne, G. C., & Morgan, R. D. (1983). Participant descriptions of guilt and shame. *Motivation and Emotion, 7,* 25–39.

Wiederman, M. W. (1993). Evolved gender differences in mate preferences: Evidence from personal advertisements. *Ethology and Sociobiology, 14,* 331–352.

Wiederman, M. W., & Allgeier, E. R. (1992). Gender differences in mate selection criteria: Sociobiological or socioeconomic explanation? *Ethology and Sociobiology, 13,* 115–124.

Wiederman, M. W., & Kendall, E. (1999). Evolution, sex, and jealousy: Investigation with a sample from Sweden. *Evolution and Human Behavior, 20,* 121–128.

Wiessner, P. (2002). Hunting, healing, and *hzaro* exchange: A long-term perspective on !Kung (Ju/'hoansi) large-game hunting. *Evolution and Human Behavior, 23,* 407–436.

Wilkinson, G. W. (1984). Reciprocal food sharing in the vampire bat. *Nature, 308,* 181–184.

Willerman, L. (1979). *The psychology of individual and group differences.* San Francisco: Freeman.

Willerman, L., Loehlin, J. C., & Horn, J. M. (1992). An adoption and a cross-fostering study of the Minnesota Multiphasic Personality Inventory (MMPI) Psychopathic Deviate scale. *Behavior Genetics, 22,* 515–529.

Williams, G. C. (1957). Pleiotropy, natural selection, and the evolution of senescence. *Evolution, 11,* 398–411.

Williams, G. C. (1966). *Adaptation and natural selection.* Princeton, NJ: Princeton University Press.

Williams, G. C. (1975). *Sex and evolution.* Princeton, NJ: Princeton University Press.

Williams, G. C. (1992). *Natural selection.* New York: Oxford University Press.

Williams, G. C., & Nesse, R. M. (1991). The dawn of Darwinian medicine. *Quarterly Review of Biology, 66,* 1–22.

Williams, K. D., Cheung, C. K. T., & Choi, W. (2000). Cyberostracism: Effects of being ignored over the internet.

*Journal of Personality and Social Psychology, 79,* 748–762.

Wilson, D. S. (1994). Adaptive genetic variation and human evolutionary psychology. *Ethology and Sociobiology, 15,* 219–235.

Wilson, D. S. (1995). Sociopathy within and between small groups. *Behavioral and Brain Sciences, 18,* 577.

Wilson, D. S. (1998). Game theory and human behavior. In L. A. Dugatkin & H. K. Reeve (Eds.), *Game theory and animal behavior* (pp. 261–282). New York: Oxford University Press.

Wilson, D. S. (2007). *Evolution for everyone: How Darwin's theory can change the way we think about our lives.* New York: Delacorte Press.

Wilson, D. S., & Sober, E. (1994). Reintroducing group selection to the human behavioral sciences. *Behavioral and Brain Sciences, 17,* 585–654.

Wilson, D. S., van Vugt, M., & O'Gorman, R. (2008). Multilevel selection theory and major evolutionary transitions: Implications for psychological science. *Current Directions in Psychological Science, 17,* 6–9.

Wilson, E. O. (1975). *Sociobiology: The new synthesis.* Cambridge, MA: Harvard University Press.

Wilson, E. O. (1998). *Consilience: The unity of knowledge.* New York: Knopf.

Wilson, G. D. (1987). Male–female differences in sexual activity, enjoyment, and fantasies. *Personality and Individual Differences, 8,* 125–126.

Wilson, G. D. (1997). Gender differences in sexual fantasy: An evolutionary analysis. *Personality and Individual Differences, 22,* 27–31.

Wilson, G. D., Cousins, J. M., & Fink, B. (2006). The CQ as a predictor of speed-date outcomes. *Sexual and Relationship Therapy, 21,* 163–169.

Wilson, K., Demetrioff, S., & Porter, S. (2008). A pawn by any other name? Social information processing as a function of psychopathic traits. *Journal of Research in Personality, 42,* 1651–1656.

Wilson, M., & Daly, M. (1985). Competitiveness, risktaking, and violence: The young male syndrome. *Ethology and Sociobiology, 6,* 59–73.

Wilson, M., & Daly, M. (1992). The man who mistook his wife for a chattel. In J. Barkow, L. Cosmides, & J. Tooby (Eds.), *The adapted mind: Evolutionary psychology and the generation of culture* (pp. 289–322). New York: Oxford University Press.

Wilson, M., & Daly, M. (1993). An evolutionary psychological perspective on male sexual proprietariness and violence against wives. *Violence and Victims, 8,* 271–294.

Wilson, M., & Daly, M. (1996). Male sexual proprietariness and violence against wives. *Current Directions in Psychological Science, 5,* 2–7.

Wilson, M., Johnson, H., & Daly, M. (1995). Lethal and nonlethal violence against wives. *Canadian Journal of Criminology, 37,* 331–361.

Wilson, M., & Mesnick, S. L. (1997). An empirical test of the bodyguard hypothesis. In P. A. Gowaty (Ed.), *Feminism and evolutionary biology: boundaries, intersections, and frontiers.* New York: Chapman & Hall.

Wilson, P. R. (1968). Perceptual distortion of height as a function of ascribed academic status. *Journal of Social Psychology, 74,* 97.

Wohlrab, S., Fink, B., Kappeler, P. M., & Brewer, G. (2009). Differences in personality attributions toward tattooed and nontattooed virtual human characters. *Journal of Individual Differences, 30,* 1–5.

Wolpoff, M. H., & Caspari, R. (1996). *Race and human evolution: A fatal attraction.* New York: Simon & Schuster.

Wolpoff, M. H., Hawks, J., Frayer, D. W., & Huntley, K. (2001). Modern human ancestry at the peripheries: A test of the replacement theory. *Science, 291,* 293–297.

Wrangham, R. (2004). Killer species. *Deedalus, 133,* 25–35.

Wrangham, R., & Peterson, D. (1996). *Demonic males.* Boston: Houghton Mifflin.

Wrangham, R. W. (1993). The evolution of sexuality in chimpanzees and bonobos. *Human Nature, 4,* 47–79.

Wrangham, R. W., Jones, J. H., Laden, G., Pilbeam, D., & Conklin-Brittain, N. (1999). The raw and the stolen: Cooking and the ecology of human origins. *Current Anthropology, 40,* 567–594.

Wynne-Edwards, V. C. (1962). *Animal dispersion in relation to social behavior.* Edinburgh, UK: Oliver & Boyd.

Yamagishi, T., Tanida, S., Mashima, R., Shimona, E., & Kanazawa, S. (2003). You can judge a book by its cover: Evidence that cheaters may look different from cooperators. *Evolution and Human Behavior, 24,* 290–301.

Yerushalmy, J., & Milkovich, L. (1965). Evaluation of the teratogenic effects of meclizine in man. *American Journal of Obstetrics and Gynecology, 93,* 553–562.

Yosef, R. (1991, June). Female seek males with ready cache. *Natural History, 37.*

Young, R. R., & Thiessen, D. (1992). The Texas rape scale. *Ethology and Sociobiology, 13,* 19–33.

Yu, D. W., & Shepard, G. H. (1998). Is beauty in the eye of the beholder? *Nature, 396,* 321–322.

Yuki, M., & Yokota, K. (2009). The primal warrior: Outgroup threat priming enhances intergroup discrimination in men but not women. *Journal of Experimental social psychology, 45,* 271–274.

Zahavi, A. (1977). The costs of honesty (Further remarks on the handicap principle). *Journal of Theoretical Biology, 67,* 603–605.

Zahavi, A. (1995). Altruism as a handicap: The limitations of kin selection and reciprocity. *Journal of Avian Biology, 26,* 1–3.

Zahavi, A., & Zahavi, A. (1996). *The handicap principle.* New York: Oxford University Press.

Zerjal, T., Xue, Y., Bertorelle, G., Wells, R. S., Bao, W., Zhu, S., et al. (2003, January 17). The genetic legacy of the Mongols. *American Journal of Human Genetics.* Published electronically.

Zihlman, A. L. (1981). Women as shapers of the human adaptation. In F. Dahlberg (Ed.), *Woman the gatherer* (pp. 77–120). New Haven, CT: Yale University Press.

# INDEX

Page numbers followed by *f* indicate figures and those followed by *t* indicate tables

p. 5: North Wind Picture Archives; p. 6: Key Sanders/Getty Images, Inc.—Stone Allstock; p. 7: Neil McIntyre/Getty Images, Inc.—Taxi; p. 11: SPL/Photo Researchers, Inc.; p. 12: Courtesy of William D. Hamilton; p. 14: Courtesy of William D. Hamilton; p. 16: Roger Ressmeyer/Corbis; p. 29: USDA/Animal and Plant Health Inspection Service; p. 39: Inc. Stephen Marks/Getty Images, Inc.—Image Bank; p. 43: Courtesy of J.L. Capinera; p. 48: Gail Shumway/Getty Images, Inc.—Taxi; p. 48: Tim Davis/Photo Researchers, Inc.; p. 48: Rob Reichenfeld; p. 52 (left): M. Kulyk/Photo Researchers; p. 52 (right): Articulate Graphics/Custom Medical Stock Photo; p. 64: Jeff Greenberg/PhotoEdit; p. 73: Richard Katz/Anthro-Photo; p. 80: Marjorie Shostak/Anthro-Photo; p. 84: Marjorie Shostak/Anthro-Photo; p. 88: Jeremy Woodhouse/Getty Images, Inc.; p. 94: George Grail/National Geographic Image Collection; p. 96: istockphoto; p. 120: Creasource/Corbis; p. 122 (left): ZUMA Press/Newscom; p. 122 (right): Janet Mayer/Splash News/Newscom; p. 126: Thinkstock; p. 134: Keven Winter/Getty Images Entertainment; p. 151: Ronald Hess/Elsevier Science; p. 162: Frazer Harrison/Getty Images Entertainment; p. 165: Shutterstock; p. 207: Topham/The Image Works; p. 210: Elena Yakusheva/Shutterstock; p. 213: Michael Newman/PhotoEdit Inc.; p. 220: Simon Marcus/Corbis; p. 228: Barros & Barros/Getty Images, Inc.—Image Bank; p. 252, 278, 286: Thinkstock; p. 299: Photofusion Picture Library/Alamy; p. 303: Bill Kostroun/AP World Wide Photos; p. 313: Roger Hutchings/Alamy; p. 317: Dagli Orti/Picture Desk, Inc./Kobal Collection; p. 353: Thinkstock; p. 364: Clive Bromhall/PhotoLibrary; p. 369: Nik Wheeler/Corbis; p. 376 (left): J. Mahoney/The Image Works; p. 376 (right): Rick Mansfield/The Image Works.